TUTORIAL
LOCAL NETWORK TECHNOLOGY

Third Edition

William Stallings

COMPUTER SOCIETY ORDER NUMBER 825
LIBRARY OF CONGRESS NUMBER 87-83434
IEEE CATALOG NUMBER EH0271-7
ISBN 0-8186-0825-0
SAN 264-620X

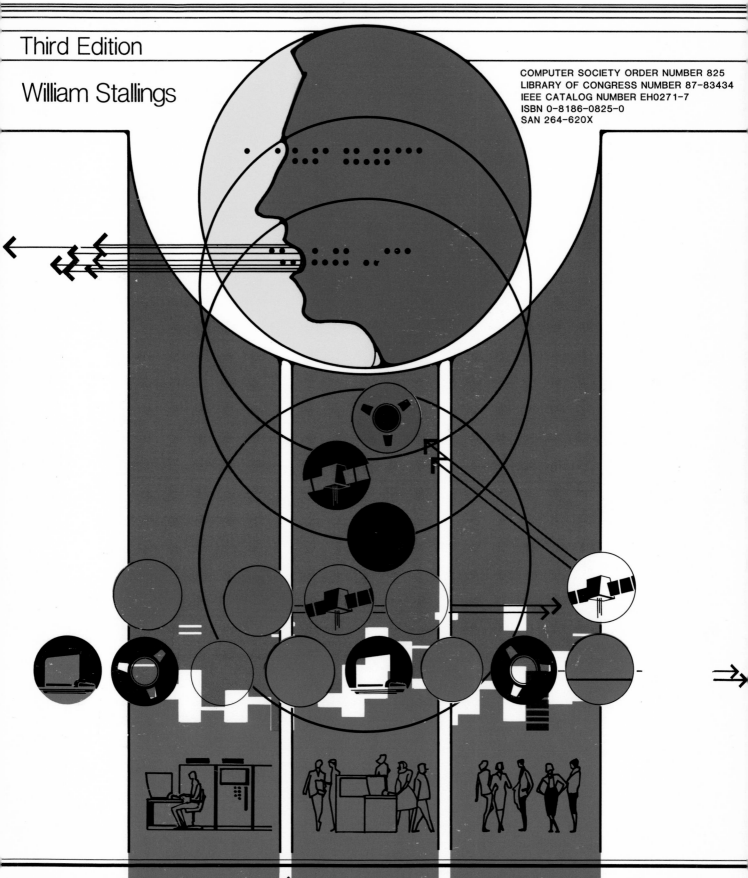

 THE COMPUTER SOCIETY
®OF THE IEEE

IEEE

THE INSTITUTE OF ELECTRICAL AND ELECTRONICS ENGINEERS, INC.

IEEE
**COMPUTER
SOCIETY
PRESS** Φ®

TUTORIAL
LOCAL NETWORK TECHNOLOGY

Third Edition

William Stallings

COMPUTER SOCIETY ORDER NUMBER 825
LIBRARY OF CONGRESS NUMBER 87-83434
IEEE CATALOG NUMBER EH0271-7
ISBN 0-8186-0825-0
SAN 264-620X

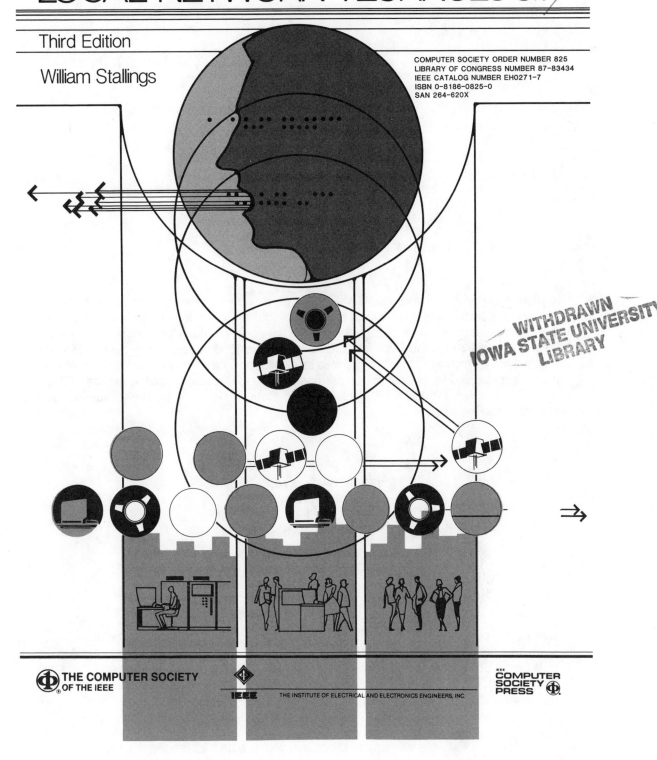

THE COMPUTER SOCIETY
OF THE IEEE

IEEE
THE INSTITUTE OF ELECTRICAL AND ELECTRONICS ENGINEERS, INC.

IEEE
COMPUTER
SOCIETY
PRESS

Published by Computer Society Press
1730 Massachusetts Avenue, N.W.
Washington, D.C. 20036-1903

Cover designed by Jack I. Ballestero

Computer Society Order Number 825
Library of Congress Number 87-83434
IEEE Catalog Number EH0271-7
ISBN 0-8186-0825-0 (Paper)
ISBN 0-8186-4825-2 (Microfiche)
SAN 264-620X

Order from:

Computer Society
Terminal Annex
Post Office Box 04699
Los Angeles, CA 90051

IEEE Service Center
445 Hoes Lane
Post Office Box 1331
Piscataway, NJ 08855-1331

Computer Society
13 Avenue de l'Aquilon
B-1200 Brussels
BELGIUM

 THE INSTITUTE OF ELECTRICAL AND ELECTRONICS ENGINEERS, INC.

Preface

Perhaps no other major innovation in data processing or data communications has been so widely discussed or so eagerly anticipated before its maturity as that of local networks. Local networks are attractive for such features as high availability and the ability to support multiple vendor equipment. Although the technology is still evolving, the principal architectural forms and design approaches have emerged.

P.1 Tutorial Focus

This tutorial focuses on the broad and rapidly evolving field of local networks. Consequently, the aims of the text, constrained by space, are dictated by concerns of breadth rather than depth. The articles and original material have been selected on the bases of topics and style to support these aims.

In terms of topics, the tutorial explores the key issues in the field in the following general categories:

- *Technology and architecture*: There is a small collection of ingredients that serves to characterize and differentiate local networks, including transmission medium, network topology, communication protocols, switching technique, and hardware/software interface.

- *Network type*: It is convenient to classify local networks into three types, based partly on technology and partly on application. These are local area network (LAN), high-speed local network (HSLN), and digital switch/digital private branch exchange (PBX).

- *Design approaches*: While not attempting to be exhaustive, the tutorial exposes and discusses important issues related to local network design.

Conspicuously missing from this list is a category with a title such as "Typical Systems." This tutorial is focused on the common principles underlying the design and implementation of all local networks and should, therefore, give the reader sufficient background to judge and compare local network products. A description of even a small sample of such systems is beyond the scope of this book. Articles about specific systems are included herein only when they are the best vehicle for communicating the concepts and principles under discussion.

In terms of style, the tutorial is primarily:

- *Descriptive*: Terms are defined, and the key concepts and technologies are discussed in some detail.

- *Comparative*: Wherever possible, alternative or competing approaches are compared, and their relative merits, based on suitable criteria, are discussed.

On the other hand, analytic and research-oriented styles are present to a much lesser degree. Virtually all of the mathematical content is confined to the section on performance, and, even there, the emphasis is on results rather than derivations.

Also, much of the material presents concepts and approaches that have moved beyond research and are commercial realities today. Both the Bibliography (Section 10) and the references contained in each article suggest additional sources for the interested reader.

P.2 Intended Audience

This tutorial is intended for a broad range of readers interested in local networks.

- *Students and professionals in data processing and data communications*: The tutorial is a convenient means of reviewing some of the important papers in the field. Its organization and the original material aid the reader in focusing on this exciting aspect of data communications and data processing.

- *Local network designers and implementors*: The tutorial discusses the critical design issues and illustrates alternative approaches to meeting user requirements.

- *Local network customers and system managers*: This text alerts the reader to some of the key issues and tradeoffs, as well as what to look for in the way of network services and performance.

Most of the material can be comfortably read with no background in data communications. The glossary and original material provide supporting information for the reprinted articles.

P.3 Organization of Material

This tutorial is a combination of original material and reprinted articles. Its organization is intended to clarify both the unifying and the differentiating concepts underlying the field of local networks. The organization of the sections is as follows:

1. *Introduction*: This section discusses local network technology, focusing on the key characteristics of transmission medium and topology. The classification of types of local networks used in this book is presented and discussed.

2. *Local Area Networks*: The term LAN is often mistakenly identified with the entire field of local networks. LANs have a general-purpose application, and most of the better-known local networks fall into this class. The major types of LANs (baseband bus, broadband bus/tree, and ring) are described and compared. The important issue of medium access control protocols is explored. The standards currently being developed for LANs are also described.

3. *High-Speed Local Networks*: This section focuses on a special-purpose high-speed type of local network and examines current technology and standards as well as possible future directions.

4. *Digital Switches and Digital Private Branch Exchanges*: Networks in this category constitute the major alternative to LANs for meeting general local interconnection needs. This section explores the technology and architecture of these devices and examines their pros and cons relative to LANs.

5. *The Network Interface*: The nature of the interface between an attached device and a LAN or an HSLN is an important design issue. This section explores some alternatives.

6. *Performance*: The purpose of this section is to give some insight into the performance problems and the differences in performance of various local networks.

7. *Internetworking*: In the majority of cases, local networks will be connected in some fashion to other networks. Some alternatives are explored.

8. *Design Issues*: The purpose of this section is to give the reader some feel for the breadth of design issues that must be addressed in implementing and operating local networks.

9. *Glossary*: Includes definitions for most of the key terms appearing in this text.

10. *Bibliography*: Provides a guide to further reading.

P.4: Related Materials

Local Networks, Second Edition (Macmillan, 1987) by William Stallings is a companion to this tutorial text, and follows the same topical organization. It is intended as a textbook as well as a reference book for professionals. *Handbook of Computer-Communications Standards, Volume II: Local Network Standards* (Macmillan, 1988) by William Stallings is a detailed examination of the IEEE 802 and FDDI standards. Both books are available from Macmillan Publishing Co., 866 Third Avenue, New York, NY 10022; 800-223-3215. The author has also prepared a videotape course on communication networks. About half of the course is devoted to local networks and the digital PBX; the remainder covers packet-switched, packet-radio, and satellite networks (available from the Association for Media-Based Continuing Education for Engineers, 500 Tech Parkway N.W., Suite 200A, Atlanta, GA 30332; 404-894-3362).

P.5: The Third Edition

The first edition of *Local Network Technology* appeared in 1983, and this is its second revision since that time. This compressed revision schedule reflects the rapid changes that are taking place in this area. The changes affect the technology, standards, internetworking strategies, and protocol design approaches for local networks. This third edition contains 24 new articles, reflecting these changes. Every section of the text has been revised, and the bibliography and glossary have been updated. The revision of this text has been an interesting and rewarding experience, and I hope that its readers find it a useful guide to this fascinating field.

Table of Contents

Section 1: Introduction

1.1 Overview

This section provides an overview of the major types of local networks and their key architectural features. As background we begin with a brief discussion of the applications of local networks. The range of applications is wide so, to give some flavor for the potential uses of local networks, we discuss four distinct types of application.

Personal Computer Networks

We start at one extreme, a system designed to support microcomputers, such as personal computers. With the relatively low cost of such systems, individual managers within organizations are independently procuring personal computers for standalone applications, such as spreadsheet programs or project management tools. Today's personal computers put processor, file storage, high-level languages, and problem-solving tools in an inexpensive, "user-friendly" package. The reasons for acquiring such a system are compelling.

However, a collection of standalone processors will not meet all of an organization's needs; central processing facilities are still required. Some programs, such as econometric forecasting models, are too big to run on a small computer. Corporate-wide data files, such as accounting and payroll, require a centralized facility but should be accessible to a number of users. Plus, there are other kinds of files that, though specialized, must be shared by a number of users. Further, there are sound reasons for connecting individual intelligent work stations not only to a central facility but also to each other. Members of a project or organization team need to share work and information. By far, the most efficient way to do so is electronically.

The capabilities of each work station can be matched to the tasks of the particular work station user. Each type of user is provided with electronic mail and word processing to improve the efficiency of creating and distributing messages, memos, and reports. Managers are also given a set of program and budget management tools. With the amount of automation that personal computers supply, the role of a secretary becomes less that of a typist and more that of an administrative assistant. Tools such as an electronic calendar and graphics support become valuable for these workers. Similarly, engineers and technical writers can be supplied with tailored systems.

Certain expensive resources, such as a disk and printer, can be shared by all users of the departmental local network. In addition, the network can tie into larger corporate network facilities. For example, the corporation may have a buildingwide local network and a long-haul corporate-wide network. A communications server can provide controlled access to these resources.

A key requirement for the success of such a network is low cost. The cost of attachment to the network for each device should be on the order of one to a few hundred dollars; otherwise, the attachment cost will approach the cost of the attached device. However, the capacity and data rate need not be high, so this is a realizable goal.

Computer Room Networks

At the other extreme from a personal computer local network is one designed for use in a computer room containing large, expensive mainframe computers. This is an example of what we refer to as a high-speed local network (HSLN). The HSLN is likely to find application at very large data processing sites. Typically, these sites will be large companies or research installations with large data processing budgets. Because of the size involved, a small difference in productivity can mean millions of dollars saved.

Consider a site that uses a dedicated mainframe computer. This implies a fairly large application or set of applications. As the load at the site grows, the existing model may be replaced by a more powerful one, perhaps by a multiprocessor system. At some sites, a single-system replacement will not be able to keep up. The facility will eventually require multiple independent computers. Again, there are compelling reasons for interconnecting these systems. The cost of system interrupt is high, so it should be possible to shift applications easily and quickly to backup systems. It must be possible to test new procedures and applications without degrading the production system. Large bulk storage files must be accessible from more than one computer. Load leveling should be possible to maximize utilization.

It can be seen that some key requirements for HSLNs are the opposite of those for personal computer networks. High data rates are required to keep up with the work, which typically involves the transfer of large blocks of data. The electronics for achieving high speeds are expensive, on the order of tens of thousands of dollars per attachment. Fortunately, given the much higher cost of attached devices, such costs are reasonable.

Office Automation

Most local network applications will fall between the two extremes of personal computer networks and computer room networks. Moderate data rates and moderate attachment costs are requirements. In some cases, the local network will support one or a few types of devices and rather homogeneous traffic. In others, it will support a wide variety of devices and traffic types.

A good generic example of the latter case is an office automation system, which can be defined as the incorporation of appropriate technology to help people manage information more effectively.

The key motivation for the move to office automation is productivity. As the percentage of white-collar workers has increased, the volume of information and paperwork has grown. In most installations, secretarial and other support functions are heavily labor intensive. Increased labor costs combined with low productivity and increasing workload have caused employers to seek effective ways of increasing the level of automation of this type of work.

At the same time, principals (managers and skilled "information workers") are faced with their own productivity bind. Work must be done faster with less wait time and waste time between segments of a job. This requires better access to information and better communication and coordination with others.

An office automation system, then, should include not only intelligent work stations but also a variety of other devices, such as minicomputers with text and data files, facsimile machines, intelligent copiers, and so forth. For this system to work and be truly effective, a local network is needed that can support the various devices and transmit the various types of information.

Integrated Voice and Data Local Networks

In virtually all offices today, the telephone system is separate from any local network that might be used to interconnect data processing devices. With the advent of digital voice technology, the capability now exists to integrate the telephone switching system of a building with the data processing equipment, providing a single local network for both.

Such integrated voice/data networks might simplify network management and control. They will also provide the required networking for the kinds of integrated voice and data devices to be expected in the future. An example is an executive voice/data work station that provides verbal message storage, voice annotation of text, and automated dialing.

Factory Local Networks

The factory environment increasingly is being dominated by automated equipment: programmable controllers, automated materials handling devices, time and attendance stations, machine vision devices, and various forms of robots. To manage the production or manufacturing process, it is essential to tie this equipment together. And, indeed, the very nature of the equipment facilitates this. Microprocessor devices have the potential to collect information from the shop floor and accept commands. With the proper use of the information and commands, it is possible to improve the manufacturing process and to provide detailed machine control.

The more that a factory is automated, the greater is the need for communications. Only by interconnecting all of the devices and by providing mechanisms for their cooperation can the automated factory be made to work. The means of interconnection is referred to as the factory local network.

To get some feeling for the requirements for a factory local network, consider the requirements developed by General Motors [STAL87a]. GM's specification of a communication network is driven by the sophisticated communication strategy it has evolved to meet its requirements. These requirements reflect those that are typical in other factory and robotics environments. Among the key areas are the following:

- Work force involvement has proven to be a valuable tool for GM's quality and cost-improvement effort. In an attempt to provide facts about the state of the business, employees are told GM's competitive position in relation to quality and costs. This information is communicated by video set-ups at numerous locations in the plant complex.

- An indirect effect on manufacturing costs has been the escalating cost of utilities. To try to control this area, GM measures usage of water, gas, pressurized air, steam, electricity and other resources—often by means of computers and programmable controllers.

- GM is investigating and, in some cases, implementing asynchronous machining and assembly systems that are much more flexible than the traditional systems of the past. To facilitate flexibility, the communication requirements increase an order of magnitude.

- To protect its large investment in facilities, GM uses closed circuit TV surveillance and computerized monitoring systems to warn of fires or other dangers.

- Accounting systems, personnel systems, material and inventory control systems, warranty systems and others use large mainframe computers with remote terminals located throughout the manufacturing facility.

- The nature of process-control and factory environments dictates that communications be extremely reliable and that the maximum time required to transmit critical control signals and alarms be bounded and known.

To interconnect all of the equipment in a facility, a local network is needed. The requirements listed above dictate the following characteristics of the local network:

- High capacity
- Ability to handle a variety of data traffic
- Large geographic extent
- High reliability
- Ability to specify and control transmission delays

1.2 Article Summary

The first article in this section, "Local Networks," serves as an overview to the entire tutorial. It lists and briefly describes the various transmission media and topologies for local networks and then defines and compares the three types of local networks as they are classified in this tutorial. They are: local area network (LAN), high-speed local network (HSLN), and digital private branch exchange (PBX). The article then expands on the technology and standards for LANs and HSLNs. The topics introduced in this article are the subject of more detailed description in the remainder of this tutorial text.

The article by Wirl also introduces topics that are referred to throughout the tutorial text. Specifically, the article is concerned with the choice of transmission medium and with the installation of various media for local networks.

Local Networks

WILLIAM STALLINGS

Honeywell Information Systems, Inc., McLean, Virginia 22102

The rapidly evolving field of local network technology has produced a steady stream of
local network products in recent years. The IEEE 802 standards that are now taking
shape, because of their complexity, do little to narrow the range of alternative technical
approaches and at the same time encourage more vendors into the field. The purpose of
this paper is to present a systematic, organized overview of the alternative architectures
for and design approaches to local networks.

The key elements that determine the cost and performance of a local network are its
topology, transmission medium, and medium access control protocol. Transmission media
include twisted pair, baseband and broadband coaxial cable, and optical fiber. Topologies
include bus, tree, and ring. Medium access control protocols include CSMA/CD, token
bus, token ring, register insertion, and slotted ring. Each of these areas is examined in
detail, comparisons are drawn between competing technologies, and the current status of
standards is reported.

Categories and Subject Descriptors: B.4.1 [**Input/Output and Data Communications**]:
Data Communications Devices—*receivers*; *transmitters*; B.4.3 [**Input/Output and Data
Communications**]: Interconnections (subsystems); C.2.5 [**Computer-Communication
Networks**]: Local Networks

General Terms: Design, Performance, Standardization

INTRODUCTION

Local networks have moved rapidly from
the experimental stage to commercial availability. The reasons behind this rapid development can be found in some fundamental trends in the data processing industry.
Most important is the continuing decrease
in cost, accompanied by an increase in capability, of computer hardware. Today's
microprocessors have speeds, instruction
sets, and memory capacities comparable to
medium-scale minicomputers. This trend
has spawned a number of changes in the
way information is collected, processed,
and used in organizations. There is an increasing use of small, single-function systems, such as word processors and small
business computers, and of general-purpose
microcomputers, such as personal computers and intelligent terminals. These
small, dispersed systems are more accessible to the user, more responsive, and easier
to use than large central time-sharing systems.

As the number of systems at a single
site—office building, factory, operations
center, etc.—increases, there is likely to be
a desire to interconnect these systems for
a variety of reasons, including

- sharing expensive resources, and
- exchanging data between systems.

Sharing expensive resources, such as
bulk storage and line printers, is an important measure for cost containment. Although the cost of data processing hardware has dropped, the cost of such essential

Computing Surveys, Vol. 16, No. 1, March 1984

• *William Stallings*

CONTENTS

---

electromechanical equipment remains high. Even in the case of data that can be uniquely associated with a small system, economies of scale require that most of that data be stored on a larger central facility: The cost per bit for storage on a microcomputer's floppy disk is orders of magnitude higher than that for a large disk or tape.

The ability to exchange data is an equally compelling reason for interconnection. Individual users of computer systems do not work in isolation and will want to retain some of the benefits provided by a central system, including the ability to exchange messages with other users, and the ability to access data and programs from several sources in the preparation of a document or the analysis of data.

A Definition

This requirement for communication, both among multiple computer systems within an organization and between those systems and shared resources, is met by the local network, which is defined as follows:

A local network is a communications network that provides interconnection of a variety of data communicating devices within a small area.

There are three significant elements in this definition. First, a local network is a communications network, not a computer network. In this paper, we deal only with issues relating to the communications network; the software and protocols required for attached computers to function as a network are beyond the scope of the paper.

Second, we broadly interpret the phrase "data communicating devices" to include any device that communicates over a transmission medium, including

- computers,
- terminals,
- peripheral devices,
- sensors (temperature, humidity, security alarm sensors),
- telephones,
- television transmitters and receivers,
- facsimile.

Of course, not all types of local networks are capable of handling all of these devices.

Third, the geographic scope of a local network is small, most commonly confined to a single building. Networks that span several buildings, such as those on a college campus or military base, are also common. A network with a radius of a few tens of kilometers is a borderline case. With the use of appropriate technology, such a system can behave like a local network.

Another element that could included in the definition is that a local network is generally a privately owned rather than a public or commercially available utility. Usually a single organization owns both the network and the attached devices.

Some of the key characteristics of local networks are

- high data rates (0.1–100 megabits per second, Mbps),

- short distances (0.1–50 kilometers),
- low error rate (10^{-8}–10^{-11}).

The first two parameters differentiate local networks from two cousins: long-haul networks and multiprocessor systems.

These distinctions between the local network and its two cousins have an impact on design and operation. Local networks generally experience much fewer data transmission errors and lower communications costs than long-haul networks, and cost–performance trade-offs therefore differ significantly. Also, it is possible to achieve greater integration between the local network and the attached devices, as they are generally owned by the same organization.

A major distinction between local networks and multiprocessors systems is the degree of coupling: Multiprocessor systems are tightly coupled, have shared memory, usually have some central control, and completely integrate the communications function, whereas local networks tend to have the opposite characteristics.

Benefits and Pitfalls

We already have mentioned resource sharing as an important benefit of local networks. This includes not only expensive peripheral devices, but also data.

A local network is also more reliable, available to the user, and able to survive failures. The loss of any one system should have minimal impact, and key systems can be made redundant so that other systems can quickly take up the load after a failure.

One of the most important potential benefits of a local network relates to system evolution. In a nonnetworked installation such as a time-sharing center, all data processing power is in one or a few systems. In order to upgrade hardware, existing applications software must be either converted to new hardware or reprogrammed, with the risk of error in either case. Even adding new applications on the same hardware, or enhancing those that exist, involves the risk of introducing errors and reducing the performance of the entire system. With a local network it is possible to gradually replace applications or systems, avoiding the "all-or-nothing" approach. Another facet of this capability is that old equipment can be left in the system to run a single application if the cost of moving that application to a new machine is not justified.

Finally, a local network provides the potential to connect devices from multiple vendors, which would give the customer greater flexibility and bargaining power.

These represent the most significant benefits of a local network. Alas, there are potential pitfalls as well.

There is a certain amount of loss of control in distributed systems; it is difficult to manage this resource, to enforce standards for software and data, and to control the information available through a network. The prime benefit of networking—distributed systems—also incorporates its prime pitfall.

It is likely that data will be distributed in a local network, or at least that access to data will be possible from multiple sources. This raises the problems of integrity of data (e.g., two users trying to update a database at the same time), security of data, and privacy.

Another pitfall might be referred to as "creeping escalation." With the dispersal of systems and ease of adding computer equipment, it becomes easier for managers of suborganizations to justify equipment procurement for their department. Although each procurement may be individually justifiable, the total may well exceed an organization's requirements.

Finally, as we mentioned, one of the significant benefits of a local network is the potential to connect devices from multiple vendors. However, the local network does not guarantee interoperability, that is, that these devices can be used cooperatively. Two word processors from different vendors can be attached to a local network, but will most likely use different file formats and control characters. Some form of format-conversion software will be required to take a file from one device and edit it on the other.

A further discussion of the applications, benefits, and pitfalls of local networks is contained in Derfler and Stallings [1983].

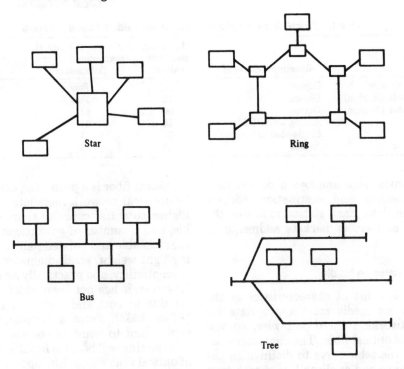

Figure 1.   Local network topologies.

1. LOCAL NETWORK TECHNOLOGY

The principle technological alternatives that determine the nature of a local network are its topology and transmission medium [Rosenthal 1982], which determine the type of data that may be transmitted, the speed and efficiency of communications, and even the kinds of applications that a network may support.

In this section we survey the topologies and transmission media that are currently appropriate for local networks, and define three types of local networks based on these technologies.

1.1 Topologies

Local networks are often characterized in terms of their topology, three of which are common (Figure 1): star, ring, and bus or tree (the bus is a special case of the tree with only one trunk and no branches; we shall use the term bus/tree when the distinction is unimportant).

In the star topology, a central switching element is used to connect all the nodes in the network. A station wishing to transmit data sends a request to the central switch for a connection to some destination station, and the central element uses circuit switching to establish a dedicated path between the two stations. Once the circuit is set up, data are exchanged between the two stations as if they were connected by a dedicated point-to-point link.

The ring topology consists of a closed loop, with each node attached to a repeating element. Data circulate around the ring on a series of point-to-point data links between repeaters. A station wishing to transmit waits for its next turn and then sends the data out onto the ring in the form of a packet, which contains both the source and destination address fields as well as data. As the packet circulates, the destination node copies the data into a local buffer. The packet continues to circulate until it returns to the source node, providing a form of acknowledgment.

The bus/tree topology is characterized by the use of a multiple-access, broadcast medium. Because all devices share a common communications medium, only one device can transmit at a time, and as with the

Table 1. Typical Characteristics of Transmission Media for Local Networks

	Signaling technique	Maximum data rate (Mbps)	Maximum range at maximum data rate (kilometers)	Practical number of devices
Twisted pair wire	Digital	1–2	Few	10's
Coaxial cable (50 ohm)	Digital	10	Few	100's
Coaxial cable (75 ohm)	Digital	50	1	10's
	Analog with FDM	20	10's	1000's
	Single-channel analog	50	1	10's
Optical fiber	Analog	10	1	10's

ring, transmission employs a packet containing source and destination address fields and data. Each station monitors the medium and copies packets addressed to itself.

1.2 Transmission Media

Table 1 is a list of characteristics of the transmission media most appropriate for local networks: twisted pair wire, coaxial cable, and optical fiber. The characteristics listed in the table serve to distinguish the performance and applicability of each type of transmission medium.

Twisted pair wiring is one of the most common communications transmission media, and one that is certainly applicable to local networks. Although typically used for low-speed transmission, data rates of up to a few megabits per second can be achieved. One weakness of twisted pair wire is its susceptibility to interference and noise, including cross talk from adjacent wires. These effects can be minimized with proper shielding. Twisted pair wire is relatively low in cost and is usually preinstalled in office buildings. It is the most cost-effective choice for single-building, low-traffic requirements.

Higher performance requirements can best be met by coaxial cable, which provides higher throughput, can support a larger number of devices, and can span greater distances than twisted pair wire. Two transmission methods, baseband and broadband, can be employed on a coaxial cable; these are explained in detail in Sections 2.2 and 2.3, respectively. The key difference is that baseband supports a single data channel, whereas broadband can support multiple simultaneous data channels.

Optical fiber is a promising candidate for future local network installations. It has a higher potential capacity than coaxial cable, and a number of advantages over both coaxial cable and twisted pair wire, including light weight, small diameter, low noise susceptibility, and practically no emissions. However, it has not been widely used thus far due to cost and technical limitations [Allan 1983]. From a technical point of view, point-to-point fiber-optic topologies like the ring will become feasible as the cost of optical fiber drops. Multipoint topologies like the bus/tree are difficult to implement with optical fiber because each tap imposes large power losses and causes optical reflections. One approach to this problem is the passive star coupler (Figure 2) [Freedman 1983; Rawson and Metcalfe 1978]. The passive star coupler consists of a number of optical fibers fused together: Light entering from one fiber on the input side is equally divided among and output through all fibers on the other side of the coupler.

1.3 Relationship between Medium and Topology

The choices of transmission medium and topology cannot be made independently. Table 2 illustrates desirable combinations.

The bus topology can be implemented with either twisted pair wire or coaxial cable.

The tree topology can be employed with broadband coaxial cable. As we shall see, the unidirectional nature of broadband signaling allows the construction of a tree architecture. The bidirectional nature of baseband signaling on either twisted pair wire or coaxial cable would not be suited to the tree topology.

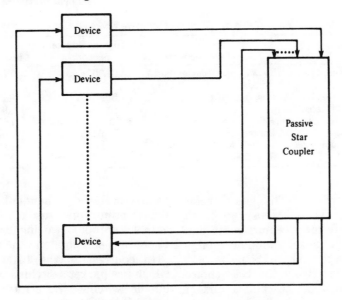

Figure 2. Optical fiber passive star configuration.

Table 2. Relationship between Transmission Medium and Topology

Medium	Topology			
	Bus	Tree	Ring	Star
Twisted pair	×		×	×
Baseband coaxial	×		×	
Broadband coaxial	×	×		
Optical fiber				×

The ring topology requires point-to-point links between repeaters. Twisted pair wire, baseband coaxial cable, and fiber all can be used to provide these links. Broadband coaxial cable would not work well in this topology, as each repeater would have to be capable, asynchronously, of receiving and retransmitting data on multiple channels. It is doubtful that the expense of such devices could be justified.

The star topology requires a single point-to-point link between each device and the central switch. Twisted pair wire is admirably suited to the task. The higher data rates of coaxial cable or fiber would overwhelm the switches available with today's technology.

1.4 Types of Local Networks

Three categories of local networks can be distinguished: local area network (LAN), high-speed local network (HSLN), and computerized branch exchange (CBX). These categories reflect differences in types of applications, possible choices of topologies and media, and, especially in the case of the CBX, differences in technology. Table 3 is a summary of representative characteristics of each category. Although we have included the CBX as a category of local network because it is an alternative means of locally interconnecting digital devices, its technology and architecture are so different from that of the LAN and HSLN that it is often not considered a local network. We mention its characteristics briefly, but in the remainder of this paper we shall concentrate on the LAN and HSLN.

1.4.1 Local Area Network

The term "local area network" (LAN) refers to a general-purpose local network that can serve a wide variety of devices. LANs support minicomputers, mainframes, terminals, and other peripheral devices. In many cases, these networks can carry not only data, but voice, video, and graphics.

The most common type of LAN is a bus or tree using coaxial cable; rings using twisted pair wire, coaxial cable, or optical

Table 3. Classes of Local Networks

Characteristics	Local area network	High-speed local network	Computerized branch exchange
Transmission medium	Twisted pair, coaxial (both), fiber	CATV coaxial	Twisted pair
Topology	Bus, tree, ring	Bus	Star
Transmission speed (Mbps)	1–20	50	0.0096–0.064
Maximum distance (kilometers)	~25	1	1
Switching technique	Packet	Packet	Circuit
Number of devices supported	100's–1000's	10's	100's–1000's
Attachment cost ($)	500–5000	40,000–50,000	250–1000

fiber are an alternative. The data transfer rates on LANs (1–10 Mbps) are high enough to satisfy most requirements and provide sufficient capacity to allow a large numbers of devices to share the network.

The LAN is probably the best choice when a variety of devices and a mix of traffic types are involved. The LAN, alone or as part of a hybrid local network with one of the other types, will become a common feature of many office buildings and other installations.

1.4.2 High-Speed Local Network

The high-speed local network (HSLN) is designed to provide high end-to-end throughput between expensive high-speed devices, such as mainframes and mass storage devices.

Although other media and topologies are possible, the bus topology using coaxial cable is the most common. Very high data rates are achievable—50 Mbps is standard—but both the distance and the number of devices are more limited in the HSLN than in the LAN.

The HSLN is typically found in a computer room setting. Its main function is to provide I/O channel connections among a number of devices. Typical uses include file and bulk data transfer, automatic backup, and load leveling. Because of the current high prices for HSLN attachment, they are generally not practical for microcomputers and less expensive peripheral devices, and are only rarely used for minicomputers.

1.4.3 Computerized Branch Exchange

The computerized branch exchange (CBX) is a digital on-premise private branch ex-change designed to handle both voice and data connections, usually implemented with a star topology using twisted pair wire to connect end points to the switch.

In contrast to the LAN and HSLN, which use packet switching, the CBX uses circuit switching. Data rates to individual end points are typically low, but bandwidth is guaranteed and there is essentially no network delay once a connection has been made. The CBX is well suited to voice traffic, and to both terminal-to-terminal and terminal-to-host data traffic.

2. THE BUS/TREE TOPOLOGY

The bus and tree topologies have been most popular to date in implementing both LANs and HSLNs. Well-known bus or bus/tree architectures include Ethernet [Metcalfe and Boggs 1976], one of the earliest local networks; HYPERchannel [Christensen 1979], the oldest and most popular HSLN; and MITRENET [Hopkins 1979], the basis of much United States government-sponsored research. Most of the low-cost, twisted pair LANs for microcomputers use a bus topology. In this section we describe key characteristics of bus and tree configurations, and present a detailed description of the two transmission techniques used in these configurations: baseband and broadband.

2.1 Characteristics of Bus/Tree LANs and HSLNs

The bus/tree topology is a multipoint configuration; that is, it allows more than two devices at a time to be connected to and capable of transmitting on the medium.

This is opposed to the other topologies that we have discussed, which are point-to-point configurations; that is, each physical transmission link connects only two devices. Because multiple devices share a single data path, only one device may transmit data at a time, usually in the form of a packet containing the address of the destination. The packet propagates throughout the medium and is received by all other stations, but is copied only by the addressed station.

Two transmission techniques are in use for bus/tree LANs and HSLNs: baseband and broadband. Baseband uses digital signaling and can be employed on twisted pair wire or coaxial cable. Broadband uses analog signaling in the radio frequency (RF) range and is employed only on coaxial cable. Some of the differences between baseband and broadband are highlighted in Table 4, and in the following two sections we explore these techniques in some detail. There is also a variant known as "single-channel broadband," which has the signaling characteristics of broadband but some of the restrictions of baseband; this technique is also covered below.

The multipoint nature of the bus/tree topology gives rise to several problems common to both baseband and broadband systems. First, there is the problem of determining which station on the medium may transmit at any point in time. Historically, the most common access scheme has been centralized polling. One station has the role of a central controller. This station may send data to any other station or may request that another station send data to the controller. This method, however, negates some of the advantages of a distributed system and also is awkward for communication between two noncontroller stations. A variety of distributed strategies, referred to as "medium access control protocols," have now been developed for bus and tree topologies. These are discussed in Section 4.

A second problem with the multipoint configuration has to do with signal balancing. When two devices exchange data over a link, the signal strength of the transmitter must be adjusted to be within certain limits.

Table 4. Bus/Tree Transmission Techniques

Baseband	Broadband
Digital signaling	Analog signaling (requires RF modem)
Entire bandwidth consumed by signal—no FDM	FDM possible—multiple data channels, video, audio
Bidirectional	Unidirectional
Bus topology	Bus or tree topology
Distance, up to a few kilometers	Distance: up to tens of kilometers

The signal must be strong enough so that, after attenuation across the medium, it meets the receiver's minimum signal strength requirements, and is strong enough to maintain an adequate signal-to-noise ratio. On the other hand, if it is too strong, the signal will overload the circuitry of the transmitter, which creates harmonics and other spurious signals. Although it is easily done for a point-to-point link, signal balancing for a multipoint configuration is complex. If any device can transmit to any other device, then the signal balancing must be performed for all permutations of stations taken two at a time. For n stations that works out to $nx(n-1)$ permutations. For example, for a 200-station network (not a particularly large system), 39,800 signal strength constraints must be staisfied simultaneously. With interdevice distances ranging from tens to possibly thousands of meters, this can become an impossible task. In systems that use RF signals, the problem is compounded, owing to the possibility of RF signal interference across frequencies. The solution to these difficulties is to divide the medium into segments within which pairwise balancing is possible (i.e., signals between pairs of devices can be balanced within each segment). Amplifiers or repeaters are used between segments to maintain signal strength.

2.2 Baseband Systems

A baseband LAN or HSLN is by definition one that uses digital signaling. The entire frequency spectrum of the medium is used to form the digital signal, which is inserted on the line as constant-voltage pulses. Baseband systems can extend only about a

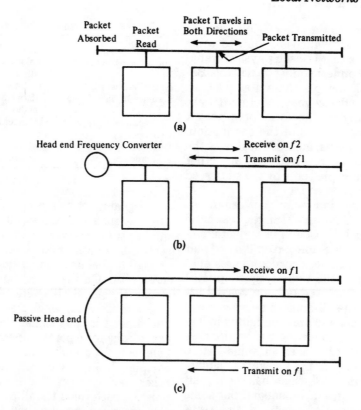

Figure 3. Baseband and broadband transmission: (a) bidirectional (baseband, single-channel broadband); (b) mid-split broadband; (c) dual cable broadband. [From W. Stallings, *Local Networks: An Introduction*, Macmillan, New York, 1984. Copyright Macmillan 1984.]

kilometer at most because the attenuation of the signal, especially at higher frequencies, causes a blurring of the pulses and a weakening of the signal to the extent that communication over longer distances is impractical. Baseband transmission is bidirectional; that is, a signal inserted at any point on the medium propagates in both directions to the ends, where it is absorbed (Figure 3a). In addition, baseband systems require a bus topology. Unlike analog signals, digital signals cannot easily be propagated through the splitters and joiners of a tree topology.

2.2.1 Baseband Coaxial

The most well-known form of baseband bus LAN uses coaxial cable. Unless otherwise indicated, this discussion is based on the Ethernet system [DEC 1983; Metcalfe and Boggs 1976; Metcalfe et al. 1977; Shoch et

al. 1983] and the almost-identical IEEE standard [IEEE 1983].

Most baseband coaxial systems use a special 50-ohm cable rather than the more common 75-ohm cable used for cable television and broadband LANs. For digital signals, the 50-ohm cable suffers less intense reflections from the insertion capacitance of the taps, and provides better protection against low-frequency electromagnetic noise.

The simplest baseband coaxial LAN consists of an unbranched length of coaxial cable with a terminator at each end to prevent reflections. A maximum length of 500 meters is recommended. Stations attach to the cable by means of a tap. Attached to each tap is a transceiver, which contains the electronics for transmitting and receiving. The distance between any two taps should be a multiple of 2.5 meters

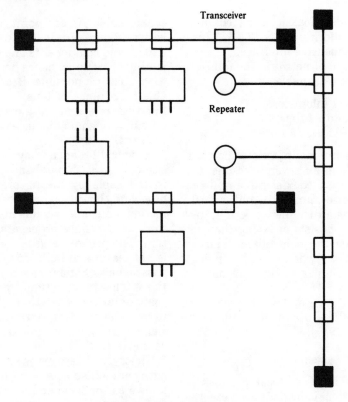

Figure 4. Baseband system.

to ensure that reflections from adjacent taps do not add in phase [Yen and Crawford 1983], and a maximum of 100 taps is recommended.

The above specifications are for a 10-Mbps data rate. They are based on engineering trade-offs involving data rate, cable length, number of taps, and the electrical characteristics of the transmit and receiver components. For example, at lower data rates the cable could be longer.

To extend the length of the network, a repeater may be used. A repeater consists, in essence, of two transceivers joined together and connected to two different segments of coaxial cable. The repeater passes digital signals in both directions between the two segments, amplifying and regenerating the signals as they pass through. A repeater is transparent to the rest of the system; since it does no buffering, it in no sense isolates one segment from another. So, for example, if two stations on different segments attempt to transmit at the same

time, their packets will interfere with each other (collide). To avoid multipath interference, only one path of segments and repeaters is allowed between any two stations. Figure 4 is an example of a baseband system with three segments and two repeaters.

2.2.2 Twisted Pair Baseband

A twisted pair baseband LAN is intended for low-cost, low-performance requirements. Although this type of system supports fewer stations at lower speeds than a coaxial baseband LAN, its cost is also far lower.

The components of the system are few and simple:

- twisted pair bus,
- terminators,
- controller interface.

The latter can simply be a standard two-wire I/O or communications interface.

Typically, the electrical signaling technique on the cable conforms to RS-422-A. This is a standard inexpensive interface.

With this kind of network, the following parameters are reasonable:

- length, up to 1 kilometer,
- data rate, up to 1 Mbps,
- number of devices, 10's.

For these requirements, twisted pair wire is a good medium for several reasons: It is lower in cost than coaxial cable and provides equal noise immunity, and virtually anyone can install the network. The task of installation consists of laying the cable and connecting the controllers. This requires only a screwdriver and a pair of pliers, and is similar to hooking up hi-fi speakers.

Examples of these systems can be found in Malone [1981], Bosen [1981], and Hahn and Belanger [1981].

2.3 Broadband Systems

Within the context of local networks, a broadband system is by definition one that uses analog signaling. Unlike digital signaling, in which the entire frequency spectrum of the medium is used to produce the signal, analog signaling allows frequency-division multiplexing (FDM). With FDM, the frequency spectrum on the cable is divided into channels or sections of bandwidth; separate channels can support data traffic, TV, and radio signals.

A special case of a broadband system is a low-cost system using only a single channel. To distinguish between the two cases, we will refer to "FDM broadband" and "single-channel broadband" in this section. In Section 2.3.1, we examine FDM broadband, describing two different physical configurations, dual cable and split cable, and three different data transfer techniques, dedicated, switched, and multiple access. In Section 2.3.2, we describe single-channel broadband.

2.3.1 FDM Broadband

Broadband systems use standard, off-the-shelf community antenna television (CATV) components, including 75-ohm

coaxial cable. All end points are terminated with a 75-ohm terminator to absorb signals. Broadband components allow splitting and joining operations; hence both bus and tree topologies are possible. Broadband is suitable for a range of tens of kilometers and hundreds or even thousands of devices. For all but very short distances, amplifiers are required.

A typical broadband system is shown in Figure 5. As with baseband, stations attach to the cable by means of a tap. Unlike baseband, however, broadband is a unidirectional medium; signals inserted onto the medium can only propagate in one direction. The primary reason for this is that it is not feasible to build amplifiers that will pass signals of one frequency in both directions. This unidirectional property means that only those stations "downstream" from a transmitting station can receive its signals. How, then, can one achieve full connectivity?

Clearly, two data paths are needed. These paths are joined at a point on the network known as the head end. For the bus topology, the head end is simply one end of the bus; for the tree topology, the head end is the root of the branching tree. All stations transmit on one path toward the head end (inbound). Signals received at the head end then are propagated along a second data path away from the head end (outbound). All stations receive on the outbound path.

Physically, two different configurations are used to implement the inbound and outbound paths (see Figure 3). On a dual cable configuration, the inbound and outbound paths are separate cables, the head end being simply a passive connector between the two. Stations send and receive on the same frequency.

In contrast, in the split configuration, the inbound and outbound paths are different frequencies on the same cable. Bidirectional amplifiers pass lower frequencies inbound and higher frequencies outbound. The head end contains a device, known as a frequency converter, for translating inbound frequencies to outbound frequencies.

The frequency converter at the head end can be either an analog or a digital device. An analog device simply translates signals

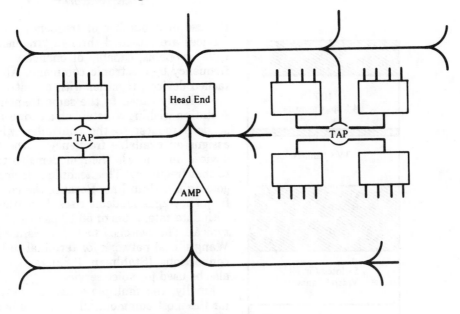

Figure 5. Broadband system.

to a new frequency and retransmits them. A digital device recovers the digital data from the head end and then retransmits the cleaned-up data on the new frequency.

Split systems are categorized by the frequency allocation to the two paths. Subsplit, commonly used by the CATV industry, provides 5–30 megahertz (MHz) inbound and 40–300 MHz outbound. This system was designed for metropolitan area TV distribution, with limited subscriber-to-central office communication. Mid-split, more suitable for LANs, provides an inbound range of 5–116 MHz and an outbound range of 168–300 MHz. This provides a more equitable distribution of bandwidth. Midsplit was developed at a time when the practical spectrum of a CATV cable was 300 MHz. Spectrums surpassing 400 MHz are now available, and either "supersplit" or "equal-split" is sometimes used to achieve even better balance by splitting the bandwidth roughly in half.

The differences between split and dual are minor. The split system is useful when a single-cable plant is already installed in a building, and the installed system is about 10–15 percent cheaper than a dual cable system [Hopkins 1979]. On the other hand, a dual cable has over twice the capacity of

mid-split, and does not require the frequency translator at the head end. A further comparison can be found in Cooper and Edholm [1983].

The broadband LAN can be used to carry multiple channels, some used for analog signals, such as video and voice, and some for data. For example, a video channel requires a 6-MHz bandwidth. Digital channels can generally carry a data rate of somewhere between 0.25 and 1 bit per second per hertz. A possible allocation of a 350-MHz cable is shown in Figure 6.

One of the advantages of the use of multiple channels is that different channels can be used to satisfy different requirements. Figure 7 depicts three kinds of data transfer techniques that can be used: dedicated, switched, and multiple access.

For dedicated service, a small portion of the cable's bandwidth is reserved for exclusive use by two devices. No special protocol is needed. Each of the two devices attaches to the cable through a modem; both modems are tuned to the same frequency. This technique is analogous to securing a dedicated leased line from the telephone company. Transfer rates of up to 20 Mbps are achievable. The dedicated service could be used to connect two devices when a heavy

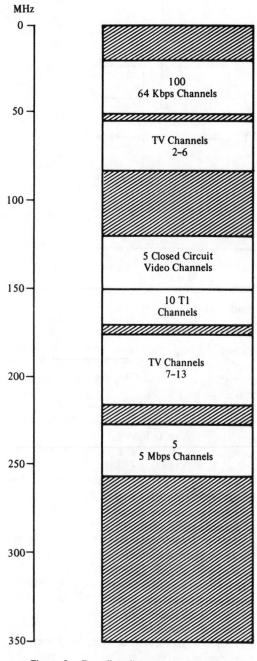

MHz

100
64 Kbps Channels

TV Channels
2-6

5 Closed Circuit
Video Channels

10 T1
Channels

TV Channels
7-13

5
5 Mbps Channels

Figure 6. Broadband spectrum allocation.

the use of a number of frequency bands. Devices are attached through "frequency-agile" modems, capable of changing their frequency by electronic command. All attached devices, together with a controller, are initially tuned to the same frequency. A station wishing to establish a connection sends a request to the controller, which assigns an available frequency to the two devices and signals their modems to tune to that frequency. This technique is analogous to a dial-up line. Because the cost of frequency-agile modems rises dramatically with data rate, rates of 56 Kbps or less are typical. The switched technique is used in Wang's local network for terminal-to-host connections [Stahlman 1982], and could also be used for voice service.

Finally, the multiple-access service, by far the most common, allows a number of attached devices to be supported at the same frequency. As with baseband, some form of medium access control protocol is needed to control transmission. It provides for distributed, peer communications among many devices, which is the primary motivation for a local network.

Further discussions of FDM broadband LANs can be found in Cooper [1982, 1983], Dineson and Picazo [1980], and Forbes [1981].

2.3.2 Single-Channel Broadband

An abridged form of broadband is possible, in which the entire spectrum of the cable is devoted to a single transmission path for analog signals. In general, a single-channel broadband LAN uses bidirectional transmission and a bus topology. Hence there can be no amplifiers, and there is no need for a head end. Transmission is generally at a low frequency (a few megahertz). This is an advantage since attenuation is less at lower frequencies.

Because the cable is dedicated to a single task, it is not necessary to ensure that the modem output is confined to a narrow bandwidth; energy can spread over the cable's spectrum. As a result, the electronics are simple and inexpensive. This scheme would appear to give comparable performance, at a comparable price, to baseband.

traffic pattern is expected; for example, one computer may act as a standby for another, and need to get frequent updates of state information and file and database changes.

The switched transfer technique requires

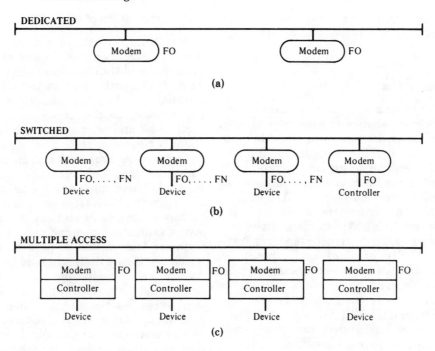

Figure 7.   Broadband data transfer services: (a) dedicated; (b) switched; (c) multiple access.

The principle reason for choosing this scheme over baseband appears to be that single-channel broadband uses 75-ohm cable. Thus a user with modest initial requirements could install the 75-ohm cable and use inexpensive single-channel components. Later, if the needs expand, the user could switch to full broadband by replacing modems, but would avoid the expense of rewiring the building with new cable.

2.4 Baseband versus Broadband

One of the least productive aspects of the extensive coverage afforded local networks in the trade and professional literature is the baseband versus broadband debate. The potential customer will be faced with many other decisions more complex than this one. The fact is that there is room for both technologies in the local network field. For the interested reader, thoughtful discussions may be found in Hopkins and Meisner [1982] and Krutsch [1981].

To briefly summarize the two technologies, baseband has the advantages of simplicity, and, in principle, low cost. The layout of a baseband cable plant is simple: A relatively inexperienced local network engineer should be able to cope with it. Baseband's potential disadvantages include limitations in capacity and distance—but these are only disadvantages if one's requirements exceed those limitations.

Broadband's strength is its tremendous capacity. Broadband can carry a wide variety of traffic on a number of channels, and with the use of active amplifiers can achieve very wide area coverage. Also, the system is based on a mature CATV technology, with reliable and readily available components. A disadvantage of broadband systems is that they are more complex than baseband to install and maintain, requiring experienced RF engineers. Also, the average propagation delay between stations for broadband is twice that for a comparable baseband system. This reduces the efficiency and performance of the system, as discussed in Section 5.

As with all other network design choices, the selection of baseband or broadband must be based on the relative cost and benefits. Neither is likely to win the LAN war.

2.5 Bus HSLNs

HSLNs using a bus topology share a number of characteristics with bus-based LANs. In particular, data are transmitted in packets, and because the configuration is multipoint, a medium access control protocol is needed. From the user's point of view, the key difference between a LAN and an HSLN is the higher data rate of the latter. Commercial HSLN products and the proposed American National Standards Institute (ANSI) standard both specify 50 Mbps, whereas 10 Mbps or less is typical for LANs. The higher data rate of the HSLN imposes cost and technical constraints, and the HSLN is limited to just a few devices (10–20) over a relatively small distance (less than 1 kilometer).

Two techniques have been used for bus HSLNs: baseband and single-channel broadband. In both cases a 75-ohm coaxial cable is used. Baseband is used for the most widely available HSLN product, HYPER-channel [Christensen 1979; Thornton 1980]. Single-channel broadband is used on CDC's product [Hohn 1980] and is the approach taken in the proposed ANSI standard [Burr 1983].

It is difficult to assess the relative advantages of these two schemes. In general, the two approaches should give comparable performance at comparable cost.

3. THE RING TOPOLOGY

The major alternative to the bus/tree topology LAN is the ring. The ring topology has been popular in Europe but is only slowly gaining ground in the United States, where Ethernet and MITRENET were largely responsible for shaping the early direction of activity. Several factors suggest that the ring may become more of a competitor in the United States: IBM has conducted research on ring LANs and is expected to announce a product, and the IEEE 802 ring LAN standard is moving toward completion.

3.1 Characteristics of Ring LANs

A ring LAN consists of a number of repeaters, each connected to two others by unidirectional transmission links to form a single closed path. Data are transferred sequentially, bit by bit, around the ring from one repeater to the next. Each repeater regenerates and retransmits each bit.

For a ring to operate as a communications network, three functions are required: data insertion, data reception, and data removal. These functions are provided by the repeaters. Each repeater, in addition to serving as an active element on the ring, serves as an attachment point for a station. Data are transmitted in packets, each of which contains a destination address field. As a packet circulates past a repeater, the address field is copied. If the attached station recognizes the address, then the remainder of the packet is copied. A variety of strategies can be used for determining how and when packets are added to and removed from the ring. These strategies are medium access control protocols, which are discussed in Section 4.

Repeaters perform the data insertion and reception functions in a similar manner to taps, which serve as station attachment points on a bus or tree. Data removal, however, is more difficult on a ring. For a bus or tree, signals inserted onto the line propagate to the end points and are absorbed by terminators, which clear the bus or tree of data. However, because the ring is a closed loop, data will circulate indefinitely unless removed. There are two solutions to this problem: A packet may be removed by the addressed repeater when it is received, or each packet could be removed by the transmitting repeater after it has made one trip around the ring. The latter approach is more desirable because: (1) it permits automatic acknowledgment, and (2) it permits multicast addressing, that is, one packet sent simultaneously to multiple stations.

The repeater then can be seen to have two main purposes: (1) to contribute to the proper functioning of the ring by passing on all the data that comes its way, and (2) to provide an access point for attached stations to send and receive data. Corresponding to these two purposes are two states (Figure 8): listen and transmit.

In the listen state, each bit that is received by the repeater is retransmitted, with a small delay to allow the repeater to perform required functions. Ideally, this delay should be on the order of one bit time (the time it takes for a repeater to transmit one complete bit onto the outgoing line). The required functions are

(1) Scan the passing bit stream for pertinent patterns, chiefly the address or addresses of attached stations. Another pattern, used in the token control strategy, is discussed in Section 4. Note that to perform the scanning function, the repeater must have some knowledge of packet format.
(2) Copy each incoming bit and send it to the attached station, while continuing to retransmit each bit. This will be done for each bit of each packet that is addressed to this station.
(3) Modify a bit as it passes by. In certain control strategies, bits may be modified, for example, to indicate that the packet has been copied. This would serve as an acknowledgment.

When a repeater's station has data to send and the repeater has permission to transmit (based on the medium access control strategy), the repeater enters the transmit state. In this state, the repeater receives bits from the station and retransmits them on its outgoing link. During the period of transmission, bits may appear on the incoming ring link. There are two possibilities, and they are treated differently:

(1) The bits could be from the same packet that the repeater is still sending. This will occur if the "bit length" of the ring is shorter than the packet. In this case, the repeater passes the bits back to the station, which can check them as a form of acknowledgment.
(2) For some control strategies, more than one packet could be on the ring at the same time. If the repeater, while transmitting, receives bits from a packet that it did not originate, it must buffer them to be transmitted later.

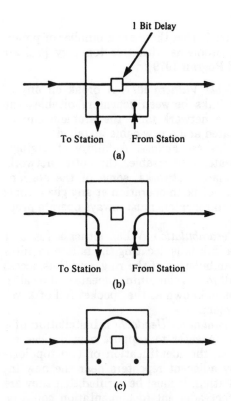

Figure 8. Ring repeater states: (a) listen state; (b) transmit state; (c) bypass state.

These two states, listen and transmit, are sufficient for proper ring operation. A third state, the bypass state, is also useful. In this state, a bypass relay can be activated, so that signals propagate past the repeater with no delay other than medium propagation. The bypass relay affords two benefits: (1) it provides a partial solution to the reliability problem, discussed later, and (2) it improves performance by eliminating repeater delay for those stations that are not active on the network.

Twisted pair wire, baseband coaxial cable, and fiber optic cable all can be used to provide the repeater-to-repeater links. Broadband coaxial cable could not be used easily, as each repeater would have to be capable of receiving and transmitting data on multiple channels asynchronously.

3.2 Potential Ring Problems

One of the principal reasons for the slow acceptance of the ring LAN in the United

States is that there are a number of potential problems with this topology [Saltzer and Pogran 1979]:

Cable Vulnerability. A break on any of the links between repeaters disables the entire network until the problem can be isolated and a new cable installed.

Repeater Failure. A failure of a single repeater also disables the entire network. In many networks, some of the stations may not be in operation at any given time; yet all repeaters must always operate properly.

Perambulation. When either a repeater or a link fails, locating the failure requires perambulation of the ring, and thus access to all rooms containing repeaters and cable. This is known as the "pocket full of keys" problem.

Installation Headaches. Installation of a new repeater to support new devices requires the identification of two topologically adjacent repeaters near the new installation. It must be verified that they are in fact adjacent (documentation could be faulty or out of date), and cable must be run from the new repeater to each of the old repeaters. There are several possible consequences: The length of cable driven by the source repeater may change, possibly requiring returning; old cable will accumulate if not removed; and the geometry of the ring may become highly irregular, exacerbating the perambulation problem.

Size Limitations. There is a practical limit to the number of stations on a ring. This limit is suggested by the reliability and maintenance problems cited earlier and by the accumulating delay of large numbers of repeaters. A limit of a few hundred stations seems reasonable.

Initialization and Recovery. To avoid designating one ring node as a controller (negating the benefit of distributed control), a strategy is required to ensure that all stations can cooperate smoothly when initialization and recovery are required. This cooperation is needed, for example, when a packet is garbled by a transient line error; in that case, no repeater may wish to assume the responsibility of removing the circulating packet.

The last problem is a protocol issue, which we discuss later. The remaining problems can be handled by a refinement of the ring topology, discussed next.

3.3 An Enhanced Architecture

The potential ring problems cited above have led to the development of an enhanced ring architecture that overcomes these problems of the ring and allows the construction of large local networks. This architecture is the basis of IBM's anticipated local network product [Rauch-Hindin 1982] and grows out of research done at IBM [Bux et al. 1982] and Massachusetts Institute of Technology [Saltzer and Clark 1981]. The result is a ring-based local network with two additions: ring wiring concentrators and bridges.

The ring wiring concentrator is simply a centralized location through which interrepeater links are threaded. The link between any two stations runs from one station into the concentrator and back out to the second station. This technique has a number of advantages. Because there is central access to the signal on every link, it is a simple matter to isolate a fault. A message can be launched into the ring and tracked to see how far it gets without mishap. A faulty segment can be disconnected and repaired at a later time. New repeaters can easily be added to the ring: Simply run two cables from the new repeater to the site of ring wiring concentration and splice into the ring.

The bypass relay associated with each repeater can be moved into the ring wiring concentrator. The relay can automatically bypass its repeater and two links for any malfunction. A nice effect of this feature is that the transmission path from one working repeater to the next is approximately constant; thus the range of signal levels to which the transmission system must automatically adapt is much smaller.

The ring wiring concentrator permits rapid recovery from a cable or repeater failure. Nevertheless, a single failure could temporarily disable the entire network. Furthermore, throughput considerations

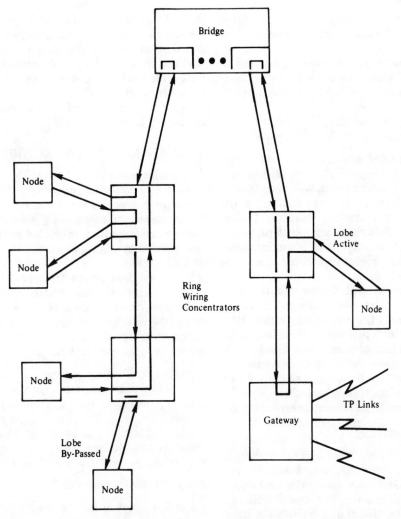

Figure 9. Star–ring architecture.

place a practical upper limit on the number of stations in a ring, since each repeater adds an increment of delay. Finally, in a spread-out network, a single wire concentration site dictates a lot of cable.

To attack these remaining problems, consider a local network consisting of multiple rings (Figure 9). Each ring consists of a connected sequence of wiring concentrators; the set of rings is connected by a bridge. The bridge routes data packets from one ring subnetwork to another on the basis of addressing information in the packet so routed. From a physical point of view, each ring operates independently of the other rings attached to the bridge. From a logical point of view, the bridge provides transparent routing between the two rings.

The bridge must perform five functions:

Input Filtering. For each ring, the bridge monitors the traffic on the ring and copies all packets addressed to other rings on the bridge. This function can be performed by a repeater programmed to recognize a family of addresses rather than a single address.

Input Buffering. Received packets may need to be buffered, either because the interring traffic is peaking, or because the output buffer at the destination ring is temporarily full.

Switching. Each packet must be routed through the bridge to its appropriate destination ring.

Output Buffering. A packet may need to be buffered at the threshold of the destination ring, waiting for an opportunity to be inserted.

Output Transmission. This function can be performed by an ordinary repeater.

Two principal advantages accrue from the use of a bridge. First, the failure of a ring, for whatever reason, will disable only a portion of the network; failure of the bridge does not prevent intraring traffic. Second, multiple rings may be employed to obtain a satisfactory level of performance when the throughput capability of a single ring is exceeded.

There are several disadvantages to be noted. First, the automatic acknowledgment feature of the ring is lost; higher level protocols must provide acknowledgment. Second, performance may not significantly improve if there is a high percentage of interring traffic. If it is possible to do so, network devices should be judiciously allocated to rings to minimize interring traffic.

3.4 Bus versus Ring

For the user with a large number of devices and high capacity requirements, the bus or tree broadband LAN seems the best suited to the requirements. For more moderate requirements, the choice between a baseband bus LAN and a ring LAN is not at all clear-cut.

The baseband bus is the simpler system. Passive taps rather than active repeaters are used. Thus medium failure is less likely, and there is no need for the complexity of bridges and ring wiring concentrators.

The most important benefit of the ring is that, unlike the bus/tree, it uses point-to-point communication links, which has a number of implications. First, since the transmitted signal is regenerated at each node, transmission errors are minimized and greater distances can be covered. Second, the ring can accommodate optical fiber links, which provide very high data rates and excellent electromagnetic interference (EMI) characteristics. Third, the electron-

ics and maintenance of point-to-point lines are simpler than those for multipoint lines. Another benefit of the ring is, assuming that the enhanced ring architecture is used, that fault isolation and recovery is simpler than for bus/tree.

Further discussion of ring versus bus is contained in Salwen [1983].

4. MEDIUM ACCESS CONTROL PROTOCOLS

All local networks (LAN, HSLN, CBX) consist of a collection of devices that must share the network's transmission capacity. Some means of controlling access to the transmission medium is needed so that any two particular devices can exchange data when required.

The key parameters in controlling access to the medium are "where" and "how." The question of where access is controlled generally refers to whether the system is centralized or distributed. A centralized scheme has the advantages of

- possibly affording greater control over access by providing such things as priorities, overrides, and guaranteed bandwidth,
- allowing the logic at each station to be as simple as possible, and
- avoiding problems of coordination,

and the disadvantages of

- a single point of failure, and
- possibly acting as a bottleneck, reducing efficiency.

The pros and cons for distributed control are mirror images of the above points.

How access is controlled is constrained by the topology and is a trade-off among competing factors: cost, performance, and complexity.

The most common medium access control protocols for local networks are categorized in Figure 10. In all cases, multiple data transfers share a single transmission medium. This always implies some sort of multiplexing, either in the time or frequency domain. In the frequency domain, any technique on a multiple-channel broadband system is by definition based on frequency-division multiplexing (FDM).

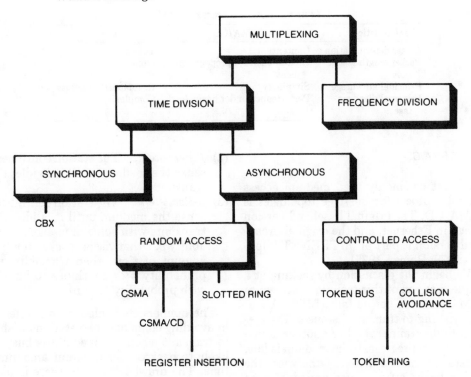

Figure 10. Local network access control techniques.

Within a single channel, however, some form of time-division multiplexing is required.

Time-division access control techniques are either synchronous or asynchronous. With synchronous techniques, a specific capacity is dedicated to a connection, as, for example, in the CBX. This is not optimal in bus/tree and ring networks: The needs of the stations are unpredictable, and the transmission capacity should be allocated in an asynchronous (dynamic) fashion in response to these needs.

Access to the medium using asynchronous time-division multiplexing (TDM) may be random (stations attempt to access the medium at will and at random times) or regulated (an algorithm is used to regulate the sequence and time of station access). The random access category includes two common bus techniques, carrier sense multiple access (CSMA) and carrier sense multiple access with collision detection (CSMA/CD), and two common ring techniques, register insertion and slotted ring.

The regulated access category includes both token bus and token ring for LANs and collision avoidance, the most common HSLN technique. All of the asynchronous techniques have found widespread application in LANs or HSLNs, and are discussed in this section.

4.1 Bus/Tree LANs

Of all the local network topologies, the bus/tree topologies present the most challenges, and the most options, for medium access control. In this section we do not survey the many techniques that have been proposed; good discussions can be found in Luczak [1978] and Franta and Chlamtec [1981]. Rather, emphasis will be on the two techniques for which standards have been developed by the IEEE 802 Committee and that seem likely to dominate the marketplace: CSMA/CD and token bus. Table 5 is a comparison of these two techniques on a number of characteristics.

Table 5. Bus/Tree Access Methods

Characteristic	CSMA/CD	Token bus
Access determination	Contention	Token
Packet length restriction	Greater than 2× propagation delay	None
Principal advantage	Simplicity	Regulated/fair access
Principal disadvantage	Performance under heavy load	Complexity

4.1.1 CSMA/CD

The most commonly used medium access control protocol for bus/tree topologies is CSMA/CD. The original baseband version is seen in Ethernet, and the original broadband version is part of MITRENET [Hopkins 1979; Roman 1977].

We begin the discussion by looking at a simpler version of this technique known as CSMA or listen before talk (LBT). A station wishing to transmit listens to the medium to determine whether another transmission is in progress. If the medium is idle, the station may transmit. Otherwise, the station backs off for some period of time and tries again, using one of the algorithms explained below. After transmitting, a station waits for a reasonable amount of time for an acknowledgment, taking into account the maximum round-trip propagation delay and the fact that the acknowledging station must also contend for the channel in order to respond.

This strategy is effective for systems in which the packet transmission time is much longer than the propagation time. Collisions only occur when more than one user begins transmitting within the period of propagation delay. If there are no collisions during the time that it takes for the leading edge of the packet to propagate to the farthest station, then the transmitting station has seized the channel and the packet is transmitted without collision.

With CSMA, an algorithm is needed to specify what a station should do if the medium is found to be busy. Three approaches or "persistence algorithms," are possible:

(1) *Nonpersistent.* The station backs off a random amount of time and then senses the medium again.

(2) *1-Persistent.* The station continues to sense the medium until it is idle, then transmits.

(3) *p-Persistent.* The station continues to sense the medium until it is idle, then transmits with some preassigned probability p. Otherwise, it backs off a fixed amount of time, then transmits with probability p or continues to back off with probability $(1 - p)$.

The nonpersistent algorithm is effective in avoiding collisions; two stations wishing to transmit when the medium is busy are likely to back off for different amounts of time. The drawback is that there is likely to be wasted idle time following each transmission. In contrast, the 1-persistent algorithm attempts to reduce idle time by allowing a single waiting station to transmit immediately after another transmission. Unfortunately, if more than one station is waiting, a collision is guaranteed! The p-persistent algorithm is a compromise that attempts to minimize both collisions and idle time.

CSMA/CD, also referred to as listen while talk (LWT), attempts to overcome one glaring inefficiency of CSMA: When two packets collide, the medium remains unusable for the duration of transmission of both damaged packets. For packets that are long in comparison to their propagation time, the amount of wasted bandwidth can be considerable. This waste is reduced with the CSMA/CD protocol: A station continues to listen to the medium while it is transmitting. Hence the following rules are added to the CSMA protocol:

(1) If a collision is detected during transmission, immediately cease transmitting the packet and transmit a brief jamming signal to ensure that all stations know there has been a collision.

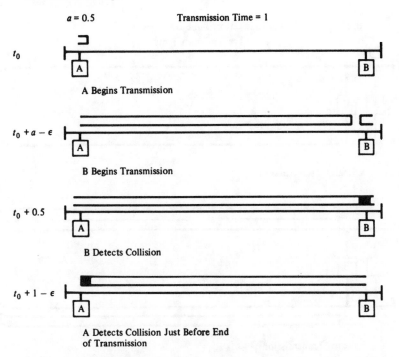

$a = 0.5$ Transmission Time = 1

t_0 — A Begins Transmission

$t_0 + a - \epsilon$ — B Begins Transmission

$t_0 + 0.5$ — B Detects Collision

$t_0 + 1 - \epsilon$ — A Detects Collision Just Before End of Transmission

Figure 11. Baseband collision detection timing (transmission time is normalized to 1; a = propagation time). [From W. Stallings, *Local Networks: An Introduction*, Macmillan, New York, 1984. Copyright Macmillan 1984.]

(2) After transmitting the jamming signal, wait a random amount of time, then attempt to transmit again, using CSMA.

When these rules are followed, the amount of wasted bandwidth is reduced to the time that it takes to detect a collision. For proper operation of the algorithm, the minimum packet size should be sufficient to permit collision detection in the worst case. For a baseband system, with two stations that are as far apart as possible (worst case), the time that it takes to detect a collision is twice the propagation delay (Figure 11). For a broadband system, in which the worst case is two stations close together and as far as possible from the head end, the wait is four times the propagation delay from the station to the head end (Figure 12).

As with CSMA, CSMA/CD employs one of the three persistence algorithms. Unexpectedly, the most common choice is 1-persistent; it is used by both Ethernet and MITRENET, and used in the IEEE 802 standard. As was mentioned, the problem with the nonpersistent scheme is the wasted idle time. Although it is more efficient, p-persistent still may result in considerable waste. With the 1-persistent scheme, that waste is eliminated at the cost of wasted collision time.

What saves the day is that the time wasted due to collisions is mercifully short if the packets are long relative to propagation delay. With random back off, two stations involved in a collision are unlikely to collide on their next tries. To ensure stability of this back off, a technique known as binary exponential back off is used. A station attempts to transmit repeatedly in the face of repeated collisions, but the mean value of the random delay is doubled after each collision. After a number of unsuccessful attempts, the station gives up and reports an error.

Although the implementation of CSMA/CD is substantially the same for baseband and broadband, there are a few differences. One difference is the means for performing carrier sense. For baseband systems, the carrier sense operation consists of detecting

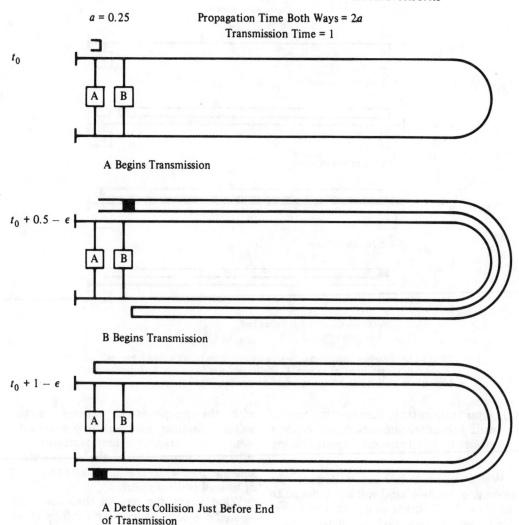

$a = 0.25$ Propagation Time Both Ways = $2a$
Transmission Time = 1

t_0

A Begins Transmission

$t_0 + 0.5 - \epsilon$

B Begins Transmission

$t_0 + 1 - \epsilon$

A Detects Collision Just Before End
of Transmission

Figure 12. Broadband collision detection timing (transmission time is normalized to 1; a = propagation time one way). [From W. Stallings, *Local Networks: An Introduction*, Macmillan, New York, 1984. Copyright Macmillan 1984.]

a stream of voltage pulses; for broadband, the RF carrier is detected.

Another difference is in collision detection (CD). In a baseband system, a collision produces higher voltage swings than those produced by a single transmitter. A transmitting transceiver detects a collision if the signal on the cable exceeds the maximum that could be produced by the transceiver alone. Attenuation presents a potential problem: If two stations that are far apart are transmitting, each station will receive a greatly attenuated signal from the other. The signal strength could be so small that

when added to the transmitted signal at the transceiver, the combined signal does not exceed the CD threshold. This is one reason that Ethernet retricts the maximum length of cable to 500 meters. Because frames may cross repeater boundaries, collisions must cross as well. Hence, if a repeater detects a collision on either cable, it must transmit a jamming signal on the other side.

There are several approaches to collision detection in broadband systems. The most common of these is to perform a bit-by-bit comparison between transmitted and received data. When a station transmits on

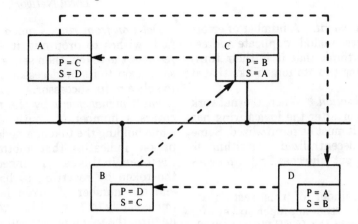

Figure 13.   Token bus.

the inbound channel, it begins to hear its own transmission on the outbound channel after a propagation delay to the head end and back. In the MITRE system, the first 16 bits of the transmitted and received signals are compared and a collision is assumed if they differ. There are several problems with this approach. The most serious is the danger that differences in signal level between colliding signals will cause the receiver to treat the weaker signal as noise, and fail to detect the collision. The cable system, with its taps, splitters, and amplifiers, must be carefully tuned so that attenuation effects and differences in transmitter signal strength do not cause this problem. Another problem for dual cable systems is that a station must simultaneously transmit and receive on the same frequency. Its two RF modems must be carefully shielded to prevent cross talk.

An alternative approach for broadband is to perform the CD function at the head end. This is most appropriate for the midsplit system, which has an active component at the head end anyway. This reduces the problem of tuning, ensuring that all stations produce approximately the same signal level at the head end, which then can detect collisions by looking for garbled data or higher-than-expected signal strength.

4.1.2 Token Bus

Token bus is a technique in which the stations on the bus or tree form a logical ring; that is, the stations are assigned positions in an ordered sequence, with the last member of the sequence followed by the first. Each station knows the identity of the stations preceding and following it (Figure 13).

A control packet known as the token regulates the right of access: When a station receives the token, it is granted control of the medium for a specified time, during which it may transmit one or more packets and may poll stations and receive responses. When the station is done, or time has expired, it passes the token on to the next station in logical sequence. Hence steady-state operation consists of alternating data transfer and token transfer phases.

Non-token-using stations are allowed on the bus, but these stations can only respond to polls or requests for acknowledgment. It should also be pointed out that the physical ordering of the stations on the bus is irrelevant and independent of the logical ordering.

This scheme requires considerable maintenance. The following functions, at a minimum, must be performed by one or more stations on the bus:

Addition to Ring.   Nonparticipating stations must periodically be granted the opportunity to insert themselves in the ring.

Deletion from Ring.   A station can voluntarily remove itself from the ring by splicing together its predecessor and successor.

Fault Management. A number of errors can occur. These include duplicate address (two stations think that it is their turn) and broken ring (no station thinks that it is its turn).

Ring Initialization. When the network is started up, or after the logical ring has broken down, it must be reinitialized. Some cooperative, decentralized algorithm is needed to sort out who goes first, who goes second, etc.

In the remainder of this section we briefly describe the approach taken for these functions in the IEEE 802 standard.

To accomplish *addition to ring*, each node in the ring is responsible for periodically granting an opportunity for new nodes to enter the ring. While holding the token, the node issues a *solicit-successor* packet, inviting nodes with an address between itself and the next node in logical sequence to request entrance. The transmitting node then waits for a period of time equal to one response window or slot time (twice the end-to-end propagation delay of the medium). If there is no request, the node passes the token to its successor as usual. If there is one request, the token holder sets its successor node to be the requesting node and transmits the token to it; the requestor sets its linkages accordingly and proceeds. If more than one node requests to enter the ring, the token holder will detect a garbled transmission. The conflict is resolved by an address-based contention scheme: The token holder transmits a *resolve-contention* packet and waits four response windows. Each requestor can respond in one of these windows, based on the first two bits of its address. If a requestor hears anything before its window comes up, it refrains from requesting entrance. If the token holder receives a valid response, it is in business; otherwise it tries again, and only those nodes that requested the first time are allowed to request this time, based on the second pair of bits in their address. This process continues until a valid request is received, no request is received, or a maximum retry count is reached. In the latter two cases, the token holder gives up and passes the token to its logical successor in the ring.

Deletion from ring is much simpler. If a node wishes to drop out, it waits until it receives the token, then sends a *set-successor* packet to its predecessor, instructing it to splice to its successor.

Fault management by the token holder covers a number of contingencies. First, while holding the token, a node may hear a packet, indicating that another node has the token. In this case, it immediately drops the token by reverting to listener mode, and the number of token holders drops immediately to 1 or 0. Upon completion of its turn, the token holder will issue a token packet to its successor. The successor should immediately issue a data or token packet. Therefore, after sending a token, the token issuer will listen for one slot time to make sure that its successor is active. This precipitates a sequence of events:

(1) If the successor node is active, the token issuer will hear a valid packet and revert to listener mode.
(2) If the issuer does not hear a valid packet, it reissues the token to the same successor one more time.
(3) After two failures, the issuer assumes that its successor has failed and issues a *who-follows* packet, asking for the identity of the node that follows the failed node. The issuer should get back a set-successor packet from the second node down the line. If so, the issuer adjusts its linkage and issues a token (back to Step 1).
(4) If the issuing node gets no response to its who-follows packets, it tries again.
(5) If the who-follows tactic fails, the node issues a solicit-successor packet with the full address range (i.e., every node is invited to respond). If this process works, a two-node ring is established and the procedure continues.
(6) If two attempts of Step 5 fail, the node assumes that a catastrophe has occurred; perhaps the node's receiver has failed. In any case, the node ceases activity and listens to the bus.

Logical *ring initialization* occurs when one or more stations detect a lack of bus activity lasting longer than a time-out value: The token has been lost. This can

Table 6. Ring Access Methods

Characteristic	Register insertion	Slotted ring	Token ring
Transmit opportunity	Idle state plus empty buffer	Empty slot	Delimiter with free indicator
Frame purge responsibility	Receiver or transmitter	Transmitter node	Transmitter node
Principal advantage	Maximum ring utilization	Simplicity	Regulated but fair access
Principal disadvantage	Purge mechanism	Bandwidth waste	Token monitor required

result from a number of causes, for example, the network has just been powered up, or a token-holding station fails. Once its time-out expires, a node will issue a *claim-token* packet. Contending claimants are resolved in a manner similar to the response-window process.

4.1.3 CSMA/CD versus Token Bus

At present, CSMA/CD and token bus are the two principal contenders for medium access control technique on bus/tree topologies. In this section we examine their comparative disadvantages and advantages.

It should be obvious that the principal disadvantage of token bus is its complexity; the logic at each station far exceeds that required for CSMA/CD. A second disadvantage is the overhead involved; under lightly loaded conditions, a station may have to wait through many fruitless token passes for a turn.

Indeed, in considering these disadvantages, it would seem difficult to make a case for token bus. Such a case can be made, however [Miller and Thompson 1982; Stieglitz 1981], and includes the following elements. First, it is easy to regulate the traffic in a token bus system; different stations can be allowed to hold the token for differing amounts of time. Second, unlike CSMA/CD, there is no minimum packet length requirement with token bus. Third, the requirement for listening while talking imposes physical and electrical constraints on the CSMA/CD system that do not apply to token systems. Finally, token bus is significantly superior to CSMA/CD under heavy loads, as discussed below.

Another advertised advantage of token bus is that it is "deterministic"; that is, there is a known upper bound to the amount of time that any station must wait

before transmitting. This upper bound is known because each station in the logical ring only can hold the token for a specified time. In contrast, the delay time with CSMA/CD can only be expressed statistically, and since every attempt to transmit under CSMA/CD can, in principle, produce a collision, there is a possibility that a station could be shut out indefinitely. For process control and other real-time applications, this "nondeterministic" behavior is undesirable. Unfortunately, in actual application there is always a finite possibility of transmission error, which can cause a lost token. This adds a statistical component to the behavior of a token bus system.

4.2 Ring LANs

Over the years, a number of different algorithms have been proposed for controlling access to the ring (surveys are presented by Penny and Baghdadi [1979] and Liu [1978]). The three most common ring access techniques are discussed in this section: token ring, register insertion, and slotted ring. In Table 6 these three methods are compared on a number of characteristics:

Transmit Opportunity. When may a repeater insert a packet onto the ring?

Packet Purge Responsibility. Who removes a packet from a ring to avoid its circulating indefinitely?

Number of Packets on Ring. This depends not only on the "bit length" of the ring relative to the packet length, but on the access method.

Principal Advantage.

Principal Disadvantage.

The significance of the table entries will become clear as the discussion proceeds.

4.2.1 Token Ring

The token ring is probably the oldest ring control technique, originally proposed in 1969 [Farmer and Newhall 1969] and referred to as the Newhall ring. This has become the most popular ring access technique in the United States. Prime Computer [Gordon et al. 1980] and Apollo both market token ring products, and IBM seems committed to such a product [Rauch-Hinden 1982]. This technique is the ring access method selected for standardization by the IEEE 802 Local Network Standards Committee [Andrews and Shultz 1982; Dixon 1982; Markov and Strole 1982].

The token ring technique is based on the use of a small token packet that circulates around the ring: When all stations are idle, the token packet is labeled as a "free" token. A station wishing to transmit waits until it detects the token passing by, alters the bit pattern of the token from "free token" to "busy token," and transmits a packet immediately following the busy token (Figure 14).

There is now no free token on the ring, and so other stations wishing to transmit must wait. The packet on the ring will make a round trip and be purged by the transmitting station. The transmitting station will insert a new free token on the ring when both of the following conditions have been met:

- the station has completed transmission of its packet, and
- the busy token has returned to the station.

If the bit length of the ring is less than the packet length, then the first condition implies the second. If not, then a station could release a free token after it has finished transmitting but before it receives its own busy token. However, this might complicate error recovery, since several packets will be on the ring at the same time. In any case, the use of a token guarantees that only one station at a time may transmit.

When a transmitting station releases a new free token, the next station downstream with data to send will be able to seize the token and transmit.

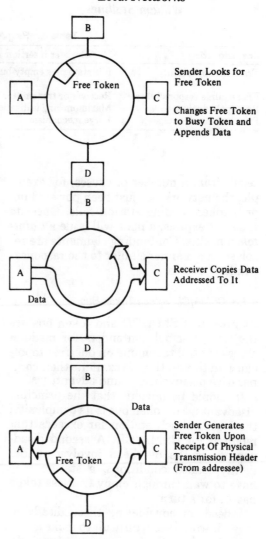

Figure 14. Token ring.

One nice feature of token ring, and all ring protocols, is this: If the source station has responsibility for removing the circulating packet, then the destination station can set bits in the packet as it goes by to inform the sender of the result of the transmission. For example, the IEEE 802 standard includes three such control bits in the packet format: address recognized (A), packet copied (C), and error (E). The A and C bits allow the source station to differentiate three conditions:

- station nonexistent/nonactive,
- station exists but packet not copied,
- packet received.

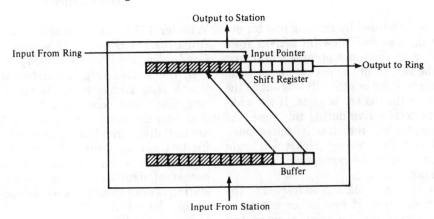

Figure 15.   Register insertion technique.

The E bit can be set by any station if an error is detected.

There are two error conditions that could cause the token ring system to break down. One is the loss of the token so that no token is circulating; the other is a persistent busy token that circulates endlessly. To overcome these problems the IEEE 802 standard specifies that one station be designated as "active monitor." The monitor detects the lost token condition using a time-out, and recovers by issuing a new free token. To detect a circulating busy token, the monitor sets a "monitor bit" to one on any passing busy token. If it sees a busy token with the bit already set, it knows that the transmitting station has failed to absorb its packet and recovers by changing the busy token to a free token.

Other stations on the ring have the role of passive monitor. Their primary job is to detect failure of the active monitor and assume that role. A contention-resolution algorithm is used to determine which station takes over.

The token ring technique shares many of the advantages of token bus. Perhaps its principal advantage is that traffic can be regulated, either by allowing stations to transmit differing numbers of data when they receive the token, or by setting priorities so that higher priority stations have first claim on a circulating token.

The principal disadvantage of token ring is the requirement for token maintenance.

The active/passive monitor system described above must be employed for error recovery.

4.2.2 Register Insertion

The register insertion strategy was originally developed by researchers at Ohio State University [Hafner et al. 1974], and is the technique used in the IBM Series 1 product [IBM 1982] and a Swiss product called SILK [Huber et al. 1983]. It derives its name from the shift register associated with each station on the ring, which is equal in size to the maximum packet length, and used for temporarily holding packets that circulate past the station. In addition, the station has a buffer for storing locally produced packets.

The register insertion ring can be explained with reference to Figure 15, which shows the shift register and buffer at one station. First, consider the case in which the station has no data to send, but is merely handling packets of data that circulate by its position. When the ring is idle, the input pointer points to the rightmost position of the shift register, indicating that it is empty. When a packet arrives along the ring, it is inserted bit by bit in the shift register, with the input pointer shifting left for each bit. The packet begins with an address field. As soon as the entire address field is in the buffer, the station can determine if it is the addressee. If not, then the

Computing Surveys, Vol. 16, No. 1, March 1984

packet is forwarded by shifting one bit out on the right as each new bit arrives from the left, with the input pointer stationary. After the last bit of the packet has arrived, the station continues to shift bits out to the right until the packet is gone. If no additional packets arrive during this time, the input pointer will return to its initial position. Otherwise, a second packet will begin to accumulate in the register as the first is shifted out.

If the arriving packet is addressed to the node in question, it can either erase the address bits from the shift register and divert the remainder of the packet to itself, thus purging the packet from the ring, or retransmit the data as before, while copying it to the local station.

Now consider the case in which the station has data to transmit. A packet to be transmitted is placed in the output buffer. If the line is idle and the shift register is empty, the packet can be transferred immediately to the shift register. If the packet consists of some length n bits, less than the maximum frame size, and if at least n bits are empty in the shift register, the n bits are parallel transferred to the empty portion of the shift register immediately adjacent to the full portion; the input pointer is adjusted accordingly.

The principal advantage of the register insertion technique is that it achieves the maximum ring utilization of any of the methods. A station may transmit whenever the ring is idle at its location, and multiple packets may be on the ring at any one time.

The principal disadvantage is the purge mechanism. Allowing multiple packets on the ring requires the recognition of an address prior to removal of a packet. If a packet's address field is damaged, it could circulate indefinitely. One possible solution is the use of an error-detecting code on the address field.

4.2.3 Slotted Ring

The slotted ring technique was first developed by Pierce [1972], and is sometimes referred to as the Pierce loop. Most of the development work on this technique was done at the University of Cambridge in England [Hopper 1977; Wilkes and Wheeler 1979], and a number of British firms market commercial versions of the Cambridge ring [Heywood 1981].

In the slotted ring, a number of fixed-length slots circulate continuously on the ring. Each slot contains a leading bit to designate the slot as empty or full. All slots are initially marked empty. A station wishing to transmit waits until an empty slot arrives, marks the slot full, and inserts a packet of data as the slot goes by. The station cannot transmit another packet until this slot returns. The slot may also contain response bits, which can be set on the fly by the addressed station to indicate accepted, busy, or rejected. The full slot makes a complete round trip, to be marked empty again by the source. Each station knows the total number of slots on the ring and can thus clear the full/empty bit that it had set as it goes by. Once the now empty slot goes by, the station is free to transmit again.

In the Cambridge ring, each slot contains room for one source and one destination address byte, two data bytes, and five control bits for a total length of 37 bits.

The Cambridge ring contains several interesting features. A station may decide that it wishes to receive data only from one other station. To accomplish this each station includes a source select register. When this register contains all ones, the station will receive a packet addressed to it from any source; when it contains all zeros, the station will not accept packets from any source. Otherwise the station is open to receive packets only from the source whose address is specified by the register.

In addition, the Cambridge ring specifies two response bits in each packet to differentiate four conditions:

- destination nonexistent/nonactive,
- packet accepted,
- destination exists but packet not accepted,
- destination busy.

Finally, the Cambridge ring includes a monitor, whose task it is to empty a slot that is persistently full.

The principal disadvantage of the slotted ring is that it is wasteful of bandwidth.

First, a slot typically contains more over-head bits than data bits. Second, a station may send only one packet per round-trip ring time. If only one or a few stations have packets to transmit, many of the slots will circulate empty.

The principal advantage of the slotted ring appears to be its simplicity. The inter-action with the ring at each node is mini-mized, improving reliability.

4.3 HSLNs

In this section, we review the only tech-nique that thus far has gained favor for HSLNs, known as prioritized CSMA. It is also referred to as CSMA with collision avoidance. The technique will be described in terms of the ANSI draft standard [Burr 1983]; the algorithm for HYPERchannel is very similar.

The protocol is based on CSMA; that is, a station wishing to transmit listens to the medium and defers if a transmission is in progress. In addition, an algorithm is used that specifically seeks to avoid collisions when the medium is found idle by multiple stations.

For this scheme, the stations or ports form an ordered logical sequence (PORT(1), PORT(2), ..., PORT(N)), which need not correspond to physical po-sition of the bus.

The scheme is initialized after each transmission by any port. Following ini-tialization, each station, in turn, may trans-mit if none of the stations in sequence before it have done so. So PORT($I + 1$) waits until after PORT(I) has had a chance to transmit. The waiting time consists of

(1) the earliest time at which PORT(I) could begin transmitting (which de-pends on the transmission opportunity for PORT($I - 1$)), plus
(2) a port delay time during which PORT(I) has the opportunity to trans-mit, plus
(3) the propagation delay between the two ports.

As we shall see, this rather simple concept becomes more complex as we consider its refinements.

The basic rule can be described as fol-lows. After any transmission, PORT(1) has the right to transmit. If it fails to do so in a reasonable time, then PORT(2) has the chance, and so on. If any port transmits, the system reinitializes.

The first refinement is to permit multi-frame dialogues. To accommodate this, an additional rule is added: After any trans-mission, the port receiving that transmis-sion has the first right to transmit. If that port fails to transmit, then it is the turn of PORT(1), and so on. This will permit two ports to seize the medium, with one port sending data frames and the other sending acknowledgment frames.

The second refinement is to accommo-date the case in which nobody has a frame to transmit. HYPERchannel solves this by entering a free-for-all period, in which col-lisions are allowed. ANSI has a more ele-gant solution: If none of the stations transmit when they have an opportunity, then the highest priority station times out and transmits a dummy frame. This serves to reinitialize the network and start over.

With these two refinements, we can de-pict the MAC protocol as a simple sequence of events:

1. Medium is active
2. Medium Goes Idle
   If Receiver Transmits,
      Then Go To 1
      Else Go To 3
3. If PORT(1) Transmits, ·
      Then Go To 1
      Else Go To 4

$$\vdots$$

N + 3. If No Port Transmits, Then Go To 1.

The third refinement has to do with bal-ancing this scheme, which at this point is biased to the lower number ports [PORT(1) *always* gets a shot, for exam-ple]. To make the scheme fair, a port that has just transmitted should not try again until everyone else has had a chance.

To concisely describe the algorithm with these three refinements, we need to define some quantities:

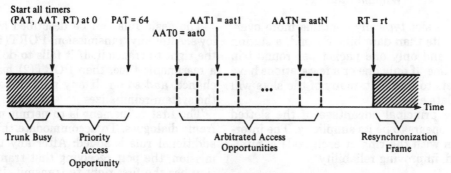

Figure 16. Operation of the ANSI medium access control protocol.

Priority Access Opportunity. A period of time granted to a port after it receives a frame. May be used to acknowledge frame and/or continue a multiframe dialogue.

Priority Access Timer (PAT). Used to time priority access opportunities: 64-bit times.

Arbitrated Access Opportunity. A period of time granted to each port in sequence, during which it may initate a transmission: 16-bit times. Assigned to individual ports to avoid collisions.

Arbitrated Access Timer (AAT). Used to provide each port with a unique, non-overlapping, arbitrated access opportunity.

Resynchronization Timer (RT). Time by which the latest possible arbitrated transmission should have been received. Used to reset all timers.

Arbiter Wait Flag (WF). Used to enforce fairness. When a port transmits, its WF is set so that it will not attempt another arbitrated transmission until all other ports have an opportunity.

Figure 16 depicts the process of this refined algorithm. For the timers listed, we use the convention that uppercase letters refer to the variable name and lowercase letters to a specific value. A timer that reaches a specified maximum value is said to have expired.

This technique seems well suited to HSLN requirements. The provision for multiframe dialogue permits rapid transfer of large files. A typical HSLN consists of only a small number of stations; under these circumstances, the round-robin ac-

cess technique will not result in undue delays.

5. COMPARATIVE PERFORMANCE OF LAN PROTOCOLS

Although there have been a number of performance studies focusing on a single protocol, there have been few systematic attempts to analyze the relative performance of the various local network protocols. In what follows, we look at the results of several carefully done studies that have produced comparative results. A lengthy survey of performance studies is found in Tropper [1981].

5.1 CSMA/CD, Token Bus, and Token Ring

One important study was done by a group at Bell Laboratories, under the sponsorship of the IEEE 802 Local Network Standards Committee [Arthurs and Stuck 1981; Stuck 1983a, 1983b]. Naturally enough, the study analyzed the three protocols being standardized by IEEE 802: CSMA/CD, token bus, and token ring. Two cases of message arrival statistics are employed. In the first case, only one out of one hundred stations has data to transmit, and is always ready to transmit. In such a case, one would hope that the network would not be the bottleneck, but could easily keep up with one station. In the second case, all one hundred stations always have data to transmit. This represents an extreme of congestion, and one would expect that the network may be a bottleneck. In both cases, the one station or one hundred stations provide enough

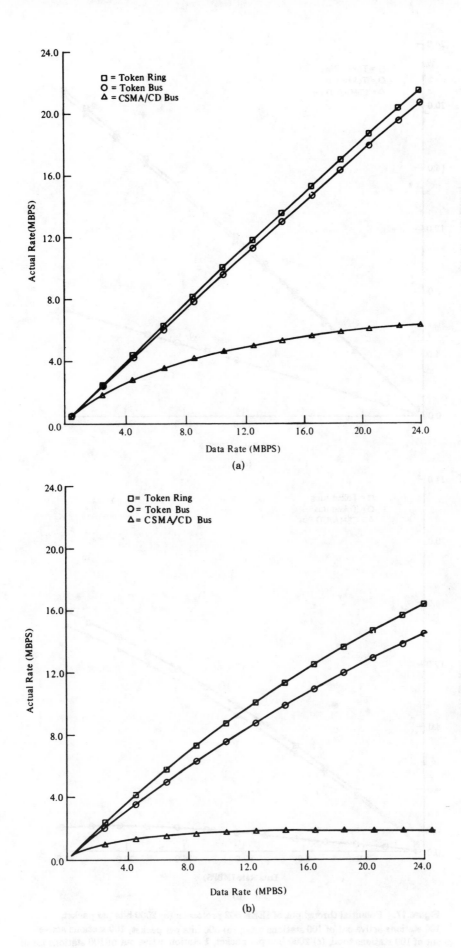

(a)

(b)

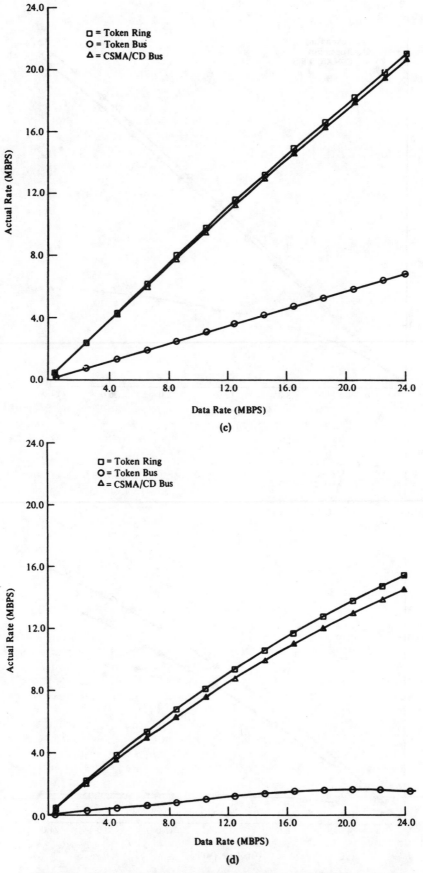

Figure 17. Potential throughput of IEEE 802 protocols: (a) 2000 bits per packet, 100 stations active out of 100 stations total; (b) 500 bits per packet, 100 stations active out of 100 stations total; (c) 2000 bits per packet, 1 station active out of 100 stations total; (d) 500 bits per packet, 1 station active out of 100 stations total.

input to fully utilize the network. Hence the results are a measure of maximum potential utilization. In addition, results were obtained by using two different packet sizes to determine the relative effect of this parameter on the three protocols. Thus a total of four different cases was analyzed.

The results are given in Figure 17, which shows the actual data transmission rate versus the transmission speed of the medium for the four cases. The length of the medium (bus or ring) is assumed to be 2 kilometers. Note that the abscissa in the plots is not offered load but the actual capacity of the medium. Three systems are examined: token ring with a 1-bit latency per station, token bus, and CSMA/CD. The analysis yields the following conclusions:

(1) For the given parameters, the smaller the mean packet length, the greater is the difference in maximum mean throughput rate between token passing and CSMA/CD. This reflects the fact that, for a given amount of data, smaller packets mean more packets and hence more collisions under CSMA/ CD.

(2) Token ring is the least sensitive to workload.

(3) CSMA/CD offers the shortest delay under light load, whereas it is most sensitive under heavy load to the workload.

Note also that in the case of a single station transmitting, token bus is significantly less efficient than the other two protocols. This is so because the assumption is made that the delay in token processing is greater for token bus than that for token ring.

Another interesting phenomenon is seen most clearly in Figure 17b. For a CSMA/ CD system under these conditions, the maximum effective throughput at 5 Mbps is only about 1.25 Mbps. If expected load is, say, 0.75 Mbps, this configuration may be perfectly adequate. If however, the load is expected to grow to 2 Mbps, raising the network data rate to 10 Mbps or even 20 Mbps will not accommodate the increase! The reason for this disparity between CSMA/CD and token passing (bus or ring)

under heavy load has to do with the instability of CSMA/CD. As offered load increases, so does throughput, until, beyond some maximum value, throughput actually declines as offered load increases. This results from the fact that there is an increased frequency of collisions: More packets are offered, but fewer successfully escape collision. Worse, those packets that do collide must be retransmitted, further increasing the load.

5.2 CSMA/CD and Ring Protocols

It is far more difficult to do a comparative performance of the three major ring protocols than to do a comparison of bus and token ring protocols, as the results depend on a number of parameters unique to each protocol, for example,

- *Token Ring.* Size of token, token processing time.
- *Slotted Ring.* Slot size, overhead bits per slot.
- *Register Insertion.* Register size.

Although there have been a number of studies on each one of the techniques, few have attempted pairwise comparisons, much less a three-way analysis. The most systematic work in this area has been done by Liu and his associates [Liu et al. 1982]. Liu made comparisons based on analytic models developed by others for token ring, slotted ring, and CSMA/CD, plus his own formulations for register insertion. He then obtained very good corroboration from simulation studies.

Figure 18 is a summary of the results, on the basis of the assumption that relatively large packets are used and that register insertion ring packets are removed by the destination station, whereas slotted ring and token ring packets are removed by the source station. This is clearly an unfair comparison since register insertion under this scheme does not include acknowledgments, whereas token ring and slotted ring do. The figure does show that slotted ring is the poorest performer, and that register insertion can carry a load greater than 1.0, since the protocol permits multiple packets to circulate.

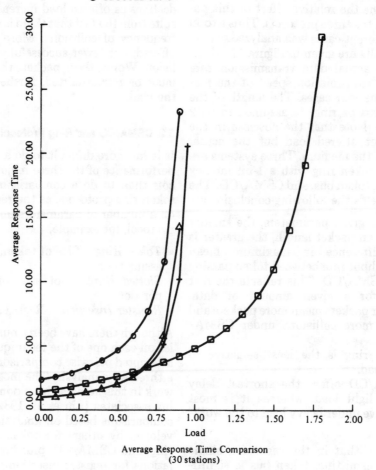

△ CSMA/CD
+ TOKEN-PASSING
□ REGISTER-INSERTION
○ SLOTTED RING

Average Response Time Comparison
(30 stations)

Figure 18. Delay for various protocols.

Bux performed an analysis comparing token ring, slotted ring, and CSMA/CD, yielding results similar to those of Liu [Bux 1981]. He confirmed several important conclusions: that token ring suffers greater delay than CSMA/CD at light load but less delay and more stable throughput at heavy loads, and further, that token ring has superior delay characteristics to slotted ring.

It is difficult to draw conclusions from the efforts made thus far. The slotted ring seems to be the least desirable over a broad range of parameter values, owing to the considerable overhead associated with each

small packet. As between token ring and register insertion, the evidence suggests that at least for some sets of parameter values, register insertion gives superior throughput and delay performance.

6. STANDARDS

6.1 Local Area Networks

The key to the development of the LAN market is the availability of a low-cost interface; the cost to connect equipment to a LAN must be much less than the cost of the actual equipment. This requirement, as

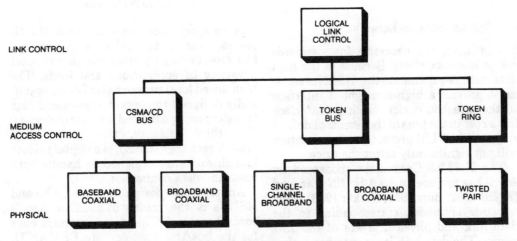

LINK CONTROL

MEDIUM
ACCESS CONTROL

PHYSICAL

Figure 19. The IEEE 802 standard.

well as the complexity of the LAN protocols, dictates a very large scale integration (VLSI) solution. However, chip manufacturers are reluctant to commit the necessary resources unless there is a high-volume market. A LAN standard would ensure that volume and also enable equipment of a variety of manufacturers to intercommunicate.

This is the rationale of the IEEE 802 committee [Clancy et al. 1982], which has developed a set of standards for LANs [IEEE 1983]. The standards are in the form of a three-layer communications architecture with a treelike expansion of options from top to bottom (Figure 19). The three layers, known as logical link control, medium access control, and physical, encompass the functionality of the lowest two layers (data link and physical) of the International Organization for Standardization (ISO) reference model.

The logical link control (LLC) layer provides for the exchange of data between service access points (SAPs), which are multiplexed over a single physical connection to the LAN. The LLC provides for both a connectionless, datagramlike service, and a connection-oriented, virtual-circuit-like service. Both the protocol and the frame format resemble HDLC.

At the medium access control layer, there are three standards: CSMA/CD has con-

verged with the Ethernet specification, which is well suited to typical office applications, and two forms of token access have been standardized, for time-critical applications, such as process control, as well as for office applications.

For CSMA/CD, a 10-Mbps baseband physical layer has been approved. Several broadband options are still under consideration, ranging in data rate per channel from 1 to 5 Mbps.

For token bus, three physical layers are provided as options. The simplest and least expensive is a single-channel broadband system using frequency shift keying (FSK) at 1 Mbps. A more expensive version of this system runs at 5 or 10 Mbps and is intended to be easily upgradable to the final option, which is multichannel broadband. The latter provides data rates of 1, 5, or 10 Mbps.

For token ring, twisted pair has been defined, which will provide data rates of 1 and 4 Mbps.

The range of options offered may be disheartening to the reader. However, the IEEE 802 Committee has at least narrowed the alternatives, and it is to be expected that the bulk of future LAN development work will be within the scope laid down by IEEE 802.

More detailed discussions of the standard may be found in Nelson [1983], Graube [1982], Allan [1982], and Myers [1982].

6.2 High-Speed Local Networks

For HSLNs, the necessity for standards seems less compelling. Because of the high data rate requirement, the HSLN vendor must provide a high-throughput interface to the attached device. Such an interface has a cost in the tens of thousands of dollars range, and a VLSI protocol implementation will not significantly affect the price.

The X.3T9.5 Committee sponsored by ANSI has prepared a draft HSLN standard [ANSI 1982; Burr 1983; Parker 1983] using a two-layer model, corresponding to the data link and physical layers of the ISO model. The data link layer specifies a simple connectionless service. The physical layer specification includes the collision-avoidance protocol discussed earlier, and it specifies a data rate of 50 Mbps.

7. SUMMARY

Local networks can be characterized, in large measure, by the transmission medium and topology employed. Common combinations are

Twisted Pair Bus or Ring. An inexpensive, easily installed network for a small number of low-cost, low-throughput devices.

Baseband Coaxial Cable Bus or Ring. A general-purpose network; supports moderate numbers of devices over moderate distances; suitable for many office applications.

High-Speed Baseband Coaxial Cable Bus. Supports a small number of high-throughput devices; suitable for computer-room requirements.

Broadband Coaxial Cable Bus. The most flexible and general-purpose network; supports a large number of devices over a wide area, and can handle a variety of traffic requirements using FDM.

Twisted Pair Star. The architecture of the CBX. Suitable for supporting at moderate cost a large number of limited throughput devices.

For descriptive clarity, and to reflect differences in standards and technology, three categories of local networks can be defined.

The category local area network (LAN) covers a variety of local networks using a bus, tree, or ring topology and that support a variety of applications and loads. The high-speed local network (HSLN) is specifically designed to support high-speed data transfer among a limited number of devices. The third category, the computerized branch exchange (CBX), is a digital private branch exchange designed to handle both voice and data connections.

An important design issue for LANs and HSLNs is the choice of medium access control protocol. The most important ones for the bus/tree topology are CSMA/CD, token bus, and collision avoidance, and, for the ring topology, token ring, register insertion, and slotted ring.

The literature on local networks is growing as rapidly as the field itself. Annotated bibliographies may be found in Shoch [1980] and Stallings [1983]. Stallings [1984] is a textbook on the subject.

REFERENCES

ALLAN, R. 1982. Local-area networks spur moves to standardize data communications among computers and peripherals. *Electron. Des.* Dec. 23, 107–112.

ALLAN, R. 1983. Local networks: Fiber optics gains momentum. *Electron. Des.* June 23.

ANDREWS, D. W., AND SCHULTZ, G. D. 1982. A token-ring architecture for local area networks: An update. In *Proceedings of COMPCON Fall 82* (Washington, D.C., Sept. 20–23). IEEE Computer Society, Los Angeles, pp. 615–624.

ANSI 1982. *Draft Proposed American National Standard Local Distributed Data Interface.* American National Standards Institute, New York.

ARTHURS, E., AND STUCK, B. W. 1981. A theoretical performance analysis of polling and carrier sense collision detection communication systems. In *Proceedings of the 7th Symposium on Data Communications* (Mexico City, Oct. 27–29). *Comput. Commun. Rev. 11*, 4, 156–163.

BOSEN, R. 1981. A low-speed local net for under $100 per station. *Data Commun. 10*, 2 (Dec.), 81–83.

BURR, W. 1983. An overview of the proposed american national standard for local distributed data interfaces. *Commun. ACM, 26*, 10 (Oct.), 554–561.

BUX, W. 1981. Local-area subnetworks: A performance comparison. *IEEE Trans. Commun. COM-29*, 10 (Oct.).

BUX, W., CLOSS, F., JANSON, P. A., KUMMERLE, K., MILLER, H. R., AND ROTHAUSER, H. 1982. A local-area communication network based on a reliable token ring system. In *Proceedings of the International Symposium on Local Computer Networks.*

CHRISTENSEN, G. S. 1979. Links between computer-room networks. *Telecommunications 13*, 2 (Feb.), 47–50.

CLANCY, G. J., et al. 1982. The IEEE 802 Committee states its case concerning its local network standards efforts. *Data Commun. 11*, 4 (Apr.), 13, 238.

COOPER, E. 1982. 13 often-asked questions about broadband. *Data Commun. 11*, 4 (Apr.), 137–142.

COOPER, E. 1983. Broadband network design: Issues and answers. *Comput. Des. 22*, 3 (Mar.), 209–216.

COOPER, E., AND EDHOLM, P. 1983. Design issues in broadband local networks. *Data Commun. 12*, 2 (Feb.), 109–122.

DEC 1980. *The Ethernet: A Local Area Network Data Link Layer and Physical Layer Specifications*, Sept. 30. Digital Equipment Corp., Intil Corp., and Xerox Corp., Digital Equipment Corp., Maynard, Mass.

DERFLER, F., AND STALLINGS, W. 1983. *A Manager's Guide to Local Networks.* Prentice-Hall, New York.

DINESON, M. A., AND PICAZO, J. J. 1980. Broadband technology magnifies local network capability. *Data Commun. 9*, 2 (Feb.), 61–79.

DIXON, R. C. 1982. Ring network topology for local data communications. In *Proceedings of COMPCON, Fall 82* (Washington, D.C., Sept. 20–23). IEEE Computer Society, Los Angeles, pp. 591–605.

FARMER, W. D., AND NEWHALL, E. E. 1969. An experimental distributed switching system to handle bursty computer traffic. In *Proceedings of the ACM Symposium on Problems in the Optimization of Data Communications.* ACM, New York.

FORBES, J. 1981. RF prescribed for many local links. *Data Commun. 10*, 9 (Sept.).

FRANTA, W. R., AND CHLAMTEC, I. 1981. *Local Networks.* Lexington Books, Lexington, Mass.

FREEDMAN, D. 1983. Fiber optics shine in local area networks. *Mini-Micro Syst. 16*, 10 (Sept.), 225–230.

GORDON, R. L., FARR, W. W., AND LEVINE, P. 1980. Ringnet: A packet switched local network with decentralized control. *Comput. Networks 3*, 373–379.

GRAUBE, M. 1982. Local area nets: A pair of standards. *IEEE Spectrum* (June), 60–64.

HAFNER, E. R., NENADAL, Z., AND TSCHANZ, M. 1974. A digital loop communications system. *IEEE Trans. Commun. COM-22*, 6 (June), 877–881.

HAHN, M., AND BELANGER, P. 1981. Network minimizes overhead of small computers. *Electronics*, Aug. 25.

HEYWOOD, P. 1981. The Cambridge ring is still making the rounds. *Data Commun. 10*, 7 (July), 32–36.

HOHN, W. C. 1980. The Control Data loosely coupled network lower level protocols. In *Proceedings of the National Computer Conference* (Anaheim, Calif., May 19–22), vol. 49. AFIPS Press, Reston, Va., 129–134.

HOPKINS, G. T. 1979. Multimode communications on the MITRENET. *Proceedings of the Local Area Communications Network Symposium* (Boston, May). Mitre Corp., McLean, Va., pp. 169–178.

HOPKINS, G. T., AND MEISNER, N. B. 1982. Choosing between broadband and baseband local networks. *Mini-Micro Syst. 16*, 7 (June).

HOPPER, A. 1977. Data ring at Computer Laboratory, University of Cambridge. In *Local Area Networking.* NBS Publ. National Bureau of Standards, Washington, D.C., pp. 500–531, 11–16.

HUBER, D., STEINLIN, W., AND WILD, P. 1983. SILK: An implementation of a buffer insertion ring. *IEEE J. Selected Areas Commun. SAC-1*, 5 (Nov.), 766–774.

IBM CORP. 1982. *IBM Series/1 Local Communications Controller Feature Description.* GA34-0142-2. IBM Corporation.

IEEE 1983. *IEEE Project 802, Local Network Standards.* Institute of Electrical and Electronic Engineers, New York.

KRUTSCH, T. E. 1981. A user speaks out: Broadband or baseband for local nets? *Data Commun. 10*, 12 (Dec.), 105–112.

LIU, M. T. 1978. Distributed loop computer networks. In *Advances in Computers*, vol. 17. Academic Press, New York, pp. 163–221.

LIU, M. T., HILAL, W., AND GROOMES, B. H. 1982. Performance evaluation of channel access protocols for local computer networks. In *Proceedings of COMPCON FALL 82* (Washington, D.C., Sept. 20–23). IEEE Computer Society, Los Angeles, pp. 417–426.

LUCZAK, E. C. 1978. Global bus computer communication techniques. In *Proceedings of the Symposium on Computer Networks* (Gaithersburg, Md., Dec.). IEEE Computer Society, Los Angeles, pp. 58–67.

MALONE, J. 1981. The microcomputer connection to local networks. *Data Commun. 10*, 12 (Dec.), 101–104.

MARKOV, J. D., AND STROLE, N. C. 1982. Token-ring local area networks: A perspective. In *Proceedings of COMPCON FALL 82* (Washington, D.C., Sept. 20–23). IEEE Computer Society, Los Angeles, pp. 606–614.

METCALFE, R. M., AND BOGGS, D. R. 1976. Ethernet: Distributed packet switching for local computer networks. *Commun. ACM 19*, 7 (July), 395–404.

METCALFE, R. M., BOGGS, D. R., THACKER, C. P., AND LAMPSON, B. W. 1977. Multipoint data communication system with collision detection. U.S. Patent 4,063,220.

MILLER, C. K., AND THOMPSON, D. M. 1982. Making a case for token passing in local networks. *Data Commun.* 11, 3 (Mar.), 79–88.

MYERS, W. 1982. Towards a local network standard. *IEEE Micro 2*, 3 (Aug.), 28–45.

NELSON, J. 1983. 802: A progress report. *Datamation* (Sept.), 136–152.

PARKER, R. 1983. Committees push to standardize disk I/O. *Comput. Des. 22*, 3 (Mar.), 30–34.

PENNY, B. K., AND BAGHDADI, A. A. 1979. Survey of computer communications loop networks. *Comput. Commun. 2*, 4 (Aug.), 165–180; 2, 4 (Oct.), 224–241.

PIERCE, J. R. 1972. Network for block switches of data. *Bell Syst. Tech. J. 51*, 6 (July–Aug.).

RAUCH-HINDIN, W. 1982. IBM's local network scheme. *Data Commun. 11*, 5 (May), 65–70.

RAWSON, E., AND METCALFE, R. 1978. Fibernet: Multimode optical fibers for local computer networks. *IEEE Trans. Commun. COM-26*, 7 (July), 983–990.

ROMAN, G. S. 1977. *The design of broadband coaxial cable networks for multimode communications.* MITRE Tech. Rep. MTR-3527. Mitre Corp., McLean, Va.

ROSENTHAL, R., Ed. 1982. The selection of local area computer networks. NBS Special Publ. 500-96, National Bureau of Standards, Washington, D.C., Nov.

SALTZER, J. H., AND CLARK, D. D. 1981. Why a ring? In *Proceedings of the 7th Symposium on Data Communications* (Mexico City, Oct. 27–29). *Comput. Commun. Rev. 11*, 4, 211–217.

SALTZER, J. H., AND POGRAN, K. T. 1979. A star-shaped ring network with high maintainability. In *Proceedings of the Symposium on Local Area Communications Network* (Boston, May). Mitre Corp., McLean, Va., pp. 179–190.

SALWEN, H. 1983. In praise of ring architecture for local area networks. *Comput. Des. 22*, 3 (Mar.), 183–192.

SHOCH, J. F. 1980. *An Annotated Bibliography on Local Computer Networks.* Xerox Palo Alto Research Center, Palo Alto, Calif., Apr.

SHOCH, J. F., DALA, Y. K., AND REDELL, D. D. 1982. Evolution of the Ethernet local computer network. *Computer 15*, 8 (Aug.), pp. 1–27.

STAHLMAN, M. 1982. Inside Wang's local net architecture. *Data Commun. 11*, 1 (Jan.), 85–90.

STALLINGS, W. 1983. *Tutorial: Local Network Technology.* IEEE Computer Society Press, Silver Spring, Md.

STALLINGS, W. 1984. *Local Networks: An Introduction.* Macmillan, New York.

STIEGLITZ, M. 1981. Local network access tradeoffs. *Comput. Des. 20*, 12 (Oct.), 163–168.

STUCK, B. 1983a. Which local net bus access is most sensitive to congestion? *Data Commun. 12*, 1 (Jan.), 107–120.

STUCK, B. 1983b. Calculating the maximum mean data rate in local area networks. *Computer 16*, 5 (May), 72–76.

THORNTON, J. E. 1980. Back-end network approaches. *Computer 13*, 2 (Feb.), 10–17.

TROPPER, C. 1981. *Local Computer Network Technologies.* Academic Press, New York.

WILKES, M. V., AND WHEELER, D. J. 1979. The Cambridge digital communication ring. In *Proceedings of the Symposium on Local Area Communications Network* (Boston, May). Mitre Corp., McLean, Va., pp. 47–62.

YEN, C., AND CRAWFORD, R. 1983. Distribution and equalization of signal on coaxial cables used in 10 Mbits baseband local area networks. *IEEE Trans. Commun. COM-31*, 10 (Oct.), 1181–1186.

Received January 1983; final revision accepted March 1984

Charles Wirl, Wilco Communications Inc., Sunnyvale, Calif.

What's the best way to wire a new building for data?

An answer for some might as well be a crystal ball, for others a dart board. But more often today, early planning pays off.

Inside wiring

Data is transmitted over so many different types of cable—coaxial, twinaxial, even triaxial, shielded and unshielded twisted pair, optical fiber—that the coexistence of multiple cable types in a single location is likely to be the rule rather than the exception. And that age-old debate over what type of wiring to run in a new building—to accommodate current and future voice and data needs—is more complex and controversial today than ever before.

Installing and operating a multiplicity of cable types clearly is something to avoid whenever possible: Effective space utilization, record keeping, and cost accounting all become increasingly more difficult. But it is getting tougher to inhibit the proliferation of transmission media, especially with the boom in local network offerings. The number of local network installations appears to be growing conversely with the time it takes to install them. Indeed, the local network has become a quick fix, a way to rapidly obtain a wideband short-distance data communications network.

Installation and planning, however, are necessarily interdependent. While the cost of any initial cabling installation must be taken into consideration, the impact and eventual cost of future changes must also be factored into the analytical equations used to select a local wiring scheme. It is not unusual today for 50 percent of the telephones and data terminals already in place to be moved each year, as offices and equipment are relocated. Moreover, the obstacles to connectivity—increased wiring complexity and loosely organized wiring plans—inherent in modern communications device designs invariably cause degradation in a network's effectiveness.

To make the task more manageable and predictable, careful early planning is an important step in selecting and installing cost-effective wiring plans that anticipate the present and future needs of voice and data users. The successful communications managers are learning this. Network designers and facilities planners are continually looking for better ways to plan and wire—and even rewire—their buildings.

Key ingredients

Proper installation planning starts with the understanding that to be used to its best advantage a building's wiring space must accommodate the tenant's short- and long-term communications requirements. Many other issues and factors, of course, will determine how well the job gets done. These factors will include the type and scope of planning resources available, time, the qualifications of the installer, and the frequently overlooked contractual relationship between the building's owner and the tenant.

Effective planning anticipates future network development and expansion. Basing design decisions on the premise that an expanding communications network will almost certainly continue to grow can never hurt. Adopting this deterministic approach not only facilitates network management but also improves cost control.

Since the cost of wiring an existing building goes up with the height of the ceiling, and rises even higher after the tenants have moved in, making the right decisions as early as possible can significantly alleviate future costs. Aside from the serious loss of productivity that results from interfering with normal working patterns, dangling cables and drifting dust create safety hazards and generally demoralize employees.

The increasingly popular method for ensuring current and future economies is prewiring—installing cabling or raceways (cable conduit) during building construction. Not only does this reduce installation costs, it also permits careful labeling and recording of cable runs and circuits, thus making future network changes much easier to effect. The final appearance or utility of wiring installed after building construction rarely equals the quality that is attainable through prewiring.

Building types

A building's design reflects and influences the type of activities that it houses. Communications station density, building codes, and communications cable distribution are all interrelated. They affect, and are affected by, the design, construction, and use of each building.

Planners should provide the highest possible degree of flexibility in cabling installations for general-purpose office buildings. Tenant activities generally exhibit high station density and medium-to-heavy communications requirements that are greatly affected by frequent changes of tenants and rearrangement of offices.

Retail buildings, by comparison, have fairly low station density, even though stations are often clustered in strategic locations within the available floor space. Cable distribution can be regarded as somewhat more stable, though it still must be flexible enough to accommodate occasional floor-space rearrangements that are intended to improve the sales environment.

Manufacturing buildings, in contrast to other types of buildings, do not usually require that the cable be hidden. Communications cabling in manufacturing environments may be comparatively stable, but this will depend on the equipment, the product line, and product-cycle factors. Because cabling is frequently run overhead or along walls, communications wiring in many manufacturing structures tends to be quite flexible.

Residential communications cabling may be characterized as accommodating telephone, television, and perhaps security equipment. For the most part, this equipment is contained in living areas of fixed size that rarely change. Cabling installed in walls and ceilings may generally be considered permanently in place.

Health-care facilities typically house heavy users of communications equipment. Communications equipment and networks in these environments are subject to frequent inspection and rigid enforcement of highly structured building and safety codes that regulate the installation and operation of primary, as well as back-up, communications facilities. Network and wiring changes are common and extensive in this environment, and highly flexible cabling plans are essential.

Building codes

A careful examination of all local and national building construction codes is a vital prerequisite to the planning process. Local codes may override or preempt nationally accepted codes, and regulations that governed the construction of existing buildings may have changed significantly by the time new construction starts.

While prewiring may be the preferred approach, it may not always be the most economically attractive.

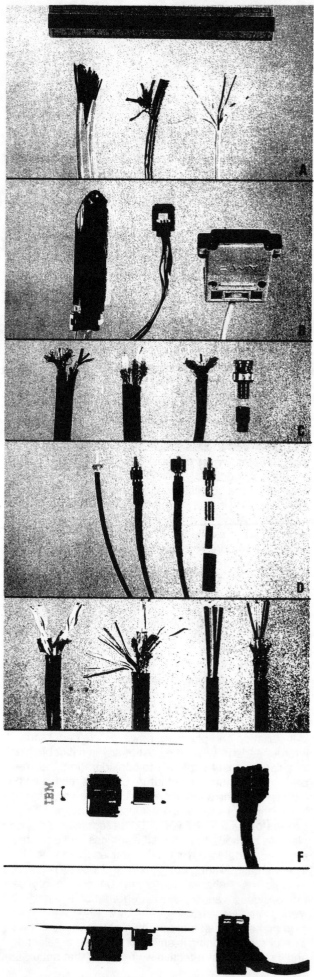

The first issue that a network planner may have to resolve is: Should a new facility be constructed and prewired, or should an existing one be rewired? In many cases, this decision will not be made unilaterally by the communications managers, though their input would likely play a major role in company determinations. Such decisions will likely also determine many subsequent issues that are within the purview of communications managers. They include:

■ Choice of networks or technologies.
■ Types of terminals and equipment.
■ Relative and real costs of installations.

Whether the network is installed in an existing building or in new construction, the need for its modification will eventually arise. Before choosing a network technology or topology, planners should determine the degree of flexibility needed for future changes. Specifically, they should answer these questions:

■ How will existing equipment, users, and peripherals be moved and new equipment be added?
■ What capabilities will be needed to expand the number of user stations?
■ Will prewired new construction use raceways, risers, or point-to-point cabling?

Plan for growth

Network growth is as inevitable as it is difficult to predict. There are, however, three basic components of such growth:

1. Expanded network utilization by the original users.
2. Extension of the network to new users.
3. Physical plant or campus modifications.

The natural growth of a network should be a primary planning consideration. This includes estimates of expansion due to business or organizational activity, such as more sales orders, invoices, productivity reports, and so on. A second aspect of natural growth is the increase in network utilization that comes with user experience and familiarity. For example, within a three-year period after initial activation, a network's inquiry and response activity per person can be expected to double.

Perhaps the biggest cause of expanded network use comes from the addition of new users. Predicting growth rates for this factor is generally more difficult than for other causes of expansion, but it is not impossible. Classic market research techniques, combined with hard data based on specific analyses, as well as the experience of other companies with similar products and services, are all good planning tools.

What is called a substitution effect usually accompanies the introduction of a newly installed communications network. If, for example, telephone inquiries from a sales office to headquarters are replaced by terminal queries, a one-for-one substitution of the traffic will occur initially, and will then probably grow only gradually. The general growth pattern for terminal-to-host activity tends to follow conventional market penetration curves (Fig. 1). A slow initial acceptance is followed by rapidly accelerated usage, which then levels off to more steady, predictable growth.

Many different materials have been exploited over

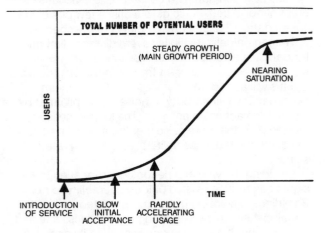

1. New service growth. *The curve shows the typical usage growth of a new computerized service over time — first slow, then rapid, and finally constant.*

the years for use as transmission media. Yet, even while the exploration of new media continues, there are really only three alternatives today — given cost, availability, and technological maturity — for use within buildings for general-purpose communications distribution:

■ Twisted pairs of copper wire, including shielded twisted pair.
■ Coaxial and twinaxial cable.
■ Optical fiber.

Other frequently used transmission media, which essentially are composites or variations of these, include flat, or under-carpet, cable and mixed-conductor cable.

Each cable type serves some application or supports certain transmission techniques better than do the others. Each, moreover, has its own cost and performance benefits.

Microwave transmission, though widely used, is unsuitable for intrabuilding data or voice communications. Infrared lightwave transmission is also making an appearance, but its use in the intrabuilding environment is still largely developmental. Neither of these technologies warrant serious consideration for local communications distribution today.

In evaluating the appropriate cable, the physical characteristics of each type should be studied with respect to its pull strength, bending radius, and weight (Table 1).

Twisted pair

Twisted copper wire, or twisted pair, is better known as common telephone cabling. Although used ubiquitously for telephony, twisted pair has several disadvantages for data transmission. It is extremely susceptible to electrical interference, which might come from sources including nearby electric typewriters, air-conditioners, X-ray equipment, or a host of other external sources. While such interference, or noise, does little to impede conventional analog voice signals, it causes two problems for data transmission that are interrelated: limitations to both speed and distance.

The sensitivity of twisted pair to noise limits the speeds at which data can be sent. This is because a burst of noise that would garble only a few bits of low-speed data will destroy many bits of high-speed data.

Twisted pair also exhibits severe distance limitations for data. An electrical signal (voice or data) grows weaker, or attenuates, as it travels. While electrical signals will attenuate on any conducting medium, twisted pair's vulnerability to noise is complicated by its capacity to act as an antenna. The longer the length of twisted pair, the more noise it gathers. After a while, the accumulated noise obliterates the attenuated signal.

Shielding the wire and periodically repeating the signal can reduce twisted pair's vulnerability to noise. Shielding—enclosing one or more twisted pairs within a metallic shell—makes twisted pair much less affected by noise, but it also adds significantly to its cost. Repeaters, which retransmit signals from one length of wire onto another, increase the distance that a signal can travel. They are, however, also expensive and can greatly increase the cost of running twisted pair.

Twisted pair, shown in Photo A, is best for low-cost, short-distance local networks, especially for small networks linking, say, microcomputers. This type of cable can carry data at rates in excess of 1 Mbit/s over distances up to several hundred feet without repeaters. The photo shows three basic twisted-pair cable types: The fat, 25-pair (50-conductor) version is the mainstay of the telephone industry. The one in the middle is a shielded length of three twisted pairs that are surrounded by a metallic foil. And the last is a basic unshielded cable containing three twisted pairs, a total of six conductors.

Photo B shows the type of termination connectors that are most commonly used with twisted pair. The 25-pair connector is a telephony standard. The middle connector, similarly, is a standard telephone wall jack: in this case, terminating three pairs, or six conductors. Most data applications employ the ubiquitous RS-232-C connector, which is used to terminate unshielded or shielded twisted pair. In the photo, the RS-232-C connector uses only six leads and terminates a three-pair twisted-pair cable. Most RS-232-C devices can be accommodated with as few as six leads, and many require only four.

Coaxial cable

Coaxial cable, or coax, is the most widely used medium today for data transmission in local networking. The cable is available in several forms, each suited to a different kind of application. All forms of coaxial cable have the same general structure (Photo C). A central conductor—the part of the cable that carries the signal—is surrounded by a dielectric, or nonconducting, insulator, then by a solid or woven metal shielding layer. The outside of the cable is encased by a protective coating. All these layers are concentric; hence, the term coaxial.

Of the three basic coaxial cable types shown in Photo C, the first is joined with a shielded twisted-pair

Table 1: Physical characteristics of communications cable types

CABLE TYPE	PULL STRENGTH (POUNDS)	BENDING RADIUS* (INCHES)	WEIGHT (POUNDS PER 1,000 FEET)	CROSS-SECTION AREA (SQUARE INCHES)
TELEPHONE CABLE				
3-PAIR	18	.22	—	0.0375
4-PAIR	24	—	—	—
6-PAIR	—	—	35 (24 AWG)	0.075
25-PAIR	150	—	—	0.220
50-PAIR	300	.69	215 (24 AWG)	0.375
DATA CABLE				
SHIELDED TWISTED PAIR (2-PAIR)	55	3.0	60 (22 AWG)	0.125
COAXIAL	22	1.0	34	0.046
TWINAXIAL	26	1.5	65	0.096

*NORMAL BEND RADIUS IS TYPICALLY FROM EIGHT TO TEN TIMES THE OUTSIDE DIAMETER

cable. The second type, in the middle of the photo, is essentially two joined coaxial cables, which constitute a twinaxial cable. The third type, a single coaxial cable, has next to it a BNC connector, which is commonly used to terminate a length of coaxial cable, especially for data transmission. The cable types in the photo all have a fine wire mesh shielding, which is less expensive—but also provides less shielding from noise—than coaxial cable that has solid, extruded-metal sheathing.

Because it is shielded, though to varying degrees depending on the specific type, coaxial cable is largely immune to electrical noise. This cable can carry data at higher rates over longer distances than twisted pair. Also, since it has been around for several decades, the techniques used to install coaxial cabling are well-established.

There are two general classifications of coaxial cable, named for the transmission techniques they support: baseband and broadband. For years controversy has flared over the relative merits of these two transmission techniques. The truth of the matter is that each serves quite different applications.

Baseband coaxial cable carries only one digital signal at a time—though typically at rates ranging from 1 to 10 Mbit/s. This bandwidth enables the time-division multiplexing of many signals. With baseband transmission, a signal is broadcast in both directions along the cable away from the sending station.

Broadband coaxial cable can carry many radio frequency (RF), or analog, signals at a time, with each signal occupying a different frequency band on the cable. Currently, practical data rates on any single channel of a broadband coaxial-cable-based network are somewhat lower than those supported by baseband transmission—generally between 1 and 5 Mbit/s. But the availability of 20 to 30 channels on a single cable—combined with time-division multiplexing—greatly increases the composite amount of data that the medium can carry.

Due to the nature of the coupling and amplification hardware that carries the RF signal, broadband signals are effectively unidirectional. Broadband transmissions, moreover, require RF modems to convert the analog signal carried over the cable to and from its original digital form.

A leading example of a broadband-based network is IBM's PC Network. The RF modem is contained on the single interface card that plugs into the back of the IBM Personal Computer. But the predominant coaxial cabling used for decades by IBM with its other devices, such as the the ubiquitous 3270 terminal family, employs baseband signaling. Xerox's Ethernet is a leading example of a coaxial-cable-based network that employs baseband signaling.

Baseband limitations

Recent studies indicate several drawbacks to baseband transmission:

- Lower aggregate data rates than with broadband.
- Serious problems from electromagnetic and RF interference.
- Higher signal loss per cable length than with optical-fiber cable at comparable data rates.

Nonetheless, baseband transmission is well-suited for small- to medium-sized data processing or office automation environments. Though more distance-limited than broadband, baseband networks may adequately cover a single building or a small campus. Broadband networks work most effectively in larger geographic configurations, where economies of scale can justify the generally higher broadband maintenance costs. A broadband network may connect the buildings on a large campus or even those in a good-sized city.

For dispersed network applications, hybrid broadband/baseband configurations are beginning to appear. In such configurations, a broadband trunk carries data among several local baseband subnetworks, along with such specialized transmissions as local videoconferencing. Hybrid networks take advantage of the best features of both technologies: They use baseband transmission to handle most of the data traffic, and they use the more accommodating broadband technology as a backbone for the multiservice network.

Optical fiber

Optical-fiber (Photo D) uses light signals, pulsed in fine glass strands (about 0.005 inches in diameter) to carry a stream of data at extremely high modulation rates. A lightweight optical-fiber cable of 144 strands can carry as many conversations as a large copper-conductor cable that would need to contain 20 times as many copper wires.

Photo D shows an unterminated single-fiber cable, along with male and female ends of a terminated optical-fiber cable. The hair-thin data-carrying fiber is barely visible, extending from the end of the cladding and insulation portion of the cable (white portion) that surrounds it as shown in the unterminated cable in the photo. An exploded view of one type of optical-fiber termination connector is also shown.

The high capacities of optical fiber are not realized. But this is not because light travels faster than electrical signals—both traverse their respective medium at effectively the speed of light—but rather because of the relative immunity of the light signal to external noise and because there is less loss of the lightwave signal compared with electrical-wire transmission over equivalent distances and with comparable modulation rates.

Light can be modulated, which is necessary for encoding data, in shorter-duration and lower-powered pulses than can electrical signals. This is inherently due to the shorter wavelength of light as compared with the wavelengths used for electrical analog-signal or pulse-coded transmission. The light-sensitive receivers used with optical-fiber transmission can, moreover, accurately decode light pulses consisting of much less residual energy than that required for, say, an analog telephone-line modem. All of these factors contribute to a much greater bandwidth—or data-carrying potential—over optical-fiber cable than with electrical-wire transmission. Optical transmission capacities today are limited only by the speed of the conventional electronics required at either end of the fiber to generate and receive the rapid on/off light pulses.

In typical configurations today, fiber can serve as a viable replacement to wire for even relatively low-speed and short-distance data transmission of the RS-232-C type. The signal integrity of the light pulses traveling through optical-fiber cable enables communications at data rates ranging from 19.2 kbit/s to 38 kbit/s over a 1,000-meter length of optical-fiber cable. This is in contrast to the 1.2-kbit/s maximum data rate supported over a 914-meter RS-232-C cable.

According to Texas Instruments Inc.'s published EIA policy, the maximum speed at which terminals and their hosts can communicate over RS-232-C-designed cable decreases in direct relation to the distance between machines (Table 2).

But not so with optical fiber. Today's typical optical-fiber transmission rates of, say, 45 kbit/s may seem very low in just a few years when "typical" transmission rates may be on the order of 400 kbit/s.

Seeing the light

The principal advantages of fiber optics are its sturdiness and its inherent security. Optical fiber is immune to both physical and electrical influences from the environment. Whereas copper corrodes, glass does not. And optical-fiber cable is almost impossible to tap surreptitiously. Current technology within the military enables operators to isolate a break, or even a significant movement, in an optical-fiber cable to within a single inch over a mile or more of cable.

Its principal disadvantages are found mainly in local all-purpose communications cabling applications, where its cost runs high and making connections is inherently difficult. The very property that makes fiber optics ideal for security reasons—its near immunity to

Table 2: RS-232-C limits

DATA RATE (BIT/S)	DISTANCE (METERS)
1.2K	914
2.4K	549
4.8K	244
9.6K	122

SOURCE: TEXAS INSTRUMENTS INC. EIA POLICY

being tapped—also makes it impractical for local network use. With coaxial cable, users have only to ensure that the conductor from the tap touches the conductor from the cable and that the connection remains adequately shielded. But multistranded optical-fiber cable requires the precise alignment of hundreds or thousands of fibers to ensure a continuous connection. New technologies, however, are simplifying the problem of connecting to an optical-fiber trunk, and future technologies are likely to simplify operations even more.

Although it is the newest medium in the commercial local-distribution communications-cabling market, optical fiber in the long run has the most potential. For now, however, it is the most limited. Currently, constrained as it is to a single channel per cable-fiber, fiber-optic technology is the equivalent of baseband coaxial cable. In addition, most optical-fiber networks require wideband multiplexers to exploit the medium's high-speed, wide-bandwidth capability.

Such new fiber-optic technologies as plastic, or acrylic, fiber will allow fiber optics to carry many times the bandwidth of broadband coaxial cable, but costs and availability still limit its use commercially. In addition, coaxial cable remains a more traceable medium. The diagnostic and maintenance procedures for electrical-wire cabling—finding breaks or shorts, making connections—are cheap and well understood by most.

The use of light to transmit information is hardly a new idea. In 1888, Alexander Graham Bell patented his Photophone, the first attempt to use light to transmit sound. The device employed a vibrating reflector and made use of the varying resistance of selenium in response to light intensity.

Several more recent approaches and technologies nave emerged as ways of providing line-of-sight communications, with many interconnecting links covering a relatively large physical area. Included among these are infrared, visible light, and ultraviolet communications links.

Of these approaches, infrared communications has been under development the longest. Still, the design and installation of infrared local networks remain very complex and highly dependent on the physical layout of an office or building environment. Infrared can span a couple of miles with very high data rates, but some difficulties have been reported when transceivers are used close to such seemingly innocuous heat generators as coffee pots or incandescent lights.

Still immature, infrared technology may yet come into wide use in the future as more implementation experience is gained. Even now, it can be used for short-distance communications point-to-point, though its application for ubiquitous local voice and data distribution remains, at best, questionable.

Microwave

Digital microwave radio may be used between two points with an unobstructed line-of-sight path between them. For relatively short distances (less than 10 miles), low bit error rates at relatively high bandwidths (at or above T1) can be obtained. Equipment capable of operating reliably in the 18-to-23-GHz range, and even higher, is readily available commercially.

Today, microwave is an ideal medium where large volumes of high-speed data must be transmitted between two fixed, relatively close locations. This cannot, of course, accommodate the needs of general communications distribution within buildings, though several vendors are planning to implement local distribution networks using 10-GHz transceivers with a time-division multiple access scheme to connect several nodes within a metropolitan area.

The same general deployment rules for microwave also apply to satellite communications, except that the distance between transmitter and receiver essentially becomes irrelevant, and certain unique transmission factors—most notably propagation delay and echoes—need to be taken into account.

As hardware costs decrease, growth in satellite transmission will increase. As with microwave transmission, satellite transmission may be used for several high-speed applications—PBX-to-PBX traffic, videoconferencing, bulk data transfer, and high-speed facsimile—but its near-term use for local communications distribution will probably remain somewhat limited.

Costs for communications distribution cabling are subject to a broad range of variables, and comparisons are somewhat difficult due to their essential differences. In addition, as the market grows and changes, costs for certain new transmission technologies will continue to decline rapidly. A few general rules apply to pricing for local communications distribution:
■ Established communications technologies are usually less expensive than state-of-the-art and experimental technologies.
■ Off-the-shelf equipment costs less than a customized network configuration.
■ A direct correlation exists between level of service and overall network price.
■ Price, speed, and performance move upward together.

Average price per workstation connection Is sometimes used as a comparison tool. But the price per connection for, say, local networks may vary greatly depending on what components and services are included (software, for example) and the type of transmission medium used. As a method of comparison, therefore, price per connection is likely to be useful only when one vendor's price is matched against

Table 3: Price per foot of cable (cents): 1981-1989

TYPE OF CABLE	YEAR								
	1981	1982	1983	1984	1985	1986	1987	1988	1989
COAXIAL	10	10.1	10.2	10.3	10.5	10.7	10.9	11.0	11.1
FIBER OPTIC	17.2	17.0	14.0	12.0	11.0	8.7	7.7	6.5	6.0
FLAT CABLE	6.25	6.5	6.8	7.1	7.25	8.0	8.1	8.5	8.9
TWISTED PAIR	–	–	–	–	–	–	–	–	–

another's for an identical network product. Even then, factors such as installation may make all the difference.

The relative cost of the transmission media is another way of measuring and comparing local network cost. This approach is especially valid since media has a major influence on both long-term operating costs as well as initial network price. Table 3 compares historic and projected prices of the transmission media that are currently available for communications distribution wiring.

The most readily available of all transmission media—because it is in constant, high-volume production for voice telephony—is twisted pair. This cable is the easiest to install and can be run along a baseboard in a matter of minutes. Prices today range from $0.05 to $0.25 per foot, depending on wire gauge, number of wire pairs, insulation, and so on. Nowadays, optical-fiber cable is the most expensive communications-distribution medium available. As it comes into wider use for telephone applications, however, it will eventually become the cheapest. The reasons are clear: The copper used in twisted pair and coaxial cable is a scarce resource. Silicon, on the other hand, is the most abundant element on earth.

For the foreseeable future, copper-wire prices will remain reasonably stable. Although ironic, the widespread deployment of optical fiber could open a new source of raw copper supply—the vast amounts of copper cable that are likely to be replaced by fiber. This might actually result in a small drop in copper prices, but this would not significantly alter the role of either transmission medium in the future.

Coaxial cable is currently the medium of choice for many local network applications, but its use for local general-purpose voice and data communications distribution is virtually nonexistent. Still, promoted for years as the IBM mainstay, coaxial cable for data is now in wide use. Available implementations today offered by a variety of vendors support from point-to-point to shared-channel wideband service.

Still, baseband coaxial cable, which costs from $0.50 cents to $3 per foot, is much more expensive than broadband cable, costing typically between $0.35 and $1 per foot. Baseband coax, moreover, may have to be run in hard conduit (such as a metal pipe) in order to comply with fire regulations in some areas. Broadband cable, on the other hand, comes already clad in a rigid aluminum sheathing. Also, baseband cable cannot extend more than a few thousand feet

without expensive digital repeaters, whereas broadband cable can span many kilometers using only inexpensive amplifiers.

While baseband cable is easy to install, requiring almost no maintenance, broadband data networks require a staff of trained RF technicians for design, day-to-day maintenance, and careful tuning of components to handle the specific range of frequencies. Both the cable itself and the broadband connecting hardware are extremely sensitive to temperature changes and variations in humidity.

Connection and splicing costs for optical-fiber cabling may outweigh the medium's inherent high-speed and wideband potential. Additionally, buildings that are "wired" with fiber could become crammed with abandoned or discarded optical cable as a result of terminal and equipment transfers and moves.

Still, the small diameter of optical-fiber cabling is bound to make it the leading contender where severe space limitations exist. By comparison, the ducting demands of coaxial cable may, in the end, cost more in architectural demands than its potential flexibility warrants.

Wiring management

As terminals and peripherals begin to appear in nearly every workspace, their interconnection becomes increasingly complex. Overcrowded raceways, time lost due to downtime, and increasing installation costs are forcing alternative approaches. The solution might be called wire management.

Keeping track of wires on, in, around, and under today's computer-topped desks will become an art in the future. Such record keeping may involve tagging and labeling boxes, pipes, closets, panels, and so on. Wiring and connection concerns have become so disruptive, given the relative technical unsophistication of many computer users, that some computer manufacturers have taken to building numerous wire and cabling options into their equipment, rather than leaving to the user the chore of finding, among other things, the right jack, cable, connector, or pin assignments. Wiring management, or cabling, plans currently in use fall into three general categories: direct cabling, wired office furniture, and distribution centers or networks.

Direct, or point-to-point, cabling is the oldest and most common type of wire management. Sometimes called the spaghetti-model, point-to-point cabling is an evolutionary solution, dating back to a time before the introduction of such concepts as distributed processing or networking. The logic of direct cabling is impeccable: Given a computer with a certain number of ports located in one place, and the same number of peripherals scattered about in various locations, simply run a cable from Port A to Peripheral A—regardless of cost, obstacles, or distance.

More to accommodate cosmetic and safety concerns than from any functional imperative, this method usually then entails the installation of false floors, walls and ceilings, many ducts—as well as the generalized construction of an internal life-support system to contain the corporate data processing organism.

Practical though it may be, direct cabling almost always necessitates running a new cable to the latest location of the workstation that needs access to a computer port. Given the labor cost of retrieving, measuring, resplicing, and reinstalling existing cable—often significantly more than the value of the cable—long cable runs are left buried in what is affectionately called "left-over spaghetti."

Considering how frequently workstations are moved, with the cost of relocating just one terminal as much as $1,500—not counting associated downtime while the work gets done—point-to-point wiring is something less than the optimal wiring management solution. The net impact on operations balance sheets hardly compares with the effect on network facilities managers over time.

Wired office furniture

A variant of the direct-cabling solution has been developed by office furniture vendors. Ever responsive to the office manager's desire for a neat, well-ordered, and safe environment, office furniture designers have taken the needs of computer users into their design considerations.

Conventional desks, tables, computer workstations, and printer stands now are commercially available with factory-installed or designed-in wire channels or wiring. Even the movable panels used in open-office environments can be purchased prewired at the factory. The first of these—a two-wire design—was introduced as early as 1976. A three-circuit panel followed in 1979, and more complex wiring architectures are on the way.

Wired furniture helps clean up the immediate workstation area itself, but it does little else that is different from the spaghetti approach in solving the intrabuilding cabling problem.

Wiring closets

Sometime shortly after World War II, what was called simply the Telephone Co., taking a lesson from electricians, began to run its wiring into central distribution points within an office or a building. Individual telephones were then connected to distribution panels within a wiring closet, thereby saving a long wire run to a singular external connection point.

This concept has been further refined by the telephone companies with the introduction of modular connectors. With the wire-it-once, or prewiring, concept and the availability of almost universally interchangeable connectors, a growing number of users are slowly digging their way out of the spaghetti pot.

Wiring closets are used to distribute cabling to voice and data communications workstations from terminal blocks and devices. In addition, they may serve to facilitate wiring electrical circuits, housing power supplies and special control devices, and so on. The wiring-closet design has, of course, been strongly influenced by the architecture of voice communications networks. But as data communications networks grow and proliferate in business, wiring-closet design and construction will change accordingly, along with integrated voice and data cable-distribution schemes.

The wiring-closet concept offers many advantages:
■ It allows communications network installation, alteration, and maintenance without affecting normal business operations or the appearance of offices or buildings.
■ Noise generated by communications equipment or by those working on it can be contained and controlled.
■ The internal environment of the wiring-closet area can be more easily managed and controlled.
■ Network security is easier to ensure—the closets can be locked.
■ During initial building construction, wiring closets can be located in areas that will provide optimum, or shortest-length, cable distribution to user equipment.

If, as trends indicate, voice and data networks will merge, "integrated" wiring closets will almost certainly be designed to serve both needs.

The floor area served by any given wiring closet is limited by the space available for cables to enter and leave the closet. This usually limits the area that can be served to about 10,000 square feet. In any case, no more than about 50,000 square feet of floor area should be served by any one closet.

Having multiple closets on each floor, while each then serves a smaller area, helps reduce cable-drop lengths, facilitates the addition of more drops, and generally helps make the rearrangement of cabling installations easier.

The wiring closet should be located at the point offering the best access to the cabling distribution. Within the closet, carpeting or uncovered concrete should be avoided. Carpets create static electricity, while concrete is a source of dust. The light source should be overhead and arranged to distribute a shadowless light. Walls of three-quarter-inch plywood for mounting telephone punch-down blocks and strain-relief cabling should be installed. Floor space should be open, without center posts. Doorways should be at least 36 inches wide, 80 inches high, and without doorsills. All doors should open outward and be equipped with locks.

Data communications wiring closets generally mount patch panels on EIA-standard 19-inch racks with universal hole spacings. These are often bolted to the floor but may alternately be mounted on the walls. A minimum-sized closet provides one rack for each 100 drops, along with space for one additional rack for future expansion.

Raceways and ducts

Cabling between wiring closets, workstations, and other devices is linked according to a cable-distribution plan. Cable distribution is generally achieved via one or more of the following techniques: underfloor ducts with headers, cellular floors with trench headers, raised or unlimited-access floors, open or closed ceilings (depending on codes), conduit, surface raceways, grid systems, and cable trays.

Often, when cabling is to be installed in a new building, too little consideration is given to the installation, and subsequent expansion, of cabling raceways. In existing buildings, the best cable raceway plan must sometimes be ruled out simply because no allowance was made for future growth during the initial planning process.

Underfloor raceways, for example, should be accessible not only during the initial installation, but also later for subsequent expansion. In some cases, structural elements of multistory buildings may prevent the construction of vertical passageways between floors. The opposite, however, is also true: Certain raceway designs will actually dictate the building's architecture. Since these passageways are often integral parts of the structure, the building must literally be built around them.

An underfloor duct network usually is assembled and installed during building construction using feeder and distribution ducts, junction boxes, and other modular components of various sizes. Such construction offers great flexibility and low initial cost, but these benefits may be offset by the impact that an underfloor duct network may have on the structural design of the building, which must accommodate the duct system. Adding underfloor ducts to an existing building is virtually impossible.

Another alternative is the so-called cellular floor. An integral and vital part of the building support structure, and serving as the structural floor, this floor is made up of distribution cells and a feeder duct or trench header. Distribution cells may be of steel or concrete.

A trench header is a specially manufactured metallic trough with a cover that fits flush with the finished floor. A trench header is normally used as a feeder duct for cellular or underfloor configurations. The maximum usable depth is only about 2.5 inches, as any greater depth makes the removal of cables for maintenance difficult.

The raised, or unlimited-access, floor is assembled from a series of square metallic plate modules resting on pedestals cemented to the floor, which are superimposed above an existing floor area. It provides unlimited access to space under the floor and is used frequently for computer rooms as well as offices. Metallic raised floors may be covered with carpet tile but must always be grounded.

Ceiling distribution

Cables and wires may be placed within ceiling space and brought down to user locations inside poles or in partitions. Ceiling distribution, or open wiring, provides a great deal of flexibility and keeps cable lengths to a minimum. Such distribution can, however, expose office employees to dirt, safety hazards, and work interruptions when installers or maintenance personnel are working on ladders in the area.

There is also the ceiling grid arrangement, which is similar to an underfloor configuration except that it uses header and distribution ducts mounted in the ceiling space.

Yet another method is to use surface metal raceways for cabling distribution. These are cable troughs mounted on walls at baseboard or desk height around the perimeter of offices or rooms. All communications devices are then served from the wall.

2. Voice and data. *IBM's Cabling System transmits voice and data over separate shielded and unshielded twisted pairs within the same cable.*

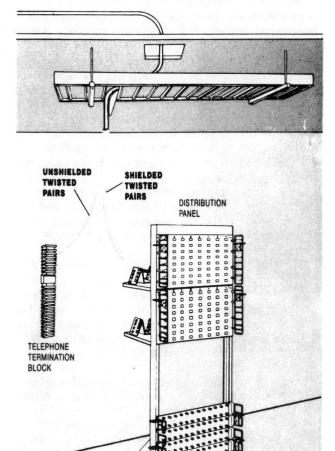

UNSHIELDED TWISTED PAIRS

SHIELDED TWISTED PAIRS

DISTRIBUTION PANEL

TELEPHONE TERMINATION BLOCK

SOURCE: IBM CABLING SYSTEM DESCRIPTION

Where permitted by code, cable trays or racks may also be useful for containing large quantities of cable that run horizontally.

Several different cable-distribution methods have been developed and introduced—most notably by such industry heavyweights as IBM and AT&T. Some, such as AT&T's, take advantage of existing telephone-line wiring and ducting. Others are designed to be installed when the electrical, PBX and telephone, or other wiring is run.

IBM Cabling System

While the type of cabling medium prescribed is often directly related to a specific local-network technology and/or product, most cable-distribution schemes being installed today are based on twisted-copper pairs. A few installations feature hybrid combinations of the three most popular transmission media and address combinations through adapters. This, in large part, is the approach taken with IBM's Cabling System.

Only recently introduced as the first element of the

company's planned token ring local network, the IBM Cabling System is apparently intended to do away with the need for coaxial cables.

The IBM Cabling System is designed to let users permanently wire buildings with two types of balanced twisted-pair cables (Photo E) in a star topology. It then eliminates the need to run cables every time new terminals or small computers are installed or moved. The Cabling System provides an outlet into which peripherals can be plugged, using connectors of IBM's proprietary design (Photos F and G, front and side views). The office outlets connect to a distribution panel in a wire closet via shielded twisted-pair wire. The panels, in turn, connect to the central computer room.

Connection of devices is accomplished by plugging the device into the wall connector, thus eliminating a special run of cable for each station. Changing the device requires that the unit be unplugged, moved to its new location, and plugged in again. Patch cords at the distribution/patch panel enable easy changes from one port to another.

The IBM cabling types (Photo E) are configured as two or six twisted-copper pairs—two pairs, within the metallic foil shielding, are reserved for data; the others are for voice communications. Versions with one or two optical fibers, with and without additional twisted pairs, are also available. Coaxial and twinaxial adapters are available from IBM to attach the Cabling System to currently installed equipment.

Able to run at multimegabit rates when it is part of the IBM token ring local network, IBM claims its cable is suitable for transmitting not only voice and data but, at some point in the future, video-image data as well.

Prices for the transmission cable used in the IBM Cabling System start at $0.50 per foot. The more flamboyant fiber and shielded twisted-pair combination cables can cost as much as $4 per foot, and availability may be a concern. Faceplates with connectors for the outlets (Photos E and F) currently sell for less than $5 each, while 64-wire distribution panels cost $273. Devices to convert from coaxial cable to the Cabling System's shielded twisted pair range in price from $45 to $155, depending on the type of device to be connected.

IBM's Cabling System calls for integrated voice and data communications via the combined shielded and unshielded twisted-pair cable combinations. At the wiring closet (Fig. 2), these would be separated, with the two shielded pair routed to the distribution/patch panel. The voice pairs would be routed to a telephone-type termination block.

Other firms have predicated their cable-distribution plans on well-established and inexpensive unshielded twisted-pair cabling.

The twisted-pair distribution scheme uses ubiquitous RJ11-type and RS-232-C telephone connectors (Fig. 3) and twisted-pair cabling consisting of three or four pairs, plus common 25-pair cabling for distribution. It can readily be installed in an existing building, or during the construction of new facilities.

One wiring plan uses a multiplug octopus wiring harness to link a multiport computer with a distribution

3. Wiring. *In-place telephone cabling may be adapted to accommodate data and voice. Modified wiring will support RS-232-C asynchronous transmission.*

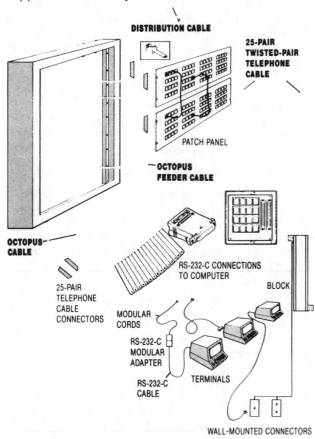

panel, usually located in or near the computer room. Each harness connects 16 computer ports to standard telephone modular connectors, coaxial or other connectors at the wall-mounted patch panel.

Wires terminating in modular connectors run from the central location to distribution blocks installed in selected areas within the facility. Discrete wiring and modular outlets can be installed in any suitable location—floor, ceiling, wall, post, or furniture. Plug-compatible wires are connected to the outlets at each workstation. Interconnection is made at the floor and central stations by unplugging cables or devices and replugging them into the appropriate plugs.

By using RS-232-C, BNC, RJ11, and optical-fiber modular connectors, such a cabling approach can allow a high degree of flexibility between existing and future telephone, computer, and terminal equipment.

Whatever alternatives the user may evaluate, it is worth remembering that transmission media and installation will play an important role in network cost, expansion, and flexibility. ■

Charles Wirl has been president of his own communications firm for the past eight years. He has almost 20 years experience in communications network construction, engineering, installation, and central offices. Wirl formerly was a contract engineer to the Bell System.

Section 2: Local Area Networks

2.1 Overview

The term local area network (LAN) is generally used to refer to a general-purpose local network that can serve a wide variety of devices over a large area. LANs support mini computers, mainframes, terminals, and other peripherals. In many cases, these networks can carry not only data but also voice, video, and graphics transmissions.

A LAN (rather than a high speed local network (HSLN) or a digital PBX) is probably the best choice when a variety of devices and a mix of traffic types are involved. The LAN, alone or as part of a hybrid local network with one of the other types, will become a common feature of many office buildings and other installations.

This section looks at the major alternative architectural approaches to LANs and focuses on some key design issues. As was described in Section 1, the key technology aspects of a LAN are transmission medium, topology, and medium access control technique. The current status of standards for LANs is also described.

2.2 LAN Transmission Media

To date, the transmission media most commonly used for LANs have been twisted pair and coaxial cable. Baseband transmission is used on twisted pair; baseband or broadband transmission is used on coaxial cable. Baseband and broadband technologies were introduced in Section 1 and are examined in greater detail in the articles of this section.

In recent years, there has been increasing interest in the use of optical fiber as a LAN transmission medium. In the remainder of this subsection, we first describe the medium and then discuss its use to construct a LAN.

Physical Description

An optical fiber is a thin (50-100 μm), flexible medium capable of conducting an optical ray. Various glasses and plastics can be used to make optical fibers. The lowest losses have been obtained by using fibers of ultrapure fused silica. Ultrapure fiber is difficult to manufacture; higher-loss multi-component glass fibers are more economical and still provide good performance. Plastic fiber is even less costly and can be used for short-haul links, for which moderately high losses are acceptable.

For a single optical fiber, the glass or plastic fiber, having a high index of refraction, is surrounded by a cladding layer of a material with slightly lower index. The cladding layer isolates the fiber and prevents crosstalk with adjacent fibers.

Fiber optic cable consists of a bundle of fibers, sometimes with a steel core for stability. Stacked ribbon cable is an alternative method of bundling; the cable consists of a stack of flat ribbons, each with a single row of fibers.

Benefits

One of the most significant technological breakthroughs in data transmission has been the development of practical fiberoptic communications systems. Optical fiber already enjoys considerable use in long-distance telecommunications, and its use in military applications is growing. The continuing improvements in performance and decline in prices, together with the inherent advantages of optical fiber, will result in new areas of application, such as local networks and short-haul video distribution. The following characteristics distinguish optical fiber from twisted pair and coaxial cable.

- *Greater bandwidth*: The potential bandwidth and, hence, data rate of a medium increases with frequency. At the immense frequencies of optical fiber, data rates of 2 Gbps over tens of kilometers have been demonstrated. Compare this to the practical maximum of hundreds of Mbps over about 1 km for coaxial cable and just a few Mbps over 1 km for twisted pair.

- *Smaller size and lighter weight*: Optical fibers are considerably smaller than coaxial cable or bundled twisted pair cable, at least an order of magnitude smaller in diameter for comparable data transmission capacity. For cramped conduits in buildings and underground along public right-of-way, the advantage of small size is considerable. The corresponding reduction in weight reduces structural support requirements.

- *Lower attenuation*: Attenuation is significantly lower for optical fiber than for coaxial cable or for twisted pair and is constant over a wide range.

- *Electromagnetic isolation*: Optical fiber systems are not affected by external electromagnetic fields. Thus, the system is not vulnerable to interference, impulse noise, or crosstalk. By the same token, fibers do not radiate energy, causing little interference with other equipment and providing a high degree of security from eavesdropping; in addition, fiber is inherently difficult to tap.

- *Greater repeater spacing*: Fewer repeaters mean lower cost and fewer sources of error. Bell Labs has successfully tested a 119-km repeaterless link at 420 Mbps

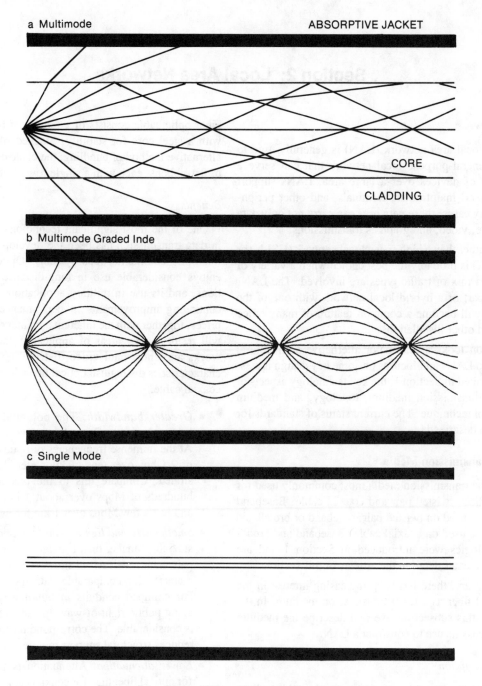

a Multimode

ABSORPTIVE JACKET

CORE

CLADDING

b Multimode Graded Inde

c Single Mode

Figure 2.1   Optical Fiber Transmission Modes

with a bit error rate of 10^{-9}. Coaxial and twisted-pair systems generally have repeaters every few kilometers.

Transmission Characteristics

Optical fiber transmits a signal-encoded beam of light by means of total internal reflection. Total internal reflection can occur in any transparent medium that has a higher index of refraction than the surrounding medium. In effect, the optical fiber acts as a waveguide for frequencies in the range 10^{14}-10^{15} Hz, which covers the visible spectrum and part of the infrared spectrum.

Figure 2.1 shows the principle of optical fiber transmission. Light from a source enters the cylindrical glass or plastic core. Rays at shallow angles are reflected and propagated along the fiber; other rays are absorbed by the surrounding material. This form of propagation is called multimode, referring to the variety of angles that will reflect. When a fiber core radius is reduced, fewer angles will reflect. By reducing the radius of the core to the order of a wavelength, only a single angle or mode can pass: the axial ray. Table 2.1 compares these two modes. The reason for

Table 2.1 Comparison of Single-Mode and Multimode Optical Fiber

SINGLE-MODE	MULTIMODE
Used for long distances and high data rates	Used for short distances and low data rates
Expensive	Inexpensive
Narrow core: requires laser light source	Wide core: gathers light well
Difficult to terminate	Easy to terminate
Minimum dispersion; very efficient	Large dispersion; inefficient

Table 2.2: Medium Access Control Techniques

	CENTRALIZED	DISTRIBUTED
ROUND-ROBIN	Polling	Token Bus Token Ring Collision Avoidance
RESERVATION	Centralized Reservation	Distributed Reservation
CONTENTION		CSMA/CD Slotted Ring Register Insertion

the superior performance of single-mode is this. With multimode transmission, multiple propagation paths exist, each with a different path length and hence time to traverse the fiber. This causes signal elements to spread out in time and limits the rate at which data can be accurately received. Since there is a single transmission path with single-mode transmission, such distortion cannot occur. Finally, by varying the index of refraction of the core, a third type of transmission, known as multimode graded index, is possible. This type is intermediate between the other two in characteristics. The variable refraction has the effect of focusing the rays more efficiently than ordinary multimode.

Two different types of light source are used in fiber optic systems: the light-emitting diode (LED) and the injection laser diode (ILD). The LED is a solid-state device that emits light when a current is applied. The ILD is a solid-state device that works on the laser principle in which quantum electronic effects are stimulated to produce a superradiant beam of narrow bandwidth. The LED is less costly, operates over a greater temperature range, and has a longer operational life than the ILD. The ILD is more efficient and can sustain greater data rates.

The detector used at the receiving end to convert the light into electrical energy is a photodiode. Two solid-state devices have been used: the PIN detector and the APD detector. The PIN photodiode has a segment of intrinsic (I) silicon between the P and N layers of a diode. The APD, avalanche photodiode, is similar in appearance but uses a stronger electric field. Both devices are basically photon counters. The PIN is less expensive and less sensitive than the APD.

Of course, only analog signaling is possible in optical fiber, since only light waves may be transmitted. With appropriate modulation, either digital or analog data may be carried.

LAN Applications

The application of fiber to LANs has lagged its use in other areas because of cost and technical concerns, which include difficulties in tapping a signal from the fiber, connecting fibers to other LAN components, and splicing. The article by Finley accurately captures the current status and most promising technical approaches for fiber LANs.

2.3 LAN Topologies

The topologies that have been most commonly used for LANs are bus/tree and ring. Again, these were introduced in Section 1 and are examined in greater detail in this section. To date, efforts at standardization have focused on these two topologies.

A more recent topology, which might be termed the star-LAN or centralized bus, has been introduced by AT&T and is under consideration by the IEEE 802 standards committee (see Section 2.5). This architecture is similar to the more traditional LAN bus. The difference is that in this case the bus is very short and, consequently, the connecting cable to the attached device may be very long. The short bus allows for a simplified access control protocol and for efficient centralized control. This architecture is explored in the paper by Acampora and Hluchyz.

2.4 Medium Access Control

With all types of local networks, a key technical issue is that of access control. An access control technique is required to regulate the use of the shared medium. The key parameters in any medium access control technique are where and how. "Where" refers to whether control is exercised in a centralized or distributed fashion. In a centralized scheme, a controller is designated that has the authority to grant access to the network. A station wishing to transmit must wait until it receives permission from the controller. In a decentralized network, the stations collectively perform a medium access control function to dynamically determine the order in which stations transmit.

IEEE 802 REFERENCE MODEL RELATIONSHIP TO OSI MODEL

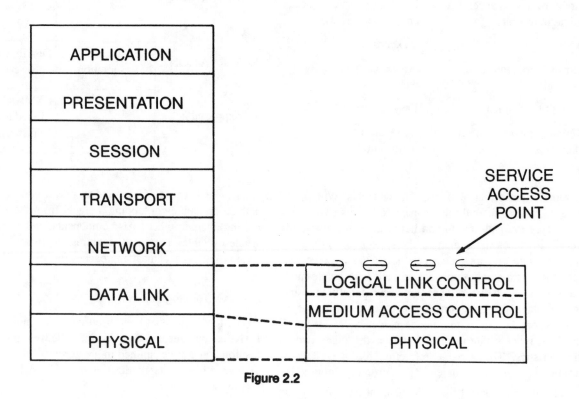

Figure 2.2

A centralized scheme has certain advantages, such as, (1) It may afford greater control over access for providing such things as priorities, overrides, and guaranteed bandwidth, (2) It allows the logic at each station to be as simple as possible, and (3) It avoids problems of coordination. Its principal disadvantages are that (1) It results in a single point of failure; (2) It may act as a bottleneck, reducing efficiency; and (3) If propagation delay is high, the overhead may be unacceptable. The pros and cons for distributed control are mirror images of the points made above.

The second parameter, "how," is constrained by the topology and is a tradeoff among competing factors: cost, performance, and complexity. In general, we can categorize access control techniques as being either synchronous or asynchronous. With synchronous techniques, a specific capacity is dedicated to a connection. We see this in the digital PBX. Such techniques are not optimal in broadcast networks because the needs of the stations are generally unpredictable. It is preferable to be able to allocate capacity in an asynchronous (dynamic) fashion, more or less in response to immediate needs. The asynchronous approach can be further subdivided into three categories: Round robin, Reservation, and Contention.

Round Robin

Round robin techniques are conceptually simple, being based on the philosophy of "give everybody a turn." Each station in turn is given an opportunity to transmit. During that opportunity the station may decline to transmit or may transmit subject to a certain upper bound, usually expressed as a maximum amount of data or time for this opportunity. In any case, the station, when it is finished, must relinquish its turn, and the right to transmit passes to the next station in logical sequence. Control of turns may be centralized or distributed. Polling on a multidrop line is an example of a centralized technique.

When many stations have data to transmit over an extended period of time, round robin techniques can be very efficient. If only a few stations have data to transmit at any give time, other techniques may be preferable, largely depending on whether the data traffic is "stream" or "bursty." Stream traffic is characterized by lengthy and fairly continuous transmissions. Examples are voice communication, telemetry, and bulk file transfer. Bursty traffic is characterized by short, sporadic transmissions. Interactive terminal-host traffic fits this description.

Reservation

For stream traffic, reservation techniques are well suited. In general for these techniques, time on the medium is divided into slots, much as with synchronous TDM. A station wishing to transmit reserves future slots for an extended or indefinite period. Again, reservations may be made in either a centralized or distributed fashion.

Contention

For bursty traffic, contention techniques are usually appropriate. With these techniques, no control is exercised to determine whose turn it is; all stations contend for time in a way that can be, as we shall see, rather rough and tumble. These techniques are of necessity distributed in nature. Their principal advantage is that they are simple to implement and, under light to moderate load, efficient. For some of these techniques, however, performance tends to collapse under heavy load.

Although both centralized and distributed reservation techniques have been implemented in some LAN products, round robin and contention techniques are the most common. Specific examples are shown in Table 2.2.

2.5 Standards

Standards for LANs have been developed by a committee set up by The Institute of Electrical and Electronics Engineers, Inc., known as the IEEE 802 committee. The task of the IEEE 802 was to specify the means by which devices could communicate over a local area network. The committee characterized its work in this way:

> A Local Network is a data communications system which allows a number of independent devices to communicate with each other. This Standard defines a set of interfaces and protocols for the Local Network.
>
> A Local Network is distinguished from other types of data networks in that the communication is usually confined to a moderate size geographic area such as a single office building, a warehouse or a campus. The network can generally depend on a communications channel of moderate to high data rate which has a consistently low error rate. The network is generally owned and used by a single organization. This is in contrast to long distance networks which interconnect facilities in different parts of the country or are used as a public utility. The Local Network is also different from networks which interconnect devices on a desktop or components within a single piece of equipment.
>
> The objective of the Local Network Standard is to ensure compatibility between equipment made by different manufacturers such that data communications can take place between the devices with a minimum effort on the part of the equipment users or the builders of a system containing the equipment. To accomplish this, the Standard will provide specifications which establish common interfaces and protocols for local area data communications networks.

Two conclusions were quickly reached. First, the task of communication across the local network is sufficiently complex that it needs to be broken up into more manageable subtasks. Second, no single technical approach will satisfy all requirements.

The first conclusion is reflected in a "local network reference model," compared in Figure 2.2 to the better-known open systems interconnection (OSI) model. The model has three layers:

- *Physical*: The layer is concerned with the nature of the transmission medium, and the details of device attachment and electrical signaling.

- *Medium access control*: A local network is characterized by a collection of devices all needing to share a single transmission medium. A means to control access is needed so that only one device attempts to transmit at a time.

- *Logical link control*: This layer is concerned with establishing, maintaining, and terminating a logical link between devices.

The second conclusion was reluctantly reached when it became apparent that no single standard would satisfy all committee participants. There was support for both ring and bus topologies. Within the bus topology, there was support for two access methods (CSMA/CD and token bus) and two media (baseband and broadband). The response of the committee was to standardize all serious proposals rather than to attempt to settle on just one.

The work of the IEEE 802 Committee is currently organized into the following subcommittees:

- 802.1: High Level Interface
- 802.2: Logical Link Control
- 802.3: CSMA/CD Networks
- 802.4: Token Bus Networks
- 802.5: Token Ring Networks
- 802.6: Metropolitan Area Networks
- 802.7: Broadband Technical Advisory Group
- 802.8: Fiber Optic Technical Advisory Group
- 802.9: Integrated Data and Voice Networks

The High Level Interface subcommittee deals with issues related to network architecture, internetworking, and network management for local networks.

The initial work on LLC, CSMA/CD, token bus, and token ring was completed and joint ANSI/IEEE standards were issued in 1985. Some minor changes and additions were made and a revised set of standards were issued in 1987. Work continues on additional options and features in each of the four subcommittees.

The work on metropolitan area networks (MANs) is just beginning to make progress. The subcommittee is attempting to develop a small number of reasonable alternatives for further study. However, the FDDI standard, described in Section 3, satisfies many of the requirements for a MAN.

The purpose of 802.7 and 802.8 is to provide technical guidance to the other subcommittees on broadband and optical fiber technology, respectively. The 802.7 subcommittee is producing a recommended practices document for broadband cabling systems. The 802.8 subcommittee is investigating the use of optical fiber as an alternative transmission medium for 802.3, 802.4, and 802.5. It is also considering installation recommendations and a tutorial on fiber optic standards and related information.

The newest subcommittee, for Integrated Data and Voice Networks, was chartered in November of 1986. It is developing a standard for interfacing desktop devices to both 802 LANs and to Integrated Services Digital Networks (ISDNs), utilizing twisted-pair wiring to carry both voice and data.

The acceptance of the IEEE 802 standards has been remarkably widespread. The National Bureau of Standards, which issues Federal Information Processing Standards for U.S. government procurements, has adopted the LLC and CSMA/CD standards as FIPS 107. The others (802.4 and 802.5) will probably follow. The International Organization for Standardization (ISO) has adopted the 1987 version of 802.2 through 802.5 as international standards 8802/2 through 8802/5. The effect of these standardization activities is to encourage both vendors and customers to employ 802-based LANs.

2.6 Article Summary

The first two articles deal with a specific baseband LAN, Ethernet. Developed jointly by Xerox, DEC, and Intel, Ethernet is a widely-used baseband LAN and is very similar to one of the options of 802.3, which is based on the Ethernet specification. These articles were chosen because of the importance and popularity of Ethernet and because of the breadth of description of the baseband approach that they provide. The article by Shoch et al. discusses the evolution of Ethernet from its initial 3-Mbps experimental version to the final 10-Mbps version, and analyzes many of the technical design details. The article by Leong examines Ethernet from the customer's perspective, discussing issues relating to installation and device attachment.

The next two articles deal with broadband LANs. As the title implies, ''Design Considerations for Broadband Coaxial Cable Systems'' is a product-independent look at the technology and design of broadband LANs. Next, ''Broad-Band Personal Computer LAN's'' discusses the requirements for supporting personal computers on a broadband LAN and examines the approach taken by Sytek, which is a representative broadband LAN.

An alternative for supporting personal computers, of course, is an inexpensive baseband system. The article by Gandhi looks at one of the most promising such systems, StarLAN, which uses twisted-pair with a star topology. StarLAN has been incorporated as an option under IEEE 802.3.

The next two articles deal with ring LANs. The article by Strole describes in considerable detail IBM's approach to the ring, which heavily influenced the 802.5 ring standard and is in conformance to that standard. The article deals with the architectural approach, the token ring protocol, and the measures employed to enhance system availability. Next, ''How to Design and Build a Token Ring LAN'' examines the IEEE 802.5 LAN from a customer's perspective, discussing issues relating to installation and device attachment.

The next article, ''Local Area Network Standards,'' provides a good, detailed description of the 802 standards, plus an examination of related issues, such as device attachment, network management, and internetworking.

Finally, ''Fiber-Optic Local Area Network Topology'' examines alternative architectures for optical fiber LANs and HSLNs.

Evolution of the Ethernet Local Computer Network

John F. Shoch, Yogen K. Dalal, David D. Redell, and
Ronald C. Crane

Evolution of the Ethernet Local Computer Network

As it evolved from a research prototype to the specification of a multi-company standard, Ethernet compelled designers to consider numerous trade-offs among alternative implementations and design strategies.

John F. Shoch, Yogen K. Dalal, and David D. Redell, Xerox
Ronald C. Crane, 3Com

With the continuing decline in the cost of computing, we have witnessed a dramatic increase in the number of independent computer systems used for scientific computing, business, process control, word processing, and personal computing. These machines do not compute in isolation, and with their proliferation comes a need for suitable communication networks—particularly local computer networks that can interconnect locally distributed computing systems. While there is no single definition of a local computer network, there is a broad set of requirements:

- relatively high data rates (typically 1 to 10M bits per second);
- geographic distance spanning about one kilometer (typically within a building or a small set of buildings);
- ability to support several hundred independent devices;
- simplicity, or the ability "to provide the simplest possible mechanisms that have the required functionality and performance";[1]
- good error characteristics, good reliability, and minimal dependence upon any centralized components or control;
- efficient use of shared resources, particularly the communications network itself;
- stability under high load;
- fair access to the system by all devices;
- easy installation of a small system, with graceful growth as the system evolves;
- ease of reconfiguration and maintenance; and
- low cost.

One of the more successful designs for a system of this kind is the Ethernet local computer network.[2,3] Ethernet installations have been in use for many years. They support hundreds of stations and meet the requirements listed above.

In general terms, Ethernet is a multi-access, packet-switched communications system for carrying digital data among locally distributed computing systems. The shared communications channel in an Ethernet is a passive broadcast medium with no central control; packet address recognition in each station is used to take packets from the channel. Access to the channel by stations wishing to transmit is coordinated in a distributed fashion by the stations themselves, using a statistical arbitration scheme.

The Ethernet strategy can be used on many different broadcast media, but our major focus has been on the use of coaxial cable as the shared transmission medium. The Experimental Ethernet system was developed at the Xerox Palo Alto Research Center starting in 1972. Since then, numerous other organizations have developed and built "Ethernet-like" local networks.[4] More recently, a cooperative effort involving Digital Equipment Corporation, Intel, and Xerox has produced an updated version of the Ethernet design, generally known as the Ethernet Specification.[5]

One of the primary goals of the Ethernet Specification is compatibility—providing enough information for different manufacturers to build widely differing machines in such a way that they can directly communicate with one another. It might be tempting to view the Specification as simply a design handbook that will allow designers to develop their own Ethernet-like network, perhaps cus-

Reprinted from *Computer*, August 1982, pages 10-26. Copyright © 1982 by The Institute of Electrical and Electronics Engineers, Inc.

tomized for some specific requirements or local constraints. But this would miss the major point: Successful interconnection of heterogeneous machines requires equipment that precisely matches a single specification.

Meeting the Specification is only one of the necessary conditions for intermachine communication at all levels of the network architecture. There are many levels of protocol, such as transport, name binding, and file transfer, that must also be agreed upon and implemented in order to provide useful services.[6-8] This is analogous to the telephone system: The common low-level specifications for telephony make it possible to dial from the US to France, but this is not of much use if the caller speaks only English while the person who answers the phone speaks only French. Specification of these additional protocols is an important area for further work.

The design of any local network must be considered in the context of a distributed system architecture. Although the Ethernet Specification does not directly address issues of high-level network architecture, we view the local network as one component in an *internetwork* system, providing communication services to many diverse devices connected to different networks.[6,9] The services provided by the Ethernet are influenced by these broader architectural considerations.

As we highlight important design considerations and trace the evolution of the Ethernet from research prototype to multicompany standard, we use the term Experimental Ethernet for the former and Ethernet or Ethernet Specification for the latter. The term Ethernet is also used to describe design principles common to both systems.

General description of Ethernet-class systems

Theory of operation. The general Ethernet approach uses a shared communications channel managed with a distributed control policy known as *carrier sense multiple access with collision detection*, or CSMA/CD. With this approach, there is no central controller managing access to the channel, and there is no preallocation of time slots or frequency bands. A station wishing to transmit is said to "contend" for use of the common shared communications channel (sometimes called the Ether) until it "acquires" the channel; once the channel is acquired the station uses it to transmit a packet.

To acquire the channel, stations check whether the network is busy (that is, use *carrier sense*) and defer transmission of their packet until the Ether is quiet (no other transmissions occurring). When quiet is detected, the deferring station immediately begins to transmit. During transmission, the transmitting station listens for a collision (other transmitters attempting to use the channel simultaneously). In a correctly functioning system, collisions occur only within a short time interval following the start of transmission, since after this interval all stations will detect carrier and defer transmission. This time interval is called the *collision window* or the *collision interval* and is a function of the end-to-end propagation delay. If no collisions occur during this time, a transmitter has ac-

quired the Ether and continues transmission of the packet. If a station detects collision, the transmission of the rest of the packet is immediately aborted. To ensure that all parties to the collision have properly detected it, any station that detects a collision invokes a *collision consensus enforcement procedure* that briefly jams the channel. Each transmitter involved in the collision then schedules its packet for retransmission at some later time.

To minimize repeated collisions, each station involved in a collision tries to retransmit at a different time by scheduling the retransmission to take place after a random delay period. In order to achieve channel stability under overload conditions, a controlled retransmission strategy is used whereby the mean of the random retransmission delay is increased as a function of the channel load. An estimate of the channel load can be derived by monitoring the number of collisions experienced by any one packet. This has been shown to be the optimal strategy among the options available for decentralized decision and control problems of this class.[10]

Stations accept packets addressed to them and discard any that are found to be in error. Deference reduces the probability of collision, and collision detection allows the timely retransmission of a packet. It is impossible, however, to guarantee that all packets transmitted will be delivered successfully. For example, if a receiver is not enabled, an error-free packet addressed to it will not be delivered; higher levels of protocol must detect these situations and retransmit.

Under very high load, short periods of time on the channel may be lost due to collisions, but the collision resolution procedure operates quickly.[2,11-13] Channel utilization under these conditions will remain high, particularly if packets are large with respect to the collision interval. One of the fundamental parameters of any Ethernet implementation is the length of this collision interval, which is based on the round-trip propagation time between the farthest two points in the system.

Basic components. The CSMA/CD access procedure can use any broadcast multi-access channel, including radio, twisted pair, coaxial cable, diffuse infrared, and fiber optics.[14] Figure 1 illustrates a typical Ethernet system using coaxial cable. There are four components.

Station. A station makes use of the communication system and is the basic addressable device connected to an Ethernet; in general, it is a computer. We do not expect that "simple" terminals will be connected directly to an Ethernet. Terminals can be connected to some form of terminal controller, however, which provides access to the network. In the future, as the level of sophistication in terminals increases, many terminals will support direct connection to the network. Furthermore, specialized I/O devices, such as magnetic tapes or disk drives, may incorporate sufficient computing resources to function as stations on the network.

Within the station there is some interface between the operating system environment and the Ethernet controller. The nature of this interface (often in software) depends upon the particular implementation of the controller functions in the station.

Controller. A controller for a station is really the set of functions and algorithms needed to manage access to the channel. These include signaling conventions, encoding and decoding, serial-to-parallel conversion, address recognition, error detection, buffering, the basic CSMA/CD channel management, and packetization. These functions can be grouped into two logically independent sections of each controller: the transmitter and the receiver.

The controller functions are generally implemented using a combination of hardware, microcode, and software, depending on the nature of the station. It would be possible, for example, for a very capable station to have a minimal hardware connection to the transmission system and perform most of these functions in software. Alternatively, a station might implement all the controller functions in hardware, or perhaps in a controller-specific microprocessor. Most controller implementations fall somewhere in between. With the continuing advances in LSI development, many of these functions will be packaged in a single chip, and several semiconductor manufacturers have already announced plans to build Ethernet controllers. The precise boundary between functions performed on the chip and those in the station is implementation-dependent, but the nature of that interface is of great importance. As many of the functions as possible should be moved into the chip, provided that this preserves all of the flexibility needed in the construction and use of system interfaces and higher level software.

The description of the controller in this article is functional in nature and indicates how the controller must behave independent of particular implementations. There is some flexibility in implementing a correct controller, and we will make several recommendations concerning efficient operation of the system.

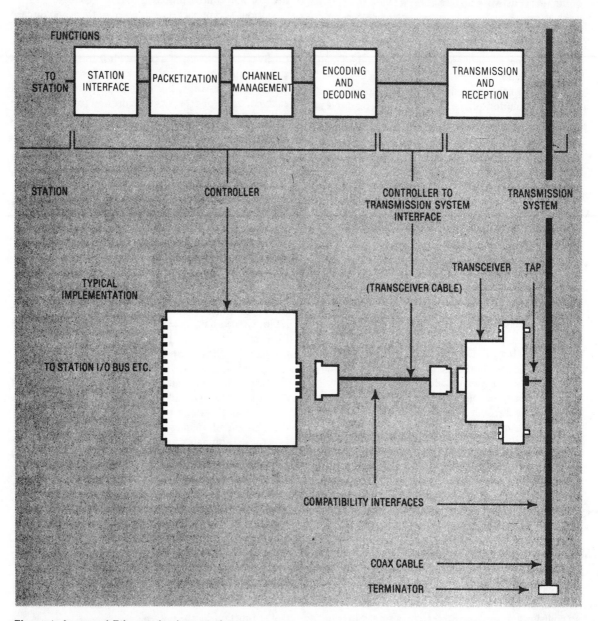

Figure 1. A general Ethernet implementation.

Transmission system. The transmission system includes all the components used to establish a communications path among the controllers. In general, this includes a suitable broadcast transmission medium, the appropriate transmitting and receiving devices—transceivers—and, optionally, repeaters to extend the range of the medium. The protocol for managing access to the transmission system is implemented in the controller; the transmission system does not attempt to interpret any of the bits transmitted on the channel.

The broadcast transmission medium contains those components that provide a physical communication path. In the case of coaxial cable, this includes the cable plus any essential hardware—connectors, terminators, and taps.

Transceivers contain the necessary electronics to transmit and receive signals on the channel and recognize the presence of a signal when another station transmits. They also recognize a collision that takes place when two or more stations transmit simultaneously.

Repeaters are used to extend the length of the transmission system beyond the physical limits imposed by the transmission medium. A repeater uses two transceivers to connect to two different Ethernet segments and combines them into one logical channel, amplifying and regenerating signals as they pass through in either direction.[15] Repeaters are transparent to the rest of the system, and stations on different segments can still collide. Thus, the repeater must propagate a collision detected on one segment through to the other segment, and it must do so without becoming unstable. A repeater makes an Ethernet channel longer and as a result increases the maximum propagation delay of the system, meaning delay through the repeater and propagation delay through the additional segments. To avoid multipath interference in an Ethernet installation, there must be only one path between any two stations through the network. (The higher level internetwork architecture can support alternate paths between stations through different communications channels.)

Controller-to-transmission-system interface. One of the major interfaces in an Ethernet system is the point at which the controller in a station connects to the transmission system. The controller does much of the work in managing the communications process, so this is a fairly simple interface. It includes paths for data going to and from the transmission system. The data received can be used by the controller to sense carrier, but the transmission system normally includes a medium-specific mechanism for detecting collisions on the channel; this must also be communicated through the interface to the controller. It is possible to power a transceiver from a separate power source, but power is usually taken from the controller interface. In most transmission systems, the connection from the controller is made to a transceiver, and this interface is called the transceiver cable interface.

Two generations of Ethernet designs. The Experimental Ethernet circa 1972 confirmed the feasibility of the design, and dozens of installations have been in regular use since then. A typical installation supports hundreds of stations and a wide-ranging set of applications: file transfer, mail distribution, document printing, terminal access to timesharing systems, data-base access, copying disks, multimachine programs, and more. Stations include the Alto workstation,[16] the Dorado (an internal research machine),[17] the Digital Equipment PDP-11, and the Data General Nova. The system has been the subject of extensive performance measurements confirming its predicted behavior.[12,13]

Based upon that experience, a second-generation system was designed at Xerox in the late 1970's. That effort subsequently led to the joint development of the Ethernet Specification. Stations built by Xerox for this network include the Xerox 860, the Xerox 8000 Network System Processor, and the Xerox 1100 Scientific Information Processor (the "Dolphin").

The two systems are very similar: they both use coaxial cable, Manchester signal encoding, and CSMA/CD with dynamic control. Some changes were made based on experience with the experimental system or in an effort to enhance the characteristics of the network. Some of the differences between the systems are summarized in Table 1.

An "Ethernet Technical Summary," which brings together the important features of Version 1 of the joint specification on two pages, is included for reference (pp. 14-15). (In building a compatible device or component, the full Ethernet Specification[5] remains the controlling document. In describing the Ethernet Specification, this article corresponds to Version 1.0; Version 2.0, including extensions and some minor revisions, will be completed later this year.)

Figure 2 is a photograph of some typical components from the Experimental Ethernet, including a transceiver and tap, transceiver cable, and an Alto controller board. Figure 3 is a photograph of similar components based on the Ethernet Specification. Note that both controller boards have been implemented with standard MSI circuits.

Transmission system design

A number of design issues and trade-offs emerged in the development of the Ethernet transmission system, and several lessons were learned from that experience.

Coaxial cable subsystem. In addition to having favorable signaling characteristics and the ability to handle multimegabit transmission rates, a single coaxial

**Table 1.
Comparison of Ethernet systems.**

	Experimental Ethernet	Ethernet Specification
Data rate	2.94M bps	10M bps
Maximum end-to-end length	1 km	2.5 km
Maximum segment length	1 km	500 m
Encoding	Manchester	Manchester
Coax cable impedance	75 ohms	50 ohms
Coax cable signal levels	0 to +3V	0 to −2V
Transceiver cable connectors	25- and 15-pin D series	15-pin D series
Length of preamble	1 bit	64 bits
Length of CRC	16 bits	32 bits
Length of address fields	8 bits	48 bits

Ethernet 1.0 Technical Summary

Packet Format

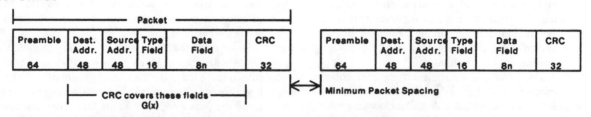

Stations must be able to transmit and receive packets on the common coaxial cable with the indicated packet format and spacing. Each packet should viewed as a sequence of 8-bit bytes; the least significant bit of each byte (starting with the preamble) is transmitted first.

Maximum Packet Size: 1526 bytes (8 byte preamble + 14 byte header + 1500 data bytes + 4 byte CRC)

Minimum Packet Size: 72 bytes (8 byte preamble + 14 byte header + 46 data bytes + 4 byte CRC)

Preamble: This 64-bit synchronization pattern contains alternating 1's and 0's, ending with two consecutive 1's.
The preamble is: 10101010 10101010 10101010 10101010 10101010 10101010 10101010 10101011.

Destination Address: This 48-bit field specifies the station(s) to which the packet is being transmitted. Each station examines this field to determ whether it should accept the packet. The first bit transmitted indicates the type of address. If it is a 0, the field contains the unique address of the destination station. If it is a 1, the field specifies a logical group of recipients; a special case is the broadcast (all stations) address, which is all

Source Address: This 48-bit field contains the unique address of the station that is transmitting the packet.

Type Field: This 16-bit field is used to identify the higher-level protocol type associated with the packet. It determines how the data field is interpre

Data Field: This field contains an integral number of bytes ranging from 46 to 1500. (The minimum ensures that valid packets will be distinguisha from collision fragments.)

Packet Check Sequence: This 32-bit field contains a redundancy check (CRC) code, defined by the generating polynomial:

$$G(x) = x^{32} + x^{26} + x^{23} + x^{22} + x^{16} + x^{12} + x^{11} + x^{10} + x^{8} + x^{7} + x^{5} + x^{4} + x^{2} + x + 1$$

The CRC covers the address (destination/source), type, and data fields. The first transmitted bit of the destination field is the high-order term of message polynomial to be divided by G(x) producing remainder R(x). The high-order term of R(x) is the first transmitted bit of the Packet Check Seque field. The algorithm uses a linear feedback register which is initially preset to all 1's. After the last data bit is transmitted, the contents of this regi (the remainder) are inverted and transmitted as the CRC field. After receiving a good packet, the receiver's shift register contains 11000111 00000 11011101 01111011 (x^{31}, ... ,x^{0}).

Minimum Packet Spacing: This spacing is 9.6 usec, the minimum time that must elapse after one transmission before another transmission may begin.

Round-trip Delay: The maximum end-to-end, round-trip delay for a bit is 51.2 usec.

Collision Filtering: Any received bit sequence smaller than the minimum valid packet (with minimum data field) is discarded as a collision fragment.

Control Procedure

The control procedure defines how and when a station may transmit packets into the common cable. The key purpose is fair resolution of occasio contention among transmitting stations.

Defer: A station must not transmit into the coaxial cable when carrier is present or within the minimum packet spacing time after carrier has end

Transmit: A station may transmit if it is not deferring. It may continue to transmit until either the end of the packet is reached or a collision detected.

Abort: If a collision is detected, transmission of the packet must terminate, and a *jam* (4-6 bytes of arbitrary data) is transmitted to ensure that all o participants in the collision also recognize its occurrence.

Retransmit: After a station has detected a collision and aborted, it must wait for a random *retransmission delay*, defer as usual, and then attempt retransmit the packet. The random time interval is computed using the backoff algorithm (below). After 16 transmission attempts, a higher level (software) decision is made to determine whether to continue or abandon the effort.

Backoff: Retransmission delays are computed using the *Truncated Binary Exponential Backoff* algorithm, with the aim of fairly resolving contention am up to 1024 stations. The delay (the number of time units) before the nth attempt is a uniformly distributed random number from [0 to $2^{n}-1$] for $0 < n \leq$ (n = 0 is the original attempt). For attempts 11-15, the interval is *truncated* and remains at [0 to 1023]. The unit of time for the retransmission delay 512 bit times (51.2 usec).

Channel Encoding

Manchester encoding is used on the coaxial cable. It has a 50% duty cycle, and insures a transition in the middle of every bit cell ("data transition"). The first half of the bit cell contains the complement of the bit value, and the second half contains the true value of the bit.

Bit Cell
1   1   0
High (also quiescent s
Low
|← 100 nS →|
0.75   1.25
Logic High: 1 = 0 mA = 0 V
Logic Low: 0 = -82 mA = -2.05 V
Cable has 0 volts in quiescent sta
Determination of Carrier at receiver.

Data Rate

Data rate is 10 M bits/sec = 100 nsec bit cell ± 0.01%.

Carrier

The presence of data transitions indicates that carrier is present. If a transition is not seen between 0.75 and 1.25 bit times since the center of the bit cell, then carrier has been lost, indicating the end of a packet. For purposes of deferring, carrier means any activity on the cable, independent being properly formed. Specifically, it is any activity on either receive or collision detect signals in the last 160 nsec.

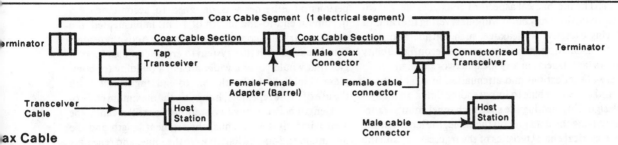

ax Cable

edance: 50 ohms ± 2 ohms (Mil Std. C17-E). This impedance variation includes batch-to-batch variations. Periodic variations in impedance of up ± 3 ohms are permitted along a single piece of cable.

le Loss: The maximum loss from one end of a cable segment to the other end is 8.5 db at 10 MHz (equivalent to ~500 meters of low loss cable).

elding: The physical channel hardware must operate in an ambient field of 2 volts per meter from 10 KHz to 30 MHz and 5 V/meter from 30 MHz to Hz. The shield has a transfer impedance of less than 1 milliohm per meter over the frequency range of 0.1 MHz to 20 MHz (exact value is a function frequency).

und Connections: The coax cable shield shall not be connected to any building or AC ground along its length. If for safety reasons a ground nection of the shield is necessary, it must be in only one place.

sical Dimensions: This specifies the dimensions of a cable which can be used with the standard tap. Other cables may also be used, if they are to be used with a tap-type transceiver (such as use with connectorized transceivers, or as a section between sections to which standard taps are nected).

ter Conductor:	0.0855" diameter solid tinned copper
e Material:	Foam polyethylene or foam teflon FEP
e O.D.:	0.242 " minimum
ld:	0.326" maximum shield O.D. (>90% coverage for outer braid shield)
ket:	PVC or teflon FEP
ket O.D.:	0.405"

ax Connectors and Terminators

x cables must be terminated with male N-series connectors, and cable sections will be joined with female-female adapters. Connector shells shall be lated such that the coax shield is protected from contact to building grounds. A sleeve or boot is acceptable. Cable segments should be terminated a female N-series connector (can be made up of a barrel connector and a male terminator) having an impedance of 50 ohms ± 1%, and able to pate 1 watt. The outside surface of the terminator should also be insulated.

ansceiver

NECTION RULES

to 100 transceivers may be placed on a cable segment no closer together than 2.5 meters. Following this placement rule reduces to a very low (but zero) probability the chance that objectionable standing waves will result.

X CABLE INTERFACE

ut Impedance: The resistive component of the impedance must be greater then 50 Kohms. The total capacitance must be less than 4 picofarads.

ninal Transmit Level: The important parameter is average DC level with 50% duty cycle waveform input. It must be -1.025 V (41 mA) nominal with ange of -0.9 V to -1.2 V (36 to 48 mA). The peak-to-peak AC waveform must be centered on the average DC level and its value can range from 1.4 -P to twice the average DC level. The voltage must never go positive on the coax. The quiescent state of the coax is logic high (0 V). Voltage surements are made on the coax near the transceiver with the shield as reference. Positive current is current flowing out of the center conductor of coax.

e and Fall Time: 25 nSec ± 5 nSec with a maximum of 1 nSec difference between rise time and fall time in a given unit. The intent is that dV/dt uld not significantly exceed that present in a 10 MHz sine wave of same peak-to-peak amplitude.

nal Symmetry: Asymmetry on output should not exceed 2 nSec for a 50-50 square wave input to either transmit or receive section of transceiver.

NSCEIVER CABLE INTERFACE

nal Pairs: Both transceiver and station shall drive and present at the receiving end a 78 ohm balanced load. The differential signal voltage shall be volts nominal peak with a common mode voltage between 0 and +5 volts using power return as reference. (This amounts to shifted ECL levels rating between Gnd and +5 volts. A 10116 with suitable pulldown resistor may be used). The quiescent state of a line corresponds to logic high, ch occurs when the + line is more positive than the - line of a pair.

lision Signal: The active state of this line is a 10 MHz waveform and its quiescent state is logic high. It is active if the transceiver is transmitting another transmission is detected, or if two or more other stations are transmitting, independent of the state of the local transmit signal.

ver: +11.4 volts to +16 volts DC at controller. Maximum current available to transceiver is 0.5 ampere. Actual voltage at transceiver is determined the interface cable resistance (max 4 ohms loop resistance) and current drain.

LATION

impedance between the coax connection and the transceiver cable connection must exceed 250 Kohms at 60 Hz and withstand 250 VRMS at 60 Hz.

ansceiver Cable and Connectors

imum signal loss = 3 db @ 10 MHz. (equivalent to ~50 meters of either 20 or 22 AWG twisted pair).

nsceiver Cable Connector Pin Assignment

Shield*		
Collision +	9.	Collision -
Transmit +	10.	Transmit -
Reserved	11.	Reserved
Receive +	12.	Receive -
Power Return	13.	+ Power
Reserved	14.	Reserved
Reserved	15.	Reserved

eld must be terminated to connector shell.

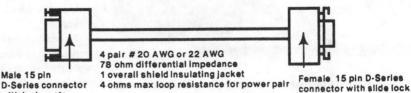

4 pair # 20 AWG or 22 AWG
78 ohm differential impedance
1 overall shield Insulating jacket
4 ohms max loop resistance for power pair

Male 15 pin
D-Series connector
with lock posts.

Female 15 pin D-Series
connector with slide lock
assembly.

cable can support communication among many different stations. The mechanical aspects of coaxial cable make it feasible to tap in at any point without severing the cable or producing excessive RF leakage; such considerations relating to installation, maintenance, and reconfigurability are important aspects in any local network design.

There are reflections and attenuation in a cable, however, and these combine to impose some limits on the system design. Engineering the shared channel entails trade-offs involving the data rate on the cable, the length of the cable, electrical characteristics of the transceiver, and the number of stations. For example, it is possible to operate at very high data rates over short distances, but the rate must be reduced to support a greater maximum length. Also, if each transceiver introduces significant reflections, it may be necessary to limit the placement and possibly the number of transceivers.

The characteristics of the coaxial cable fix the maximum data rate, but the actual clock is generated in the controller. Thus, the station interface and controller must be designed to match the data rates used over the cable. Selection of coaxial cable as the transmission medium has no other direct impact on either the station or the controller.

Cable. The Experimental Ethernet used 75-ohm, RG-11-type foam cable. The Ethernet Specification uses a 50-ohm, solid-center-conductor, double-shield, foam dielectric cable in order to provide some reduction in the magnitude of reflections from insertion capacitance (introduced by tapping into the cable) and to provide better immunity against environmental electromagnetic noise. Belden Number 9880 Ethernet Coax meets the Ethernet Specification.

Terminators and connectors. A small terminator is attached to the cable at each end to provide a termination impedance for the cable equal to its characteristic impedance, thereby eliminating reflection from the ends of the cable. For convenience, the cable can be divided into a number of sections using simple connectors between sections to produce one electrically continuous segment.

Figure 2. Experimental Ethernet components: (a) transceiver and tap, (b) tap-block, (c) transceiver cable, and (d) Alto controller board.

Segment length and the use of repeaters. The Experimental Ethernet was designed to accommodate a maximum end-to-end length of 1 km, implemented as a single electrically continuous segment. Active repeaters could be used with that system to create complex topologies that would cover a wider area in a building (or complex of buildings) within the end-to-end length limit. With the use of those repeaters, however, the maximum end-to-end length between any two stations was still meant to be approximately 1 km. Thus, the segment length and the maximum end-to-end length were the same, and repeaters were used to provide additional flexibility.

In developing the Ethernet Specification, the strong desire to support a 10M-bps data rate—with reasonable transceiver cost—led to a maximum segment length of 500 meters. We expect that this length will be sufficient to support many installations and applications with a single Ethernet segment. In some cases, however, we recognized a requirement for greater maximum end-to-end length in one network. In these cases, repeaters may now be used not just for additional flexibility but also to extend the overall length of an Ethernet. The Ethernet Specification permits the concatenation of up to three segments; the maximum end-to-end delay between two stations measured as a distance is 2.5 km, including the delay through repeaters containing a point-to-point link.[5]

Taps. Transceivers can connect to a coax cable with the use of a *pressure tap,* borrowed from CATV technology. Such a tap allows connection to the cable without cutting it to insert a connector and avoids the need to interrupt network service while installing a new station. One design uses a tap-block that is clamped on the cable and uses a special tool to penetrate the outer jacket and shield. The tool is removed and the separate tap is screwed into the block. Another design has the tap and tap-block integrated into one unit, with the tap puncturing the cable to make contact with the center conductor as the tap-block is being clamped on.

Alternatively, the cable can be cut and connectors fastened to each piece of cable. This unfortunately disrupts the network during the installation process. After the connectors are installed at the break in the cable, a T-connector can be inserted in between and then connected to a transceiver. Another option, a connectorized transceiver, has two connectors built into it for direct attachment to the cable ends without a T-connector.

Experimental Ethernet installations have used pressure taps where the tap and tap-block are separate, as illustrated in Figure 2. Installations conforming to the Ethernet Specification have used all the options. Figure 3 illustrates a connectorized transceiver and a pressure tap with separate tap and tap-block.

Transceiver. The transceiver couples the station to the cable and is the most important part of the transmission system.

The controller-to-transmission-system interface is very simple, and functionally it has not changed between the two Ethernet designs. It performs four functions: (1) transferring transmit data from the controller to the transmission system, (2) transferring receive data from the transmission system to the controller, (3) indicating to the controller that a collision is taking place, and (4) providing power to the transmission system.

It is important that the two ground references in the system—the common coaxial cable shield and the local ground associated with each station—not be tied together, since one local ground typically may differ from another local ground by several volts. Connection of several local grounds to the common cable could cause a large current to flow through the cable's shield, introducing noise and creating a potential safety hazard. For this reason, the cable shield should be grounded in only one place.

It is the transceiver that provides this ground isolation between signals from the controller and signals on the cable. Several isolation techniques are possible: transformer isolation, optical isolation, and capacitive isolation. Transformer isolation provides both power and signal isolation; it has low differential impedance for signals and power, and a high common-mode impedance for isolation. It is also relatively inexpensive to implement. Optical isolators that preserve tight signal symmetry at a competitive price are not readily available. Capacitive coupling is inexpensive and preserves signal symmetry but has poor common-mode rejection. For these reasons transformer isolation is used in Ethernet Specification transceivers. In addition, the mechanical design and installation of the transceiver must preserve this isolation. For example, cable shield connections should not come in contact with a building ground (e.g., a cable tray, conduit, or ceiling hanger).

The transceiver provides a high-impedance connection to the cable in both the power-on and power-off states. In addition, it should protect the network from possible internal circuit failures that could cause it to disrupt the network as a whole. It is also important for the transceiver to withstand transient voltages on the coax between the center conductor and shield. While such voltages should not occur if the coax shield is grounded in only one place, such isolation may not exist during installation.[1]

Negative transmit levels were selected for the Ethernet Specification to permit use of fast and more easily integrated NPN transistors for the output current source. A current source output was chosen over the voltage source used in the Experimental Ethernet to facilitate collision detection.

The key factor affecting the maximum number of transceivers on a segment in the Ethernet Specification is the input bias current for the transceivers. With easily achievable bias currents and collision threshold tolerances, the maximum number was conservatively set at 100 per segment. If the only factors taken into consideration were signal attenuation and reflections, then the number would have been larger.

Controller design

The transmitter and receiver sections of the controller perform signal conversion, encoding and decoding, serial-to-parallel conversion, address recognition, error detection, CSMA/CD channel management, buffering,

and packetization. Postponing for now a discussion of buffering and packetization, we will first deal with the various functions that the controller needs to perform and then show how they are coordinated into an effective CSMA/CD channel management policy.

Figure 3. Ethernet Specification components: (a) transceiver, tap, and tap-block, (b) connectorized transceiver, (c) transceiver cable, (d) Dolphin controller board, and (e) Xerox 8000 controller board.

Signaling, data rate, and framing. The transmitter generates the serial bit stream inserted into the transmission system. Clock and data are combined into one signal using a suitable encoding scheme. Because of its simplicity, Manchester encoding was used in the Experimental Ethernet. In Manchester encoding, each bit cell has two parts: the first half of the cell is the complement of the bit value and the second half *is* the bit value. Thus, there is always a transition in the middle of every bit cell, and this is used by the receiver to extract the data.

For the Ethernet Specification, MFM encoding (used in double-density disk recording) was considered, but it was rejected because decoding was more sensitive to phase distortions from the transmission system and required more components to implement. Compensation is not as easy as in the disk situation because a station must receive signals from both nearby and distant stations. Thus, Manchester encoding is retained in the Ethernet Specification.

In the Experimental Ethernet, any data rate in the range of 1M to 5M bps might have been chosen. The particular rate of 2.94M bps was convenient for working with the first Altos. For the Ethernet Specification, we wanted a data rate as high as possible; very high data rates, however, limit the effective length of the system and require more precise electronics. The data rate of 10M bps represents a trade-off among these considerations.

Packet framing on the Ethernet is simple. The presence of a packet is indicated by the presence of carrier, or transitions. In addition, all packets begin with a known pattern of bits called the *preamble*. This is used by the receiver to establish bit synchronization and then to locate the first bit of the packet. The preamble is inserted by the controller at the sending station and stripped off by the controller at the receiving station. Packets may be of variable length, and absence of carrier marks the end of a packet. Hence, there is no need to have framing flags and "bit stuffing" in the packet as in other data-link protocols such as SDLC or HDLC.

The Experimental Ethernet used a one-bit preamble. While this worked very well, we have, on rare occasions, seen some receivers that could not synchronize with this very short preamble.[18] The Ethernet Specification uses a 64-bit preamble to ensure synchronization of phase-lock loop receivers often used at the higher data rate. It is necessary to specify 64 bits to allow for (1) worst-case tolerances on phase-lock loop components, (2) maximum times to reach steady-state conditions through transceivers, and (3) loss of preamble bits owing to squelch on input and output within the transceivers. Note that the presence of repeaters can add up to four extra transceivers between a source and destination.

Additional conventions can be imposed upon the frame structure. Requiring that all packets be a multiple of some particular byte or word size simplifies controller design and provides an additional consistency check. All packets on the Experimental Ethernet are viewed as a sequence of 16-bit words with the most significant bit of each word transmitted first. The Ethernet Specification requires all packets to be an integral number of eight-bit bytes (exclusive of the preamble, of course) with the least significant bit of each byte transmitted first. The order in which the bytes of an Ethernet packet are stored in the memory

of a particular station is part of the controller-to-station interface.

Encoding and decoding. The transmitter is responsible for taking a serial bit stream from the station and encoding it into the Manchester format. The receiver is responsible for decoding an incoming signal and converting it into a serial bit stream for the station. The process of encoding is fairly straightforward, but decoding is more dif-

---

During transmission a controller must recognize that another station is also transmitting.

---

ficult and is realized in a *phase decoder*. The known preamble pattern can be used to help initialize the phase decoder, which can employ any of several techniques including an analog timing circuit, a phase-locked loop, or a digital phase decoder (which rapidly samples the input and performs a pattern match). The particular decoding technique selected can be a function of the data rate, since some decoder designs may not run as fast as others. Some phase decoding techniques—particularly the digital one—have the added advantage of being able to recognize certain phase violations as collisions on the transmission medium. This is one way to implement collision detection, although it does not work with all transmission systems.

The phase decoders used by stations on the Experimental Ethernet included an analog timing circuit in the form of a delay line on the PDP-11, an analog timing circuit in the form of a simple one-shot-based timer on the Alto, and a digital decoder on the Dorado. All stations built by Xerox for the Ethernet Specification use phase-locked loops.

Carrier sense. Recognizing packets passing by is one of the important requirements of the Ethernet access procedure. Although transmission is baseband, we have borrowed the term "sensing carrier" from radio terminology to describe the detection of signals on the channel. Carrier sense is used for two purposes: (1) in the receiver to delimit the beginning and end of the packet, and (2) in the transmitter to tell when it is permissible to send. With the use of Manchester phase encoding, carrier is conveniently indicated by the presence of transitions on the channel. Thus, the basic phase decoding mechanism can produce a signal indicating the presence of carrier independent of the data being extracted. The Ethernet Specification requires a slightly subtle carrier sense technique owing to the possibility of a saturated collision.

Collision detection. The ability to detect collisions and shut down the transmitter promptly is an important feature in minimizing the channel time lost to collisions. The general requirement is that during transmission a controller must recognize that another station is also transmitting. There are two approaches:

(1) *Collision detection in the transmission system.* It is usually possible for the transmission system itself to recognize a collision. This allows any medium-dependent technique to be used and is usually implemented by comparing the injected signal with the received signal. Comparing the transmitted and received signals is best done in the transceiver where there is a known relationship between the two signals. It is the controller, however, which needs to know that a collision is taking place.

(2) *Collision detection in the controller.* Alternatively, the controller itself can recognize a collision by comparing the transmitted signal with the received signal, or the receiver section can attempt to unilaterally recognize collisions, since they often appear as phase violations.

Both generations of Ethernet detect collisions within the transceiver and generate the collision signal in the controller-to-transmission-system interface. Where feasible, this can be supplemented with a collision detection facility in the controller. Collision detection may not be absolutely foolproof. Some transmission schemes can recognize all collisions, but other combinations of transmission scheme and collision detection may not provide 100-percent recognition. For example, the Experimental Ethernet system functions, in principle, as a wired OR. It is remotely possible for one station to transmit while another station sends a packet whose waveform, at the first station, exactly matches the signal sent by the first station; thus, no collision is recognized there. Unfortunately, the intended recipient might be located between the two stations, and the two signals would indeed interfere.

There is another possible scenario in which collision detection breaks down. One station begins transmitting and its signal propagates down the channel. Another station still senses the channel idle, begins to transmit, gets out a bit or two, and then detects a collision. If the colliding station shuts down immediately, it leaves a very small collision moving through the channel. In some approaches (e.g., DC threshold collision detection) this may be attenuated and simply not make it back to the transmitting station to trigger its collision detection circuitry.

The probability of such occurrences is small. Actual measurements in the Experimental Ethernet system indicate that the collision detection mechanism works very well. Yet it is important to remember that an Ethernet system delivers packets only with high probability—not certainty.

To help ensure proper detection of collisions, each transmitter adopts a *collision consensus enforcement* procedure. This makes sure that all other parties to the collision will recognize that a collision has taken place. In spite of its lengthy name, this is a simple procedure. After detecting a collision, a controller transmits a *jam* that every operating transmitter should detect as a collision. In the Experimental Ethernet the jam is a phase violation, while in the Ethernet Specification it is the transmission of four to six bytes of random data.

Another possible collision scenario arises in the context of the Ethernet Specification. It is possible for a collision to involve so many participants that a transceiver is incapable of injecting any more current into the cable. During such a collision, one cannot guarantee that the waveform on the cable will exhibit any transitions. (In the extreme case, it simply sits at a constant DC level equal to the saturation voltage.) This is called a *saturated collision.* In this situation, the simple notion of sensing carrier by detecting transitions would not work anymore. In particular, a station that deferred only when seeing transitions would think the Ether was idle and jump right in, becoming another participant in the collision. Of course, it would immediately detect the collision and back off, but in the extreme case (everyone wanting to transmit), such jumping-in could theoretically cause the saturated collision to snowball and go on for a very long time. While we recognized that this form of instability was highly unlikely to occur in practice, we included a simple enhancement to the carrier sense mechanism in the Ethernet Specification to prevent the problem.

We have focused on collision detection by the transmitter of a packet and have seen that the transmitter may depend on a collision detect signal generated unilaterally by its receiving phase decoder. Can this receiver-based collision detection be used just by a receiver (that is, a station that is not trying to transmit)? A receiver with this capability could immediately abort an input operation and could even generate a jam signal to help ensure that the collision came to a prompt termination. With a reasonable transmitter-based collision detection scheme, however, the collision is recognized by the transmitters and the damaged packet would come to an end very shortly. Receiver-based collision detection could provide an early warning of a collision for use by the receiver, but this is not a necessary function and we have not used it in either generation of Ethernet design.

CRC generation and checking. The transmitter generates a cyclic redundancy check, or CRC, of each transmitted packet and appends it to a packet before transmission. The receiver checks the CRC on packets it receives and strips it off before giving the packet to the station. If the CRC is incorrect, there are two options: either discard the packet or deliver the damaged packet with an appropriate status indicating a CRC error.

While most CRC algorithms are quite good, they are not infallible. There is a small probability that undetected errors may slip through. More importantly, the CRC only protects a packet from the point at which the CRC is generated to the point at which it is checked. Thus, the CRC cannot protect a packet from damage that occurs in parts of the controller, as, for example, in a FIFO in the parallel path to the memory of a station (the DMA), or in the memory itself. If error detection at a higher level is required, then an end-to-end software checksum can be added to the protocol architecture.

In measuring the Experimental Ethernet system, we have seen packets whose CRC was reported as correct but whose software checksum was incorrect.[18] These did not necessarily represent an undetected Ethernet error; they usually resulted from an external malfunction such as a broken interface, a bad CRC checker, or even an incorrect software checksum algorithm.

Selection of the CRC algorithm is guided by several concerns. It should have sufficient strength to properly detect virtually all packet errors. Unfortunately, only a limited set of CRC algorithms are currently implemented in LSI chips. The Experimental Ethernet used a 16-bit CRC, taking advantage of a single-chip CRC generator/checker. The Ethernet Specification provides better error detection by using a 32-bit CRC.[19,20] This function will be easily implemented in an Ethernet chip.

Addressing. The packet format includes both a source and destination address. A local network design can adopt either of two basic addressing structures: *network-specific* station addresses or *unique* station addresses.[21] In the first case, stations are assigned network addresses that must be unique on *their* network but may be the same as the address held by a station on another network. Such addresses are sometimes called *network relative* addresses, since they depend upon the particular network to which the station is attached. In the second case, each station is assigned an address that is unique over all space and time. Such addresses are also known as absolute or universal addresses, drawn from a flat address space.

To permit internetwork communication, the network-specific address of a station must usually be combined with a unique network number in order to produce an unambiguous address at the next level of protocol. On the other hand, there is no need to combine an absolute station address with a unique network number to produce an unambiguous address. However, it is possible that internetwork systems based on flat (internetwork and local network) absolute addresses will include a unique network number at the internetwork layer as a "very strong hint" for the routing machinery.

If network-specific addressing is adopted, Ethernet address fields need only be large enough to accommodate the maximum number of stations that will be connected to one local network. In addition, there must be a suitable administrative procedure for assigning addresses to stations. Some installations will have more than one Ethernet, and if a station is moved from one network to another it may be necessary to change its network-specific address, since its former address may be in use on the new network. This was the approach used on the Experimental Ethernet, with an eight-bit field for the source and the destination addresses.

We anticipate that there will be a large number of stations and many local networks in an internetwork. Thus, the management of network-specific station addresses can represent a severe problem. The use of a flat address space provides for reliable and manageable operation as a system grows, as machines move, and as the overall topology changes. A flat internet address space requires that the address space be large enough to ensure uniqueness while providing adequate room for growth. It is most convenient if the local network can directly support these fairly large address fields.

For these reasons the Ethernet Specification uses 48-bit addresses.[22] Note that these are station addresses and are not associated with a particular network interface or controller. In particular, we believe that higher level routing and addressing procedures are simplified if a station connected to multiple networks has only one identity which is unique over all networks. The address should not be hard-wired into a particular interface or controller but should be able to be set from the station. It may be very useful, however, to allow a station to read a unique station identifier from the controller. The station can then choose whether to return this identifier to the controller as its address.

In addition to single-station addressing, several enhanced addressing modes are also desirable. *Multicast* addressing is a mechanism by which packets may be targeted to more than one destination. This kind of service is particularly valuable in certain kinds of distributed applications, for instance the access and update of distributed data bases, teleconferencing, and the distributed algorithms that are used to manage the network and the internetwork. We believe that multicast should be supported by allowing the destination address to specify either a physical or logical address. A logical address is known as a *multicast ID. Broadcast* is a special case of multicast in which a packet is intended for all active stations. Both generations of Ethernet support broadcast, while only the Ethernet Specification directly supports multicast.

Stations supporting multicast must recognize multicast IDs of interest. Because of the anticipated growth in the use of multicast service, serious consideration should be given to aspects of the station and controller design that reduce the system load required to filter unwanted multicast packets. Broadcast should be used with discretion, since all nodes incur the overhead of processing every broadcast packet.

Controllers capable of accepting packets regardless of destination address provide *promiscuous* address recognition. On such stations one can develop software to observe all of the channel's traffic, construct traffic matrices, perform load analysis, (potentially) perform fault isolation, and debug protocol implementations. While such a station is able to read packets not addressed to it, we expect that sensitive data will be encrypted by higher levels of software.

CSMA/CD channel management

A major portion of the controller is devoted to Ethernet channel management. These conventions specify procedures by which packets are transmitted and received on the multi-access channel.

Transmitter. The transmitter is invoked when the station has a packet to send. If a collision occurs, the controller enforces the collision with a suitable jam, shuts down the transmitter, and schedules a retransmission.

Retransmission policies have two conflicting goals: (1) scheduling a retransmission quickly to get the packet out and maintain use of the channel, and (2) voluntarily backing off to reduce the station's load on a busy channel. Both generations of Ethernet use the *binary exponential back-off algorithm* described below. After some maximum number of collisions the transmitter gives up and reports a suitable error back to the station; both generations of Ethernet give up after 15 collisions.

The binary exponential back-off algorithm is used to calculate the delay before retransmission. After a collision takes place the objective is to obtain delay periods that will reschedule each station at times quantized in steps at least as large as a collision interval. This time quantization is called the *retransmission slot time*. To guarantee quick use of the channel, this slot time should be short; yet to avoid collisions it should be larger than a collision interval. Therefore, the slot time is usually set to be a little longer than the round-trip time of the channel. The real-time delay is the product of some retransmission delay (a positive integer) and the retransmission slot time.

Collisions on the channel can produce collision fragments, which can be eliminated with a fragment filter in the controller.

To minimize the probability of repeated collisions, each retransmission delay is selected as a random number from a particular retransmission interval between zero and some upper limit. In order to control the channel and keep it stable under high load, the interval is doubled with each successive collision, thus extending the range of possible retransmission delays. This algorithm has very short retransmission delays at the beginning but will back off quickly, preventing the channel from becoming overloaded. After some number of back-offs, the retransmission interval becomes large. To avoid undue delays and slow response to improved channel characteristics, the doubling can be stopped at some point, with additional retransmissions still being drawn from this interval, before the transmission is finally aborted. This is referred to as *truncated binary exponential back-off*.

The truncated binary exponential back-off algorithm approximates the ideal algorithm where the probability of transmission of a packet is $1/Q$, with Q representing the number of stations attempting to transmit.[23] The retransmission interval is truncated when Q becomes equal to the maximum number of stations.

In the Experimental Ethernet, the very first transmission attempt proceeds with no delay (i.e., the retransmission interval is [0-0]). The retransmission interval is doubled after each of the first eight transmission attempts. Thus, the retransmission delays should be uniformly distributed between 0 and $2^{\min(\text{retransmission attempt, 8})} - 1$. After the first transmission attempt, the next eight intervals will be [0-1], [0-3], [0-7], [0-15], [0-31], [0-63], [0-127], and [0-255]. The retransmission interval remains at [0-255] on any subsequent attempt, as the maximum number of stations is 256. The Ethernet Specification has the same algorithm with ten intervals, since the network permits up to 1024 stations; the maximum interval is therefore [0-1023]. The back-off algorithm restarts with a zero retransmission interval for the transmission of every new packet.

This particular algorithm was chosen because it has the proper basic behavior and because it allows a very simple implementation. The algorithm is now supported by empirical data verifying the stability of the system under heavy load.[12,13] Additional attempts to explore more sophisticated algorithms resulted in negligible performance improvement.

Receiver. The receiver section of the controller is activated when the carrier appears on the channel. The receiver processes the incoming bit stream in the following manner:

The remaining preamble is first removed. If the bit stream ends before the preamble completes, it is assumed to be the result of a short collision, and the receiver is restarted.

The receiver next determines whether the packet is addressed to it. The controller will accept a packet in any of the following circumstances:

(1) The destination address matches the specific address of the station.
(2) The destination address has the distinguished broadcast destination.
(3) The destination address is a multicast group of which the station is a member.
(4) The station has set the controller in promiscuous mode and receives all packets.

Some controller designs might choose to receive the entire packet before invoking the address recognition procedure. This is feasible but consumes both memory and processing resources in the controller. More typically, address recognition takes place at a fairly low level in the controller, and if the packet is not to be accepted the controller can ignore the rest of it.

Assuming that the address is recognized, the receiver now accepts the entire packet. Before the packet is actually delivered to the station, the CRC is verified and other consistency checks are performed. For example, the packet should end on an appropriate byte or word boundary and be of appropriate minimum length; a minimum packet would have to include at least a destination and source address, a packet type, and a CRC. Collisions on the channel, however, can produce short, damaged packets called collision fragments. It is generally unnecessary to report these errors to the station, since they can be eliminated with a fragment filter in the controller. It is important, however, for the receiver to be restarted promptly after a collision fragment is received, since the sender of the packet may be about to retransmit.

Packet length. One important goal of the Ethernet is data transparency. In principle, this means that the data field of a packet can contain any bit pattern and be of any length, from zero to arbitrarily large. In practice, while it is easy to allow any bit pattern to appear in the data field, there are some practical considerations that suggest imposing upper and lower bounds on its length.

At one extreme, an empty packet (one with a zero-length data field) would consist of just a preamble, source and destination addresses, a type field, and a CRC. The Experimental Ethernet permitted empty packets. However, in some situations it is desirable to enforce a minimum overall packet size by mandating a minimum-length data field, as in the Ethernet Specification. Higher level protocols wishing to transmit shorter packets must then pad out the data field to reach the minimum.

At the other extreme, one could imagine sending many thousands or even millions of bytes in a single packet. There are, however, several factors that tend to limit packet size, including (1) the desire to limit the size of the buffers in the station for sending and receiving packets, (2) similar considerations concerning the packet buffers that are sometimes built into the Ethernet controller itself, and (3) the need to avoid tying up the channel and increasing average channel latency for other stations. Buffer management tends to be the dominant consideration. The maximum requirement for buffers in the station is usually a parameter of higher level software determined by the overall network architecture; it is typically on the order of 500 to 2000 bytes. The size of any packet buffers in the controller, on the other hand, is usually a design parameter of the controller hardware and thus represents a more rigid limitation. To insure compatibility among buffered controllers, the Ethernet Specification mandates a maximum packet length of 1526 bytes (1500 data bytes plus overhead).

Note that the upper and lower bounds on packet length are of more than passing interest, since observed distributions are typically quite bimodal. Packets tend to be either very short (control packets or packets carrying a small amount of data) or maximum length (usually some form of bulk data transfer).[12,13]

The efficiency of an Ethernet system is largely dependent on the size of the packets being sent and can be very high when large packets are used. Measurements have shown total utilization as high as 98 percent. A small quantum of channel capacity is lost whenever there is a collision, but the carrier sense and collision detection mechanisms combine to minimize this loss. Carrier sense reduces the likelihood of a collision, since the acquisition effect renders a given transmission immune to collisions once it has continued for longer than a collision interval. Collision detection limits the duration of a collision to a single collision interval. If packets are long compared with the collision interval, then the network is vulnerable to collisions only a small fraction of the time and total utilization will remain high. If the average packet size is reduced, however, both carrier sense and collision detection become less effective. Ultimately, as the packet size approaches the collision interval, system performance degrades to that of a straight CSMA channel without collision detection. This condition only occurs under a heavy load consisting predominantly of very small packets; with a typical mix of applications this is not a practical problem.

If the packet size is reduced still further until it is less than the collision interval, some new problems appear. Of course, if an empty packet is already longer than the collision interval, as in the Experimental Ethernet, this case cannot arise. As the channel length and/or the data rate are increased, however, the length (in bits) of the collision interval also increases. When it becomes larger than an empty packet, one must decide whether stations are allowed to send tiny packets that are smaller than the collision interval. If so, two more problems arise, one affecting the transmitter and one the receiver.

The transmitter's problem is that it can complete the entire transmission of a tiny packet before network acquisition has occurred. If the packet subsequently experiences a collision farther down the channel, it is too late for the transmitter to detect the collision and promptly schedule a retransmission. In this situation, the probability of a collision has not increased, nor has any additional channel capacity been sacrificed; the problem is simply that the transmitter will occasionally fail to recognize and handle a collision. To deal with such failures, the sender of tiny packets must rely on retransmissions invoked by a higher level protocol and thus suffer reduced throughput and increased delay. This occasional performance reduction is generally not a serious problem, however. Note that only the sender of tiny packets encounters this behavior; there is no unusual impact on other stations sending larger packets.

While occasional collisions should be viewed as a normal part of the CSMA/CD access procedure, line errors should not. One would therefore like to accumulate information about the two classes of events separately.

The receiver's problem with tiny packets concerns its ability to recognize collision fragments by their small size and discard them. If the receiver can assume that packets smaller than the collision interval are collision fragments, it can use this to implement a simple and inexpensive fragment filter. It is important for the receiver to discard collision fragments, both to reduce the processing load at the station and to ensure that it is ready to receive the impending retransmission from the transmitter involved in the collision. The fragment filter approach is automatically valid in a network in which there are no tiny packets, such as the Experimental Ethernet. If tiny packets can occur, however, the receiver cannot reliably distinguish them from collision fragments purely on the basis of size. This means that at least the longer collision fragments must be rejected on the basis of some other error detection mechanism such as the CRC check or a byte or word alignment check. One disadvantage of this approach is that it increases the load on the CRC mechanism, which, while strong, is not infallible. Another problem is that the CRC error condition will now be indicating two kinds of faults: long collisions and genuine line errors. While occasional collisions should be viewed as a normal part of the CSMA/CD access procedure, line errors should not. One would therefore like to accumulate information about the two classes of events separately.

The problems caused by tiny packets are not insurmountable, but they do increase the attractiveness of simply legislating the problem out of existence by forbidding the sending of packets smaller than the collision interval. Thus, in a network whose collision interval is longer than an empty packet, the alternatives are

(1) *Allow tiny packets.* In this case, the transmitter will sometimes fail to detect collisions, requiring retransmis-

sion at a higher level and impacting performance. The receiver can use a partial fragment filter to discard collision fragments shorter than an empty packet, but longer collision fragments will make it through this filter and must be rejected on the basis of other error checks, such as the CRC check, with the resultant jumbling of the error statistics.

(2) *Forbid tiny packets.* In this case, the transmitter can always detect a collision and perform prompt retransmission. The receiver can use a fragment filter to automatically discard all packets shorter than the collision interval. The disadvantage is the imposition of a minimum packet size.

Unlike the Experimental Ethernet, the Ethernet Specification defines a collision interval longer than an empty packet and must therefore choose between these alternatives. The choice is to forbid tiny packets by requiring a minimum data field size of 46 bytes. Since we expect that Ethernet packets will typically contain internetwork packet headers and other overhead, this is not viewed as a significant disadvantage.

Controller-to-station interface design

The properties of the controller-to-station interface can dramatically affect the reliability and efficiency of systems based on Ethernet.

Turning the controller on and off. A well-designed controller must be able to (1) keep the receiver on in order to catch back-to-back packets (those separated by some minimum packet spacing), and (2) receive packets a station transmits to itself. We will now look in detail at these requirements and the techniques for satisfying them.

Keeping the receiver on. The most frequent cause of a lost packet has nothing to do with collision or bad CRCs. Packets are usually missed simply because the receiver was not listening. The Ethernet is an asynchronous device that can present a packet at any time, and it is important that higher level software keep the receiver enabled.

The problem is even more subtle, however, for even when operating normally there can be periods during which the receiver is not listening. There may, for instance, be turnaround times between certain operations when the receiver is left turned off. For example, a receive-to-receive turnaround takes place after one packet is received and before the receiver is again enabled. If the design of the interface, controller, or station software keeps the receiver off for too long, arriving packets can be lost during this turnaround. This occurs most frequently in servers on a network, which may be receiving packets from several sources in rapid succession. If back-to-back packets come down the wire, the second one will be lost in the receive-to-receive turnaround time. The same problem can occur within a normal workstation, for example, if a desired packet immediately follows a broadcast packet; the workstation gets the broadcast but misses the packet specifically addressed to it. Higher level protocol software will presumably recover from these situations, but the performance penalty may be severe.

Similarly, there may be a transmit-to-receive turnaround time when the receiver is deaf. This is determined by how long it takes to enable the receiver after sending a packet. If, for example, a workstation with a slow transmit-to-receive turnaround sends a packet to a well-tuned server, the answer may come back before the receiver is enabled again. No amount of retransmission by higher levels will ever solve this problem!

It is important to minimize the length of any turnaround times when the receiver might be off. There can also be receive-to-transmit and transmit-to-transmit turnaround times, but their impact on performance is not as critical.

Sending to itself. A good diagnostic tool for a network interface is the ability of a station to send packets to itself. While an internal loop-back in the controller provides a partial test, actual transmission and simultaneous reception provide more complete verification.

The Ethernet channel is, in some sense, half duplex: there is normally only one station transmitting at a time. There is a temptation, therefore, to also make the controller half duplex—that is, unable to send and receive at the same time. If possible, however, the design of the interface, controller, and station software should allow a station to send packets to itself.

Recommendations. The Ethernet Specification includes one specific requirement that helps to solve the first of these problems: There must be a minimal interpacket spacing on the cable of 9.6 microseconds. This requirement applies to a transmitter getting ready to send a packet and does not necessarily mean that all receivers conforming to the Specification must receive two adjacent packets. This requirement at least makes it possible to build a controller that can receive adjacent packets on the cable.

Satisfying the two requirements described earlier involves the use of two related features in the design of a controller: full-duplex interfaces and back-to-back receivers. A full-duplex interface allows the receiver and the transmitter to be started independently. A back-to-back receiver has facilities to automatically restart the receiver upon completion of a reception. Limited back-to-back reception can be done with two buffers; the first catches a packet and then the second catches the next without requiring the receiver to wait. Generalized back-to-back reception can be accomplished by using chained I/O commands; the receiver is driven by a list of free input buffers, taking one when needed. These two notions can be combined to build any of the following four interfaces: (1) half-duplex interface, (2) full-duplex interface, (3) half-duplex interface with back-to-back receive, and (4) full-duplex interface with back-to-back receive.

The Experimental Ethernet controller for the Alto is half duplex, runs only in a transmit or receive mode, and must be explicitly started in each mode. The need to explicitly start the receiver (there is no automatic hardware turnaround) means that there may be lengthy turnaround times in which packets may be missed. This approach allows sharing certain components, like the CRC function and the FIFO.

Experimental Ethernet controllers built for the PDP-11 and the Nova are full-duplex interfaces. The transmit-to-receive turnaround has been minimized, but there is no provision for back-to-back packets.

The Ethernet controller for the Xerox 8000 processor is a half-duplex interface with back-to-back receive. Although it cannot send to itself, the transmit-to-receive turnaround delay has been avoided by having the hardware automatically revert to the receive state when a transmission is completed.

The Experimental Ethernet and Ethernet Specification controllers for the Dolphin are full-duplex interfaces with back-to-back receivers. They are the ultimate in interface organization.

Our experience shows that any one of the four alternatives will work. However, we strongly recommend that all interface and controller designs support full-duplex operation and provide for reception of back-to-back packets (chained I/O).

The controller-to-station interface defines the manner in which data received from the cable is stored in memory and, conversely, how data stored in memory is transmitted on the cable.

Buffering. Depending upon the particular data rate of the channel and the characteristics of the station, the controller may have to provide suitable buffering of packets. If the station can keep up with the data rate of the channel, only a small FIFO may be needed to deal with station latency. If the station cannot sustain the channel data rate, it may be necessary to include a full-packet buffer as part of the controller. For this reason, full compatibility across different stations necessitates the specification of a maximum packet length.

If a single-packet buffer is provided in the controller (a buffer that has no marker mechanism to distinguish boundaries between packets), it will generally be impossible to catch back-to-back packets, and in such cases it is preferable to have at least two input buffers.

Packets in memory. The controller-to-station interface defines the manner in which data received from the cable is stored in memory and, conversely, how data stored in memory is transmitted on the cable. There are many ways in which this parallel-to-serial transformation can be defined.[24] The Ethernet Specification defines a packet on the cable to be a sequence of eight-bit bytes, with the least significant bit of each byte transmitted first. Higher level protocols will in most cases, however, define data types that are multiples of eight bits. The parallel-to-serial transformations will be influenced by the programming conventions of the station and by the higher level protocols. Stations with different parallel-to-serial transformations that use the same higher level protocol must make sure that all data types are viewed consistently.

Type field. An Ethernet packet can encapsulate many kinds of client-defined packets. Thus, the packet format includes only a data field, two addresses, and a type field. The type field identifies the special client-level protocol that will interpret the data encapsulated within the packet. The type field is never processed by the Ethernet system itself but can be thought of as an escape, providing a consistent way to specify the interpretation of the rest of the packet.

Low-level system services such as diagnostics, bootstrap, loading, or specialized network management functions can take advantage of the identification provided by this field. In fact, it is possible to use the type field to identify all the different packets in a protocol architecture. In general, however, we recommend that the Ethernet packet encapsulate higher level internetwork packets. Internetwork router stations might concurrently support a number of different internetwork protocols, and the use of the type field allows the internetwork router to encapsulate different kinds of internetwork packets for a local network transmission.[25] The use of a type field in the Ethernet packet is an instance of a principle we apply to all layers in a protocol architecture. A type field is used at each level of the hierarchy to identify the protocol used at the next higher level; it is the bridge between adjacent levels. This results in an architecture that defines a layered tree of protocols.

The Experimental Ethernet design uses a 16-bit type field. This has proved to be a very useful feature and has been carried over into the Ethernet Specification.

Summary and conclusions

We have highlighted a number of important considerations that affect the design of an Ethernet local computer network and have traced the evolution of the system from a research prototype to a multicompany standard by discussing strategies and trade-offs between alternative implementations.

The Ethernet is intended primarily for use in such areas as office automation, distributed data processing, terminal access, and other situations requiring economical connection to a local communication medium carrying bursts of traffic at high peak data rates. Experience with the Experimental Ethernet in building distributed systems that support electronic mail, distributed filing, calendar systems, and other applications has confirmed many of our design goals and decisions.[26-29]

Questions sometimes arise concerning the ways in which the Ethernet design addresses (or chooses not to address) the following considerations: reliability, addressing, priority, encryption, and compatibility. It is important to note that some functions are better left out of the Ethernet itself for implementation at higher levels in the architecture.

All systems should be reliable, and network-based systems are no exception. We believe that reliability must be addressed at each level in the protocol hierarchy; each level should provide only what it can guarantee at a reasonable price. Our model for internetworking is one in which reliability and sequencing are performed using end-to-end transport protocols. Thus, the Ethernet provides a "best effort" datagram service. The Ethernet has been designed to have very good error characteristics, and, without promising to deliver all packets, it will deliver a very large percentage of offered packets without error. It includes error detection procedures but provides no error correction.

We expect internetworks to be very large. Many of the problems in managing them can be simplified by using absolute station addresses that are directly supported within the local network. Thus, address fields in the Ethernet Specification seem to be very generous—well beyond the number of stations that might connect to one local network but meant to efficiently support large internetwork systems.

Our experience indicates that for practically all applications falling into the category "loosely coupled distributed system," the average utilization of the communications network is low. The Ethernet has been designed to have excess bandwidth, not all of which must be utilized. Systems should be engineered to run with a sustained load of no more than 50 percent. As a consequence, the network will generally provide high throughput of data with low delay, and there are no priority levels associated with particular packets. Designers of individual devices, network servers, and higher level protocols are free to develop priority schemes for accessing particular resources.

Protection, security, and access control are all system-wide functions that require a comprehensive strategy. The Ethernet system itself is not designed to provide encryption or other mechanisms for security, since these techniques by themselves do not provide the kind of protection most users require. Security in the form of encryption, where required, is the responsibility of the end-user processes.

Higher level protocols raise their own issues of compatibility over and above those addressed by the Ethernet and other link-level facilities. While the compatibility provided by the Ethernet does not guarantee solutions to higher level compatibility problems, it does provide a context within which such problems can be addressed by avoiding low-level incompatibilities that would make direct communication impossible. We expect to see standards for higher level protocols emerge during the next few years.

Within an overall distributed systems architecture, the two generations of Ethernet systems have proven to be very effective local computer networks. ∎

Acknowledgments

Many people have contributed to the success and evolution of the Ethernet local computer network. Bob Metcalfe and David Boggs built the Experimental Ethernet at the Xerox Palo Alto Research Center, and Tat Lam built and supplied the many transceivers. Since then, Ed Taft, Hal Murray, Will Crowther, Roy Ogus, Bob Garner, Ed Markowski, Bob Printis, Bob Belleville, Bill Gunning, and Juan Bulnes have contributed to the design and implementation of the Ethernet. Cooperation among Digital Equipment Corporation, Intel, and Xerox also produced many important contributions to the Ethernet Specification.

References

1. R. C. Crane and E. A. Taft, "Practical Considerations in Ethernet Local Network Design," *Proc. 13th Hawaii Int'l Conf. Systems Sciences,* Jan. 1980, pp. 166-174.

2. R. M. Metcalfe and D. R. Boggs, "Ethernet: Distributed Packet Switching for Local Computer Networks," *Comm. ACM,* 19:7, July 1976, pp. 395-404.

3. R. M. Metcalfe, D. R. Boggs, C. P. Thacker, and B. W. Lampson, "Multipoint Data Communication System with Collision Detection," US Patent No. 4,063,220, Dec. 13, 1977.

4. J. F. Shoch, *"An Annotated Bibliography on Local Computer Networks"* (3rd ed.), Xerox Parc Technical Report SSL-80-2, and IFIP Working Group 6.4 Working Paper 80-12, Apr. 1980.

5. *The Ethernet, A Local Area Network: Data Link Layer and Physical Layer Specifications,* Version 1.0, Digital Equipment Corporation, Intel, Xerox, Sept. 30, 1980.

6. D. R. Boggs, J. F. Shoch, E. A. Taft, and R. M. Metcalfe, "PUP: An Internetwork Architecture," *IEEE Trans. Comm.,* Apr. 1980, pp. 612-624.

7. H. Zimmermann, "OSI Reference Model—The ISO Model of Architecture for Open Systems Interconnection," *IEEE Trans. Comm.,* Apr. 1980, pp. 425-432.

8. Y. K. Dalal, "The Information Outlet: A New Tool for Office Organization," *Proc. On-line Conf. Local Networks and Distributed Office Systems,* London, May 1981, pp. 11-19.

9. V. G. Cerf and P. K. Kirstein, "Issues in Packet-Network Interconnection," *Proc. IEEE,* Vol. 66, No. 11, Nov. 1978, pp. 1386-1408.

10. F. C. Shoute, "Decentralized Control in Computer Communication," Technical Report No. 667, Division of Engineering and Applied Physics, Harvard University, Apr. 1977.

11. R. M. Metcalfe, "Packet Communication," Thesis Harvard University, Project MAC Report MAC TR-114, Massachusetts Institute of Technology, Dec. 1973.

12. J. F. Shoch and J. A. Hupp, "Performance of an Ethernet Local Network—A Preliminary Report," *Local Area Comm. Network Symp.,* Boston, May 1979, pp. 113-125. Revised version *Proc. Compcon Spring 80,* San Francisco, pp. 318-322.

13. J. F. Shoch and J. A. Hupp, "Measured Performance of an Ethernet Local Network," *Comm. ACM,* Vol. 23, No. 12, Dec. 1980, pp. 711-721.

14. E. G. Rawson and R. M. Metcalfe, "Fibernet: Multimode Optical Fibers for Local Computer Networks," *IEEE Trans. Comm.,* July 1978, pp. 983-990.

15. D. R. Boggs and R. M. Metcalfe, Communications network repeater, US Patent No. 4,099,024, July 4, 1978.

16. C. P. Thacker et al., "Alto: A Personal Computer," Xerox Palo Alto Research Center Technical Report CSL-79-11, Aug. 1979.

17. "The Dorado: A High-Performance Personal Computer," Three Reports, Xerox Palo Alto Research Center, CSL-81-1, Jan. 1981.

18. J. F. Shoch, *Local Computer Networks,* McGraw-Hill, in press.

19. J. L. Hammond, J. E. Brown, and S. S. Liu, "Development of a Transmission Error Model and an Error Control Model," Technical Report RADC-TR-75-138, Rome Air Development Center, 1975.

20. R. Bittel, "On Frame Check Sequence (FCS) Generation and Checking," ANSI working paper X3-S34-77-43, 1977.

21. J. F. Shoch, "Internetwork Naming, Addressing, and Routing," *Proc. Compcon Fall 78,* pp. 430-437.

22. Y. K. Dalal and R. S. Printis, "48-bit Internet and Ethernet Host Numbers," *Proc. Seventh Data Comm. Symp.,* Oct. 1981.

23. R. M. Metcalfe, "Steady-State Analysis of a Slotted and Controlled Aloha System with Blocking," *Proc. Sixth Hawaii Conf. System Sciences,* Jan. 1973. Reprinted in *Sigcom Review,* Jan. 1975.

24. D. Cohen, "On Holy Wars and a Plea for Peace," *Computer,* Vol. 14, No. 10, Oct. 1981, pp. 48-54.

25. J. F. Shoch, D. Cohen, and E. A. Taft, "Mutual Encapsulation of Internetwork Protocols," *Computer Networks,* Vol. 5, No. 4, July 1981, pp. 287-301.

26. A. D. Birrell et al., "Grapevine: An Exercise in Distributed Computing," *Comm. ACM,* Vol. 25, No. 4, Apr. 1982, pp. 260-274.

27. H. Sturgis, J. Mitchell, and J. Israel, "Issues in the Design and Use of a Distributed File System," *ACM Operating Systems Rev.,* Vol. 14, No. 3, July 1980, pp. 55-69.

28. D. K. Gifford, "Violet, an Experimental Decentralized System," Xerox Palo Alto Research Center, CSL-79-12, Sept. 1979.

29. J. F. Shoch and J. A. Hupp, "Notes on the 'Worm' Programs—Some Early Experiences with a Distributed Computation," *Comm. ACM,* Vol. 25, No. 3, Mar. 1982, pp. 172-180.

Yogen K. Dalal is manager of services and architecture for office systems in the Office Products Division of Xerox Corporation. He has been with the company in Palo Alto since 1977. His research interests include local computer networks, internetwork protocols, distributed systems architecture, broadcast protocols, and operating systems. He is a member of the ACM and the IEEE. He received the B. Tech. degree in electrical engineering from the Indian Institute of Technology, Bombay, in 1972, and the MS and PhD degrees in electrical engineering and computer science from Stanford University in 1973 and 1977, respectively.

David D. Redell is a staff scientist in the Office Products Division of Xerox Corporation. He was previously on the faculty of the Massachusetts Institute of Technology. His research interests include computer networks, distributed systems, information security, and computer architecture. He received his BA, MS, and PhD degrees in computer science from the University of California at Berkeley.

John F. Shoch is deputy general manager for office systems in the Office Products Division of Xerox Corporation. From 1980 to 1982, he served as assistant to the president of Xerox and director of the corporate policy committee. He joined the research staff at the Xerox Palo Alto Research Center in 1971. His research interests have included local computer networks (such as the Ethernet), internetwork protocols, packet radio, and other aspects of distributed systems. In addition, he has taught at Stanford University, is a member of the ACM and the IEEE, and serves as vice-chairman (US) of IFIP Working Group 6.4 on local computer networks. Shoch received the BA degree in political science and the MS and PhD degrees in computer science from Stanford University.

Ronald C. Crane, a founder of 3Com Corporation in Mountain View, California, now heads advanced engineering for the firm. From 1977 to 1980 he served as a technical staff member and subsequently a consultant to Xerox's Office Products Division in Palo Alto where he was a principal designer of the Digital, Intel, Xerox Ethernet system. His research interests have included adaptive topology packet networks, digital broadcasting systems (Digicast), and baseband transmission systems. He is a member of the ACM and IEEE. He received the BS degree in electrical engineering from the Massachusetts Institute of Technology in 1972 and the MS degree in electrical engineering from Stanford University in 1974.

A Practical Guide to Ethernet

John Leong

Director, Networking and Communications
Carnegie Mellon University

Introduction

Four years ago, I wrote an article about the nuts-and-bolts of Ethernet installation and operation. The article was eventually published in the September 1985 issue of *Data Communications* magazine. Since then, Ethernet has practically become the standard local area networking technology for the scientific and engineering community with a large and well established install base. There are now a wide and increasing range of products from a host of vendors.

This paper is a complete re-write of the original article. It takes into consideration our additional experiences and the developments in the market over the past few years. A major change since the publication of the nuts-and-bolts article is our view on Ethernet configuration. We have now come to the conclusion that a bus type network can be very troublesome from a network management point of view and is not suitable for a network of any significant size.

This paper will again focuses on the practical aspects of Ethernet configuration, installation and management. It assumes that the reader is reasonably familiar with the principle of Ethernet. Definitive description of the network can be found in the rather dense IEEE publication *IEEE802.3 Carrier-Sense Multiple Access With Collision Detection (CSMA/CD)*.

This paper is organized in 3 parts. The first deals with Ethernet in general. The second describes various components of the network. The third rounds up the paper with miscellaneous topics.

Background

Carnegie Mellon University has one of the largest collections of heterogeneous and highly interconnected local area networks in the world. We differ significantly from most commercial organizations in that we support multiple LAN technologies as well as a diverse range of computers from various vendors. By the end of 1987, we had over 2,500 nodes attached to the networks. More than 1,200 of these nodes are on Ethernets while around 1,000 nodes are on the IBM token rings. The rest are connected to the rapidly growing Appletalk networks for the Macintoshes. Over and above the local area networks, there is a 3,000 ports asynchronous, circuit switched, terminal network. This network is slowly being down-sized as terminals are replaced by personal computers or workstations. Furthermore, circuit switched technology turns out to be inappropriate for a distributed computing environment.

We have been involved with Ethernet since its early days. As a matter of fact, we still have a very active 75 Ohm, 3 Mbps experimental Ethernet in service. Our Ethernet operation has been evolving over the years as new products become available and as we learn from our mistakes.

Part 1: General

Is Ethernet for You ?

In quite a number of cases, one really has no choice. Some machines will only support Ethernet. Example of these are the low cost, diskless SUN and VAX workstations. On the other hand, if you have purchased one of the older and closed Macintoshes, Ethernet is not an option. For machines with a public domain or standard bus architecture, a potential choice exists. A vendor, however, will often bias the machines to a particular LAN technology in the form of software support. Hence DEC and SUN favor Ethernets while IBM favors token ring. As of today, the only machine where one really has a choice of LAN is the IBM PC and its clones.

In our experience, both Ethernet and Token Ring have high performance and are generally very reliable. Token ring offers better network management capabilities and is generally easier to maintain and trouble shoot. This is particularly true when comparing the token ring with the standard bus topology Ethernet. The gap narrows somewhat if the Ethernet is configured in the form of a star or interconnected stars.

Besides reliability and ease of maintenance, another factor to be considered is the bandwidth. There are numerous papers and discussions about the "true" bandwidth of Ethernet. This uncertainty is due to the non-deterministic nature of the CSMA/CD algorithm. Under a heavy load situation caused by numerous stations contending for bandwidth, the high rate of collision can make the network unstable. Then, there are the few and

special applications where raw bandwidth in excess of 10 Mbps is needed. In general, we found Ethernet performance to be consistent with most of our current requirements. We did have problems with some of our networks, particularly those heavily populated with diskless SUN 3 workstations. These have been overcome through careful network planning and segmentation.

Over the years, I have often been asked a somewhat surprising question: "I have a 3-Plus Ethernet from 3COM. Can I use that Ethernet to support VAX stations running DECNET also?" The products quoted here are for example only. They could well be network packages from Ungermann-Bass, Novell, SUN or whatever. The answer is "Yes." Thanks to standardization, one can pick and choose any combination of equipment and software as long as it conforms to Ethernet specifications. It should all peacefully coexist on the same Ethernet cable. A good analogy is the phone system. One can attach AT&T, Panasonic or other types of sets to the network as long as they conform to specifications. Similarly, one can use Ethernet transceivers and controllers from any company. Furthermore, the phone system itself does not care whether you speak English, French or Swahili. It supports simultaneous conversations using different languages. For meaningful communication, however, the person at the other end of the line should understand the language you are using! In the case of Ethernet, it does not matter what protocol is encapsulated within the packet—whether it is TCP/IP, XNS or DECNET. Again, it helps if the station you are communicating with has the necessary software to process the protocol you are using.

Ethernet Version 1, Version 2 and 802.3

There have been 3 10 Mbps Ethernet specifications since it was launched. The original, Ethernet version 1, was defined by Digital Equipment Corporation (DEC), Intel and Xerox back in 1980. This group of three companies are sometimes referred to as DIX. In 1982, a draft official specification was introduced by the IEEE. This is the 802.3 specification, which was approved as an IEEE standard in 1984. In response, the DIX group revised the version 1 specification to be compatible with IEEE. This is Ethernet version 2.

Today, all vendors produce products according to the 802.3 standard. Some will also provide version 1 compatibility. Ethernet version 2 is practically the same as 802.3 except for a few minor additions. Although the network management enhancements are useful, they are rarely implemented. For all practical purposes, Ethernet version 2 is being ignored.

The main differences between the 802.3 (and Ethernet version 2) specifications and the Ethernet version 1 specification lie in the controller to transceiver interface. Examples are the different ground pins assignment, timing of the collision present test and the change of the line idle state voltage from 0.7V to 0V.

In practice, since the signalling convention within the coaxial trunk cable is the same for both versions, we have had no problem mixing version 1 with 802.3 transceivers on the same cable. We have had problems, however, connecting version 1 transceivers to 802.3 controllers or vice versa. The problem does not show up all the time and the symptoms can be quite maddening — the attached station can communicate with some stations but not others. This mixed versions problem does not exist if one is installing a new Ethernet since, presumably, one will be using all 802.3 equipment. It applies only to operations with an installed base of version 1 components.

Configuration: Star or Bus?

The generic configuration of an Ethernet is a bus. Typically, it consists of a coax trunk cable running above the ceilings of a building. Transceivers are attached to the trunk at various locations. To install a new station on the network, one needs to attach a transceiver to the nearest and most accessible location of the trunk cable. Then one can connect the transceiver with the station with a transceiver or drop cable. This is a relatively easy exercise if one can locate the coaxial trunk cable. However, this ease of installation can translate into a potential maintenance nightmare for the future.

An Ethernet can fail in 2 modes. It can experience a hard failure such that the network is completely disabled. This happens when the trunk cable is either shorted or not terminated. Location and correction of the problem is generally straightforward. The other mode of failure is a soft failure. This happens when a certain network component malfunctions and starts to interfere intermittently with normal network operation. The typical symptom is a substantial reduction of effective network bandwidth due to an excessive amount of collisions and errors. This is by far the more difficult failure to locate and resolve. Quite often, one has to resort to the low tech, trial and error approach of detaching stations from the network until one can identify the link that is causing the problem. This can be a tedious exercise when one has over a hundred stations connected to a long and winding Ethernet. Typically, the task is complicated by lack of access to some rooms and by the presence of stations attached to, or removed from, the network without the knowledge of network maintenance personnel.

On the other hand, if the network is configured as a star, virtually all the trouble shooting can be done at the hub. This can significantly reduce the time required to locate and isolate the problem. Furthermore, the network can be quickly reconfigured at the hub if required. Additionally, the hub can be located in a room requiring key access. This allows networking personnel greater control over what is connected to or removed from the network. The small down side of a star topology network is the longer aggregate cable runs. This translates into both higher cabling cost as well as longer installation time for the attachment of a new node. A compromise can be made by having a number of interconnected and strategically located stars instead of a single large one. In general, the long term maintenance benefit one can derive from a star configuration is well worth any overhead cost.

There are at least 3 ways to create a star shaped Ethernet. They are described below. Details about the components used in the configurations can be found in later sections.

A simple approach is to use a multiport transceiver as the hub and connect stations to it using standard Ethernet drop cables. The down side of this approach is that the distance between the multiport transceiver and a station is limited to 50 meters. For larger network, one can attach multiport transceivers instead of stations to a multiport transceiver. This is known as cascading. It increases the number of attachment ports as well as overcomes the 50 meters limitation. However, in view of the fact that the transceiver cable is both expensive and bulky, it is not really all that desirable to create a large network using those cables.

The second approach is to connect a station to a hub using the more common 2 shielded twisted pairs instead of the 4 pairs transceiver cable. SynOptic markets a product called LattisNet that supports such a configuration. Essentially, a station is connected to a proprietary transceiver which presents a standard 802.3 interface to the station. The transceiver is connected to a controller in the hub via either a pair of fibre optic cables or 2 shielded twisted pairs.

The third approach is with thin Ethernet. In this case, a multiport thin Ethernet repeater is positioned in the hub. A station with a built-in thin Ethernet transceiver is connected to the hub using the thin, flexible and inexpensive RG58 Ethernet coax cable. This is the approach championed by DEC and will be described in a later section. Other supporters are HP and 3COM. The main disadvantage is the requirement for the installation of the thin Ethernet cables. Unlike the shielded or unshielded twisted pairs, this cable has little potential use other than Ethernet.

A variation on the second and third approaches is the recent development of supporting Ethernet over unshielded twisted pairs (a.k.a. phone pairs). DEC, 3COM, HP, SynOptics and Ungermann- Bass are working toward that goal. Again, more about this can be found in a later section. In general, if one has an excess amount of "recently" installed and well documented phone pairs, one may consider using them for this purpose. However, if one needs to install additional cables, it is worth spending the extra dollars for shielded twisted pairs instead since they tend to have better performance characteristics and greater potential.

Part 2 : Ethernet Components

The following sections describe various Ethernet components. It is based on our experiences as well as those of our colleagues. It is important to bear in mind that the data reflects the status of year end 1987. While most of the observations should remain valid for a while, certain product specific data may have a much shorter life span. As an example, the original as well as the first few drafts of this article refers to products from a company called American Photonics. That company is now history!

The Ethernet Trunk Coax

There are two types of Ethernet trunk cables: standard cable and plenum cable.

Plenum space is the space used as part of the air circulation system of a building. Typically, it is located above the ceiling panel. Quite often, the whole area above the ceiling is one massive plenum area. Check with the people responsible for the building.

According to fire codes, only plenum cable may be installed in the plenum space. The problem with most standard cable is that the jacket gives out poisonous fumes when ignited. This can be deadly within an air circulation system. Plenum rated cables are typically teflon coated and do not have such undesirable characteristics. They are, however, much more expensive. Furthermore, they are stiffer and more difficult to work with. The alternative is to install a cable tray outside the plenum space or conduits. This can be both difficult as well as expensive.

When installing or working on an Ethernet trunk cable, bear in mind that all the specifications call for grounding the coax shielding at one and only one point. Connectors and terminators on the cable should be installed with plastic boots or sleeves to provide ground isolation. Note that the CATV industry takes the opposite approach with regards to grounding. It recommends the cable shield to be grounded as often as possible for safety reasons. Since Ethernet trunk cable is grounded at only one point, care should be taken during installation and maintenance. Specifically, the cable should not be run in between buildings. Besides potentially affecting reliable communications, accidental and improper grounding can also be a health hazard. Details on safety related issues can be found in the 802.3 specification.

On the subject of trunk cable installation, it is a good idea to have the cable marked at 2.5 meters intervals. This will facilitate transceiver placement. Furthermore, it is also a good idea to sequentially label those intervals. This can be very useful when it comes to trouble shooting with a Time Domain Reflectometer (TDR) as described in the section on diagnostic tools.

Ethernet trunk cable can be purchased from Ethernet equipment vendors such as DEC or from cable dealers and manufacturers such as Anexter, Black Box and Beldon.

Transceiver or Drop Cable

At one stage, we used to make our own cable in order to reduce costs. We have since given up on that practice. Numerous problems surfaced due to poor quality control with connector fixtures. This type of problem is particularly troublesome since it is typically very difficult and time consuming to locate.

Drop cables from vendors come in a variety of lengths. Some vendors offer both standard as well as a thinner and more flexible cable for easier installation. The thinner cable has higher attenuation and is usually shorter. As with Ethernet trunk cable, if a drop cable runs through plenum space, it needs to be a plenum cable.

Some cables come with connectors molded into them. These connectors are generally sturdier in construction but cannot be disassembled. This can be a problem since disassembly may be required if the cable has to be pulled through a narrow conduit. Secure attachment of the drop cable to the transceiver or station is important. We have had our share of problems resulting from bad connections.

Transceivers

Over the past few years, quite a number of manufacturers have gotten into the transceiver business. Virtually all the transceivers on the market today are the non-invasive variety. Thus one does not need to cut the Ethernet cable into two in order to insert the transceiver in line with the cable. The transceiver is clamped onto the Ethernet cable itself. This approach minimizes the down time of the trunk cable during the installation process.

Ease of installation is an important consideration for a transceiver since it is typically located in areas difficult to get at (e.g. above ceiling panels). In general, installation of transceivers on plenum Ethernet trunk cable is a lot more difficult than on standard Ethernet cable since the teflon jacket is more difficult to penetrate.

A well designed transceiver must have the proper mechanics to ensure that it is clamped onto the trunk cable securely. Improper installation can cause shorting. Worse still, it can cause intermittent problems that will affect not only the attached station, but the whole network. Form factor of the transceiver can also be an important. A bulky unit is a potential obstruction in a cable tray and it has a higher probability of getting pulled loose when additional cables are run next to it at a later date.

When attaching a drop cable to a transceiver, it is good practice to tie the drop cable to the trunk at a location close to the connector — 9 inches or so away. This provides additional stress relief to the securing clip of the connector.

In the earlier days, we experienced a fair amount of compatibility problems between transceiver and controller. This problem has been substantially reduced as designers began using off-the-shelf front end chip for the controller rather than doing custom design.

While "heart beat" or "collision present test" is part of the official specification, some vendors provide transceivers without such a signal. The function of the heart beat signal is as follows: after the transceiver blasts out a packet, it should do a quick self check to ensure that the collision detect logic is functional. If it is, an "all's well" signal is sent on the collision detect line back to the controller within a short and specific period of time after the transmission of the packet. While most controllers and driver software tend to ignore this signal, there is really no reason to get a transceiver without the heart beat feature. The exception is for an obscure application described in the multiport transceiver section.

Today, all vendors produce transceivers according to the 802.3 standard. Some vendors also produce version 1 transceiver or those that can work with either specification.

We have quite an installed base of TCL and DEC transceivers. The TCL transceivers are easy to install. However, they can be twisted loose relatively easily. The DEC transceiver, on the other hand, can be mounted much more securely on the trunk cable but it is a bit bulky. We have not purchased many standard transceivers lately since we have been focusing on star shaped Ethernet. If we are in the market for transceiver today, we will also consider products from 3COM and Siecor. The Siecor transceiver is relatively new. It is remarkably compact. This is made possible through the use of a VLSI transceiver chip that has only become available recently.

DELNI

If one needs to connect a cluster of stations to an Ethernet, one should consider using a multiport repeater. Instead of putting a number of transceivers onto the Ethernet cable, one can tap the cable with one transceiver and connect a multiport transceiver to it. The stations can then be connected to the multiport transceiver. Not only will this reduce the overall connection cost, it will also increase the reliability and maintainability of the network by reducing the number of taps on the trunk cable and hence the source of potential failures. All multiport transceivers may be used in the mode described above or in a standalone mode.

In the standalone mode, the multiport transceiver is essentially an Ethernet-in-a-box. Typically, one can cascade the multiport unit to form a much larger standalone network. This is quite convenient for a small to medium size network that is not scattered over a large area.

As a fan-out expansion unit to a coax attached transceiver, most multiport transceiver vendors advise against cascading. Some Ethernet controllers have the ability to check the distance between controller and transceiver. The accumulative latency due to the cascaded multiport transceivers can make the test fail. In practice, this is not a requirement of any Ethernet specification and while the capability exists, virtually none of the driver software invokes the test. However, if one cascades the multiport transceivers in this mode, the additional latency has to be taken into the slot time calculation.

Multiport transceivers come in 2 common configurations. DEC and Cabletron's units come as complete units of 8 ports. TCL sells their units in the form of a basic chassis and port modules allowing one to buy port modules as required. Nearly all the multiport transceivers are designed for the attachment of 8 or more ports. In most office environments, a cost effective, 2 or 3 ports fan out unit is what is really needed. While it is possible for one to purchase expandable units, they are typically bulky and carry a relatively high startup cost.

Some multiport transceiver units have indicator lights showing traffic status on each port. The unit from Cabletron is an example. Status indicators can be useful in network management and diagnostics.

Expanding the Network Coverage

Local Repeater: The maximum length of a standard Ethernet segment is specified to be 500 meters. This is a function of the power output of the transceiver. This limitation can be overcome by using repeaters to connect segments. Most Ethernet equipment vendors produce such devices. Examples are DEC, Ungermann-Bass and TCL.

A good repeater should be able to prevent hard problems on one segment from bringing down the other. If one segment is shorted and rendered inoperable, the repeater should automatically disconnect it from the other segment. When the problem has been resolved, it should reconnect the segment back automatically. Another good feature to look for is status indicators. There should be LED's showing traffic and collisions for each segment.

We have had reasonably good experiences with our repeaters. One problem we had in the earlier days was repeaters failing to isolate problems

effectively. We also had some repeaters failing to reliably relay packets greater than 1200 bytes. A potential problem, brought to our attention by vendors, concerns the preamble. A repeater typically uses up the first few bits of an incoming packet's preamble to get into synchronization. Some repeaters will relay the packet without making up the lost bits while others will. If one has a lot of repeaters that do not regenerate the preambles arranged in series, there may not be enough preamble bits left by the time a packet gets to the furthest reach of the network. Generally this is not a problem since the number of repeaters one tends to use in series are not that many. The specification recommends a maximum of 2.

As mentioned in a previous section, a repeater cannot be connected to most multiport transceivers. The problem is with the lack of special logic by the multiport transceiver to properly handle heart beat. After a packet is transmitted, the heart beat signal from a standard transceiver is relayed to all the attached stations. While the station initiating the transmission will interpret it correctly as a heart beat signal, the other stations, with the exception of the repeater, will treat it as a collision notification and ignore it. The repeater, on the other hand, will carry out collision reinforcement onto the other Ethernet. This translates to a big waste of bandwidth. It is possible to by-pass the problem by attaching the multiport transceiver to a transceiver that does not generate heart beat. But then one has to ensure that all the other attached stations do not require heart beat. In general, it is simpler to handle the repeater separately.

As in the case of multiport transceiver, there are multiport repeaters. Since this is mainly related with thin Ethernet, it will be dealt with in that section.

Remote Repeaters: If two Ethernet segments to be connected are more than 100 meters or 2 drop cable lengths apart, one has to use a pair of remote repeaters. A remote repeater is essentially a repeater cut in two and joined back together using a pair of fibre cables. Typically, the fibre run can be up to 1 km in length. The signalling convention used between the two half repeaters has not been standardized. Thus one cannot mix and match remote repeaters from different vendors.

Initially, we experienced a lot of problems with remote repeaters. The first product we used 3 years ago had a defect with the fibre driver and the receiver module resulting in an error rate of over 30%! Then we had a problem with our fibre optic plant itself. The plant was installed with 50 micron fibres while most vendor equipment is designed for 100 microns. More about this can be found in the fibre Ethernet section. Once the problems were resolved, the remote repeaters were very reliable.

An alternative to using remote repeaters is to attach segments together using either a broadband or a fibre Ethernet. These are described in separate sections.

Theoretically, one can keep chaining segments together indefinitely using repeaters to regenerate signals at appropriate locations. This is not feasible, however, since the collision detect algorithm defines a slot time constraint such that no two stations in an Ethernet can be more than 51.2 micro seconds of signal propagation time apart. This loosely translate to 2.5 km in distance. If one requires a larger configuration, one has to construct separate Ethernets and connect them together with bridges.

Bridge: Whereas a repeater is a bit-by-bit, real-time relaying device, a bridge will receive a complete packet from one Ethernet and queue it for transmission to another Ethernet. Besides acting as a packet forwarding agent, most bridges will also do filtering. Instead of forwarding all packets from one net to another, forwarding is done on an "as needed" basis. This is a tremendous advantage over a repeater since the traffic load of the connected networks are not summed. In general, if the price of a bridge is comparable to that of a repeater, there is really no reason to purchase the latter. Like repeaters, bridges come in both local and remote versions.

A local bridge can be used to connect two or more Ethernets as long as they are within 2 drop cable length. To connect Ethernets that are farther apart, remote bridges can be used. A pair of bridges can be connected by a variety of communications media ranging from fibre optic, 56K synchronous line, T1, microwave as well as satellite links. Indeed, NCAR (National Center for Atmospheric Research) operates a bridge network in the sky linking together a number of Ethernets scattered across the U.S.

Bridge operation is very I/O and processor intensive since every packet on both networks has to be captured and handled. A bridge must also have sufficient memory for buffers since it does not necessarily get control of bandwidth when needed to forward a packet. This is particularly true for remote bridges with a relatively slow interconnecting link.

Besides acting as a topology and traffic controlling tool, bridges can play an important role in network management. A number of bridges allow stations with appropriate software to remotely control its operation and query it for information. The type of information of interest is the traffic load on the connected networks, number of packets that it fails to relay, effectiveness of its filtering and a list of stations residing on the networks.

The type of control that one may wish to assert is the explicit filtering of packets by address and other parameters such as protocol types.

The three most significant vendors of bridges are DEC, Bridge and Vitalink. DEC's products have the highest performance since they employ hardware assist. Vitalink has the largest range of products particularly for wide area interconnection using 56K, T1 or Satellite links. If "right of way" is a potential problem, a microwave based remote bridging system called Etherwave from Microwave Bypass may be worth considering.

Fibre Optic Ethernet

Besides using fibre optic cables as part of a remote repeater or bridge, one can construct an Ethernet using fibre. This is particularly useful if security is a big consideration or the network transverses very electrically noisy environments.

There are two types of fibre ethernet. Both have star shape topologies and both use 1 pair of fibre for station connection. One fibre cable is used to transmit and the other to receive. The station is connected to the fibre pair through a special transceiver which has a standard controller-transceiver interface on one side and a proprietary fibre interface on the other. The difference between the two types of fibre Ethernet is in the hub.

One type of fibre ethernet has a passive hub. Conceptually, it is all done by mirrors. Light coming in from one leg of the star is reflected into all the other legs. This approach is simple and relatively inexpensive. The flux loss in the hub, however, can be substantial. This approach is really only suitable for a very small network. The other type of fibre network uses an active hub which contains logic to carry out collision detection as well as signal regeneration. This is a more reliable approach even though it costs more. SynOptics's LattisNet and SIECOR's Active Star are examples of such a network.

Interesting variations on the theme are FibreWay from Artel and WhisperLAN from FibreCom. These two companies produce network products that have Ethernet transceiver interfaces but uses fibre token ring technology internally. In the case of the Artel product, the data rate of the internal fibre network is actually 100 Mbps. Strategically, both companies pledge allegiance to FDDI — whenever it becomes a commercial reality.

A point to watch out for with fibre Ethernet is the type of fibre cable to install. In the past, virtually all data communications equipment vendors used the 100 micron multi-mode fibre while the telecommunications industry, Bell and their suppliers, used 50 micron cable. When one connects a 100 micron output to a 50 micron cable, only 25% of the light makes it into the cable. This represents a tremendous signal loss. Depending on the flux budget of one's data equipment and depending on the length and number of connectors on one's fibre cable, this loss can be fatal. The good news is that both the data and telecommunications industries are converging to the 62.5 micron fibre. On the other hand, the telecommunications industry is also pushing a new single mode 8 micron cable for their long line operation. This fibre will definitely not work with any of the existing LAN equipment and it is questionable whether it will be adopted by the data communications industry in the future.

Ethernet over Broadband

The generally perceived advantages of broadband networks are (a) multimedia capability, (b) lots of channels, (c) large geographical coverage and (d) mature technology with lots of operational experience. On close examination, most of these advantages fall short of expectations, particularly in the Ethernet context.

While there are lots of channels in a broadband system, consistencies in channel definition and assignment have been some what lacking across the industry. This is despite the existence of a standard concerning channel allocation for data services. Quite a number of broadband network operators have resorted to using separate cables for different services, defeating the multi-media, multi-channel capability of the technology.

The large geographical coverage of broadband is typically constrained by the 51.2 micro slot time requirement of Ethernet. Furthermore, collision detection on broadband network has posed quite a technical challenge. Some earlier broadband "Ethernet" equipment simply did not bother with collision detection! This problem has been resolved, but at a cost.

Most of the broadband experience comes from the cable TV industry. There are significant differences between operating a single source, simplex network from that of a duplex data network with hundreds of transmitting stations — all having the potential of interfering with the noraml operation of the whole network. That kind of operational experience is not very common.

In general, we prefer the use of fibre optic rather than broadband for data networking and we will be staying with standard switching technology for voice. For those who are interested in broadband Ethernet, ChipCom seems to be the purveyor of the technology. Other vendors are DEC and Ungermann-Bass.

Thin Ethernet or CheaperNet

Thin Ethernet started out as a sort of poor man's Ethernet. One of the first products was 3COM's Ethernet card for the PC. The big savings comes from the fact that the transceiver is built into the controller. Thus one needs not purchase an external transceiver. The station is connected directly to the thin, 50 Ohm RG58 Ethernet cable. The cable is physically very similar to the popular 75 Ohm RG59 coax of the video world. It is very cheap, flexible and easy to handle.

Note that the savings above assumes the station is equipped with the built-in thin Ethernet transciever. Otherwise, it has to be attached to the thin Ethernet using a special transceiver such as the one marketed by DEC called the DESTA.

There are two down sides with the thin Ethernet approach. First of all, the attenuation of the thin cable is much higher than standard cable. Segment length is reduced substantially. Secondly, the thin Ethernet cable has to be run all the way into the back of a station. If the cable is damaged or disconnected by mistake, the whole network will go down. In the case of a standard Ethernet, the trunk cable is usually hidden away in the ceiling. Damage to a drop cable will generally affect only the attached station.

This problem has been resolved recently. DEC, HP and 3COM have introduced multiport thin Ethernet repeaters. Instead of daisy chaining stations on one thin Ethernet cable, a star topology network is used. At the hub of the star is the multiport repeater. A station is connected to each port through a thin Ethernet cable.Essentially, we have one station per Ethernet segment. In general, a very limited amount of diasy chaining per segment is also allowed. This provides a very convenient and low cost expansion option for an office environment.

With the multiport repeater, problems such as shorting on one segment is automatically isolated from the others. Earlier versions of this product have been known to fail to do so properly. As a result, if one leaves a port or segment open accidentally without a terminator, all the attached segments will fail including the main trunk. This serious problem has been resolved.

Ethernet over Phone Pairs

During the past year, the development that has the highest profile is the operation of Ethernet over unshielded twisted pairs. The intent is to use the ubiquitous phone wires. The technical challenge is to push high speed data over non-optimum cables for reasonable distances without incurring too high a signal to noise ratio and staying within the FCC radiation guideline.

Two groups of companies have proposed different solutions. DEC and 3COM have an approach, which is essentially an extension of their thin Ethernet multiport transceiver concept. They provide a special balun to be put on each end of the twisted pair and turn it into a coax. A regular balun will not work since the transformer will not pass on the DC collision signal. SynOptics and HP use a different approach with 2 twisted pairs. It can support a longer cable. In practice, neither solution works that well with the old phone wires one finds in the older buildings. Typically, there are rarely any documentation showing the cable runs. Quite often, the cable are patched through all over the place. In practice, even the telephone people will prefer to pull new cable rather than use the questionable old wires for basic voice service. Running Ethernet over unshielded twisted pair is generally worth considering only if one has recently installed new phone cables. Even then, they need to be verified as to their length, impedances and other characteristics. 3COM has a device that allows one to check if a particular cable run is acceptable to work with their thin Ethernet multiport repeater.

Part 3: Miscellaneous

Network Problems, Trouble Shooting and Tools

As described in an earlier section, Ethernet can have either a hard or soft mode of failure. Hard failure is when the network is completely dead. This is typically caused by shorting or the lack of termination in the trunk cable. Soft failure is when a significant, but not all, of the network bandwidth is destroyed due to some abnormal event. This can be caused by intermittent problems of components and can be very difficult to track down. As mentioned earlier, one has typically ended up with the crude, trial and error approach of detaching stations from the network in order to isolate the problem.

There is actually a third class of "pseudo" failure. This happens when the station software is malfunctioning. While it is not really a network problem, it typically gets the blame anyway since most users do not really know what is going on with the software! Hence if a network file server gets really congested or malfunctions, all the stations using that server will be affected. Users can easily jump to the wrong conclusion that the network is chewing up packets and hence every station is having problem. Other software related or induced problems such as poison packets, broadcast storm, etc. can also give one the illusion of a network problem since the result is abnormal bursts of network traffic or wide spread station failures. An interesting article on this topic is "Problems in Large LANS" by L. Bosack and C. Hedrick in the January 1988 issue of *IEEE Network* magazine. Note that unlike the telecommunications world, stations are typically connected to a LAN without going through any hardware or software certification process. Indeed, in a university environment, a high percentage of the stations could well be using software under development. As a result, the range of "pseudo" problems is unbounded. The conclusion is that in order to operate and manage a sizable local area network, it is not sufficient just to have tools and expertise dealing with the physical and link layer protocols. Having a reasonable understanding of the higher level protocols issue can be very useful.

A problem with Ethernet's design is the lack of network management capability. In contrast, the 802.5 token ring has a significant amount of management functions defined and actually built into the chip set. This ensures that all stations will participate to some extent in network management activities. The closest thing in Ethernet is the reasonably good algorithm in the version 2 specification. Unfortunately, it has not found its way into 802.3 and is ignored by virtually all the vendors.

In the early days of Ethernet, there were few trouble shooting or status monitoring tools. The first sign of trouble often came from users who were experiencing problems with their computers. While the number of Ethernet operational tools has been increasing in the past years, they tend to be focused on general monitoring rather than trouble shooting. It is surprising the number of times we still find ourselves resorting to the trial and error approach when confronted with a soft failure. Quite often, the problem is "resolved" when it simply just disappeared.

The following are some tools that have been useful to us. A number of them are actually free.

"Prevention is the best medicine" is applicable in networking as in other activities. A good network configuration can minimize impact of failures and help with problem determination. Once again, one should use star configuration instead of bus for ease of maintenance. It is also a good idea to put in plenty of "fire walls" such as repeaters and bridges. For those who have been following the current debate about bridges and routers, an even better fire wall is a router although they are protocol specific devices. See the January 1988 issue of the *IEEE Network* magazine for more information.

An invaluable network planning and trouble shooting tool is a good set of cable plant documentation. This should indicate clearly at least the locations of connectors, terminators and repeaters. It will also be very desirable to have the tap locations documented. Another very valuable document is an operational log book. Very often problems are the result of work that has been done most recently to the network. The log book will provide an excellent lead to such problems.

If an Ethernet is totally inoperable, there is a good probability that the trunk cable has either been shorted or left opened. This type of problem happens most frequently after some work has been done to the cable. Hence an improper installation of a transceiver can leave the trunk cable shorted while a loose or missing terminator will cause an open. The typical symptom of these problems is that the network appears to be continuously jammed. The best trouble shooting tool for this class of problem is a Time Domain Reflectometer (TDR). A TDR is not an Ethernet specific tool. It was actually developed for the general telecommunications industry and has been around for decades. It can be used with a large variety of cable plants. The TDR will "sweep" the cable with a signal and the resultant display will show the presence of any short, open and attachments to the cable.

The first time we used the TDR in earnest was a learning experience. The device quickly told us that we had a short 300 meters away. The question then was "where is 300 meters away" in an Ethernet cable that twisted and turned over 3 floors? Now our cable was marked up every 2.5 meters so as to facilitate transceiver placement. But that did not help. We have learned from this that the markers should also be sequentially numbered. In that case, if we are TDR'ing from marker 10 and a problem is indicated 250 meters away, we can translate that to be near marker 110 (10 + 250/2.5). Given this information, it is much easier to zero in on the problem location.

The TDR we use is a compact and self-contained unit from Tektronix. It comes with an optional built in printer. Tektronix also makes TDR add-on modules for some of their scopes. Note that a TDR is typically used only when a network is already down since most TDR testing will interfere with network operation. It would be useful to be able to conduct TDR testing on an active network.

Another good basic tool is a network status indicator. Quite often, they come free as part of an Ethernet component such as repeater and bridge. Occasionally they can be found in multiport transceivers. Of interest are traffic status and collisions. An operator who is familiar with the "typical" traffic pattern of a particular Ethernet can tell by the LED's if the network is behaving abnormally.

At Carnegie Mellon, we have a home built, very low cost device consisting of a Z80 processor with a small piece of software in ROM that samples a drop cable continuously. It displays three values on an LED: load as in the percentage utilization of the network, collisions and packets per second or other time intervals. We found these three indications to be very useful to the operators. Generally, any significant deviation from the norm spells trouble. This applies to individual values as well as combinations. Hence if a 5% load typically equates 150 packets, a display of 5% with 450 packets may signal a problem even though 450 packets per second by itself is not alarming. Conversely, a 30% load with 100 packets can also be a warning. Again, an experienced operator will pick up the characteristic values of a particular Ethernet. He/she may even be able to recognise from experience signature values for specific recurring problems. Besides the LED, the monitor also has an asynchronous port such that monitored data may also be logged by a remote machine for further analysis. An unusual feature of this monitor is that it does not rely on an Ethernet chip set. Unlike most other monitors, it will pick up all sorts of noise that may be destroying bandwidth correctly as load even though they may not be legitimate Ethernet packets.

A portable PC fitted with an Ethernet card togther with appropriate software can be a very useful tool. We have a small collection of programs for network monitoring and diagnostics. Most of these programs are in the public domain. Some are imported, particularly from MIT, while others are developed locally at Carnegie Mellon. The most basic test program allows one to send and receive packets to and from the Ethernet. This tells us from a particular vantage point whether the network is at least functional. For example, we can instruct the program to blast out 1,000 packets to some non existing address. If the network or the local link (drop cable and transceiver) is having problems we will get continuous or a lot of collisions. A small feature we have added to our software is the option to signal collision by a bell. This is particularly useful when the technician is working on a transceiver up in the ceiling while the PC is on the floor. Other programs, designed mainly for the TCP/IP world, allow us to send echo packets to remote stations as well as selectively monitoring network traffic. From the commercial world, Excelan sells a product called the Lanalyser which can do both load and packet monitoring. It comes with a rather costly but full featured board to be inserted into a PC.

The portable PC is the main diagnostic tool used by our technicans. Our only complain is with its weight.

Some system vendors such as DEC and SUN also provide software that can perform network monitoring functions on their standard work stations and computers. Such programs tend to have fancier display interfaces since, unlike the dedicated monitoring equipment, they run on top of more powerful platforms and operating environments. Besides regular features such as load, collision and such, these programs can typically display other potentially useful information such as the top group of network users, packet size distribution etc., on a real time basis.

Problem Determination

In the past, problem determination procedures were quite crude. If only one user complained, it was probably a problem with a station or its software. If users of a specific server complained, then it was likely a server problem. If lots of users complained, then there might be a real network problem. Since then, we have been working on better monitoring tools such that we may be able to detect the onset of a problem before the phone rings. In practice, the progress has really not been that impressive. The following are extracts from my September 1985 article in the *Data Communications* magazine. They are still applicable today.

No network communications: This can be detected by various monitoring tools such as packets per second count being zero, network traffic indicator showing no sign of traffic, etc. This can be confirmed by trying to send some packets into the network. They will fail due to collision. This is typically a "hard" problem due to short or open of the Ethernet cable as described earlier. The best approach to track down the source of the problem is to use a TDR. In case of a large network, one can localize the problem into a smaller segment first if that has not already been done automatically by the "fire walls."

Abnormal network traffic: This is the catch all for "soft" failures. The possible symptoms are high network load, large number of collisions, large number of packets with CRC error and possibly a large amount of packet per seconds — particularly of small or "dribble" packets. Dribble or packets of less than 64 bytes, the minimum permissible length of an Ethernet packet, is typically the result of a collision between a legitimate packet with one that originates from a station with a malfunctioning CSMA implementation.

This type of problem can be very difficult to locate except by the trial and error of detaching stations from the network approach. This is where star configuration comes in very handy. If the configuration consists of layering of stars configuration, one can carry out do step-wise trial and error approach. That way, one can quickly locate and disconnect the star containing the culprit from the network. The problem star can then be examined in greater detail while the rest of the network is once again in operation.

Station not communicating: This is a problem when a station is not able to communicate while the rest of the network seems to be functioning properly. The problem can be with the station software or hardware, the drop cable, the transceiver or a combination of the above. The simplest approach is to take a portable PC to the drop cable and if it works, then the problem lies with the station. Otherwise, one can, by process of elimination, check out the drop cable and transceiver. Note that if one has a temporary drop cable connector problem, the problem may simply disappear during the diagnostic process!

Station not able to communicate with some other stations: This can be a real frustrating problem. The symptom is that a station cannot communicate with some stations in the network but have no problems with the others. The problem can be caused by a misconfigured topology such that there are stations that are more than 51.2 micro seconds of propagation time apart. The only way to see if that is indeed the case is to have a good network configuration diagram. One can also confirm that with TDR and optical TDR if fibre links are involved.

The other potential cause of this problem is a version mismatch between the controller and the transceiver. This is the 802.3 and version 1 problem described in an earlier section.

Bandwidth and All That

In terms of bandwidth, we found that Ethernet has sufficient bandwidth for most of our applications even in our heavily distributed processing environment. There are, of course, exceptions. A typical example is the support of diskless workstations, especially if the stations do not have a lot of memory and require constant paging. Our experience shows that 20 diskless SUN-3 can make the network performance intolerable. This brings us to the question, "At what load will an Ethernet becomes saturated or unusable?" 20%? 50%? The practical answer is, "It depends on the appli-

cation mix of the attached work stations." On the one hand, we can have a handful of processors doing file system backups across the network, creating a high load in the process. Potentially, no one will complain since a lot of these heavy data transfer applications have a tendency to synchronize into a non-competitive mode of bandwidth demands. On the other hand, we can have a few dozen highly active and interactive stations on the network. Their asynchronous and competitive bandwidth demand characteristics may cause the network to be deemed "saturated" at a relatively moderate load. In our Ethernet, there are typically 3 high load periods: late morning, afternoon and late at night. The morning and afternoon loads are due to people using their stations. The late night load which is the heaviest of the three is due to file servers backup. High collisions occur during the first two periods but not the last, despite the heavier traffic. When a network performance becomes intolerable, it can be segmented using bridges. To be really effective, however, one needs to have a good understanding of the traffic patterns between stations so that the 80/20 rule can be applicable — i.e. 80% of the traffic can be serviced within the local net and only 20% needs to be sent to the remote network. With careful traffic monitoring and network planning, the segmentation strategy can extend the usefulness of the Ethernet technology.

What about the future? Ethernet has established a very strong hold in the scientific and engineering market. It will be around for quite a few years to come. While there are developments in the much higher speed networks such as the much publicized 100 Mbps FDDI, the cost of new network interfaces as well as the indirect cost of software changes will be high enough to deter any rapid cut over. The higher speed networks will establish themselves gradually in niche applications as well as the backbone arena.

Last words: Finally, we have had a lot of good experience with Ethernet. It is a cost effective and reliable technology with a solid product base. The only problem we have with it is that unless the network is star configured, when a problem arise, trouble shooting can range from tricky to very difficult.

Brief Curriculum Vitae of Author

John Leong is the Director of the Networking and Communications Department, Carnegie Mellon University. He is responsible for the development and provision of data and voice communication services to Carnegie Mellon University. John Leong has held a variety of management and technical positions with Philips Information Systems, Bell Northern Software Research, Globe and Mail and University of Liverpool. Projects range from ISO-CCITT protocol products development, distributed data bases to newspaper systems. B.Sc. and M.Sc., both in Computer Science, from the University of Manchester, England.

Design Considerations for Broadband Coaxial Cable Systems

Richard N. Dunbar

Broadband coaxial cable LAN's utilize existing Community Antenna Television (CATV) technology to implement large-scale communication networks that provide video, voice, and data services to groups of users.

L ocal Area Networks (LAN's) are a new addition to the field of data communications. Broadband coaxial cable LAN's utilize existing Community Antenna Television (CATV) technology to implement large-scale communication networks that provide video, voice, and data services to groups of users typically located within a campus or large office building. In Metropolitan Area Networks (MAN's), the CATV services have been operational for many years, and voice and data services are added as the technology and need arise. Whether the system is designed as a LAN or a CATV system, the cable plant design issues are related, and, in fact, the CATV issues are a subset of the LAN issues. A LAN may be operated as a CATV system without any changes, but a CATV system must usually be redesigned or retrofitted in order to operate as a LAN. The major engineering design problems and solutions involved in both types of systems and their applications toward MAN's are discussed. A glossary of terms and abbreviations is provided at the end of the article.

Terminology and Definitions

Where a broadband LAN is constructed using a conventional (metropolitan) CATV-network structure, signals travel from the transmitter to the head-end, and then from the head-end to the receiver (see Fig. 1). The reverse or return direction (inbound) is from the transmitter to the head-end, and the forward direction (outbound) is from the head-end to the receiver. The head-end is the physical location where all the coaxial cables are combined into a single cable for distribution or processing. A CATV system often has only a forward direction, whereas a LAN always has both directions with a substantial reverse bandwidth (at least 100 MHz). The reverse direction is significantly more difficult to design, because signal levels must be matched from every reverse path for optimum performance.

LAN's may be dual cable, where a separate cable is used for each direction of transmission, or single cable, where Frequency Division Multiplexing (FDM) is used to provide the different directions of transmission. A single cable LAN may be sub-split, mid-split, or high-split, depending on the amount of reverse direction bandwidth required. Dual cable CATV systems consist of two sub-split single cable systems with a reverse bandwidth of 5–30 MHz and a forward bandwidth of 50–450 MHz on each cable.

A "path" is the components, including cable, through which a signal must travel to get from the transmitter to the head-end (reverse path), or from the head-end to a receiver (forward path). An end-to-end path is any combination of reverse and forward paths. Unless otherwise designated, a "path" in this article is an end-to-end path.

A Bus Interface Unit (BIU) is the hardware which physically attaches the user devices (terminals, hosts, printers, etc.) to the broadband Radio Frequency (RF) cable. The BIU function is to implement the physical, data link, and network layers of the International Standards Organization (ISO) Open Systems Inter-

Reprinted from *IEEE Communications Magazine*, Volume 24, Number 6, June 1986, pages 24-37. Copyright © 1986 by The Institute of Electrical and Electronics Engineers, Inc.

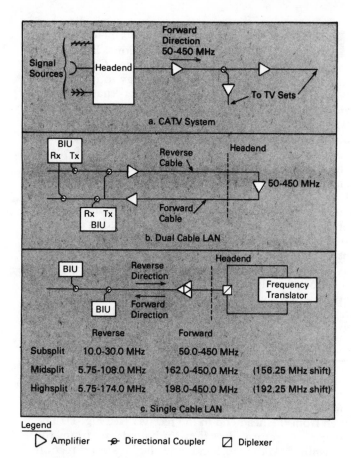

Fig. 1. Several Broadband Cable Configurations.

connection (OSI) Reference Model. The microprocessor-based BIU contains the RF modem and electrical interface to the digital baseband data equipment.

A MAN is an interconnection of LAN's and CATV systems that service an entire Metro Area. CATV systems are constructed according to the franchise agreement which varies from county to county. Within a county there may be different agreements from city to city. Since a Metro Area may consist of several counties, the end result is a multitude of independently owned and operated cable companies. The interconnection of these systems into a MAN is discussed further in this article.

Performance

The overall system performance depends upon the cable plant performance as well as the transceiver performance. All receivers have two common design requirements: signal level and signal-to-noise ratio. The receiver operational window (or dynamic range) is defined by the maximum and minimum signal voltage levels into the receiver. Too high a level may produce internal intermodulation (IM), distortion, or clipping. Too low a level will produce insufficient signal quality or result in signal levels below the receiver sensitivity threshold. The cable plant must be designed to support the receiver requirements. Typical cable plant performance parameters are shown in Table I. Systems that have been designed for these parameters

are capable of yielding a grade 2 Television Allocations Study Organization (TASO) video signal (noise just perceptible) and Bit Error Rates (BER's) less than one in one billion.

For both LAN and CATV systems, the RF transmission bandwidth is critical if the entire available bandwidth is to be utilized. The transmitting signal should be at least 46 dB down at the channel boundary to prevent interference with adjacent channels. The transmitters should also be well filtered to keep out-of-band signals at least 55 dB below the carrier. The receiver bandwidth should be kept as small as possible to increase sensitivity and decrease susceptibility to interference. Although the transmission bandwidth is standardized for National Television Standards Committee (NTSC) video systems, this is not the case for data modems, since they use different modulation techniques with different spectral efficiencies.

The values for video in Table I were determined by human perception of picture quality, and therefore vary slightly (1 or 2 dB) depending on the source.

The values for data in Table I were determined under the assumption that a 30 dB composite Carrier-to-Noise Ratio (CNR) is required, and that data modems are insensitive to the type of interference. Tests on data modems have shown this insensitivity assumption to be valid, except when the interfering signal bandwidth is much less than that of the desired signal. In this

TABLE I.
TYPICAL CABLE PLANT PERFORMANCE PARAMETERS

Parameter	Video	Data
Carrier to Composite Noise Ratio	(1)	30 dB
Carrier to Thermal Noise Ratio	40 dB	33 dB
Carrier to Second Order Distortion	55 dB	40 dB
Carrier to Third Order Distortion	55 dB	40 dB
Carrier to Hum Modulation	2 percent	2 percent
Carrier to Spurious	55 dB	40 dB
Channel Bandwidth (60 dB points)	6 MHz	(2)
System Bandwidth	400 MHz	400 MHz
Device Transmit Level	+50 dBmV	+45 dBmV (3)
Device Receive Level	+5 dBmV	0 dBmV (3)
System Loss	45 ± 5 dB	45 ± 5 dB
Reverse Signal Level Variation	(1)	6 dB
System Frequency Response	±5 dB	±5 dB
Channel Frequency Response	±1.5 dB	±1.5 dB
Propagation Delay	(1)	100 μsec
Group Phase Delay	50 ηsec	40 ηsec

(1) Not specified.

(2) Depends upon data rate and modulation technique.

(3) The values for other data channels are referenced to the 6 MHz data channel level by 10log(Bandwidth Ratio).

case, the interferor starts to look like continuous wave (CW) interference. The impact of CW interference on modem performance becomes significant when the CW signal lies exactly on one of the modulated carrier sidebands (a harmonic of the clock rate). Intermodulation products from modulated signals spread in frequency; thus, the interfering signals must have extremely narrow bandwidths (such as pilot tones) for this to actually degrade performance. Since the majority of signals are modulated, CW effects can in general be ignored. If the modem is sensitive to the type of interference, then the requirements must be specified by the modem manufacturer. In addition, the narrowband carrier power levels are reduced by 10log (Bandwidth Ratio) to reduce amplifier loading and to minimize interference effects.

As shown in Fig. 2, the 30 dB composite CNR (all noise sources combined) can be divided into two approximately equal contributors: thermal and other noise. Thermal noise is broadband, and is generally the main contributor of noise in broadband coaxial cable systems. Since 10log(2) = 3 dB, both contributors must be kept 3 dB down or at 33 dB. The other noise can be divided into four approximately equal contributors: second order, third order, hum mod, and other (spurious and higher order IM). Since 10log(4)=6 dB, each of these contributors must be kept $33 + 6 = 39$ dB below the carrier. The hum modulation is specified at 34 dB (two percent), since this is sufficient for video.

Table I shows separate specifications for video and data. If both services are to be operated on the same

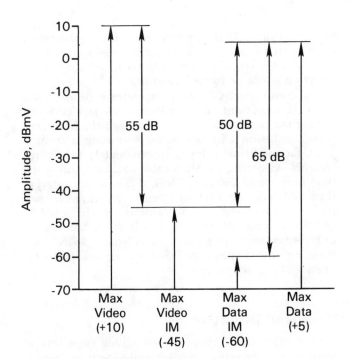

Fig. 3. CNR Relationship for Concurrent Video and Data.

cable, then the system must be designed for the more stringent requirements of video. If data levels are reduced 5 dB below video levels, then the data thermal CNR will be 35 dB, and the IM produced by data signals will be 65 dB (assuming a "well-behaved amplifier") below the data carriers, provided that the system has been designed for video. The system must also be designed to meet the minimum requirements under the worst-case situation. Since the frequency response is flat, the maximum and minimum loss paths represent physically different paths. The minimum loss path will be the minimum for both video and data, and has the same relationship as the maximum values shown in Fig. 3.

There are two additional data design parameters which are non-existent for video: propagation delay and collision detection window. Due to the FM capture effect, signal levels presented to Frequency Shift Keyed (FSK) receivers using in-band Carrier Sense Multiple Access with Collision Detection (CSMA/CD) techniques must not vary by more than 6 dB; otherwise, a collision may not be detected. This could result in a drastic reduction in throughput for certain users, since the error rate will increase due to undetected collisions. If error detection is implemented, then the number of retransmissions will increase, which again reduces throughput. Thus, the reverse signal level variation is not as important in CATV systems, where reverse traffic is very light. In MAN's, the data channels are usually point-to-point channels such as T1 links, rather than contention data channels.

The propagation delay is specified, since there is usually a minimum system delay requirement. It will also seriously affect performance if the cable plant propagation delay is of the same or greater magnitude than that of the mean "back-off" time of the RF

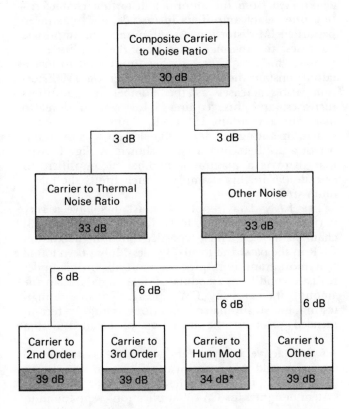

* Video Specification

Fig. 2. Data Performance Parameters.

modem (when CD is implemented). The propagation delay is significant in broadband networks only if the cable plant is large, such as in MAN's, and if collision detection is not performed continuously.

For continuous CD, only the reverse propagation delay is important. If a collision has not occurred during the packet transmission through the head-end, then a collision will not occur. Assuming a 20-mile path, the total time delay is approximately 140 microseconds. Assuming a 2 Mb/s cable data rate, this is the time to transmit 280 bits. Thus, if the packet is larger than 280 bits, the BIU will begin receiving its own packet prior to the end of transmission. In a MAN, additional time delays will result from the digital interconnection equipment. In a small LAN (one building), the propagation delay is often less than 5 bit times and can be ignored.

Noise and Distortion

External noise (ingression) may come from several sources. Components installed improperly or which have become corroded may exhibit poor RF isolation resulting in ingression. Routing of cables near heavy electrical machinery or high-voltage cables may lead to interference through electromagnetic coupling. Quad shield coaxial drop cable or coaxial trunk cable is normally used in these cases, and the interference can be controlled by proper cable routing and grounding.

In LAN's and CATV systems, the head-end is often located near RF generating equipment, such as computer equipment. Unterminated cables (such as test points) are susceptible to ingression if the center conductor is exposed (such as male F-connectors). This ingression can degrade the entire system, and, in a LAN, the interference may propagate in both directions, making it difficult to isolate. Patch panels with female F-connectors should be used in these areas to minimize interference during testing.

The Principle of Reciprocity implies that RF isolation is the same for ingression as for egression. Thus, signals' leaking in implies that signals are also leaking out, and the converse. Due to the relatively high internal noise levels, ingressive signals are often buried in the internal noise level; however, the degree of interference depends upon the internal noise level and bandwidth, the interfering signal level and bandwidth, and the cable or component RF isolation at the point of ingression. Egressive signals may lead to Federal Communications Commission (FCC) fines and can be a public safety hazard. In government LAN's, undetected RF emanations could lead to the compromise of classified information.

In most CATV cases, external interference usually occurs at the head-end antenna prior to the signal injection into the cable plant, rather than to signal ingression. This is also possible for LAN's, which are connected via an atmospheric link. If the atmospheric signal is degraded prior to injection, the received signal will have at least the same degradation, regardless of the cable plant performance. If digital repeaters are employed, this degradation may result in an increase in error rate, and thus repeaters are not always the solution.

In both LANs and CATV systems the amplifiers are the main contributor of internal noise. In single cable LAN's the frequency translators (upconverters) are usually the limiting factor on CNR performance. However, the signal degradation may be controlled during the design process in order to meet the required CNR performance in all types of systems. The video and data transmitter characteristics will also affect system performance.

A common technique used in CATV system design is the application of the "unity gain concept." This requires that the cable loss between amplifiers be equal to the gain of the amplifier. Thus, the net loss through the cable and amplifier is 0 dB, or a ratio of 1:1. This technique maximizes the cable spans between amplifiers, which minimizes cost. Since fewer amplifiers are used, system performance can be optimized. Since the net loss between amplifiers is 0 dB, the signal input level into each amplifier is the same for a cascade of identical amplifiers.

The amplifier operating window is the maximum and minimum signal levels allowed at the input to the amplifier in order to meet the performance requirements. Signals below the minimum will not provide a sufficient thermal CNR. Signals above the maximum will create IM distortion and thus will not provide a sufficient IM CNR. The minimum input level is determined from the thermal noise floor, amplifier noise figure, number of amplifiers, and minimum required thermal CNR. The maximum input level is determined from the amplifier distortion characteristics, number of amplifiers in cascade, and maximum permitted IM distortion. As the number of amplifiers increases, the thermal noise from the amplifiers increases which requires a higher input level to maintain a constant thermal CNR. However, the IM distortion also increases as the number of amplifiers increases, and this requires a lower input level to maintain a constant IM CNR. Thus the amplifier system operating window range decreases as the number of amplifiers increases, as shown in Fig. 4. Note that there is a maximum number of amplifiers in cascade (56 in this example), which limits the maximum size.

The LAN data frequency translators have a very narrow window under fully loaded conditions (all channels in use), which typically limits the maximum CNR in the passband to 40 dB or less. It has been found that most translators produce more distortion under realistic conditions (modulated data signals) than the amount indicated by CW testing. Thus, thorough testing under simulated conditions is highly recommended prior to the initiation of detailed design efforts.

Other active components will also contribute to distortion and may warrant consideration. Pin diodes used as on/off RF switches in an addressable tap system designed for CATV applications were found to create severe port-to-port harmonic distortion when operated at the BIU transmit level. The taps had to be modified prior to production to provide acceptable

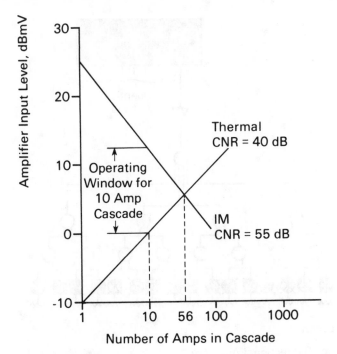

Gain = 20 dB
Noise Figure = 9 dB
Intermodulation is -55 dBmV at a 30 dBmV Output
Cable Loss Between Amplifiers = 20 dB

Fig. 4. System Operating Window.

distortion levels. All components will contribute to distortion, though in varying amounts. It is recommended that components be thoroughly tested to confirm specifications for the intended application as well as vendor specification sheets (which have been known to contain errors).

Design Considerations

Design calculations are performed on a worst case basis to ensure that the minimum performance parameters are met in every channel.

Although TV performance has been standardized, data modem performance has not. IEEE 802 is an attempt at standardization, but the market and technology have been advancing too fast for the approval process to keep pace. Thus the commercial market is filled with data modems that differ in performance, yet the cable plant must be designed to accommodate as many types as possible.

Once the data modem is designed (as in off-the-shelf), the performance is fixed and characterized by a CNR vs. BER curve. Since BER performance is also a function of signal level, the CNR vs. BER becomes a family of curves. The cable plant must be designed to provide a CNR greater than that required by the modem to deliver the required error rate at the minimum signal level.

The tradeoffs between dual cable and single cable LAN's are cost vs. performance. Dual cable LAN's will provide better performance and a much larger available bandwidth due to the current limitations of the single cable frequency translators and the advanced level of state-of-the-art amplifiers. If a single cable LAN will meet the performance requirements, then the tradeoffs become cost vs. size. For small systems, dual cable is cheaper, but single cable becomes more cost effective as the size increases (see Fig. 5). The initial cost difference depends on the required bandwidth (number of different translators) and the cost of the translators and redundant translators (if needed).

The design objectives are to make the system loss and CNR constant for all channels on any end-to-end path. This will enhance system flexibility and optimize system performance. When possible, the unity gain concept should be applied, since this maximizes efficiency, which minimizes cost. However, this is usually not possible in a single cable LAN due to different operating windows of components for the reverse and forward directions. The cable plant design should put all operating levels at the high end of the operational window, since signal levels are always easily reduced after installation, but additional gain is usually costly.

If the system must support wideband data (arbitrarily chosen as requiring more than 6 MHz of bandwidth), consideration must be given to the cable plant wideband frequency response. Wideband modems which utilize double sideband modulation must have mirror image sidebands similar in amplitude for proper demodulation. Designs for narrowband modems typically do not share this problem, since the 6 MHz channel frequency response can usually be kept small.

In LAN's the area to be covered is usually smaller than a CATV system, but the port density is significantly higher. This results in most of the loss being due to the components (flat loss) rather than the cable (sloped loss), a higher number of components in cascade, and a shorter spacing between components.

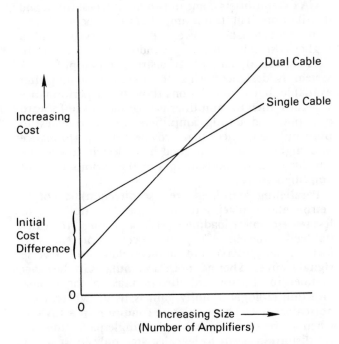

Fig. 5. LAN Cable Plant Cost Versus Size Comparison.

Since each component has a manufacturing tolerance, the cascading of components results in the accumulation of tolerances and a potentially large signal level variance. This variation is not easily controllable (the only control being the exchanging of components), and must be tolerated in the cable plant design by the BIU operational window. The reverse level variation consists of design variation (reverse path to reverse path) and manufacturing tolerance variation. The variation window is fixed at the head-end and will slide up and down in the BIU operational window for each forward path.

Since identical components tend to have similar frequency profiles, the cascading of components tends to reinforce the hills and valleys (poles and zeros) in the system frequency response. Therefore, in order to maximize the system frequency flatness, the number of identical components in cascade should be minimized. In single cable systems, the frequency profile is usually different for the high and low portions of the frequency band and thus each direction may be treated separately.

In single cable LAN's the components are transversed twice; therefore, the smallest signal level change is twice that of a component. The quantizing of taps and attenuators (in 3 dB increments) compounds this problem, making it more difficult to maintain a small signal level variation from tap to tap in a single cable LAN design.

The topology which is best suited toward the LAN design goals, but not necessarily the easiest to install, is a tree-bus topology as shown in Fig. 6. The tree, which is made up of two- and four-way splitters, provides four major benefits for both dual and single cable systems. It maximizes reverse signal level matching and signal power distribution efficiency (thus minimizing the number of amplifiers); and minimizes design and testing efforts, and the number of components in cascade.

CATV amplifiers come in two main types: trunk and distribution. The trunk amplifiers have better distortion characteristics, lower operating levels, and a higher cost. The operating windows of trunk amplifiers are usually larger than distribution amplifiers. A system is designed using the lowest cost amplifier available, but if calculations show better performance is needed, then the amplifier is upgraded. Feed-forward and power doubling amplifiers are alternatives to push-pull amplifiers that provide better performance at a higher cost. For a good brief description of the advantages and disadvantages of the various types of amplifiers see [7].

Paralleling amplifiers (reverse direction) is not as detrimental as placing them in cascade (series), due to less reverse power loading (reverse amplifiers, typically not having the entire frequency spectrum present as do forward amplifiers) and non-correlation of reverse signal sources. Thermal noise accumulates in the exact manner in the forward direction as in the reverse direction (10logN if unity gain is used), whereas IM noise does not. The worst case condition in a LAN is when all reverse signals travel a single path; thus the IM distortion needs to be calculated only for a single cascade string of amplifiers (the longest in the system),

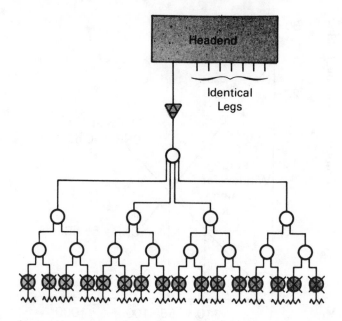

Legend:

⯈ Bidirectional Amplifier

⎤O⎡ Two-way Splitter/Combiner

⊗ Four-way Multi-tap

⎨ Terminator

⊐O⊏ Four-way Splitter/Combiner

Fig. 6. Tree-bus Topology for Single Cable LAN.

and the IM contribution from the paralleled amplifiers may be ignored. The spurious noise (including harmonics) from the transmitters may or may not accumulate on a power basis, depending on the correlation of the sources.

Frequency agility in LAN's makes the design parameters more critical and complicates operability. A constant system loss for all channels for any path becomes mandatory, since the BIU's may change frequency but not location. The BIU performance specifications must be maintained at all frequencies. The most difficult aspect, however, is operability, since the users may now be on any one of a number of different channels. The network controller must keep track of which devices are on which channel so that users may be advised. In many cases this information is privileged, so that the controller must track access rights as well. In addition, modem hardware performance is difficult to maintain as the operational frequency band increases. The advantage of frequency agility is that the user may easily switch to uncongested or priority channels under heavy traffic conditions.

CATV systems typically require Automatic Gain Control (AGC) and Automatic Slope Control (ASC) to compensate for temperature variations, since the cable is outside, and cable lengths are long (several miles). In a LAN, AGC and ASC are often not needed if the cable plant is indoors and thus not subject to the same temperature extremes. If the outdoor sections of cable are short, then AGC and ASC may still not be required, since the net variation depends upon the temperature change and exact cable length.

Standards and Practices

When operating data and video signals on the same cable, the data levels should be reduced below video levels. If the data signal has a 6 MHz channel bandwidth, then the data level should be 5 dB below the video level. Reducing the data level will not impact the BER, since the CNR will still be above the minimum requirement of 33 dB due to the 40 dB CNR required for video. However, reducing the data levels will improve intermodulation distortion, which improves system performance.

When operating data signals with a bandwidth other than 6 MHz, the narrowband data levels should be reduced by 10log(Bandwidth Ratio). This will make the equivalent noise power across the frequency band approximately constant and will provide uniform amplifier loading. Since the thermal noise floor also obeys the derating formula, this provides a constant CNR regardless of bandwidth, provided that the transmit and receive levels are related by the same formula. For example, if a 6 MHz data signal transmits at 45 dBmV and receives at 0 dBmV, then a 300 kHz data signal would transmit at 45 dBmV—13 dB = 32 dBmV, and receive at −13 dBmV; the system loss is constant. If the 6 MHz data channel has a 33 dB thermal CNR, then the 300 kHz data signal will also have a 33 dB thermal CNR (provided that the signals have taken the same path). If the data signal has a bandwidth greater than 6 MHz, the same formula applies and the levels are increased.

LAN channel frequency designations usually start from the recommendations shown in Table II and are modified according to application. The channel spacing reverts to the standard CATV assignments at TV channel 2, so that off-the-air signals may be injected directly into the head-end. Adhering to the standard Incrementally Related Carrier (IRC) or Harmonically Related Carrier (HRC) frequency plan will maximize the use of off-the-shelf equipment.

The IRC system reassigns off-the-air channels 5 and 6 to provide a more efficient utilization of bandwidth between channels 4 and 5 and the FM band. The HRC system does the same, but also shifts every signal away from the standard assignment. Thus, off-the-air signals require additional processing equipment. Both IRC and HRC systems allow signal levels to be slightly higher (3 dB) in order to extend the cascade. The IEEE 802.4 Recommendation indicates that transmit and receive levels for BIU's which have different bandwidths should be related by 10log(Bandwidth Ratio). Again, this makes the equivalent noise power spectral density approximately constant across the cable plant frequency spectrum.

Problems and Solutions

The most typical problem with newly installed LAN's and CATV systems is a lack of adequate quality

TABLE II.
BASIC LAN FREQUENCY PLAN

Channel Designation	Frequency Range (MHz)	LAN use
T7	5.75–11.75	
T8	11.75–17.75	
T9	17.75–23.75	
T10	23.75–29.75	Data channels
T11	29.75–35.75	
T12	35.75–41.75	
T13	41.75–47.75	
T14	47.75–53.75	
—	53.75–54	Guardband
2	54–60	
3	60–66	Off-air video
4	66–72	channels
53 IRC	72–78	
54 IRC	78–84	Off-air video
55 IRC	84–90	(Ch. 5,6),
56 IRC	90–96	IRC video
57 IRC	96–102	channels, or
58 IRC	102–108	FM band (88–108
59 IRC	108–114	MHz)
60 IRC	114–120	
A	120–126	
B	126–132	
C	132–138	
D	138–144	CATV video
E	144–150	channels
F	150–156	
G	156–162	
H	162–168	
I	168–174	Data channels for midsplit (156.25 MHz shift)
7	174–180	
8	180–186	
9	186–192	
10	192–198	Off-air video channels
11	198–204	
12	204–210	
13	210–216	Data channels for highsplit (192.25 MHz shift)
J	216–222	
K	222–228	
L	228–234	
M	234–240	
N	240–246	
O-up	246–up	CATV video or additional data

assurance testing. Unless the entire system is tested, there can be no assurance that all paths meet the minimum requirements. A method which minimizes testing for LAN's takes advantage of the similarity in frequency profiles of identical components and the bus-tree topology. Since the frequency profile is similar from path to path, each forward and reverse path is tested once at a single frequency (during installation). The maximum signal level indicates the minimum loss path and the minimum signal level indicates the maximum loss path. The minimum loss reverse and forward path combination determines the minimum system loss, and the maximum loss reverse and forward path combination determines the maximum system loss. Thus the system loss extreme can be validated from two secondary measurements. If all the reverse amplifiers operate at the same level and all the forward amplifiers operate at the same level (they will if unity gain was applied), then only the maximum and minimum loss paths for the longest cascade of amplifiers need to be tested for thermal CNR and IM CNR. All other path combinations in the system will have values between these paths.

The thermal CNR is tested for the maximum loss reverse path, and the maximum loss forward path for the longest cascade of forward amplifiers. The IM CNR is measured for the minimum loss reverse path in the longest reverse cascade and the minimum loss forward path in the longest forward cascade. All other path combinations will have CNR's greater than those measured, provided that the number of amplifiers is the same or less and that the bus-tree topology is used.

In many cases the system is CATV-based and data services were added at a later time, usually incrementally. These additions are engineered on a case-by-case basis, and external attenuators and filters are often required. In addition, the systems do not have the flexibility of location changes (they may not need it), since the path losses are not constant. However, if properly engineered, the systems can usually support the additional services adequately without major reinvestment.

The only effect a receiver has on the cable plant system is due to low return loss or a poor Voltage Standing Wave Ratio (VSWR). VSWR can affect system performance by creating reflected signals. The reflections can cause collisions for data signals and ghosts for video signals. In some rare cases, the incoming video signal has mixed with the TV Intermediate Frequency (IF) Local Oscillator (LO) and then been reflected to produce out-of-band interference. In most cases, a device with poor VSWR (up to 5:1) can be compensated for by a tap or pad value of 8 dB or more which has good VSWR performance. Tests have shown that reflected signals can essentially be eliminated by using high tap values that have a high return loss and high port-to-port isolation.

Conversely, the transmitters will affect almost all of the cable plant performance parameters. BIU filtering will affect the transmission bandwidth as well as harmonics and spurious signals. The BIU on/off ratio determines the amount of noise when the transmitter is not transmitting, and may accumulate in the reverse direction.

In government LAN's, RF emanations are critical if the network carries classified information. To solve this problem, an automatic RF leakage detection system was developed using off-the-shelf equipment. The system continuously monitors the RF emanations and triggers security alarms which indicate the location when an RF leak occurs.

If the availability of the system is critical, then automatic diagnostics may be engaged to reduce the time to detect and localize faults. An addressable tap system which turns the RF ports on and off (instead of

scrambling) can be used to facilitate this process.

In MAN's, the LAN's are often not interconnected due to the proprietary nature of the data. Private industry LAN owners prefer to have complete control over the accessibility and performance of the system, and in government LAN's this is often mandatory. BIU encryption techniques are still under development, are costly, and are not 100 percent secure. Thus, MAN's are limited to providing public service type interconnections.

Conclusions

Due to the limitations of CATV amplifiers and other limitations discussed in this article, it is not technically possible to design a LAN using only CATV equipment that will cover an entire metropolitan area with one cable system. In any system, there is a maximum number of amplifiers in cascade which is set by the performance characteristics of the amplifiers and system topology. There is a direct correspondence between the density of users and the maximum possible coverage area. For a typical push-pull trunk amplifier, the maximum number of amplifiers is about 56. For a 21 dB gain amplifier and one-half inch trunk cable (1.04 dB/100 ft at 400 MHz), this would be a distance (or diameter) of about 20 miles, provided that the loss consisted only of cable loss. If the system consisted of half cable loss and half tap loss, then the distance would be ten miles, and due to the paralleling affects of amplifiers, the reverse noise limitation would set the actual limit at about five miles. Thus, the only way to cover an entire Metro Area is through the interconnection of LAN's which are isolated in terms of analog noise. This must be implemented by the use of digital repeaters, bridges, or gateways, and is accomplished on a channel-by-channel basis. The IEEE 802.6 recommendation specifies a Media Access Control (MAC) protocol to perform this interconnection.

The major design considerations for CATV systems are the head-end location, quality of signal sources, noise accumulation, amplifier selection and operating levels, passive component characteristics, receiver characteristics, and cost. Although the receivers are always TV sets, their typical performance characteristics vary among TV manufacturers. In particular, some TV sets have very poor adjacent channel rejection resulting in poor-quality signals on all channels when connected to a CATV system utilizing adjacent channels. In order to limit this variability and provide a method of protecting pay channels, a cable TV converter/descrambler is often used.

For LAN's, the reverse direction is the primary concern and warrants consideration of the reverse signal level variation, transmitter characteristics, topology, redundancy, and amplifier configuration, in addition to the CATV considerations. Since transmitters can be located anywhere in the network, the transmission bandwidth, on/off ratio, VSWR, and out-of-band performance can all affect the design or utilization of a LAN. Since the density of users (outlets per square foot) in a LAN is much greater than in a CATV system, there is a greater number of passive components in cascade. Thus the component characteristics are more critical in a LAN and must be examined carefully.

The primary challenge of the future for LAN's is the industry standardization of cable plant RF design characteristics. Due to the wide variations in RF modems, it is impossible to design a cable system that will simultaneously satisfy all of the system and modem performance considerations for every manufacturer (in particular the BIU operating levels and adjustment according to bandwidth). A design standard which is more stringent than IEEE 802 with regard to cable plant specifications must be adopted in order to allow the complete operability of different modems on the same cable plant. A more stringent standard will allow the purchaser the flexibility of a larger variety of services in addition to increased competition among manufacturers. The current trend of cable plant designers associated with a modem manufacturer is to design a cable plant which will only support the manufacturers' modem.

The hardware challenges for both CATV and LAN systems are to increase the bandwidth and maximum size capabilities. The CATV industry is extremely competitive in this area, and advances are made on a continual basis. Many passive components are now available with a 600 MHz upper frequency, and active components are exceeding 450 MHz. An increase in size in order to accomodate metropolitan areas would require improved amplifier performance for better noise figures, less IM distortion at higher input levels, and flatter frequency responses. In addition, manufacturing tolerances must be tightened for passive components in order to increase cascade length. Products oriented toward LAN's, such as stand alone status monitors, on/off RF switches, and attenuation values in 1 dB increments, need to be developed by more CATV manufacturers if they intend to compete in the LAN market.

Glossary of Terms and Abbreviations

AGC—*Automatic Gain Control*—a feature of CATV amplifiers which allows automatic control of the amplifier gain to compensate for temperature fluctuations. Implemented by monitoring the level of a pilot tone.

ASC—*Automatic Slope Control*—a feature of CATV amplifiers which allows automatic control of the amplifier frequency response to compensate for temperature fluctuations. Implemented by monitoring the levels of two pilot tones at different frequencies.

BER—*Bit Error Rate*—The frequency of bit errors. The cable plant CNR determines the BER depending on the modem characteristics.

BIU—*Bus Interface Unit*—the device which physically attaches the data equipment to the LAN. Also called an Interface Unit (IU) or Network Interface Unit (NIU).

Bus-tree Topology—a topology which physically resembles the branches of a tree. The transmission media is shared in a bus contention fashion.

CATV—*Community Antenna Television*—A communications service which provides TV signals to a large community through cable. Commonly referred to as cable TV. Governed by FCC Rules and Regulations Part 76.

CNR—*Carrier to Noise Ratio*—The ratio of the RMS RF carrier level to the RMS RF noise level. In CATV systems a 4.5 MHz noise bandwidth is usually used.

Cross modulation—a form of third order intermodulation where a signal is modulated by another signal.

CSMA/CD—*Carrier Sense Multiple Access with Collision Detection*—a bus contention method in which the BIU monitors the transmission media for activity prior to transmitting. When a collision is detected the BIU pauses and then re-transmits the packet.

CTB—*Composite Triple Beat*—the interference created by the third order intermodulation term $\pm f1 \pm f2 \pm f3$. Typically measured with CW carriers.

CW—*Continuous Wave*—a sinusoidal RF signal which has a constant amplitude and frequency.

F-connectors—a connector used in the CATV industry for connecting drop cable to components and TV sets. A threaded metal fitting which grasps the outside of the drop cable and connects to the cable shield. The connector is hollow to allow the cable dielectric and center conductor to extend through the connector.

FDM—*Frequency Division Multiplexing*—a method of permitting the simultaneous use of a common RF media by assigning the different services to different frequency bands in the available frequency spectrum.

FSK—*Frequency Shift Keying*—a digital FM modulation technique.

Head-end—the physical point in the system where all the cables join together for distribution, collection or both.

HRC—*Harmonically Related Carrier*—a frequency plan which makes all the carriers uniformly spaced in frequency. A comb generator is used to phase lock the TV carriers.

Hum modulation—low frequency (60 Hz) amplitude modulation of the carrier by AC power supplies and other disturbances.

IEEE 802—the committee assigned by the IEEE to provide a standard for LAN's.

IM—*Intermodulation*—interference created from the input signals by the non-linearities in the amplifier gain.

IRC—*Incrementally Related Carrier*—a frequency plan which reassigns TV channels similar to the HRC system. A comb generator is used to phase lock the TV carriers.

ISO OSI Reference Model—*International Standards Organization Open Systems Interconnection Reference Model*—the network architecture proposed by ISO for international standardization of protocols.

LAN—*Local Area Network*—a communications service which provides connectivity for network users in a given area.

NTSC—*National Television Standards Committee*—the signal format used for broadcasting television signals in the U.S.

Path—any physical cable route from any transmitter to any receiver.

Quad shield coaxial drop cable—center conductor embedded in dielectric with inner shield of metal tape bonded to the dielectric and covered with braided wire sheath; the whole cable further shielded with another layer of metal tape and another layer of braided wire; plastic jacket overall.

Return Loss—the logarithmic ratio between the incident and reflected signals. The return loss is directly related to the voltage reflection coefficient which is directly related to the VSWR.

Tap or **multi-tap**—a directional coupler with two trunk cable connections and multiple (typically 2, 4, or 8) drop cable connections. The insertion loss between the trunk cable ports is usually 1 dB or less. The tap loss from the trunk port to a drop port is available in 3 dB increments from about 7 dB to 25 dB.

TASO—*Television Allocations Study Organization*—studied the effects of noise on perceived signal quality and published a report to the FCC in 1959.

Trunk cable—center conductor embedded in dielectric with outer sheath of seamless metal, plastic jacket overall optional.

TV IF LO—*Television Intermediate Frequency Local Oscillator*—the mixer inside the TV which converts the RF signal to an intermediate frequency (typically 46 to 48 MHz) for processing.

VSWR—*Voltage Standing Wave Ratio*—the linear voltage ratio between the incident and reflected standing waves.

References

[1] Edward Cooper, *Broadband Network Technology*, Sytek, Inc., 1984.
[2] Ken Simons, *Technical Handbook for CATV Systems*, Jerrold Electronics Corporation, 1968.
[3] Andrew S. Tanenbaum, *Computer Networks*, Prentice-Hall, 1981.
[4] R. Simpson and R. Houts, *Fundamentals of Analog and Digital Communication Systems*, Allyn and Bacon, Inc., 1971.
[5] K. Sam Shanmugam, *Digital and Analog Communication Systems*, John Wiley & Sons, Inc., 1979.
[6] Members of the Technical Staff, *Transmission Systems for Communications*, Bell Telephone Laboratories, Inc., 1982.
[7] Constance Warren, "Amplifier technology evolves," *CED Magazine*, Dec. 1984.
[8] FCC Rules and Regulations Part 76, Oct. 1982.
[9] IEEE Standards for Local Area Networks: Token Passing Bus Access Method and Physical Layer Specifications, Institute of Electrical and Electronics Engineers, Inc. (ANSI/IEEE Std 802.4-1985, ISO Draft International Standard 8802/4), 1985.
[10] Draft of Proposed IEEE Standard 802.6, Metropolitan Area Network (MAN), Media Access Control, Revision E, Oct. 4, 1985.
[11] T. McGarty and G. Clancy, Jr., "Cable-based metro area networks," *IEEE Jour. on Sel. Areas in Comm.*, Nov. 1983.

Richard Dunbar received the B.S. degree in Physics (minor in Mathematics) and the M.S. degree in Electrical Engineering (Communications) from Virginia Polytechnic Institute and State University in 1979 and 1984 respectively.

From 1980 to 1982 he was a systems design engineer for Telcom, Inc. and performed the design, installation, and test of commercial microwave communication systems.

In 1982 he joined Contel Information Systems (Government Systems Division) and is responsible for the design and test of broadband coaxial cable communication systems. He performed design research into the hardware performance of cascaded CATV components including the theoretical prediction and measurement of noise and distortion on a system basis. This included analyses of Gaussian noise and intermodulation distortion accumulation. He has performed consulting services to the U.S. government in developing LAN specifications and to the U.S. House of Representatives' House Information System (HIS LAN) in recommending LAN channel allocations. He is currently managing Contel staff engineers in the design and test of communication systems for LAN's.

He is a member of Sigma Pi Sigma Physics Honor Society. ∎

Reprinted from *IEEE Journal on Selected Areas in Communications*, Volume
SAC-3, Number 3, May 1985. Copyright © 1985 by The Institute of Electrical and Electronics Engineers, Inc.

Broad-Band Personal Computer LAN's

CARL A. SUNSHINE AND GREGORY ENNIS

Abstract—Broad-band technology provides several advantages for personal computer local area networks (PC LAN's) including mature readily available transmission technology, large total bandwidth, support for multiple services, and cost-effective expansion from very small to very large systems. This paper presents an overview of basic broad-band technology, hardware, software, and protocols needed for PC LAN's. Gateways and network management are also considered. Recent PC LAN products are compared, with a more detailed case study of the PC LAN developed by IBM and Sytek.

I. INTRODUCTION

WHILE the interconnection of personal computers (PC's) with a local area network (LAN) has been common for some time, the use of broad-band LAN's for this purpose is relatively new. As well as being an attractive technology for stand-alone PC LAN's, broad-band promises to integrate PC communications into a broader spectrum of local communications. This paper presents some of the design tradeoffs and system issues that must be considered to make most effective use of broad-band technology for PC LAN's.

We first discuss the motivation for PC LAN's, with an emphasis on the requirements that must be met to support them on broad-band systems. We next present an overview of broad-band technology and its advantages for PC LAN's.

To meet PC LAN requirements, all aspects of a LAN design must be considered. In particular, we discuss alternative approaches and design tradeoffs for hardware, software and protocols, bridging and gateways, and network control. Examples from current product offerings are cited whenever possible.

After this overview of general issues, we present a particular broad-band PC LAN architecture in greater detail as a case study. A short table comparing commercially available equipment and some comments on standardization conclude the paper.

II. PERSONAL COMPUTER LAN'S

Personal computers have until recently been used primarily in a "stand-alone" fashion. Stand-alone PC's obviously provide considerable value as evidenced by their market success. However, to be really useful, the personal computer must be able to exchange information with other machines. Information exchange can take place through manual transport of removable storage (floppy disks), or via the ubiquitous low-speed RS-232 asynchronous interface and a modem, but neither is ideal. Hence, one major motivation for the introduction of local networks for PC's has been to improve such machine-to-machine communications capabilities.

Another major factor has been the cost justification of "resource sharing." Rather than require that each PC have its own hard disk, printer, etc., a LAN for PC's makes it possible to share resources among multiple users.

These two primary benefits of a PC LAN—increased function and decreased cost—are equally valid for the small installation and the large. However, most PC LAN systems available today are specifically oriented towards the simpler small installation solution. Although many (if not most) PC LAN's will be small, a substantial number of installations will require the attachment of hundreds or even thousands of PC's and associated servers. For example, universities are encouraging the proliferation of personal computers on campus, and many large time-sharing installations are gradually replacing their terminals with personal computers.

A successful PC LAN architecture must address the needs of both the small and large user. As with the PC industry itself, the existence of substantial application software for a particular LAN will be the determining factor in most user's installation requirements. Such application software will be developed only for those networks which for technical reasons seem to fit a wide variety of user environments in a cost-effective manner. As a communication medium that can service the whole range of PC LAN environments, from the very small to the very large, broad-band appears to be the most promising PC LAN technology.

In fact, the large and the small PC LAN installation seem to merge in what is likely to be a dominant type of network: the "department" PC net, procured and managed by a small piece of a larger organization, involving a significant communication requirement with the rest of the larger installation. Broad-band has advantages in such an environment due to its ability to support multiple "logical" networks on different frequency bands of the same communication medium.

From the above brief discussion of typical PC LAN environments, we can derive some requirements for a broad-band LAN architecture for personal computers.

- It must support small installations. This implies that

Manuscript received October 5, 1984; revised January 24, 1985.
C. A. Sunshine is with Sytek, Inc., Culver City, CA 90230.
G. Ennis is with Sytek, Inc., Mountain View, CA 94043.

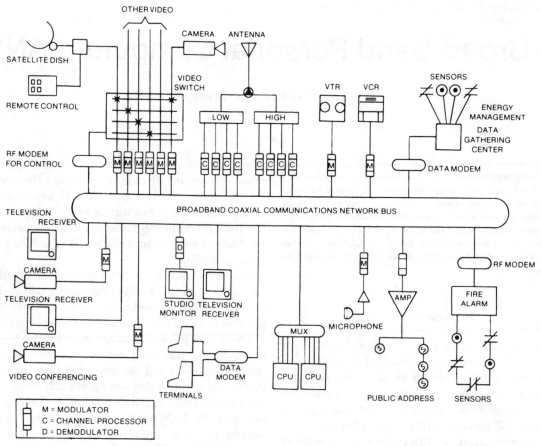

OTHER VIDEO

SATELLITE DISH

REMOTE CONTROL

CAMERA ANTENNA

VIDEO SWITCH

LOW   HIGH

VTR   VCR

SENSORS

ENERGY MANAGEMENT

DATA GATHERING CENTER

RF MODEM FOR CONTROL

M M M M M M   C C C C   C C C C   M   M

DATA MODEM

TELEVISION RECEIVER

BROADBAND COAXIAL COMMUNICATIONS NETWORK BUS

M

RF MODEM

CAMERA

M

D

M

FIRE ALARM

TELEVISION RECEIVER

STUDIO MONITOR   TELEVISION RECEIVER

CAMERA

M

MUX

MICROPHONE

AMP

VIDEO CONFERENCING

DATA MODEM

TERMINALS

CPU CPU

PUBLIC ADDRESS   SENSORS

M = MODULATOR
C = CHANNEL PROCESSOR
D = DEMODULATOR

Fig. 1.   Multiple services using a broad-band network.

the architecture must be simple enough to be cost-effectively used in small systems, which cannot justify the expense of specialized network control equipment.

- It must support large installations. Not only must large networks be supportable, but the architecture must include mechanisms which provide for the interconnection of separate networks into a unified system.

- It must provide a rich set of communications services. The full power of communicating personal computers can only be realized if the underlying network provides a set of protocols powerful enough to support true distributed applications.

- It must provide adequate performance. This means both total channel capacity adequate for low delay transmission of large packets (1–5 Mbits/s), and an interface to each individual PC sufficient to match its I/O capabilities (several hundred kbits/s).

III. BROAD-BAND COMMUNICATION

Broad-band LAN technology is based on the same 75 Ω coaxial cable used by the cable television industry (this is different from the 50 Ω cable used by baseband Ethernets). Broad-band technology also differs from baseband in its ability to support multiple simultaneous channels as in CATV systems which provide multiple video channels on a single cable. Broad-band LAN's enhance this concept to provide multiple data channels as well as video and even voice. Hence, a variety of services can be carried over a common transmission medium by using industry standard interface equipment (Fig. 1).

The physical topology of broad-band installations is a tree, with the main trunk emanating from a "headend," and splitters to branch cables, each of which may have numerous taps to drop cables providing attachment points for user equipment [7]. Such cable systems can include amplifiers which extend the range of transmission beyond 20 miles; nevertheless, it is possible to install very inexpensive broadband systems in an area as small as a single room.

Information signals (video or data) are placed on a broad-band cable system by modulation of a carrier. The use of different carrier frequencies allows multiple such information signals to share the same cable, thereby creating the multiple channels. Signals on any given channel must propagate on a broad-band cable system in a single direction. Thus two-way broad-band systems can be created by using two parallel cables, one for "return" traffic from users to headend, and the other for "forward" traffic from headend to users. In such dual cable systems, the headend simply repeats signals from the return cable onto the forward cable.

Another popular method for creating two-way systems uses frequency translation at the headend to avoid the need for dual cables. By installing appropriate directional couplers, amplifiers, and filters, the frequency space on a single cable can be divided so that signals in the lower frequency range are sent to the headend, and those in the high range are sent from headend to users. The headend creates bidirectional channels by frequency translating the signals on each return channel to a corresponding forward channel (Fig. 2). This method provides a little less than half the bandwidth of a dual cable, but provides a major savings in cable installation and material costs. If many channels are in use, multiple frequency translators at the headend may be needed.

Each user node on a broad-band system must include a radio frequency (RF) modem. In the dual cable system, the transmitter must be attached to the return cable and the receiver to the forward cable, both operating at the same frequency. In single cable systems, both transmitter and receiver are attached to the same cable, but they operate at different frequencies. Many nodes may be set to operate on the same channel, in which case all receivers will hear whatever signal is being transmitted (after it is passed through the headend). Thus the system provides a logically fully connected, full-duplex broadcast medium on each return/forward channel pair.

The system may be divided into various numbers of channels, each operating at different data rates. The data rate may be selected for maximum cost-effectiveness for each type of use (e.g., 9.6 kbits/s for a dedicated peripheral channel, 128 kbits/s for inexpensive shared access by many low-speed terminals, or 1–5 Mbits/s for PC interconnection). Traffic can be forwarded between different channels if desired by "bridges" or routers (discussed below) to create an integrated system providing very large total capacity, with each portion operating at the best data rate.

In summary, broad-band may be seen to have the following advantages for use in PC LAN's.

- It provides mature readily available transmission technology (CATV) with highly competitive suppliers.
- It provides adequate bandwidth for the total data communication needs of the vast majority of sites.
- It allows multiple independent communication facilities to share the same physical transmission facility ("coexistence").
- It allows high total capacity with cost-effective equipment by using multiple lower speed channels in an integrated system.
- It supports inexpensive entry level systems, but expands easily to large distances and/or user population.

IV. HARDWARE

The hardware for attachment of PC's to LAN's typically consists of an adaptor card (or cards) which are mounted internally to the PC chassis. This provides a high-speed interface to the PC's internal bus. The card typically contains a specialized controller to handle the physical and

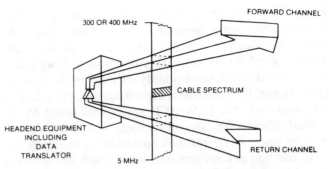

Fig. 2. Frequency translation at headend.

link level procedures (e.g., CSMA/CD, token passing), and may have an additional processor for higher level protocol processing. For broad-band systems, the LAN interface must include a modem.

These components may be packaged in various combinations. For lowest cost and space consumption, everything can be packaged together on a single card, as in the IBM and Wang products (see Section IX for product descriptions). Alternatively, the modem may be packaged on a separate board, still housed within the PC as in the Ungermann–Bass (UB) product, or may be housed externally, This makes it possible to use different modems for different types of channel, at an increase in cost and space required.

Finally, the bulk of the network interface equipment may be housed externally in a separate network interface module, with a short high-speed interface back to one or more PC's, each containing a simplified device interface module. This latter approach opens the possibility of sharing the cost of the network interface module, or of attaching relatively unintelligent devices (such as printers or terminals) directly to the network.

Early broad-band modem designs included a large number of analog components, leading to relatively large board areas and high cost. As in other areas, volume production provides justification for development of special purpose devices and more efficient designs, leading to reduced size and cost. The modem portion of the IBM product occupies only 25 in^2 for example.

As noted above, a key component of the hardware is a specialized controller chip to perform physical and link control functions. Broad-band products available now have taken advantage of controllers originally designed for baseband systems. The IBM unit and the highend UB unit (NIU) include the Intel 82586 "Ethernet" chip; the lowend UB unit (NIC) includes the Fujitsu Ethernet chip set; and the Wang unit includes the Advanced Microsystems 9026 "RIM" chip. These chips typically need some specialized additional logic to properly interface to the broad-band modem (e.g., for frame delimiting and collision detection in CSMA/CD).

A long-standing controversy over the relative merits of CSMA/CD and token passing techniques for sharing a channel has carried over into the broad-band LAN environment [11, p. 28]. Advantages cited for CSMA/CD are lower delay for large populations of "bursty" traffic sources, and simpler more robust management (no problems with node entry/exit or token loss). The major advantage cited for token passing is bounded delay under high load (although lower priority stations may be shut out [10]). Hence, the ideal choice depends on the application to be supported, but CSMA/CD seems best suited to the typical office automation environment, while token passing may be desirable for real-time control or for steady traffic.

In addition to a network interface for each user device, a broad-band system requires a cable system including a headend as described above. Normally this is a standard "commercial" CATV system supporting multiple services as shown in Fig. 1. Such cable systems must be designed and installed to maintain proper signal levels at all points. With proper design, they are relatively easy to expand to greater distances and/or more access taps. Headend equipment is available from several manufacturers, typically in increments of 6 MHz channel slots.

To support modest sized stand-alone broadband PC LAN's, several vendors provide do-it-yourself cable kits and low cost headends. These systems can support 50–250 PC's over a distance of several thousand ft. They provide predetermined cable layout options that can be easily assembled by PC users and that guarantee proper signal levels without requiring any design calculations.

V. SOFTWARE AND PROTOCOLS

To provide full general purpose communication capabilities, all layers of the ISO protocol hierarchy (or vendor specific equivalent) should be provided. A major question is how to partition this set of protocols between the PC and the network adaptor. As noted above, the physical level includes a modem in broad-band systems, often supported along with the link level by a specialized controller located in the adaptor. One tempting solution (from the network vendor's point of view) is to relegate the remaining protocol functions to the PC, allowing a relatively simple and inexpensive network adaptor. This is the approach taken in the Wang and UB NIC products. Unfortunately, this often yields low performance since the computational engine in the PC generally has modest power and must be shared with other activities.

The alternative is to place more of the protocol processing in the network adaptor, typically supported by an additional microprocessor. At least network, transport, and session level functions can be performed in the adaptor, providing a general purpose communication service to the PC itself. This is the approach taken in the IBM unit using Sytek LocalNet (TM) protocol technology. Since presentation level functions are intimately connected with the specifics of file system conventions and screen display formats, placing these functions within the network adaptor requires more device-specific code and risks mixing application and communication functions, but does provide the potential for further offloading the PC processor. This approach is taken in the UB NIU unit.

Wherever the higher level protocols are placed, they must provide a rich enough set of communication services to fully support distributed processing. Hence, we next present a summary of necessary functions at these levels in a broad-band LAN for PC's.

Network: The network layer is responsible for routing of packets between different channels and/or cables to provide an integrated fully connected communication service to higher level protocols. Unfortunately, it is often omitted in simpler LAN systems designed for a single baseband channel with a limited population of nodes. Support for routing is particularly important in broad-band systems, where use of multiple channels on a single cable as well as use of multiple cables is a key feature. Typically some network layer processing is needed in end-user nodes, while additional routing functions must be implemented by the packet forwarding nodes that interconnect channels (bridges).

Transport: The transport protocols are responsible for end-to-end data transfers. "End-to-end" implies that the transport protocols need not be implemented within any intermediate packet routing nodes, but are implemented at the endpoints of all data transfers. The major transport protocol in the LAN context provides reliable flow-controlled "virtual circuit" type service between a pair of users. Other important transport protocols provide for the best-effort transmission of a single message or "datagram" to one or more users ("broadcast"), and a single request/response transaction.

Session: Protocols within the session layer are involved in the management of the network services in more user-oriented manner than the lower layers provide. For example, the transport layer protocols may identify destinations using complex network addresses, whereas the user would rather refer to destinations using meaningful symbolic names. The session layer in this context is responsible for performing the necessary mappings between names and addresses and allowing users to register new names. Another session service is identification of logical message boundaries. Several sessions may be needed simultaneously by PC applications.

Access to these communication services must be provided to PC applications in a convenient fashion. Typically this access is via a set of operating system calls or a network "driver" (e.g., the IBM NETBIOS). The full range of services specified by ISO should be provided, plus additional management functions appropriate in an LAN environment. To support open systems, the PC LAN vendor should clearly define this network command set, and make it available to application developers over the full range of network interfaces.

VI. BRIDGES AND GATEWAYS

Various forms of data forwarding are particularly important in broad-band systems with their potential to cover large areas and user populations. At the physical level, the RF technology of cable splitters, combiners, taps, amplifiers, and even point-to-point links to remote subheadends are used to provide channels over a wide area [7].

At the network level, packets are selectively forwarded from one channel to another, tying the system into a single logical network. As long as the source and destination user nodes have compatible higher level protocols, the "bridges" functioning at this level need not perform any higher level protocol functions. However, the routing problem itself is quite a challenging one.

A. Bridges

In one approach to routing common in baseband systems [8], packets are routed by tables in the bridges based on an explicit address of the destination subnetwork which the sending user must supply in each packet. This requires procedures for the bridges to maintain current routing tables and for user nodes to determine destination network addresses.

In another approach, the first transmission to a new destination causes a "discovery" procedure to be invoked which sets up a path through the bridges to the destination [9], [12]. This path is remembered by the bridges and used for subsequent packets between the same users. This simplifies the sending user and bridge processing considerably at the cost of the initial discovery procedure. Sytek holds the basic patent for broad-band bridge technology [4], and has fielded a number of products in this area.

Bridges may also play a roll in network control. This may include call establishment by name lookup or filtering, accounting data collection, performance data collection, and fault isolation.

A variety of coverage strategies involving bridges can be used in broad-band systems. Thanks to their branching tree structure, a single physical cable plant can be used to cover over 1000 nodes anywhere within a radius of several kilometers of the headend. Several different frequency channels may be used globally to support even more nodes, with the channels connected by bridges.

More distributed approaches are also possible. Separate cable segments, each with its own headend, can be joined by bridges, allowing reuse of the same frequency channel on each segment. This multiplies both the separation distance and number of nodes that can be supported. Individual "local" cable segments in each building, floor, or department may also be linked through bridges to a site-spanning trunk system (Fig. 3). The trunk channel(s) may even use a different speed and/or protocol (e.g., token bus) than the local segments.

A hybrid scheme is also possible with a global physical cable plant reaching all users. Some channels are used to provide global service for trunking, popular servers, video, etc. Other channels are terminated locally via filters and subnetwork headends (Fig. 4), and are connected by bridges to the global trunk channels. This provides the benefits of a centrally maintained cable plant and global services plus

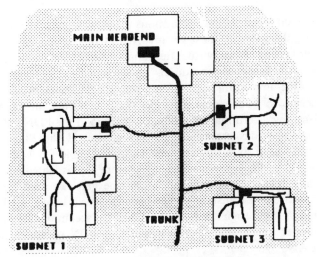

Fig. 3. Main trunk and subnet segments.

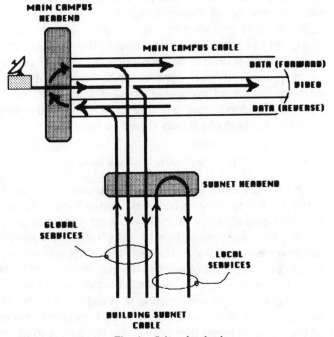

Fig. 4. Subnet headend.

the greater efficiency of local traffic separation via frequency reuse.

B. Gateways

If the higher level protocols in the user nodes on different channels are not compatible, then the forwarding node also must terminate and translate the appropriate protocols on either side. A node performing this more complex processing is usually called a gateway [1]. Common examples are gateways to public data networks or specific vendor systems.

The complexity of the gateway depends on the number of protocol layers involved. If the presentation/application levels are compatible in the user nodes (e.g., a common file transfer procedure), then the gateway needs to merely concatenate transmission services at network, transport, or session levels. If the applications themselves are incompatible, the gateway must get involved at this level also (e.g., converting from virtual terminal protocol to a vendor specific terminal procedure).

One important type of gateway for PC nets provides access to public data networks (PDN's). Often the PC is running a terminal emulation program, and the PDN gateway provides essentially a PAD service. If the PDN is being used as a link between two compatible PC LAN's, then the PC's may be running a more sophisticated common higher level application and the gateway need only concatenate transmission services. However, care must be taken to design such applications to accommodate the longer delays and lower capacities of PDN compared to LAN.

Another important type of gateway is to a vendor-specific mainframe "network" system. Here the gateway is likely to emulate some set of known devices to the vendor system, such as cluster controller or RJE station. Again, the complexity of the gateway is determined by how support for the emulation is divided between gateway and PC's. In the future, hosts and other servers should begin to directly support distributed processing oriented toward PC nets, and provide direct attachments to PC LAN's, so that the need for this type of gateway should be reduced.

VII. Network Management

Small systems can get by with minimal manual informal network management procedures. Broad-band systems, with the potential for multiple channels and large user population, can benefit from a wide range of network management functions. As for any large LAN, accounting access control, queueing, performance monitoring, and fault isolation are important to support with automated tools.

A major management function in broad-band LAN's is assignment of nodes with frequency agile modems to one of the many channels they can access. The goal is to place calling and called nodes on the same channel, or if this is impossible (multiple concurrent sessions must share the same modem), minimize the path length. This may be done relatively statically based on long-term usage statistics. It may also be done dynamically at the time a session is formed if the modem is software tunable as in the Sytek LocalNet/20 system [2], [3].

Another management function unique to broad-band is fault diagnosis and recovery in the RF plant. Portable cable testers are available that can be attached to any tap to test for proper signal levels through the headend and back. Individual modem degradation can be detected by counting errors in packet transmission and reception at individual nodes and reporting when a threshold is exceeded. Screaming modems are largely prevented by a maximum activity cutoff in the final output stage.

Overall channel noise problems are indicated by monitoring all packets on a channel for total error rates. Noise sources can then be isolated by selectively switching off branches of the cable plant via remotely controlled RF components.

VIII. Case Study of IBM PC LAN

The IBM PC Network is IBM's local network for their family of personal computers. This broad-band network has as its primary component a "Network Adapter" card which plugs into a single slot in the chassis of the AT, XT, PC, and Portable personal computers. The Network Adapter card includes a connector for attachment of standard 75 Ω coaxial cable.

Most small installations of the IBM PC Network will likely use the simple "do-it-yourself" cable kit which allows for the attachment of up to 72 nodes over a distance of 1000 ft. Larger installations will typically involve the use of a custom-engineered broad-band cable system installed throughout a campus or large facility.

A. Basic Network Adapter Hardware

The IBM Network Adapter card contains a broad-band modem, specialized local network controller chips, a microprocessor with associated RAM and ROM, and a specialized chip which manages the interface to the PC system bus (Fig. 5).

The broad-band modem for the IBM PC Network uses FSK (frequency shift keying) to transmit digital signals at a 2 Mbit/s rate. FSK is a simple and robust modulation technique, and its use allows for the design of a compact and inexpensive modem. This modem is built out of common analog components and resides on the Network Adapter card itself, encased in a metal shield which serves as protection against interference and emanation problems.

The modem transmits in a 6 MHz channel centered at 50.75 MHz, and receives in a 6 MHz channel centered at 219.00 MHz. By configuring the broad-band cable system with an IBM Translator Unit (a simple headend), all signals on the cable within the transmit band will be "upconverted" to the corresponding receive frequencies, allowing each Network Adapter card to receive the transmissions of other cards. Thus all nodes on this pair of transmit and receive channels are logically connected to a common "bus."

This logical bus is operated according to the CSMA/CD access method. To accomplish this on broad-band, the Network Adapter card uses a standard commercial CSMA/CD controller (the Intel 82586) together with a custom VLSI chip designed by Sytek called the "serial interface controller" (SIC). The SIC chip's primary responsibility is to perform the actual collision detection function. On broad-band this is accomplished by comparing the bits received over the receive channel to those which were transmitted, looking for discrepancies which would indicate the occurrence of a collision (simultaneous transmission by multiple stations).

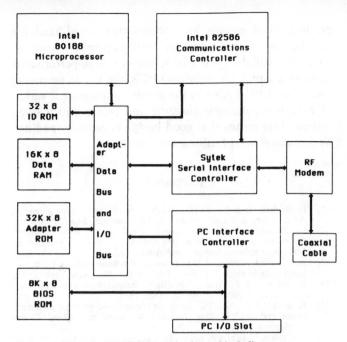

Fig. 5.   IBM PC network adapter block diagram.

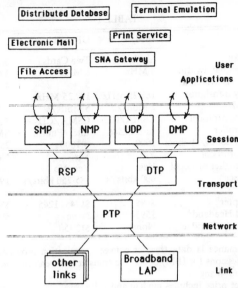

Fig. 6.   Sytek LocalNet/PC protocol architecture.

The Network Adapter card includes a 16 bit micro-processor (the Intel 80188), which executes higher level protocol software from a 32 kbyte ROM. Sixteen kbytes of RAM are used for temporary variable storage and packet buffers. An additional 8 kbyte ROM is used for interface software which is used in conjunction with another custom VLSI "host interface controller" (HIC) chip to manage the transfer of commands and data between the PC and its local Network Adapter card.

B. Software and Protocols

The software which is executed by the Network Adapter card's 80188 microprocessor is an implementation of Sytek's LocalNet/PC (TM) high-level protocol architecture (Fig. 6) [5]. The LocalNet/PC protocols provide up through the session level of ISO Open Systems Interconnection services.

The lowest level of the IBM Network Adapter implements the basic physical transmission of the broad-band modem and the CSMA/CD access method. Above this resides the LocalNet/PC network-level protocol called "PTP" (the Packet Transfer Protocol). PTP supports the "discovery" method of pathfinding and provides for packet routing through bridges which may connect multiple broad-band channels or multiple cables. This protocol is designed specifically to handle the presence of frequency-agile modems on the cable system.

Above PTP, the two transport-level protocols are RSP (Reliable Stream Protocol), which provides for multiple flow-controlled reliable virtual connections, and DTP (Datagram Transport Protocol), which provides a simple best-effort datagram service.

Four protocols are included in the LocalNet/PC session-layer. NMP (the Name Management Protocol) allows applications to register symbolic names via which they may be called on the network. SMP (the Session Management Protocol) provides for management of multiple sessions between named applications, performing the actual packetization function in a manner transparent to the user program. The User Datagram Protocol (UDP) provides for datagram exchanges between named users. The Diagnostic and Monitoring Protocol (DMP) allows for the remote gathering of node status and network statistics.

These session-level protocols within the Network Adapter make their services available to application software on the personal computer through the "NETBIOS" command interface. The NETBIOS is IBM's standard interface for personal computer communications, consisting of a specified set of command formats and procedures between the PC host processor and an attached Network Adapter card. Through the NETBIOS interface to the LocalNet/PC session-level services, software designers will be developing distributed applications to run on the IBM PC Network. IBM has also announced their intent of supporting the NETBIOS for personal computers which will attach to their future token-ring network.

IX. PRODUCT SUMMARY

As of this writing, three vendors provide broad-band LAN products specifically oriented towards the PC market. These are the IBM PC Network described above, the Ungermann–Bass Net/One Personal Connection (TM), and the Wang Professional Computer WangNet Option.

The UB product consists of a separate broadband modem card and two alternate controller cards, a highend Network Interface Unit (NIU), and a lowend Network Interface Controller (NIC), all designed to fit within the IBM PC. The NIU has an Intel 80186 microprocessor and 128 kbyte RAM to perform higher level protocol processing, while the NIC has no microprocessor and only 16 kbyte RAM for packet buffering, relying on the PC to perform higher level protocol processing. The software includes integrated file server, print server, and electronic mail functions.

The Wang product consists of a single WangNet Option card that fits within the Wang Professional Computer. This

TABLE I

	IBM/Sytek	UB (NIU/NIC)	Wang
Form factor	Single Card	Two Cards	Single Card
RF channel bandwidth	6 MHz	6 MHz	3.6 MHz
No. channels available	1	5	4
Frequency translation	168.25 MHz	192.25 MHz	None
Link speed	2 Mbits/s	5 Mbits/s	2.5 Mbits/s
Link access protocol	CSMA/CD	CSMA/CD	Token Bus
Link controller	Intel 82586	Intel/Fujitsu	SM 9026
Maximum nodes/channel	1000	>1000	255
Network protocol	Yes	Yes	No
Onboard higher protocol	Yes	Yes/No	No
Performance[a]	600 kbits/s	185-250 kbits/s	195 kbits/s
Price			
PC adapter[b]	$695	$1745/1245	$800
Limited Headend[c]	$595	None	$995
Two-channel bridge	None	$12750	None

[a]Performance is data transfer between application programs on two PC's via sessions for IBM/Sytek; file transfer between disks on two PC's for UB and Wang.

[b]Adapter price includes modem and software.

[c]IBM Sytek headend includes frequency translation; Wang does not. A "commercial" grade single-channel headend is available from UB and Sytek for $3500.

system uses a token-passing link control strategy implemented in a specialized controller, and leaves higher level protocol processing to the PC. The network software that runs in the PC includes integrated file server and print server functions [6].

Table I gives a brief summary and comparison of major product features.

X. STANDARDS

Although each of the broad-band PC LAN products mentioned incorporates some form of protocol hierarchy that corresponds approximately to the ISO Open Systems Interconnection (OSI) model, none of them implements the actual ISO protocol standards at any level. This is partly due to the unavailability of the standards at the time these products were being developed, and partly due to the desire of LAN vendors to optimize performance for the LAN environment (the ISO standards have been largely oriented towards long-haul networks so far).

The CSMA/CD access method used by IBM and UB is similar to the IEEE 802.3 baseband standard (Ethernet), and the development of a broad-band standard along these lines is now in progress within the IEEE 802.3 committee. No PC products making use of the other IEEE broad-band LAN standard (802.4 token bus) have been developed yet, and this will probably have to await the availability of VLSI controller chips for this protocol.

At the higher levels, broad-band (and other) LAN's will probably begin to make use of the ISO protocol standards as they become more widely used and accepted. This will likely be done initially with gateways translating from vendor protocol sets to the ISO standards, and later by directly implementing the ISO protocols in LAN interface equipment.

XI. CONCLUSIONS

Broad-band systems seem to offer unique advantages for large area systems with many thousands of users. Recent product developments have shown that broad-band can also be very cost-effective for small networks. Going beyond the availability of a basic low-cost high-performance network adapter for individual PC's, the key to success of broad-band PC LAN's is the ability to integrate a variety of devices on multiple channels and cables into a single system. This means that good bridging, gateway, and network management facilities are a must.

REFERENCES

[1] E. Benhamou and J. Estrin, "Multilevel internetworking gateways: Architecture and applications," *IEEE Computer*, Sept. 1983.

[2] M. Bernstein, C. Sunshine, and D. Kaufman, "A network control center for broadband local area networks," in *Proc. Localnet 83*. London, England: Online Conferences, Ltd.

[3] K. Biba, "LocalNet: A digital communications network for broadband coaxial cable," in *Proc. COMPCON 81*. New York: IEEE.

[4] K. Biba and J. Picazo, "Multiple channel data communication system," U.S. Patent 4 365 331, Dec. 1982.

[5] K. Biba, "LocalNet/PC: Integrated broadband personal communication services," in *Proc. Localnet 84* London, England: Online Conferences, Ltd.

[6] T. Casten, "Local area networks: Concept and recent developments of WangNet—Meeting the requirements of the user," presented at Networks 84, Online Conferences, Ltd., London, England.

[7] E. Cooper, *Broadband Network Technology*. Mountain View, CA: Sytek Press, 1984.

[8] Y. Dalal, "Use of multiple networks in Xerox' network system," in *Proc. COMPCON*, Feb. 1982.

[9] G. Ennis and P. Filice, "Overview of broad-band local area network protocol architecture," *IEEE J. Select. Areas Commun.*, Nov. 1983.

[10] G. LeLann, "On real-time distributed computing," in *Proc. IFIP Congress 1983*, R. Mason, Ed. Amsterdam, The Netherlands: North-Holland.

[11] W. Stallings, "LocalNetworks," *ACM Comput. Surveys*, Mar. 1984.

[12] C. Sunshine et al., "Interconnection of broadband local area networks," in *Proc. 8th Data Commun. Symp.*, Oct. 1983.

Carl A. Sunshine received the Ph.D. degree in computer science from Stanford University, Stanford, CA, in 1975, where he helped develop the ARPA internet protocols during his graduate studies.

He has worked at the Rand Corporation and the University of Southern California's Information Sciences Institute on various military, commercial, and public data network projects, and has done research in the area of formal protocol verification. He is currently Manager of Systems Architecture, Sytek Incorporated, Culver City, CA, engaged in developing protocols and products for broad-band local area networks.

Dr. Sunshine is chairman of IFIP WG 6.1 (the Internet Working Group) on Network Architectures and Protocols, serves on the editorial boards of *Computer Networks* and the IEEE TRANSACTIONS ON COMMUNICATIONS, and is active in network standards groups.

Gregory Ennis received the A.B. degree in mathematics from the University of California, Berkeley, in 1974, the M.S. degree in mathematics from the University of Wisconsin, Madison, in 1976, and the M.S. degree in computer engineering from Stanford University, Stanford, CA, in 1979.

Since 1979, he has been with Sytek, Incorporated, Mountain View, CA, where he is currently Director of Network Applications. His responsibilities include network architecture, development, protocol design, and performance analysis for Sytek's local network product family. His previous work at Sytek included participation in the DoD Protocol Standardization Program in the areas of protocol specification and validation. He is the convenor of the IEEE 802 Broad-Band CSMA/CD Task Force, and his current interests include metropolitan broad-band networks, personal computer networks, and network management.

StarLAN

S. Gandhi

7.2 StarLAN

StarLAN is a low cost 1 Mb/s networking solution aimed at office automation applications. It uses a star topology with the nodes connected in a point-to-point fashion to a central HUB. HUBs can be connected in a hierarchical fashion. Up to 5 levels are supported. The maximum distance between a node and the adjacent HUB or between two adjacent HUBs is 800 ft. (about 250 meters) for 24 gauge wire and 600 ft. (about 200 meters) for 26 gauge wire. Maximum node-to-node distance with one HUB is 0.5 km, hence IEEE 802.3 designation of type 1BASE5. 1 stands for 1 Mb/s and BASE for baseband. (StarLAN doesn't preclude the use of more than 800 ft wiring provided 6.5 dB maximum attenuation is met, and cable propagation delay is no more than 4 bit times).

One of the most attractive features of StarLAN is that it uses telephone grade twisted pair wire for the transmission medium. In fact, existing, installed telephone wiring can also be used for StarLAN. Telephone wiring is very economical to buy and install. Although use of telephone wiring is an obvious advantage, for small clusters of nodes, it is possible to work around the use of building wiring.

Factors contributing to low cost are:

1) Use of telephone grade, unshielded, 24 or 26 gauge twisted pair wire transmission media.

2) Installed base of redundant telephone wiring in most buildings.

3) Buildings are designed for star topology wiring. They have conduits leading to a central location.

4) Availability of low cost VLSI LAN controllers like the 82588 for low cost applications and the 82586 for high performance applications.

5) Off-the-shelf, Low cost RS-422, RS-485 drivers/receivers compatible with the StarLAN analog interface requirements.

7.2.1 StarLAN Topology

StarLAN, as the name suggests, uses a star topology. The nodes are at the extremities of a star and the central point is called a HUB. There can be more than one HUB in a network. The HUBs are connected in a hierarchical fashion resembling an inverted tree, as shown in Figure 7-1, where nodes are shown as PCs. The HUB at the base (at level 3) of the tree is called the Header Hub (HHUB) and others are called Intermediate HUBs (IHUB). It will become apparent, later in this section, that topologically, this entire network of nodes and HUBs is equivalent to one where all the nodes are connected to a single HUB. Also StarLAN doesn't limit the number of nodes or HUBS at any given level.

7.2.1.1 TELEPHONE NETWORK

StarLAN is structured to run parallel to the telephone network in a building. The telephone network has, in fact, exactly the same star topology as StarLAN. Let us now examine how the telephone system is typically laid out in a building in the USA. Figure 7-2 shows how a typical building is wired for telephones. 24 gauge unshielded twisted pair wires emanate from a Wiring Closet. The wires are in bundles of 25 or 50 pairs. The bundle is called D inside wiring (DIW). The wires in these cables end up at modular telephone jacks in the wall. The telephone set is either connected directly to

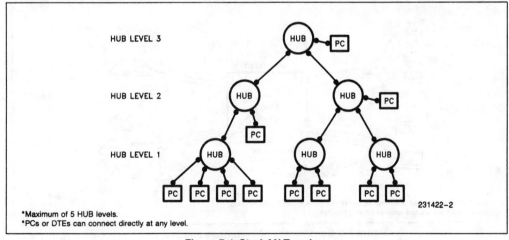

*Maximum of 5 HUB levels.
*PCs or DTEs can connect directly at any level.

Figure 7-1. StarLAN Topology

the jack or through an extension cable. Each telephone generally needs one twisted pair for voice and another for auxilliary power. Thus, each modular jack has 2 twisted pairs (4 wires) connected to it. A 25 pair DIW cable can thus be used for up to 12 telephone connections. In most buildings, not all pairs in the bundle are used. Typically, a cable is used for only 4 to 8 telephone connections. This practice is followed by telephone companies because it is cheaper for install extra wires initially, rather than retrofitting to expand the existing number of connections. As a result, a lot of extra, unused wiring exists in a building. The stretch of cable between the wiring closet and the telephone jack is typically less than 800 ft. (250 meters). In the wiring closet the incoming wires from the telephones are routed to another wiring closet, a PABX or to the central office through an interconnect matrix. Thus, the wiring closet is a concentration point in the telephone network. There is also a redundancy of wires between the wiring closets.

7.2.1.2 StarLAN AND THE TELEPHONE NETWORK

StarLAN does not have to run on building wiring, but the fact that it can, significantly adds to its attractiveness. Figure 7-3 shows how StarLAN piggybacks on telephone wiring. Each node needs two twisted pair wires to connect to the HUB. The unused wires in the 25 pair DIW cables provide an electrical path to the wiring closet, where the HUB is located. Note that the telephone and StarLAN are electrically isolated. They only use the wires in the same bundle cable to connect to the wiring closet. Within the wiring closet, StarLAN wires connect to a HUB and telephone wires are routed to a different path. Similar cable sharing can occur in connecting HUBs to one another. See Figure 7-4 for a typical office wired for StarLAN through telephone wiring.

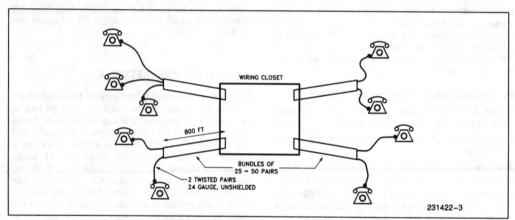

Figure 7-2. Telephone Wiring in a Building

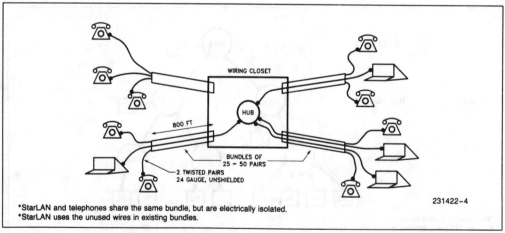

*StarLAN and telephones share the same bundle, but are electrically isolated.
*StarLAN uses the unused wires in existing bundles.

Figure 7-3. Coexistence of Telephone and StarLAN

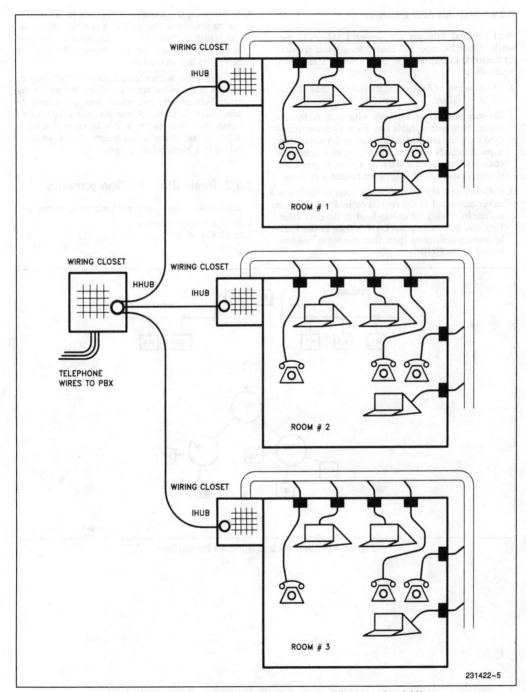

Figure 7-4. A Typical Office Using Telephone Wiring for StarLAN

231422-5

7.2.1.3 StarLAN AND Ethernet

StarLAN and Ethernet are similar CSMA/CD networks. Since Ethernet has existed longer and is better understood, a comparison of Ethernet with StarLAN is worthwhile.

1. The data rate of Ethernet is 10Mb/s and that of Star-LAN is 1 Mb/s.

2. Ethernet uses a bus topology with each node connected to a coaxial cable bus via a 50 meter transceiver cable containing four shielded twisted pair wires. StarLAN uses a star topology, with each node connected to a central HUB by a point to point link through two pairs of unshielded twisted pair wires.

3. Collision detection in Ethernet is done by the transceiver connected to the coaxial cable. Electrically, it is done by sensing the energy level on the coax cable. Collision detection in StarLAN is done in the HUB by sensing activity on more than one input line connected to the HUB.

4. In Ethernet, the presence of collision is signalled by the transceiver to the node by a special collision detect signal. In StarLAN, it is signalled by the HUB using a special collision presence signal on the receive data line to the node.

5. Ethernet cable segments are interconnected using repeaters in a non-hierarchical fashion so that the distance between any two nodes does not exceed 2.8 kilometers. In StarLAN, the maximum distance between any two nodes is 2.5 kilometers. This is achieved by wiring a maximum of five levels of HUBs in a hierarchical fashion.

7.2.2 Basic StarLAN Components

A StarLAN network has three basic components:

1. StarLAN node interface
2. StarLAN HUB
3. Cable

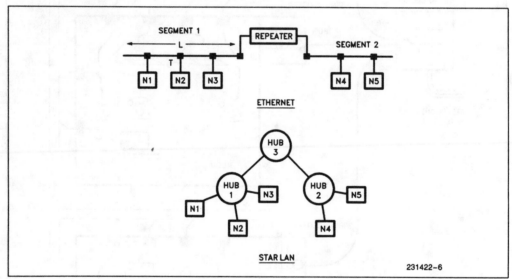

Figure 7-5. Ethernet and StarLAN Similarities

7.2.2.1 A StarLAN NODE INTERFACE

Figure 7-6 shows a typical StarLAN node interface. It interfaces to a processor on the system side. The processor runs the networking software. The heart of the node interface is the LAN controller which does the job of receiving and transmitting the frames in adherence to the IEEE 802.3 standard protocol. It maintains all the timings—like the slot time, interframe spacing etc.—required by the network. It performs the functions of framing, deferring, backing-off, collision detection which are necessary in a CSMA/CD network. It also does Manchester encoding of data to be transmitted and clock separation—or decoding—of the Manchester encoded data that is received. These signals before going to the unshielded twist pair wire, may undergo pulse shaping (optional) pulse shaping basically slows down the fall/rise times of the signal. The purpose of that is to diminish the effects of cross-talk and radiation on adjacent pairs sharing the same bundle (digital voice, T1 trunks, etc). The shaped signal is sent on to the twisted pair wire through a pulse transformer for DC isolation. The signals on the wire are thus differential, DC isolated from the node and almost sinusoidal (due to shaping and the capacitance of the wire).

NOTE:

Work done by the IEEE 802.3 committee has shown that no slew rate control on the drivers is required. Shaping by the transformer and the cable is sufficient to avoid excessive EMI radiation and crosstalk.

The squelch circuit prevents idle line noise from affecting the receiver circuits in the LAN controller. The squelch circuit has a 600 mv threshold for that purpose. Also as part of the squelch circuitry an envelope detector is implemented. Its purpose is to generate an envelope of the transitions of the RXD line. Its output serve as a carrier sense signal. The differential signal from the HUB is received using a zero-crossing RS-422 receiver. Output of the receiver, qualified by the squelch circuit, is fed to the RxD pin of the LAN controller. The RxD signal provides three kinds of information:

1) Normal received data, when receiving the frame.

2) Collision information in the form of the collision presence signal from the HUB.

3) Carrier sense information, indicating the beginning and the end of frame. This is useful during transmit and receive operations.

7.2.2.2 StarLAN HUB

HUB is the point of concentration in StarLAN. All the nodes transmit to the HUB and receive from the HUB. Figure 7-7 shows an abstract representation of the HUB. It has an upstream and a downstream signal processing unit. The upstream unit has N signal inputs and 1 signal output. And the downstream unit has 1 input and N output signals. The inputs to the upstream unit come from the nodes or from the intermediate HUBs (IHUBs) and its output goes to a higher level HUB. The downstream unit is connected the other way around; input from an upper level HUB and the outputs to nodes or lower level IHUBs. Physically each input and output consist of one twisted pair wire carrying a differential signal. The downstream unit essentially just re-times the signal received at the input, and sends it to all its outputs. The functions performed by the upstream unit are:

1. Collision detection
2. Collision Presence signal generation
3. Signal Retiming
4. Jabber Function
5. Start of Idle protection timer

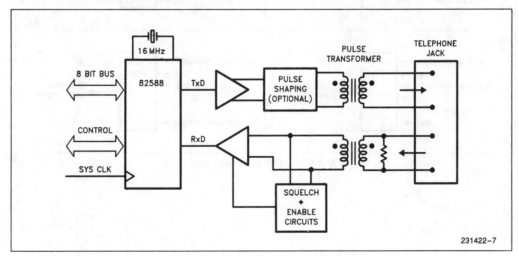

Figure 7-6. 82588 Based StarLAN Node

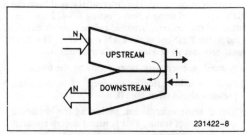

Figure 7-7. A StarLAN HUB

The collision detection in the HUB is done by sensing the activity on the inputs. If there is activity (or transitions) on more than one input, it is assumed that more than one node is transmitting. This is a collision. If a collision is detected, a special signal called the Collision Presence Signal is generated. This signal is generated and sent out as long as activity is sensed on any of the input lines. This signal is interpreted by every node as an occurrence of collision. If there is activity only on one input, that signal is re-timed—or cleaned up of any accumulated jitter—and sent out. Figure 7-8 shows the input to output relations of the HUB as a black box.

If a node transmits for too long the HUB exercises a Jabber function to disable the node from interfering with traffic from other nodes. There are two timers in

the HUB associated with this function and their operation is described in section 7-6.

The last function implemented by the HUB is the start of Idle protection timer. During the end of reception, the HUB will see a long undershoot at its input port. This undershoot is a consequence of the transformer discharging accumulated charge during the 2 microseconds of high of the idle pattern. The HUB should implement a protection mechanism to avoid the undesirable effects of that undershoot.

Figure 7-9 shows a block diagram of the HUB. A switch position determines whether the HUB is an IHUB or a HHUB (Header HUB). If the HUB is an IHUB, the switch decouples the upstream and the downstream units. HHUB is the highest level HUB; it has no place to send its output signal, so it returns its output signal (through the switch) to the outputs of the downstream unit. There is one and only one HHUB in a StarLAN network and it is always at the base of the tree. The returned signal eventually reaches every node in the network through the intermediate nodes (if any). StarLAN specifications do not put any restrictions on the number of IHUBS at any level or on number of inputs to any HUB. The number of inputs per HUB are typically 6 to 12 and is dictated by the typical size of clusters in a given networking environment.

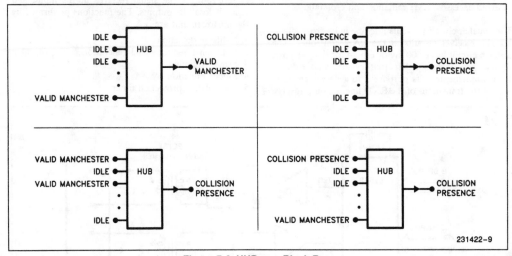

Figure 7-8. HUB as a Black Box

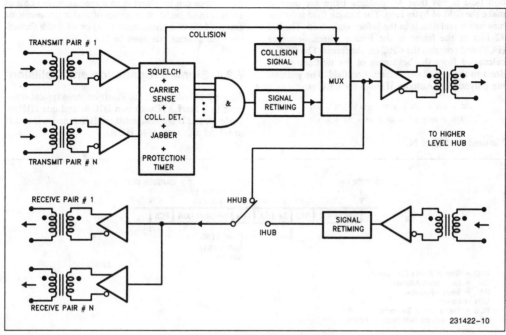

Figure 7-9. StarLAN HUB Block Diagram

7.2.2.3 StarLAN CABLE

Unshielded telephone grade twisted pair wires are used to connect a node to a HUB or to connect two HUBs. This is one of the cheapest types of wire and an important factor in bringing down the cost of StarLAN.

Although the 24 gauge wire is used for long stretches, the actual connection between the node and the telephone jack in the wall is done using extension cable, just like connecting a telephone to a jack. For very short StarLAN configurations, where all the nodes and the HUB are in the same room, the extension cable with plugs at both ends may itself be sufficient for all the wiring. (Extension cables must be of the twisted pair kind, no flat cables are allowed).

The telephone twisted pair wire of 24 gauge has the following characteristics:

Attenuation	: 42.55 db/mile @ 1 MHz
DC Resistance	: 823.69 Ω/mile
Inductance	: 0.84 mH/mile
Capacitance	: 0.1 μF/mile
Impedance	: 92.6Ω, −4 degrees @ 1 MHz

Experiments have shown that the sharing of the telephone cable with other voice and data services does not cause any mutual harm due to cross-talk and radiation, provided every service meets the FCC limits.

Although it is outside the scope of the IEEE 802.3 1BASE5 standard, there is considerable interest in using fiber optics and coaxial cable for node to HUB or HUB to HUB links especially in noisy and factory environments. Both these types of cables are particularly suited for point-to-point connections. Even mixing of different types of cables is possible (this kind of environments are not precluded).

NOTE:

StarLAN IEEE 802.3 1BASE5 draft calls for a maximum attenuation of 6.5 dB between the transmitter and the corresponding receiver at all frequencies between 500 KHz to 1 MHz. Also the maximum allowed cable propagation delay is 4 microseconds.

7.2.3 Framing

Figure 7-10 shows the format of a 802.3 frame. The beginning of the frame is marked by the carrier going active and the end marked by carrier going inactive. The preamble has a 56 bit sequence of 101010 . . . . ending in a 0. This is followed by 8 bits of start of frame delimiter (sfd) − 10101011. These bits are transmitted with the MSB (leftmost bit) transmitted first. Source and destination fields are 6 bytes long. The first byte is the least significant byte. These fields are transmitted with LSB first. The length field is 2 bytes long and gives the length of data in the Information field. The entire information field is a minimum of 46 bytes and a maximum of 1500 bytes. If the data content of the Information field is less than 46, padding bytes are used to make the field 46 bytes long. The Length field indicates how much real data is in the Information field. The last 32 bits of the frame is the Frame Check Sequence (FCS) and contains the CRC for the frame. The CRC is calculated from the beginning of the destination address to the end of the Information field. The generating polynomial (Autodin II) used for CRC is:

$$X^{32} + X^{26} + X^{23} + X^{22} + X^{16} + X^{12} + X^{11} +$$
$$X^{10} + X^8 + X^7 + X^5 + X^4 + X^2 + X + 1$$

No need for Figure N.

The frames can be directed to a specific node (LSB of address must be 0), to a group of nodes (multicast or group—LSB of address must be 1) or all nodes (broadcast—all address bits must be 1).

7.2.4 Signal Propagation and Collision

Figure 7-11 will be used to illustrate three typical situations in a StarLAN with two IHUBs and one HHUB. Nodes A and B are connected to HUB1, nodes C and D to HUB2 and node E to HUB3.

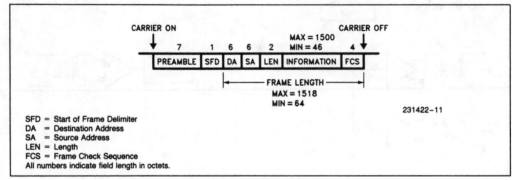

Figure 7-10. Framing

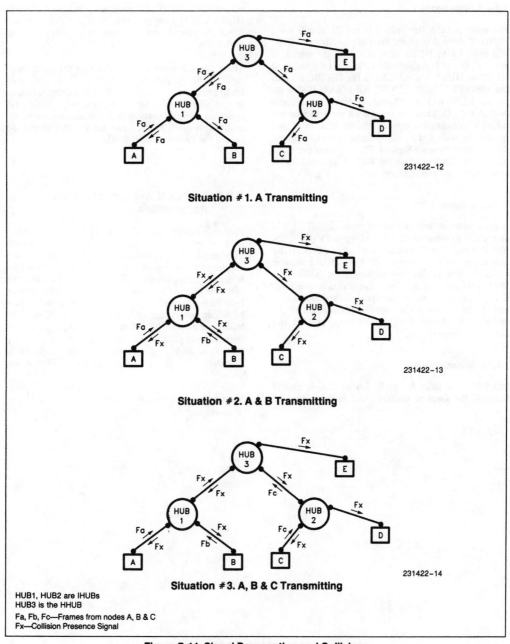

Situation # 1. A Transmitting

231422-12

Situation # 2. A & B Transmitting

231422-13

Situation # 3. A, B & C Transmitting

231422-14

HUB1, HUB2 are IHUBs
HUB3 is the HHUB

Fa, Fb, Fc—Frames from nodes A, B & C
Fx—Collision Presence Signal

Figure 7-11. Signal Propagation and Collisions

7.2.4.1 Situation #1

Whenever node A transmits a frame Fa, it will reach HUB1. If node B is silent, there is no collision. HUB1 will send Fa to HUB3 after re-timing the signal. If nodes C, D and E are also silent, there is no collision at HUB2 or HUB3. Since HUB3 is the HHUB, it sends the frame Fa to HUB1, HUB2 and to node E after re-timing. HUB1 and HUB2 send the frame Fa to nodes A, B and C, D. Thus, Fa reaches all the nodes on the network including the originator node A. If the signal received by node A is a valid Manchester signal and not the Collision Presence Signal (CPS) for the entire duration of the slot time, then the node A assumes that it was a successful transmission.

7.2.4.2 Situation #2

If both nodes A and B were to transmit, HUB1 will detect it as a collision and will send signal Fx (the Collision Presence Signal) to the HUB3—Note that HUB1 does not send Fx to nodes A and B yet. HUB 3 receives a signal from HUB1 but nothing from node E or HUB2, thus it does not detect the situation as a collision and simply re-times the signal Fx and sends it to node E, HUB2 and HUB1. Fx ultimately reach all the nodes. Nodes A and B detect this signal as CPS and call it a collision.

7.2.4.3 Situation #3

In addition to nodes A and B, if node C were also to transmit, the situation at HUB1 will be the same as in situation #2. HUB2 will propagate Fc from C towards HUB3. HUB3 now sees two of its inputs active and hence generates its own Fx signal and sends it towards each node.

These situations should also illustrate the point made earlier in the chapter that, the StarLAN network, with nodes connected to multiple HUBs is, logically, equivalent to all the nodes connected to a single HUB (Yet there are some differences between stations connected at different HUB levels, those are due to different delays to the header hub HHUB).

7.2.5 StarLAN System and Network Parameters

Preamble length (incl. sfd) .... 64 bits
Address length .... 6 bytes
FCS length CRC (Autodin II) .... 32 bits
Maximum frame length .... 1518 bytes
Minimum frame length .... 64 bytes
Slot time .... 512 bit times
Interframe spacing..................... 96 bit times
Minimum jam timing .... 32 bit times
Maximum number of collisions 16
Backoff limit 10
Backoff method .... Truncated binary exponential
Encoding .... Manchester

Clock tolerance .... ±0.01% (100 ppm)
Maximum jitter per segment .... ±62.5 ns

Robert D. Love and Thomas Toher, IBM, Research Triangle Park, N. C.

How to design and build a token ring LAN

What cable should be used? What are the choices? How many wiring concentrators are needed? How about repeaters? And what happens when a ring device fails?

How to

The implications of the IEEE 802.5 token-passing local area network design are just beginning to be explored. And as with any new technology, there are many variant methods of implementation. Described here are some of the different design solutions that can be employed in a typical single, multistory establishment.

For most of this discussion the transmission medium is assumed to be shielded twisted-pair wire conforming to the IEEE 802.5 requirements. This medium is produced by many manufacturers and is commonly referred to as types 1 and 2 cable (using 22-gauge wire) and type 9 (26 gauge). Type 2 contains an additional four twisted pairs for telephone use. All three types consist of solid (unstranded) wire. Patch cables, using 26-gauge stranded-wire (for flexibility), are also generally available.

In general, ring configurations covering a small geographical area can be designed and implemented without concern for wire lengths or overall signal-drive capability. For example, a ring may serve up to 260 devices from a single wiring closet, as long as the length of cable from the wiring closet to each of the 260 devices does not exceed 330 feet (Fig. 1). For rings covering larger geographical areas, periodic signal amplification, done with repeaters, may be required. The repeaters are usually installed in wiring closets.

The physical dimensions of a ring are limited by the amount of attenuation that is caused by cables, connectors, and multistation access units (MAUs). (The MAU's function is to isolate its attached devices from the main path—discussed later—of the ring, so that a problem that occurs on the device side of the MAU will not usually affect the operation of the entire ring.) The principle followed in developing the planning rules is that a single device gaining access to the ring must be able to receive its own transmitted signal. In the event that the attenuation is too

large, signal repeaters are used to reshape and retransmit the signal.

Figure 1 shows a typical token ring network with MAUs and terminals (devices), but without repeaters. At any given time, some of the terminals are active (operational on the ring) and some are not. The MAU enables the bypassing of each of, typically, eight devices by activating the bypass circuitry of the attached device's interface card.

The signal propagates from one active terminal to the next one. Assume stations B and C are inactive. The signal travels from terminal A along lobe a, through MAU 2, to MAU 3, to the next lobe (d) with an active terminal, and to the next active station (D). (A lobe is a section of cable that connects an attaching device—such as a workstation—via its adapter or ring-interface card, to an MAU.)

Receive and retransmit

Each active station participates in the process of receiving and regenerating the signal for retransmission on the ring, whether or not the station is using the information being transmitted. A ring-interface card automatically carries out the receive and retransmit functions without involving its host workstation, and without using any of that workstation's processing or storage capacity.

Since the signal is regenerated at each active station, the transmission requirement for the ring is that the signal must always be able to reach the next active station coherently (without excessive attenuation). Transmission design, therefore, must ensure that the distance between transmitting and receiving stations will always be within the allowable limits, no matter what stations are active or inactive.

At the start of a business day, the configuration might consist of only one active station—say A (Fig. 1). This station must establish a valid signal path around the entire ring, in preparation for other stations becoming active on

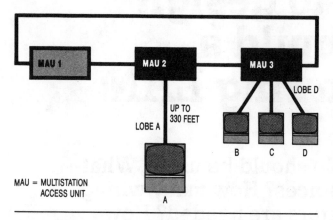

***1. Typical layout.** At any given time, some terminals are operational on the ring and some are not. The access unit enables the bypassing of the inactive ones.*

MAU = MULTISTATION ACCESS UNIT

the ring. For this case, the signal must propagate along the station's lobe wiring, through each MAU, through each length of wire connecting the access units together as well as those connecting the wiring closets, and finally, back down the lobe wire to the station.

This case provides the longest unregenerated path length and the greatest signal attenuation for a normal configuration. It would establish the transmission design requirement if any abnormal conditions did not have to be taken into account.

Continued operation

However, network design is based on the ring's ability to operate with any single fault, after bypassing or removing the faulty section. In the event of a faulty device or faulty lobe wiring, bypassing that lobe allows the network to continue operation. Most lobe problems cause the attaching device to be bypassed automatically, without any user intervention. If an MAU, or a patch cable interconnecting the MAUs, is faulty, then bypassing the faulty MAU or replacing the faulty component allows the remaining portion of the network to continue to operate. If a section of wire between two wiring closets fails, the maintenance person disconnects that wire segment at both ends. With the broken cable removed from the circuit, the maintainer can confirm that the wrap (self-shorting) capability at the MAU's input and output connectors is properly activated. The network is then permitted to operate on the built-in backup path.

Therefore, the transmission requirement for the configuration shown in Figure 2 is that the signal must be able to go from any station, around the ring, to a wiring closet output where the output wire ("ring out" in the forward path) has been disconnected. The backup path is activated by the disconnection (see "Multistation access units"). The signal travels along the backup path to the input of an MAU (disconnected from its normal input cable), and back on the main path until the signal reaches the station originally transmitting it.

Based on this configuration, the longest transmission path occurs when the station attached to the longest lobe is transmitting back to itself, with the shortest segment between wiring closets removed.

When a ring is large enough to require repeaters, or contains optical fiber links that use converters (to transform optical-light levels to electrical-current levels, and vice versa), then the transmission requirements for each ring segment are examined separately. A ring segment is defined as a portion of the ring bounded by—and including—repeaters or converters.

Simple drive requirements

There are two types of ring segments that do not contain MAUs: optical fiber links (bounded by converters) and copper wire links (bounded by repeaters). The drive requirements for these links is simply that the signal must be able to travel from transmitter to receiver within the allowable attenuation limits of the design. The maximum distance between repeaters is 2,525 feet with type-1 or type-2 copper media. The maximum distance between optical fiber converters is 6,500 feet with 100/140-micron optical fiber cable.

There are two separate conditions that must be met for each ring segment containing MAUs. The first is that the longest transmission path in the segment must be operable with the repeaters removed. For this case, the longest lobe must be able to send a signal around the segment and back to itself. The second condition is that the input (or output) repeaters must be able to send a signal around the segment with the output (or input) repeaters removed, and with no attaching devices active in that segment.

The maximum transmission distance for a ring segment or for a multiple-wiring-closet ring without repeaters is shown in Table 1. This table takes into account the signal loss through the MAUs, the patch cables connecting the MAUs to each other, and the input and output cables in the main ring path. The table gives the total allowable length of cable in the transmission path. Since each section of cable is passed through twice, the distances are one-half of the signal's total transmission distance. For a ring without repeaters, the maximum transmission distance is the adjusted ring length (ARL) plus the longest lobe length. ARL is the total main-ring-path length, less the shortest interwiring-closet length (refer again to Fig. 2).

Computation examples

For a ring with repeaters, the lengths in Table 1 represent the ring-segment drive distance (the distance that a signal can travel without being regenerated). Figure 3 shows two simple examples of ring segments with the computation of the maximum transmission length for each.

In Figure 3a, the ring-segment drive distance is the sum of the longest lobe length plus the length of all the cables (not including patch cables in wiring closets) between MAUs in the ring segment. Because the length of cable between the repeaters and the nearest MAUs is *less* than the length of the longest lobe, these former cable lengths are not part of the drive distance calculation.

When one or both lengths of cable between the repeaters and the MAUs are *greater* than the length of the longest lobe, the ring segment drive distance is the sum of the cable lengths between MAUs plus the longer of the two cables between the repeaters and the MAUs (Fig. 3b). The 150 feet between the workstation and the MAU is the lobe length.

continued

2. Multipath transmission. *The signal must go from any station, around the ring, to a wiring closet output where the output wire has been disconnected. The backup path is* *activated by the disconnection. The signal travels along the backup path to the input of an access unit, then back onto the main path.*

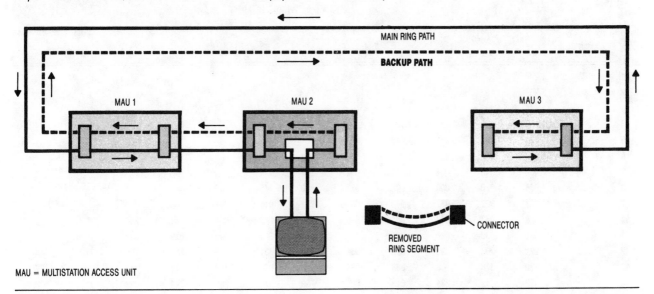

MAU = MULTISTATION ACCESS UNIT

All ring segments that contain MAUs fall into one of the two cases illustrated in Figure 3. Each ring segment drive distance must be checked using one of these two methods.

In the initial stages of a token ring network design, the user may not know if repeaters are necessary. To determine if the maximum lobe length plus ARL is within the allowable bounds, the appropriate table for the wire type can be used. To obtain the required parameters for the table, the user must determine the locations of the wiring closets, the cable lengths between them, the maximum number of MAUs used in each wiring closet, and the longest lobe length. If the sum of the maximum lobe length plus the ARL is not within allowable bounds, then repeaters will be necessary.

Implementation tactics

Factors affecting the need for repeaters also include choice of cable and the way the network is divided into rings. The following discussion illustrates the extensive choice of options available to the network designer, using as an example a hypothetical local area network design in a multistory building.

A seven-story office building (Fig. 4) has been wired with type 9 (26-gauge) cable. Type 9 cable was selected for its smaller size and lower cost. Each floor has two wings with a wiring closet in each wing. The wiring closets are vertically stacked. The distance separating the stacks of wiring closets is 500 feet. The wiring between floors is 30 feet. Each wiring closet services an area with a longest wiring run not exceeding 250 feet. There are 10 to 15 users per wiring closet that need to be connected together in a network. First, let's assume that all the stations are connected together on a single ring.

Since type-9 cable has about one-and-one-half times the attenuation of types 1 or 2 (22-gauge), refer to Table 2 to determine if repeaters are needed for this network. Assume the wiring closets are connected together as shown

in Figure 4. To accommodate 10 to 15 users per wiring closet, two MAUs per closet will be required. The total number of MAUs in the 14 closets is therefore 28, which is one more than the allowable number of MAUs per ring without using repeaters. Therefore, the ring must be divided into multiple ring segments separated by repeaters.

The installation site of a repeater is not mandated. The final choice may be influenced by such factors as ease of installation and service and consideration for future expan-

Multistation access units

Token ring networks use multistation access units to form a star-wired-ring topology. The MAU is an unpowered device containing both a main ring path and a backup path for transmitting signals onto the network. Typically, each MAU provides ring access to a maximum of eight devices (such as workstations) via its relays. The accessing device's adapter (interface) card performs a self-check and, if the results are positive, transmits a voltage to the MAU relay via the lobe cable (the connecting cable to the main ring path). The resultant relay action switches the device from its bypassed mode to its ring-access mode. When the device is to be deleted from the ring, the voltage is removed, and the relay changes state again to bypass the lobe.

"Ring in" and "ring out" terminations are used to connect the main ring path and the backup path in each MAU to other MAUs. The self-shorting feature of the data connectors used in the MAUs and on all the cables allows the main ring path to be "wrapped" to the backup path when the connector is not mated with another connector (Fig. 2). The built-in backup path allows a properly configured ring to operate with an inter-MAU-cable segment completely removed from the ring.

Table 1: Type-1 or -2 cable distances

NUMBER OF MAUs	NUMBER OF WIRING CLOSETS											
	1	2	3	4	5	6	7	8	9	10	11	12
1	1,235											
2	1,207	1,192										
3	1,178	1,163	1,148									
4	1,150	1,135	1,120	1,104								
5	1,121	1,106	1,091	1,076	1,061							
6	1,093	1,078	1,062	1,047	1,032	1,017						
7	1,064	1,049	1,034	1,019	1,004	989	974					
8	1,036	1,020	1,005	990	975	960	945	930				
9	1,007	992	977	962	947	932	916	901	886			
10	979	963	948	933	918	903	888	873	858	843		
11	950	935	920	905	890	874	859	844	829	814	799	
12	921	906	891	876	861	846	831	816	801	786	770	755
13	860	878	863	848	833	817	802	787	772	757	742	727
14	832	849	834	819	804	789	774	759	744	729	713	698
15	803	821	806	791	775	760	745	730	715	700	685	670
16	774	792	777	762	747	732	717	702	687	671	656	641
17	746	764	749	733	718	703	688	673	658	643	628	613
18	717	735	720	705	690	675	660	645	629	614	599	584
19	689	707	691	676	661	646	631	616	601	586	571	556
20	660	678	663	648	633	618	603	587	572	557	542	527
21	632	649	634	619	604	589	574	559	544	529	514	499
22	603	621	606	591	576	561	545	530	515	500	485	470
23	575	592	577	562	547	532	517	502	487	472	457	441
24	546	564	549	534	519	503	488	473	458	443	428	413
25	485	502	520	505	490	475	460	445	430	415	399	384
26	456	474	492	477	461	446	431	416	401	386	371	356
27	428	445	463	448	433	418	403	388	373	357	342	327

MAXIMUM TRANSMISSION DISTANCE IN FEET

MAU = MULTISTATION ACCESS UNIT

REPRINTED WITH PERMISSION OF IBM

sion. The placement choice for the first pair of repeaters can sometimes affect the total number of repeaters needed on the ring. Generally, repeaters are placed at the input or output of wiring closets, both to minimize the required number of repeaters, and for convenience in expanding the network.

One good starting point for repeater placement is at one end of a long intercloset wiring run. For this example (Figure 4 shows the basic building layout; Figure 5, the first discussed solution), assume that the first pair of repeaters is placed at the output of wiring closet 7 on the first floor of the west wing. Since the 500-foot length from wiring closet 7 to wiring closet 8 is greater than any of the lobe distances, the first ring segment we design will be limited by the total wiring distance between MAUs in the segment plus 500 feet.

First we may ask "Can we keep all the repeaters in the west wing?" To do this, the ring segment in the east wing would include seven wiring closets with 14 MAUs, and intercloset spacing of 30X6=180 feet. With repeaters at the output of wiring closet 7 and at the input of wiring closet 1, the distance from repeaters to MAU is 500 feet for either pair. Therefore, the distance we would need is 500 + 180 (680 feet) for seven wiring closets and 14 MAUs. Table 2 shows a maximum distance for 7 wiring closets and 14 MAUs of 516 feet. Therefore, we cannot keep all the repeaters in the west wing.

If we put a pair of repeaters at the input side of wiring closet number 12, then our first ring segment will include MAUs in wiring closets 8, 9, 10, and 11, or four wiring closets with eight MAUs. The inter-closet wiring between wiring closets 8 and 9, 9 and 10, and 10 and 11, totals 90 feet (3X30). The ring-segment drive distance is 590 feet. Table 2 shows that for four wiring closets and eight MAUs we are allowed 660 feet.

Note that an attempt to move the repeaters to the output side of wiring closet number 12 would include wiring closet number 12 in the segment and add the 30 feet of wiring from 11 to 12. The requirement would then be for five wiring closets with 10 MAUs and 500+120=620 feet. Table 2 indicates that 612 feet is the maximum allowed. Therefore, the first segment is from the output of wiring closet 7 to the input of wiring closet 12.

Another possible solution is to place the repeaters between the first and second MAU in wiring closet 12. This solution is numerically correct but inadvisable because exact cable lengths may not be known. Furthermore, such an optimized solution leaves no room for additional MAUs in the ring segment without adding repeaters.

The next pair of repeaters can be placed at least as far away as the input to wiring closet 1. Looking at a placement at the output of wiring closet 1, wiring closets with MAUs in the second segment are 12, 13, 14, and 1. The ring-segment drive distance is $30+30+500=560$ feet. The maximum lobe length is 250 feet, so we need to check the table for four wiring closets with eight MAUs and $560+250$ feet$=810$ feet. But four wiring closets with eight MAUs only allows 660 feet. Therefore, this solution exceeds the allowable drive limits. Note that by placing the third pair of repeaters at the input to wiring closet 1, the ring segment length to be compared with the number in the table is 60 feet plus the maximum of the 500 foot run or the 250 foot maximum lobe length, resulting in 560 feet. (Refer to Figures 3b and 5: The choice is either the distance between repeaters and MAU or the length of the largest lobe, whichever is greater.) This is a reduction of 250 feet compared with moving the repeaters to the output of wiring closet 1.

Next, determine if the third ring segment formed by placement of the third pair of repeaters is within the allowable limits. This segment contains wiring closets 1

through 7 with a main ring-path length of $30X6=180$ feet. The maximum lobe length is 250 feet for a total of 430 feet. Looking at the table for seven wiring closets and 14 MAUs, the maximum allowable length is 516 feet. Therefore, the third segment is within the design guidelines, and the ring is designed.

Placement solution

Figure 5 shows the ring with repeaters in place at the top and bottom of the west wing and at the input of the east wing's wiring closet 12. (A repeater installation is in pairs—one for each transmission direction.) Note that the repeaters in the east wing could have been placed anywhere from the output of wiring closet 10 to their present location, based on ease of access, availability of space and power, or expected growth of the ring.

While this solution is relatively straightforward, it is not the only one that is available—particularly if the building wiring is still in the planning stages or can be conveniently changed. For example, the two 500-foot lengths of type-9 cable interconnecting the vertical stacks of wiring closets could be replaced by 100/140-micron optical fiber cable. Optical-fiber converters would be required to transform the signal from electrical to optical at one end of each optical fiber and from optical to electrical at the other. A total of four converters would be needed, one at the top and bottom of each vertical stack.

Since the drive distance capability on optical fiber is over 6,000 feet, all that remains to be checked is the ring

3. Repeaters added. *In A, the ring segment drive distance is the sum of the longest lobe length plus the length of all the cables between MAUs in the ring segment. The ring seg-* *ment drive distance is the sum of the cable lengths between MAUs plus the longer of the two cables between the repeaters and the MAUs (B).*

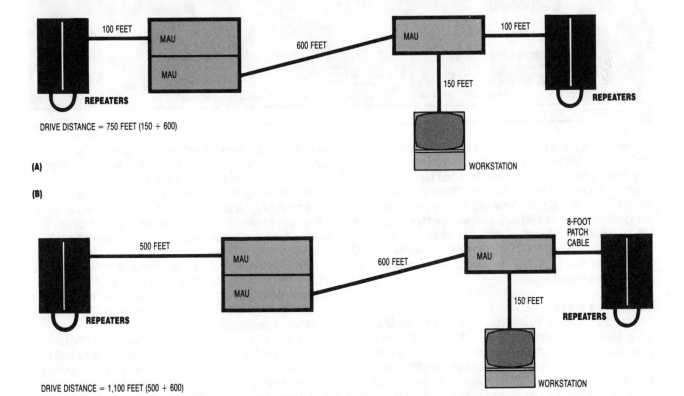

Data Communications/May 1987

115

4. Wiring a building. *To accommodate 10 to 15 users per wiring closet, two MAUs per closet will be required. The total number of MAUs is therefore 28, which is one more than the allowable number of MAUs per ring without using repeaters. Therefore, the ring must be divided into multiple ring segments separated by repeaters.*

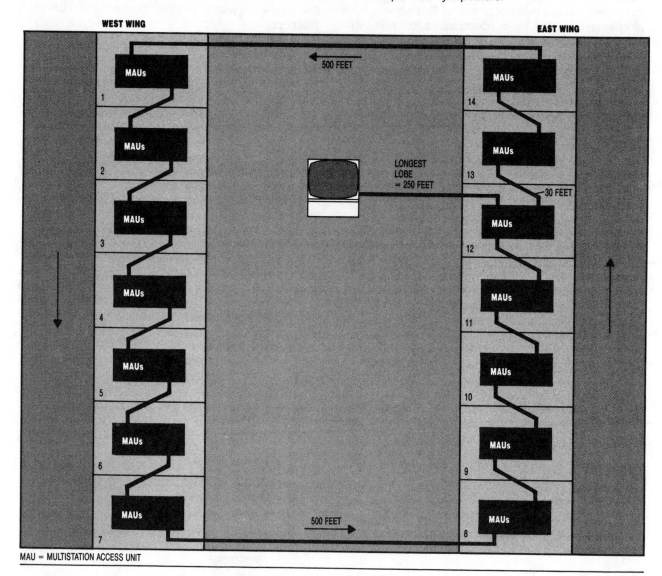

WEST WING

EAST WING

500 FEET

LONGEST LOBE = 250 FEET

30 FEET

500 FEET

MAU = MULTISTATION ACCESS UNIT

segment drive distance for the two identical stacks of wiring closets. As stated previously, the total amount of type 9 cable between wiring closets is 180 feet and the length of the longest lobe is 250 feet. The ring segment drive distance is 430 feet. For a ring segment with seven wiring closets and 14 MAUs, the allowable drive distance is 516 feet. Each of the vertical stacks of wiring closets would not require any converters. Furthermore, an additional MAU could be installed in each of the wiring closets without adding repeaters.

Mixing wire sizes

Another alternative is to use type 1 cable between all the wiring closets, while continuing to use the smaller and less expensive type 9 on lobes. When mixing types 1 and 9 in an installation, computation of equivalent transmission distance for a length of type 9 cable is done by converting the type 9 lengths into equivalent type 1 lengths based on the increased loss in the type 9 cable. Specifically, convert

the 250-foot lobe length to its type 1 equivalent by multiplying 250 by 3/2, which equals 375 feet. Then place the repeaters on the ring using Table 1.

Next, place the first pair of repeaters at the output of wiring closet 7. The second pair of repeaters can be placed at the input to wiring closet 1. The ring-segment drive distance for the segment between the repeaters encompassing the two 500-foot cables and wiring closets 8 through 14 is the sum of the cable lengths between MAUs (6X30 = 180 feet) plus 500 feet for a total of 680 feet. The length of the longest lobe is discounted in this case because the 375-foot lobe length is less than 500 (refer to the earlier discussion of Figure 3B).

Table 1 shows an allowable drive distance of 774 feet for a segment containing seven wiring closets and 14 MAUs. The ring-segment drive distance for that segment encompassing wiring closets 1 through 7 is the sum of the cable lengths between MAUs (6X30 = 180) plus the length of the longest lobe (375) for a total of 555 feet. This, too, is less

Table 2: Type-9 cable distances

NUMBER OF MAUs	NUMBER OF WIRING CLOSETS											
	1	2	3	4	5	6	7	8	9	10	11	12
1	823											
2	804	794										
3	785	775	765									
4	766	756	746	736								
5	747	737	727	717	707							
6	728	718	708	698	688	678						
7	709	699	689	679	669	659	649					
8	690	680	670	660	650	640	630	620				
9	671	661	651	641	631	621	611	601	591			
10	652	642	632	622	612	602	592	582	572	562		
11	633	623	613	603	593	583	573	563	553	543	533	
12	614	604	594	584	574	564	554	544	534	524	514	503
13	573	585	575	565	555	545	535	525	515	505	494	484
14	554	566	556	546	536	526	516	506	496	486	475	465
15	535	547	537	527	517	507	497	487	477	466	456	446
16	516	528	518	508	498	488	478	468	458	447	437	427
17	497	509	499	489	479	469	459	449	438	428	418	408
18	478	490	480	470	460	450	440	430	419	409	399	389
19	459	471	461	451	441	431	421	410	400	390	380	370
20	440	452	442	432	422	412	402	391	381	371	361	351
21	421	433	423	413	403	393	383	372	362	352	342	332
22	402	414	404	394	384	374	363	353	343	333	323	313
23	383	395	385	375	365	355	344	334	324	314	304	294
24	364	376	366	356	346	335	325	315	305	295	285	275
25	323	335	347	337	327	316	306	296	286	276	266	256
26	304	316	328	318	307	297	287	277	267	257	247	237
27	285	297	309	299	288	278	268	258	248	238	228	218

MAXIMUM TRANSMISSION DISTANCE IN FEET

MAU = MULTISTATION ACCESS UNIT

than the allowed distance of 774 feet.

The resulting configuration permits keeping all of the repeaters in one wing of the building for ease of maintenance and repair. Note that by substituting type 1 cable for type 9 cable between wiring closets, two less repeaters are used, compared with an all-type-9 ring.

A practical solution
Finally, if the users in the east wing and the users in the west wing communicate with each other only occasionally (such as separate departments in each wing might do), two small rings, each consisting of seven wiring closets and 14 MAUs joined together by a bridge midway between the stacks of wiring closets, may offer the most practical solution. (A bridge is a device, attached to two rings, across which messages can be sent.) What makes this solution so practical is: If trouble occurs in one ring, only half the users lose network access; small rings are easier to administer than large ones; and repeaters are eliminated,

increasing the average mean time between failures per ring.

Additional type 9 cable—each 180 feet long—would have to be run from wiring closet 1 to 7 and from 8 to 14. The two 500-foot cables would not be needed. The adjusted ring length for each of these two rings would be 180 + 180 + 250 - 30 = 580 feet (180 = 6X30). Table 2 shows that the allowable adjusted ring length for seven wiring closets and 14 MAUs is 516 feet. Two pairs of repeaters would have to be used in each wing.

If type 1 cable is used rather than type 9 between wiring closets, the adjusted ring length would be 180 + 180 + 375 - 30 = 705 feet. Note that the 250-foot lobe length of type-9 cable must be treated as 3/2X250 = 375 feet of equivalent type-1 cable when using Table 1. The allowable drive lengths in Table 2 have already been reduced to account for the increased loss of type-9 cable. According to Table 1, the allowable adjusted ring length for these type-1 cable configurations is 774 feet. The rings in both stacks of wiring

5. Repeaters in place. *For this typical installation, the east wing's repeaters could have been placed from the output of wiring closet 10 to their present location, based on ease of access, availability of space and power, or expected ring growth. A repeater installation is in pairs—one for each transmission direction.*

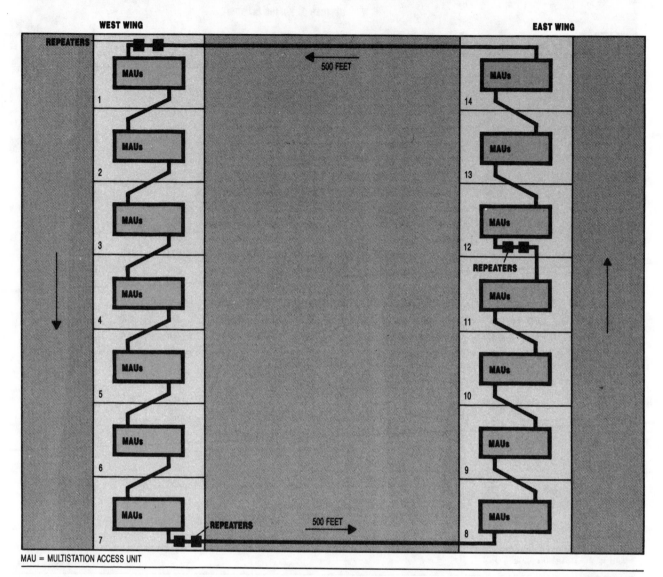

MAU = MULTISTATION ACCESS UNIT

closets can be run without repeaters if type-1 cable is used between wiring closets.

Yet another solution would be to substitute 100/140-micron optical fiber cable for the type 9 cable between wiring closets 1 and 7 and closets 8 and 14. Two optical fiber converters would be required for each ring. If this option were selected, up to four MAUs could be added to each ring without need for additonal repeaters.

In this example, a good place for a bridge might be in a centrally located room between the two stacks of wiring closets. This solution is particularly attractive if the devices on the rings are largely workstations and file and print servers that are communicating with each other rather than with a host computer.

However, if users need access to a host computer, the network implementer should consider a third ring consisting of a single MAU. Connecting this backbone ring via bridges to the two rings in the stacked wiring closets and to a gateway (which interconnects two dissimilar entities)

connected to a host computer may be the most appropriate network design. For ease of maintenance and network management, the bridges should—if possible—be located in the computer room with the host and the MAU.

There are, of course, other possible configurations that might better suit the needs of a particular user than the ones presented here. Employing the methodology presented in developing these design solutions, users have a chance to design physical layouts calculated to suit both their immediate and projected needs. ■

Bob Love, an advisory engineer at IBM's transmission system technology department, holds two chip patents. He received his B. S. E. E. from Columbia University and an M. S. in electrophysics from the Brooklyn Polytechnic Institute. Tom Toher is a senior associate information developer in the network products information development department. Toher received B. A. and M. A. degrees in English from, respectively, Hobart College and Clark University.

Norman C. Strole

A Local Communications Network Based on Interconnected Token-Access Rings: A Tutorial

Local area networks are expected to provide the communications base for interconnecting computer equipment and terminals over the next decade. The primary objective of a local area network (LAN) is to provide high-speed data transfer among a group of nodes consisting of data-processing terminals, controllers, or computers within the confines of a building or campus environment. The network should be easily accessible, extremely reliable, and extendible in both function and physical size. The rapid advances in computing and communications technology over the last two decades have led to several different transmission schemes and media types that could be used in these networks. The star/ring wiring topology with token-access control has emerged as a technology that can meet all of these objectives. The requirements of small networks with just a few nodes, as well as those of very large networks with thousands of nodes, can be achieved through this one architecture. This paper is a tutorial of the fundamental aspects of the architecture, physical components, and operation of a token-ring LAN. Particular emphasis is placed on the fault detection and isolation capabilities that are possible, as well as the aspects that allow for network expansion and growth. The role of the LAN relative to IBM's Systems Network Architecture (SNA) is also discussed.

Introduction

A local area network (LAN) can be defined as an information transport system for high-speed data transfer among a group of nodes consisting of office or industrial system terminals and peripherals, cluster controllers, or computers, via a common interconnecting medium within the bounds of a single office building, building complex, or campus [1]. The geographical constraints together with advanced transmission technologies enable data transfer rates of many millions of bits per second within the local network. These transmission rates, coupled with a reliable access control scheme, permit a large number of devices to share a common physical interconnection link with minimum interference to one another, while allowing large blocks of data to be transferred with simple error-recovery procedures and data management protocols.

This paper is a tutorial of a LAN communication system based on a ring topology with token-access control. The concepts presented here have been the subjects of research investigations on token-ring local area networks conducted at the IBM Research Laboratory in Zurich, Switzerland [2–4] and at IBM's Research Triangle Park laboratory in North

Carolina [5–9]. A brief historical perspective on the evolution of teleprocessing and a description of some basic LAN topologies, control schemes, and transmission techniques are presented. A discussion of the criteria that should be considered in designing a LAN is followed by a functional description of several of the key physical components that comprise a token-ring network. The token-access control protocol for regulating data flow on the ring is explained, including the data frame format and addressing structure, and mechanisms for ensuring token integrity and uniform token access to all attached nodes. The implementation of a LAN in the context of IBM's Systems Network Architecture (SNA) [10] is also discussed. Finally, some of the fault detection and isolation capabilities that enhance the overall reliability of the token-access ring LAN are presented.

Historical perspective

The factors influencing the present surge in office automation and the use of computer terminal equipment in industry have arisen as a natural outgrowth of the revolution in technology that has occurred during the last twenty-five years in both computing and communications. Through the

1960s, large host computers were used primarily in batch processing modes, with punched cards or magnetic tape as the primary input medium. In 1964, one of the first commercial interactive systems, known as the Semi-Automatic Business-Related Environment (SABRE), became fully operational for handling airline passenger information and reservations. This project introduced a new era in telecommunications and contained many significant innovations in the areas of line control, multiplexors, and real-time operating systems [11]. In 1968, one of the earliest and largest nationwide nonmilitary computer networks was established for air-route traffic control using the IBM 9020 system [12]. Data concerning each flight are established at the point of takeoff and are passed from one control sector to the next in the path as the flight progresses. This system introduced new concepts in hardware and software reliability, having such features as a distributed data base, a failsafe system design with gradual degradation, and highly interactive application programs.

The 1970s brought new technologies to both computing and communications that enabled more and more users to have direct access to a computing facility. Advances in microelectronics led to the development of minicomputers which offered good performance capabilities at substantially lower cost. Also, interactive processing came into general use with the advent of the keyboard/printer and keyboard/display terminals as costs decreased and as operating systems shifted to allow both batch mode and interactive processing. The introduction of commercial distributed processing permitted multiple users to share access to common data bases and remote input/output equipment. Distributed processing has now expanded to a global level with the advent of satellite communications and packet-switching. The ARPANET is one of the better-known examples of a nationwide computer communications network [13]. Structured communications functions, such as those implemented in SNA [10, 14], provide well-defined protocols for the reliable exchange of information between network nodes. At the local level, the increased installation of terminals and workstations has resulted in a steady growth in the volume of information that must be transferred over the communications network. High-speed local networks are emerging to meet this growing demand as it becomes economically feasible to implement networking within an establishment. New technologies, such as very-large-scale integrated (VLSI) circuits, have greatly reduced the cost of implementing high-speed transmission and sophisticated communication functions that are necessary to interface a large number of devices to the local area networks.

Current LAN concepts

● *LAN configurations and control schemes*
A fundamental understanding of the basic LAN configurations and control schemes that are prevalent today will enable the reader to comprehend the more detailed discussions in subsequent sections of this paper. There are basically three network configurations that are particularly suited to LANs, namely the *ring,* the *bus,* and the *star* [15]. There are also a number of control schemes that can be implemented with each of these network configurations for regulating access among the network nodes.

Ring A ring network configuration consists of a series of nodes that are connected by unidirectional transmission links to form a closed path. Information signals on the ring pass from node to node and are regenerated as they pass through each node. The application of ring communication systems as local networks has been the object of significant research investigations including such projects as the Distributed Computing System (DCS) [16], the Pierce ring [17], the MIT ring [18], the Cambridge ring [19], and the experimental ring network at the IBM Research Laboratory in Zurich, Switzerland [3].

The Pierce ring and the Cambridge ring utilize a slotted-ring control scheme in which several fixed-length data "slots" flow continuously around the ring. Any node can place a data packet in one of the empty slots, along with the appropriate address information. Each node on the ring examines the address information in each packet and copies those frames that are directed to that node. A "message received bit" can be set by the receiving node to indicate to the originator that the message was received. The originating node must remove the packet from the ring when it returns, thus freeing that slot on the ring.

A second control scheme applicable to ring systems is known as *register insertion.* Each node must load the frame it wishes to transmit into a shift register and insert the entire contents of the register into the ring whenever the ring becomes idle. The shift register, in effect, becomes a part of the ring. The frame is shifted out onto the ring and any incoming frame is shifted into the register temporarily until it too is shifted onto the ring. A frame may be purged (removed from the ring) by either the sending or the receiving node. The sending node can only remove its register from the ring whenever the register contains only idle characters (i.e., no frame data) or the returned original frame itself. A new message cannot be loaded into the shift register until it has been removed from the ring. The IBM local communications controller for Series/1 uses a control scheme based on the register insertion concept [20].

A third control scheme, known as *token-access* control, has been implemented in the DCS, the MIT ring, and the Zurich ring. A unique bit sequence, called a *token,* is passed from one node to another. If a node has no data to transmit, the token is simply passed on to the next node. The receipt of a token gives permission to the receiving node to initiate a transmission. Upon completion of the transmission, the token is passed implicitly (without addressing information) to the next node on the ring.

In all three of the above ring control schemes, the sending node can determine on its own when it may begin transmitting based on the status of the ring at the time. This is contrasted with other ring (or loop) control schemes in which a single master node is responsible for initiating all data transfers. An example of this is the IBM 8100 communication loop. Here, the master node polls the nodes around the loop, allowing each of them in turn to send data if they have any waiting when they are polled.

Bus   The *bus* provides a bidirectional transmission facility to which all nodes are attached [15]. Information signals propagate away from the originating node in both directions to the terminated ends of the bus. Each node is tapped into the bus and copies the message as it passes that point in the cable. One bus control scheme that is particularly suited for LAN systems is carrier sense, multiple access, with collision detection (CSMA/CD) [21]. With this scheme, any node can begin transmitting data whenever it detects that the bus is idle. The node continues to monitor the bus for interference from another node that may have begun transmitting at about the same time. Any "collisions" will be detected by all transmitting nodes, causing those nodes to halt transmission for a short random time period before attempting to transmit again.

The token control scheme can also be employed on a bus system. The operation is similar to that for a ring except that an explicit token (containing a specific node address) is employed for a bus, resulting in a logical ordering of the nodes that resembles a ring [5]. Polling can also be used in multidrop-bus configurations where a master controller polls each node to initiate data transfers.

Star   The *star* topology, which derives its name from the radial or star-like connection of the various nodes to a centralized controller or computer, is implemented in point-to-point communication schemes that enable each node to exchange data with the central node. This topology is also used in private branch exchanges (PBXs) or computerized branch exchanges (CBXs) where the central node acts as a high-speed switch to establish direct connections between pairs of attached nodes. CBX systems are well suited for voice communications, and they can also accommodate the transfer of data between two nodes. Transmission speeds are presently in the 56-kb/s or 64-kb/s range, which is much less than the multiple-megabit-per-second rates achievable with ring and bus LAN systems.

The bus and ring network topologies are examples of what are called "shared-access links." That is, all nodes share access to a common communications facility, and any signal that is generated at a node propagates to all other active nodes. However, for a meaningful and reliable exchange of data to take place, two nodes must establish a logical, point-to-point link with one another [1]. The physical network thus provides a mechanism for moving the information between nodes that have established logical connections.

● *Transmission techniques*
The various transmission techniques that are implemented within LANs can be generally categorized by the signaling scheme used to transfer the electrical energy onto the medium. The digital information to be transmitted over the medium must first be electrically encoded such that the bits (*1*s and *0*s) are distinguishable at the receiving node(s). The rate at which the encoded bit information is applied to the medium by a sending node is referred to as the transmission speed, expressed in bits per second. The encoded information is applied to the medium in one of two basic methods, commonly referred to as *baseband* and *broadband* signaling.

Baseband   In *baseband* signaling, the simpler of the two methods, the encoded signal [22] is applied directly to the medium as a continuous stream of voltage transitions on a copper medium or as a stream of light pulses on an optical fiber medium. One node at a time may apply signals to the medium, resulting in a single channel over which signals from multiple nodes must be time-multiplexed to separate the energy. Baseband data rates exceeding 100 million bits per second (Mb/s) are possible. However, practical limitations, such as the rates at which the attached nodes can continuously send or receive information and the maximum signal drive distance for a given data rate and medium, result in typical LAN data rates of up to 16 Mb/s. Baseband signals must be periodically repeated over a long distance to avoid data loss or interference due to signal degradation. The maximum distance between repeaters is a function of the properties of the transmission medium, use of intermediate connectors, and the data rate. In general, a decrease in the distance between repeaters is needed as the data rate is increased [7].

Broadband   *Broadband* transmission schemes, unlike baseband, employ analog signals and multiplexing techniques on the LAN medium to permit more than one node to transmit at a time. Multiple channels or frequency bands can be created by a technique known as frequency division multiplexing (FDM). A typical broadband system has a bandwidth of 300 megahertz (MHz) which can be divided into multiple 6-MHz channels (as used in cable television signal distribution) with pairs of channels designated for bidirectional communications over a single cable. A standard 6-MHz channel can readily accommodate data rates up to 5 Mb/s. Two adjacent 6-MHz channels can be used to provide a single 12-MHz channel for data rates up to 10 Mb/s [23]. Access to a channel that is shared by a large number of nodes must be regulated by some type of control scheme, such as token passing or CSMA/CD. Broadband operation requires that a modulate/demodulate function be performed by radio-frequency modulator/demodulators (rf modems) at the sender and receiver, respectively, resulting in a higher cost per attachment than with baseband schemes. However, this enables broadband signals to be transmitted for longer distances between repeaters over a specially designed broadband cable.

• *Data frames or packets*

The control scheme that is selected for a particular topology governs the access of the various nodes to the network. In all of the transmission control schemes, the data being transferred from one node to another must be transmitted in a particular format that is recognizable by the receiving node. The actual format of a packet or frame varies depending upon the specific communication requirements. In addition to the data (information) field, the frame contains some type of delimiter field that is distinguishable from all other fields to mark the beginning and end of the frame. There may also be some control fields that contain status information, specific commands, format qualifiers, or the frame length. Most of the schemes require that the frame contain address information to identify the sender (source) and intended receiver (destination). Finally, one or more check bits are normally included to enable the receiver to detect possible errors that may have occurred after the sender transmitted the frame. A more complete description of a frame format is given later.

Selection criteria for a LAN

There are a number of factors that must be considered when selecting or designing a LAN. Each of the LAN configurations and control schemes described earlier has both strong and weak points, requiring the designer or user to make trade-offs in selecting the appropriate system design. One criterion that may be used is a comparison of the information transfer characteristics of the various schemes. The performance characteristics of several LAN transmission schemes, including token-access rings, slotted rings, and CSMA/CD buses, were evaluated by Bux [24]. He compared their data-throughput characteristics as affected by system parameters such as transmission rate, cable length, packet lengths, and control overhead. He concluded that the token ring performs well at high throughputs and transmission speeds of 5 and 10 Mb/s. The CSMA/CD bus also performed well at these speeds as long as the ratio of propagation delay to mean packet transmission time was on the order of 2 to 5%. The requirement to minimize propagation delay on a bus restricts the length of the bus in a LAN system, a factor that is not as critical in a token ring system.

Another performance study by Stuck [25] showed the token ring to be the least sensitive to workload, offering short delays under light load and controlled delays under heavy load. The token bus was shown to be not as efficient as the token ring under heavy load and to have greater delay under light load. Stuck also found the CSMA/CD bus to have the shortest delay under light load, but to be quite sensitive to heavy workload, and to be sensitive to the bus length and message length, performing better with a shorter bus and longer messages.

A primary criterion in selecting a LAN is to minimize the cost of installing, operating, and maintaining the system without sacrificing network performance and reliability. In general, a baseband token-access communication scheme can be implemented with low-cost interface adapters and does not require the more sensitive rf modems associated with broadband systems. Also, the token-access ring wiring medium can be installed within a building using a radial (star) wiring scheme. Star wiring implies that the transmission cable is installed from concentration points within a building to the various user work areas, such as offices or laboratories. Wall outlets in each of these areas can provide physical interfaces to the network to permit fast, reliable attachment or relocation of the nodes.

Another design criterion is that any network faults or disruptions should be quickly detected and isolated to restore normal operation. The wiring concentration points provide centralized access to some of the primary network components to enhance the maintenance and reliability aspects of the overall system [18]. In addition, the flow of data and control signals around a closed ring provides an inherent capability for monitoring normal token operation from a single point on the ring and enables ring faults (such as a break in a segment of the ring) to be quickly detected. A more comprehensive discussion of the fault detection and isolation capabilities within a token-ring LAN is presented later in this paper.

The above LAN design criteria and others are incorporated into the token-ring architecture described here. This description is intended to give the casual reader an understanding of the fundamental aspects of a token-ring system while providing enough detail to permit further comparison with other LAN architectures.

Token-ring topology and network components

A star/ring wiring scheme combines the basic star wiring topology with the unidirectional, point-to-point signal propagation of the ring configuration. A major benefit of radial wiring is the capability of isolating those links that have failed, or are not in use, from the network [18]. Also, additional links may be added at any time. Major components of a two-ring system are represented in Fig. 1 and described next.

• Ring interface adapter

The term *node* encompasses a wide variety of machine types that can attach to and communicate over the local network. The primary functions associated with token recognition and data transmission are distributed to each node within the network. Advances in VLSI technology make it possible to delegate a large portion of this communication function to a ring interface adapter within each node, thus freeing the node from this processing. The adapter handles the basic transmission functions that are described later, including frame recognition, token generation, address decoding, error checking, buffering of frames, and link fault detection.

There may be instances where a device with an incompatible communication interface is to be attached to the local network. In this case a separate interface converter may be attached between the device and the token ring to perform the protocol and timing conversions that are required to send and receive data over the local network.

• Wiring concentrators

Wiring concentrators which contain a series of electronic relays are the central elements for structuring the star/ring wiring layout. Wiring lobes, consisting of two pairs of conductors for separate send and receive paths, emanate from the wiring concentrators to the various network interface points (e.g., wall outlets) at each of the node locations throughout a building. The lobes are physically connected within the concentrators to form a serial link, with the wiring concentrators then being interconnected in a serial fashion to complete the ring (Fig. 1). A lobe is only included in the ring path when the node is active; otherwise, an electronic relay within the wiring concentrator causes that lobe to be bypassed [4, 26]. Nodes may easily be moved from one location to another without requiring the installation of a new cable. The wiring is segmented at the wiring concentrators rather than being a continuous cable, thus permitting the intermixing of transmission media. For example, shielded twisted-pair wire can be used to interconnect the wiring concentrators to nodes, while optical fibers can be used for transmission links between wiring concentrators.

The wiring concentrators provide points within the star/ring network that facilitate reconfiguration and maintenance, thus enhancing network reliability. As described earlier, electronic relays within the wiring concentrators are activated whenever a node is powered on to bring that node and the associated wiring lobe into the active ring. Should the attached adapter detect a fault within either its own components or the wiring lobe between itself and the wiring concentrator, it can deactivate the relay and remove itself

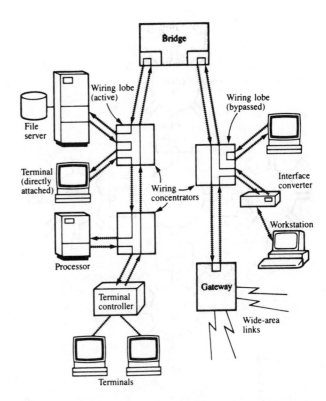

Figure 1 Wiring topology and components of a two-ring network. *Wiring concentrators* are the central elements for structuring a star/ring wiring layout. *Bridges* provide high-speed links between multiple rings. *Gateways* are used to access wide-area networks for long-distance communications.

from the ring. This lobe-bypass function may also be accomplished by manually deactivating the faulty node in case a faulty adapter is unable to remove itself from the ring. Passive concentrators contain electronic relays but no active elements, such as processing logic or power supplies, and require only enough power from an attached node to activate the relays to insert a node into the ring [18, 26]. Active wiring concentrators, on the other hand, contain processing logic and their own power supplies, and thus have the ability to detect and bypass faults that occur in the ring segments between concentrators. Active concentrators may also be remotely activated through the receipt of appropriate network management commands to bypass faults.

• Bridge function

Multiple rings may be required in a LAN when the data transfer requirements exceed the capacity of a single ring or when the attached nodes are widely dispersed, as in a multifloor building or campus environment. Therefore, large networks may typically have several rings with 100 to 200 nodes per ring. Two rings can be linked together by a high-speed switching device known as a *bridge* (Fig. 1). A

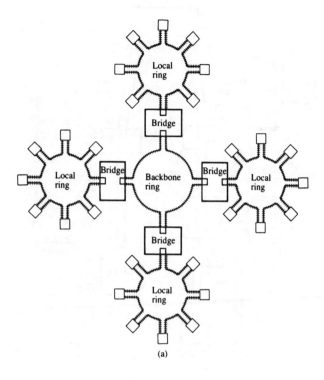

(a)

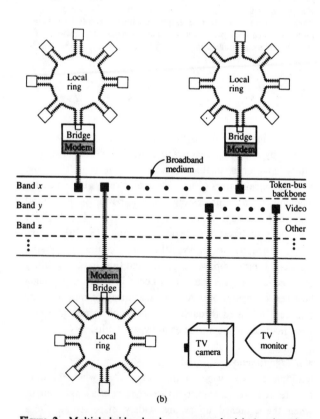

(b)

Figure 2 Multiple-bridge local area network: (a) A token-ring backbone wherein the bridges provide a logical routing of frames among rings and perform a speed conversion between the local rings and the backbone ring; (b) A broadband-bus backbone in which the bridges switch the ring data onto a channel of the broadband medium.

bridge is capable of providing a logical routing of frames between the rings based on the destination address information contained in the headers of the frames. An additional capability of the bridge is to perform transmission speed changes from one ring to another. Each ring retains its individual identity and token mechanism, and can therefore stand alone in the event the bridge or another ring is disrupted. The bridge's interface to a ring is the same as any other node's, except that it must recognize and copy frames with a destination address for one of the other rings within the network. Also, several frames may be temporarily buffered in the bridge while awaiting transfer to the next ring.

The local network can be further expanded to meet larger data capacity requirements by interconnecting multiple bridges. This results in a hierarchical network in which multiple rings are interconnected via bridges to a separate high-speed link known as a *backbone*. The backbone itself may be a high-speed token ring, Fig. 2(a), or it may be a token-access bus link, such as a channel within a broadband CATV system, Fig. 2(b). The address field format described later is structured to designate the specific ring to which a node is attached, thereby facilitating the routing of packets through bridges [17].

● *Gateway function*

In today's networking environment, a growing number of users require access to nationwide communication links as well as to the local network. For example, the primary host processing system may be located in another city or state, requiring that access be provided over a geographically dispersed area. A *gateway* node provides an interface between a LAN and a wide-area network for establishing long-distance communications between nodes within the LAN and nodes that are within other LANs or that are accessible directly on the wide-area network. Wide-area networks include private and commercial satellite links, packet-switching networks, leased lines, or other terrestrial links. They generally operate at lower transmission rates than most LANs, usually in the kb/s transmission range. A gateway can perform the necessary address translations as well as provide the speed and protocol conversions that are required to interface the LAN to these various transmission facilities. There may also be applications where a gateway could be used as an intermediate node between a token-ring LAN and a node in either a CSMA/CD- or PBX-based LAN.

● *Transmission media in a ring network*

The most prevalent LAN wiring media today are twisted-pair copper wire and coaxial cable. However, the use of optical fiber media in LAN systems will certainly increase in the coming years. Unshielded twisted-pair copper medium is used extensively for normal voice communications. However, voice transmission frequencies are much lower than those of local networks, and the impact of environmental noise is not as detrimental to analog voice signals as it could be to digital LAN traffic. Thus, "voice-grade" twisted-pair media cannot satisfy all of the requirements of a high-speed LAN. A high-quality "data-grade" twisted-pair medium has a higher characteristic impedance and is shielded to reduce the external electromagnetic interference (EMI), as well as the outward electromagnetic radiation from the cable itself. Also, the data-grade pair is a balanced medium (i.e., both wires have the same impedance to ground) which, in combination with the shielding, reduces the crosstalk interference from other twisted pairs within the same cable. (See Park and Love [27].) Thus, a well-designed twisted-pair cable can provide a reliable transmission medium for a local network system operating at baseband data rates of 1 to 10 Mb/s [7].

Optical fibers offer several advantages over copper media for use in LANs, including low susceptibility to electromagnetic interference and low signal attenuation over long distances at speeds greater than 100 Mb/s [7]. As this technology matures, lower-cost splicing techniques, as well as lower production costs, will make the use of optical fibers more economical than it is today. As noted earlier, the token-ring control scheme and the radial wiring topology enable optical fibers to be used within the LAN. For example, optical fibers could be used between buildings where lightning poses a hazard that requires additional protection with metallic media but not with optical fiber. Fibers could also be used in industrial environments where higher levels of EMI are found.

Broadband coaxial cable systems can be incorporated within a LAN for transmitting both analog video and digital data signals. While television systems do not play a major role in the office today, they may do so in the future. As noted earlier, standard CATV channels could be used for data transmission between rings by means of broadband bridges or for the interconnection of LANs via appropriate gateways.

● *Differential Manchester encoding scheme*
The binary data that originate within a node must be encoded for effective transmission over the ring. Many different encoding schemes are possible, including 8B/10B encoding [28] and differential Manchester encoding [22]. The differential Manchester code is being considered by the IEEE Project 802 Local Area Network Committee as the standard scheme for baseband ring transmission [29]. This code allows for simpler receive/transmit and timing recovery circuitry and offers a smaller delay per station than do block codes. Also, the differential Manchester code allows for the interchanging of the two wires of a twisted pair without introducing data errors [4]. A series of contiguous *1*s and *0*s

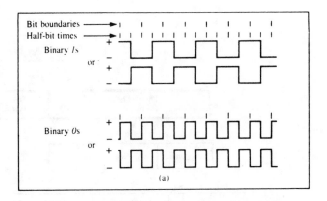

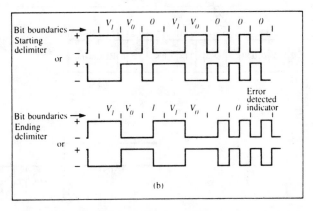

Figure 3 Differential Manchester encoding: (a) A *1* is distinguished from a *0* by the presence or absence of a polarity change at the bit boundary followed by a polarity change at the half-bit time of the synchronous signal on the medium; (b) Starting and ending delimiters contain code violations to distinguish them from data for delineating a frame.

(bits) would appear as shown in Fig. 3 when encoded. Each bit is encoded as a two-segment signal, with a signal transition (polarity change) at the middle or half-bit time. This transition at the half-bit time effectively cancels the dc component of the signal and provides a signal transition for clock synchronization at each adapter. The *1*s are differentiated from the *0*s at the leading bit boundary; a value of *1* has no signal transition at the bit boundary, while a value of *0* does. In decoding the signal, only the presence or absence of the signal transition, and not the actual polarity (positive or negative), is detected.

A code violation results if no signal transition occurs at the half-bit time. Code violations can be intentionally created to form a unique signal pattern that can be distinguished from normal data (*1*s and *0*s) by the receiving adapter(s). Such unique signal patterns can be inserted to mark the start and end of a valid data frame. Four code violations are used in pairs to maintain the dc balance, as well as to prevent spurious signals from being recognized as valid delimiters.

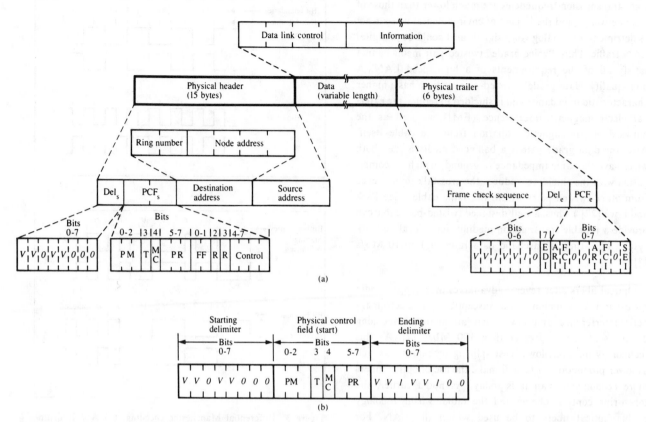

Figure 4 (a) Overall frame format. (b) Free token frame format. The abbreviations used are as follows: ARI = address-recognized indicator; Del$_e$ = ending delimiter; Del$_s$ = starting delimiter; EDI = error-detected indicator; FCI = frame-copied indicator; FF = frame format; MC = monitor count; PCF$_e$ = ending physical control field; PCF$_s$ = starting physical control field; PM = priority mode; PR = priority reservation; R = reserved; SEI = soft error indicator; T = token: *1* means busy, *0* means free; V = code violation.

Also, within each violation pair, the first is a violation of the normal *1* bit, V_1 (i.e., no signal transition at the leading bit boundary), while the second is a violation of the normal *0* bit, V_0 (i.e., signal transition occurs at the leading bit boundary). Thus the bit pattern $V_1 V_0 0 V_1 V_0 0$ is used to denote the starting delimiter, while the pattern $V_1 V_0 1 V_1 V_0 1$ is used to denote the ending delimiter (Fig. 3). These code patterns comprise the first six bit-times of either delimiter, leaving two bit-times within the byte (eight bit-times) for other uses. Any other code violations that occur are assumed to be transmission errors.

Token-ring architecture

• Data frame format
The general format for transmitting information on the ring, called a frame, is shown in Fig. 4(a). The "data" portion of the frame is variable in length (up to a fixed maximum) and contains the information that the sender is transferring to the receiver. The data field is preceded by a physical header, which contains three subfields. The first is a starting delimiter (Del$_s$) that identifies the start of the frame. The starting delimiter is a unique signal pattern that includes pairs of

code violations of the differential Manchester encoding scheme as described earlier. Next, a starting physical control field (PCF$_s$) is defined for controlling the access to the transmission facility and for passing encoded information to the adapters. This two-byte field includes a one-bit token indicator that indicates whether the token is free (*0*) or busy (*1*). The frame format shown in Fig. 4(a) would contain a busy token indication. A free token, on the other hand, contains only the first byte of the PCF$_s$ and the starting and ending delimiters [Fig. 4(b)]. A token priority mode, in conjunction with the priority reservation indicators within the first byte of the PCF$_s$, provides different priority levels of access to the ring. The monitor count bit is used in conjunction with a token monitor function to maintain the validity of the token. Both the priority access scheme and the token monitor function are described subsequently. The second byte of the PCF$_s$ contains a two-bit frame format (FF), two reserved bits, and a four-bit control indicator. The FF bits enable the receiving node to determine whether the information within the data field of the frame contains medium-access control (MAC) information (FF = *00*) or user data (FF = *01*). MAC frames may optionally include frame status information or other urgent ring management information within the control indicator subfield. Finally, the header includes a field containing the address of the node that originated the information and the address of the node (or nodes) destined to receive the information. Both address fields contain six bytes, with the first two bytes indicating the specific ring number (in multiple ring networks) and the last four bytes indicating the unique node address.

The data field itself may be subdivided to include a data link control subfield as well as the user information field. Data link control information is necessary for the higher-level protocols that are normally used within data communication networks [14].

The dàta field is followed by a physical trailer which is also composed of three subfields. The first portion of the trailer contains a four-byte frame check sequence (FCS) that is calculated by the source node and used for detecting errors that occur during transmission within the second byte of the physical control field, the address fields, or the data field itself. The FCS is a 32-bit cyclic redundancy check (CRC) that is calculated using a standard generator polynomial [29]. Next, an ending delimiter (Del$_e$) is provided to identify the end of the frame. This delimiter also contains pairs of code violations such as were found in the starting delimiter, but with *1*s following the violations to distinguish the Del$_e$ from the Del$_s$. The last bit of the Del$_e$ is designated as the error-detected indicator (EDI). This indicator is always *0* during error-free ring operation, but is set to *1* by any intermediate ring adapter that detects an error with the FCS of a frame. The Del$_e$ is followed by an ending physical control field (PCF$_e$), which is also employed for certain physical control functions. The PCF$_e$ contains bits that can be modified while the frame is traversing the ring and is therefore not included in the calculation of the FCS character. For this reason the frame-copied indicator (FCI) and the address-recognized indicator (ARI) bits are duplicated to provide a redundancy check to detect erroneous settings. The uses of the FCI, the ARI, and the soft error indicator (SEI) within the PCF$_e$ are discussed later.

● *Token-access control protocol*

The token-access control mechanism for regulating data flow in a ring topology is based on the principle that permission to use the communications link, in the form of a "free" token, is passed sequentially from node to node around the ring. The "free" token, as described earlier, contains a one-bit indication that the token is "free" (T = *0*). With the token-access control scheme, a single free token circulates on the ring (Fig. 5), giving each node in turn an opportunity to transmit data when it receives the token. Each node introduces into the ring approximately a one-bit delay as the time to examine, copy, or change a bit as necessary. A node having data to transmit can change the token indicator from free (*0*) to busy (*1*) and begin data transmission by appending the

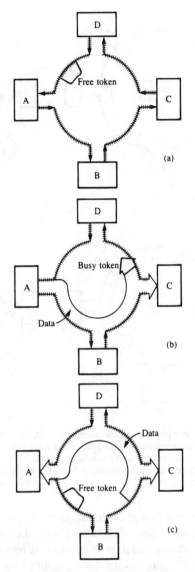

Figure 5 Token-ring access control protocol. (a) Sender (node A) looks for a *free* token, then changes *free* token to *busy* and appends data. (b) Receiver (node C) copies data addressed to it; token and data continue around the ring. (c) Sender (node A) generates free token upon receipt of physical header and completion of transmission, and continues to remove data until receipt of the physical trailer.

remainder of the physical header field (second byte of PCF$_s$ and destination/source address fields), the data field, and the physical trailer. The node that initiates a frame transfer must remove that frame from the ring and issue a free token upon receipt of the physical header, allowing other nodes an opportunity to transmit. If a node finishes transmitting the entire frame prior to receiving its own physical header, it continues to transmit idle characters (contiguous *0*s) until the header is recognized. This ensures that only one token (free or busy) is on the ring at any given time. The single-token protocol is thus distinguished from a multiple-token protocol in which a new free token is released immediately

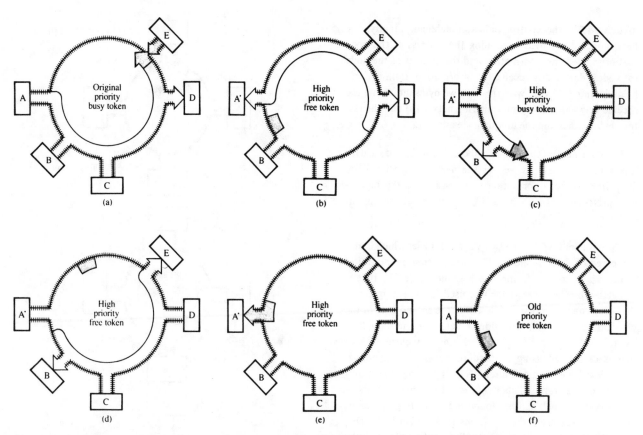

Figure 6 Priority with "uniform access." (a) "A" is in the process of sending to "D." "E" makes a higher priority level reservation. (b) "A" generates a higher priority level free token and saves the original priority level. Since "B" is at a lower priority level, it cannot use the higher level token. (c) "E" uses the free token to send data to "B." (d) "E" generates a free token at the current (higher) priority level. (e) "A" sees the higher priority level free token and generates a free token at the saved preempted priority level. (f) Now "B" is given the chance it missed earlier to use the free token.

following the last byte of the trailer. Only one free token is permitted in either case, with multiple busy tokens (frames) possible in the latter case if the length of a data frame is short compared to the time that it takes the leading busy token to travel completely around the ring. However, multiple-token error recovery is much more complex, while performance improvements of a multiple-token protocol over a single-token protocol are marginal when adapter delays are small [24].

Note that the ARI bits in the physical trailer of a frame are set by a node whenever it recognizes its own address within the destination field of that frame. The FCI bits are set by a node whenever it copies a frame from the ring. If a node cannot copy a frame from the ring, only the ARI bits are set, indicating to the sending node that the destination node is active but did not copy the frame. The ARI and FCI bits are used only for passing status information on a ring and do not provide an end-to-end acknowledgment of frame transfer in a multiple ring network.

The token-access control protocol provides uniform access to the ring for all nodes. A node must release a free token after each transmission and is not allowed to transmit

continuously (beyond a maximum frame size or preset time limit) on a single token. All other nodes on the ring will have a chance to capture a free token before that node can capture the token again. In some system configurations, it may be necessary for selected nodes, such as bridges or synchronous devices, to have priority access to the free tokens. The priority mode and reservation indicators in the PCF$_s$ are used in regulating this access mechanism. Various nodes may be assigned priority levels for gaining access to the ring, with the lowest priority being *000*. This means that a selected node can capture any free token that has a priority mode setting equal to or less than its assigned priority. The requesting node can set its priority request in the reservation field of a frame if the priority of that node is higher than any current reservation request (Fig. 6). The current transmitting node must examine the reservation field and release the next free token with the new priority mode indication, but retain the interrupted priority level for later release. A requesting node uses the priority token and releases a new token at the same priority so that any other nodes assigned that priority can also have an opportunity to transmit. When the node that originally released the priority free token recognizes a free token at that priority, it then releases a new free token at the level that was interrupted by the original request. Thus, the lower-priority token resumes circulation at the point of interruption.

Network addressing and frame routing The local network environment is expected to be changing frequently as nodes are added to a ring, moved from one ring to another, or removed completely [6]. The addressing and routing schemes for transferring frames from the source node to the destination node must be efficient and reliable in this changing environment. There are three types of addresses that could be used to identify a particular node. One type of identification is an identifier address that could be preset by hardware components within a node and remain unique no matter where the node is located within the network. Another type of address could be assigned to the specific wall outlet or wiring concentrator lobe to which the node is attached, denoting the physical location of the node within the network. A third logical address could be assigned to a node by a separate address server whenever the node becomes active in the network. The important point is that an address exists that distinguishes one particular node from all the others. This address is appended to the ring number to form the complete source or destination address that is included in each frame [Fig. 4(a)].

Certain addresses can be defined to be "all-stations" or "all rings" addresses that can be used when a frame is to be sent to all nodes in the network or on a particular ring. Otherwise the sender must determine at least the unique portion of the intended receiver's address before the first message can be sent. This information could be obtained from a central address management function or from a published source (similar to a telephone book). The sender then transmits a special MAC frame, known as an *address resolution request* frame, containing the unique portion of the destination address and an "all-rings" address, since the sender does not yet know which ring the destination node is attached to, or even if that node is currently active. If the target node is active, it will receive the address resolution request and respond to the requesting source node with another MAC frame containing its full address information (including ring number). Both nodes then know the complete address of the other and can continue communicating. Saltzer describes how a similar scheme could be used to determine the exact route through the network that the resolution request frame traversed in reaching the destination node [30].

The ring number portion of the destination address within frames is examined by a bridge and those frames that are directed to another ring are transferred within the bridge to the appropriate destination ring (if multiple rings are attached to a single bridge) or to the backbone. A frame is removed from the backbone by a bridge only if the destination ring number can be reached directly through that bridge or if the frame contains a general "all-rings" broadcast address.

A communication path between a node, A, within the local network and another node, B, in a separate network is established through an intermediate gateway node. Node A can communicate directly with the gateway node using the addressing scheme described above. However, the address information that identifies node B must be contained within the information portion of the frames which the gateway node examines to route the frames. Thus, routing through a gateway node can be associated with those functions performed at the path control layer of an SNA node or the network control layer of the ISO model [10].

Token monitor function Normal token operation is monitored by a special function, known as the token monitor, that is always active in a single node on each ring. This function can be performed by any node on the ring and is necessary to initiate the proper error recovery procedure if normal token operation is disrupted. This includes the loss of a free token or the continuous circulation of a busy token, both of which prevent further access to the ring [3]. It is important to note that this monitor function exists only for token recovery and does not play an active role in the normal exchange of data frames.

The monitor count flag in the physical control field of a frame is employed by the active token monitor to detect the continuous circulation of a busy token. When a busy token is first observed by the active monitor, the monitor count flag is set to *1* as the frame passes by. The failure of the transmitting node to remove the frame causes it to pass the token monitor a second time. The token monitor, observing the monitor count flag set, removes the frame from the ring and issues a free token. The active monitor also maintains a timer which is reset upon the passage of either a busy token or a free token. Loss of the token due to interference or noise causes the timer to expire, prompting the token monitor to reinitialize the ring with a free token.

The capability to be an active monitor exists in all active nodes attached to a ring. These other nodes maintain a standby monitor status and are prepared to become the new active monitor should a failure in the current active monitor occur. The standby monitors are essentially monitoring the ring to detect abnormal ring operation that could occur whenever the active monitor has failed. The detection of an error condition by any standby monitor initiates a recovery procedure that allows it or one of the other nodes to become the new monitor [3].

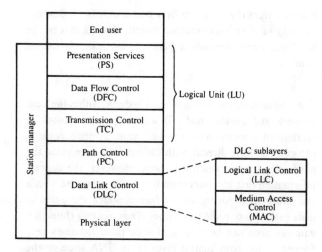

Figure 7 Systems Network Architecture (SNA) layers. Local network protocols and transmissions are performed at the data link control (DLC) and physical layer functional layers of SNA. DLC functions can be further subdivided into logical link control and medium access control sublayers.

Extension of token-access protocol for synchronous applications The token-access control protocol, in conjunction with the priority reservation scheme described earlier, provides a basis for incorporating synchronous data transfer over a token ring [1, 3, 6]. Synchronous operations require that data packets be transmitted and/or received at periodic intervals rather than asynchronously. However, the token-access mechanism is basically an asynchronous control scheme. Synchronous operations, such as real-time digitized voice transfer, can be accomplished by periodically making the ring available only for synchronous data transfer. A special function node, known as a synchronous bandwidth manager, can maintain an internal clock to provide the correct time interval. At the end of each time interval, the synchronous bandwidth manager raises the priority of the circulating free token via the reservation scheme described earlier. This unique priority frame is available only to those nodes requiring synchronous data transfer. The token remains at this priority until all synchronous nodes have had an opportunity to transmit one data frame. The synchronous bandwidth manager then releases a free token at the original priority. The synchronous bandwidth manager must be involved in the establishment of any synchronous communication connections to regulate the synchronous load added to the network so as to avoid excessive delays in the asynchronous traffic.

Token-ring architecture relative to SNA

• Overview
A LAN provides a basic transport mechanism for data transfer among nodes within the network. However, the

LAN by itself does not provide all of the functions that are necessary for two nodes to manage and conduct a meaningful two-way exchange of information. The same higher-level communication protocols that are implemented to control data transfer across public data networks [31] are also applicable to data transfer across a LAN. IBM's Systems Network Architecture (SNA) and the International Organization for Standardization (ISO) reference model separate network functions into layers to facilitate the description of the protocols as well as their implementation [10, 32, 33]. SNA protocols can be implemented for managing the flow of information within a local network as in any other SNA environment [8]. The basic SNA layers are depicted in Fig. 7. The functions of the lowest layer, known as the *physical layer*, are unique to the particular transport mechanism that is implemented, whether it be a communications loop, a multidrop bus, or a token ring. The next higher layer, *data link control* (DLC), is traditionally independent of the actual physical transport mechanism and performs the functions that are necessary to ensure the integrity of the data that reach the layers above DLC. A modification of this concept that would allow the DLC layer to share physical access functions with the physical layer is presented later. Network flow control and message unit routing functions are provided at the next higher layer, known as *path control* (PC). The composite of the functions at the DLC and PC layers of all of the nodes within an SNA network comprises the path control subnetwork, the fundamental transport mechanism for transferring data from a source SNA node to a destination SNA node.

An end user within an SNA environment may be a person engaged in interactive work at a display terminal or an application software function that is active within a host. The end user in an SNA node is represented to the network by a *logical unit* (LU). A logical unit comprises the functions of the upper three layers of SNA, transmission control (TC), data flow control (DFC), and presentation services (PS). Two end users communicate within an SNA network by establishing a logical path, called a session, between their respective LUs. The LU-LU session provides a temporary connection for moving the data between the end users, utilizing the services of the PC subnetwork. A more detailed discussion of the logical unit functions relative to local area networks can be found in [8]. The functions of the physical layer and the data link control layer are discussed in more detail next.

• Physical layer
The physical layer of the model encompasses the basic functions associated with placing the electrical signals onto the transmission medium. This includes such fundamental operations as signal generation, phase timing along the ring, and the encoding of the signal information using the differen-

tial Manchester scheme. These operations are performed within the ring interface adapter at each active node in the network.

• *Data link control*

Data link control (DLC) is the next layer above the physical layer in SNA. The IEEE Project 802 Committee on Local Area Networks and the European Computer Manufacturers Association (ECMA) have proposed that for local networks, the data link layer of the ISO model, which corresponds to the DLC layer of SNA, be further subdivided into two functional sublayers: logical link control (LLC) and medium-access control (MAC), as depicted in Fig. 7 [29, 34]. This functional decomposition essentially separates those DLC functions that are hardware dependent from those that are hardware independent, thereby possibly reducing the cost of developing data equipment to interconnect to different types of physical transmission interfaces [35].

Medium-access control sublayer The medium-access control (MAC) sublayer of DLC includes those functions associated with frame and token transmission which can be, but are not necessarily, performed by the interface adapter in each node. The actual functions performed at this sublevel depend upon the LAN architecture that is being implemented. The functions for a token-ring LAN include the following:

• Token protocols—basic token access and generation, including token priority reservation scheme.
• Address recognition—copying of frames from ring based on destination address in physical header.
• Frame delimiters—identifying beginning and ending of frames (transmit and receive) via unique delimiters.
• Frame check sequence (FCS)—calculation and verification of cyclic redundancy check (CRC) for each frame.
• Token monitor—performance of all functions associated with active or standby token monitors.

Logical link control sublayer The second sublayer, logical link control (LLC), includes those functions unique to the particular link control procedures that are associated with the attached node and not the medium access. This permits various logical link protocols to coexist on a common network without interfering with one another. Logical links are established primarily to ensure data integrity to the higher layers. For example, HDLC employs a frame-sequencing protocol for verifying that frames have successfully reached their destination, with the appropriate retransmission of lost frames [14].

Multiple appearances of LLC may exist within each node. In these instances, a link multiplex function within the LLC layer directs incoming frames to the appropriate LLC task and also provides the correct address information for outgoing frames. Each LLC appearance is logically associated

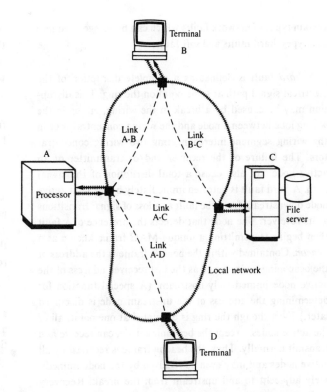

Figure 8 Logical link connectivity. The local network provides the physical transport mechanism for the transfer of data between nodes that have established a logical link connection.

with one other LLC appearance in another node. Models of four nodes are shown in Fig. 8, with examples of some of the logical links that may exist. Each link within the figure is identified by the pair of addresses of the nodes at the ends of the logical link. Thus, the point-to-point connectivity discussed earlier is provided by the LLC sublayer of the DLC layer of the architecture.

• *Station manager*

The station manager function interfaces to both sublayers of the DLC layer, as well as to the higher layers of SNA. The overall function of the station manager can be partitioned according to the various levels of the architecture, such as PC manager or MAC manager functions. The MAC manager performs operations relative to fault diagnosis and statistics collection within the LAN that are described next.

Ring fault detection and isolation

The topological structure of a star/ring configuration, in conjunction with the token-access control protocol, provides an extremely reliable communication link [5]. The unidirectional propagation of information (electrical signals and data frames) from node to node provides a basis for detecting certain types of network faults which can be categorized into two types: hard faults and soft faults.

A *hard* fault is defined as a complete disruption of the electrical signal path at some point on the ring. This disruption may be caused by a break in the wiring, either in the wiring lobe between a node and the wiring concentrator or in the wiring segment interconnecting two wiring concentrators. The failure of the receiver and/or transmitter of an active node can also cause a total disruption of the signal path. A hard fault is detected immediately by the next active node downstream from the fault as a loss of signal transitions at its receiver. The node that detects the presence of a fault then begins transmitting a unique MAC frame known as a *beacon*. Contained within the beacon frame is the address of the beaconing node as well as the last received address of the active node immediately upstream. (A special function for determining the address of the upstream node is discussed later.) Even though the ring is disrupted at one point, all of the active nodes, except the beaconing node, can receive and transmit normally. Thus, the beacon frame is received by all active nodes and may even be received by the node immediately adjacent to and upstream from the break. Recovery actions at the wiring concentrator might include removing from the ring the beaconing node or the node upstream from the beaconing node, or else switching to an alternate ring, as discussed later.

A *soft* fault is characterized by intermittent errors, usually caused by a degradation in the electrical signal or environmental electromagnetic interference. The frame check sequence (FCS) of all frames is calculated and verified by all intermediate nodes as the frames are repeated. The first node on the ring that detects an FCS error can set the error-detected indicator (EDI) bit in the physical trailer of the frame as an indication to all other nodes that the error has been detected. That node also logs the occurrence of the error by maintaining a count of the errors it has detected. If a predetermined threshold of FCS errors is reached over a given time interval at any one node, an indication of the condition can be reported to a special ring network management (RNM) function. The error report message that is sent to the ring network manager contains information that can be used in locating the source of the soft errors. The node detecting the FCS errors can also send a frame with the SEI bit set to *1* to all other nodes on the ring to inform them that a soft error condition exists on the ring.

The RNM node is a special function node within the local network that is capable of monitoring the network operation and configuration. For example, the RNM node could compile error statistics on the occurrence of FCS errors throughout the network or notify an operator of an excessive number of soft errors at a particular node [6]. With this information, the operator or a software application within the RNM node could initiate an appropriate ring reconfiguration action via a command to an active wiring concentrator to bypass a faulty ring segment or node. The RNM node can also maintain an up-to-date list of what nodes are active on any given ring within the network. Network management functions may be distributed over several RNM nodes in large networks if required.

As described earlier, the ARI bits are set by a node whenever it recognizes its own address within the destination field of that frame. If two nodes on a ring were inadvertently assigned the same address, one of the nodes would detect that the ARI bits had been set by the other node. This condition is reported as an error to the RNM node for action.

The isolation of a fault is enhanced if the node detecting and reporting it can also identify the address of the next active upstream node from the fault. This address information can be considered in conjunction with the address of the reporting node to expedite the isolation of a fault, such as was described in the beaconing and soft error procedures earlier. Thus, periodically, the active monitor issues a broadcast frame called a roll-call-poll MAC frame [1]. The first active node downstream from the monitor node sets the ARI bits and copies the source address. Other nodes on the ring do not copy the address information in this particular broadcast frame when the ARI bits are set. The node that received the roll-call-poll frame then issues a roll-call-repeat MAC frame containing its own source address whenever a free token is observed. This frame is recognized and copied by the next downstream active node. This process continues around the ring until the active monitor receives the roll-call-repeat MAC frame without the ARI bits set. At that time, each node has copied and saved the specific address of the adjacent node immediately upstream. This information is transmitted with all beacon frames and soft error report frames, thereby allowing the RNM node to log the general location of the fault.

Once the general location of a fault (hard or soft) has been determined, some action is necessary to eliminate the faulty segment(s) from the ring so that normal operation can resume. The wiring concentrators provide concentration points for bypassing such faults, as was discussed earlier with lobe bypass. A separate technique is necessary if reconfiguration is required as a result of faults occurring within the ring segments interconnecting wiring concentrators. Alternate backup links can be installed between the wiring concentrators in parallel with the principal links (Fig. 9). If a fault occurs in the ring segment between two wiring concentrators, wrapping of the principal ring to the alternate ring within the two wiring concentrators restores the physical path of the ring. This wrapping function, like the lobe bypass function, may be activated manually or via automatic switching logic, or may be command initiated from an RNM node. The figure shows four wiring concentrators as they would be configured to bypass such a fault with both a principal and an alternate ring. The signals on the alternate ring are propagated in the direction opposite to those on the principal ring, thus maintaining the logical order of the nodes on the ring. In other words, node N remains immediately downstream from node M. Consequently, configuration tables associated with the network management functions do not have to be altered [1]. In addition to the procedure for bypassing faults, each node can perform self-diagnostic tests of its own circuitry and wiring lobe to ensure that it does not disrupt the signal path when it is inserted into the ring. If these tests indicate a potential problem, the node is not inserted into the ring until after the situation is remedied [6].

Summary

This tutorial has highlighted many of the key aspects of a token-ring local area network. The star/ring topology with token-access control offers a network architecture that can satisfy today's requirements while allowing for future growth and expansion. Wiring concentrators provide points throughout a building for a radial wiring scheme in which any node can be isolated from the network in case of failure. This concept forms the basis for a network management scheme that should provide quick isolation and recovery from both hard faults and soft faults. Token-ring networks are extendible in that additional token-controlled rings may be added to the network through the use of bridges. Furthermore, a hierarchical network structure can be implemented in a large building or a campus environment by interconnecting multiple bridges via a high-speed backbone. The backbone link may utilize the token-access control scheme on either another baseband ring or a channel within a broadband communication system (e.g., CATV). A token-ring LAN provides the basic transport mechanism for the transfer of data among nodes within the LAN. Higher-level communication protocols, such as those within SNA, must be implemented to ensure meaningful and reliable information exchange across the network.

Acknowledgments

The author wishes to acknowledge Roy C. Dixon, Don W. Andrews, and James D. Markov for their contributions and suggestions in preparing this tutorial, and Frank P. Corr and Edward H. Sussenguth for their technical review and comments. Several IBM researchers have contributed to the overall token-ring concepts presented here. The basic research within IBM that led to the development of this token-ring LAN architecture was conducted at the IBM Research Laboratory in Zurich, Switzerland.

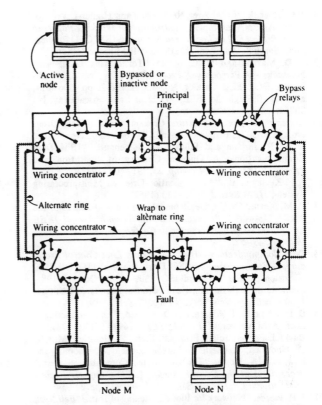

Figure 9   Ring reconfiguration with alternate ring. A fault on the ring between two wiring concentrators can be bypassed by wrapping the connections within the wiring concentrators, thereby using the alternate path and maintaining the same node ordering that existed before the fault occurred.

References

1. R. C. Dixon, N. C. Strole, and J. D. Markov, "A Token-Ring Network for Local Data Communications," *IBM Syst. J.* **22**, 47–62 (1983).
2. W. Bux, F. Closs, P. A. Janson, K. Kümmerle, and H. R. Müller, "A Reliable Token Ring System for Local-Area Communication," *Proceedings of the National Telecommunications Conference,* November 1981, pp. A.2.2.1–A.2.2.6.
3. W. Bux, F. Closs, P. A. Janson, K. Kümmerle, H. R. Müller, and E. H. Rothauser, "A Local-Area Communication Network Based on a Reliable Token Ring System," *Proceedings of the International Symposium on Local Computer Networks,* Florence, Italy, April 1982, pp. 69–82.
4. H. R. Müller, H. Keller, and H. Meyer, "Transmission in a Synchronous Token Ring," *Proceedings of the International Symposium on Local Computer Networks,* Florence, Italy, April 1982, pp. 125–147.
5. R. C. Dixon, "Ring Network Topology for Local Data Communications," *Proc. COMPCON Fall '82,* Washington, DC, IEEE Catalog No. 82CH1796-2, pp. 591–605, available through the IEEE, 445 Hoes Lane, Piscataway, NJ 08854.
6. D. W. Andrews and G. D. Schultz, "A Token-Ring Architecture for Local-Area Networks—An Update," *Proc. COMPCON Fall '82,* Washington, DC, IEEE Catalog No. 82CH1796-2, pp. 615–624, available through the IEEE, 445 Hoes Lane, Piscataway, NJ 08854.
7. P. Abramson and F. E. Noel, "Matching the Media to Local Network Requirements," *Data Communications* **12**, No. 7, pp. 115–123 (July 1983).

8. J. G. Rusnak, "Local-Area Networking and Higher-Level Protocols: An SNA Example," *Contribution of Working Papers to IEEE Project 802 on Local Area Networks*, IBM CPD Publication, March 8, 1982; available through IBM branch offices.

9. J. D. Markov and N. C. Strole, "Token Ring Local Area Networks—A Perspective," *Proc. COMPCON Fall '82*, Washington, DC, IEEE Catalog No. 82CH1796-2, pp. 606–614, available through the IEEE, 445 Hoes Lane, Piscataway, NJ 08854.

10. *Systems Network Architecture: Concepts and Products*, Order No. GC30-3072, available through IBM branch offices.

11. David R. Jarema and Edward H. Sussenguth, "IBM Data Communications: A Quarter Century of Evolution and Progress," *IBM J. Res. Develop.* **25**, 391–404 (1981).

12. J. F. Keeley et al., "An Application-Oriented Multiprocessing System," *IBM Syst. J.* **6**, 78–133 (1967).

13. P. M. Karp, "Origin, Development and Current Status of the ARPA Network," *Proceedings of the Seventh Annual IEEE Computer Society International Conference*, San Francisco, 1973, pp. 49–52.

14. *Data Communication—High-Level Data Link Control Procedures—Frame Structure*, ISO Draft Proposal ISO/DP 3309 (Revision of ISO Standard ISO/3309-1976), October 1981; available through the American National Standards Institute, 1430 Broadway, New York, NY 10018.

15. D. D. Clark, K. T. Pogran, and D. P. Reed, "An Introduction to Local Area Networks," *Proc. IEEE* **66**, 1497–1517 (1978).

16. David J. Farber, Julian Feldman, Frank R. Heinrich, Marsha D. Hopwood, Kenneth C. Larson, Donald C. Loomis, and Lawrence A. Rowe, "The Distributed Computing System," *Proceedings of the Seventh Annual IEEE Computer Society International Conference*, San Francisco, 1973, pp. 31–34.

17. J. R. Pierce, "Network for Block Switching of Data," *Bell Syst. Tech. J.* **51**, 1133–1145 (1972).

18. J. H. Saltzer and K. T. Pogran, "A Star-Shaped Ring Network with High Maintainability," *Proceedings of the Local Area Communications Network Symposium*, Boston, May 1979, pp. 179–189.

19. M. V. Wilkes and R. M. Needham, "The Cambridge Model Distributed System," *ACM Oper. Syst. Rev.* **14**, 21–29 (1980).

20. *IBM Series/1 Local Communications Control, General Information*, Order No. GA27-3093, available through IBM branch offices.

21. R. M. Metcalfe and D. R. Boggs, "Ethernet: Distributed Packet Switching for Local Computer Networks," *Commun. ACM* **19**, 395–404 (1976).

22. "A Survey of Digital Baseband Signaling Techniques," *NASA Technical Memorandum X-64615*, University of Tennessee, June 1971.

23. "Token-Passing Bus Access Method and Physical Layer Specifications," *IEEE Standard 802.4*, Draft D, Sections 14–15, December 1982; available from the Director of Standards, IEEE, 345 East 47th St., New York, NY 10017.

24. W. Bux, "Local-Area Subnetworks: A Performance Comparison," *IEEE Trans. Commun.* **29**, 1465–1473 (1981).

25. B. W. Stuck, "Calculating the Maximum Mean Data Rate in Local Area Networks," *Computer* **16**, No. 5, 72–76 (1983).

26. K. Kümmerle and M. Reiser, "Local-Area Communication Networks—An Overview," *J. Telecommun. Networks* **1**, 349–370 (1982).

27. D. I.-H. Park and R. D. Love, "An Analysis of the Tolerance to Crosstalk Noise of a Pulse Width Modulation System," *IBM J. Res. Develop.* **27**, 432–439 (1983, this issue).

28. A. X. Widmer and P. A. Franaszek, "A DC-Balanced, Partitioned-Block, 8B/10B Transmission Code," *IBM J. Res. Develop.* **27**, 440–451 (1983, this issue).

29. *IEEE Project 802, Local Network Standard, Draft C*, May 1982; available from the Director of Standards, IEEE, 345 East 47th St., New York, NY 10017.

30. J. H. Saltzer, D. P. Reed, and D. D. Clark, "Source Routing for Campus-Wide Internet Transport," *Local Networks for Computer Communications*, North-Holland Publishing Co., New York, 1981, pp. 1–23.

31. F. P. Corr and D. H. Neal, "SNA and Emerging International Standards," *IBM Syst. J.* **18**, 244–262 (1979).

32. *ISO Reference Model of Open-Systems Interconnection* ISO/TC97/SC16, DP 7498; available from the American National Standards Institute, 1430 Broadway, New York, NY 10018 (Rev., January 1983).

33. P. François and A. Potocki, "Some Methods for Providing OSI Transport in SNA," *IBM J. Res. Develop.* **27**, 452–463 (1983, this issue).

34. Standard ECMA-80-81-82, Local Area Networks: Coaxial Cable System—Physical Layer—Link Layer, September 1982.

35. K. N. Larson and W. R. Chestnut, "Adding Another Layer to the ISO Net Architecture Reduces Costs," *Data Communications*, 215–222 (1983).

Received March 29, 1983; revised June 28, 1983

Norman C. Strole   *IBM Communication Products Division, P.O. Box 12195, Research Triangle Park, North Carolina 27709.* Dr. Strole is a staff engineer at the Research Triangle Park laboratory, where he is currently involved in the performance evaluation and analysis of local area network systems. He joined IBM in 1973 and prior to his current assignment worked in the development and performance evaluation of the IBM supermarket/retail store systems. His research activities have included the development of a simulation methodology for the performance evaluation of shared-resource computer architectures. Dr. Strole received a B.S. in electrical engineering from North Carolina State University, Raleigh, in 1973. He received the M.S. and Ph.D. in electrical engineering from Duke University in 1975 and 1980, respectively. He currently holds an adjunct appointment in the School of Electrical Engineering at Duke University and is a member of Eta Kappa Nu, the Institute of Electrical and Electronics Engineers, and Tau Beta Pi.

Chapter 9

Local Area Network Standards

by
David C. Wood

Dr. David C. Wood is a Department Head at the MITRE Corporation in McLean, Virginia. He is responsible for prototype local network projects and for providing support to the government in the
acquisition of large systems and networks. He has published numerous articles on networking and has taught courses on networks and
protocols for The Johns Hopkins University, The George Washington
University, the ACM, and the IEEE.

Dr. Wood is Secretary of the ACM and a member of the ACM
Council, a past Chairman of the ACM Special Interest Group on Data
Communication (SIGCOMM), and a past chairman of the Washing-
ton, D.C. chapter of ACM. Dr. Wood holds a B.Sc. and Ph. D., both in mathematics, from
the University of Manchester, United Kingdom.

9.1 INTRODUCTION

The purpose of this chapter is to describe current and proposed standards for
local area networks (LANs). The protocols used within a LAN are placed in the
context of the Open Systems Interconnection (OSI) reference model. The evolution of LAN standards is described, starting with Ethernet and evolving to the
IEEE 802 standards. The various local network standards encompassed by IEEE
802 are defined.

Protocols and standards for LANs involve much more than just the protocols
internal to the local network represented by IEEE 802. Standards for interfacing

stand-alone terminals and computers to the LAN are also necessary. Moreover, an operational system also requires protocols for network management and control functions. Finally, depending on the applications supported on the LAN, transport and higher-level protocols are likely to be required. The chapter concludes with a summary of the current status of LAN standards and an assessment of future directions.

9.1.1 LAN Protocols and the OSI Model

In terms of the OSI reference model (see Chapter 5), the protocols internal to a local network occupy the two lower layers: the data link layer and the physical layer. These correspond, for example, to HDLC and RS-232, respectively, in point-to-point communications lines (Table 9-1).

Table 9-1. Local Network Protocols and the OSI Reference Model

Reference Model Layer	Point-to-Point Circuits	Local Area Networks
Data Link	HDLC	CSMA/CD or Token
Physical	RS-232	Baseband or Broadband Signaling

Data link layer protocols provide functions, such as error control and access control, on a logical data link (see Chapter 4). HDLC does this by using a cyclic redundancy checksum (CRC) for error detection and polling to control which station has access to a multipoint link. In the case of local networks, with many stations sharing a common communications channel, two access-control schemes are prevalent: a contention scheme known as *carrier-sense multiple access with collision detection* (CSMA/CD) and a token scheme rather similar to polling. In other respects, local network protocols resemble HDLC at the data link layer.

Physical layer protocols are concerned with mechanical, electrical, functional, and procedural functions. RS-232 defines the familiar standard 25-pin connector, the electrical signal levels, assignment of functions to the pins, and procedures for initializing communications, sending and receiving data, etc. Local network protocols support a variety of combinations of topology, transmission medium, signal encoding technique, and data rate.

9.1.2 Evolution of LAN Standards

The first major step in the evolution of LAN standards occurred in 1980 with the publication of the Ethernet specification by DEC, Intel, and Xerox.[10] The published Ethernet specification was derived from many years of research and development at the Xerox Palo Alto Research Center. An experimental Ethernet was first publicly described in 1976.[6]

The 1980 Ethernet specification encompasses the two lower protocol layers. At the data link layer, the specification defines a contention-based channel-access protocol known as carrier-sense multiple access with collision detection (CSMA/CD). This layer also defines a frame structure for messages similar to that used in HDLC. At the physical layer, the specification defines the medium as a particular type of shielded coaxial cable with a topology known as a branching nonrooted tree. Baseband signaling is employed at a data rate of 10 million bits per second (Mbps). This contrasts with the earlier experimental Ethernet that used 3-Mbps signaling.

Ethernet configurations are illustrated in Figs. 9-1 and 9-2. Fig. 9-1 shows a

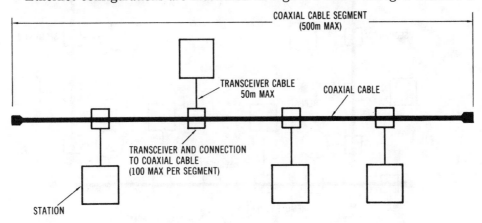

SOURCE: ETHERNET SPECIFICATION

Fig. 9-1. Minimal Ethernet configuration.

minimal configuration consisting of a single segment of coaxial cable that is up to 500 meters in length. User devices, or *stations*, such as workstations or host computers, are connected to the main cable by an *access* or *transceiver cable* that can be up to 50 meters in length. The transceiver cable connects to the main cable via a *transceiver*, a small box that essentially performs the signal transmission and reception. Most of the Ethernet protocol logic is implemented in the workstation. A single segment can contain up to 100 stations.

For a local network extending more than 500 meters, multiple segments are required. These are interconnected by *repeaters*, as shown in Fig. 9-2. A repeater is connected as a regular station to two segments. However, every transmission on one segment is automatically retransmitted by the repeater onto the second segment with a very tiny delay and, conversely, in the other direction. The repeaters essentially overcome the distance limitation of a single segment that results from the baseband signaling employed. Up to 1024 stations can be on the local network. All the interconnected segments are one space as far as the CSMA/CD contention protocol is concerned. At most, two repeaters can be in the path between any two stations. However this allows for large configurations; for example, in a high-rise office building, one segment could be vertical up a utility shaft, with segments off on each floor. To connect segments that may be some distance away in adjacent buildings, a point-to-point link is allowed. This can be up to 1000 meters in length and will appear as a repeater divided into two parts.

The rationale for many of the design decisions for the Ethernet specification is contained in *Evolution of the Ethernet Local Computer Network* by J.F. Shoch.[9] Xerox's goal in publishing the specification was to get it accepted as a de facto standard for local area networks that other vendors would adopt, thus leading to open systems; i.e., interoperability among different vendor's equipment. Ethernet was widely accepted and, as a result, board-level implementations of Ethernet controllers became available in about 1982 from vendors such as Intel, Interlan,

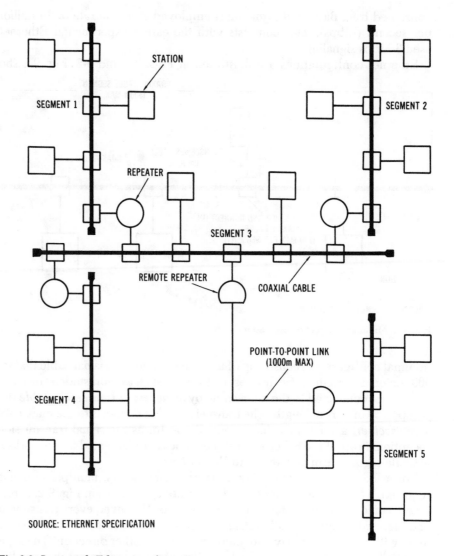

STATION

SEGMENT 1

SEGMENT 2

REPEATER

SEGMENT 3

REMOTE REPEATER

COAXIAL CABLE

POINT-TO-POINT LINK
(1000m MAX)

SEGMENT 4

SEGMENT 5

SOURCE: ETHERNET SPECIFICATION

Fig. 9-2. Large-scale Ethernet configuration.

and 3Com. Chip-set implementations, using very large-scale integration, started to come on the market in 1983 from Intel and Fujitsu.

Ethernet was incorporated as one of the options within the IEEE 802 local network standards with just a few changes from the 1980 specification. Xerox Corp. agreed to these changes and revised their specification accordingly.[12] The final Ethernet-based specification is described in more detail in the next section as part of the IEEE 802 standard.

9.2 IEEE 802 LOCAL AREA NETWORK STANDARDS

The IEEE established project 802 on local area network standards in 1980. The scope of the standard development activity is illustrated in Fig. 9-3. It encompasses the two lower layers of the OSI reference model and an interface to the network layer. The data link layer is divided into two sublayers: a *logical link control* sublayer similar to HDLC and a *medium access control* sublayer such as the CSMA/CD protocol used in Ethernet. An *access unit interface* is defined between the component containing both the link layer and physical signaling and the physical medium attachment to the transmission media. This is analogous to the transceiver cable in Ethernet.

The IEEE 802 standard that has emerged is, in fact, a family of standards. As shown in Fig. 9-4, the standard consists of a common portion at the logical link-control sublayer, together with three major options encompassing the medium access control sublayer and the physical layer. These options are the CSMA/CD access protocol on a bus topology, a token access protocol on a bus topology, and a token access protocol on a ring topology. (A *token* access protocol is one in which permission to transmit, known as the token, is systematically passed from node to node around the network. A particular node may transmit only when it possesses the token.)

Even within these three major options, there are many suboptions concerning transmission medium, signaling method, and data rate. Table 9-2 summarizes the options that have appeared at least in draft form.

Some parts of the standard were approved by the IEEE Standards Board during 1983. The approved standards are:

IEEE 802.2 Logical Link Control (IEEE 802.2)
IEEE 802.3 CSMA/CD for Baseband (IEEE 802.3)
IEEE 802.4 Token Bus (IEEE 802.4)

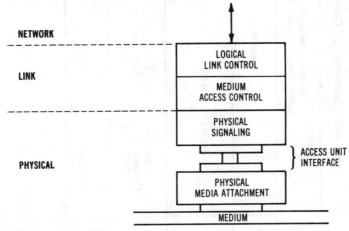

Fig. 9-3. IEEE 802 Protocol Model.

Work continues on other parts of the standard, such as the token ring and CSMA/CD for broadband systems.

International standards based on the 802.2 and 802.3 were undergoing final approval late in 1984 in the International Organization for Standardization (ISO). The 802.4 specification was subject to some revision prior to acceptance as an international standard. The approved standards, and those for which fairly stable drafts have appeared, are described in the remainder of this section.

9.2.1 Logical Link Control Sublayer

The scope of the logical link control sublayer consists of an interface service specification to the network layer above, the logical link control procedures them-

Table 9-2. Summary of Options in IEEE 802

		Connectionless Service (Connection-Oriented Optional)				
CSMA/CD		**Token Bus**			**Token Ring**	
Baseband Coax 50 Ω	Broadband Coax 75 Ω	Single Channel Coax 75 Ω		Broadband Coax 75 Ω	Baseband Twisted Pair 150 Ω	Baseband Coax 75 Ω
Manchester	TBD*	Phase Continuous FSK	Phase Coherent FSK	Multilevel Duobinary AM/PSK	Differential Manchester	Differential Manchester
10 Mb/s	2, 10 Mb/s (TBD*)	1 Mb/s	5, 10 Mb/s	1, 5, 10 Mb/s	1, 4 Mb/s	4, 20, 40 Mb/s

* To be determined.

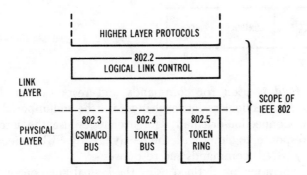

Fig. 9-4. Major components of IEEE 802.

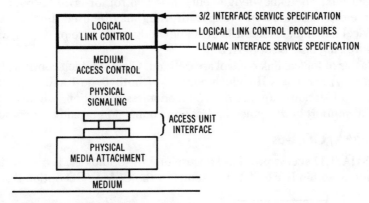

Fig. 9-5. Logical link control sublayer.

selves, and an interface service specification to the medium access control sublayer below (Fig. 9-5).

The interface service specification to the network layer defines the calls for an unacknowledged connectionless service; i.e., a datagram style of service in which stations exchange data units without establishment of a data link connection and without acknowledgements. A connection-oriented service is optional.

The logical link control procedures are based on HDLC and ADCCP (ANSI X3.66)[1] and, in particular, the asynchronous balanced mode of those standards. However, HDLC/ADCCP is extended for the multistation, multiaccess environment of a local network. In a local network, a logical data link is possible between any pair of stations. This contrasts with the point-to-point or multipoint configurations supported by HDLC/ADCCP in which all transmissions are to and from a primary station. Moreover, in the local network, a single station can be included in multiple data exchanges simultaneously with multiple different stations. Within a single station, these multiple exchanges are identified by a *service access point* which can be viewed as a port address to a higher-level protocol within that station.

The format of the logical link-control protocol data unit is shown in Fig. 9-6. The *destination service access point* (DSAP) and *source service access point* (SSAP) represent an individual address as described previously. The DSAP is also usable as a group address.

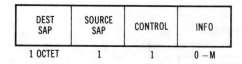

DEST SAP	SOURCE SAP	CONTROL	INFO
1 OCTET	1	1	0 — M

Fig. 9-6. Logical link control frame format.

The *control field* is used for commands and responses in the sense of HDLC/ADCCP. Connectionless data exchanges use the unnumbered information (UI) command. Connection-oriented data exchanges use the information (I) command and response, together with the receive ready (RR), reject (REJ), and receive not ready (RNR) commands and responses.

Two types of operation are defined using the logical link-control procedures: Type 1 (operation that is connectionless) and Type 2 (operation that is connection-oriented). In Type 1 operation, there is no need for establishment of a logical data link; no acknowledgement, flow control, or error recovery is provided and either individual or group addressing may be used. In Type 2 operation, a logical data link is established, acknowledgements are provided, and individual addressing only is supported.

Two classes of logical link control are defined: Class I (which consists of Type 1 operation only) and Class II (which consists of both Type 1 and Type 2 operation). Thus, all stations support the connectionless operation, whereas, Class II stations can support both connectionless and connection-oriented operation.

9.2.2 CSMA/CD Bus

The CSMA/CD access protocol, for use on bus topologies, is one of the three major options within IEEE 802. The scope of the CSMA/CD option is shown in

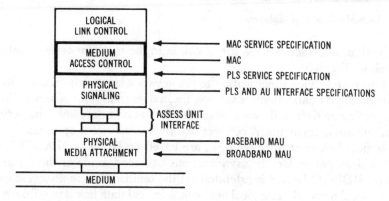

Fig. 9-7. CSMA/CD bus option.

Fig. 9-7. It consists of the media access control (MAC) service specification, the MAC sublayer itself using CSMA/CD, a physical signaling layer (PLS) service specification, and the PLS and access unit (AU) specification itself. All these parts of the standard are independent of the transmission medium. Finally, the physical medium attachment unit (MAU) defines two suboptions: baseband and broadband. The baseband version is based on the Ethernet specification.

9.2.2.1 Media Access Control Sublayer

The services provided by the MAC sublayer allow the local LLC sublayer entity to exchange LLC data units with peer LLC sublayer entities. The MAC sublayer defines the MAC frame structure and the procedures of the CSMA/CD protocol. The MAC frame format is shown in Fig. 9-8. The *preamble* is a 7-octet field of

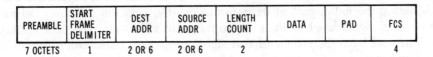

Fig. 9-8. CSMA/CD media access control frame format.

alternating ones and zeros which are used both for synchronization and to allow the PLS circuitry to reach its steady-state condition. The *start frame delimiter* field is the sequence 10101011; it immediately follows the preamble pattern and indicates the start of a valid frame.

Next follows the *destination address* and the *source address* for the frame. The address fields can contain either 2 or 6 octets. This is an implementation option; however, the source and destination addresses must be the same size for all stations on a particular local network. The destination address can designate either an individual or a group address. There are two kinds of group address: a multicast-group address associated with a group of logically related stations and a broadcast address denoting the set of all stations. In the case of 6-octet addresses, they may be locally or globally administered. Global addresses will be unique among any local network conforming to the standard. They are assigned by Xerox Corporation pending the designation of a standards organization to administer address registration.

The *length* field is a 2-octet field whose value indicates the number of LLC data octets in the data field. The *data* field itself contains a LLC protocol data unit (i.e., destination SAP, source SAP, control, and information) shown previously in Fig. 9-6. If the length of the data unit is less than a minimum required by a particular implementation of the protocol, then the data field is extended by extra octets known as *pad*. In the case of a 10-Mbps baseband system, the minimum frame size is 512 bits. Finally, the *frame check sequence* (FCS) field contains a 32-bit cyclic redundancy check (CRC) computed as a function of the destination address, source address, length, LLC data, and pad fields.

This MAC frame format is similar to the original Ethernet specification, but with a few differences. The addresses are always 6 octets in the Ethernet specification. Instead of the length field, there is a type field that is also 2 octets that is used to identify a higher-level protocol.

The functions provided by the MAC sublayer are equivalent to the major functions provided in a data link layer protocol. The MAC sublayer provides data encapsulation: that is, framing, addressing, and error detection. It also provides medium access management; medium allocation is performed using collision avoidance mechanisms and a contention resolution capability handles collisions.

The *carrier-sense multiple access with collision detection* (CSMA/CD) protocol operates as follows. The MAC sublayer constructs the frame from the LLC-supplied data. The carrier-sense signal provided by the physical layer is monitored and, if there is passing traffic, then transmission is deferred. When the medium is clear, frame transmission is initiated after a brief interframe delay (9.6 microseconds for a 10-Mbps system) to provide recovery time for other stations.

During transmission, the physical layer also monitors the medium and turns on the collision-detect signal in the event of a collision.

A *collision* occurs when multiple stations attempt to transmit at the same time and their signals interfere with each other. A given station can experience a collision during the initial part of its transmission (the *collision window*) before its transmitted signal has had time to propagate to all stations on the CSMA/CD medium and have the effects of that signal propagate back. Once the collision window has passed, the station is said to have acquired the medium; subsequent collisions are avoided, since all other stations can be assumed to have noticed the signal and be deferring to it. The time to acquire the medium is thus based on the round-trip propagation time of the physical layer.

In the event of a collision, the physical layer of the transmitting station notices the interference on the medium and turns on the collision detect signal. This is noticed by the MAC sublayer and collision handling begins. First, a bit sequence called the *jam* (32 bits for a 10-Mbps system) is transmitted to ensure that the duration of the collision is sufficient to be noticed by the other transmitting stations. After the jam is sent, transmission is terminated and a retransmission attempt is scheduled after a randomly selected delay. In the event of repeated collisions, retransmission is still attempted repeatedly, but the interval in which the random delay is selected is doubled with each attempt. This is known as a *binary exponential backoff*. However, the retransmission attempt is abandoned after 16 attempts and an error condition is signaled.

The retransmission delay is controlled by a parameter known as the *slot time* which exceeds the round-trip propagation time and the jam time. For a 10-Mbps baseband system, the slot time equals 512 bit times. The *backoff delay* is always an integral number of slot times. The number of slot times to delay before the nth retransmission is a random integer r, where

$$0 \leq r \leq 2^k$$

and

$$k = \min(n, 10)$$

In other words, the delay interval is doubled for each of the first ten retransmissions, but then stays the same up to the 16th retransmission.

9.2.2.2 *Physical Signaling and Attachment Unit Interface*

The MAC sublayer communicates with the physical signaling (PLS) sublayer using primitives defined in the PLS service specification. The Data Terminal Equipment (DTE) containing the data link and higher-level protocols may be physically separate from the *Medium Attachment Unit* (MAU) that connects to the transmission medium. The DTE and MAU are connected by a cable whose specifications are known as the *Attachment Unit Interface* (AUI). This is illustrated in Fig. 9-9. The AUI is also used to enable the DTE to be independent of the transmission media; e.g., baseband coaxial cable or broadband coaxial cable.

The AUI is capable of supporting one or more of the specified data rates of 1, 5, 10, or 20 Mbps. The physical signaling is capable of driving an AUI cable up to 50 meters in length. The interface permits the DTE to test the AU interface, the AU interface cable, the MAU, and the medium. The AUI consists of four signal circuits providing separate data and control circuits in each direction, together with power and ground. A standard 15-pin connector is used.

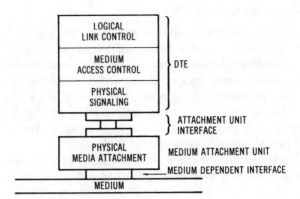

Fig. 9-9. CSMA/CD Attachment Unit Interface.

Manchester encoding is used for the transmission of data across the AUI. Manchester encoding is a binary signaling mechanism that combines data and clock into a single bit stream. The signal state during the first half of the bit period indicates the data value; a transition to the inverse state always occurs in the middle of each bit period. Manchester encoding is shown in Fig. 9-10.

Fig. 9-10. Manchester encoding.

The same framing and preamble are used for the transmission of data across the AUI as defined in the MAC sublayer. Signals on the control circuit are based on frequency.

9.2.2.3 Baseband Medium Attachment Unit

The Medium Attachment Unit (MAU) is specific to the transmission medium. The MAU for a baseband coaxial transmission system follows closely the original Ethernet specification. Signaling is at a data rate of 10 Mbps. The MAU is capable of driving up to 500 meters of coaxial cable in a single segment. Multiple segments may be coupled together using *repeater units* to form a bus topology as described previously for Ethernet. Up to two repeater units may be in the path between any two MAUs. Allowing for a point-to-point link, the maximum cable connection path is 2500 meters. The data propagation delay for a repeater unit is specified to be less than 7.5 bit times.

The MAU detects a collision on the coaxial cable when the signal level on the cable equals or exceeds that produced by two transmitters. The coaxial cable has a 50-ohm characteristic impedance and may have a jacket of polyvinyl chloride or fluoropolymer. The cable jacket is marked with annular rings in a contrasting color every 2.5 meters. MAUs should only be attached at these 2.5-meter marks to ensure that signal reflections do not add in-phase to a significant degree. The total number of MAUs on a segment cannot exceed 100. The MAU-to-cable connection may be designed either such that the cable is severed to install the MAU or such that a piercing tap connector is used without severing the cable. The shield of the trunk coaxial cable should be effectively grounded at only one point along the length of the cable.

9.2.2.4 Broadband Medium Attachment Unit

The MAU specification for broadband coaxial-cable systems has not been finalized at the time of this writing. The following description, based on draft material, is intended only to illustrate the general characteristics of broadband systems.

Broadband local area networks use the same types of coaxial cable and components as are used in community antenna television (CATV) systems which are used for tv distribution in towns and apartment buildings. Such cable systems are capable of carrying analog signals over a wide range of frequencies: up to 300 MHz and, for newer systems, even up to 400 MHz.

Broadband systems are arranged in a tree-like topology using splitters (Fig. 9-11). The root of the tree is known as the *head-end*. Signals are applied to the

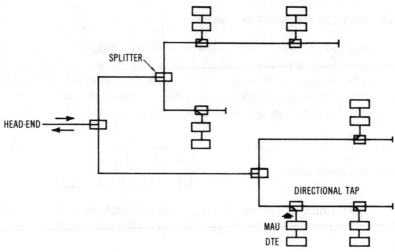

Fig. 9-11. Typical broadband configuration.

cable at directional taps and travel in a single direction. Broadband local area networks may use either a dual-cable or a single-cable system. In a dual-cable system, two parallel cables are used throughout the tree-like structure, looped together at the head-end. An MAU transmits on the inbound cable toward the head-end, where the signal is looped onto the outbound cable and broadcast to all MAUs.

In a single-cable system, different frequencies are used for each direction of transmission. In a mid-split system, the lower half of the frequency range is used for inbound transmissions and the upper half is used for outbound transmissions. A remodulator at the head-end shifts all inbound signals up in frequency and retransmits them on the outbound cable. Thus, the transmitter and receiver of an MAU will be on separate frequencies for a single-cable system. A dual-cable system could also incorporate a head-end remodulator and separate transmitter and receiver frequencies, but there is generally no reason to do this.

Broadband systems use 75-ohm coaxial cable. The trunk cable is generally aluminum sheathed. When a broadband system is designed, signal levels are calculated based on the attenuation of the cable, taps, and splitters. Amplifiers are inserted periodically in the cable system to maintain signal levels. With appropriate amplifiers, cable systems can be designed with a maximum length of several kilometers from the head-end.

Collision detection based on signal levels cannot be performed in broadband systems because of the variation in signal level at different points on the cable. Collision detection is, therefore, usually performed using a bit comparison. That is, a transmitting MAU keeps a copy of its transmitted frame and compares this with the received frame. If they match for the duration required to acquire the cable, it is assumed no other MAU is transmitting.

The specific modulation techniques remain to be defined. Data rates in the range from 1 to 10 Mbps have been proposed in various drafts of the standard. Frequency allocation is performed in units of 6 MHz, corresponding to tv channel bandwidths.

One proposal under consideration is for a 10-Mbps data channel that uses 18 MHz of bandwidth. This scheme is attachment unit interface compatible with a broadband interface unit. Another scheme under consideration is for a 2-Mbps data rate using a scheme that is optimized for broadband rather than emphasizing compatibility with baseband systems.

9.2.3 Token Bus

The use of a token access protocol on a bus topology is the second of the three major options within IEEE 802. The scope of the token option, shown in Fig. 9-12,

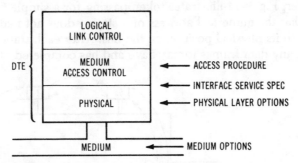

Fig. 9-12. Token bus option.

is similar to the CSMA/CD option but without a distinct MAU physically separate from the DTE.

9.2.3.1 Media Access Control Sublayer

The frame format used in the token bus MAC sublayer is quite similar to that used in the CSMA/CD bus (Fig. 9-13). The *preamble* is used by the receiving modem to acquire signal level and phase lock. The preamble pattern depends on the modulation scheme and data rate; the duration must be at least two microseconds. The *start delimiter* consists of one octet that is distinguishable from data. The *frame control* octet determines the class of frame being sent: MAC control frames concerned with the token, LLC data frames, and MAC management data frames.

Each token frame contains two address fields: the destination address field and the source address field. Addresses are either 2 or 6 octets in length; all addresses on a given LAN are the same length. Six octet addresses may be globally administered. The destination address may be an individual, group, or broadcast address. The source address is always an individual address.

Depending on the bit pattern specified in the frame's Frame Control octet, the MAC Data Unit field can contain an LLC protocol data unit, MAC management

PREAMBLE	START FRAME DELIMITER	FRAME CONTROL	DEST ADDR	SOURCE ADDR	MAC INFO	FCS	END FRAME DELIMITER
1 OR MORE OCTETS	1	1	2 OR 6	2 OR 6	0 TO 8191	4	1

Fig. 9-13. Token bus media access control frame format.

data, or a value specific to one of the MAC control frames. The *frame check sequence* is the same as used in other IEEE 802 options. Finally, there is an *end delimiter* that is always distinguishable from data and determines the position of the frame check sequence.

9.2.3.2 Token Bus Access Procedure

The right to transmit, the *token*, passes among all the stations in a logically circular fashion. Each participating station knows the address of its *predecessor*: the station it got the token from. It knows its *successor*: who the token should be sent to next. It also knows its own address. These predecessor and successor addresses are dynamically determined and maintained.

The token is passed from station to station in numerically descending station address order. Fig. 9-14 illustrates token passing for a simple 6-node configuration. Note that the numerical address of a station does not necessarily bear any relationship to its physical position on the bus. After each station has completed transmitting any data frames it may have and has completed other maintenance

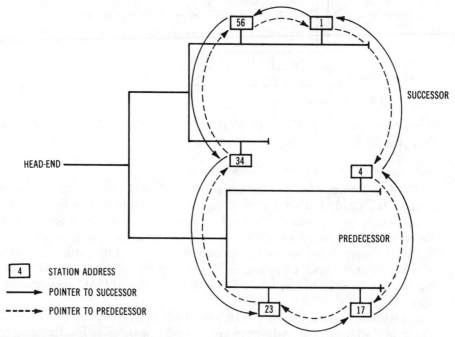

Fig. 9-14. Token passing in the token bus.

functions, the station passes the token to its successor. After sending the token frame, the station listens to make sure that its successor hears the token frame and is active. If the sender hears a valid frame following the token, it assumes that its successor has the token and is transmitting. If the token sender does not hear a valid frame from its successor, it must assess the state of the network.

If the token holder does not hear a valid response after sending the token the first time, successive *fall back steps* are taken to recover the token. First, the token-pass operation is repeated a second time. If the successor still does not respond, the sender assumes the successor has failed.

The sender now sends a *who follows* frame with its successor's address in the data field of the frame. All stations compare the value of the data field of a who_follows frame with the address of their predecessor. The station whose predecessor is the successor of the sending station responds to the who_follows frame by sending its address in a set_successor frame. The station holding the token thus establishes a new successor, bridging the failed station from the logical ring.

If the sending station hears no response to a who_follows frame, it repeats the frame a second time. If there is still no response, the station tries another strategy to reestablish the logical ring.

The station now sends a solicit_successor_2 frame, with itself as destination, asking any station in the system to respond to it. If there are any operational stations that can hear the request, they respond and the logical ring is reestablished using the response window process discussed next.

New stations are added to the logical ring through a controlled-contention process called *response windows*. A response window is a controlled interval of time after transmission of a MAC control frame in which the station sending the frame pauses and listens for a response. If the station hears a transmission start during the response window, the station will continue to listen to the transmission, even after the response window time expires, until the transmission is complete. Thus, the response windows define the time interval during which a station must hear the beginning of a response from another station.

All stations in the ring periodically send *solicit successor* frames specifying a range of station addresses between the frame source and the destination address. Stations whose address falls within this range who wish to enter the ring respond to the frame.

The sender of a solicit successor frame transmits the frame and then waits, listening for a response in the response window following the frame. Responding stations send the frame sender requests needed to become the next station in the logical ring. If the frame sender hears a valid request, it allows the new station to enter the ring by changing the address of its successor to the new station and passes its new successor the token.

If multiple stations respond to a solicit successor frame, only unrecognizable noise may be heard during the response period. The soliciting station then sequences through an arbitration algorithm to identify a single responder by sending a *resolve contention* frame. The stations which had responded to the earlier solicit successor frame choose a 2-bit value and listen for 0, 1, 2, or 3 slot-times. This process is repeated iteratively until there is a single responder.

Initialization is handled as a special case of adding new stations triggered by a timer.

An optional priority mechanism allows data frames to be assigned a *service class* representing one of four priorities. To prevent any single station from monopolizing the network, a parameter known as the *high-priority token hold time* limits the number of highest-priority frames that can be transmitted before passing the token.

The object of the priority system is to allocate network bandwidth to the higher-priority frames and only send lower-priority frames when there is sufficient bandwidth. The network bandwidth is allocated by timing the rotation of the token around the logical ring. Each access class is assigned a target *token rotation time*. For each access class, the station measures the time it takes the token to circulate around the logical ring. If the token returns to a station in less than the target rotation time, the station can send frames of that access class until the target rotation time has expired. If the token returns after the target rotation time has been reached, the station cannot send frames of that priority on this pass of the token.

9.2.3.3 *Physical Layer and Medium*

Three particular types of physical layer and medium are specified for the token bus. They are:

Single-channel phase-continuous FSK,
Single-channel phase-coherent FSK,
Broadband bus.

9.2.3.3.1 Single-Channel Phase-Continuous FSK

Phase-continuous FSK is a particular form of frequency-shift keying where the translation between signaling frequencies is accomplished by a continuous change of frequency, as opposed to the discontinuous replacement of one frequency by another.

The communications medium consists of a long unbranched trunk cable which connects to stations via tee connectors and very short, stubbed, drop cables. Extension of the topology to a branched trunk usually is accomplished via active regenerative repeaters which are connected to span the branches. The tee connectors are nondirectional so a station's signal propagates in both directions along the trunk cable. The trunk cable is 75-ohm CATV-type coaxial cable. The drop cable is 35- to 50-ohm cable and is not more than 35 cm in length.

The data-signaling rate is 1 Mbps using differential Manchester encoding. The modulation scheme uses a carrier frequency of 5 MHz, varying smoothly between the signaling frequencies of 3.75 MHz and 6.25 MHz with transition times of 100 nanoseconds.

9.2.3.3.2 Single-Channel Phase-Coherent FSK

Phase-coherent FSK is a particular form of FSK where the two signaling frequencies are integrally related to the data rate, and transitions between the two signaling frequencies are made at zero crossings of the carrier waveform.

The communications medium consists of a 75-ohm CATV-like trunk and drop structure, with branching using splitters. The trunk cable is connected to the drop cable by nondirectional taps. Extension of the topology is accomplished via active regenerative repeaters connected in the trunk cabling.

The data-signaling rates are 5 Mbps and 10 Mbps. The 5-Mbps data rate uses signaling frequencies of 5 MHz and 10 MHz. The 10-MHz data rate uses signaling frequencies of 10 MHz and 20 MHz.

9.2.3.3.3 Broadband Bus

The communication medium consists of a 75-ohm CATV-like broadband coaxial-cable system. A single-cable mid-split configuration is recommended. A dual cable is also permitted. In both cases, signals are transmitted toward the head-end, where they are retransmitted on the outbound cable or channel.

The modulation scheme used is multilevel duobinary AM/PSK. AM/PSK is a form of modulation in which a radio-frequency (rf) carrier is both amplitude modulated (am) and phase-shift keyed (PSK). *Duobinary signaling* is a method of representing information that is to be transmitted with pulses shaped so as to reduce the frequency spectrum required to signal the information. *Multilevel duobinary AM/PSK* uses more than two distinct amplitude levels to represent information. A three-level duobinary AM/PSK system is specified that is capable of signaling at about 1 bit/Hz.

Standard data-signaling rates are 1 Mbps, 5 Mbps, and 10 Mbps. The 1-Mbps data rate requires a 1.5-MHz channel bandwidth. The 5-Mbps data rate requires a standard 6-MHz channel bandwidth. A data rate of 10 Mbps requires a 12-MHz channel bandwidth. Standard frequency channel pairings have a difference of 192.25 MHz between the inbound and outbound channels.

9.2.4 Token Ring

The third major option within IEEE 802 is the token ring; that is, the use of a token medium access control with a ring topology in contrast to the bus topology of the other options. The token ring is not an approved standard at the time of this writing, so the following description is based on drafts of the standard.

The scope of the token ring is illustrated in Fig. 9-15. It encompasses a MAC

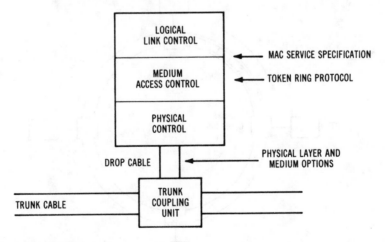

Fig. 9-15. Token ring option.

service specification, medium access control using the token ring protocol, physical control, and physical layer and medium options. The trunk coupling unit is inserted in the trunk cable.

9.2.4.1 MAC Sublayer

The *Media Access Control* frame format for the token ring is shown in Fig. 9-16. The format is very similar to the token bus. The starting delimiter is a unique bit pattern indicating the start of a frame. The access control field identifies the frame as for medium access control or logical link control data; the token is passed using a particular bit pattern in this field. The destination and source addresses may be 2 or 6 octets, but all stations on a local network must have the same address length. Six octet addresses may be globally or locally administered. The destination address may be an individual or group address. The information field contains the LLC data, or parameters in the case of a control frame. The same 32-bit CRC is used for the frame check sequence as in other options. Finally, the ending frame delimiter indicates the end of a frame. Two bits in the ending frame delimiter

STARTING DELIMITER	ACCESS CONTROL	DESTR ADDR	SOURCE ADDR	INFO	FCS	ENDING FRAME DELIMITER
2 OCTETS	1	2 OR 6	2 OR 6	0 TO 4099	4	2

Fig. 9-16. Token ring option access control frame format.

have special significance. When the frame is repeated by a station whose address matches the destination address, then the *address recognized* bit in the ending frame delimiter is turned on. If the frame is copied successfully at the destination address and the FCS balances, then the *frame copied* bit is turned on.

The operation of the token ring is illustrated in Fig. 9-17. The physical connectivity of the medium establishes the logical connectivity of active stations on the ring. The token gives a station the opportunity to transmit frames. Each station around the ring repeats the data that it receives. Thus, a frame travels the full circle of the ring back to the source station which takes the frame off. A station

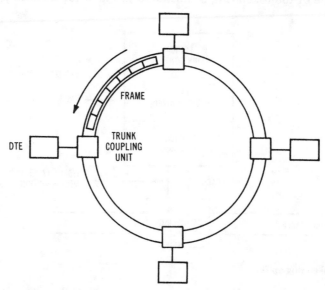

Fig. 9-17. Token ring operation.

passes the token to its physical successor when it has no more data to transmit, or when a token-holding timer has expired.

If the destination address matches the address of a receiving station, then that station sends the frame to its LLC layer. The frame is repeated on the ring, but 2 bits are set in the ending frame delimiter as previously described.

9.2.4.2 Physical Layer and Medium

Two physical layer and medium options are in the process of being defined for the token ring. One option uses 150-ohm shielded twisted pair. Data rates of 1 Mbps or 4 Mbps are specified. Baseband signaling is used with differential Manchester encoding.

A second option for higher data rates uses coaxial cable. Data rates of 4 Mbps, 20 Mbps, and 40 Mbps are specified. Baseband signaling with differential Manchester encoding is also employed.

9.3 OTHER PROTOCOL ISSUES

In Section 9.2, we discussed communication between stations on a LAN using various medium access control mechanisms: CSMA/CD and tokens, and various physical configurations. The many options defined within the IEEE 802 LAN standard all fit within the two lowest layers of the OSI reference model. IEEE 802 defines both the interface between the network layer and the data link control layer and the internal operation of the data link and physical layers.

However, many additional protocols are necessary for the total operation of a local network than just simply protocols to control access to a shared piece of cable. These additional protocols are the subject of this section. They will be discussed in five major areas: terminal interfacing, host interfacing, network management and control, internetting, and higher-level protocols. The relationship of these protocols is illustrated in Fig. 9-18.

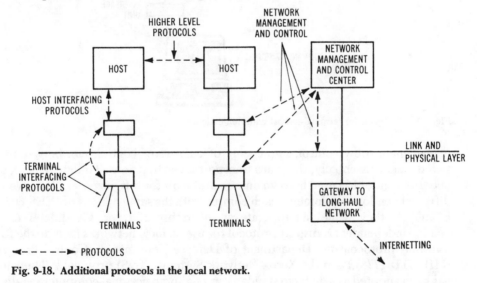

Fig. 9-18. Additional protocols in the local network.

9.3.1 Terminal Interfacing

Terminals connected to a local network need to be able to establish connections to various host computers on the network. A terminal command language provides for the opening and closing of connections. Once a connection is open, the terminal will be in a transparent mode in which characters entered at the terminal are forwarded to the host. An escape character must be available to return to the command mode. Other terminal commands will typically support setting parameters and determine the status of parameters and connections. Parameters can be set to manage such terminal- and host-dependent variables as echoing, data forwarding, padding, and speed. In addition, an interrupt capability is needed to convey an urgent signal to the host computer that bypasses the regular input-data stream. This is equivalent to the "break" key or other special character on a hard-wired terminal that will interrupt a program, stop output, etc.

The preceding features are similar to those provided by CCITT Recommendations X.3, X.28, and X.29 for interfacing asynchronous terminals to long-haul packet-switching networks. However, at present, there is no equivalent standard for terminal interfaces to local area networks.

When a connection is opened from a terminal to a particular host, a virtual circuit will generally be established between the terminal interface unit and the host interface unit (Fig. 9-19). The virtual circuit protocol will coordinate buffer

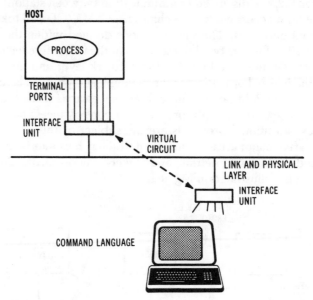

Fig. 9-19. Protocols for terminal-to-host communication.

management, flow control, sequencing of data, error control, etc. between the two devices. Essentially, these are transport layer functions. To date, each local network vendor has used his own unique protocols for this purpose. Thus, even if different vendors' equipments each comply with the same options of IEEE 802, it is unlikely they would interoperate at the transport layer. Candidates for a vendor-independent transport protocol for use on local networks include the ISO transport protocol,[2] the Department of Defense Transmission Control Protocol (MIL-STD 1778),[8] and the Xerox Network Systems (XNS) protocol.[11] The latter has been adopted as a de facto standard among some personal computer vendors, operating on top of Ethernet.

Stand-alone interface units implementing the preceding protocol can be used to connect terminals to a local network. A standard RS-232 connection is used between the terminal and the interface unit. Interface units supporting a cluster of several terminals can reduce the unit cost per terminal connection. In the future, the local network interface will increasingly be built into the terminal, and certainly into more intelligent workstations. The adoption of standards and the availablity of large-scale integration implementations, such as has already occurred for Ethernet, will make this economically attractive. However, it should be recognized that a standard transport-level protocol will also need to be built into the workstation if interoperability is to be attained.

9.3.2 Host Interfacing

Two fundamentally different approaches exist to interfacing host computers to a local network: terminal emulation and high-speed multiplexed interfaces.

With a terminal emulation approach, the local network interface unit is connected to separate physical terminal ports (Fig. 9-19). Thus, the network just looks to the host like a collection of terminals, each on its own port. When a terminal opens a connection, it is assigned an available port by the interface unit. The advantage of this approach is that it can be achieved without changes to any host that supports terminals. However, it is necessary that the host support flow control on the terminal ports, either by using the ASCII XON/XOFF flow control signals, or the RS-232 RTS/CTS modem control signals. The limitation of this approach is that it limits the functionality of the network to terminal access. That is, the host cannot initiate connections or communicate with other hosts.

With a multiplexed host interface, many logical connections can be supported over a single high-speed connection (Fig. 9-20). The hardware interface will pro-

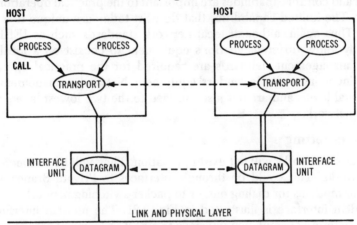

Fig. 9-20. Multiplexed host interface for process-to-process communication.

vide access to the host's channel or bus, and thus will be specific to that particular host. Appropriate software is required in the host to demultiplex the various connections. This software must be compatible with the transport and session layer protocols of the remote devices communicating with the host. However, such interfaces permit process-to-process applications, such as file transfers between hosts on a local network.

Terminal emulation interfaces are obviously the easiest to develop and most early local network products in the marketplace supported only terminal-to-host communications using such interfaces. However, high-speed interfaces are starting to appear, particularly those using Ethernet on the local network side and popular buses, such as Unibus and Multibus, on the host side.

9.3.3 Network Management and Control

The practical operation of a local network requires network management and control capabilities. Mature network technologies, such as multiplexers and packet-switching networks, have extensive capabilities built in for fault isolation, maintenance, and statistics reporting. In the case of local networks, such capabilities are still rather limited.

Fault isolation and diagnosis is clearly important for an operational system. This is necessary to locate faults in a backbone of a broadband or baseband cable system. It is also necessary to be able to detect faulty interface units.

To operate and maintain a system, capabilities are required to modify software in interface units, change parameters, etc. For example, new releases of software might need to be installed, or the address of a particular station changed. These changes could be performed either locally at an individual station or remotely from a network control center. The latter capability is desirable for a large operational network.

Network management functions include statistics collection and also, possibly, access control. For example, a network management center could control who is allowed to communicate with whom. It could also administer the issuing of session keys to two devices that want to encrypt data, using a unique key for the duration of a session.

It should be apparent from the preceding discussion that various network management and control capabilities are important to the practical operation of a local network. The limited capabilities that do exist today are unique to a particular vendor. Thus again, although local network standards such as IEEE 802 will potentially allow different vendor's equipment to coexist on a local network, network management standards are required for the practical operation of a network involving multiple vendors' equipment. Network management protocols span several layers and are not just confined to the two lowest layers internal to the local network.

9.3.4 Internetting

Local area networks will not exist in isolation. They will be connected to long-haul networks. This could be through interfaces to Private Branch Exchanges (PBXs), or modems for dialing out, or to packet-switching networks.

A modem interface is illustrated in Fig. 9-21. The modem interface is very similar to a terminal emulation interface to a host. A terminal user can establish a virtual connection to the modem interface. Then, by issuing additional commands to the modem interface itself, a circuit-switched connection can be established to a remote host or other local network. The modem interface will have to buffer data and will have to manage flow control.

When interconnecting packet-oriented local area networks with long-haul packet-switching networks, a fundamental choice is the protocol level in the gateway between the two networks. The gateways can operate at the datagram level, treating each packet as a self-contained entity and forwarding it on to the next network. This is also known as a *nontranslating gateway*. Alternatively, the gateway can operate at the virtual circuit level, essentially joining together virtual circuits through the two networks. In this case, the gateway is concerned with error control, sequencing, etc. of the data on a virtual circuit. This is known as a *translating gateway*.

Issues that have to be dealt with by a gateway include message size, addressing, routing, flow control, acknowledgements, and recovery. The approach to many of these issues is determined by the choice of a datagram or virtual circuit gateway.

Fig. 9-22 illustrates the connection of a local network to a long-haul network via

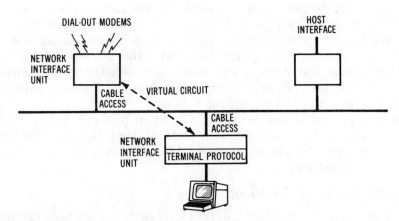

Fig. 9-21. Internetting using dial-out modems.

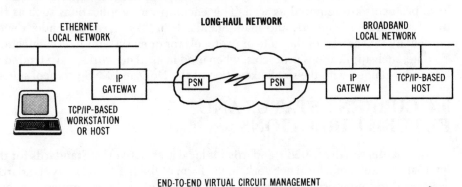

Fig. 9-22. Interconnection of datagram networks using IP gateways.

a datagram gateway. In this case, compatible protocols at the transport level and above are used in the two networks. Virtual circuit management, such as sequencing, retransmission, duplicate detection, and flow control, is performed on an end-to-end basis. The gateway operates at the internet level, routing each packet independently.

Fig. 9-23 illustrates the connection of a local network to a long-haul network via a virtual circuit gateway. In this case, incompatible transport-level protocols may be used in the two networks. The two virtual circuits are joined end-to-end in the

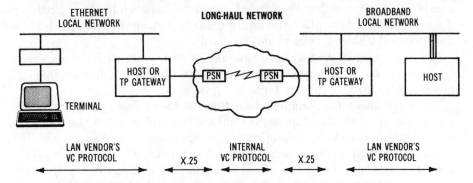

Fig. 9-23. Interconnection of virtual circuit networks using transport-level gateways.

gateway. Thus, the gateway is responsible for sequencing, retransmission, duplicate detection, and flow control. Any significant differences in the two protocols, such as in handling resetting, may be difficult for the gateway to deal with. Virtual circuit gateways, performing translation, may suffice for low-speed terminal-to-host connections, where there is a terminal user who can intervene in any unusual circumstances. However, their resilience remains to be demonstrated when used for process-to-process communication between hosts.

Datagram gateways with compatible transport protocols have been demonstrated using both the DoD and XNS protocol suites. However, the subject of routing between gateways, and the general control of large numbers of gateways, remains a research area.

9.3.5 Higher-Level Protocols

The importance of standard transport layer protocols has been discussed earlier. For fully interoperable open systems on a local network, standard higher-level protocols are required as well. This encompasses applications such as file transfer, remote file access, and mail. Standards in these areas are under development by ISO as part of the suite of protocols for open systems interconnection. To date, such applications protocols, when used in local networks, have tended to be vendor-unique with the small exception of the DoD and XNS protocol suites.

9.4 CURRENT STATUS AND FUTURE DIRECTIONS

This chapter has described standards for local area networks. Standards for the internal operation of a local network, in the form of the IEEE 802 LAN standards, are becoming established. However, the number of different options encompassed by IEEE 802 will result in incompatible local networks; just how many will be determined by the marketplace. Ethernet's early lead as a de facto standard has resulted in LSI and VLSI implementations and constantly dropping prices.[7] Consequently, more commercial local network products based on the Ethernet-based option of IEEE 802 have appeared than for any of the other IEEE 802 options. This includes not only terminal interfaces, but also boards for personal computers and for providing high-speed host interfaces to various computer buses.

Although a large number of CSMA/CD broadband systems are installed, the delay in arriving at a standard for these systems has inhibited their market. This is because the modems remain relatively expensive in the absence of large-scale integration which will only occur once standards are agreed. Moreover, there are competing approaches for broadband standards, between the type already predominant in the marketplace and an approach that maximizes compatibility with the approved CSMA/CD baseband standard.

Products based on the token bus have also started to appear in the marketplace. However, as more implementation experience is obtained, it appears that refinements will be made to the standard.

There are also a few products based on the token ring concept, though not necessarily precisely the same as the standard that will emerge. The token ring is eventually expected to be a significant influence because of its support by IBM.

However, even where compatible local networks are used, interoperability cannot be assumed. As was discussed in Section 9.3, compatible transport protocols are needed for interoperability among various devices on a local network.

For interoperability between the local network and a long-haul network, compatible transport-level protocols should be used in both networks. A few commercial local networks support the DoD TCP transport protocol, and somewhat more products use the XNS protocol at the transport level. Eventually, it is expected that the ISO transport protocol will become widely used. Translating gateways may be able to bridge between incompatible transport protocols, but their performance and reliability remains to be proven.

Standards at the internetting layer are particularly important if local networks are to be widely interconnected to long-haul networks. Internetwork standards will need to deal with such issues as addressing and routing. Internetwork standards are under development by ISO.

Higher-level protocol standards are needed for interoperability of applications systems even with a local network. This includes file transfer, remote file access, and mail systems. Standards for open systems interconnection in this area, being developed by ISO, should be applicable to local area networks.

9.5 REFERENCES

1. *ANSI X3.66*, ANSI X3.66—1979, Advanced Data Communications Control Procedures.

2. *DIS 8073*, Open Systems Interconnection—Connection-Oriented Transport Protocol Specification.

3. *IEEE 802.2*, IEEE 802.2—1983, Logical Link Control.

4. *IEEE 802.3*, IEEE 802.3—1983, CSMA/CD Access Method and Physical Layer Specifications.

5. *IEEE 802.4*, IEEE 802.4—1983, Token-Passing Bus Access Method and Physical Layer Specifications.

6. Metcalfe, R.M. and Boggs, D.R., Ethernet: Distributed Packet Switching for Local Computer Networks, *Comm. ACM*, July 1976, pp. 395-404.

7. Mier, E.E., Who's on Board for Ethernet?, *Data Communications*, May 1984, pp. 46-47, 62.

8. *MIL-STD 1778*, Transmission Control Protocol.

9. Shoch, J.F. et al, Evolution of the Ethernet Local Computer Network, *Computer*, August 1982, pp. 10-26.

10. Xerox Corporation, *Ethernet Specification*, September 1980.

11. Xerox Corporation, *Internet Transport Protocols*, December 1981.

12. Xerox Corporation, *Ethernet Specification*, *Revision 2.0*, December 1982.

Fiber-Optic Local Area Network Topology

S. Y. Suh

S. W. Granlund

S. S. Hegde

This article reviews the fundamental limitations of fiber optic links in the LAN environment and addresses the criteria for selecting a suitable topology for a fiber optic based LAN. It also discusses how the shortcomings of a bus topology can be circumvented by centralized star-like wiring topology. This centralized wiring topology is shown to be sufficiently flexible and well suited to fiber optic based LAN architectures

Network topologies suitable for local area networks (LAN's) are categorized briefly as bus, ring, and star. In the past few years, many different proposals for LAN architectures using combinations of the above basic topologies have appeared in the literature, and a variety of different protocols have been proposed for the transmission of data packets over these networks. In bus topology, coaxial cables or twisted-pair lines are commonly used as the transmission media. When a bidirectional broadcast channel is implemented, an Ethernet-type network using distributed controlled access protocols can be constructed. When a large number of terminals is connected to the network, signal losses and reflections at each connection cause critical problems in designing a stable system. Ring topologies allow very high data transmission rates to be used because of the point-to-point transmission in each link. However, rings have reliability problems due to the large number of active repeaters in the communication path. Reliability can be significantly enhanced by using counter-rotating double rings and/or active bypass switches to overcome the loss of power. In a counter-rotating double ring, the stations can be switched to an identical ring moving in the opposite direction when there is a break in the ring. Another reasonable way to increase reliability is to consolidate the repeaters into a central location. This eases the management and maintenance of each repeater, and changes the topology into a star. The central hub in the star has the function of collecting and delivering signals, as in a communication satellite. This centralized topology does raise another reliability issue in that a single point of failure may be totally unacceptable for some applications, for example, a military communication network.

Fiber-optic LAN's have begun to receive increasing attention as the technology for optical point-to-point data transmission matures [1,2]. Fiber-optic links have been used in the experimental LAN configurations mentioned below:

1) ring-configured networks [3]
2) passive star-configured networks such as Fibernet [4] and Codenet [5]
3) active star-configured networks [6]
4) cascade star network [7]
5) Hubnet [8]
6) broadband LAN's [9]

However, fiber optics is not a technology in widespread use in the LAN market today. Fiber optics has not been considered a suitable medium for LAN's, primarily due to its relatively high cost compared to metallic-based media. Fiber-optic networks were justifiable only for specialized applications, where one or more of the following applied:

1) long distance
2) high data rate
3) noisy environment (EMI)
4) ground loop
5) hazardous area (high voltage)
6) harsh environment (high temperature and high humidity)

Reprinted from *IEEE Communications Magazine*, Volume 24, Number 8, August 1986, pages 26-32. Copyright © 1986 by The Institute of Electrical and Electronics Engineers, Inc.

Rapid advances in fiber optic components and subsystems as well as standardization efforts are changing the criteria for using fiber optics in LAN's. As typical work stations become more powerful in processing speed and user-interface sophistication, the need for a high-bandwidth technology is inevitable; fiber-optic LAN's are likely to become commonplace in the near future. Rapid growth in the number of data processing users can cause a wiring congestion problem [10], and since wiring a building is an expensive operation, it is desirable to wire the building to last as long as the building stands. Thus, planners choose wiring which can handle large bandwidth signals and which is adaptable to future applications. Suitability for future use is itself a sufficient driving force to use fiber-optic technology as a cost-effective successor to today's metallic-based wiring technology.

In this paper, the salient features of fiber-optic technology are carefully evaluated for a LAN application. A centralized star topology that is well suited for a fiber optic LAN is identified and discussed.

Characteristics of Fiber-optic Media Relevant to LAN Applications

The signal-transporting characteristics of fiber-optic media are significantly different from those of electrical signals in copper cables, so that a mere replacement of copper wires by optical fibers does not make sense. Fiber-optic media offer many desirable properties over conventional metallic media, namely high bandwidth, low loss, noise immunity, physical size (weight), potentially low cost, etc. Among these, we will focus our attention on the specific characteristics which play a major role in determining a fiber-optic LAN topology.

Bandwidth Advantage of Fiber-optic Media

In the classical finite-state machine, input information is processed according to the stored instructions in the memory cells attached to the processor. As the processor becomes more powerful, the instructions to be stored in the memory increase proportionally, requiring an increased number of memory cells. This results in wiring congestion between the memory block and the processor. Use of a common bus between the memory block and the processor eliminates the wiring congestion, but introduces a new problem; namely, the bus does not allow simultaneous access from the memory cells. This access time limitation is known as the Von Neumann bottleneck.

Figure 1 illustrates this problem in a communication system wherein a large number of nodes share a common medium. This problem can be overcome by an efficient communication protocol and/or high link bandwidth. As network complexity and message exchange volume increase, the bandwidth of the medium will eventually be exceeded. In general, the greater the bandwidth of the physical medium, the larger the LAN that can be built and the greater the volume of messages that can be exchanged. Moreover, high bandwidth allows the use of a simple protocol which, though not efficient, can be implemented in cost-effective software. In this case, fiber-optic technology is well suited to support the high bandwidth required by a complex or busy LAN.

Low Attenuation Characteristics of Fiber-optic Media

A transmission system's capability is determined by balancing the available power budget, governed by the difference between transmitter (T) launch power and receiver (R) sensitivity, against transmission losses such as media attenuation, connector loss, power splitting loss, etc. In this section, we will concern ourselves with media attenuation versus the T/R pair power budget, ignoring all other sources of loss.

It is straightforward to compare the available transmitter-launched power of representative electronic and optical systems. A diode laser launches perhaps 1 mW into optical fibers, while an ECL line driver will deliver approximately 20 mW into a 50 Ω terminated coaxial cable. Indeed, an electronic power level of several watts is entirely practical; for example, a radio frequency (RF) power amplifier used in citizens band (CB) radio can provide five watts of power.

The difference between electronic and optical receiver sensitivities is more dramatic. Suppose that amplifiers and load resistors were noise free, such that the performance of either receiver would be limited by the noise associated with random photon arrival. Under these conditions, some 21 photons per bit are required for 10^{-9} BER [11]. The energy (E) of a photon can be calculated as

$$E = \frac{hc}{\lambda} \qquad (1)$$

where h is Plank's constant (6.6×10^{-34} joule sec), c is speed of light (3×10^{10} cm/sec), and λ is wavelength of photon. The power (P) contained in a digital data stream containing n photons per bit is

$$P = rnE = \frac{rnhc}{\lambda} \qquad (2)$$

where r is the data rate. With $r = 30$ Mbit/s, $n = 21$, and $\lambda = 1$ μm for the optical photons, we obtain an

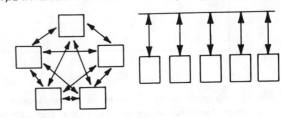

N(N—1)/2 INTERCONNECTIONS   N(N—1)/2 TIME SLOTS

- PARALLEL   • SERIAL
- NO ADDRESSES   • ADDRESS-ORIENTED
  - • TRADES TIME FOR INTERCONNECTIONS

Fig. 1. Broadcast bus bottleneck. Trade N(N—1)/2 time slots for N(N—1)/2 interconnections.

optical receiver sensitivity of −70 dBm. With frequency of electronic photon to be 30 MHz (same as the data rate of optical photons) and $\lambda = 10$m, we obtain an electronic receiver sensitivity of −140 dBm.

Thus, the ideal electronic receiver will be 70 dB more sensitive than the optical one, when producing the same receiver output signal intensity. Of course, practical receiver designs must include consideration of thermal noise and amplifier shot noise. The magnitude of thermal noise sources is on the order of kT, where k is the Boltzmann constant (1.38×10^{-23} joules/K), and T is the absolute temperature. At room temperature, $kT = 4 \times 10^{-21}$ joules. The energy of a 30 MHz electronic photon is 2×10^{-26} joules (using equation 1). This is several orders of magnitude less than the thermal electronic energy (4×10^{-21} joules) in the electronic circuits. This implies that thermal noise will completely dominate in the electronic receiver, but have little impact on the photonic one. Actually, it is more likely that thermal noise and, even more so, amplifier shot noise will dominate in both optical and electronic receivers. Thus, for electronic receivers, practical sensitivities are closer to −75 dBm at 30 MHz, while for fiber-optic PIN photodiode receivers, one can expect sensitivities of about −45 dBm at 30 MHz [12,13]. An avalanche photo detector (APD) receiver would add about 10 dB more to the above sensitivity, because of the avalanche gain of the APD [12,13].

The available power budget for an electronic transmission system will be at least +13 dBm − (−75 dBm) = 88 dB compared to a laser/PIN budget of 0 dBm − (−45 dBm) = 45 dB. The attenuation of a copper transmission line is typically 30 dB/Km at 30

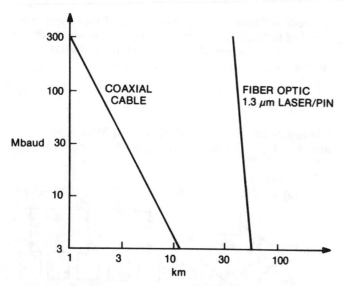

Fig. 2. *Representation bit rate vs. point-to-point link distance limitations for coaxial cable and fiber-optic transmission systems. Calculations are based on the following assumptions: Electronic transmitter power = 30 dBm. Electronic receiver sensitivity at 30 MHz = −75 dBm. Ethernet coaxial cable attenuation at 30 MHz = 30 dB/Km. 1.3 μm laser transmitter power = 0 dBm. PIN receiver sensitivity at 30 MHz = −45 dBm. Fiber attenuation (neglect dispersion) = 1 dB/Km.*

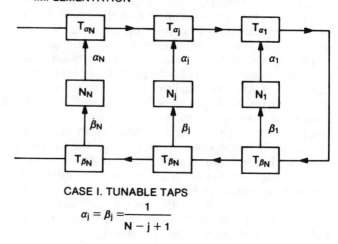

IMPLEMENTATION

CASE I. TUNABLE TAPS
$$\alpha_i = \beta_i = \frac{1}{N - j + 1}$$

CASE II. ARBITRARILY FIXED TAPS
$$\alpha_i = \beta_i = \gamma$$

Fig. 3. *Optical bus. α_j (β_j) is the tap ratio launching (splitting) the power from the jth node onto (from) the bus.*

MHz (Ethernet 50 Ω coaxial cable) and scales roughly as the square root of the bit rate. The attenuation of an optical fiber at a wavelength of 1.3 μm is 1 dB/Km, almost independent of bit rate (neglecting dispersion). Representative performance limits of electronic and optical transmission systems are plotted in Fig. 2. Available power budget is equated with transmission loss to determine the bit rate versus link distance trade off. Receiver sensitivity is specified for a specific bandwidth, and it is assumed that bandwidth trades off with sensitivity on a one-to-one basis.

The very low attenuation of optical fiber more than compensates for the limited power budget. This explains why the initial fiber-optic application has been mostly in long-distance telecommunication links. However, the long-distance capability of fiber optics is of little value in LAN designs, because the size of a LAN is limited by the maximum allowed network propagation delay, as determined by the access protocol, and thus a LAN is usually no larger than 1-2 Km.

Limitations of Fiber Optics in Tapped Bus Networks

One of the prerequisites to sharing a common communication medium is the broadcasting capability of the transmission system. Can fiber-optic technology support a short-distance multidrop broadcast-type network? For such a network, optical taps, as shown in Fig. 4, are required to split or combine optical power. For lossless ideal optical taps, the output powers are

$$P_o^\alpha = (1 - \alpha) P_I^\alpha + \alpha P_T^\alpha \qquad (3)$$

for a power-combining tap, T_α; and

$$P_o^\beta = (1 - \beta) P_I^\beta \qquad (4)$$

and

$$P_R^\beta = \beta P_I^\beta \qquad (5)$$

for a power-splitting tap, T_β, as a result of energy conservation and lightwave propagation reciprocity. The notations used in Eqs. 3–5 are described in the caption of Fig. 4. Applying these relationships to the tapped optical bus shown in Fig. 3, it is straightforward to compute the available power budget between any pair of nodes in a tapped bus system.

Figure 5 shows the numerical results of the power budget calculation for two extreme cases: in case I, α and β have been chosen to optimize the system performance, and in case II α and β have been assigned arbitrary fixed values ($\alpha = \beta = 1/5$). The calculation is based on the lossless condition. Case I represents the theoretical upper limit of the tapped optical bus capability, and indicates that the maximum allowable network size is no greater than about 30 nodes. However, this number reduces quickly to about 10 nodes for a more realistic situation, that is, a fixed-tap ratio (case II). In addition, the required optical receiver dynamic range increases very rapidly as the number of nodes increases (Fig. 5). Of course, in a real system, transmission losses (connector loss, splice loss, fiber attenuation, dispersion penalty, etc.) have to be included. Therefore, without using an expensive laser at each node, the number of nodes in a practical fiber-optic tapped bus network will be few (10 or less).

By including a head-end repeater, depicted in Fig. 6, the system performance constraint imposed by tap reciprocity is avoided. Without a head-end repeater, the optical signal is attenuated twice; once when launched (T_α) onto the bus, and once when tapped off (T_β). With a head-end repeater, the optical signal is still attenuated when launched, but it is regenerated before being

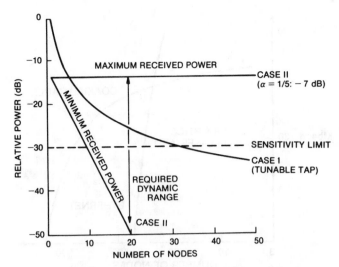

Fig. 5. Inherent loss characteristics of tapped optical bus. The sensitivity limit is calculated based on the following assumption: Launched optical power = 100 μW. Required number of photon/bit = 1000 photons. Wavelength = 1 μm. Data rate = 500Mb/s. Case I: continuously tunable tap. Case II: arbitrarily fixed tap ($\alpha = \beta = 1/5$).

tapped off. Effectively, the receiver can be designed as if all power were launched onto the bus, and there is no head-end repeater. It is now more appropriate to plot bandwidth against number of nodes and assume some fixed network extent, such as 1 Km.

Figure 7 plots performance limits for a tapped bus without a head-end repeater (example, Ethernet) and for a tapped bus with a head-end repeater (0.8-μm wavelength laser/APD detector). As implied in Fig. 7, fiber optics is still limited in a tapped bus by the available power budget balanced against the 0.25 dB splice loss and uneven power tapping along the bus. Even lasers and APD's do not provide enough power budget to compete with an electronic transceiver at rates less than 100 Mbaud. When the connectors are included in the system, the head-end repeated tapped optical bus becomes practically useless for a LAN application.

Star Topology for Fiber-optic LAN

The limited power budget, together with the unavoidably high total loss of tapping/launching optical

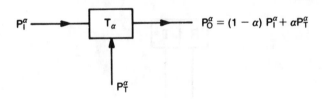

1) POWER COMBINING TAP (T_α)

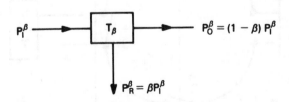

2) POWER SPLITTING TAP (T_β)

Fig. 4. Ideal optical tap. 1. Power-combining tap (T_α). P_I^α (P_T^α) is the power injection from the bus (node) to the power-combining tap, Tα. P_o^α is the total power injection onto the bus from the tap, T_α. 2. Power-splitting tap (T_β). P_I^β is the power injection from the bus to the power-splitting tap, T_β. P_o^β (P_R^β) is the power injection from the tap, T_β, onto the bus (node).

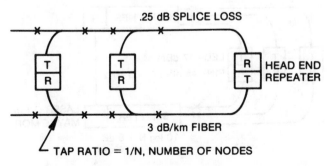

Fig. 6. Tapped bus with head-end repeater.
T = transmitter. R = receiver.

August 1986—Vol. 24, No. 8
IEEE Communications Magazine

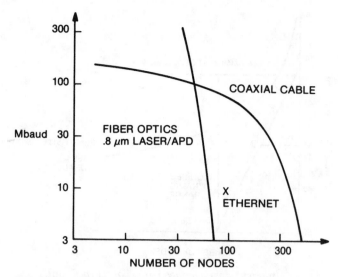

Fig. 7. *Representative bit rate vs. number of node limitations for coaxial cable and fiber-optic tapped buses. Calculations are based on the following assumptions: Electronic transmitter power = 30 dBm. Electronic receiver sensitivity at 30 MHz = 30 dB/Km. Ethernet coaxial cable attenuation at 30 MHz = 30 dB/Km. 0.82 μm laser transmitter power = 0 dBm. APD receiver sensitivity at 30 MHz = −58 dBm. Fiber attenuation (neglecting dispersion) = 3 dB/Km. Link distance = 1 Km.*

power with reciprocal couplers, sharply limits the use of fiber for bus-type LAN's. However, star geometries are very attractive when implemented optically, because the loss due to many connectors can be avoided and they use point-to-point communication links. In this section, we will examine how this centralized, star-like wiring scheme can be used to implement a variety of optical LAN architectures.

Simple Active Star Bus

Figure 8 depicts an optical star topology bus. Figure 9 shows the network performance limitations of the optical star represented in Fig. 8. An active repeater-star optical network makes it practical to use LED's at the nodes. At the star's center, a laser's output is distributed into a bundle of fibers. Alternatively, a large-area, presumably high-power LED could be butt-

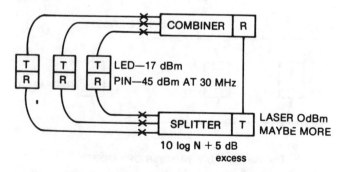

Fig. 8. *Optical star network topology. T = optical transmitter. R = receiver.*

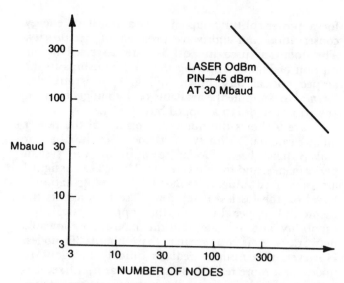

Fig. 9. *Representative bit rate vs. number of node limitations for fiber-optic star bus. Calculations are based on the same assumptions used in Fig. 7, except that the receiver sensitivity is assumed to be −45 dBm (PIN receiver).*

coupled to the fiber bundle, or an LED array could be coupled to ribbon cable. By interconnecting active stars of moderate size (about 20 fibers), reasonably large (several hundred nodes) optical networks would be practical.

In addition, an active star can include intelligence at its hub, so the network access protocol is simplified. In this way, the total cost of network interface equipment

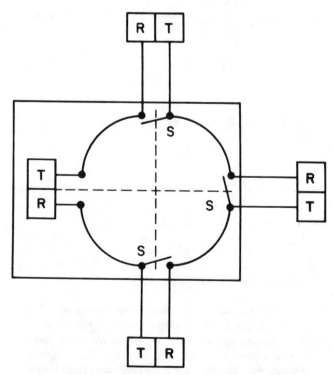

Fig. 10. *Centralized ring. T = optical transmitter. R = optical receiver. S = optical bypass switch.*

is minimized. Furthermore, the central intelligence facilitates network maintainability and provides network security (for example, denying unauthorized resource access), as well as ease of billing, broadcasting network information, etc.

Centralized Fiber-optic Ring

Figure 10 shows a centralized ring. By providing active bypass switches at the center of the ring, the reliability of the ring network can be greatly enhanced. Since the ring uses only point-to-point-type communication links, the fundamental limitations of fiber-optic technology discussed above do not apply.

Repeated Star

When all fibers at the star center are terminated by n number of T/R pairs, as shown in Fig. 11 (n is the number of nodes), signal combining and splitting or switching can be done in the electronic domain, and the fiber-optic topology becomes essentially point-to-point. This method offers several advantages: (1) collision detection can be done at the hub; (2) the network can be expanded gracefully; and (3) crosspoint circuit switching can be implemented. Furthermore, buffer memory may be allocated to the nodes and the hub so that each node may transmit at any time and the hub interrogate its memory either sequentially or by priority. In this design, there is an immense potential for point-to-point data links.

Conclusion

The application of fiber-optic technology to local area networks has been discussed. Because fiber-optic data links have a limited available power budget compared to electronic data links, fiber-optic networks can only support a limited number of stations. Nonetheless, it is practical to build large networks, provided a star topology with active repeating of the optical signals at the hub is used. The advantages of this centralized active hub scheme include the use of fiber-optic technology to its fullest capability as point-to-point links and the convenience of central data processing, data base storage, and maintenance services.

The centralized wiring topology proposed in this paper is sufficiently flexible and well suited for the design of an optical-fiber network to accommodate the various incompatible requirements imposed by offices of the future, fully automated factory floors, and hospital information systems.

Acknowledgment

The authors acknowledge useful discussions with D. A. Snyder, C. J. Daniels, and D. E. Tamburino, and the encouragement of W. A. Stocker, P. I. Slicks, and F. S. Welsh, III.

References

[1] S. D. Personick, "Applications for fiber optics in local area networks," *Proceedings of the 8th European Conference on Optical Fibers*, Cannes, p. 425, Sept. 1982.

[2] N. L. Rhodes, "Interacting a network design and fiber optic components design in local area networks," *IEEE J. Selected Areas in Comm.*, vol. sac-1, 489, 1983.

[3] W. F. Giozza and G. Noguez, "FIPNET: A 10 MBPS fiber-optics local network," *ACM Comput. Commun. Rev.*, vol. 12, pp. 6–20, Apr. 1982.

[4] E. G. Rawson, "Optical fibers for local computer networks," *Tech. Dig. Topical Mtg. Opt. Fiber Commun.*, Washington, D.C., Paper WEI, Mar. 1979.

[5] J. R. Jones, J. S. Kennedy, and F. W. Scholl, "A prototype CSMA/CD local area network using fiber optics," *Proc. Local Area Networks*, Los Angeles, CA, pp. 78–92, Sept. 1982.

[6] R. V. Schmidt, E. G. Rawson, R. E. Norton, Jr., S. B. Jackson, and M. D. Bailey, "Fibernet II: a fiber optic ethernet," *IEEE J. Selected Areas in Commun.*, vol. sac-1, no. 5, pp. 702–711, Nov. 1983.

[7] T. Tamura, M. Nakamura, S. Ohshima, T. Ito, and T. Ozeki, "Optical cascade star network—a new configuration for a passive distribution system with optical collision detection capability," *J. Lightwave Technol.*, vol. 1t-2, no. 1, pp. 61–65, Feb. 1984.

[8] E. S. Lee and P. I. P. Boulton, "The principles and performance of Hubnet: a 50 Mbit/s glass fiber local area network," *IEEE J. Selected Areas in Commun.*, vol. sac-1, no. 5, pp. 711–720, Nov. 1983.

[9] E. Hara, "A fiber optic broadband LAN/OCS using a PBX," *IEEE Communications Mag.*, pp. 22–27, Oct. 1983.

[10] M. Akhtar, "Evaluating a building-wide local area network," *Proc. Local Net '83*, New York, NY, p. 61, Sept. 1983.

[11] S. E. Miller and A. G. Chynoweth (ed.), "Optical fiber telecommunications," Academic Press, pp. 630–632, 1979.

[12] D. R. Smith, R. C. Hooper, P. P. Smythe, and D. Wake, "Experimental comparison of a Germanium avalanche photodiode and InGaAs PIN/FET receiver for longer wavelength optical communications systems," *Electron. Lett.*, vol. 18, no. 10, pp. 453–454, 1982.

[13] R. G. Smith, C. A. Brackett, H. W. Reinbold, "Atlanta fiber system experiment: optical detector package," *Bell Syst. Tech. J.*, vol. 57, no. 6, pp. 1809–1822, July–Aug., 1978.

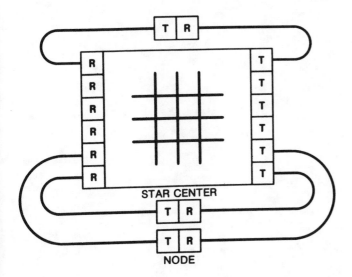

Fig. 11. Terminated active star. T = optical transmitter. R = optical receiver.

S. Y. Suh received a B.S. in chemistry from Seoul National University in 1968, an M.S. in physical chemistry from the University of Minnesota in 1977, and a Ph.D in analytical chemistry from the University of Michigan, Ann Arbor, MI, in 1980.

In 1980, he joined AT&T Bell Laboratories at Allentown, PA, where he worked on the characterization and fabrication of optical recording materials and the design of fiber optic communication devices.

Stephen W. Granlund received a B.S. in Physics from Moravian College, Bethlehem, PA, in 1980 and an M.S. in Electrical Engineering from Lehigh University, Bethlehem, PA, in 1985.

He joined AT&T Bell Laboratories in 1980 and has been working on the design of passive optical devices for fiber-optic communications.

Shankar S. Hegde is a Member of Technical Staff at AT&T Bell Laboratories in Holmdel, New Jersey, working on the product architecture, requirements, design, and development of a radiology information (text and images) movement and management system.

Prior to joining Bell Laboratories, he worked at CGR Medical Corporation, General Electric Company, and Westmoreland Coal Company. At CGR, he was an engineering manager for digital subtraction angiography product development. At GE, he designed and developed image processing software for Multispectral scanner and then led the development of Thematic Mapper Image Processing System (LANDSAT-4 Satellite System). At Westmoreland Coal Company, he designed and developed interactive graphics packages related to mine simulation.

He received a Ph.D from Purdue University in 1977 and then spent a year at Brown University as a post-doctoral research fellow. He has published several articles and is a senior member of the I.E.E.E. ∎

Section 3: High-Speed Local Networks

3.1 Applications

High-speed local networks are intended to meet a variety of requirements and to be used for applications where the higher cost of a high-speed local network (compared to the IEEE 802 variety) is justified. Three general areas of application are addressed by HSLNs:

- Backend local network
- High-speed office networks
- Backbone local networks

Backend Local Networks

Backend local networks are used in a computer-room environment to interconnect mainframe computers and mass storage devices [THOR79]. The key requirement here is for bulk data transfer among a limited number of devices in a small area. High reliability is also a requirement. Typical characteristics include:

- *High data rate:* To keep up with the high-volume demand, data rates of 50 to 100 Mbps are needed.
- *High-speed interface:* File transfer operations are typically performed through high-speed paralled I/O interfaces, rather than slower communications interfaces. Thus the physical link between station and network must be high speed.
- *Distributed access:* For reasons of reliability and efficiency, a distributed medium access control (MAC) technique is used.
- *Limited distance:* Generally, a backend local network will be employed in a computer room or a small number of rooms.
- *Limited number of devices:* The number of expensive mainframes and mass storage devices found in the computer room is generally in the 10s of devices.

In addition to the need for high data rate, the backend network introduces a performance requirement that relates to the type of traffic to be handled. The backend network is more likely to see the file transfer application as opposed to interactive usage. For efficient operation, the MAC protocol should permit sustained use of the medium either by permitting transmissions of unbounded length or permitting a pair of devices to seize the channel for an indefinite period. The former has not in practice been used because it is not desirable to send long blocks of data; a single error necessitates the retransmission of the entire block. The latter technique, which is used in a number of networks, including HYPERchannel and FDDI, permits a multiframe dialogue between two devices, with no other data allowed on the medium for the duration of the dialogue. This permits a long sequence of data frames and acknowledgments to be interchanged. An example of the utility of this feature is its use to read from or write to high-performance disks. Without the ability to seize the network temporarily, only one section of the disk could be accessed per revolution—a totally unacceptable performance.

High-Speed Office Networks

Traditionally, the office environment has included a variety of devices with low to medium-speed data transfer requirements. The requirements of such an environment can be met in a cost-effective manner by the type of local network specified in the IEEE 802 standards. However, new applications in the office environment are being developed for which the limited speeds (1 to 10 Mbps) of the typical local area network (LAN) are inadequate. Desktop image processors could soon increase network data flow by an unprecedented amount [BEVA86]. Examples of these applications include fax machines, document image processors, and graphics programs on personal computers. Resolutions as high as 400×400 per page are standard for these applications. Even with compression techniques, this will generate a tremendous load. Table 3.1 compares the load generated by image processing and some other office applications. In addition, optical disks are beginning to reach technical maturity and are being developed toward realistic desktop capacities exceeding 1 Gbyte. These new demands will require local networks with high speed that can support the larger numbers and greater geographic extent of offices systems as compared to computer room networks.

Backbone Local Networks

The increasing use of distributed processing applications and personal computers has led to a need for a flexible strategy for local networking. Support of premises-wide data communications requires a networking and communications service that is capable of spanning the distances involved and that interconnects equipment in a single (perhaps large) building or a cluster of buildings. While it is possible to develop a single local network to interconnect all the data processing equipment of a premises, this is probably not a practical alternative in most cases. There are several drawbacks:

- *Reliability:* With a single local network, a service interruption, even of short duration, could result in major disruption for users.

Table 3.1: Comparison of Load Generated by Various Devices

Traffic Type	Size in Bits
Compressed page image (400 × 400)	600,000
Compressed page image (200 × 200)	250,000
Word processing page	20,000
Typical memo (electronic mail)	3,500
Data processing transaction	500

- *Capacity:* A single local network could be saturated as the number of devices attached to the network grows over time.

- *Cost:* A single network technology is not optimized for the diverse requirements for interconnection and communication. The presence of large numbers of low-cost microcomputers dictates that network support for these devices be provided at low cost. Local networks that support very low cost attachment will not be suitable for meeting the overall requirement.

A more attractive alternative is to employ lower-cost, lower-capacity local networks within buildings or departments and to link these networks with a higher-capacity (and therefore higher-cost) local network. This latter network is referred to as a backbone local network.

Although many studies have shown that intradepartmental and intrabuilding communications greatly exceed interdepartmental and interbuilding communications, it is to be expected that the backbone local network in a large distributed processing environment will have to sustain high peak loads and, as the demand for communications grows over time, high sustained loads. Thus a major requirement for the backbone is high capacity.

3.2 Coaxial-Cable HSLNs

Until recently, HSLN technology has been dominated by the coaxial-cable bus architecture used in a backend application. These HSLNs share a number of characteristics with bus-based LANs. In particular, a packet-broadcasting technique is used and, because the medium is multi-access, a medium access control technique is needed to regulate the right of transmission.

Two signaling approaches have been used with bus topology HSLNs. The single-channel broadband is the basis for a pending ANSI standard referred to as Local Distributed Data Interface (LDDI); it is also the technique used in Control Data's Loosely Coupled Network product. The baseband technique is used in the oldest and most widely used HSLN, Network System Corporation's HYPERchannel. These approaches have much in common, including the following characteristics:

- *Data rate of 50 Mbps:* At this speed, the cost of the HSLN attachment is significantly greater than that of a LAN.

- *Maximum length of about 1 km:* This limit is dictated by the data rate and medium access control technique, but is adequate for computer-room requirements.

- *Maximum number of stations in the tens:* Again, this is dictated by the data rate, and is adequate for computer-room requirements.

- *Provisions for multiple (up to four) cables:* This increases throughput and reliability.

A somewhat similar approach is found in DEC's VAX-cluster product, which is physically a passive star but logically a bus. This approach is one of the physical-layer options for LDDI. One of the papers in this section examines this HSLN.

3.3 Fiber HSLNs

Because of the potentially high data rate of optical fiber, this medium is attractive for implementing an HSLN. As with fiber LANs, fiber HSLNs have been slow in developing. The same ANSI committee that has worked on LDDI has produced an optical fiber ring standard known as Fiber Distributed Data Interface (FDDI). The committee felt that the ring offered fewer technical problems than the bus and thus concentrated on this topology for the fiber medium. Two of the articles in this section deal with FDDI.

Although a true optical-fiber bus HSLN is not yet commercially feasible, there is considerable research in this area, and products will eventually appear. One of the articles in this section deals with such HSLNs.

3.4 Article Summary

The first article deals with the DEC HSLN product, VAXcluster. The technology used in this product is a 70-Mbps passive star coupler. With this scheme, a transmission into the central node is retransmitted out along all attached links via transformer coupling. A transmission from one station is received by all other stations, and only one station at a time can successfully transmit. Thus, the configuration is physically a star but logically a bus. This configuration is one of the alternatives in the draft ANSI LDDI standard.

The next two papers deal with the optical-fiber HSLN standard developed by ANSI: the fiber distributed data interface (FDDI), which is a 100-Mbps token ring. This is the first fiber HSLN standard, and the first commercially feasible fiber HSLN technology, and reflects the fact that fiber optic technology is reaching maturity for local network applications. The first of the two articles, by Joshi, is an overview of the entire standard. The article discusses application areas, the physical layer, reliability mechanisms, medium access control, and capacity allocation. The next article, "The FDDI Optical Data Link," concentrates on the physical layer of FDDI, and examines the technology of optical fiber as applied to a ring local network.

The final article in this section deals with a just-emerging area: the optical fiber bus. "Tokenless Protocols for Fiber Optic Local Area Networks" examines the critical problem of minimizing overhead in performing medium access control on a high-speed bus. If the overhead is high, then the benefit of the high data rate is lost. The authors describe and compare a number of approaches.

VAXclusters: A Closely-Coupled Distributed System

NANCY P. KRONENBERG, HENRY M. LEVY, and WILLIAM D. STRECKER
Digital Equipment Corporation

A VAXcluster is a highly available and extensible configuration of VAX computers that operate as a single system. To achieve performance in a multicomputer environment, a new communications architecture, communications hardware, and distributed software were jointly designed. The software is a distributed version of the VAX/VMS operating system that uses a distributed lock manager to synchronize access to shared resources. The communications hardware includes a 70 megabit per second message-oriented interconnect and an interconnect port that performs communications tasks traditionally handled by software. Performance measurements show this structure to be highly efficient, for example, capable of sending and receiving 3000 messages per second on a VAX-11/780.

Categories and Subject Descriptors: C.2.5 [**Computer Communications Networks**]: Local Networks—*buses*; D.4.3 [**Operating Systems**]: File Systems Management—*distributed file systems*; D.4.4 [**Operating Systems**]: Communications Management; D.4.5 [**Operating Systems**]: Reliability—*fault-tolerance*; D.4.7 [**Operating Input/Output Systems**]: Organization and Design—*performance*

General Terms: Design, Performance, Reliability

Additional Key Words and Phrases: Device control protocols, distributed database management, intersystem communication protocols, network protocols, resource locking

1. INTRODUCTION

Contemporary multicomputer systems typically lie at the ends of the spectrum delimited by tightly-coupled multiprocessors and loosely-coupled distributed systems. Loosely-coupled systems are characterized by physical separation of processors, low-bandwidth message-oriented interprocessor communication, and independent operating systems [1, 2, 5, 13]. Tightly-coupled systems are characterized by close physical proximity of processors, high-bandwidth communication through shared memory, and a single copy of the operating system [7, 9, 15].

An intermediate approach taken at Digital Equipment Corporation was to build a "closely-coupled" structure of standard VAX computers [16], called *VAXclusters*. By closely-coupled, we imply that a VAXcluster has characteristics of both loosely- and tightly-coupled systems. On one hand, a VAXcluster has separate processors and memories connected by a message-oriented interconnect, running separate copies of a distributed VAX/VMS operating system. On the

Authors' addresses: N. P. Kronenberg and W. D. Strecker, Digital Equipment Corporation, 295 Foster Street, Littleton, MA 01460; H. M. Levy, Department of Computer Science, University of Washington, Seattle, WA 98195.

ACM Transactions on Computer Systems, Vol. 4, No. 2, May 1986, Pages 130–146.

other hand, the cluster relies on close physical proximity, a single (physical and logical) security domain, shared physical access to disk storage, and high-speed memory-to-memory block transfers between nodes.

The goals of the VAXcluster multicomputer system are high availability and easy extensibility to a large number of processors and device controllers. In contrast to other highly available systems [3, 4, 10, 11], VAXcluster is built from general-purpose, off-the-shelf processors and a general-purpose operating system. A key concern in this approach is system performance. Two important factors in the performance of a multicomputer system are the software overhead of the communications architecture and the bandwidth of the computer interconnect. To address these issues, several developments were undertaken, including:

(1) A simple, low-overhead communications architecture whose functions are tailored to the needs of highly available, extensible systems. This architecture is called SCA (System Communication Architecture).
(2) A very high speed message-oriented computer interconnect, termed the CI (Computer Interconnect).
(3) An intelligent hardware interface to the CI, called the CI Port, that implements part of SCA in hardware.
(4) An intelligent, message-oriented mass storage controller that uses both the CI and the CI Port interface.

This paper describes the new communications hardware developed for VAXclusters, the hardware-software interface, and the structure of the distributed VAX/VMS operating system. The developments described in this paper are part of Digital's VAXcluster product; there are, as of early 1985, approximately 2000 VAXcluster systems in operation.

2. VAXcluster HARDWARE STRUCTURE

Figure 1 shows the topology of an example VAXcluster. The components of a VAXcluster include the CI, VAX hosts, CI Ports, and HSC-50 mass storage (i.e., disk and tape) controllers. For high reliability applications, a cluster must contain a minimum of two VAX processors and two mass storage controllers with dual-ported devices. The preferred method of attaching terminals is through a Local Area Terminal server (not shown in the figure), which allows a terminal to connect to any host in a VAXcluster.

The CI is a dual path serial interconnect with each path supporting a 70 Mbit/s transfer rate. The primary purpose of the dual paths is to provide redundancy in the case of path failure, but when both paths are available they are usable concurrently. Each path is implemented in two coaxial cables: one for transmitted and one for received signals. Baseband signaling with Manchester encoding is employed.

While the CI is logically a bus, it is physically organized as a star topology. A central hub called the Star Coupler connects all of the nodes through radial CI paths of up to 45 meters. The current coupler is a passive device that supports a maximum of 16 nodes; node addresses are 8 bits providing an architectural limit of 256 nodes.

The selection of a star topology was chosen over a conventional linear topology for several reasons. First, the efficiency of a serial bus is related to the longest

ACM Transactions on Computer Systems, Vol. 4, No. 2, May 1986.

171

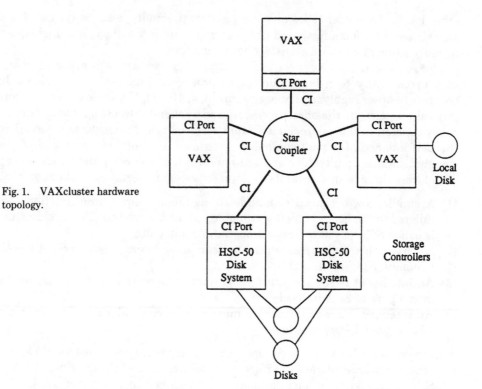

Fig. 1. VAXcluster hardware topology.

transit time between nodes. The star permits nodes to be located within a 45 meter radius (about 6400 square meters) with a maximum node separation of 90 meters. Typically, a linear bus threaded through 16 nodes in the same area would greatly exceed 90 meters. Second, the central coupler provides simple, electrically and mechanically safe addition and removal of nodes.

The CI port is responsible for arbitration, path selection, and data transmission. Arbitration uses carrier sense multiple access (CSMA) but is different from the arbitration used by Ethernet [12]. Each CI port has a node-specific delay time. When wishing to transmit, a port waits until the CI is quiet and then waits its specific delay time. If the CI is still quiet the node has won its arbitration and may send its packet. This scheme gives priority to nodes with short delay times. To ensure fairness, nodes actually have two delay times—one relatively short and one relatively long. Under heavy loading, nodes alternate between short and long delays. Thus, under light loading the bus is contention driven and under heavy loading it is round robin.

When a port wins an arbitration, it sends a data packet and waits for receipt of an acknowledgement. If the data packet is correctly received, the receiving port immediately returns an acknowledgement packet *without* rearbitrating the CI. This is possible because the CI port can generate an acknowledgement in less time than the smallest node-specific delay. Retries are performed if the sending CI port does not receive an acknowledgement.

To distribute transmissions across both paths of the dual-path CI, the CI port maintains a *path status table* indicating which paths to each node are currently

ACM Transactions on Computer Systems, Vol. 4, No. 2, May 1986.

good or bad. Assuming that both paths are marked good, the CI port chooses one randomly. This provides statistical load sharing and early detection of failures. Should repeated retries fail on one path, that path is marked bad in the status table and the other path is tried.

3. THE CI PORT ARCHITECTURE

Each cluster host or mass storage controller connects to the CI through a CI port. CI ports are device specific and have been implemented for the HSC-50 mass storage controller and the VAX 11/750, VAX 11/780, VAX 11/782, VAX 11/785, and VAX/8600 hosts. All CI ports implement a common architecture, whose goals are to:

(1) Offload much of the communications overhead typically performed by nodes in distributed systems.
(2) Provide a standard, message-oriented software interface for both interprocessor communication and device control.

The design of the CI port is based on the needs of the VMS System Communications Architecture. SCA is a software layer that provides efficient communications services to low-level distributed applications (e.g., device drivers, file services, and network managers). SCA supports three communications services: datagrams, messages, and block data transfers.

SCA datagrams and messages are information units of less than 4 kbytes sent over a connection. They differ only in reliability. Delivery of datagrams is not guaranteed; they can be lost, duplicated, or delivered out of order. Delivery of messages is guaranteed, as is their order of arrival. Datagrams are used for status and information messages whose loss is not critical, and by applications such as DECNET that have their own high-level reliability protocols. Messages are used, for example, to carry disk read and write requests.

To simplify buffer allocation, hosts must agree on the maximum size of messages and datagrams that they will transmit. VAXcluster hosts use standard sizes of 576 bytes for datagrams and 112 bytes for messages. These sizes are keyed to the needs of DECNET and the lock management protocol, respectively.

To ensure delivery of messages without duplication or loss, each CI port maintains a virtual circuit with every other cluster port. A virtual circuit descriptor table in each port indicates the status of its port-to-port virtual circuits. Included in each virtual circuit descriptor are sending and receiving sequence numbers. Each transmitted message carries a sequence number enabling duplicate packets to be discarded.

Block data is any contiguous data in a process' virtual address space. There is no size limit except that imposed by the virtual and physical memory constraints of the host. CI ports are capable of copying block data directly from process virtual memory on one node to process virtual memory on another node.

Delivery of block data is guaranteed. The sending and receiving ports cooperate in breaking up the transfer into data packets and ensuring that all packets are correctly transmitted, received, and placed in the appropriate destination buffer. Virtual circuit sequence numbers are used on the individual packets, as with messages. Thus, the major differences between block data and messages are the

ACM Transactions on Computer Systems, Vol. 4, No. 2, May 1986.

size of the transfer and the fact that block data does not need to be copied by the host operating system. Block data transfers are used, for example, by disk subsystems to move data associated with disk read and write requests.

3.1 CI Port Interface

The VAX CI Port interface is shown in Figure 2. The interface consists of a set of seven queues: four command queues, a response queue, a datagram free queue, and a message free queue. The queues and queue headers are located in host memory. When the port is initialized, host software loads a port register with the address of a descriptor for the queue headers.

Host software and the port communicate through queued command and response packets. To issue a port command, port driver software queues a command packet to one of the four command queues. The four queues allow for four priority levels; servicing is FIFO within each queue. An opcode within the packet specifies the command to be executed. The response queue is used by the port to enqueue incoming messages and datagrams, while the free queues are a source of empty packets for incoming messages and a sink for transmitted message packets.

For example, to send a datagram, software queues a SEND DATAGRAM packet onto one of the command queues. The packet contains an opcode field specifying SEND DATAGRAM, a port field containing the destination port number, the datagram size, and the text of the datagram. The packet is doubly linked through its first two fields. This structure is shown in Figure 3.

If host software needs confirmation when the packet is sent, it sets a *response queue* bit in the packet. This bit causes the port to place the packet in the response queue after the packet has been transmitted. The response packet is identical to the SEND DATAGRAM packet, except that the status field indicates whether the send was successful. Had the response queue flag bit been clear in the SEND DATAGRAM command (as it typically is), the port would instead place the transmitted command packet on the datagram free queue.

When a CI port receives a datagram, it takes a packet from its datagram free queue. Should the queue be empty, the datagram is discarded. Otherwise, the port constructs a DATAGRAM RECEIVED packet that contains the datagram text and the port number of the sending port. This packet is then queued on the response queue.

Messages operate in a similar fashion, except that they have a different opcode and message buffers are dequeued from the message free queue. If the message free queue is empty when a message arrives, the port generates an error interrupt to the host. High level SCA flow control ensures that the message free queue does not become empty.

Block transfer operations are somewhat more complicated. Each port has a data structure called a *buffer descriptor table*. Before performing a block transfer, host software creates a buffer descriptor that defines the virtual memory buffer to be used. The descriptor contains a pointer to the first VAX page table entry mapping the virtually contiguous buffer. In addition, the descriptor contains the offset (within the first page) of the first byte of the buffer, the length of the buffer, and a 16-bit key. The data structures for a block transfer are illustrated in Figure 4.

ACM Transactions on Computer Systems, Vol. 4, No. 2, May 1986.

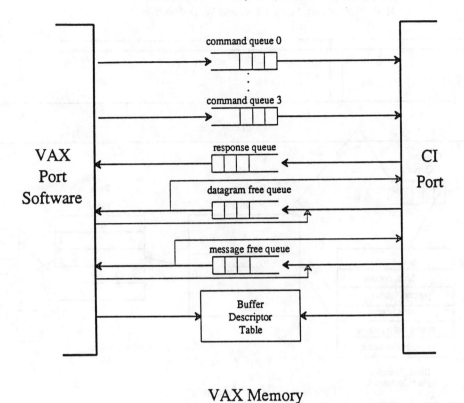

VAX Memory

Fig. 2.   CI Port interface.

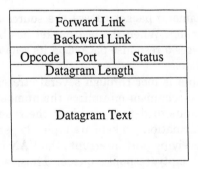

Fig. 3.   Example CI Port command packet.

Each buffer has a 32-bit *name*. The name consists of a 16-bit buffer descriptor table index and the 16-bit buffer key. The key is used to prevent dangling references and is modified whenever a descriptor is released. To transfer block data, the initiating software must have the buffer names of the source and destination buffers. The buffer names are exchanged through a high level message protocol. A host can cause data to be moved either to another node (SEND DATA) or from another node (REQUEST DATA). A SEND DATA or REQUEST DATA command packet contains the names of both buffers and the length of the transfer. In

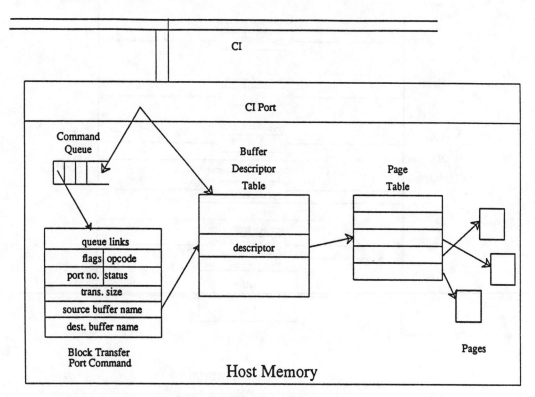

Fig. 4.   CI Port block data memory mapping.

either case (send or request), a single command packet causes the source and destination ports to perform the block transfer. When the last packet has been successfully received, the initiating port places a response packet on its response queue indicating that the transfer is complete.

The goal of reducing VAX host interrupts is met through several strategies and mechanisms. First, the block transfer mechanism minimizes the number of interrupts necessary to transfer large amounts of data. Second, at the sending port, DATAGRAM SENT/MESSAGE SENT confirmation packets are typically generated only when a failure occurs. Third, a receiving port interrupts the VAX only when it queues a received packet on an empty response queue. Thus, when software dequeues a packet in response to an interrupt, it always checks for more packets before dismissing the interrupt.

4. MASS STORAGE CONTROL

The move from Control and Status Register activated storage devices to message-oriented storage devices offers several advantages, including:

(1) Sharing is simplified. Several hosts can queue messages to a single controller. In addition, device control messages can be transmitted to and executed by hosts with local disks.

ACM Transactions on Computer Systems, Vol. 4, No. 2, May 1986.

(2) Ease of extension to new devices. In contrast to conventional systems, where there is a different driver for every type of disk and disk interface, a single *disk class driver* simply builds message packets and transmits them using a communications interface. The disk class driver is independent of drive specifics (e.g., cylinders and sectors). New disk and tape devices and controllers can be added with little or no modification to host software.

(3) Improved performance. The controller can maintain a queue of requests from multiple hosts and can optimize disk performance in real time. The controller can also handle error recovery and bad block replacement.

The HSC-50 (Hierarchical Storage Controller), shown in Figure 1, is the first CI-based controller for both disks and tapes. A single HSC controller can handle up to 24 disk drives. Multiple HSCs with dual-ported disks provide redundancy in case of failures.

The protocol interpreted by the HSC is called the Mass Storage Control Protocol (MSCP). The MSCP model separates the flow of control and status information from the flow of data. This distinction has been used in other systems to achieve efficient file access [6] and corresponds to the CI port's message and block data mechanisms; messages are used for device control commands while block transfers are used for data.

For example, to perform a disk read, the disk class driver transmits an MSCP READ message to the controller using a CI port SEND MESSAGE command. The read request contains the device type and unit number, the device media address (e.g., the disk logical block number), the 32-bit buffer name of the requester's buffer, and the length of the transfer. To process the request, the controller reads the specified data from disk and transmits it directly to host memory using a CI port SEND DATA command. When the data is successfully transferred, the controller sends a message to the host driver indicating the completion status of the request.

The same control protocol is used to provide cluster-wide access to CI-based controllers such as the HSC, and to Unibus or Massbus disks connected privately to a VAX node. Messages are routed from the disk class driver in the requesting node to an MSCP server on the node with the private disk. This server then parses the MSCP message, issues requests to its local disk, and initiates the block transfer through its SCA interface.

5. VAXcluster SOFTWARE

From a user's point of view, a VAXcluster is a set of nodes cooperating through VAX/VMS distributed operating system software to provide sharing of resources among users on all nodes. Shared resources include devices, files, records, and batch and print services. Typically, user account and password information resides in a single file shared by all cluster nodes. A user obtains the same environment (files, default directory, privileges, etc.) regardless of the node to which he or she is logged in. In many respects the VAXcluster feels like a single system to the user.

Figure 5 shows an example of a small VAXcluster and some of the major software components. At the highest level, multiple user processes on each node

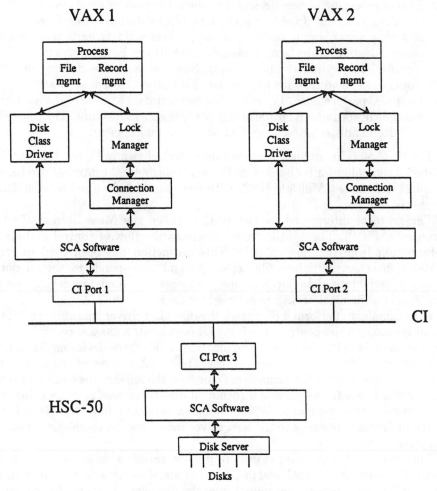

Fig. 5. VAXcluster software structure.

execute in separate address spaces. File and record management services are implemented as procedure-based code within each process.

The file and record services rely on lower level primitives such as the *lock manager* and *disk class driver*. The lock manager is the foundation of all resource sharing in both clustered and single-node VMS systems. It provides services for naming, locking, and unlocking cluster-wide resources. The disk class driver, mentioned earlier, uses MSCP to communicate with disk servers. The disk class driver runs in both clustered and nonclustered environments and contains no knowledge of the VAXcluster. SCA software below the driver is responsible for routing driver messages to the correct device controller.

Cluster *connection managers* are responsible for coordinating the cluster. Connection managers on all cluster nodes collectively decide upon cluster membership, which varies as nodes leave and join the cluster. Connection managers recognize recoverable failures in remote nodes; they provide data transfer services that handle such failures transparently to higher software levels.

ACM Transactions on Computer Systems, Vol. 4, No. 2, May 1986.

5.1 Forming a Cluster

A VAXcluster is formed when a sufficient set of VAX nodes and mass storage resources become available. New nodes may boot and join the cluster, and members may fail or shut down and leave the cluster. When a node leaves or joins, the process of reforming the cluster is called a *cluster transition*. Cluster transitions are managed by the connection managers.

In an operating cluster, each connection manager has a list of all member nodes. The list must be agreed upon by all members. A single node can be a member of only one VAXcluster; in particular, the same resource (such as a disk controller) cannot be shared by two clusters or the integrity of the resources could not be guaranteed. Therefore, connection managers must prevent the partitioning of a cluster into two or more clusters attempting to share the same resources.

To prevent partitioning, VMS uses a quorum voting scheme. Each cluster node contributes a number of votes and the connection managers dynamically compute the total votes of all members. The connection managers also maintain a dynamic quorum value. As transitions occur, the cluster continues to run as long as the total votes present equals or exceeds the quorum. Should the total votes fall below the quorum, the connection managers suspend process activity throughout the cluster. When a node joins and brings the total votes up to the quorum, processes continue.

Initial vote and quorum values are set for each node by a system manager, and can be used to determine the smallest set of resources needed to operate as a VAXcluster. In order to start the cluster, each node contains an initial estimate of what the quorum should be. However, as nodes join, connection managers increase the quorum value, if necessary, so it is at least $(V + 2)/2$, where V is the current vote total.

A cluster member may have a recoverable error in its communications, that is, one that leaves the node's memory intact and allows the operating system to continue running after the error condition has disappeared. Such errors can cause termination of a virtual circuit and a corresponding loss in communication. When cluster members detect the loss of communication with a node, they wait for a short period for the failing member to reestablish contact. The waiting period is called the *reconnect interval* and the system manager sets it, usually to about a minute. If the failing member recovers within the reconnect interval, it rejoins the cluster. During the time the failing member is recovering, some processes experience a delay in service. If the failing member does not rejoin within the reconnect interval, surviving members remove it from the cluster and continue if sufficient votes are present. A node that recovers after it has been removed from the cluster is told to reboot by other connection managers.

5.2 Shared Files

The VAXcluster provides a cluster-wide shared file system to its users. Cluster accessible files can exist on CI-based disk controllers or on disks local to any of the cluster nodes (e.g., connected via Unibus or Massbus). Each cluster disk has a unique name. A complete cluster file name includes the disk device name, the directory name, and the file name. Using the device name for a file, cluster

ACM Transactions on Computer Systems, Vol. 4, No. 2, May 1986.

179

software can locate the node (either CPU or disk controller) on which the file resides.

Cluster file activity requires synchronization: exclusive-write file opens, coordination of file system data structures, and management of file system caches are a few examples. However, despite the fact that files can be shared cluster wide, file management services are largely *unaware* of whether they are executing in a clustered environment. The file managers synchronize through the VMS lock manager, to be described below. It is the lock manager that handles locking and unlocking of resources across the cluster. At the level of the file manager, then, cluster file sharing is similar to single-node file sharing. Lower levels handle cluster-wide synchronization and routing of physical-level disk requests to the correct device.

5.3 Distributed Lock Manager

As previously described, the VMS lock manager is the basis for cluster-wide synchronization. Several goals influenced the design of the lock manager for a distributed environment. First, programs using the lock manager must run in both single node and cluster configurations. Second, lock services must be efficient to support system-level software that makes frequent requests. Therefore, in a VAXcluster, the lock manager must minimize the number of SCA messages needed to manage locks. In a single node configuration, the lock manager must recognize the simpler environment and bypass cluster-specific overhead. Finally, the lock manager must recover from failures of nodes holding locks so that surviving nodes can continue to access shared resources in a consistent manner.

The VMS lock manager services allow cooperating processes to define shared resources and synchronize access to those resources. A resource can be any object an application cares to define. Each resource has a user-defined name by which it is referenced. The lock manager provides basic synchronization services to request a lock and release a lock. Each lock request specifies a locking mode, such as exclusive access, protected read, concurrent read, concurrent write, null, etc. If a process requests a lock that is incompatible with existing locks, the request is queued until the resource becomes available.

The lock manager provides a *lock conversion* service to change the locking mode on an existing lock. Conversions are faster than new lock requests because the database representing the lock already exists. For this reason, applications frequently hold a null lock (a no access place holder) on a resource and then convert it to a more restricted access mode later.

In many applications resources may be subdivided into a resource tree, as illustrated in Figure 6. In this example, the resource Disk Volume contains resources File 1 through File 3; resource File 3 contains resources Record 1 and Record 2, and so on. The first locking request for a resource can specify the parent of the resource, thereby defining its relationship in a tree. A process making several global changes can hold a high-level lock (e.g., the root) and make them all very efficiently; a process making a small low-level change (e.g., a leaf) can do so while still permitting concurrent access to other parts of the tree [8].

ACM Transactions on Computer Systems, Vol. 4, No. 2, May 1986.

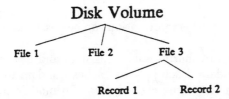

Disk Volume

File 1   File 2   File 3

Record 1   Record 2

Fig. 6.   VAXcluster locking structure.

The lock manager's implementation is intended to distribute the overhead of lock management throughout the cluster, while still minimizing the inter-node traffic needed to perform lock services. The database is therefore divided into two parts—the resource lock descriptions and the resource lock directory system—both of which are distributed. Each resource has a *master node* responsible for granting locks on the resource; the master maintains a list of granted locks and a queue of waiting requests for that resource. The master for all operations for a single tree is the node on which the lock request for the root was made. While the master maintains the lock data for its resource tree, any node holding a lock on a resource mastered by another node keeps its own copy of the resource and lock descriptions.

The second part of the database, the resource directory system, maps a resource name into the name of the master node for that resource. The directory database is distributed among nodes willing to share this overhead. Given a resource name, a node can trivially compute the responsible directory as a function of the name string and the number of directory nodes.

In order to lock a resource in a VAXcluster, the lock manager sends a lock request message via SCA to the directory for the resource. The directory responds in one of three ways:

(1) If the directory is located on the master node for the resource, it performs the lock request and sends a confirmation response to the requesting system.
(2) If the directory is not on the master node but finds the resource defined, it returns a response containing the identity of the master node.
(3) If the directory finds the resource to be undefined, it returns a response telling the requesting node to master the resource itself.

In the best cases (1 and 3) two messages are required to request a lock, whereas case 2 takes four messages. An unlock is executed with one message. If the lock request is for a subresource in a resource tree, the requesting process will either be located on the master node (i.e., the request is local) or will know who the master for its parent is, allowing it to bypass the directory lookup. In all cases, the number of messages required is independent of the number of nodes in the VAXcluster.

In addition to standard locking services, the lock manager supports data caching in a distributed environment. Depending on the frequency of modifications, caching of shared data in a distributed system can substantially reduce the I/O and communications workload.

A 16-byte block of information, called a *value block*, can be associated with a resource when the resource is defined to the lock manager. The value in the value block can be modified by a process releasing a lock on the resource, and read by

ACM Transactions on Computer Systems, Vol. 4, No. 2, May 1986.

a process when it acquires ownership. Thus, this information can be passed along with the resource ownership.

As an example, assume two processes are sharing some disk data and use the value block as a version number of the data. Each process caches the data in a local buffer and holds the version number of the cached data. To modify the data, a process locks it and compares the latest version returned with the lock with the version of the cached data. If they agree, the cache is valid; if the versions disagree, then the cache must be reloaded from disk. After modifying the data, the process writes the modified data back to disk and releases the lock. Releasing the lock increments the version number.

Another mechanism useful for caching data with deferred writeback is a software interrupt option. This is similar to the Mesa file system call-back mechanism [14], but is used for a different purpose. When requesting an exclusive lock, a process can specify that it should be notified by software interrupt if another lock request on the resource is forced to block. Continuing the example of cached disk data, a process owning the lock can cache and repeatedly modify the data. It writes the data back to disk and releases the lock when notified that it is blocking another process.

In the case of cluster transitions (e.g., failure of a node), the connection manager notifies the lock manager that a transition has started. Each lock manager performs recovery action, and all lock managers must complete this activity before cluster operation can continue.

As the first step in handling transitions, a lock manager deallocates all locks acquired on behalf of other systems. Only local lock and resource information is retained. Temporarily, there are no resource masters or directory nodes. In the second step, each lock manager reacquires each lock it had when the cluster transition began. This establishes new directory nodes based on a new set of eligible cluster members and rearranges the assignment of master nodes. If a node has left the cluster, the net result is to release locks held by that node. If no node has left the cluster but nodes have joined, this recovery is not necessary from an integrity point of view. However, it is performed to distribute directory and lock mastering overhead more fairly.

Some resources, depending on how they are modified, can be left in an inconsistent state by a cluster transition. One method of handling this problem would be to mark the locks for such resources to prevent access following a transition. A special process can then search for such locks and perform needed consistency checks before releasing them.

5.4 Batch And Print Services

In a VAXcluster, users may either submit a batch job to a queue on a particular node (not necessarily their own node), or submit a job to a cluster-wide batch queue. Jobs on the cluster-wide queue are routed to queues attached to specific nodes for execution. The algorithm for assigning jobs to specific nodes is a simple one based on the ratio of executing jobs compared to the job limit of the queue.

Management of batch jobs is the responsibility of a VMS process called the job controller. Each VMS node runs a job controller process. The process acquires work from one or more batch queues. Batch queues are stored in a disk file that may be shared by all nodes. Synchronization of queue manipulation is handled with lock manager services.

Print queues are similar to batch queues. Users may queue a request for a specific printer (not necessarily physically attached to their own node) or may let the operating system choose an available printer from those in the cluster.

Both batch and print jobs can be declared restartable. If a node fails, restartable jobs are either requeued to complete on another node in the cluster, or will execute when the failed node reboots (for jobs that required to execute on a specific node).

6. TERMINAL SUPPORT

The optimum method for connecting users' terminals to a VAXcluster is through the Local Area Terminal Server (LAT). Terminals are connected to LAT, which is attached to VAXs by Ethernet. Users command LAT to connect them to a specific node or to any node in the cluster. The ease of switching nodes leads users to find and use the least busy node. It also allows users to quickly move from a failed node to one that is still running. If LAT is directed to select a node, it attempts to find the least busy node. Its choice is based on node CPU type (a measure of processing power) and recent idle time.

7. PERFORMANCE

Performance of the system communications architecture (SCA) and the underlying hardware interconnect was measured using operating system processes running on clustered VAX nodes. By operating system processes, we mean that these programs run at the same level as the connection manager shown in Figure 5. These processes measured the datagram, message, and block transfer throughput for various message sizes. All numbers are approximate, as performance may vary due to different command options.

Table I shows the CPU time used on a VAX 11/780 to send and receive a reply to a 576-byte datagram and a 96-byte message. These sizes were used because they were representative of the sizes used by VMS. The CPU time to initiate a block transfer and receive the response is the same as that for a sequenced message (i.e., 320 μs) independent of the transfer size. Round trip elapsed time is also shown. In general, for a given transfer size the performance of datagrams and messages is approximately the same. The results also depend on the amount of buffering and the number of messages queued to the port before waiting for a response.

Table II shows the number of message round trips per second achieved on a cluster with between 2 and 12 communicating nodes. Each node was communicating with one other node; for example, in the 12 node case there were 6 pairs of communicating nodes, each pair engaged in sending and receiving a single stream of 112-byte messages. These experiments were run on VAX 11/785 nodes. As can be seen from Table II, the total number of messages increases nearly linearly. Once again, performance depends on the number of messages queued at a time. While one message was queued at a time in this experiment, previous experiments have shown that by queueing four messages at a time, it is possible to achieve 3000 message round trips per second on two VAX 11/780s.

ACM Transactions on Computer Systems, Vol. 4, No. 2, May 1986.

Table I

	Datagram	Message
Send/receive CPU time	290 μs (576 byte)	320 μs (96 byte)
Send/receive Round trip Elapsed time	1500 μs (576 byte)	1000 μs (96 byte)

Table II

Number of nodes	Cluster round-trip (messages/s)
2	1090
4	2170
6	3250
8	4330
10	5420
12	6480

Table III

Number of nodes	Cluster block transfer thruput (mbytes/s)
2	2.65
4	5.28
6	7.70

Table IV

	Single-CPU system	Clustered system
Request lock	400 μs	3000 μs
Convert lock	250 μs	1000–2300 μs
Release lock	300 μs	700 μs

Throughput results are shown in Table III. In this experiment, 4 streams of 64-kbyte block transfers were initiated between 2, 4, and 6 VAX 11/785 nodes. Again, throughput increases almost linearly. Throughput measurements for datagrams and messages show that a throughput of about 2.4 Mbytes per second can be achieved between two VAX 11/780 nodes sending 900-byte messages or datagrams.

These throughputs do not represent real workloads, which produce less traffic than the contrived test programs. It is clear that the 8.75 Mbyte per second (per path) CI is not the bottleneck. For this test, we believe that the limiting factor is the speed of the CI port and the memory bandwidth of the host. Of course, the reason for having a high-speed interconnect is to provide bandwidth for multiple hosts.

This performance provides a basis for efficient execution of higher level distributed services, such as the lock manager. Table IV lists approximate

ACM Transactions on Computer Systems, Vol. 4, No. 2, May 1986.

performance values for lock operations in both clustered and nonclustered environments. As previously stated, lock conversions are faster than new lock requests because the database already exists. The measured elapsed time for a conversion depends upon the existing mode and new mode.

8. CONCLUSIONS

A principal goal of VAXclusters was the development of an available and extensible multicomputer system built from standard processors and a general-purpose operating system. Much was gained by the joint design of distributed software, communications protocols, and hardware aimed to meet this goal. For example:

(1) The CI interconnect supports fast message transfer needed by system software.
(2) The CI port implements many of the functions needed by SCA software.
(3) The HSC-50 with its message protcol and request queueing optimization logic provides direct network access to a large pool of disks for multiple hosts.

Designing hardware and software together allows for system-level tradeoffs; the software interface and protocols can be tuned to the hardware devices.

An important simplifying aspect of the VAXcluster design is the use of a distributed lock manager for resource synchronization. In this way, higher level services such as the file system do not require special code to handle sharing in a distributed environment. However, performance of the lock manager becomes a crucial factor. Distributed lock manager performance has been attacked with the design of a locking protocol requiring a fixed number of messages, independent of the number of cooperating nodes.

Finally, we believe that the performance measurements presented show the extent to which the VAXcluster system has succeeded in implementing an efficient communications architecture. These numbers are particularly impressive when considering that VMS is a large, general-purpose operating system.

ACKNOWLEDGMENTS

VAXclusters are the result of work done by many individuals in several engineering groups at Digital Equipment Corporation. We would particularly like to acknowledge the contributions of Richard I. Hustvedt.

We wish to thank Bill Laing, Steve Neupauer, and Stan Amway for performance measurements reported in this paper, and Steve Beckhardt, Liz Hunt, Jim Krycka, Christian Saether, and Dave Thiel for reviews of earlier versions of the paper.

REFERENCES

1. ALMES, G. T., BLACK, A. P., LAZOWSKA, E. D., NOE, J. D.   The eden system: A technical review. *IEEE Trans. Softw. Eng. SE-11*, 1 (Jan. 1985), 43–59.
2. APOLLO COMPUTER CORP.   *Apollo domain architecture.* Tech. Rep. Apollo Computer Corporation, North Billerica, Mass., 1981.
3. BARTLETT, J. F.   A nonstop kernel. In *Proceedings of the 8th Symposium on Operating Systems Principles* (Pacific Grove, Calif., Dec. 14–16), ACM, New York, 1981, pp. 22–29.

4. BORG, A., BAUMBACH, J., AND GLAZER, S.   A message system supporting fault tolerance. In *Proceedings of the 9th Symposium on Operating Systems Principles* (Bretton Woods, N.H., Oct. 11–13), ACM, New York, 1983, pp. 90–99.

5. BROWNBIRDGE, A., MARSHALL, A., AND RANDELL, A.   The newcastle connection or unixes of the world unite! *Softw.—Pract. Exp. 12* (1982), 1147–1162.

6. CHERITON, D., AND ZWAENEPOEL, W.   The distributed V kernel and its performance for diskless workstations. In *Proceedings of the 9th Symposium on Operating Systems Principles* (Bretton Woods, N.H., Oct. 11–13), ACM, New York, 1983, pp. 129–140.

7. FIELLAND, G., AND RODGERS, D.   32-bit computer system shares load equally among up to 12 processors. *Elect. Des.* (Sept. 1984), 153–168.

8. GRAY, J. N., LORIE, R. A., PUTZOLU, G. R., AND TRAIGER, I. L.   Granularity of locks and degrees of consistency in a shared data base. In *Modelling in Data Base Management Systems.* Nijssen, G. M., Ed., North Holland, Amsterdam, 1976.

9. HWANG, K., AND BRIGGS, F. A.   *Computer Architecture and Parallel Processing.* McGraw-Hill, New York, 1984.

10. KATSUKI, D., ELSAM, E. S., MANN, W. F., ROBERTS, E. S., ROBINSON, J. G., SKOWRONSKI, F. S., WOLF, E. W.   Pluribus—An operational fault-tolerant multiprocessor. In *Proceedings of the IEEE 66,* 10 (Oct. 1978), 1146–1159.

11. KATZMAN, J. A.   The Tandem 16: A fault-tolerant computing system. In *Computer Structures: Principles and Examples,* Siewiorek, D. P., Bell, C. G., and Newell, A., Eds., McGraw-Hill, New York, 1982, pp. 470–480.

12. METCALFE, R. M., AND BOGGS, D. R.   Ethernet: Distributed packet switching for local computer networks. *Commun. ACM 19,* 7 (July 1976), 395–404.

13. POPEK, G., WALKER, B., CHOW, J., EDWARDS, D., KLINE, C., RUDISIN, G., THIEL, G.   LOCUS: A network transparent, high reliability distributed system. In *Proceedings of the 8th Symposium on Operating Systems Principles* (Pacific Grove, Calif., Dec. 14–16), ACM, New York, 1981, pp. 169–177.

14. REID, L. G., AND KARLTON, P. L.   A file system supporting cooperation between programs. In *Proceedings of the 9th Symposium on Operating Systems Principles* (Bretton Woods, N.H., Oct. 11–13), ACM, New York, 1983, pp. 20–29.

15. SATYANARAYANAN, M.   *Multiprocessors: A Comparative Study.* Prentice-Hall, Englewood Cliffs, N.J., 1980.

16. STRECKER, W. D.   VAX-11/780: A virtual address extension to the DEC PDP-11 family. In *Proceedings of AFIPS NCC,* 1978, pp. 967–980.

Received July 1985; revised December 1985; accepted December 1985

High-Performance Networks: A Focus on the Fiber Distributed Data Interface (FDDI) Standard

Sunil P. Joshi
Advanced Micro Devices

A new standard provides a high-performance LAN solution for the quick transfer of large amounts of data.

As the computing power of computers and the storage capacity of disk media increase with each passing day, there is increasing demand on communication links to transfer large amounts of data with minimum delay. The emerging Fiber Distributed Data Interface (FDDI) is a standard that provides a high-performance local area network solution for such high-end applications.

The FDDI standard is being defined by the American National Standards Institute committee X3T9.5, which is responsible for high-speed local area networks. FDDI is a fiber-optic token-ring network operating at a data rate of 100 megabits per second. The FDDI protocol has used the IEEE 802.5 token-ring protocol[1] as a starting point and enhanced it to enable cost-effective, high-speed implementation. The Institute of Electrical and Electronic Engineers and ANSI X3T9.5 work closely to prevent overlaps in activities. IEEE is defining standards at data rates below 50M bps, while the X3T9.5 committee is looking at speeds above that.

The initial FDDI specifications, referred to as the FDDI-1 standard, are better suited for data traffic than voice traffic. Those aspects of FDDI-1 that affect hardware implementation are already frozen as a standard. As an enhancement to FDDI-1 the committee has just begun work on a new definition called FDDI-2, which will provide a better interface for both data and voice traffic.

The FDDI-1 specification consists of four documents specifying the data-link layer and physical layer of the seven-layer Open Systems Interconnect model (see Figure 1).[2] The Physical Media Dependent (PMD) document

deals with the fiber-optic cable, connectors, and jitter specifications at the electro-optic interface. The Physical Layer (PHY) document specifies the clock recovery and encoding mechanism. The Media Access Control (MAC) document specifies the token-passing protocol, and the Station Management (SMT) document deals with network management issues.[3]

Why fiber optics?

FDDI decided to use fiber optics as a transmission medium for a variety of reasons:

- *Bandwidth*. Fiber cable provides a very high capacity for carrying information. The data rate can be in the range of several hundred megabits per second.
- *Attenuation*. Fiber provides low attenuation resulting in efficient communication over several kilometers without repeaters.
- *Noise susceptibility*. Fiber cables transmit information as light and neither generate nor are affected by electromagnetic interference.
- *Security*. Since it is not easy to tap a fiber-optic cable without interrupting communication, fiber is more secure from malicious interception.
- *Cost*. The cost of fiber-optic cable has fallen considerably over the last two years, and fiber is projected to become cheaper than coaxial cable in a year or so. Since fiber is lightweight and thinner than coaxial cable, it is easier to pull through overcrowded ducts, which results in lower installation costs. In fact, the additional cost of putting a second fiber in the same cable is negligible; hence, FDDI has

Reprinted from *IEEE Micro*, June 1986, pages 8-14. Copyright © 1986 by The Institute of Electrical and Electronics Engineers, Inc.

opted for a duplex fiber cable and provided a high level of fault tolerance through this added redundancy.

In the past the cost of the laser diodes or avalanche photo diodes to interface with the fiber has been high. However, technological advances have provided low-cost LEDs and pin-diodes that can operate at the 100M-bps rate specified by FDDI.

Key application areas

The requirements and characteristics of a network vary, depending on the applications they try to support. Broadly speaking, one can identify four major application areas: the office floor, the computer room, the factory floor, and campus interconnections. Figure 2 illustrates the way a variety of applications could coexist in a typical company environment.

Office floor. A typical office environment is characterized by the proliferation of word processors, desktop personal computers, facsimile machines, terminals, and

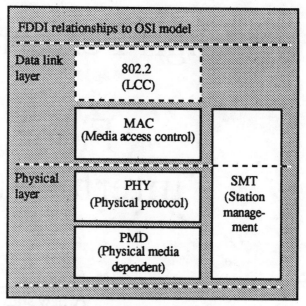

Figure 1. Scope of FDDI specifications.

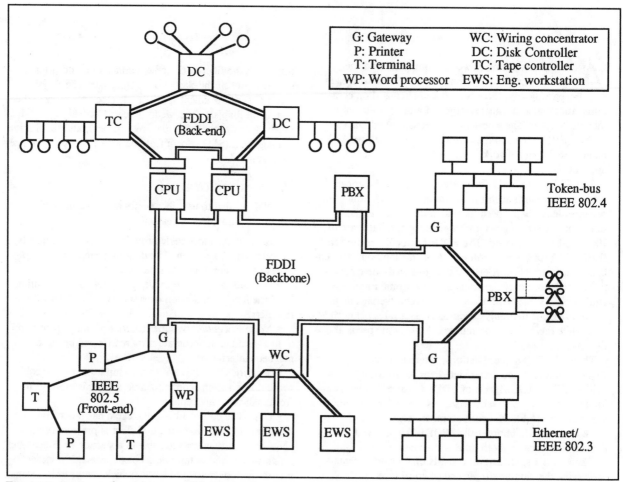

Figure 2. A view of a company-wide network.

June 1986

printers. Most of these are low-cost, medium-performance devices that feature direct user interfaces. Because humans are fairly slow at data entry or display tasks, the computing power of such devices is ususally not a concern. Networks for such applications are often referred to as front-end networks.

A local area network for these applications needs to support hundreds of nodes but does not necessarily have to run at a high data rate. The LAN may cover a single floor, or an entire building, depending on the number of nodes.

A variety of LAN alternatives are suitable for this environment. These include front-end networks such as Cheapernet/Ethernet, low-speed token-rings, PC-Net, Apple-Talk, and Starlan. For terminals or PCs working in the terminal mode, it may be desirable to use a modem over the PBX connection to interface with a remote mainframe. The cost of the network interface is a prime concern for such devices and choosing a scheme involves cost/performance trade-offs.

In addition to these applications, offices in the engineering environment will have engineering workstations, computer-aided design equipment, graphics or imaging machines, and multiuser micro- or minicomputers. The need to handle computation-intensive operations, such as moving large blocks of data, sets this equipment apart from PC devices. The performance of the network is crucial when hundreds of millions of bytes of graphics data are being moved, and as a result these devices can tolerate slightly higher network interface costs than terminals or PCs. Presently, Ethernet LANs are being used to link engineering workstations, but once higher performance solutions such as FDDI become available at reasonable cost, these applications will utilize the higher data rate.

Computer room. The computer room can be visualized as a collection of very high performance mainframes or minicomputers connected over a back-end network to peripheral controllers, communications controllers, file servers, and database machines. The peripheral controllers in turn can be attached to individual disk drives or tape drives. In addition, high-speed laser printers may be attached on the back-end network.

Usually the back-end networks in a computer room do not span large distances, but they must operate at a very high data rate and be extremely reliable or fault tolerant. In the past nonstandard networks such as Hyperchannel have been used for computer room connections. Also, parallel interconnect schemes such as the Intelligent Peripheral Interface, or IPI, have been used, since the distance limitation is not a concern. Now FDDI is emerging as an alternative that offers increased performance.

Factory floor. Networking is an essential element of the automated factory. A typical factory floor will include many kinds of controllers (for numerical, robotic, and process control functions) as well as data acquisition and display devices and imaging and computing equipment.

Deterministic access to the network is the key requirement of a factory network. Process control applications, such as nuclear reactors, need periodic updating of control information with a guaranteed access time.

The first-generation factory network will be the IEEE 802.4 token-bus network, which forms a subset of the large Manufacturing Automation Protocol, or MAP, being defined by several companies in the US. MAP networks will use a combination of baseband and broadband transmission on the cable.

However, FDDI shows promise as a second-generation factory network due to its deterministic token-ring protocol and the fiber-optic medium, which is immune to the electromagnetic interference present in a factory environment.

Campus LANs. The backbone LAN can connect the different networks in various buildings on a campus spanning a few miles.

The connections to the backbone network can be gateways or bridges. A gateway provides an interface between two dissimilar LANs while a bridge connects two similar LANs. A backbone network, however, does not have to merely connect smaller networks. It could very well have a direct interface to the mainframe computers in each building. Also, it is desirable to interconnect distributed PBXs carrying both voice and data using the same backbone. If the transmission of real-time voice is needed, the network has to be able to provide some circuit-switched capability in addition to packet switching. Once this is possible, transmission of real-time video also is easy to provide.

Since a campus network is a backbone network, it should have a high data rate and operate over extended distances.

FDDI topology and protocol

FDDI provides a considerable amount of flexibility in configuring its topology and also provides a protocol suitable for a variety of applications.

Configuration limits. The FDDI specification places no lower limits on the number of nodes and the distance between the nodes. There are also no absolute upper limits. For example, for the sake of calculation of default timer values and to keep the ring latency down to a few milliseconds, a system is assumed to include up to 1000 nodes on the ring, with up to two kilometers between adjacent nodes and up to 200 kilometers of total fiber length. However, these parameters can be traded off to produce the optimum configuration for the chosen application; for instance, more nodes can be allowed over shorter distances.

A dual-ring approach. The FDDI ring is a combination of two independent counterrotating rings, each running at a 100M-bps data rate. If both rings operate simultaneously, the effective throughput is 200M bps. It is also possible to have configurations where one ring connects all

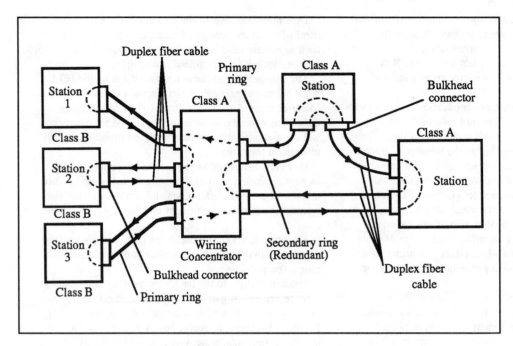

Figure 3.
FDDI dual rings.

the nodes and a second counterrotating ring connects only a few select nodes.

Figure 3 shows a possible FDDI configuration with fiber-optic cables interconnecting to form the rings; the paths through which the data circulates around the ring are also depicted. The primary ring reaches all the nodes. The secondary ring carries data in the opposite direction, which is useful during ring reconfiguration. The advantage of having two rings is that if one ring fails, the network can reconfigure using the other ring and still keep operating.

Class A and Class B stations. The nodes connecting to the FDDI rings are divided into two categories: Class A and Class B. Class A stations connect to two rings simultaneously, and Class B stations connect to only one of the rings.

The two classes help tailor the complexity of systems to meet cost objectives. Since Class B stations need to connect to only one ring, they can be implemented at lower cost. The disadvantage is that the Class B station is isolated if its link fails. Class A stations, on the other hand, require additional hardware to connect to dual rings but are protected against failure. If there is a link failure, they can keep operating in a reconfigured ring.

Typically those systems that need more fault tolerance will be configured as Class A. Less critical stations can be configured as Class B stations. Another kink of Class A interconnect is a wiring concentrator (WC).

Wiring concentrator. A wiring concentrator, as the name implies, is a hub node through which several other stations can be connected. A WC allows a physical ring to be maintained easily, as is done in star networks. The WC

can be a service point, and several WCs can be established at various distributed locations from which shorter connections can be taken out to individual stations. A WC is always a Class A station, and other Class A and B stations can connect to it.

The way the fiber cable is packaged makes the concept of WCs very attractive. The fiber cable in FDDI contains two physical fibers packaged in one jacket with a bulkhead connector on either end. The same cable is used for all Class A and Class B connections. For example, for the dual ring connecting the Class A stations each jacketed cable would contain one fiber for the primary ring and one for the secondary ring; for Class B stations the identical cable would carry the incoming and outgoing signals on the same ring. Hence, when a Class B station has to be connected to a WC, only one physical cable has to be routed between the two. Because it carries two fibers, a ring path is physically established.

Multimedia implementation. Although the use of a combination of media, such as optical fiber and coaxial cable, is not a part of FDDI, combined media can be implemented easily. For example, a dual-ring scheme connecting Class A stations can be built using fiber, but the shorter connections between a WC and the Class B stations that attach to it can be coaxial cable. As long as the data rate is maintained and the protocol is adhered to, the existence of multiple media in a ring is transparent to the network.

Fault tolerance in FDDI. Several levels of fault tolerance are possible in FDDI. Some types of cable faults may cause the ring to reconfigure. Loss of power on certain nodes may switch an optical relay in place.

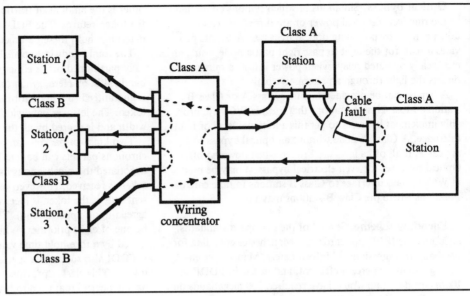

Figure 4. Ring reconfiguration.

Ring configuration. The most likely faults in a network are caused by either failed components or broken cables. Even if a connection is not fully broken, there may be a substantial degradation, which shows up as an increase in the bit-error rate. Figure 4 shows a ring reconfiguring its data paths when a link (or a pair of links in a cable) in the dual ring becomes inoperative. The stations sense the breakage and use the appropriate paths on the secondary ring to keep the network running. In FDDI this reconfiguration happens automatically, within a few milliseconds. FDDI defines a station management interface for this even-

tuality. When a broken ring is restored, the station management handshake will allow the ring to go back to its original state.

The effect of a second failure in the dual ring is interesting too. Figure 5 shows how a network can split into two smaller independent networks, which both remain operative internally.

If there is a cable fault in the cable going to a Class B station, this station is cut off from the network, and the WC provides a bypass for the node.

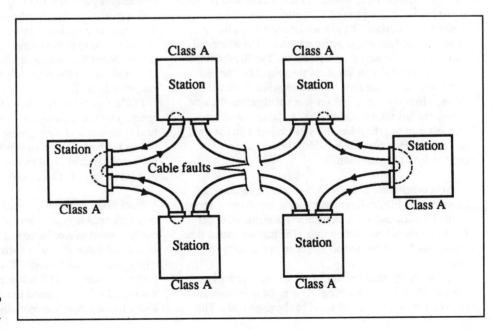

Figure 5. A ring with two cable faults.

Optical bypass. Situations in which stations connected to the ring lose electrical power or are turned off can be taken care of by providing optical bypasses. A bypass provides a path for the light to pass right past a node, using an electrically operated relay; when power is lost, a mirror directs the light through an alternative path.

A bypass can be provided in either Class A or Class B stations. Most Class A stations that include WCs will probably implement bypasses to get this additional level of fault tolerance. A Class A node without an optical bypass will appear as if all of its links are broken when powered off. Optical bypasses (or even electrical bypasses) may be used in WCs at their interface to Class B stations to take care of situations where the Class B stations may fail.

Encoding scheme. Several of the low-speed standards, including the IEEE standards, use Manchester encoding for baseband transmissions.[4] Unfortunately, Manchester encoding is only 50 percent efficient, and its use in FDDI's 100M-bps data rate would have required 200 megabauds on the medium, with the LEDs and pin receivers operating at 200 MHz.

FDDI uses a more efficient encoding scheme, called 4B/5B, to keep the baud rate down.[5,6] In 4B/5B, the encoding is performed on four bits at a time to create a five-cell "symbol" on the medium. It is 80 percent efficient, and at 100M bps the baud rate becomes 125 megabauds. The advantage is that inexpensive LEDs and pin diode receivers, which only have to operate at 125 MHz, can be used.

Token-passing ring

FDDI uses a token-passing ring consisting of stations serially connected by a transmission medium to form a closed loop. The packets are transmitted sequentially from one station to the next, where they are retimed and regenerated before they are passed on to the following (or downstream) station. The idle stations can either be bypassed or can function as active repeaters. The addressed station copies the packet as it passes by. Finally, the station that transmitted the packet strips the packet off the ring.

A station gains the right to transmit when it has the token, which is a special packet that circulates on the ring behind the last transmitted packet. A station wanting to transmit captures the token, puts its packet(s) on the ring, and then issues a new token, which the next station can capture for its transmission.

Access scheme. Using an access scheme called timed-token access, FDDI allows each node a fair share of access to the network and at the same time maintains an upper bound on the token-rotation time. The token-rotation time determines how often the nodes get an opportunity to transmit.

To satisfy the requirements of various applications, a node needs to know two things. One is the maximum latency before the token returns again to the given node. The other is the amount of traffic that the node can send once the token returns. The FDDI protocol allows the node to determine both these parameters through negotiation.

The total bandwidth available on the ring can be dynamically partitioned off as either synchronous or asynchronous bandwidth.[5,6] Here, synchronous refers to bandwidth that is guaranteed to a node for its use, every time it gets the token. The leftover bandwidth is the asynchronous bandwidth and is shared by all the nodes.

Two kinds of packets can be transmitted on FDDI. Synchronous packets can be sent by the nodes that have negotiated the synchronous bandwidth, every time the token is received. However, asynchronous packets can be sent only if the token is received early (that is, within the agreed-upon upper bound). The asynchronous packets can be one of eight priorities. Which priority to send is determined by a threshold time value.

FDDI also supports a special token class called restricted tokens. This class is provided mainly for back-end networks having devices that need to hog the network for data streaming.

Benefits to various applications

As shown in Figure 1, FDDI can be used as back-end, backbone, and front-end networks. Different features of FDDI make it attractive for each application.

Back-end network. For a back-end network in a computer room, reliability and performance are the important considerations. In this environment, it is desirable for two stations to maintain unimpaired operation, even if up to six intervening stations are powered down (causing their optical bypass relays to be in the active connection path between the communication stations). FDDI is projected to meet this constraint when the total fiber length between communication stations is less than 300 meters.

The dual rings, by reconfiguring, provide additional fault tolerance. In a back-end network most nodes will be Class A nodes talking to both rings. If the 100M-bps data rate is not sufficient in this application, an additional 100M bps is also available on the secondary ring as long as the ring is not reconfigured.

FDDI also supports a class of service called restricted token. This sets up a master/slave connection between the host computer and a peripheral controller, allowing the two to hog the network and stream data between them. Although the restricted token violates the deterministic access of a token ring, it is acceptable in a back-end environment.

Backbone network. A backbone network stretching over a campus may span several kilometers. The backbone can be viewed as a collection of trunk lines connecting several computer rooms or individual networks in the office environment or distributed PBXs. A high bandwidth on the backbone ensures that it is not a bottleneck during internetworking. FDDI is designed to allow links at least two kilometers in length between adjacent nodes with no optical bypasses on either end. The total allowable fiber-path length to satisfy the default-timer values and ring-latency constraints is 200 kilometers. Since duplex cable is used, the actual length of cable in the entire ring is 100 kilometers. The 100M-bps data rate provides ample bandwidth for this application.

Another concern during internetworking is station addressing. Since FDDI permits both 16-bit and 48-bit addresses with physical and logical addressing support for both as well as broadcast capability, the addressing translation across gateways and bridges is simplified.

For supporting distributed PBXs, a circuit-switched or time-slotted access method is desirable. The ANSI X3T9.5 committee is starting preliminary work on the FDDI-2 specification, which will implement a combination of circuit- and packet-switched traffic. This will make it easy to provide a gateway to the telephone network or to the ISDN.

Front-end network. In the office-floor situation FDDI is suitable as a front-end network. The cost of connection can be minimized by having a preponderance of Class B stations. These Class B stations can be attached to wiring concentrators, which in turn will provide Class A connections to the backbone FDDI network.

Because wiring concentrators generally are powered, the need for optical bypassing is minimized. Class B connections lower the cost of the connection since the duplicate physical layer logic is not needed. At the same time, they still form a part of the main ring and can transfer data at the 100M-bps data rate.

FDDI provides for a separation of up to 500 meters between a Class B station and a wiring concentrator. When any of the Class B stations is powered down or its link is broken, the wiring concentrator can bypass it electrically very easily. The wiring concentrator also provides a convenient maintenance point.

T he FDDI committee has made reasonable trade-offs to ensure that the technology needed for implementing FDDI is presently available and that the standard will not be obsolete in the next several years. The standard's authors have kept in mind upgradability to higher speeds and additional services that will be necessary in the future.

The emergence of FDDI as a popular standard is spurring integrated circuits development from semiconductor vendors. The use of dedicated VLSI to support FDDI will lower the cost of an FDDI interface dramatically.

References

1. Sunil Joshi, "Session Overview: A look at Standards Committees," *Proc. Wescon 84,* Oct.-Nov. 1984, pp. 1-5.

2. David Berry, "Standardizing Upper-Level Network Protocols," *Computer Design,* Feb. 1984, pp. 174-190.

3. *Draft Proposed American National Standard FDDI Physical Layer Protocol* (*PHY*), ANSI X3T9/85-39, X3T9.5/83-15; *FDDI Media Access Control* (*MAC*), ANSI X3T9/84-100, X3T9.5/83-16; *FDDI Physical Medium Dependent Layer* (*PMD*), ANSI X3T9/85, X3T9.5/84-48; and *FDDI Station Management* (*SMT*), ANSI X3T9/85-, X3T9.5/84-49; American National Standards Institute, New York, 1979.

4. V. Iyer and S. Joshi, "Hardware Considerations in Local Area Networks," *Proc. Midcon 82,* Nov. 1982.

5. Sunil Joshi, "Making the LAN Connection with a Fiber Optic Standard," *Computer Design,* Sept. 1985, pp. 64-69.

6. S. Joshi and V. Iyer, "New Standards for Local Networks Push Upper Limits for Lightware Data," *Data Communications,* July 1984, pp. 127-138.

Sunil P. Joshi is the section manager for local area networks at Advanced Micro Devices. His duties include the planning and specification of high-speed LAN products. During the past six years at AMD he has participated in the design and development of several Am2900-family microprogrammable products, the Ethernet chip set, and the Supernet chip set designed to implement FDDI.

Joshi holds a BSEE from the Indian Institute of Technology, Bombay, and an MSEE from Rensselaer Polytechnic Institute, Troy, New York.

Questions about this article can be directed to Joshi at Advanced Micro Devices, Inc., 901 Thompson Place, PO Box 453, Sunnyvale, CA 94086.

The FDDI Optical Data Link

W. E. Burr

This article focuses on the Physical Medium Dependent (PMD) layer of the FDDI

In another paper in this issue Floyd Ross describes the overall structure of the proposed Fiber Distributed Data Interface (FDDI) standard(s). FDDI will consist of a number of separate, compatible layered standards which will implement a 100 Mb/s ring network. This article focuses on the Physical Medium Dependent (PMD) layer of the FDDI. The PMD layer of the FDDI corresponds to the lowest sublayer of Layer 1 of the Open Systems Interconnection Reference Model [1] and defines the optical transmission medium used to link two FDDI stations. While FDDI is a ring network, most of the characteristics of the FDDI PMD could also be applied to other network topologies which can be implemented in terms of point-to-point duplex links.

Any standard such as FDDI is a compromise between the highest possible performance and the need to accommodate a wide range of components and implementations. This article discusses the choices made in FDDI to achieve reliable operation between stations made by different vendors using different components. The effort to complete PMD began in earnest in Accredited Standards Committee X3T9.5 in December 1984, and has since gathered intensity. The major choices in PMD have now been made, and the draft proposed American National Standard should be completed in 1986.

The Institute for Computer Sciences and Technology of the National Bureau of Standards has been a major contributor to the FDDI standards and is planning to develop a laboratory to investigate the FDDI technology as it applies in the open systems interconnection architecture.

The Interface Point

The FDDI Physical Medium Dependent interface is specified at the station optical bulkhead connector. Only properties which can be observed through that connector are specified. Figure 1 illustrates the block function design of a typical FDDI station, and the interface between PMD and the next highest sublayer, the Physical Protocol (PHY) sublayer. The PHY sublayer specifies the 4 of 5 code used in FDDI. The PMD standard will specify the bulkhead connector optical transmitter output, the bulkhead connector receiver input and the cable plant. It is not absolutely necessary to specify the FDDI cable plant in the standard, because it can be inferred from the station specifications. However, many users needing to specify a cable plant would have difficulty deriving a specification, so one is provided.

It is necessary to consider the internal design of stations to arrive at a practical interface, but the standard should not unnecessarily restrict internal station design. A poor choice of interface specifications could unnecessarily eliminate sound components or designs.

Specific Goals

The FDDI data link performance goals are 100 Mb/s (125 Mbaud) through up to 2 km of cable with a bit error rate of less than one in 2.5×10^{10} transmitted bits.

Reprinted from *IEEE Communications Magazine*, Volume 24, Number 5, May 1986, pages 8-23. Copyright © 1986 by The Institute of Electrical and Electronics Engineers, Inc.

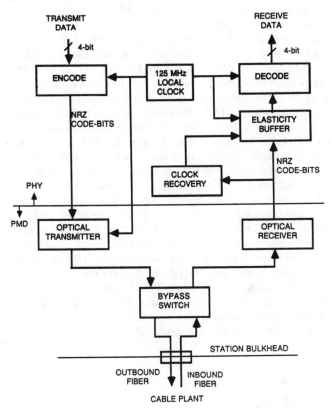

Fig. 1. *FDDI Physical Layer Block Diagram.*

The rate of 100 Mbit/s is as fast as the higher level protocols of FDDI stations can be made to operate for a reasonable cost. This rate seems to satisfy most computer system needs. The 2 km link distance covers most local network needs and should not require the use of premium grade optical fibers. The error rate is determined by estimates of what is required to meet overall network goals.

A second goal is to specify the PMD so that links can be implemented using components which are relatively inexpensive and are commercially available in 1986. No interface standard can succeed until it can be inexpensively implemented.

Why Optical Fiber?

Currently available silica glass fiber optic waveguides are remarkably good, inexpensive products, offering dramatic cost and performance advantages over electrical waveguides. In long haul communication networks optical fiber has long since supplanted coaxial cable as the medium of choice for high bandwidth, long distance data links. The costs of such links are dominated by the costs of installing the waveguide. Since other optical components such as transmitters, receivers and connectors are much less mature products than their electrical alternatives, local networks, such as FDDI, with much shorter average distances, have generally used electrical media.

As stated, the design goal of the FDDI is 100 Mb/s over a maximum link distance of 2 km. While it is possible to achieve this design goal over electrical media, fiber optic waveguides have impressive advantages for such links. In particular, the electrical media

required would be bulky solid sheath coaxial cables, which are much more difficult to install than optical fibers. Although the bulk of FDDI links will probably be much shorter than 2 km, and electrical media would have a near term cost advantage for shorter links, optical media have several other advantages, even for very short distances. Unlike electrical media, optical fibers are essentially immune to electrical interference, do not radiate, and reduce electrical safety concerns. Part of the purpose of a standard such as FDDI is to help markets develop and thereby bring down prices through high volume production of components.

Single vs. Multimode Fiber

Two types of optical fiber waveguides are in common use today: single mode and multimode (see Fig. 2). In single mode fiber there is a single propagation mode directly along the axis of the fiber. In multimode fiber there are a number of different propagation modes; the "low order" modes being nearly parallel to the axis of the fiber, and the "high order" modes diverging more from the axis of the fiber. Light in the higher order modes will travel a longer path causing modal dispersion in these multimode fibers, and limiting their bandwidth. Consequently, single mode fiber has largely supplanted multimode fiber in long haul telecommunications applications.

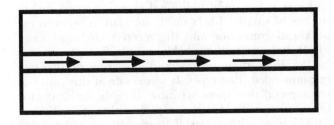

a) Single Mode Fiber

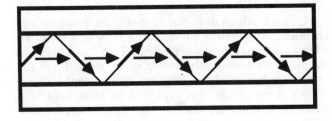

b) Multimode Fiber

Fig. 2. *Single and Multimode Fiber.*

While single and multimode mode fibers have similar costs per meter, single mode transmitters, switches and connectors are all more expensive than their multimode equivalents, and are not needed to meet the FDDI performance goals. Since some of the cost advantages of multimode fiber seem irreducible (they require less precise control of dimensions and are easier to couple power into), FDDI will use multimode fiber.

While there are a number of types of multimode fiber developed over the years, only graded index silica glass fibers meet the performance needs of FDDI. Such fibers are conventionally identified by an inner or core diameter and an outer or cladding diameter, both expressed in microns. Virtually all high bandwidth graded index multimode fiber commercially available today use one of four sizes:

> 50/125
> 62.5/125
> 85/125
> 100/140

In general, the smaller the core size, the easier it is to make a high bandwidth fiber; the bigger the core size, the easier it is to couple optical power into the fiber and (given similar mechanical tolerances) the less the losses in connectors and switches. Both power coupling and bandwidth are important in FDDI and these four sizes represent somewhat different tradeoffs. While it will be possible to use FDDI stations with any of these sizes of fiber, 62.5/125 and 85/125 seem the best overall compromise for the FDDI application. Consequently the standard is being specified using either of these rather similar fibers. When used with 100/140 fiber, FDDI stations may or may not be able to take advantage of the its greater power coupling potential and may suffer some additional insertion losses due to the use of smaller fibers inside the station between the bulkhead connector and the receiver. In most cases FDDI stations will probably couple less power into 50/125 fiber than they would into one of the two recommended fiber types. It seems safe at this point to recommend that those wishing to cable buildings for future use with FDDI, employ either 62.5/125 or 85/125 fiber with a modal bandwidth of at least 400 MHz·km and an attenuation not greater than 2.5 dB per km. Cables containing such fibers are widely available.

The Window

Figure 3 illustrates characteristic attenuation and chromatic dispersion curves for a typical multimode fiber as a function of wavelength. Two "windows" in the fiber are commonly used, one at around 850 nm and the other at about 1300 nm. Wavelengths in the 1550 nm range are also exploited in long haul telecommunications applications, but LED sources in the 1550 nm range are not commercially available. The second window at around 1300 nm typically has a lower attenuation per unit length than the first and, more significantly, the chromatic dispersion curve passes through zero in the second window, at a point conventionally called, "Lambda Zero." Since LED's have comparatively wide spectra, chromatic dispersion is one of the primary effects which limit link bandwidth. The fiber simply works better at the longer wavelength than at 850 nm.

Nevertheless, 850 nm operation, or both 850 and 1300 nm operation were seriously considered for FDDI, because first window AlGaAs LED's devices can be made with a somewhat simpler process and cost somewhat less than second window InGaAsP devices and because more sensitive detectors are also available for the first window. At the FDDI rate of 125 Mbaud, however, chromatic dispersion would limit short wavelength operation to distances of a few hundred meters. Although many FDDI links will span such distances or less, the confusion created by two incompatible types of FDDI links was felt to be not worth any savings which might result. It would not be practical to change high frequency transmitters and detectors in the field on a routine basis, and if both wavelengths were allowed in the same network the result would be an administrative nightmare. There could even be a need for as many as four kinds of stations (short receive/long transmit, long receive/short transmit, long receive/long transmit and short receive/short transmit). Long wavelength devices do the whole job, and by sticking to them any FDDI link can be up to 2 km long. In most buildings link distances will always be less than 2 km, so the network can be configured without much additional concern.

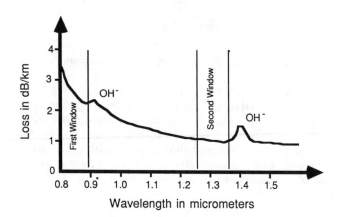

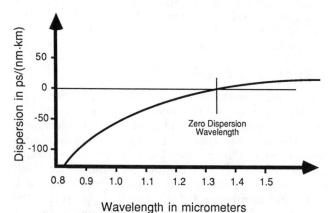

Fig. 3. *Fiber Attenuation and Dispersion.*

Transmitters: LED vs. Laser

Two types of transmitters can be used with multimode fiber: light emitting diodes (LED's) and lasers. Lasers generate more power and have much narrower spectral widths or "linewidths" than LED's. Both characteristics are advantages. On the other hand, lasers are significantly more complex devices than LED's and therefore cost more and fail more frequently. Moreover, they do not appear to be necessary for the FDDI application. Finally, there is the perception that it may be possible to damage the retina of an eye by looking directly into the end of a fiber driven by a laser. Though the safety hazards associated with laser fiber optics are probably less than those associated with common electrical cables, FDDI will be used in workstations and the cables will be accessible to untrained users. For these reasons PMD is written to allow use of LED's. Still, lasers can also clearly meet PMD specifications, and could offer greater link distances, while preserving compatibility with all stations at distances less than 2 km.

Receivers: PIN Diodes vs. APD's

Two general types of optical detectors are in use: PIN diodes or Avalanche Photo Diodes (APD's). APD's are considerably more sensitive, and the FDDI link power budget (the difference between minimum transmitter output and receiver sensitivity) is a concern. However, while first window APD's are comparatively well developed commercial products, second window APD's are not yet commodity products. The use of APD's is therefore ruled out for FDDI because of the component availability and cost goals of FDDI.

Power Budget

One of the consequences of the choices outlined above is that the power budget for FDDI links suffers, particularly from the choice of LED's rather than lasers, and PIN diodes rather than APD's. In the current draft standard the proposed transmitter minimum peak output is −16 dBm into either 62.5/125 or 85/125 fibers, while the minimum receiver input power for a bit error rate of one bit error in 2.5×10^{10} transmitted bits is specified to be −27 dBm. The total link power budget is 11 dB. The launched power will be measured using a precision test fiber and connector plug, so the full 11 dB is available for cable plant loss. These numbers are reasonable and can be maintained in the face of changes in temperature and component aging. Since 2 km of good quality fiber will have a loss of less than 5 dB, this leaves at least 6 dB for other loss elements, including splices, connectors, and switches.

One factor which affects the power budget is the unbalanced code specified in PHY. FDDI uses a 4 of 5 code, that is a code with 4 data bits for every 5 code bits. Such a code has an efficiency of 80 percent, in contrast to the "Manchester" codes used in many other networks, which are 1 of 2 codes with an efficiency of 50 percent. There is, however, no perfectly balanced non-adaptive 4 of 5 code. This means that for some code values there are more ones than zeroes or vice versa. The code chosen for FDDI has a maximum plus or minus 10 percent DC unbalance. Experimental work done in the development of the standard indicates that this causes about a 1 dB link power penalty for equivalent error rates when a long sequence of worst case code values is transmitted. Since the balanced alternatives either have lower code efficiencies, or, in the case of an 8 of 10 code, require a significantly more complex decoder and encoder, this seems a good tradeoff. It will require the use of worst case code value patterns to test receiver sensitivity and must be allowed for in the sensitivity specification.

Loss Elements

PMD will specify a "footprint" for a duplex connector receptacle to be used at the bulkhead of stations. This will be a dry, lensless connector, capable of using either a straight ferrule or a "dual wheelbase" ferrule. Fibers will typically be epoxied into the ferrule and the ends polished for smoothness. Connector losses will not be specified in the standard, but a precision test plug and fiber will be defined for measuring the output power of FDDI stations. Connector loss measurements do not necessarily yield figures for individual connector losses which can be summed across all the connectors in the link to accurately estimate total connector loss. This is in part because many connectors and switches seem to differentially attenuate high order modes more than lower order modes; once the first few connectors or switches have largely stripped off the high order modes, attenuation decreases. Connectors of the type chosen for FDDI stations exhibit losses between .2 dB or less and 1 dB. Any kind of connectors may be used in FDDI cable plants (as opposed to the stations themselves) as long as total link losses are kept under 11 dB.

When station bypass switches are contained in the cable plant, no loss figure is specified; the cable plant designer must simply see that, when stations are bypassed, the total link loss does not exceed 11 dB for any intended operating configuration. When bypass switches are included in stations, however, a maximum inbound to outbound loss of 3 dB is specified for the station bypass condition.

There is little cost advantage to the use of optical fibers with a loss greater than 2.5 dB per km. Fiber losses can therefore easily be held to 5 dB or less at 2 km.

Jitter

Signal jitter arises from a variety of phenomena. Jitter can be broken down into a data dependent component, and a random component. The data dependent component arises in part from the limited channel bandwidth. A major cause of random jitter is thermal noise in the receiver. Random jitter components can be summed together in "RMS" fashion (that is, as a square root of a sum of squares), but data dependent jitter can not be added in any straightforward fashion, because the various jitter terms are correlated to the data. While PMD does not specify jitter allocation inside stations, but rather draws the line at the station optical bulkhead, it is necessary to analyze all jitter components and sources between the encoder and decoder, to determine reasonable specifications at the station bulkhead.

The design of the FDDI receiver is further complicated because the receiver will see weak signals with comparatively high exit bandwidths (when losses are primarily due to connectors and switches) and with low bandwidths (when long optical fibers are used). This limits what can be done to compensate for channel bandwidth with filters in the receiver. With an 8 ns code-bit cell, an error will occur whenever the instantaneous jitter exceeds plus or minus 4 ns. A series of experiments are being conducted with a number of PIN diode receivers to determine reasonable bulkhead jitter specifications for FDDI using available components. This work is not complete, but preliminary indications are that the budget will be tight, but workable. The determination of the jitter budget involves trading off source rise times and fiber bandwidth, as well as the source spectrum. There are a number of dependent variables which must be assigned values, so that FDDI stations can be implemented using a broad range of components and designs, while still maintaining compatibility between stations.

Conclusion

FDDI will establish a standard for 100 Mb/s optical data links of up to 2 km. In general, FDDI will allow the use of the lowest cost components which can satisfy this goal. It is expected that the standard will help to develop the market for these components, and that, as the market grows, prices will fall. FDDI is expected to serve an anticipated broad demand for the interconnection of large computers, storage servers and high performance work stations, as well as for trunk connections between lower bandwidth networks.

It is possible, by carefully matching fiber, transmitter and receiver, to use components of the types chosen for FDDI in data links which significantly exceed the 100 Mb/s at 2 km goal of FDDI. The norm for local networks, however, is that stations are made by dif-

ferent vendors who use a variety of different commodity components. FDDI will be intended to permit use of a wide range of such components and this will help to reduce network costs. The FDDI PMD standard will be a reasonable compromise between maximum performance and the need to reliably accommodate heterogeneous stations.

References

[1] International Standard 7498, "Information Processing Systems—Open systems Interconnection—Basic Reference Model," International Organization for Standardization, Geneva, 1984.

William E. Burr is a graduate of the Ohio State University (BEE '67). In his early career he was a system programmer. While working for the U.S. Army Communications Research and Development Command he organized a research program in the measurement of computer instruction-set architecture, and is the author of several papers on the subject. Since 1978 he has worked for the National Bureau of Standards on the development of input/output interface standards for computer mass storage devices. This has led to his interest in high speed "backend" networks. Mr. Burr is the chairman of American National Standards Committee X3T9.2 (presently doing a standard for the Small Computer System Interface), and vice chairman of ANSC X3T9, which has overall preview over IO interface standards activities. He led the effort which resulted in the formation of ANSC X3T9.5, which does standards for high bandwidth back-end networks, and participates in both the Local Distributed Data Interface and Fiber Distributed Data Interface standards projects for very high bandwidth back-end network standards. He is the author of several papers on back-end networks and a member of the IEEE Communications and Computer Societies.

Spectral Complications

A principal indicator of the quality of the signal at a receiver is its optical input rise time. With an 8 ns bit cell, FDDI receiver rise times should be held to under 4 ns, to simplify the receiver design. Even with second

window LED's, chromatic dispersion is a significant factor in determining the rise time seen after a rising edge has traversed a km or two of fiber.

LED product data sheets typically specify a peak or

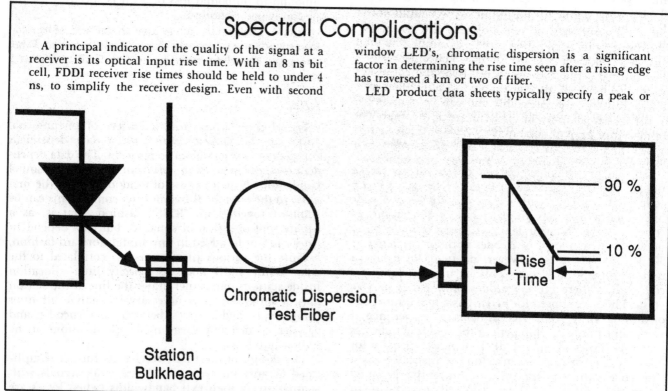

Station
Bulkhead

Chromatic Dispersion
Test Fiber

90 %

10 %

Rise
Time

center wavelength, a "full width, half max." spectral width and a rise time. Most available LED sources have a center wavelength on the low (short wavelength) side of the zero dispersion wavelength. Available LED's vary considerably in their spectral width. The source spectrum and pulse shape, along with the fiber chromatic and modal dispersion determine the overall channel bandwidth and rise times seen by the receiver.

Any simple three number worst case specification for transmitter rise time, center wavelength and spectral width will either rule out many devices which would work perfectly well, or will allow devices which would not work.

A more direct approach would be to specify a worst case spectral dispersion curve and fiber bandwidth, representing the fiber characteristics of the worst case intended link (this is required in any event) and then specify and measure rise times after the signal had traversed such a fiber. Any source which gives the desired rise time then meets the standard, whatever its spectrum and rise time going into the fiber.

There are some obvious practical problems to this approach, however. One is simply the need for a source of carefully calibrated test fibers. Another possible approach, which may be adopted, at least as an interim solution, is to assume that LED's have a spectrum with a normal distribution (this is not necessarily so), and calculate the chromatic dispersion term from center wavelength and spectral width data published on component data sheets. This could then be combined with the published rise time to calculate the expected exit rise time or channel bandwidth seen by a receiver at the end of a 2 km link. Because of the approximations involved, this is obviously less satisfying than the direct measurement suggested above, but it would allow designers to work from data already available to them.

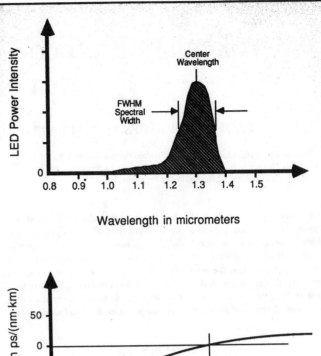

Tokenless Protocols for Fiber Optic Local Area Networks

PAULO RODRIGUES, LUIGI FRATTA, MEMBER, IEEE, AND MARIO GERLA, MEMBER, IEEE

Reprinted from *IEEE Journal on Selected Areas in Communications*, Volume SAC-3, Number 6, November 1985, pages 928-940. Copyright © 1985 by The Institute of Electrical and Electronics Engineers, Inc.

Abstract —A family of LAN (Local Area Network) protocols is presented. The LAN consists of a pair of unidirectional fiber optic buses to which stations are connected via passive taps. The protocols provide round-robin bounded delay access to all stations. Contrary to most round-robin access schemes, the protocols do not require transmission of special packets (tokens); rather, they simply rely on the detection of bus activity at each station. The performance of these protocols in various traffic conditions and system configurations is evaluated via analysis and simulation.

I. INTRODUCTION

RECENT years have witnessed a rapid growth in local area communications needs due to the increase in user demands and the emergence of new applications such as real-time voice and video, high-speed printers, and graphics. LAN designers are being urged to provide systems able to handle very high throughput among users several kilometers apart, while still satisfying delay constraints which become severe when real-time traffic is involved. A suitable choice of transmission medium, topology, and access protocol is necessary to meet these demands.

Among the possible transmission media, optical fiber appears to be the most cost-effective and promising technology. Fiber offers high bandwidth, immunity against electrical and magnetic interference, and protection against signal leakage. Other attractive features are its ease of installation due to light weight and small size, and low attenuation compared to coaxial cable.

Fiber optics topologies can be configured in three basic ways: ring, star, and bus. In the ring, access is generally provided by a token scheme. Ring implementations require active repeaters and substantial logic working at channel speed (e.g., address recognition and flag setting) at each station. Cost and reliability, in spite of some fail-safe node proposals [1], may pose limits to the use of ring interfaces

Manuscript received November 13, 1984; revised July 19, 1985. This paper was presented in part at ICC '84, Amsterdam, The Netherlands, April 1984. This work was supported in part by the United States Defense Advanced Research Projects Agency under Contract MDA903-82-C-0064, the U.S. Army Research Office under Contract DAAG 29-85-K-0101, the National Science Foundation under Contract E-CS-80-20300, the Italian National Research Council under Contract C-NET No. 104520.97.8007745, and by the Brazilian Research Council under Contract 200.123/79.

P. Rodrigues is with the Nucleo de Computacáo Eletrônica, Federal University of Rio de Janeiro, Brazil.

L. Fratta is with the Department of Electrical Engineering, Politecnico di Milano, Milano, Italy.

M. Gerla is with the Department of Computer Science, University of California, Los Angeles, CA 90024.

at very high speed. Furthermore, special procedures are needed to maintain synchronization, to recover from token loss or duplication, and to avoid nonrecognized packets circulating endlessly in the ring.

Star topologies can be built by connecting several stations via an optical coupler. Star-configured networks have been implemented using either passive [6] or active [7] components. Most star implementations use the CSMA-CD access protocol which was successfully used in ETHERNET. Unfortunately, CSMA-CD performance becomes very poor when end-to-end propagation delay on the bus is comparable to (or larger than) packet transmission time [9].

Bus topology is the third alternative. Since optical fibers are unidirectional in nature, a unidirectional-bus system (UBS) must be used. In UBS, each station is connected to the bus and signals propagate in only one direction. To achieve broadcast communication two separate buses are needed where signals propagate in opposite directions, or the same bus must be folded in order to visit all stations twice. In recent years, extensive research has been conducted on UBS local area networks and some efficient protocols have been proposed. Expressnet [2] is based on a folded unidirectional bus and achieves conflict-free transmissions and bounded delay by means of a completely distributed implicit token protocol. A simple modification of Expressnet, D-net [10] uses central control to regenerate the token at each cycle.

U-net [3], Buzz-net [4], and Fasnet [5] are examples of UBS local area networks based on the twin-bus architecture. U-net and Buzz-net are asynchronous networks which use special patterns to implement the signaling scheme to control the channel. The need to recognize different transmission patterns may cause difficulties in the implementation. Fasnet is a synchronous slotted network, where slot generation and clock synchronization are the responsibility of the physical end stations. In Fasnet, stations must maintain bit synchronization with the bus at all times.

All the above mentioned systems can be implemented on either optical fiber or coaxial cable. When optical fibers are used, insertion loss is the major limitation to the maximum number of stations, N, which can be passively connected to the network. In view of this constraint, the twin-bus architecture is preferable to the folded-bus architecture since each segment must support N (instead of $2N$) passive taps. Furthermore, the twin bus presents fewer techni-

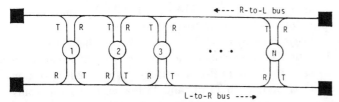

Fig. 1. Dual-bus architecture.

cal problems for cable installation and further network expansion.

This paper presents a family of protocols suitable for twin unidirectional-bus architectures. These protocols are innovative because they provide round-robin access to active stations (as any token-based scheme does), without using a token. In fact, the only required control feature at the interface is the ability to detect bus activity. For this reason the protocols are named Tokenless.

The basic operating principles of the Tokenless protocols are given in Section II, while details of different versions are described in Section III. Recovery and joining procedures are described in Section IV. Analytical and simulation results are presented in Sections V and VI.

II. PRINCIPLES OF OPERATION

The tokenless protocol (TLP) runs on the twin-bus architecture shown in Fig. 1. Stations are connected to each bus via two passive taps, a *receive* tap and *transmit* tap. Stations receive packets and monitor channel activity through the receive tap. Specifically, the receive tap can observe presence or absense of activity (i.e., data) and detect events such as EOA (end of activity) and BOA (beginning of activity).

The transmit tap transmits (data) packets or an activity signal (AS). The activity signal keeps the downstream part of the channel busy. Its implementation (modulated or unmodulated carrier, random bits, continuous sequence of 1's, etc.) can be chosen according to the low-level encoding utilized for transmission on the channel.

A maximum reaction delay d is assumed between the time a station senses EOA on one bus and the time it can start transmission on either bus. Likewise, there is a maximum delay d between the sensing of activity from an upstream station and the interruption of an ongoing transmission. Moreover, an activity burst of duration d is the minimum amount of energy reliably detected at any interface. The actual value of the parameter d depends on the speed and transmission delays of the detection logics in the hardware implementation. Laboratory experiments show that detection of activity in optical fibers can be done reliably in nanosecond intervals.

A transmitting station always defers to an upstream transmission by aborting its own. The upstream transmission proceeds with only the first few bits corrupted by deferrals, regardless of the number of downstream stations attempting to transmit. If the preamble is sufficiently long, this feature guarantees that a packet which has been completely transmitted by a station is correctly received by all (downstream) stations.

Apart from the corruption of the first few bits in the preamble, the TLP protocols are generally collision free. The only exception is one version of the protocol, TLP-4, where, as we shall see, conflict may occur when an idle station becomes active and attempts to acquire channel synchronization. The conflict, however, is resolved in finite time. For this case, we assume that an interface detects a packet even when the packet is immediately preceded by a truncated transmission. The underlying assumption is that the beginning-of-packet flag cannot be replicated within the packet data nor contained in the activity signal described above. Flags can be implemented as reserved bit patterns (in which case bit stuffing is required to preserve data transparency), or as code violations on the bit encoding level.

The goal of the protocol is to guarantee round-robin transmissions among all back-logged stations, and to achieve good throughput/delay performance for a variety of traffic conditions and station placement. Furthermore, the need to detect special packets (e.g., tokens) is avoided, and control is completely distributed. These goals are achieved by EOA events propagating in the two buses alternatively. EOA events can be viewed as virtual tokens that allow stations to transmit packets in a round-robin fashion. One advantage of controlling the channel only through EOA events is the simple, reliable, and low-cost implementation even at very high speeds. Another advantage is the easy implementation of initialization and recovery procedures.

III. THE PROTOCOL

The protocol basically consists of five procedures. Each of these procedures has a specifically defined purpose and is represented by a set of states in the protocol's state diagram. The *probing* procedure enables a station to recognize its turn to transmit in a round. The *election* procedure enables a station to determine whether it is an extreme (leftmost or rightmost active) station. The *round-restart* procedure enables an extreme station to initiate a round in the reverse direction. The *recovery* procedure provides recovery when illegal events are detected. The *initialization* procedure enables a newly active station to synchronize with other active stations, if any, or through the recovery procedure, to initialize the round-robin cycle in an empty net. An active station is a station that is neither idle nor powered off.

Different parameters and options may be chosen when specifying the full protocol. Before exploring the details of the different implementations, the common foundation of the various versions of tokenless protocol is presented below.

A. Basic Tokenless Protocol

In describing the basic protocol, A is a variable designating one channel and $\overline{A}$ designates the opposite channel. Events on channel A are indicated by $EVENT(A)$.

The first procedure, or *probing*, enables a station to probe the end of the train of packets (which has been forming on one bus) and to append its packet to the train. Assume channel A has been sensed busy by backlogged station S_i. S_i then waits for $EOA(A)$. If $EOA(A)$ occurs, S_i starts transmitting an activity signal on channel A. Otherwise, after time-out d, S_i assumes that it has found the end of the train and it starts packet transmission on both channels.

The above procedure prevents station S_i from starting transmission on channel $\bar{A}$ during an interpacket gap, before the end of the train. In fact, if a burst of activity were sent on channel $\bar{A}$ during an interpacket gap, a collision with an upstream (with respect to channel A) transmitting station may occur. With the proposed procedure, actual packet transmission starts on both channels only when the end of a train of packets is detected. Prior to that, a signal is transmitted only on channel A. Thus, only the first few bits of the incoming packet on channel A may be corrupted.

After completing the transmission of a packet, station S_i the *election* procedure to determine whether it is an extreme station (i.e., leftmost or rightmost station on the channel). In order to do that, S_i sets time-out TES (extreme station) and continuously transmits the activity signal on channel $\bar{A}$ until either a $BOA(\bar{A})$ is detected or time-out TES occurs. If $BOA(\bar{A})$ is detected, S_i cancels time-out TES and repeats the probing procedure with A and $\bar{A}$ reversed. If TES is reached, S_i realizes it is an extreme station and executes the *round-restart* procedure. The *round-restart* procedure enables the extreme station to initiate a round in the opposite direction. Different versions of TLP take slightly different actions at the end of a round. The details are discussed separately for each TLP version.

If both channels are initially idle, the *initialization* procedure is invoked. Namely, each station S_i sets time-out ND (Network Dead) and waits for the first of two events: BOA on either channel or time-out ND. If BOA occurs on channel A, S_i cancels time-out ND and performs as if channel A were initially sensed busy. Alternatively, if time-out ND occurs (no other station is active in the network), S_i begins the *recovery* procedure to initialize the idle network.

The *recovery* procedure is also invoked during normal operation when illegal events are detected on the channels. Illegal events may be symptomatic of a temporary malfunction in one interface, or may be caused by a station out of synchronism. A thorough discussion of recovery and joining procedures is given in Section IV.

B. Various Implementations

The several ways to specify round restart, initialization, and to choose parameters ND and TES lead to different versions of TLP. Two versions, TLP-1 and TLP-3, require all powered-on stations to be active in the network. TLP-2 and TLP-4 require only backlogged stations to be active. Moreover, TLP-3 and TLP-4 use additional status variables to improve performance. All versions are completely distributed, follow the basic protocol described in the previous section, and use the same recovery procedure.

These four versions, TLP-1, TLP-2, TLP-3, and TLP-4, constitute the family of tokenless protocols.

1) Definitions: A station is *idle* if it is in the IDLE state. A station that is neither idle nor powered off is called an *active* station. In TLP-1, and TLP-3, a powered-on station is always active. In TLP-2 and TLP-4, an idle station only becomes active when a packet backlog is formed.

Variable A denotes the channel where EOA is expected, or where the station is currently transmitting the activity signal. Channel A is called the synchronizing channel. The identity of A changes during the execution of the protocol and is assigned value 0 or 1 depending on whether the synchronizing channel is, respectively, channel L to R (Left to Right) or channel R to L.

Parameter $R = 2\tau + 2d$ is fundamental in the implementation of the protocols. τ is the end-to-end propagation delay. R may be interpreted as the interval of time needed for EOA to be propagated from one end station to the opposite end station (τ), detected at the latter station and regenerated as a BOA on the other channel (reaction delay d), propagated back to the former station (τ), and finally detected (d).

The EOA signal at the end of a "train" can be viewed as a virtual token circulating on the bus between end stations. A station physically located inside the present sweep of the virtual token is called an *inside station*. Similarly, a station physically located outside the present sweep of the virtual token is called an *outside station*. An outside station may be an idle station (in TLP-2 or TLP-4) or a station which has just been powered on.

2) TLP-1: TLP-1 is described below in detail. This description includes background information which also pertains to TLP-2, TLP-3, and TLP-4. The state diagram shown in Fig. 2 defines the TLP-1 operation.

States ON and I at the left of the figure represent the *initialization* procedure. Also at the left, states R1 and R2 represent the *recovery* procedure. R is a pseudostate which simplifies the drawing of state transitions into recovery. States WFT, TTT, ST, and TXP represent the *probing* and *transmission* procedures. State ES executes the *round-restart* procedure.

A station enters ON only when it is powered-on. If one of the channels is busy (i.e., bus is busy, or BIB in Fig. 2) A is set to the value of that channel (0 or 1) and the state moves to WFT (Wait For Token) where the station waits for the synchronizing signal $EOA(A)$ as described in Section II. If both channels are idle (i.e., Both Buses Idle, or BBI), S_i sets time-out $ND = R + d$ and moves to state I. ND guarantees that if any station is active in the network it will be heard before any other action is taken. The reason for setting ND to the given value will be clear after the *round-restart* procedure is explained. If activity is sensed in a channel (BOA detection) before time-out ND is reached, A is set to the corresponding channel, and the station leaves the *initialization* procedure moving to state WFT. Otherwise, when ND is reached, the *recovery* procedure is executed by states R1 and R2. In the state diagram, the dotted lines which converge toward R1 (through R) repre-

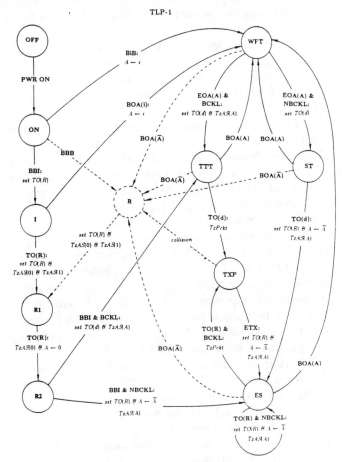

Fig. 2. TLP-1 state diagram.

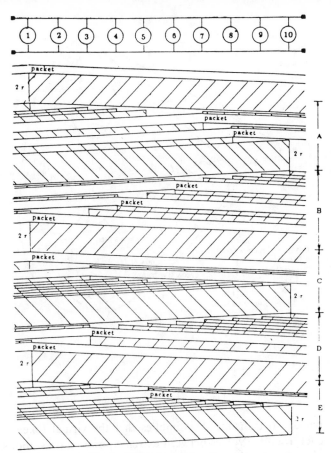

Fig. 3. TLP-1 Space–time diagram.

sent transitions due to illegal events. The *recovery* procedure is standard for all versions of TLP and will be explained in Section IV.

States WFT, TTT, ST, and TXP allow a station to identify its turn and transmit a backlogged packet at the proper time. When in WFT, the station waits for $EOA(A)$ as described in Section III-A. If there is a backlogged packet in the station, detection of $EOA(A)$ causes a move to state TTT (Try To Transmit) after setting time-out d. In TTT the station transmits activity signal AS for an interval d. The purpose of TTT is to detect the end of a train of packets with an interpacket gap of, at most, d. If no $BOA(A)$ is detected before time-out d expires, the state moves to TXP (Transmit Packet) and the first packet in the queue is transmitted on both channels. At the end of packet transmission, (i.e., ETX), the state moves to ES (End-Station Detection mode) and the activity signal is transmitted on channel $\bar{A}$.

If $BOA(A)$ was detected while in TTT, the state moves back to WFT.

If the station has no backlog, it moves from WFT to ST (Set Time-Out). State ST performs as TTT except that no packet transmission occurs. Consequently, the state changes directly from ST to ES, without passing through TXP.

The *round-restart* procedure is performed in state ES. In this state, the station transmits the activity signal in the channel opposite of the channel where the virtual token is propagating. If the station senses $BOA(A)$, then it concludes it is not an end station and moves to state WFT. If the station does not sense a $BOA(A)$ within the interval R,

then it realizes it is an extreme station. If the extreme station has a backlogged packet, it moves to TXP immediately. Otherwise, it remains in state ES and behaves accordingly after inverting the identity of the synchronizing channel.

Observe that if only one station is active in the network, then the periods of activity in either channel are separated by idle intervals of duration R. Also note that any new active station must wait for $ND = R + d$ seconds in state I before starting recovery. Thus, the new joining station will be automatically synchronized with the network if there is another active station since $ND > R$.

An example of the operation of TLP-1 for a network with 10 stations is given in the space–time diagram shown in Fig. 3. The time intervals, A, B, C, D, and E represent rounds. In round A, the virtual token propagates from left to right, stations 1, 3, 4, 5, 7, 8, 9, and 10 are powered on, and stations 7 and 8 transmit packets. In round B, the virtual token propagates from right to left, station 6 is powered on, and stations 6, 4, and 1 transmit packets. Rounds C, D, and E are similar.

TLP-1's greatest advantage is simplicity. Only the first station which finds the network dead must execute the initialization procedure. All other stations detect activity when they come alive and gracefully join the set of active stations. Ease of network joining is a consequence of time-out R enforced at the end of each round. However, performance is impaired by this extra overhead.

Performance also degrades under other special circumstances. In TLP-1 a powered-on station always performs activity on the channel even if the station has no

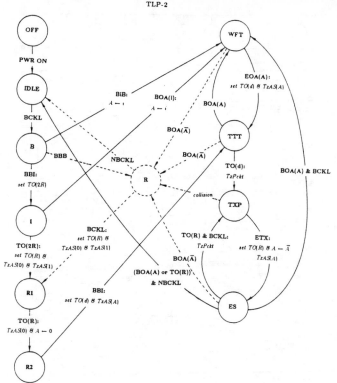

Fig. 4. TLP-2 state diagram.

packet to transmit. This implies that the virtual token in each round revolves between extreme powered-on stations. If traffic load is unbalanced and only a few stations are actually transmitting, this mode of operation introduces unnecessary delay because the virtual token must sweep the entire bus, rather than only the section of the bus containing the stations involved in transmission.

In an attempt to remove some of the TLP-1 limitations other versions of the protocol have been investigated. These versions are described below.

3) TLP-2: In TLP-2, the unnecessary propagation delay observed in TLP-1 is eliminated by allowing the virtual token to sweep only between extreme stations which have a packet to transmit. This efficiency is achieved by forcing a station with no backlog to idle. Fig. 4 shows the state diagram for TLP-2.

As a difference from TLP-1, state ST is no longer necessary (only backlog stations are active) and ON is replaced by states IDLE and B (i.e., Backlogged). IDLE is initially entered when a station is powered on. While in IDLE, transition to B only occurs when a packet is backlogged. Upon leaving ES, the system moves back to IDLE if no backlogged packet is present.

Transitions from B are similar to those from ON in TLP-1, except that time-out ND is set to $2R$, allowing newly backlogged stations to smoothly join the other active stations [8].

In terms of state-diagram complexity, TLP-1 and TLP-2 are very similar. Performance, however, may differ substantially. When the active stations are confined to a small section of the network and remain busy for several rounds, TLP-2 is preferred to TLP-1. The virtual-token sweep is confined only to the span of the network covering the active stations, and stations do not incur initialization

overhead since the channels are constantly busy. At heavy load, when all the stations are backlogged, TLP-1 and TLP-2 perform identically. If the load is light, TLP-2 shows inferior performance because the channel often becomes idle, and a newly backlogged station must execute the *initialization* procedure before transmitting on an idle channel.

4) TLP-3: A substantial contribution to overhead in both previous versions of the protocol is given by time-out R enforced between rounds. This delay can be reduced by observing that in TLP-1, if a station is an extreme station in a round, then in the next round the station is likely to be an extreme station again. TLP-3 works similarly to TLP-1, with the exception that an extreme station starts a new round in the opposite direction as soon as time-out $2d$ has elapsed since the last action of the station on the channel. Time-out $2d$ in TLP-3 is generally negligible compared to time-out R used in TLP-1. The result is a substantial performance improvement. Time-out $2d$ is sufficient to guarantee that a new powered-on outside station joins the set of active stations in a finite time. This joining procedure is explained in more detail in Section IV.

The state diagram for TLP-3 is shown in Fig. 5. As a difference from TLP-1, TLP-3 substitutes state ES with states ES0 and ES1. In addition, a flag $E(A)$ signals whether or not a station is the most upstream active station in channel A. ES0 is entered after a packet transmission if flag $E(\overline{A})$, corresponding to the future synchronizing channel $\overline{A}$ is 0. ES0 performs similarly to ES. However, if time-out R is reached while in ES0, $E(A)$ is set to 1, indicating that the station is currently an extreme station on that channel. Transition from ES0 to recovery-state R only occurs if activity on channel $\overline{A}$ [i.e., $BOA(\overline{A})$] is detected. If $BOA(A)$ occurs, the state moves to WFT, as in the normal procedure.

ES1 is entered after a packet transmission if flag $E(\overline{A})$, corresponding to the future synchronizing channel $\overline{A}$, is 1. ES1 performs similarly to ES0 except that time-out $2d$ is used instead of time-out R and any activity on either channel (while in ES1), triggers recovery. Transition into recovery resets $E(0)$ and $E(1)$ to 0.

Transition from ES0 to ES1 occurs when time-out R expires, if $E(\overline{A}) = 1$ and there is no backlog. If $E(\overline{A}) = 0$ and there is no backlog, the state remains in ES0. In case of backlog, the state moves back to TXP. The reverse is true for transitions from ES1 to ES0 if time-out $2d$ is substituted for R.

TLP-3 is always superior to TLP-1 except in unrealistic cases where stations turn on and off continuously. In such a situation, collisions could force additional recovery delays of up to $2R + d$ per round (see Section IV). Under this circumstance TLP-1 performs better because overhead (not including propagation delay) is kept at R per round.

The cost of this improved performance is a more complex state diagram and the additional use of status flags. These flags are needed as internal hardware variables, thus requiring more elaborate implementation.

5) TLP-4: TLP-4 combines features of both TLP-2 and TLP-3. The token sweep is confined between the most widely separated backlogged active stations, as in TLP-2.

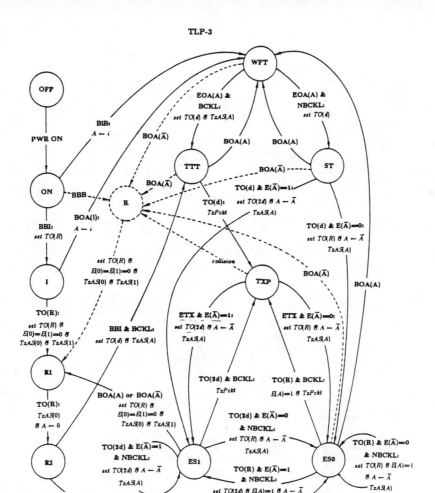

Fig. 5. TLP-3 state diagram.

Extreme stations preserve their status in flag variables set in the same manner as in TLP-3. The extreme-station flag variable allows round reversal with a minimum overhead of $2d$.

Fig. 6 shows the state diagram for TLP-4. As in TLP-2, state ST is unnecessary, because only backlogged stations are active. Also, transitions between ES0 and ES1 do not exist because absence of backlog moves the state to IDLE. The need for state WT is explained in Appendix I. Essentially, it prevents a lock-up condition which could cause infinite delays in accessing the network.

Because flag variable status is preserved when the station returns to IDLE, initialization delay is reduced by allowing a station with a channel flag set to 1 to transmit immediately on the corresponding channel, if both channels are sensed idle at packet arrival. If the station is an extreme station on both channels, the last value of A determines the synchronizing channel. This procedure is executed concurrently with the transition from B to TTT. Also different from the initialization in TLP-2, a station does not start recovery if both channels are sensed busy while in B. Sensing both channels busy probably means that a recovery is occurring. There is no need to cause additional delay by starting a new recovery. The station simply remains in state B waiting for a channel to become idle.

Then, the station moves to state WFT synchronized on the busy channel. The busy channel flag is also reset to 0.

At heavy load, when all stations are active, TLP-4 performs identically to TLP-3. There are no collisions or initializations. Overhead between rounds is kept at $2d$ seconds.

At light load, first stations go through the initialization procedure. However, the extreme-station flag corresponding to the synchronizing channel is set to 1 after the first successful transmission on that channel, when the station is the current extreme station. Subsequently, the station can access the network, as in random mode, without any delay. If the station has a large packet backlog, the packets will be transmitted one after the other with interpacket gaps of $2d$ seconds. While no collision occurs, stations access the network freely. Delay at light load is decreased to almost zero.

At intermediate load, TLP-4 performance may degrade considerably. The token sweep may become confined to a small section of the network, so that a station outside this section must force a collision to get in. Furthermore, a station may join the network synchronized by one channel; then, if it has a flag set for the other channel, it reverses the round at the end of its packet transmission, even if there is another active station upstream. This premature round

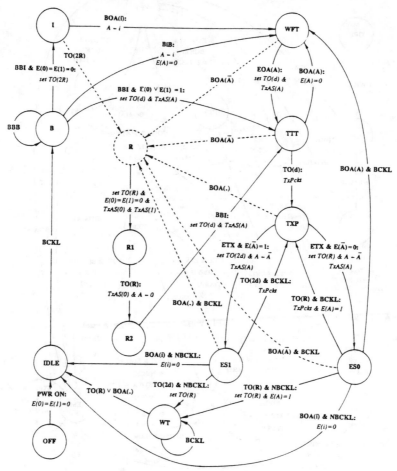

Fig. 6. TLP-4 state diagram.

reversal causes a collision with the upstream station transmission, triggering recovery and causing extra delay. This occurence becomes more frequent as the ratio τ/T increases (T is the packet length).

When leaving state B and going to state I, time-out ND is set to $2R$, as in TLP-2.

TLP-4 outperforms the other protocol versions under light-load conditions, in which case access delay becomes negligible. At heavy load, TLP-4 and TLP-3 both perform optimally. At intermediate-load levels an uneven distribution of the pattern with large backlog at only a few stations may favor TLP-4 over the other versions, as simulation results in Section VI show. For very large networks, the improvement may be considerable.

IV. RECOVERY AND JOINING

For all TLP versions, the recovery procedure is executed by states R1 and R2. R is a pseudostate which simplifies the drawing of state transitions to recovery. These transitions are drawn in dotted lines to distinguish them from transitions between regular states.

TLP protocols are structured so that stations sense only one channel busy at any one time. Furthermore, while the channels are "synchronized," packet transmission is collision free and BOA events are expected only on the channel which is currently busy, or on which the station is presently transmitting an activity signal.

Transition into R1 is triggered by detection of simultaneous activity on both channels or by detection of upstream activity during packet transmission (collision). Either condition may be caused by station malfunctioning, or newly powered-on stations (TLP-3 and TLP-4), or newly backlogged stations (TLP-4).

Newly active inside stations are always transparently absorbed by the network (the joining process occurs without extra overhead). State ON (TLP-1, TLP-3) or B (TLP-2, TLP-4) guarantees the correct behavior by moving the station to state WFT when one of the channels is initially sensed busy. The variable A is set to the busy channel.

A newly active outside station is still transparently absorbed in TLP-1 and TLP-2 because of delay R between rounds. This station detects end-of-train in the synchronizing channel, and its transmission reaches the current extreme station before the round is reversed. It then becomes the new extreme station.

However, in TLP-3 and TLP-4, a newly active outside station can join the active network only after recovery is executed. In fact, the extreme station situated upstream of the joining station reverses the round before the joining station can transmit successfully. In both versions, the delay $2d$ in round reversal forces a collision following the joining station attempt to transmit at the end-of-train in the round. Recovery then takes place.

Stations perform the recovery procedure in a distributed fashion. The recovery is completed in a finite time. The following steps are executed during recovery:

a) detection of abnormal condition and transition into R1,

b) transmission of activity on both channels for $R = 2\tau + 2d$ while in state R1; after R has expired, move to R2, and

c) in R2, continue to transmit activity on channel L to R. After both channels are sensed idle, the station executes the standard procedure as if channel L to R had been initially detected busy. In TLP-2 and TLP-4, the state moves from R2 to TTT because a backlog always exists. In TLP-1 and TLP-3, if a backlog exists, the state moves from R2 to TTT. Otherwise, the state moves to ES or ES0, respectively, where the station checks whether or not it is an extreme station.

In Appendix I we show that recovery is completed in $2R + d$ seconds in the worst case, for any of the protocol versions.

V. Performance Analysis

In this section we develop analytic models for TPL performance. These models differ from conventional polling models in that the stations with backlogged packets transmit in sequential order from 1 to N and from N to 1, alternatively. This alternate operation makes channel-access time dependent on the position of the station on the bus. In fact, if stations are uniformly spaced and traffic is balanced, only the central station can access the network at uniformly distributed time intervals. All other stations observe alternatively shorter and longer access-time intervals. This asymmetry in time-access distribution introduces some unfairness in delay performance but does not affect station throughput, which is the same for all stations.

Before introducing the models, some definitions are in order.

N	Number of stations connected to the network.
M	Number of active stations with heavy backlog.
T	Packet transmission time (includes preamble overhead). This time is assumed constant.
$\tau_{ij} = \tau_{ji}$	Propagation delay between stations i and j. Stations are assumed to be uniformly spaced along the buses.
$\tau = \tau_{i1} + \tau_{iN}$	End-to-end propagation delay on the bus.
S_r	Rightmost active station.
S_l	Leftmost active station.
S_i	ith station.
T_{ES}	Round-restart time out.
d	Reaction time.

A. Network Utilization

Under equilibrium conditions, network utilization $U_i(M)$ is defined as the ratio between the time in a round spent for packet transmissions and the round duration, given that M stations are active and always transmitting in each round. The subscript i refers to TLP version i.

The round duration, $R(M)$, defined as the time between the detection of the end of round at one end station and the detection of the next end of round at the other end station, is given by $R(M) = M(T + 2d) + T_{ES} + \tau_{lr}$.

In reviewing this expression, we note that $R(M)$ is maximum when S_1 and S_N are the extreme stations ($\tau_{lr} = \tau_{1N} = \tau$). Station reaction time is usually equal to a few bit times and, therefore, $2d \ll T$. T_{ES} represents the time needed for a station to discover that it is an extreme station and is equal to the time-out set during the *round-restart* procedure. In TLP-1 and TLP-2, T_{ES} is R seconds. In TLP-3 and TLP-4, T_{ES} may be assumed $2d$ at heavy load. In fact, at heavy load the identity of the extreme stations does not change; thus, no extra overhead is incurred due to initialization.

Based on the above considerations we find

$$U_{1,2}(M, a) = \cfrac{1}{1 + \cfrac{3a}{M} + \cfrac{2d}{T}} \cong \cfrac{1}{1 + \cfrac{3a}{M}} \qquad (1)$$

and

$$U_{3,4}(M, a) = \cfrac{1}{1 + \cfrac{a}{M} + \cfrac{2d}{T} \cdot \cfrac{M+1}{M}} \cong \cfrac{1}{1 + \cfrac{a}{M}} \qquad (2)$$

where $a = \tau/T$.

Maximum network utilization is achieved for $M = N$ (i.e., all the stations are active).

B. Delay Performance

Delay in this section is defined as the average insertion delay (ID), namely, the interval between the time when the packet reaches the head of the transmitting queue and the time when the successful transmission begins. The average is over all stations and over time. Analytic expressions for ID at light load (IDL) and at heavy load (IDH) are derived. Results for general load can be obtained only via simulation and are presented in Section VI.

1) Light Load: In TLP-4, insertion delay at light load is negligible. The first packet transmitted after power-on suffers a delay $3R$ due to network initialization, but all subsequent packets are transmitted immediately after arrival. In case of multipacket traffic at a single station, packets are transmitted with an interpacket gap of $2d$ seconds. The probability of collision during message transmission is assumed negligible.

In TLP-2 insertion delay is the time needed to initialize the idle network, which is $3R$. All single packets suffer this delay. In case of multipacket messages, the first packet suffers delay $3R$ and subsequent packets are transmitted with an interpacket gap R.

For TLP-1 and TLP-3 all stations are assumed powered on. Therefore, S_1 and S_N are the extreme stations. Consider station S_i. At light load, access instants for S_i are alternatively separated by x_i and y_i time intervals where $x_i = n(x_i)(T+2d) + T_{ES} + 2\tau_{1i}$ and $y_i = n(y_i)(T+2d) + T_{ES} + 2\tau_{iN}$. Here, $n(\cdot)$ represents the number of packets transmitted in the corresponding interval.

The average insertion delay for packets generated at station S_i at random points in time is

$$IDL_i = \frac{x_i}{2}\,\text{Prob}\,\{\text{arrival in } x_i\}$$
$$+ \frac{y_i}{2}\,\text{Prob}\,\{\text{arrival in } y_i\}$$
$$= \frac{x_i}{2}\frac{x_i}{x+y} + \frac{y_i}{2}\frac{y_i}{x+y}$$
$$= \frac{(T_{ES}+2\tau_{1i})^2 + (T_{ES}+2\tau_{iN})^2}{2(2T_{ES}+2\tau)}. \qquad (3)$$

Maximum IDL occurs at the end stations and minimum IDL occurs at the central station(s).

TLP-1 shows $(3/2)\tau \leqslant IDL_i \leqslant (5/3)\tau$, and TLP-3 shows $(1/2)\tau \leqslant IDL_I \leqslant \tau$, which demonstrates that the difference in IDL among stations is always less than $\tau/2$. Averaging over all stations yields

$$IDL_{\text{TLP }1,3} = \frac{1}{N}\sum_{i=1}^{N} IDL_i$$
$$= \frac{1}{T_{ES}+\tau}\left[\frac{T_{ES}^2}{2} + T_{ES}\tau + \frac{\tau^2}{3}\left(2+\frac{1}{N-1}\right)\right]. \qquad (4)$$

2) Heavy Load: At heavy load, stations always have a packet to transmit, and the time intervals between consecutive access rights at station S_i are alternatively

$$x_i + (2(N-i)+1)(T+2d) + T_{ES} + 2\tau_{iN},$$

and

$$y_i(2(i-1)+1)(T+2d) + T_{ES} + 2\tau_{i1}.$$

The average insertion delay is

$$IDH_i = \frac{x_i+y_i}{2} - T = (N-1)T + 2Nd + T_{ES} + \tau = IDH.$$

IDH is independent of station location and increases linearly with the number of stations. As expected, ID is bounded for any value of offered traffic.

VI. SIMULATION RESULTS

As discussed in the previous section, analytic results can be obtained only for extreme load conditions (either light or heavy) and for symmetric traffic pattern. For a thorough evaluation and comparison of the various TLP versions, a more general set of traffic conditions must be tested. This is possible only via simulation.

In this section, we report the results corresponding to three different simulation experiments. In the first two experiments, the input rate is uniform over all the stations. The difference is in the length of the cable (1000 m in the first case, and 10 000 m in the second case). In the third experiment, an unbalanced traffic situation is considered; namely, one station has high input rate, while the remaining $N-1$ stations offer light background load.

The first two experiments permit us to validate the analysis in Section V in light and heavy load conditions. As we shall see, the agreement is very good. In addition, the experimental results are used to understand the tradeoffs between the different versions of TLP protocols in various traffic conditions.

All experiments assume a network with 15 stations ($N = 15$), infinite buffers per station, channel speed of 1 Gbit/s, fixed packet length of 1000 bits, and packet interarrival time exponentially distributed. The preamble in each packet is 100 bits. The length of the cable is assumed to be 1000 m in the first experiment and 10 000 m in the second and third experiment. Propagation delay in the medium is assumed to be 5 μs/km. The reaction time d is set to 10 ns (i.e., 10 bits at 1 Gbit/s). In collecting simulation results, 95 percent confidence intervals are obtained through batch runs. Trial runs were used to identify and exclude the transient phase of each run.

A. Equally Loaded Stations — 1000 m Span

This experiment is used to compare the behavior of the various TLP protocols in a uniform traffic environment. In addition, a validation of the analytic models is possible at light and heavy loads.

The experiment consists of a sequence of runs executed for different values of the (uniform) station-input rate, ranging from very light load to saturation load. For each run, insertion delay (ID) and bus utilization are monitored and are plotted in Fig. 7. (Note: bus utilization excludes preamble O/H.)

First, we wish to validate the analytic results of Section V. Recall that the value of the parameter a ($= \tau/T$) in this case (1000 m, 1000 bits per packet, and 1 Gbit/s channel) is 5. The parameter a has a critical impact on network performance. At very light load, the analytic models provide the following values of insertion delay.

TLP-1: $IDL_1 = 1.56\,\tau = 7.8\,\mu$s

TLP-2: $IDL_2 = 3R = 30\,\mu$s

TLP-3: $IDL_3 = 0.69\,\tau = 3.45\,\mu$s

TLP-4: $IDL_4 = 0$

The experimental values for zero load (extrapolated from the measurements in Fig. 7) show excellent agreement with the above analytic results.

At heavy load, the analytic models provide the following values of insertion delay IDH and bus utilization.

	IDH	U
TLP-1	30.7 μs	0.47

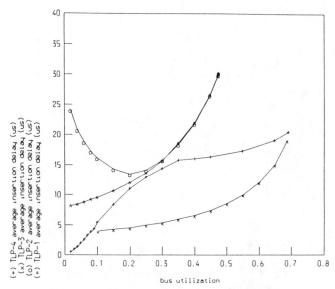

Fig. 7. TLP delay versus bus utilization (span = 1000 m).

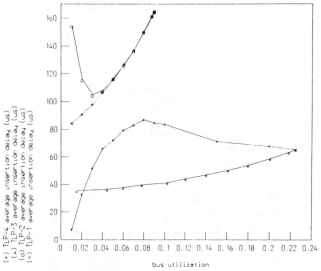

Fig. 8. TLP delay versus bus utilization (span = 10 000 m).

TLP-2	30.7 μs	0.47
TLP-3	20.7 μs	0.69
TLP-4	20.7 μs	0.99

Again, the agreement with the analytic models is excellent.

At intermediate loads, we observe two interesting effects. First, the insertion delay of TLP-2 decreases for an initial increase in load. This is due to the fact that at very light load, each packet transmission requires channel initialization. This explains the high delay at zero load. As load increases, more and more stations become active. Thus, the channel tends to be synchronized most of the time and does not require initialization. This explains the reduction in section delay for increase in load.

Secondly, the insertion delay for TLP-4 increases sharply for an initial increase in load, and then levels off for higher loads. This is due to the fact that at very light load, each station can transmit immediately. However, as load builds up, collisions occur which force reinitialization and thus introduce additional delay. At intermediate loads, the situation stabilizes and the channel becomes permanently synchronized, thus drastically reducing the frequency of collisions.

From this experiment we conclude that TLP-3 offers the lowest delay for a very wide range of channel utilizations. As for the effective throughput on the channel, TLP-3 and TLP-4 are tied at 70 percent utilization, and definitely outperform TLP-1 and TLP-2.

B. Equally Loaded Stations — 10 000 m Span

This experiment is identical to the previous one except for the length of the network, which is now 10 000 m. The purpose of the experiment is to evaluate the effect of the parameter a on performance. In the previous experiment, we had $a = 5$. Now we have $a = 50$.

The results of the simulation experiment are shown in Fig. 8. First, we validate the analytic model in Section V. At very light load, the model predictions are

$$\text{TLP-1: } IDL_1 = 78 \ \mu s$$

$$\text{TLP-2: } IDL_2 = 300 \ \mu s$$

$$\text{TLP-3: } IDL_3 = 34.5 \ \mu s$$

$$\text{TLP-4: } IDL_4 = 0$$

Again, we observe good agreement with simulation results. At heavy load, the analysis predicts the following.

	IDH	U
TLP-1	165.7 μs	0.091
TLP-2	165.7 μs	0.091
TLP-3	65.7 μs	0.23
TLP-4	65.7 μs	0.23

Agreement with the experimental results is excellent.

Comparing the results in Fig. 8 to those in Fig. 7, we note that the relative ranking of the various TLP schemes is the same: TLP-3 is still the best, except for the very light load region where TLP-4 prevails. We also observe a maximum in the TLP-4 insertion delay. As explained earlier, this is due to the fact that conflict and reinitialization overhead first increases, then decreases with increasing load.

The overall effect on performance of the increase of a from 5 to 50 is quite dramatic. Insertion delays increase by a factor of 5 to 10; throughput is reduced by a factor of 3 to 5. The throughput degradation is most significant for TLP-1 and TLP-2, as expected, since these schemes introduce a gap of 2τ s between each round. TLP-3 and TLP-4 do not introduce this overhead, thus, are less sensitive to the increase in end-to-end propagation delay.

C. Single Heavy-Loaded Station with Uniform Background Traffic

In this experiment, the input rate of one of the stations is progressively increased from zero to saturation while the remaining stations offer a fixed background load of 5 Mbits/s. This background load is very light, considering the fact that channel speed is 1 Gbit/s. The network span is 10 000 m.

The purpose of this experiment is to reproduce an unbalanced load situation which is fairly common in high-speed networks, namely, one or a few stations involved in very high data-rate transfers (e.g., digitized video or image), while the remaining stations are transmitting a more conventional type of traffic.

In this experiment, we are interested in monitoring overall throughput and delay performance as well as the impact of heavy station-rate increase on background stations' delays.

The results are displayed in Figs. 9, 10, 11 and in Table I. Fig. 9 shows insertion delay ID and queueing delay QD for the heavy station (station no. 8 in our example) as a function of increasing offered load for protocols TLP-1, TLP-2, and TLP-3. Insertion delay ID was already defined before. Queueing delay QD is the total time spent by a packet in the station input buffer. We note that at light load ID and QD coincide, as expected, since there is practically no wait in the input buffer. Also, ID at light load is consistent with the values reported in Fig. 8. As the load at station 8 increases, ID increases slightly (or even decreases, as is the case for TLP-2) while QD increases asymptotically as the bus becomes saturated. We note that TLP-3 can practically double the throughput of the other two schemes, due to the fact that the gap between rounds is eliminated.

Fig. 10 shows ID and QD values for the background stations for TLP-1, TLP-2, and TLP-3, as a function of increasing load at station 8. We note that ID and QD practically coincide, that is, no queueing occurs in station input buffers due to the light background load. Furthermore, the insertion delay does not seem to be affected by the increase in station 8 load, thus confirming the fairness of the TLP protocols.

Fig. 11 shows ID and QD for TLP-4. A separate diagram was necessary since TLP-4 throughput performance is one order-of-magnitude better than the performance of the previous schemes. In Fig. 11, the performance of both heavy station (i.e., station 8) and background stations are shown. We note that at light load the insertion delay is comparable to that reported in Fig. 8 for the uniform load experiment. As load increases, the background station delay remains approximately constant, while the delay for the heavy station decreases dramatically. This is explained by the fact that in TLP-4, when a station is transmitting alone on the bus, it can transmit packets one immediately after the other with practically no gap in between.

Table I summarizes the throughput performance (expressed in terms of maximum bus utilization) of the various TLP protocols for this experiment. TLP-4 exhibits a performance one order-of-magnitude better than the other schemes. Total bus utilization of TLP-4 is in excess of 20 percent. This is a surprisingly good result, considering the fact that the upper bound for TLP-4 with uniform load is 22 percent, as shown in Fig. 8.

D. Comparing TLP Versions

TLP-3 and TLP-4 decisively outperform TLP-1 and TLP-2 in all examples. For equally loaded and symmetrically spaced stations, TLP-3 outperforms TLP-4, and TLP-1

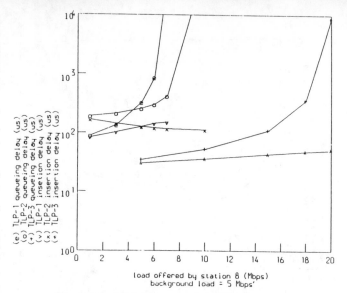

Fig. 9. Station 8 delay versus load (TLP-1, 2, and 3).

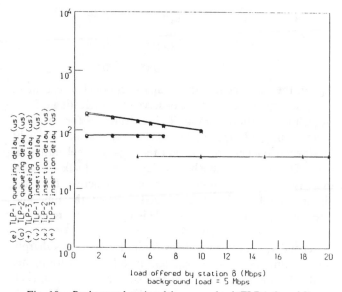

Fig. 10. Background station delay versus load (TLP-1, 2, and 3).

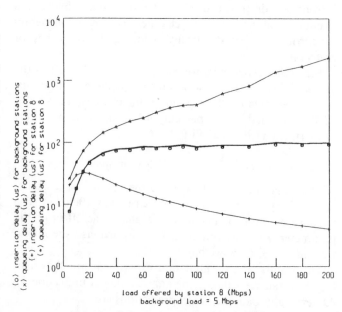

Fig. 11. Delays versus station 8 load (TLP-4).

TABLE I
Maximum Bus Utilization in Single Heavy-Loaded Station Experiment

EXAMPLE 1	
PROTOCOL	MAX BUS UTILIZATION
TLP-1	0.012
TLP-2	0.014
TLP-3	0.024
TLP-4	>0.20

outperforms TLP-2. However, single heavy-load station and asymmetrical placement favor the adaptive versions TLP-2 and TLP-4.

TLP-4 is the only version to show no deterioration of performance for single heavy-loaded traffic. The achieved maximum utilization of TLP-4 in this cases is more than 10 times better than the next best maximum utilization (TLP-3).

For all protocols, background stations are unaffected by the heavy-load traffic. This tolerance is valuable because it guarantees a fair share of resources. Furthermore, bounded delays are inherent to all protocols.

The fact that TLP-4 provides much lower queueing delays than the other protocols makes TLP-4 an excellent choice for applications where bursty high-bandwidth traffic occurs (file transfers, graphics, etc.). The insensitivity of background performance to heavy traffic from a single source guarantees proper service to interactive and priority traffic.

VII. CONCLUSIONS

This paper has described four versions of tokenless protocols for dual-bus architectures. The control operation of the protocols is solely based on the detection of activity on the channel and is completely distributed. The protocols are such that the circuitry needed at line speed is simple and small. The network can support 20–30 stations connected via passive taps, providing reliable operation.

Access is collision free in TLP-1, TLP-2, and TLP-3. In TLP-4, collisions may occur when a previously idle station becomes active. Even in this case, however, the collision is resolved in a finite time (on the order of the round-tip delay) and packet delay remains bounded.

Joining and recovery actions have been analyzed and TLP behavior under adverse conditions was proved correct. Exact expressions for behavior at light and heavy load were derived. Results for unbalanced message traffic were obtained via simulation and were found to agree with analytic results. The analysis of the results shows that TLP-4 outperforms the other versions under most conditions. Background traffic has been shown to be relatively insensitive to foreground heavy traffic. The above findings indicate that TLP is a suitable choice for implementation of very high speed local area networks.

APPENDIX I

Claim: Steps a), b), and c) in Section IV guarantee complete recovery within $2R + d$ seconds in the worst case.

Proof: Assume that station S_i is the first station to start recovery at time t_o. Define $T_i[EVENT_j(A)]$ as the time that event $EVENT$ detected or originated at S_j tap on channel A reaches S_i tap on the same channel. Hence, $t_o = t_i[BOA_i(\cdot)]$.

S_i activity signal, transmitted on both buses, hits another station S_j at $t_j[BOA_i(\cdot)] = t_o + \tau_{ij}$. Here, if S_j is not yet in recovery, it moves to state WFT and waits for EOA in the normal procedure. Otherwise, S_j starts recovery. In the latter case, the activity signal transmitted on both channels by S_j starts at $t_j[BOA_j(\cdot)] = t_o + \tau_{ij} + d$. R seconds later, S_j activity on channel R to L stops, and S_j moves to R2. Any active station S_k, between S_i and S_j, not yet in recovery, moves into recovery at $t_k[BOA_j(\cdot)] = t_o + \tau_{ij} + \tau_{jk} + d$ when S_j activity signal is detected (observe that the other channel has been busy with S_i activity signal). In this event, S_k activity signal starts d seconds later and S_k activity on channel R to L stops at $t_k[EOA_k(RL)] = t_o + \tau_{ij} + \tau_{jk} + 2d + R$, and S_k moves to R2.

Assume S_l, $l \leq i$, and S_r, $r \geq i$, are, respectively, the leftmost and the rightmost stations on recovery. S_l starts recovery at most by time $t_{R1} = t_i[BOA_i(RL)]$ and enters state R2 by time $t_{R2} = t_{R1} + d + r = t_o + \tau_{il} + d + R$. Nevertheless, S_l can only detect channel R to L idle by

$$t_{\text{idle}} = \max\{t_l[EOA_k(RL)] \mid S_k \text{ in recovery}\}$$
$$= \max\{t_o + \tau_{ir} + \tau_{rk} + \tau_{kl} + 2d + R \mid$$
$$\cdot l \leq k \leq r, S_k \text{ in recovery}\}$$
$$= \{t_o + \tau_{ir} + \tau_{rl} + 2d + R\},$$

which depends only on the position of the extreme stations involved in recovery.

From the expressions above, $t_{\text{idle}} \geq t_{R2}$. Therefore, S_l starts packet transmission at the latest by $t_x = t_{\text{idle}} + d$. The worst case for t_x occurs for $i = l = 1$ and $r = N$.

Therefore,

$$\max\{t_x\} = t_o + 2\tau + 3d + R$$
$$= t_o + 2R + d,$$

and complete recovery occurs within $2R + d$ from the detection of illegal events on the channels.

Now the need for state WT in TLP-4 is explained. Assume for a moment that transitions to WT go directly to IDLE. Following recovery in TLP-4, if S_r has only one backlogged packet it can return to idle after leaving ES0 and setting $E(RL) = 1$. However, if S_r receives another packet before it detects activity on channel L to R, S_r may transmit and cause another recovery before stations on the left of S_l have the opportunity to transmit. This behavior may repeat following each succeeding round, possibly preventing the low-numbered stations from transmitting packets.

State WT prevents such a lock up from occurring. After the transmission from the next active downstream station reaches S_r (at most, R s after S_r leaves ES0), S_r is in synchronism again. Consequently, a station leaves WT and goes to IDLE after $BOA(\cdot)$ has been detected or time-out R has expired. Time-out R is set when state WT is entered.

REFERENCES

[1] A. Albanese, "Fail-safe nodes for lightguide digital networks," *Bell Syst. Tech. J.*, vol. 61, no. 2, pp. 247–256, Feb. 1982.

[2] F. A. Tobagi, F. Borgonovo, and L. Fratta, "Expressnet: A high-performance integrated-services local area network," *IEEE J. Select. Areas Commun.*, vol. SAC-1, pp. 898–912, Nov. 1983.

[3] M. Gerla, P. Rodrigues, and C. Yeh, "U-Net: A unidirectional fiber bus network," in *Proc. FOC-LAN Conf.*, Las Vegas, NV, Sept. 1984, pp. 295–299.

[4] M. Gerla, P. Rodrigues, and C. Yeh, "BUZZ-NET: A hybrid random access/virtual token local network," in *Proc. 1983 IEEE Global Telecommun. Conf.* (*Globecom '83*), vol. 3, San Diego, CA, Nov. 28–Dec. 1, 1983, pp. 1509–1513.

[5] J. O. Limb and C. Flores, "Description of Fasnet—A unidirectional local area communications network," *Bell Syst. Tech. J.*, vol. 61, no. 7, pp. 1413–1440, Sept. 1982.

[6] E. G. Rawson, "Optical fiber for local computer networks," *Proc. Digest Topical Meeting on Opt. Fiber Commun.*, Washington, DC, March 1974.

[7] E. G. Rawson and R. V. Schmidt, "FIBERNET II: An ETHERNET-compatible fiber optic local area network," in *Proc. '82 Local Net*, Los Angeles, CA, 1982, pp. 42–46.

[8] P. H. A. Rodrigues, "Access protocols for high speed fiber optics local networks," Ph. D. dissertation, Dep. Comput. Sci., Univ. of California, Los Angeles, CA, CS Rep. 840050.

[9] F. A. Tobagi and V. B. Hunt, "Performance analysis of carrier sense multiple access with collision detection," *Computer Network*, vol. 4, no. 5, pp. 245–259, Oct. 1980.

[10] C. Tseng and B. Chen, "D-Net: A new scheme for high data rate optical local area networks," in *Proc. Globecom '82*, Miami, FL, Nov.–Dec. 1982, pp. 949–955.

Luigi Fratta (M'74) received the Doctorate in electrical engineering from the Politecnico di Milano, Milano, Italy, in 1966.

From 1967 to 1970, he worked at the Laboratory of Electrical Communications, Politecnico di Milano. As a Research Assistant at the Department of Computer Science, University of California, Los Angeles, CA, he participated in data network design under the ARPA project from 1970 to 1971. From November 1975 to September 1976, he was with the Computer Science Department of the IBM Thomas J. Watson Research Center, Yorktown Heights, NY, working on modeling, analysis, and optimization techniques for teleprocessing systems. In 1979 he was a Visiting Associate Professor at the Department of Computer Science, University of Hawaii, Honolulu, HI. In the Summer of 1981 he was at the Computer Science Department, IBM Research Center, San Jose, CA, working on local area networks. At present, he is a full Professor at the Dipartimento di Elettronica of the Politecnico di Milano. His research interests concern communication networks.

Dr. Fratta is a member of the Association for Computing Machinery and the Italian Electrotechnical and Electronic Association.

Paulo Rodrigues received the M.Sc. degree from COPPE, Rio de Janeiro, Brazil in 1977 and the Ph.D. degree from the University of California, Los Angeles, CA, in 1984, both in computer science. He has been a consulting computer analyst and professor at the Federal University of Rio de Janeiro (UFRJ), Brazil, since 1975, where he actively participated in the development of micro systems and peripheral devices. In 1978, he was director of EBC, a Brazilian computer industry, and in 1979, he joined the Ph.D. program at UCLA where he worked as a research assistant in high-speed fiber optic local area network research. He is presently in the research division of the Computer Center (NCE) at UFRJ. His current technical interests are in design and performance analysis of computer networks, local area networking supporting integrated services, interconnection of computer networks, and distributed operating systems.

Mario Gerla (M'75) received the graduate degree in engineering from the Politecnico di Milano, Milano, Italy, in 1966, and the M.S. and Ph.D. degrees in engineering from University of California, Los Angeles, CA, in 1970 and 1973, respectively.

From 1973 to 1976, he was Network Planning Manager at Network Analysis Corporation, New York, and led several computer network design projects for both government and industry. From 1976 to 1977, he was with Tran Telecommunications, Los Angeles, CA, where he participated in the development of an integrated packet and circuit network. In 1977 he joined the University of California, Los Angeles, and is now a Professor in the Department of Computer Science. His research interests include the design and control of distributed computer communication systems and networks, and the development of protocols for high-speed local area networks.

Section 4: Digital Switches And Digital Private Branch Exchanges

4.1 Overview

The digital switch and the digital private branch exchange (PBX) are major alternatives to the LAN for handling a wide variety of local networking requirements. Some of the typical characteristics of these systems are as follows:

- Stations are connected by twisted pair to a central switching unit (star topology).

- Circuit switching is used. The switch establishes a dedicated communications path between two devices wishing to communicate. Bandwidth (data rate) is fixed and guaranteed.

- The switch is actively involved during the call setup phase. During the data transfer phase, data passes transparently through the switch, with only propagation delay.

- Data rates for individual devices are typically limited to about 64 kbps.

- The total capacity, however, may be quite high. A digital PBX may have a total throughput potential in the neighborhood of 500 Mbps.

The digital PBX differs from the digital switch in that it is intended to handle voice traffic as well as data traffic. Additional typical characteristics are as follows:

- Voice is digitized; that is, it is encoded as a digital bit stream. The encoding is done by a device called a codec (coder-decoder), and this function is either dispersed (at the phone) or concentrated (at the switch).

- A hierarchical star topology is often used. In this case, one or more satellite switches are attached to a central switch. This architecture increases system capacity and availability.

Modern digital switches and digital PBXs are based on the use of synchronous time-division multiplexing (TDM). This technique involves preassigning time slots to communicating devices on a shared transmission medium. Since the slots are preassigned, no overhead control or address bits are needed. The slots recur frequently enough to provide the desired data rate.

4.2 Digital Data Switching Devices

The digital switching techniques discussed above have been used to build a variety of digital switching products designed for data-only applications. These devices do not provide telephone service and are generally cheaper than a digital PBX of comparable capacity.

The variety of devices is wide and the distinction between types are blurred. For convenience, we categorize them as follows: (1) Terminal/port-oriented switch, and (2) Data switch.

Before defining these categories, let us look at the functions associated with data switching. The most basic, of course, is the making of a connection between two attached lines. These connections can be preconfigured by a system operator, but more dynamic operation is often desired. This leads to two additional functions: port contention and port selection.

Port contention is a function that allows a certain number of designated ports to contend for access to a smaller number of ports. Typically, this is used for terminal-to-host connection thereby allowing a smaller number of host ports to service a larger number of terminal ports. When a terminal user attempts to connect, the system will scan through all host ports in the contention group. If any port is available, a connection is made.

Port selection is an interactive capability. It allows a user (or an application program in a host) to select a port for connection. This is analogous to dialing a number in a telephone system. Port selection and port contention can be combined by allowing the selection, by name or number, of a contention group. Port selection devices are becoming increasingly common. A switch without this capability only allows connections that are preconfigured by a system operator. If one knows in advance what interconnections are required, fine. Otherwise, the flexibility of port selection is usually worth the additional cost.

An interactive capability carries with it an additional responsibility: The control unit of the switch must be able to talk to the requesting port. This can be done in two ways. In some cases, the manufacturer supplies a simple keypad device that attaches to and shares the terminal's line. The user first dials a connection by using the keypad. Once the connection is made, communication is by the terminal. As an alternative, the connection sequence can be effected through the terminal itself. A simple command language dialogue is used. However, this technique requires that the system understand the code and protocol being used by the terminal. Consequently, this feature is generally limited to asynchronous ASCII devices.

We can now describe the distinction between terminal/ port-oriented switches and data switches. In the former, switch attachment points are designated as either terminal or host. Connections are only allowed between a terminal and a host port. For a data switch, there is no such distinction; any attached device can connect to any other attached device.

4.3 The Digital Private Branch Exchange

Evolution of the Digital PBX

The digital PBX is a marriage of two technologies: digital switching and telephone exchange systems. A PBX is an on-premise facility, owned or leased by an organization, that interconnects the telephones within the facility and provides access to the public telephone system. Typically, a telephone user on the premises dials a three- or four-digit number to call another telephone on the premises and dials one digit (usually an 8 or a 9) to get a dial tone for an "outside line," which allows the caller to dial a number in the same fashion as a residential user would dial.

The original private exchanges were manual, with one or more operators required to make all connections from a switchboard. Back in the l920's, these began to be replaced by automatic systems, called private automatic branch exchanges (PABX), that did not require attendant intervention to place a call. These first-generation systems used electro-mechanical technology and analog signaling. Data connections could be made through modems. That is, a user with a terminal, a telephone, and a modem or acoustic coupler in the office could dial an on-site or remote number that reached another modem, and data could be exchanged.

The second-generation PBXs were introduced in the mid 1970's. These systems use electronic rather than electro-magnetic technology and the internal switching is digital. Such a system is referred to as digital PBX, or computerized branch exchange (CBX). These systems were primarily designed to handle analog voice traffic, with the codec function built into the switch so that digital switching could be used internally. (The codec is the opposite of a modem; it converts analog voice signals into digital data and vice versa.) The systems were also capable of handling digital data connections without the need for a modem.

The third-generation systems are touted as "integrated voice-data" systems, although the differences between third and upgraded second-generation systems are rather blurred. Perhaps a better term is "improved digital PBX." Some of the characteristics of these systems that differ from those of earlier systems include:

- *Use of digital phones*: This permits integrated voice/ data workstations.

- *Distributed architecture*: Multiple switches in a hierarchical or meshed configuration with distributed intelligence provide enhanced reliability.

- *Nonblocking configuration*: Typically, dedicated port assignments are used for all attached phones and devices.

It is worthwhile to summarize the main reasons why the evolution described above has occurred. To the untrained eye, analog and digital PBXs would seem to offer about the same level of convenience. The analog PBX can handle telephone sets directly and uses modems to accommodate digital data devices; the digital PBX can handle digital data devices directly and uses codecs to accommodate telephone sets. Some of the advantages of the digital approach are:

- *Digital technology*: By handling all internal signals digitally, the digital PBX can take advantage of low cost LSI and VLSI components. Digital technology also lends itself more readily to software and firmware control.

- *Time-division multiplexing (TDM)*: Digital signals lend themselves readily to TDM techniques, which provide efficient use of internal data paths, access to public TDM carriers, and TDM switching techniques, which are more cost effective than older, cross-bar techniques.

- *Digital control signals*: Control signals are inherently digital and can be integrated easily into a digital transmission path by use of TDM. The signaling equipment is independent of the transmission medium.

- *Encryption*: This is more easily accommodated with digital signals.

Digital PBX Architecture

A variety of architectures has been developed by PBX manufacturers. Since these are proprietary, the details are not generally known in most cases. Here, we attempt to present the general architectural features common to all digital PBX systems.

Figure 4.1 presents a generic digital PBX architecture. Except for features specifically supportive of voice communication, this also depicts a digital data switch architecture. The heart of the system is some kind of digital switching network. The switch is responsible for the manipulation and switching of TDM digital signal streams, using the techniques described in the articles in this section.

Attached to the switch is a series of interface units that provide access to/from the outside world. Typically, an interface unit will perform a synchronous TDM function to accommodate multiple incoming lines. On the other side, the unit requires two lines into the switch for full duplex operation. For input to the switch, the unit performs a multiplex operation. Each incoming line is sampled at a specified rate. For n incoming lines each of data rate x, the unit must achieve an input rate of nx. The incoming data is buffered and organized into chunks of time-slot size. Then, according to the timing dictated by the control unit, individ-

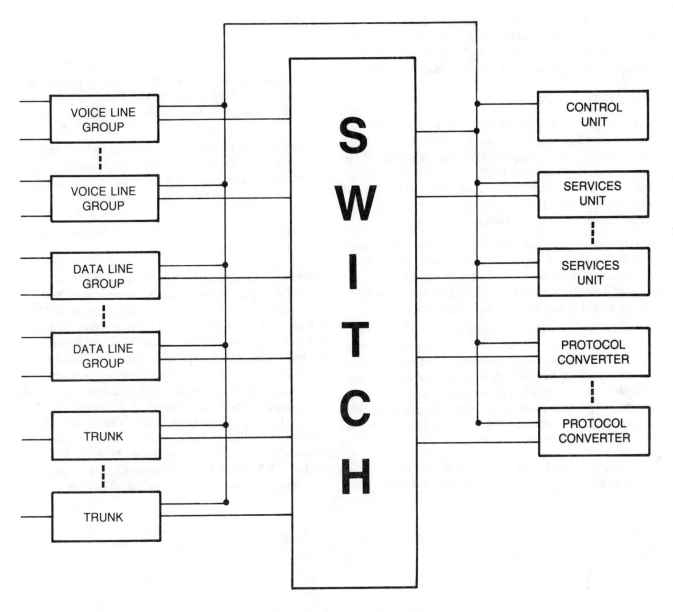

Figure 4.1   Generic CBX Architecture

ual chunks are sent out into the switch at the internal digital PBX data rate, which may be in the range of 50-500 Mbps. In a nonblocking switch, *n* time slots are dedicated to the interface unit for transmission, whether or not they are used. In a blocking switch, time slots are assigned for the duration of a connection. In either case, the time-slot assignment is fixed for the duration of the connection, and synchronous TDM techniques may be used. For output from the switch, the interface unit accepts data from the switch during designated time slots.

Several types of interface units are used. A data-line group unit handles data devices. An analog voice-line group handles a number of twisted pair phone lines. The interface unit must include codecs for digital-to-analog (input) and analog-to-digital (output) conversion. A separate type of unit may be used for an integrated digital voice/data work station, which presents digitized voice at 64 kbps and data at

the same or a lower rate. The range of lines accommodated by interface units is typically 8 to 24. In addition to multiplexing interface units that accommodate multiple lines, trunk interface units are used to connect to offsite locations. These may be analog voice trunks or digital trunks, which may carry either data or digitized voice.

The other boxes in Figure 4.1 can be briefly explained. The control unit operates the digital switch and exchanges control signals with attached devices. For this purpose, a separate bus or other data path is used; control signals generally do not propagate through the switch itself. As part of this or a separate unit, network administration and control functions are implemented. Service units would include such things as tone and busy-signal generators and dialed-digit registers. Some digital PBX systems provide protocol converters for connecting dissimilar lines. A connection is made from each line to the protocol converter.

It should be noted that this generic architecture lends itself to a high degree of reliability. The failure of any interface unit means the loss of only a small number of lines. Key elements such as the control unit can be made redundant.

Fourth-Generation PBX

We spoke earlier of the evolution of the digital PBX up through a third generation. As new features and technologies are employed, incremental improvements make difficult the continuing classification of PBXs into generations. Nevertheless, it is worth noting recent advances that will soon begin to show up in PBX products and that, together, might be considered to constitute a fourth generation:

- *Integrated LAN link*: This capability provides a direct high-speed link to a LAN. This allows an optimum distribution of lower-speed devices (terminals) on the PBX and higher-speed devices (computers) on the LAN in a fashion that is fully transparent to the user.

- *Dynamic bandwidth allocation*: Typically, a PBX offers one or only a small number of different data rate services. The increased sophistication of capacity allocation within the PBX allows it to offer virtually any data rate to an attached device. This allows the system to grow as user requirements grow. For example, full-motion color video at 448 kbps or advanced codecs at 32 kbps could be accommodated.

- *Integrated packet channel*: This allows the PBX to provide access to an X.25 packet-switched network.

4.4 Article Summary

The articles in this section are intended to provide the reader with an understanding of how digital switches and digital PBXs work, plus an overview of the various types of devices.

The first article explains the technology and architecture underlying all these types of systems, and explores the key concepts of synchronous time-division multiplexing, space-division switching, and time-division switching.

The next article, by Kane, discusses various types of data-only digital switches.

The remainder of the articles discuss the digital PBX. "The ABCs of the PBX;" is an interesting discussion of the evolution of the digital PBX and its likely future direction. "The Evolution of Data Switching for PBX's" analyzes the different traffic requirements of voice and data communications. The role of the PBX in supporting data traffic is then discussed. Next, the article by Coover examines approaches to voice-data integration using the PBX; the requirements of the various devices to be supported are discussed. "Office Communications and the Digital PBX" details the requirements for intra-office communications and discusses the satisfaction of these requirements by the digital PBX. The final article, "PBX versus LAN" compares the two, and concludes that both are needed in the typical office environment.

Time Division Switching

J. Bellamy

1.3 THE INTRODUCTION OF DIGITS

Voice digitization and transmission first became feasible in the late 1950s when the economic, operational, and reliability features of solid state electronics became available. In 1962 Bell System personnel established the first commercial use of digital transmission when they began operating a T1 carrier system for use as a trunk group in a Chicago area exchange [23]. Since that time a whole family of T-carrier systems (T1, T1C, T1D, T2, T4) has been developed—all of which involve time division multiplexing of digitized voice signals. Following the development of T-carrier systems for interoffice transmission, Western Electric and numerous independent manufacturers developed digital pair-gain systems for long customer loop applications. However, the pair-gain systems have not been used nearly as extensively as T-carrier systems. Projections for T-carrier usage indicate that 50% of the exchange area trunks will be digital by 1985 [24].

The world's first commercially designed digital microwave radio system was established in Japan by Nippon Electric Company (NEC) in 1968 [25]. In the early 1970s digital microwave systems began to appear in the United States for specialized data transmission services. Foremost among these systems was a digital network developed by Data Transmission Company (Datran).* The first digital microwave link in the U.S. public telephone network was supplied by NEC of Japan for a New York Telephone link between Brooklyn and North Staten Island in 1972 [25]. Digital microwave systems have since been developed and installed by several U.S. manufacturers for use in intermediate length toll and exchange area circuits.

In addition to transmission systems, digital technology has proven to be equally useful for implementing switching functions. The first country to use digital switching in the public telephone network was France in 1970 [26]. The first application of digital switching in the public network of the United States occurred in early 1976 when the Bell System began operating its No. 4ESS [27] in a class 3 toll office in Chicago. Two months after that Continental Telephone Company began operation in Ridgecrest, California of an IMA2 digital toll switch supplied by TRW-Vidar [28]. The first digital end office switch in the United States became operational in July of 1977 in the small town of Richmond Hill, Georgia [29]. This switch was supplied by Stromberg-Carlson for Coastal Utilities, Inc., a small independent telephone company.

1.3.1 Voice Digitization

The basic voice coding algorithm used in T-carrier systems, and most other digital voice equipment in telephone networks around the world, is shown in Figure 1.25. The first step in the digitization process is to periodically sample the waveform. As discussed at length in Chapter 3, all of the information needed to reconstruct the original waveform is contained in the samples—if the samples occur at an 8 kHz rate. The second step in the digitization process involves quantization: identifying which amplitude interval of a group of adjacent intervals a sample value falls into. In essence the quantization process replaces each con-

---

*The Datran facilities were taken over in 1976 by another specialized common carrier: Southern Pacific Communications.

"Time-Division Switching" by J. Bellamy from *Digital Telephony* by J. Bellamy, 1982, pages 47-51 and 242-259. Copyright © 1982 by John Wiley & Sons, Inc.

tinuously variable amplitude sample with a discrete value located at the middle of the appropriate quantization interval. Since the quantized samples have discrete levels, they represent a multiple level digital signal.

For transmission purposes the discrete amplitude samples are converted to a binary code word. (For illustrative purposes only, Figure 1.26 shows 4 bit code words.) The binary codes are then transmitted as binary pulses. At the receiving end of a digital transmission line the binary data stream is recovered, and the discrete sample values are reconstructed. Then a low-pass filter is used to "interpolate" between sample values and recreate the original waveform. If no transmission errors have occurred, the output waveform is identical to the input waveform except for a small amount of quantization distortion: the difference between a sample value and its discrete representation. By having a large number of quantization intervals (and hence enough bits in a code word to encode them), the quantization intervals can be small enough to effectively eliminate quantization effects.

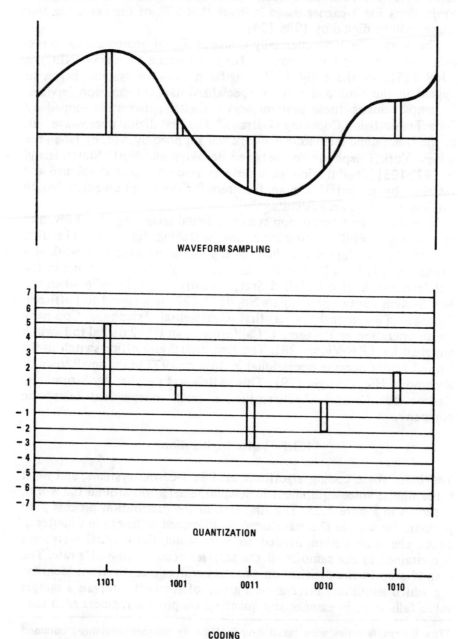

WAVEFORM SAMPLING

QUANTIZATION

| 1101 | 1001 | 0011 | 0010 | 1010 |

CODING

Figure 1.25 Voice digitization process.

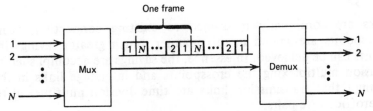

Figure 1.26 Time division multiplexing.

It is worth noting that the bandwidth requirements of the digital signal increase as a result of the binary encoding process. If the discrete, multiple-amplitude samples are transmitted directly, the bandwidth requirements are theoretically identical to the bandwidth of the original signal. When each discrete sample is represented by a number of individual binary pulses, the signal bandwidth increases accordingly. The two-level pulses, however, are much less vulnerable to transmission impairments than are the multiple-amplitude pulses (or the underlying analog signal).

1.3.2 Time Division Multiplexing

Basically, time division multiplexing (TDM) involves nothing more than sharing a transmission medium by establishing a sequence of time slots during which individual sources can transmit signals. Thus the entire bandwidth of the facility is periodically available to each user for a restricted time interval. In contrast, FDM systems assign a restricted bandwidth to each user for all time. Normally, all time slots of a TDM system are of equal length. Also, each subchannel is usually assigned a time slot with a common repetition period called a frame interval. This form of time division multiplexing (as shown in Figure 1.26) is sometimes referred to as synchronous time division multiplexing to specifically imply that each subchannel is assigned a certain amount of transmission capacity determined by the time slot duration and the repetition rate. In contrast, another form of TDM (referred to as "statistical or asynchronous time division multiplexing") is described in Chapter 8. With this second form of multiplexing, subchannel rates are allowed to vary according to the individual needs of the sources. All of the backbone digital links of the public telephone network (T-carrier and digital microwave) use a synchronous variety of TDM.

Time division multiplexing is normally associated only with digital transmission links. Although TDM can be used conceivably for analog signals by interleaving samples from each signal, the individual samples are usually too sensitive to all varieties of transmission impairments. In contrast, time division switching of analog signals is more feasible than analog TDM transmission because noise and distortion of the switching equipment is more controllable. As discussed in Chapter 5, analog TDM techniques are used in some PBXs.

5.3 TIME DIVISION SWITCHING

As evidenced by multiple stage switching, sharing of individual crosspoints for more than one potential connection provides significant savings in implementation costs of space division switches. In the cases demonstrated, the crosspoints of multistage space switches are shared from one connection to the next, but a crosspoint assigned to a particular connection is dedicated to that connection for its duration. Time division switching involves the sharing of crosspoints for shorter periods of time so that individual crosspoints and their associated interstage links are continually reassigned to existing connections. When the crosspoints are shared in this manner, much greater savings in crosspoints can be achieved. In essence, the savings are accomplished by time division multiplexing the crosspoints and interstage links in the same manner that transmission links are time division multiplexed to share interoffice wire pairs.

Time division switching is equally applicable to either analog or digital signals. Analog time division switching is attractive when interfacing to analog transmission facilities, since the signals are only sampled and not digitally encoded. However, large analog time division switches experience the same limitations as do analog time division transmission links: the PAM samples are particularly vulnerable to noise, distortion, and crosstalk. In digital switches, the voice signals are regenerated every time they pass through a logic gate. Thus at some point in switching sizes, the cost of digitizing PAM samples is mandated by the need to maintain end-to-end signal quality. As the cost of digitization continues to decline, digital switching of analog signals is more and more competitive for small switch sizes. If a sufficient number of the signals to be switched are already digital or will be converted to digital at a future date, digital switching becomes more attractive than analog switching, even for the smallest PBXs.

5.3.1 Analog Time Division Switching

A vast majority of PBXs presently available in the United States use time division technology for the switching matrix. Of these, approximately one-half use analog time division switching while the other half use digital time division switching. Figure 5.14 depicts a particularly simple analog time division switching structure. A single switching bus supports a multiple number of connections by interleaving PAM

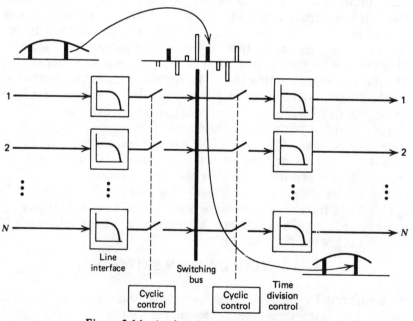

Figure 5.14 Analog time division switching.

samples from receive line interfaces to transmit line interfaces. The operation is depicted as though the receive interfaces are separate from the respective transmit interfaces. When connecting two-wire analog lines, the two interfaces are necessarily implemented in a common module. Furthermore, in some PAM-PBX systems, analog samples are simultaneously transferred in both directions between the interfaces [9].

Included in Figure 5.14 are two cyclic control stores. The first control store controls gating of inputs onto the bus one sample at a time. The second control store operates in synchronism with the first and selects the appropriate output line for each input sample. A complete set of pulses, one from each active input line, is referred to as a frame. The frame rate is equal to the sample rate of each line. For voice systems the sampling rate ranges from 8 to 12 kHz. The higher sampling rates are used to simplify the band-limiting filter and reconstructive filters in the line interfaces.

5.3.2 Digital Time Division Switching

The analog switching matrix described in the preceding section is essentially a space division switching matrix. By continually changing the connections for short periods of time in a cyclic manner, the configuration of the space division switch is replicated once for each time slot. This mode of operation is referred to as time multiplexed switching. While this mode of operation can be quite useful for both analog and

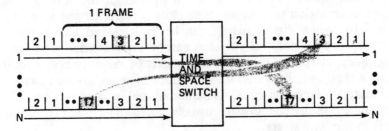

Figure 5.15 Time and space division switching.

digital signals, digital time division multiplexed signals usually require switching between time slots, as well as between physical lines. This second mode of switching represents a second dimension of switching and is referred to as time switching.

In the following discussion of digital time division switching it is assumed, unless otherwise stated, that the switching network is interfaced directly to digital time division multiplex links. This assumption is generally justified since, even when operating in an analog environment, the most cost-effective switch designs multiplex groups of digital signals into TDM formats before any switching operations take place. Thus most of the following discussion is concerned with the internal structures of time division switching networks, and possibly not with the structure of an entire switching complex.

The basic requirement of a time division switching network is shown in Figure 5.15. As an example connection, channel 3 of the first TDM link is connected to channel 17 of last TDM link. The indicated connection implies that information arriving in time slot 3 of the first link is transferred to time slot 17 of the last link. Since the voice digitization process inherently implies a four-wire operation, the return connection is required and realized by transferring information from time slot 17 of the last input link to time slot 3 of the first link. Thus each connection requires two transfers of information: each involving translations in both time and space.

A variety of switching structures are possible to accomplish the transfers indicated in Figure 5.15. All of these structures inherently require at least two stages: a space division switching stage and a time division switching stage. As discussed later, larger switches use multiple stages of both types. Before discussing switching in both dimensions, however, we discuss the characteristics and capabilities of time switching alone.

A Digital Memory Switch

Primarily owing to the low cost of digital memory, time switching implementations provide digital switching functions more economically than space division implementations. Basically, a time switch operates

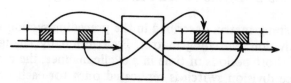

Figure 5.16 Time slot interchange operation.

by writing data into and reading data out of a single memory. In the process the information in selected time slots is interchanged as shown in Figure 5.16. When digital signals can be multiplexed into a single TDM format, very economical switches can be implemented with time switching alone. However, practical limitations of memory speed limit the size of a time switch so that some amount of space division switching is necessary in large switches. As demonstrated in later sections, the most economical multistage designs usually perform as much switching as possible in the time stages.

The basic functional operation of a memory switch is shown in Figure 5.17. Individual digital message circuits are multiplexed and demultiplexed in a fixed manner to establish a single TDM link for each direction of travel. The multiplexing and demultiplexing functions can be considered as part of the switch itself, or they may be implemented in remote transmission terminals. If the multiplexing functions are implemented locally, the multiplexer and demultiplexer may be connected in parallel, directly to the memory. Otherwise, a serial-to-parallel converter is used to accumulate the information in a time slot before it is written into the memory. In either case, a memory write access is required for each incoming time slot, and a memory read access is required for each outgoing time slot.

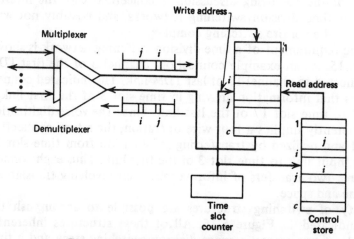

Figure 5.17 Time slot interchange circuit.

The exchange of information between two different time slots is accomplished by a time slot interchange (TSI) memory. In the TSI of Figure 5.17 data words in incoming time slots are written into sequential locations of the memory. Data words for outgoing time slots, however, are read from TSI addresses obtained from a control store. As indicated in the associated control store, a full-duplex connection between TDM channel i and TDM channel j implies that TSI address i is read during outgoing time slot j and vice versa. The TSI memory is accessed twice during each link time slot. First, some control circuitry (not shown) selects the time slot number as a write address. Second, the content of the control store for that particular time slot is selected as a read address.

Since a write and a read is required for each channel entering (and leaving) the TSI memory, the maximum number of channels c that can be supported by the simple memory switch is

$$c = \frac{125}{2t_c} \tag{5.12}$$

where 125 is the frame time in microseconds for 8 kHz sampled voice, and t_c is the memory cycle time in microseconds.

As a specific example, consider the use of a 500 ns memory. Equation 5.12 indicates that the memory switch can support 125 full-duplex channels (62 connections) in a strictly nonblocking mode of operation. The complexity of the switch (assuming digitization occurs elsewhere) is quite modest: the TSI memory stores one frame of data organized as c words by 8 bits each. The control store also requires c words, but each word has a length equal to $\log_2(c)$ (which is 7 in the example). Thus both memory functions can be supplied by 128 × 8 bit random access memories (RAMs). The addition of a time slot counter and some gating logic to select addresses and enable new information to be written into the control store can be accomplished with a handful of conventional integrated circuits (ICs).

This switch should be contrasted to a space division design that requires 7,680 crosspoints for a nonblocking three-stage switch. Although modern integrated circuit technology might be capable of placing that many digital crosspoints in a few integrated circuits, they could never be reached because of pin limitations. As mentioned in Chapter 2, one of the main advantages of digital signals is the ease with which they can be time division multiplexed. This advantage arises for communication between integrated circuits as well as for communication between switching offices.

If the multiplexer and demultiplexer combination in Figure 5.17 is enhanced to provide concentration and expansion, the system can service much greater numbers of input lines, depending on the average circuit utilization. For example, if the average line is busy 10% of the time, a concentrator/memory switch/expandor operation could support 1000 circuits with a blocking probability of less than .002. The concentration and expansion operations, however, imply a significant increase in the complexity of the system. In fact, these equipments essentially represent time multiplexed space division switches that must be controlled accordingly. The concentrator/memory switch/expandor structure essentially becomes a simple form of a space-time-space (STS) switch discussed later.

Time Stages in General

Time switching stages inherently require some form of delay element to provide the desired time slot interchanges. Delays are most easily implemented using random access memories that are written into as data arrives and read from when data is to be transferred out. If one memory location is allocated for each time slot in the TDM frame format, the information from each TDM channel can be stored for up to one full frame time without being overwritten.

There are two basic ways in which the time stage memories can be controlled: written sequentially and read randomly, or written randomly and read sequentially. Figure 5.18 depicts both modes of operation and indicates how the memories are accessed to translate information from time slot 3 to time slot 17. Notice that both modes of operation use a cyclic control store that is accessed in synchronism with the time slot counter.

The first mode of operation in Figure 5.18 implies that specific memory locations are dedicated to respective channels of the incoming TDM link. Data for each incoming time slot is stored in sequential locations within the memory by incrementing a modulo-c counter with

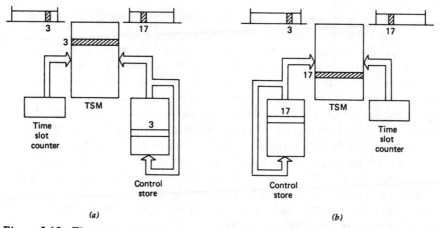

Figure 5.18 Time stage modes of operation. (*a*) Sequential writes/random reads. (*b*) Random writes/sequential reads.

every time slot. As indicated, the data received during time slot 3 is automatically stored in the third location within the memory. On output, information retrieved from the control store specifies which address is to be accessed for that particular time slot. As indicated, the seventeenth word of the control store contains the number 3, implying that the contents of time stage memory (TSM) address 3 is transferred to the output link during outgoing time slot 17.

The second mode of operation depicted in Figure 5.18 is exactly the opposite of the first one. Incoming data is written into the memory locations as specified by the control store, but outgoing data is retrieved sequentially under control of an outgoing time slot counter. As indicated in the example, information received during time slot 3 is written directly into TSM address 17 where it is automatically retrieved during outgoing TDM channel number 17. Notice that the two modes of time stage operation depicted in Figure 5.18 are forms of output-associated control and input-associated control, respectively. In a multiple stage design example presented later, it is convenient to use one mode of operation in one time stage and the other mode of operation in another time stage.

5.4 TWO-DIMENSIONAL SWITCHING

Larger digital switches require switching operations in both a space dimension and a time dimension. There are a large variety of network configurations that can be used to accomplish these requirements. To begin with, consider a simple switching structure as shown in Figure 5.19. This switch consists of only two stages: a time stage T followed by a space stage S. Thus this structure is referred to a time-space TS switch.

The basic function of the time stage is to delay information in arriving time slots until the desired output time slot occurs. At that time the delayed information is transferred through the space stage to the appropriate output link. In the example shown the information in incoming time slot 3 of link 1 is delayed until outgoing time slot 17 occurs. The return path requires that information arriving in time slot 17 of link N be delayed for time slot 3 of the next outgoing frame. Notice that a time stage may have to provide delays ranging from one time slot to a full frame.

Associated with the space stage is a control store that contains the information needed to specify the space stage configuration for each individual time slot of a frame. This control information is accessed cyclically in the same manner as the control information in the analog time division switch. For example, during each outgoing time slot 3, control information is accessed that specifies interstage link number 1

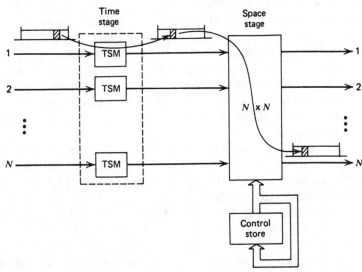

Figure 5.19 Time-space (TS) switching matrix.

is connected to output link N. During other time slots, the space switch is completely reconfigured to support other connections.

As indicated, a convenient means of representing a control store is a parallel end-around-shift register. The width of the shift register is equal to the number of bits required to specify the entire space switch configuration during a single time slot. The length of the shift register conforms to the number of time slots in a frame. Naturally, some means of changing the information in the control store is needed so that new connections can be established. In actual practice, the control stores may be implemented as random access memories with counters used to generate addresses in a cyclic fashion.

Implementation Complexity of Time Division Switches
In previous sections, alternative space division switching structures were compared in terms of the total number of crosspoints required to provide a given grade of service. Other factors that should be considered in a comprehensive analysis are: modularity, pathfinding requirements,

effects of failures, serviceability, wiring or interconnection requirements, electrical loadings, and others. Despite the need to assess these other considerations, a crosspoint count is a useful, single measure of a space division switch cost, particularly with electromechanical crosspoints.

In the case of solid state electronic switching matrices, in general, and time division switching, in particular, the number of crosspoints alone is a less meaningful measure of implementation cost. Switching structures that utilize integrated circuits with relatively large numbers of internal crosspoints are generally more cost effective than other structures that may have fewer crosspoints but more packages. Hence a more relevant design parameter for solid state switches would be the total number of integrated circuit packages. If alternate designs are implemented from a common set of integrated circuits, the number of packages may closely reflect the number of crosspoints.

Another useful cost parameter is the total number of IC pin-outs required in a particular implementation. Although this parameter is obviously related closely to the total number of packages, it is generally more useful since it more accurately reflects package cost and circuit board area requirements. Pin-out measurements also provide a direct indication of implementation reliability, since external interconnections are generally less reliable than internal connections of an IC.

Medium scale integrated (MSI) circuits typically provide the equivalent of one crosspoint (AND gate) for $1\frac{1}{2}$ external pins to access the crosspoint. Thus when MSI technology is used, the total number of crosspoints is a useful indication of the total number of pins. We therefore continue to use crosspoints as an implementation cost measurement with the understanding that medium scale integration would be used in all comparative designs. To do so we must be sure that all systems operate at about the same speed, since higher speeds require lower levels of integration.

In addition to the number of crosspoints in space division stages, a digital time division switch uses significant amounts of memory that must be included in an estimate of the overall cost.* The memory count includes the time stage memory arrays and the control stores for both the time stages and the space stages. In the following analyses we assume that 100 bits of memory corresponds to $1\frac{1}{2}$ IC interconnections. (A 1024 bit random access memory typically requires 14 pins.) With this assumption, we can relate memory costs to crosspoint costs by a 100 bits per crosspoint factor. Hence the following analyses of implementation complexity for digital time division switching matrices include the total number of crosspoints and the total number of bits of memory divided by 100.

The implementation complexity is expressed as follows:

$$\text{complexity} = N_X + \frac{N_B}{100} \qquad (5.13)$$

where N_X = number of space stage crosspoints
N_B = number of bits of memory

EXAMPLE 5.2

Determine the implementation complexity of the TS switch shown in Figure 5.19 where the number of TDM input lines $N = 80$. Assume each input line contains a single DS-1 signal (24 channels). Furthermore,

---

*It is worth noting that digital memories are inherently implemented with at least two crosspoints per bit. In this case the crosspoints are gates used to provide write and read access to the bits. These crosspoints, however, are much less expensive than message crosspoints that are accessed from external circuits.

assume a one-stage matrix is used for the space stage.

Solution. The number of crosspoints in the space stage is determined as

$$N_X = 80^2 = 6400$$

(The crosspoints on the main diagonal are included since two channels within a single TDM input may have to be connected to each other.) The total number of memory bits for the space stage control store is determined as

$$N_{BX} = \text{(number of links)}\,\text{(number of control words)}$$
$$\text{(number of bits/control word)}$$

$$= (80)(24)(7)$$

$$= 13440$$

The number of memory bits in the time stage is determined as the sum of the time slot interchange and the control store bits:

$$N_{BT} = \text{(number of links)}\,\text{(number of channels)}$$
$$\text{(number of bits/channel)} + \text{(number of links)}$$
$$\text{(number of control words)}\,\text{(number of bits/control word)}$$

$$= (80)(24)(8) + (80)(24)(5)$$

$$= 24{,}960$$

Thus the implementation complexity is determined as

$$\text{complexity} = N_X + (N_{BX} + N_{BT})/100 = 6784 \text{ equivalent crosspoints}$$

The implementation complexity determined in Example 5.2 is obviously dominated by the number of crosspoints in the space stage. A significantly lower complexity (and generally lower cost) can be achieved if groups of input links are combined into higher-level multiplex signals before being switched. The cost of the front end multiplexers is relatively small if the individual DS-1 signals have already been synchronized for switching. In this manner, the complexity of the space stage is decreased appreciably while the overall complexity of the time stage increases only slightly. (See the problem set at the end of this chapter.) The implementation costs are reduced proportionately— up to the point that higher speeds dictate the use of a more expensive technology.

Multiple Stage Time and Space Switching

As discussed in the preceding section, an effective means of reducing the cost of a time division switch is to multiplex as many channels together as practical and perform as much switching in the time stages as possible. Time stage switching is generally less expensive than space stage switching—primarily because digital memory is much cheaper than digital crosspoints (AND gates). To repeat, the crosspoints themselves are not so expensive, it is the cost of accessing and selecting them from external pins that makes their use relatively costly.

Naturally, there are practical limits as to how many channels can be multiplexed into a common TDM link for time stage switching. When these practical limits are reached, further reductions in the implementation complexity can be achieved only by using multiple stages. Obviously, some cost savings result when a single space matrix of a TS or ST switch can be replaced by multiple stages.

A generally more effective approach involves separating the space stages by a time stage, or, conversely, separating two time stages by a space stage. The next two sections describe these two basic structures. The first structure, consisting of a time stage between two space stages, is referred to as a space-time-space (STS) switch. The second structure is referred to as a time-space-time (TST) switch.

5.4.1 STS Switching

A functional block diagram of an STS switch is shown in Figure 5.20. Each of the space switches is assumed to be a single stage (nonblocking) switch. For large switches, it may be desirable to implement the space switches with multiple stages. Establishing a path through an STS switch requires finding a time switch array with an available write access during the incoming time slot and an available read access during the desired outgoing time slot. When each individual stage (S, T, S) is nonblocking, the operation is functionally equivalent to the operation of a three-stage space switch. Hence a probability graph in Figure 5.21 of an STS switch is identical to the probability graph of Figure 5.8 for three-stage space switches. Correspondingly, the blocking probability of an STS switch is

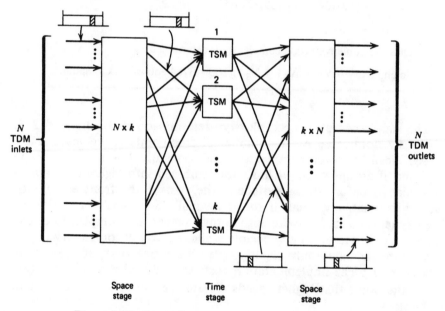

Figure 5.20 Space-time-space (STS) switching structure.

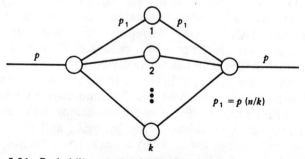

Figure 5.21 Probability graph of STS switch with nonblocking stages.

$$B = (1 - q'^2)^k \tag{5.14}$$

where $q' = 1 - p' = 1 - p/\beta$ $(\beta = k/N)$
k = number of center stage time switch arrays

Assuming the space switches are single stage arrays and that each TDM link has c message channels, we may determine the implementation complexity of an STS switch as*

complexity = (number of space stage crosspoints)
    + [(number of space stage control bits)
    + (number of time stage memory bits)
    + (number of time stage control bits)]/100

$$= 2kN + \frac{[2 \cdot k \cdot c \cdot \log_2 N + k \cdot c \cdot 8 + k \cdot c \cdot \log_2 c]}{100}$$

$$\tag{5.15}$$

EXAMPLE 5.3

Determine the implementation complexity of a 2048 channel STS switch implemented for 16 TDM links with 128 channels on each link. The desired maximum blocking probability is .002 for channel occupancies of 0.1.

Solution. The minimum number of center stage time switches to provide the desired grade of service can be determined from Equation 5.14 as $k = 7$. Using this value of k, the number of crosspoints is determined as $(2)(7)(16) = 224$. The number of bits of memory can be determined as $(2)(7)(128)(4) + (7)(128)(8) + (7)(128)(7) = 20,608$. Hence the composite implementation complexity is 430 equivalent crosspoints.

The value of implementation complexity obtained in Example 5.3 should be compared to the number of crosspoints obtained for an equivalent sized three-stage switch listed in Table 5.2. The space switch design requires 41,000 crosspoints while the STS design requires only 430 equivalent crosspoints. The dramatic savings comes about as a result of the voice signals having already been digitized and multiplexed (presumably for transmission purposes). When the STS switch is inserted into an analog environment, the dominant cost of the switch occurs in the line interface. Modern digital switches are not unlike modern digital computers. The cost of a central processing unit has become relatively small compared to the costs of peripheral devices.

5.4.2 TST Switching

A second form of multiple stage time and space switching is shown in Figure 5.22. This switch is usually referred to as a time-space-time (TST) switch. Information arriving in a TDM channel of an incoming link is delayed in the inlet time stage until an appropriate path through the space stage is available. At that time the information is transferred through the space stage to the appropriate outlet time stage where it is held until the desired outgoing time slot occurs. Assuming the time stages provide full availability (i.e. all incoming channels can be con-

---

*This derivation assumes output-associated control is used in the first stage and input-associated control is used in the third stage. A slightly different result occurs if the space stages are controlled in different manners.

nected to all outgoing channels), any space stage time slot can be used to establish a connection. In a functional sense the space stage is replicated once for every internal time slot. This concept is reinforced by the TST probability graph of Figure 5.23.

An important feature to notice about a TST switch is that the space stage operates in a time divided fashion, independently of the external TDM links. In fact, the number of space stage time slots l does not have to coincide with the number of external TDM time slots c.

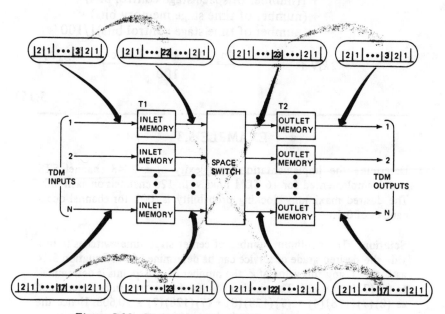

Figure 5.22 Time-space-time (TST) switching structure.

If the space stage is nonblocking, blocking in a TST switch occurs only if there is no internal space stage time slot during which the link from the inlet time stage and the link to the outlet time stage are both idle. Obviously, the blocking probability is minimized if the number of space stage time slots l is made to be large. In fact, as a direct analogy of three-stage space switches, the TST switch is strictly nonblocking if $l = 2c - 1$. The general expression of blocking probability for a TST switch with nonblocking individual stages (T, S, T) is:

$$B = [1 - q_1^2]^l \qquad (5.16)$$

where $q_1 = 1 - p_1 = 1 - p/\alpha$

α = time expansion (l/c)

l = number of space stage time slots

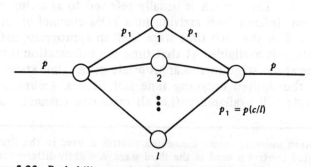

Figure 5.23 Probability graph of TST switch with nonblocking stages.

The implementation complexity of a TST switch can be derived as follows:*

$$\text{complexity} = N^2 + \frac{[N \cdot l \cdot \log_2 N + 2 \cdot N \cdot c \cdot 8 + 2 \cdot N \cdot l \log_2 c]}{100}$$

(5.17)

EXAMPLE 5.4

Determine the implementation complexity of a 2048 channel TST switch with 16 TDM links and 128 channels per link. Assume the desired maximum blocking probability is .002 for incoming channel occupancies of 0.1.

Solution. Using Equation 5.16, we can determine the number of internal time slots required for the desired grade of service as 25. Hence time concentration of $1/\alpha = 5.12$ is possible because of the light loading on the input channels. The implementation complexity can now be determined from Equation 5.17 as 656.

The results obtained in Examples 5.3 and 5.4 indicate that the TST architecture is more complex than the STS architecture. Notice, however, that the TST switch operates with time concentration whereas the STS switch operates with space concentration. As the utilization of the input links increase, less and less concentration is acceptable. If the input channel loading is high enough, time expansion in the TST switch and space expansion in the STS switch are required to maintain low blocking probabilities. Since time expansion can be achieved at less cost than space expansion, a TST switch becomes more cost effective than an STS switch for high channel utilizations. The implementation complexities of these two systems are compared in Figure 5.24 as a function of the input utilization.

As can be seen in Figure 5.24, TST switches have a distinct implementation advantage over STS switches when large amounts of traffic are present. For small switches, the implementation complexities favor STS architectures. The choice of a particular architecture may be more dependent on such other factors as modularity, testability, expandability. One consideration that generally favors an STS structure is its relatively simpler control requirements [10]. For very large switches with heavy traffic loads, the implementation advantage of a TST switch is dominant. Evidence of this fact is provided by the No. 4ESS, a TST structure that is the largest capacity switch built to date.

---

*This derivation assumes that the inlet time stage uses output-associated control (random reads) and the outlet time stage uses input-associated control (random writes). A slightly different result occurs if the time stages operate differently.

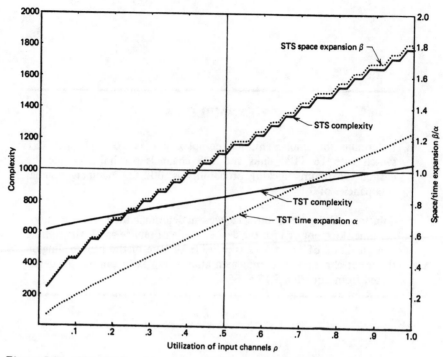

Figure 5.24 Complexity comparison of STS and TST switching structures for a blocking probability of .002.

TSSST Switches

When the space stage of a TST switch is large enough to justify additional control complexity, multiple space stages can be used to reduce the total crosspoint count. Figure 5.25 depicts a TST architecture with a three-stage space switch. Because the three middle stages are all space stages, this structure is sometimes referred to as a TSSST switch. The

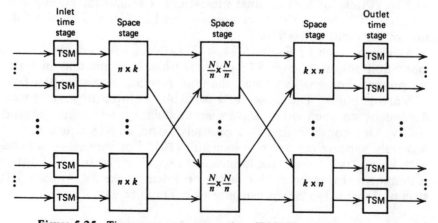

Figure 5.25 Time-space-space-space-time (TSSST) switching structure.

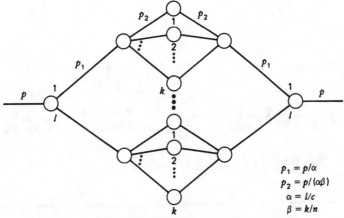

$$p_1 = p/\alpha$$
$$p_2 = p/(\alpha\beta)$$
$$\alpha = l/c$$
$$\beta = k/n$$

Figure 5.26 Probability graph of TSSST switch.

implementation complexity of a TSSST switch can be determined as follows:*

$$\text{complexity} = \frac{N_X + (N_{BX} + N_{BT} + N_{BTC})}{100} \qquad (5.18)$$

where N_X = number of crosspoints = $2 \cdot N \cdot k + k \cdot (N/n)^2$

N_{BX} = number of space stage control store bits = $2 \cdot k \cdot (N/n) \cdot l \cdot \log_2(n) + k \cdot (N/n) \cdot l \cdot \log_2(N/n)$

N_{BT} = number of bits in time stages = $2 \cdot N \cdot c \cdot 8$

N_{BTC} = number of time stage control store bits = $2 \cdot N \cdot l \cdot \log_2(c)$

The probability graph of a TSSST switch is shown in Figure 5.26. Notice that this diagram is functionally identical to the probability graph of a five-stage space switch shown in Figure 5.10. Using the probability graph of Figure 5.26, we can determine the blocking probability of a TSSST switch as

$$B = \{1 - (q_1)^2 [1 - (1 - q_2^2)^k]\}^l \qquad (5.19)$$

where $q_1 = 1 - p_1 = 1 - p/\alpha$
$q_2 = 1 - p_2 = 1 - p/\alpha\beta$

EXAMPLE 5.5

Determine the implementation complexity of a 131,072 channel TSSST switch designed to provide a maximum blocking probability of .002 under channel occupancies of 0.7. Assume the switch services 1024

---

*The assumed control orientations by stages are: output, output, output, input, input.

Data Communications Network Switching Methods

Features of multichannel intelligent data switching system permit cost-effective data switching of data communications networks

David A. Kane   Develcon Electronics Incorporated, Doylestown, Pennsylvania

Today's data communications networks are considerably more complex and larger than the systems in use just a few years ago. Too often, however, these networks have been limited in their rate of growth and usefulness due to the lack of adequate data switching facilities to interconnect system elements. More direct, selective, interterminal communications links are needed to meet the requirements of increasingly intelligent data communications systems. The technology required to effectively interconnect data in these systems has grown in proportion with the advances in data processing's state of the art.

Previously, there were two popular methods of connecting the various

hardware in the network: the dial-up lines of common carrier facilities, and dedicated channels and contention hardware. Recently a multichannel, intelligent data switch system has been developed. Connection methods are chosen depending on criteria such as the distances involved and the amount of time a device in the network must remain online with another device.

Common Carrier Facilities

The common carrier or dial-up facilities connect each device in the data processing network to separate multiline rotary exchanges (see Fig 1). This connection enables an unlimited group of users to contend for service

port groups. through the common carrier switched network—all on a first come, first serve basis.

In a typical timesharing application, the telephone rotary contention allows support of up to four terminals per computer. This permits realization of significant savings in computer port hardware. In addition, there is improved utilization of the computer ports installed. When the computer is busy or connected, the user receives these indications via the telephone rotary. Moreover, terminal users may gain access to different computer systems or support different applications programs on the same computer system, so dial-up access may be used to provide a port selection facility.

Since dial-up access is dependent upon the telephone, many of this system's advantages are negated by the ever increasing telephone and equipment costs and by limiting performance factors. Because this approach operates on a 2-wire circuit, there are data transmission speed restrictions. Even with the new modems available, the maximum speed is only 1200 baud. Controlled carrier operations with synchronous speeds up to 9600 baud are possible, however, many terminals don't have the required interface control signals for these operations.

With common carrier facilities, no statistical information as to system usage is available. There is no way to exactly determine how many users dialed but were unable to connect with the computers. There are also no statistics for the number of successful calls. If this type of information were available, computer center managers could determine more accurately the efficiency of their operations.

Another problem facing common carrier facility users is the increasingly higher tariffs charged by the

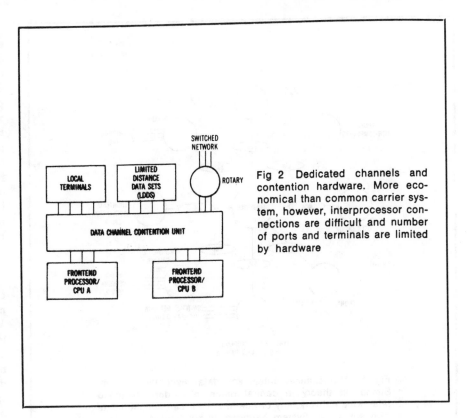

Fig 2 Dedicated channels and contention hardware. More economical than common carrier system, however, interprocessor connections are difficult and number of ports and terminals are limited by hardware

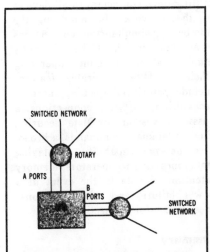

Fig 1 Common carrier system configuration. Multi-line rotary exchanges allow large numbers of users to contend for computer ports through its switched network

telephone company for use of its facilities. Originally the tariffs were based on voice usage. The typical phone call lasted three to five minutes and billings were charged for the number of these short calls. Now, since so many computer users connect to the data terminal by the switched telephone network, phone calls are much longer. Many terminal users are connected for eight or ten hours through the common carrier facility every business day.

The phone company wants to be compensated for this type of usage and now penalizes terminal users with a new tariff in which business usage is measured in increments of five minutes or less. Single message units are charged for each 5-min increment. These tariffs may adversely affect users with PABX and Centrex services. Heavier reliance on these services may result in larger systems—even though voice traffic may not warrant it.

Dedicated Channels and Contention Hardware

This method, commonly known as port contention, eliminates some of the problems associated with the dial-up access approach. Service re-

quests are hardware generated. It is more economical—channels are normally leased or owned. The response to service requests is fast. Also, statistical information on system usage may be available.

The dedicated channels and contention hardware approach (Fig 2) does have limiting factors. It presumes that associated equipment are either ports or terminals, and the hardware limits the number of ports and terminals that can be utilized. Inter-processor (port to port) connections are difficult. This method may not provide connect and busy indications.

Multichannel Intelligent Data Switch

There is yet another means of connecting terminals to computers, one that eliminates all of the shortcomings of the other two methods, as well as offers many additional advantages. The technique, called multichannel intelligent data switching, is comparable to the typical central office in a modern switched telephone network. With this approach (see Fig 3), any device in the network can access any other device in the network. Computers

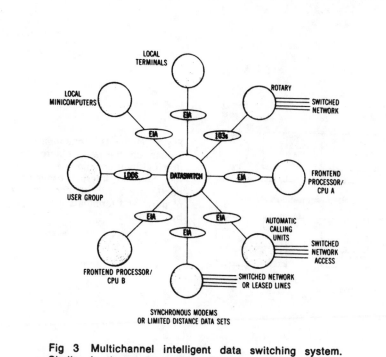

Fig 3 Multichannel intelligent data switching system. Similar in theory to central office in modern switched telephone network, any device in system can communicate with any other. System hardware is not limited

Data switching methods improve computer utilization by expanding data communications line capacities of a realtime computer system. They can be used to optimize computer port utilization for such applications as university campuses, military bases, and hospital complexes where private wires and terminal connections are often required to minimize transmission costs when dedicated channels are uneconomical due to low usage. The data switching method also circumvents the single message unit tariff imposed by the telephone company, without the use of leased or private lines.

Several considerations will insure continued cost-effectiveness, usefulness, and even growth of the system. Maximizing the number of possible terminals, ports, and subscribers will expand the data communications network. The ability to accommodate different codes and transmission speeds ranging from 1200 to 19.2k baud will also assure future growth. The highest possible synchronous and asynchronous transmission speeds will help maximize the cost-effectiveness of the system.

For a truly effective data communications network, the central switching device must be capable of permitting universal access to all devices in the network. In addition, the number of simultaneous connections at any one time should be sufficiently high to allow maximum operating efficiency. Other desirable features include prioritized queuing, account recognition, partyline connections. a password system for data security, English language commands, a broadcast message capability, displaying status messages to operators, memory retention of data in the event of a power failure, and system response to a successful connection.

Summary

A multichannel intelligent data switching system eliminates the short comings of both the common carrier dial-up facilities and the dedicated channels and contention hardware approaches to data switching. The advantages of this type of data switch help lower overall costs of data communications, improve efficiency, and enhance network performance. □

can communicate with terminals, terminals can talk with printers, printers with computers, and peripheral devices can talk with each other.

Through a unique combination of hardware and software the data switch system controls and coordinates all ports, integrating both the dial-up and dedicated access approaches. The system permits non-biased use by operating on a first come, first serve basis. All subscribers (devices in the system) have an equal opportunity to originate requests to any other subscriber. The subscribers contend for a number of incoming channels, or lines, and for computer communications interfaces (ports).

The data switch intercepts a subscriber's request for service, reviews whether the service is available, and then either completes the connection or advises the calling subscriber that the connection cannot be made. Up to 2048 subscribers may be connected, and the system will allow up to 1023 simultaneous full-duplex connections. Communications links in a data communications network incorporating a data switching system may be by dial-up, leased line with limited distance modems, by local terminals, or through any device with an EIA standard RS-232 interface.

Devices with different bit rates or character sets in the network are responded to automatically with a data switching system. A 1200-baud terminal contending for the same deck with a 2400-baud device, will automatically be connected to the first 1200-baud port available in that deck; the 2400-baud device will automatically be connected to the first 2400-baud port available. Essentially, all mixing of transmission speeds is handled by the system. Once port to port connections are made, full-duplex conversations proceed without further intervention. When one party desires to end a connection, the system disconnects both devices simultaneously.

The ABCs of the PBX

Leo F. Goeller, Jr. and Jerry A. Goldstone

Private branch exchanges aren't just for communications types anymore. Here's part two of our four-part series on these important devices.

THE ABCS OF THE PBX

by Leo F. Goeller Jr. and Jerry A. Goldstone

A PBX or private branch exchange is a switchboard for business telephones. It differs from the phone company's central office (CO) switch in two very important ways. First, it must in general have someone to say, "XYZ Company, good morning" and then complete the call. Then, if the call reaches the wrong party, some means must be provided to transfer that call to another extension.

At the smaller end of the spectrum, key telephone systems compete with PBXs. A key system may have 50 or more telephones associated with it and many advanced features. There is a philosophical difference, however, between a PBX and a key system: a PBX has a relatively high proportion of calling among telephones it serves, while a key system has most of its traffic with the outside world and is used very little for internal calling. In much larger sizes, Centrex competes, usually by using specially modified central office equipment.

A PBX system (Fig. 1) is composed of four basic parts: switching matrix, control, user terminals, and trunks. The PBX proper includes the matrix and control, along with interface units, usually called line and trunk circuits, that terminate the transmission facilities that extend to user telephones or other switches. In addition, one usually finds "service circuits" in a PBX to apply ringing and call progress tones (busy, reorder, etc.), and to assimilate caller signaling information from telephone dials and tone pads, converting this information to something the control can use.

No matter how complex a modern PBX may become internally, it still works

Excerpted with permission from the *Business Communications Review Manual of PBXs*, published by Business Communications Review, Hinsdale, Ill.

PHOTOGRAPH BY STEVE COOPER

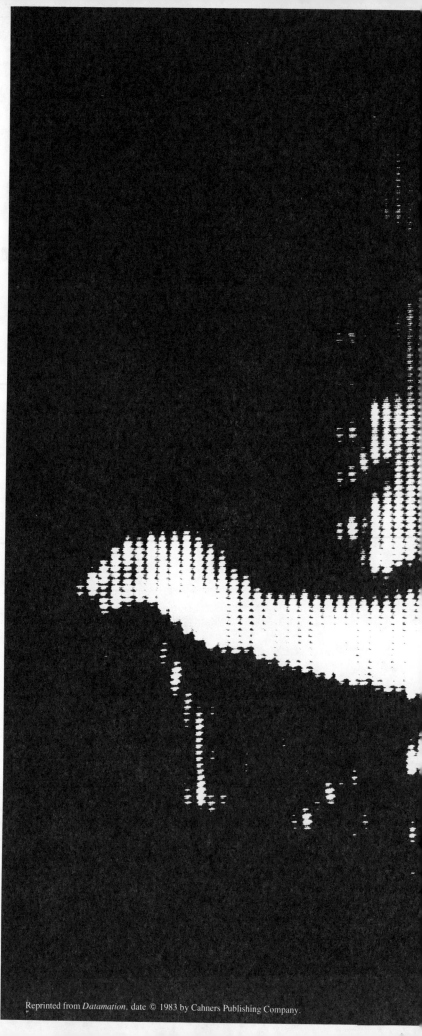

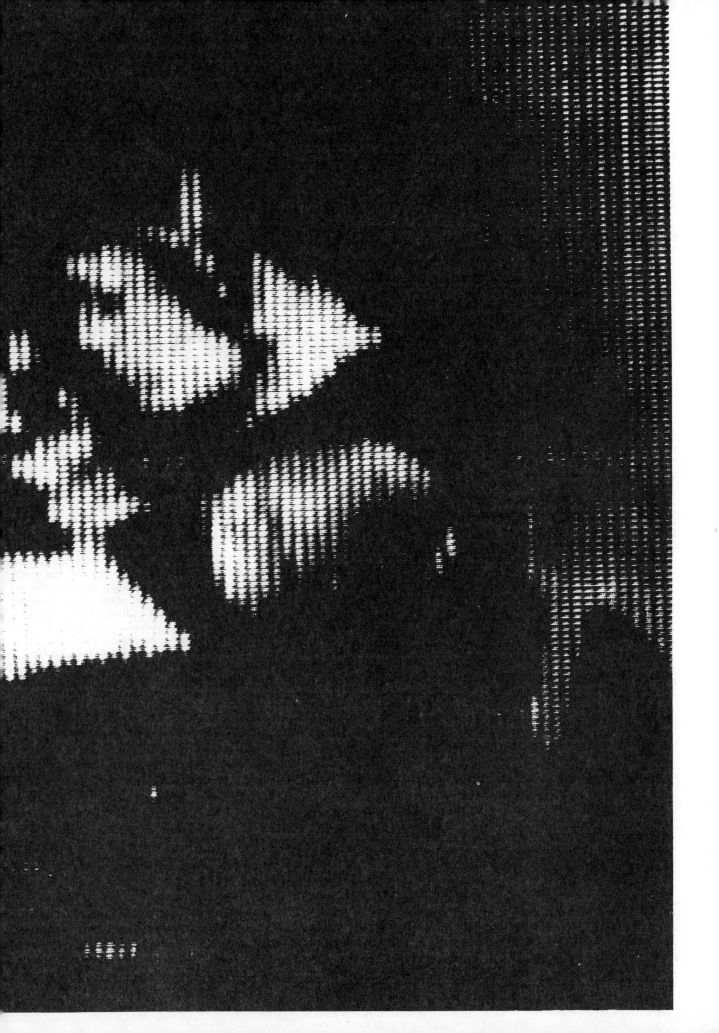

very much the way the old manual switch-
boards did. In the so-called cord board, each
line and trunk terminates in a suitable interface circuit that controls one or more signal
lamps to alert the attendant and passes the
voice path on to a jack that permits easy interconnection.

When a user picks up his phone, the
PBX supplies power to the instrument and, by
monitoring this flow of power (usually with a
line relay), knows to light a lamp to tell the
attendant that assistance is needed. The attendant has in front of him a number of pairs of
cords that can be used to make connections to
lines and/or trunks. These cords perform the
precise functions that a modern PBX performs
with its switching matrix. The attendant
plugs one cord of a particular pair into the
jack associated with the calling line and operates a switch that connects his headset to the
cord circuit. He then says something like
"Number, please" so that the caller knows
the attendant is ready to respond to his communication needs. A modern system, of
course, uses a dial tone to perform the same
function, even though many such systems
have replaced rotary dials with tone pads.

The caller then gives the attendant the
number he wishes to reach. If it is another
extension on the PBX, the attendant takes the
other cord of the pair and makes a "busy
test" on the called line to make sure it is not
busy on another call. If the called line is idle,
the attendant then completes the connection
to the appropriate jack.

Either the attendant or automatic circuitry detects an answer, terminates ringing,
and leaves the calling and called-station users
to converse. If either of them needs further
assistance, he flashes his switch-hook. That
is, he depresses and releases his switch-hook.
Each of the two cords in the pair making the
connection has a lamp associated with it. Momentary depression of the switch-hook
causes the lamp to come on momentarily.
This flash signals the attendant to reconnect
his headset to the cord circuit to see what
assistance is required. When the call is completed and the parties hang up, the cord lamps
light, letting the attendant know that the call
is over and the cords can be pulled down and
made available for another call.

There are still a few manual PBXs in
use. They serve their customers well and,
because they consist primarily of a very small
switching matrix (the cords) and simple line
and trunk circuits, they occupy little space
and are relatively inexpensive. But perhaps
their main advantage, in addition to low cost,
is their control. They have the most advanced
system control available today, one that is
quite flexible and very smart: a human being.
A human attendant at a manual switchboard
can provide almost all the modern features
associated with the new, computer-con-

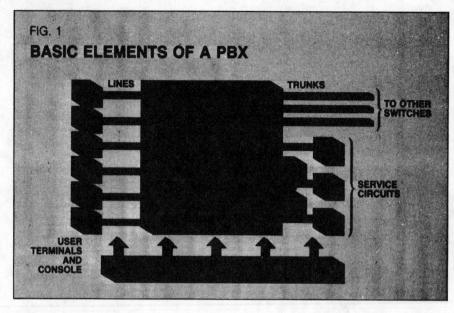

FIG. 1
BASIC ELEMENTS OF A PBX

trolled PBXs. Attendants, available in common to all lines and trunks, meet all the requirements of what is called "common control" in modern switching systems. (Common control can be contrasted with "distributed control" in step-by-step electromechanical systems where each switch has its own
control equipment and control is distributed
over the entire switching matrix. Common
control equipment, shared by all parts of the
system, eliminates a great deal of duplication
and, when done properly, reduces costs and
improves operations.)

However, people are getting more
and more expensive: they like to go to lunch
in the middle of the day, they want to go
home at night, and they require training. Humans being human, the trend today is to effect as many of the functions of the attendant
as possible with automatic equipment, often
in the form of a computer acting as a common
control.

MODERN PBX FEATURES A modern PBX still detects
the flow of power when
the telephone user picks up
his instrument. It then
makes a connection automatically through
the switching matrix to a digit receiver that
returns dial tone. The caller dials or keys the
called number into the digit receiver (sometimes called a register, a decoder, or something similar). The system responds by making sure the call is permitted and then rings
the called line. Upon detection of answer, the
calling and called parties are interconnected
via the switching matrix for conversation; the
system monitors for switch-hook flashes that
indicate the need for some additional service,
or hang up to free the portions of the switching matrix used on this call for future calls.

A major point of complexity, far

more important in PBXs than in most central
office switches, lies in terminating the call to
some line other than the one requested. Hunt-
ing is usually available and widely used in
PBXs so that if the boss's line is busy, the call
will be routed to his secretary. Modern PBXs
have added a variety of call-forwarding features that can be invoked and canceled by the
station user. Sometimes privacy features require the return of a special tone to indicate
that the called party does not wish to be dis-
turbed. Pickup is a relatively new feature that
allows any station in a previously defined
pickup group to come off hook and snatch
away a call that is ringing unanswered at another station in the group. Camp-on and call
waiting may have calls stacked up waiting for
an existing conversation to end; automatic
callback may have one or more callers waiting for an existing call to be completed so that
the system can call them back and then complete to the called party. Obviously, a call
encountering camp-on, call waiting, or call-
back at the terminating line will be dealing
with a situation that has several levels of
"busy" to contend with. A simple test to see
if the line is busy is no longer sufficient.
From all this, it is easy to see that the terminating half of the call setup procedure can be
quite complex.

Trunk calls are a little more intricate.
An outgoing call starts off exactly the same
way as an extension-to-extension call, but
now the control can complete its part of the
job by connecting to any one of several trunks
to the local central office. Further, it can, if it
wants to, do this long before the caller has
finished dialing. Traditionally, callers on a
PBX dial 9, get dial tone from the CO, and then
dial the telephone number of the called party.
This approach was very important in the early
automatic PBXs that were constructed from

With the present PBX and central office designs, it is imperative that the CO use ground start circuits.

relays and other electromechanical components. It let the PBX complete its part of the job quickly and easily and turn all the hard work over to the CO. The CO would then store the called number, set up the connection, handle the billing, etc.

The problem with this was the propensity of PBX station users to make personal calls that kept showing up in the bill from the phone company as message units, short-haul tolls, or even long-haul tolls. This led to a central office feature called toll diversion, which automatically terminated all toll calls or diverted them to the switchboard attendant. But because many COs did not have this feature, the restrictor was developed. A restrictor was a box full of switching components that attached to each trunk of the CO and could be programmed with a list of approved calling regions. As time went on, however, it became evident that the restrictor function should be incorporated in the PBX design.

A PBX that incorporates restriction knows which extension is originating the call. Thus the PBX can automatically perform restricting and routing functions based on the "class of service" assigned to the specific extension without the caller having to take any action. External restrictors must treat all calls alike since they have no way of identifying the caller, and external call routers, quite popular during the last 10 years, require the user to identify himself by dialing in an additional group of digits.

Two ways of handling outward calls became possible: cut through and register sender. With memory and control capability being relatively inexpensive in modern PBXs, the register-sender approach has much to recommend it. Many manufacturers, however, still cling to the cut-through approach. Note carefully the difference: with cut through, the system connects as soon as possible to the CO and, in certain circumstances, monitors digits as they go past, while with register-sender operation, the system takes in the entire number and performs restriction, routing, and whatever else may be appropriate and then continues with setting up the call.

In setting up an outgoing call, the PBX sometimes doesn't know when the CO is ready to receive digits, and it almost never knows when the called party answers. Further, it may not know when the call is ended by the called party hanging up. In cut-through operation, the user hears CO dial tone and, ultimately, the called-party answer (or busy tone or whatever); this relieves the PBX of the need to do anything. But the PBX must monitor the internal extension very carefully since this, in many instances, is the only source of information about adding features or ending the call. If the internal extension has been put on hold, the outside party can sometimes hang up without being detected.

When call detail recording equipment is added to or built into the PBX, the inability of the system to determine when a call is answered is a severe problem in making accurate toll bills. On the other hand, machine detection of hang-up is fairly simple if "ground start" trunks are obtained from the CO; ground start trunks also work well to provide an automatic start dialing signal in register-sender operation, although, for a variety of reasons, detection of dial tone directly has much to recommend it.

INCOMING CO CALLS DIFFER

Traditional incoming calls from the CO are quite different from the intra-PBX and outgoing calls we have examined so far. It must be recalled that a PBX trunk is, as far as the CO is concerned, a station line just like the one that goes to a telephone. Thus when the CO wants to complete a call to somebody served by a PBX, it will send ringing down the line (viewed from its end) or trunk (when viewed from the PBX end). Ringing (which is a large, high-power signal at 20Hz and 86 volts) operates a ring-up relay or similar device in the PBX's trunk circuit to make some kind of indication to the system that a CO call is coming in. This indication is forwarded to the console position where the attendant can see and respond to it.

When the attendant signals the system control that the call is to be accepted, ringing is tripped and the call is connected to the console. Tripping ringing causes the CO to put its equipment in the talking state and to start charging. Thus, the calling party pays for the call if it reaches the PBX attendant.

The attendant obtains the called extension number or, more often, the name of the called party, and instructs the control to manipulate the switching matrix to complete the call. The control applies ringing toward the called extension, generally returns audible ringing (ringback) to the calling party, and watches for answer. It is highly desirable that a PBX monitor this ringing situation and return the call to the console after a timed interval if no answer is obtained. It is also desirable that the PBX be able to monitor the trunk circuit for abandon in case the calling party hangs up. Ground start trunks are required for this to be possible. As on any call, the system must monitor the internal party for switch-hook flashes and hang-up.

In many systems, the same CO trunks used for incoming calls are used for outgoing dial 9 calls. This poses a problem that must be understood if serious trouble is to be avoided. The trouble concerns seizure of the same trunk simultaneously by both the CO and the PBX. This situation puts the PBX caller, who has just dialed 9, in direct contact with an incoming call that is almost certainly intended for someone else.

Simultaneous seizure can be minimized at the PBX if the trunk circuit involved is made busy to dial 9 calls as soon as the CO has seized the trunk from the far end. This cannot, in general, be done if all the CO does is apply ringing. Ringing, in most central offices, is on for two seconds and off for four. Thus, if the CO seized the trunk at the start of the silent interval in the ringing cycle, up to four seconds could elapse before the PBX trunk circuit would know. In a busy hour, four seconds is eternity and many dial 9 calls would have a crack at the "idle" trunk. Thus, once again ground start trunks are necessary. They tell the PBX immediately when the trunk is seized from the CO and thus allow the PBX to direct outgoing calls to other circuits. Trunks used in the outgoing direction for dial 9 and incoming for completion to the attendant are usually called combination trunks. With the present PBX and CO designs, it is imperative that the CO use ground start circuits.

Direct inward dialing (DID) is rapidly making Centrex unnecessary, and most modern PBXs offer it. As mentioned above, DID is not particularly difficult at the PBX. Any PBX that can handle dial repeating tie trunks is ready to go immediately. All that is needed is for a CO to be able to send dial pulses; this is harder to come by. In some metropolitan regions, New York City in particular, tandem offices in the public network bypass the local central offices and connect directly to DID PBXs. This lets each PBX be treated as a small central office, and everything works fine.

There are, of course, some practical details. All the old-fashioned step-by-step (SXS) PBXs were quite fast in that they could accept dial pulsing on a tie trunk as soon as the trunk was seized at the distant end. Unfortunately, most modern COs and PBXs are much slower. After detecting seizure, they must find a digit detector to attach to the trunk, or arrange their internal operation to examine the trunk circuit fast and often enough to catch all the dial pulses as they come in. This may take a while. Thus, the distant end must be held off until the PBX is ready. The technique used is called "wink start." The CO (or tandem office) is psyched up to watch for a momentary off-hook signal to be returned. At the end of this one fifth of a second interval of off-hook, the telco end knows it can start sending dial pulses.

Some modern PBXs are always watching their DID trunks (and tie trunks) for incoming dial pulses, and thus are as fast as SXS systems. However, they sometimes have to return a wink start signal anyway to make the CO happy. Thus, we have two problems here: we must know if a PBX is able to send wink start to satisfy the CO, and if it must send wink start to fend off the CO until the PBX is ready to receive digits.

The current trend in PBX design is away from the relatively inexpensive 500/2500-type sets.

When digits are sent to a PBX in a DID situation, the telco sends them at the slowest possible rate: 10 pulses per second, with something more than half a second between trains of pulses that constitute a digit. Thus, to send a four-digit extension number to a PBX, the CO will require at least four seconds. If Touch-Tone had been used, about a half a second would have been needed. There is even a standardized form of dial pulsing, long used between common control switches in the public network and between PBX attendants and common control COs, in which the time could be cut to two seconds. But, for reasons that are unknown, the slowest form

of dialing is used. This is particularly amusing in that the Bell System is installing, as rapidly as possible, a new digital method of signaling called CCIS (Common Channel Interoffice Signaling) that may, among other things, cut down signaling time in the public network. The time saved will, of course, be balanced by the slow pulsing into DID PBXs.

A DID call seizes the trunk, gets wink start (if required), and sends the PBX the extension-identifying digits it needs. The PBX then completes the call. That is, the PBX rings the called extension, sends audible ringing (or, if appropriate, busy tone) to the calling party, and monitors for answer. When the

call is answered, the answer signal is returned to the CO and the talking connection is established. Note that charging does not start on a DID call until the called party (or somebody else) answers. The telephone company, to be sure it gets paid for the call, will not make the trunk work in both directions until the answer signal is received. The trunk must work in one direction so that the caller can hear audible ringing or busy tone—but it won't work in both directions until after answer has taken place and charging begins.

THE USER INTERFACE

Telephone sets are the interface between the telephone system and the users. Consoles, in modern equipment seldom more than glorified telephone sets, fall into the same category. Additional interfaces, provided for maintenance and information exchange, are often standard teletypewriters or data terminals although sets or consoles with special displays are sometimes provided. Needless to say, the instrument and the switching system must be able to work with one another if the system is to support communications.

Telephone sets must, in general, convert acoustical energy to electrical energy and vice versa to permit voice communications. For nonvoice services, analogous requirements exist. In addition, the station user must be able to signal toward the system to "place his order," and the system must be able to signal toward the caller to let him know what the system is doing to carry out his instructions. The system must also signal toward the called party to encourage him to answer his phone and, in some instances, to tell him which line he is supposed to answer.

The basic mechanism of the 500-type telephone set, the one in present use throughout the country, was perfected just about the time transistors were announced. Thus, station apparatus has not, as yet, taken any particular advantage of developments in solid-state physics. The 2500-type telephone set, identical to the 500 except for the use of a DTMF (the generic name for AT&T's Touch-Tone trademark) pad for signaling rather than a rotary dial, does, it is true, use transistors for generating the tones. But that is sort of an add-on application.

The 500/2500-type telephone does use some rather early solid-state components to compensate for the distance between the central office and the telephone. The curious result is that the closer to the switch a telephone is, the more it upsets transmission when connecting to trunks. Or, to put it another way, the majority of PBX telephone sets are located where they will harm overall network transmission.

It happens that something less than 20% of all telephones are served by Centrex

DEPT. OF FUNNY SMELLS

EMERGENCY

J. Harris

or PBX systems, while the rest are served directly by central offices on (mostly) a single line basis. It appears, however, that the great majority of toll calls are placed from PBX and Centrex telephones, and these calls are, of necessity, made during the business day when rates are high. Thus, improving transmission at PBX telephones would seem to be one of the easiest ways to improve overall transmission on a nationwide basis. And the easiest way to improve transmission would be to make PBX systems four-wire end-to-end, including the telephone sets.

The current trend in PBX design is away from the relatively inexpensive 500/2500-type sets. The SL-1 PBX from Northern Telecom was the first to go in this direction, and Bell followed quickly with sets for Dimension. Danray also had electronic sets from the beginning. These sets require three or four pairs between the telephone set and the switch, but unfortunately all except Danray use only one pair for voice transmission. One can understand the Dimension using two-wire telephone sets, since Dimension is a two-wire switch. And one can even understand the SL-1 using two-wire telephone sets even though the switch is four-wire internally; after all, Northern Telecom is a telephone-oriented company and tradition is of considerable importance. What is really hard to understand, however, is the new Rolm electronic telephone set. The Rolm switch is four-wire, and the people who designed it were determined to innovate. But their new microprocessor controlled telephone set, the ETS 100, uses two-wire transmission.

Only Tele/Resources and Danray have, to date, seen the logic of four-wire telephone sets. The T/R System 32 is four-wire from station to station, as is the Danray. The only time they are vulnerable to transmission echo is when they connect to two-wire facilities, as when they go to off-premises stations or, more important, to CO trunks.

Conventional 500- or 2500-type telephone sets have a microphone or transmitter for converting acoustical energy to electrical energy to be transmitted via wires. Similarly, they have a receiver for making the opposite conversion. The two are connected via a network, which permits a single pair of wires to be used for transmission in each direction when two separate devices are obviously required at the telephone set to interface a caller's ear and mouth.

The "network" serves an additional purpose. It provides "sidetone." That is, it allows a certain amount of the spoken energy to be fed back to the ear of the speaker (without delay). That is necessary because we are used to hearing ourselves speak (cover both ears and speak aloud to detect the impact of not hearing yourself); if we don't, we change our speaking patterns. As it happens, the sidetone circuit feeds back slightly less sound than we hear through the air; this tends to make us talk a little louder, and provides better volume for the person on the far end of the connection.

The switch-hook, the next device we encounter, makes a path for current from the PBX or CO switch through the telephone set when the caller picks up the handset. The handset, of course, contains the transmitter and receiver, and, when not in use, sits in a cradle on the telephone base. While placed in the cradle, it operates a switch that turns off power; when lifted, the switch closes and completes the path needed for current to flow.

Note that the PBX or CO must always monitor a line for its on-hook or off-hook status. This is called supervision. The switch must know if the user is originating a call, answering a call to his phone, or terminating a call that is already in progress. In recent years, the switch-hook "flash" has regained the importance it had in manual systems. A flash is a momentary on-hook. The system detects it and knows that it is not a hang-up followed by the origination of a new call.

The purpose of the flash is to tell the system that the user wants to send an additional command, a "feature code." Particularly if the system uses DTMF, but often when dial pulsing is used as well, a digit receiver must be connected to unscramble the user's new command. Use of the switch-hook flash and as many as 20 feature codes is common in modern PBXs.

TELEPHONE SET FEATURES

Special telephone sets designed to work directly with the PBX combine PBX capabilities with user convenience. These sets, available from Northern Telecom, the Bell System, and others, usually have a group of buttons that can be either line pickup keys (as in conventional key telephone sets) or feature keys. What usually happens is depression of a selected key tells the system which key is depressed. The system looks up in a table in memory to find out what is going on, and carries out the appropriate action. If a line select key is pushed, the system connects an incoming call for the line to the tel set via the switching matrix; on an outgoing call, charging and restriction are based on the class marks of the line selected. If a feature key has been pushed (the hold button, for instance, although we now have many other possibilities), the system does whatever is required. If visual cues are required by the user, the PBX control causes an appropriate signal to be returned to light or blink the appropriate lamp, to cause the tone ringer to sound, or to provide some other suitable signal.

These modern electronic sets have a number of advantages. First, they are much easier for the user when contrasted with flashing the switch-hook, dialing a number of feature codes, and identifying a variety of call progress tones. Second, they usually need only three pairs, and three pairs will work on any kind of phone from a simple single line set to a 30-button call director. Finally, they permit complete program control of changes in lines picked up, features selected, etc. This kind of control can often be handled from remote locations via a dataset in a dial-up connection or by the customer's communication manager. The saving in OCC (other charges and credits) for moves and changes can be considerable in an active location, and the saving in aggravation and time when the communication manager can effect the change directly rather than trying to honcho an order through a reluctant vendor can hardly be appreciated until it is experienced.

One problem must be noted, however. Single line sets usually require different line cards in the PBX than do these modern sets. This shows that more than a program change is required when one goes from a single line to a multiline set. Further, it is evident that when one changes from a five-button set to a 30-button set, the sets themselves will have to be interchanged even though programming can do most of the rest. In any event, the identification required on each button must be made at the set and not with the program. Even so, the modern sets can be cost effective when properly used.

It should be possible to switch data over public and private voice networks like any other signal. Just how readily this can be done was demonstrated by Danray and taken up by Northern Telecom upon its purchase of Danray. One simply puts an RS232C interface on the electronic telephone set (there are, apparently, better or less expensive interfaces, but 232 exists in vast quantities) and plugs in a terminal or a computer. Danray uses the power pair (one of the three pairs required by their electronic set) to carry off 9,600 bps full-duplex data to a separate auxiliary data switch. The voice telephone is used to set up the connection, but once the data path is set up, the voice equipment is free for make or receive voice calls. This kind of simultaneous voice/data operation seems to be highly favored by those who normally use terminals, particularly over some version of alternate voice/data where the voice phone is tied up with the data connection.

Northern Telecom uses the same approach with the SL-1 PBX, but without a separate data matrix. The SL-1 has a digital time-division switching matrix, and can switch data directly by simply omitting the analog to digital conversion in the data line circuit. Each telephone has two appearances on the

No amount of processor duplication will save the system in the event of a power failure.

switching matrix: one for voice and one for data. Again, the voice phone is free to make and receive calls once it has the data connection established. With the long holding times of data calls (normally found with timesharing in industry), some traffic problems may develop here—but the idea seems to be quite good.

Rolm has done something different. A single voice path through the matrix is submultiplexed into as many as 40 data paths (depending on the speed of the switched data). In addition to adding switching capability with negligible degradation of the system's voice handling capability, this approach appears to be quite inexpensive compared with even relatively low-speed modems.

Many people feel that a telephone set

in a business area should have a full alphanumeric keyboard and display and a handset, along with an array of feature and line pickup buttons. This relatively dumb terminal could then interface with the switch, which could include software to permit the set to do whatever is required: be a timesharing terminal, a word processing station, an electronic mail system, or whatever. The cost of modern electronic components would seem to point in this direction.

Consoles are provided with PBXs to permit human assistance when required to complete calls. Early consoles interfaced trunks directly and, working through the trunk appearance on the switching matrix, effected call completion. Today the trend is to use something very much like an electronic telephone set as a console; the switch con-

nects calls needing assistance to the console as to any other telephone, but provides a bit more information by driving suitable displays. Consoles, like electronic telephone sets, can be arranged to have digital signaling paths to the system control to interchange information directly without using the voice path.

SYSTEM CONTROL METHODS

Most modern PBX switches today use a processor of some sort for control. Stored program approaches are now standard, but this hardly tells the whole story. We are confronted with minicomputers and microprocessors, RAM and ROM, backup tapes and disks, and separate standalone mechanisms for call data recording and processing. Like any small computer-controlled industrial system, a PBX is operated by its processor. The processor, backed with program instructions, inspects all lines, trunks, service circuits, and other portions of the system, first for supervisory information (on-hook and off-hook) and then for any additional information that may be needed to make things work (dialed addresses, feature codes, signals from feature/line buttons on electronic telephones, alarm and trouble warning information, etc.). Further, maintenance or other control information may also be coming in.

The control responds to externally generated signals and to internal signals that result from processing information in accordance with data stored in memory. That is, it checks class marks and other instructions and sets up paths through the switching matrix between lines and/or trunks, records information in memory for billing and traffic purposes, and, in general, carries out the functions of an operator at a manual switchboard.

Processors are usually not duplicated for redundancy in small systems; they almost always are in large systems. The breakpoint appears to be at about 400 lines. Duplication for reliability requires additional complexity in that both sets of memories have to be kept up to date, and the computers have to be able to decide which one is in charge. In some systems with duplicated processors, standard business programs (payroll, inventory, etc.) can be run on the standby machine; other systems use the standby machine to handle other functions (such as Rolm's electronic mail) until it is needed. With or without duplication, the system may very well have extra time and memory that could be devoted to store and forward data, etc.

No amount of processor duplication will save the system in the event of power failure. In such an instance, a backup battery is required to keep the system running (or, at least, to save the memory) until the power is restored. If batteries are not provided, some

THE DYNAMIC BUILDING

BIO-DYNAMIC PLAN	312
COMMUNICATION DYNAMICS	402
CONTROL DYNAMIC DESIGNS	105
CREATIVE DYNAMICS, INC.	107
DYNAMIC ASSOCIATES	210
DYNAMIC MANAGEMENT GROUP	220
DYNAMIC SYSTEMS, LTD.	320
DYNAMIC THERAPY INST.	115
MEDICO-DYNAMICS, INC.	405
MOTIVATIONAL DYNAMICS	120
MULTIMODAL DYNAMICS, LTD.	206
PERSONAL DYNAMICS, INC.	305
REGIONAL DYNAMIC DESIGNS	415
SPECTRUM DYNAMICS	202
VITAL DYNAMICS ASSN.	318

CARTOON BY HENRY MARTIN

One of the main advantages of computer control of switching systems is the ease with which new features can be installed.

means may be required to reprogram memory when the power comes back up. Systems using a volatile random access memory (RAM) lose their program when power is cut off, so the system must be able to reload from some reasonably permanent memory when the power is restored. Often a magnetic tape or disk contains the backup program. The backup memory does not always keep track of the calls in progress or the station-programmed features such as call forwarding. Thus, reload sometimes does not get back to the starting point.

One of the main advantages of computer control of switching systems (or other industrial equipment) is the ease with which new features can be installed, services can be upgraded, and changes can be made in the course of regular activity. Note, however, that not all stored-program processor controlled systems permit easy changes. Read only memories (ROMs) are not always changeable in the field—sometimes they have to be unplugged and replaced, while in other instances, they must be altered in a special programming device. ROM memory is quite reliable—it can't be changed by unauthorized personnel very easily, and it is non-volatile so that it is ready to go as soon as power comes back after a failure. But in most instances, the greater flexibility of making changes from a maintenance terminal, the console, or a special telephone set is of much greater importance. Usually some sort of compromise is used: program instructions that do not change are stored in ROM, while parameters that define special features and translations are keyed in, stored in memory that is easily changed but wiped out with power failure, and duplicated on the backup tape for reload with power restoral. There are almost as many variations as there are PBX systems on the market, and we haven't seen the end of it yet.

Switching matrices can be cataloged under three general headings: space division, frequency division, and time division. In space division, which includes all the older electromechanical systems and some electronic systems, the control finds a path through one or more sets of switches between the line and trunk, sets up that path, and the path, a physical connection that can be traced from point to point, is used by the caller for the duration of the call. When the call is over, the various switches are released for use by other callers.

Frequency division is seldom used, while time division is taking over the field. Unfortunately, time division can be carried out in many different ways, some analog and some digital. And even the digital techniques permit a wide variety. For example, pulse code modulation (PCM) and delta modulation are incompatible with each other, and no two

forms of a delta modulation system are compatible.

ANALOG VERSUS DIGITAL There is a great deal of discussion about the merits of digital versus analog switching. Some people feel that a switch controlled by a digital computer is a digital switch, and they point out quite correctly that most of the features of interest to users are a direct result of stored program control. But this is not what is generally meant when one speaks of digital switching. Digital vs. analog in this context refers to the way the switching matrix operates, and has little to do with the control equipment. Further, it is true that many of the features of interest to users today can be carried out quite well with a switch that has a matrix that works on analog principles.

Analog transmission means that the signal transmitted is a direct analog of the actual signal. In telephony, the actual signal is compressions and rarefactions of air—changes of air pressure that are interpreted as speech. These changes of pressure fall on the microphone or transmitter in the telephone handset, and the microphone converts pressure variations to current variations. Note that the current variations are a direct analog of the pressure variations, increasing and decreasing in exactly the same way. Note also that the power in the current variations is appreciably larger than the power in the sound pressure; there is gain or amplification available in the telephone set. This is the only way long distance telephony could have been practical 25 years before the invention of the vacuum tube.

The electric current can be transmitted over wires, and it can operate more modern equipment to make another analog of the original signal which permits transmission via radio beam. In all these instances, a view of the signal on an oscilloscope would look just the same as if the scope could read sound pressure directly.

Amplification is very important in analog transmission. A small incoming signal must control something that makes a large but directly analogous outgoing signal. The signal will be attenuated by a long cable, but can be amplified again to get back to its proper size. Unfortunately, amplification can't tell the difference between the original signal and that signal plus any noise that may have been picked up along the way. Each time amplification is used, more noise is added to the signal. Ultimately, the signal is submerged in noise. Even a very small variation in the original signal will change it, and all such changes will add up.

A digital signal cannot be continuously variable as can a pressure wave or the analogous current variations produced by the

microphone. A digital signal can only take on one of a finite number of values at any instant. It does not have to be amplified, however. The digital signal is measured, its value is determined, and a new signal is made just like the old one. All the noise is stripped off and lost.

This technique is called regeneration and is very old. It was used in telegraph systems before the telephone was invented. Telegraph pulses would be distorted by long wires, and the dots and dashes couldn't be distinguished; then somebody figured that, instead of using one long wire with a key at one end and a sounder and a huge battery at the far end, a number of short wires could be used, end to end, each powered with a smaller battery. The first wire would have a key on one end for sending, and a relay and battery at the far end for receiving. The relay would follow the key properly, and its contacts could act as a key in the next circuit to regenerate a new signal. This regeneration could go from circuit to circuit, outwitting noise and distortion. In a digital telephone system, we convert a voice signal to something that looks like a telegraph signal. Then we can use regeneration rather than amplification and be free of noise and distortion.

The characteristic of digital modulation techniques is that all of the pulses are the same in both amplitude and width. All the system has to do, then, is determine whether a pulse is present or not. A series of standard pulses (or absence of pulses) in successive time intervals can define the amplitude of a voice signal at any instant. This requires more pulses than analog modulation techniques, but simplifies pulse detection and retransmission.

Can a customer tell the difference between an analog and a digital switch? Not on a voice call. Make a connection through relays, reed switches, crossbar, or SXS switches, or with a variety of electronic techniques including the various digital modulation schemes discussed above, and a caller cannot tell which system has been used. On a per-call basis, there is no difference. Why, then, go to all this trouble? Why not stick with SXS, or even stop with 8,000 samples per second where each is of variable height or width?

There are reasons for a PBX to be digital. The public telephone network is about half digital today in an 8-bit PCM format. If these 8-bit words or bytes of PCM are kept intact when they go through switches and trunks, new frontiers open up. It just happens that ASCII uses seven bits, often plus a parity or check bit. Voice channels normally handle 8,000 eight-bit bytes per second; if they can be switched together in built-up connections ultimately extending from one telephone to another, there are possibilities for data transmission that make all present data systems,

The purchase of a digital PBX to obtain all the advantages of the digital future is a bit premature at the present.

including packet networks, seem roughly comparable to the postal service.

THE ULTIMATE PAYOFF

This is the ultimate payoff. With an all-digital network served by digital switches handling digital user stations, voice and nonvoice communications can be mixed as needed on a per-call basis. Note that nonvoice communications are particularly easy to handle: on that day in the future when there is an all-digital network, modems will not be needed. A data signal will just bypass the A/D converters required for the speech part of the telephone and get directly on the bit stream with information precoded to fit. When any dial-up connection can handle 8,000 ASCII characters/sec, new opportunities for business communications not yet even considered will be possible.

Unfortunately, there is a long way to go before such a future will be possible. Most intertoll trunks will remain analog until fiber optics becomes generally available for long-haul PCM circuits. Microwave, satellite, and coaxial cable can handle many more analog circuits than digital at the same cost or bandwidth so they will not vanish easily. Further, protocols required by various data machines to permit them to talk to one another vary from data system to system; indeed, in data communications, one of the principal functions of a node or switch is to convert from one system to another to permit connections between otherwise incompatible equipment. Finally, digital telephone systems need a variety of other signals for synchronization, supervision and control; these tend to make a universal voice/nonvoice system hard to achieve. Thus, the purchase of a digital PBX to obtain all the advantages of the digital future is a bit premature at the present time.

What can a digital switch do for a user today? A few things, some of which may be quite important in special applications. First, distributed switching is now possible with several modern switches. One can take parts of the switch, analogous to line groups in a SXS system, and put them near the telephones. Using T-Carrier techniques, these remote units can connect something like 100 extensions to the main part of the switch with two pairs; this minimizes the three-pair wiring from the remote units to the electronic telephone sets, and the overall economies are considerable in a large building or in a campus-type environment.

The second thing a digital switch can do is switch digital signals internally in digital form, without modems. A digital switch is needed, although Danray, using an analog switch, pioneered the effort as described above. A small interface box is required to take the computer or terminal's digital signal and convert it slightly to conform to the needs of the power pair, which is the channel to the switch, but this little box is relatively inexpensive compared to a high-speed modem. In the newest PBXs, A/D conversion takes place in the telephone set and not at the line card in the switch. Then the data signal can enter the digital world immediately, without the need to utilize power pairs for access.

A modern PBX, from the equipment point of view, is much simpler than the older electromechanical systems. Most of the sophistication is built into the program that instructs the control, and modern digital circuitry has simplified most of what is left. The switching matrix tends to be quite small, and new opportunities are available for convenient design of user terminals. Trunks circuits, going mostly to obsolete (two-wire analog) central offices and to analog long-haul tie trunks, have to meet the outside world on its own terms, but even they tend to take advantage of PBX control and component sophistication.

A modern PBX can do many things the older PBXs could not do, and can open the way to doing things that are done today by completely separate systems. We are right on the edge of a whole range of developments that will change the way business is conducted. But we are not there yet. Thus, one should not rush to buy the current state of the art just because it is more modern. One should understand just what is involved, and make sound decisions on the basis of rational information. And above all, be ready for change. ✳

Leo F. Goeller Jr. is an independent consultant with Communication Resources in Haddonfield, N.J. He is also on the Board of Members of the Business Communication Review.

Jerry A. Goldstone has been the editor and publisher of *Business Communications Review* for the past 12 years. Copies of the BCR manual can be obtained from the company by writing to 950 York Rd., Suite 203, Hinsdale, IL 60521.

CARTOON BY JACK CORBETT

The Evolution of Data Switching for PBX's

BRIJ BHUSHAN AND HOLGER OPDERBECK

Abstract — This paper compares and contrasts the different traffic requirements of both voice and data communications. The role of evolving PBX technology in solving data communication needs is outlined, beginning with the analog PBX's of the 1970's and the digital-switching technology of the 1980's. The evolution of packet switching, and its superiority over traditional circuit switching for solving data communications needs, is analyzed.

The paper concludes by describing a PBX implementation that takes advantage of circuit- and packet-switching technologies and thus offers a truly integrated multipurpose communications switch.

I. INTRODUCTION

THE PBX has long held immense potential as the most economical and workable solution to meet the rapidly growing voice and data communications needs of business. This potential has not gone unrecognized, but until now it has gone largely unrealized. For years, manufacturers and users of PBX's have seen that their central voice switch would also be the ideal candidate for accommodating their data-switching requirements. The points in favor of the PBX as a data switch are numerous. First, the PBX provides an existing network of installed lines that runs from every office to the central switch, creating a de facto local area network. Second, the PBX can be connected directly to long-haul transmission networks via T1 interfaces using media such as conventional cable pairs, coaxial cables, fiber optics, and satellite and terrestrial microwave links. These interfaces provide high-speed access to public and private communication networks. Third, PBX's have always provided the most sophisticated administration and maintenance capabilities which are required to optimally manage complex telecommunication systems.

The problem, therefore, was one of technology, of fulfilling the potential of the PBX in the area of data communications. Over the last five to eight years, the attempts to produce a completely integrated voice/data PBX have brought it through three basic phases of development. With each phase, the data capabilities of the PBX improved, and the true integration of voice and data moved a step closer to reality.

II. REQUIREMENTS OF VOICE/DATA TRAFFIC

The characteristics of voice and the demand it imposes on the switch have been fairly well known for a long time

Manuscript received July 9, 1984; revised March 25, 1985.
B. Bhushan is with GTE Telenet Communications Corporation, Reston, VA 22096.
H. Opderbeck is with Opderbeck Communications Consultants, Vienna, VA 22180.

TABLE I
VOICE-TRAFFIC CHARACTERIZATION AND PBX REQUIREMENTS

Holding Time	120–180 s
Traffic/Port	6–12 CCS/Station; 18–28 CCS/Trunk
Busy Hour Call Attempt	4–5/Port
Dial Tone Delay	< 3 s 98.5 Percent of the Time
Busy Hour	20 Percent of Daily Average Traffic

PBX REQUIREMENTS FOR VOICE TRAFFIC

In Switch Blocking Characteristics	P.01
	Nonblocking P0.0
	Essentially Nonblocking (At a Certain Traffic)
Intra-PBX Traffic	10–40 Percent
Inter-PBX Traffic	30–50 Percent
Off-net Traffic (For network of PBX's)	20–40 Percent

and are well documented. A summary of these is shown in Table I (for details see [1]).

Data traffic typically has three attributes that differ from voice attributes. Unlike voice, data communication generally does not occur between any two devices, e.g., data devices always tend to reach applications at a prefixed number of hosts. Thus, there is a tremendous amount of concentration that is required. This attribute has led to a number of manufacturers making concentrators, multiplexors, etc. With the advent of personal computers, this trend will change when these personal computers will generate traffic by connecting to each other and occasionally connecting to a host computer.

The second attribute of data is its bursty nature. There can be inactivity on the line for quite some time and then suddenly a burst of data at the rated speed will come through followed by a period of silence. In contrast to this phenomenon, the voice traffic generally is continuous once a connection is made.

The third is the time sensitivity of the information. Unlike voice, where one copes with busy modes (station busy or congestion busy) and attempts to either call back or queue the call, the data call demands instant connection since the information retrieval from the application/database is time-critical for the end user in some applications. This last attribute translates into a requirement of "nonblocking" switch for data applications.

Data traffic is extremely diverse and is generally application dependent. The common characteristics are outlined in Table II and can be classified into four broad categories,

Reprinted from *IEEE Journal on Selected Areas in Communications*, Volume SAC-3, Number 4, July 1985, pages 569-573. Copyright © 1985 by The Institute of Electrical and Electronics Engineers, Inc.

TABLE II
DATA-TRAFFIC CHARACTERIZATION AND PBS REQUIREMENTS

Call Holding Time	8 s–15 h
Bit-Error Rate $10^{**}-5$ to $10^{**}-8$	End-to-End
(Or Error-Free Seconds)	
Speed and Type of Transmission	
• Asynchronous and Synchronous	
• Half-Duplex versus Full-Duplex	
• Codes ASCII/EDBDIC/	
BAUDOT, etc.	
Throughput of switch	
• Bits	
• Packets	

e.g., call-holding time, speed and type of transmission, bit-error rate (or error-free seconds) and the throughput of the switch.

Call-holding times are very much dependent upon the application. The typical values may range from 8–15 s for an interactive transaction-type application to 8–15 h a day for remote job entry applications. These applications could be run on asynchronous or synchronous terminals in full- or half-duplex mode ranging in speed from 300 bits/s to 56 kbits/s and demand bit error rates of $10^{**}-5$–$10^{**}-8$.

III. ANALOG APPROACH TO DATA SWITCHING IN A PBX

The majority of PBX's that were designed and built in the late 1970's were analog PBX's, and were primarily designed for switching voice. These PBX's were built for call duration of only a few minutes which is typical for voice calls in the office environment. Although data could be switched through these early PBX's, the data stream had to be converted to a format that made it look to the PBX like a voice call, e.g., typically modem data. This conversion to voice format at the input, and back to data format at the output, was accomplished by modems. Thus, PBX handled data in the same way as the public-switched network regardless of its destination, e.g., intra-PBX or inter-PBX.

The call establishment and tear-down process was accomplished via telephone sets. These PBX's thus were unable to provide error correction or concentration of data into high-speed lines or ports. This implied that all data had to be switched on a direct line-to-line low-speed access basis (up to 9.6 kbits/s) as shown in Fig. 1. These constraints not only limit the value of the PBX for data communication capability; this cost was further compounded by the cost of lost voice capacity. In short, running data communications on the voice-only PBX of the late 1970's was an inefficient and expensive proposition.

IV. DIGITAL APPROACH TO DATA SWITCHING IN A PBX

The 1980's saw the beginning of integrated voice/data communications. When a digital local loop is used, the expensive modems are replaced by digital devices like the

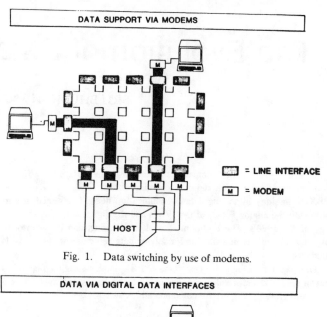

Fig. 1. Data switching by use of modems.

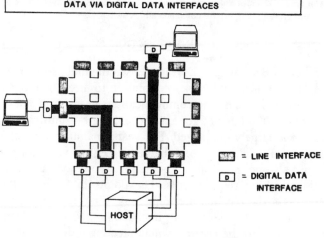

Fig. 2. Data switching utilizing DDI.

digital-device data interface (DDI) shown in Fig. 2. DDI's are capable of connecting to data terminal equipment in the same manner as the modems. The received data bits are transmitted digitally to the PBX where the bit stream is switched the same way as voice. This digital interface, however, is capable of signaling to the PBX via a message-oriented format. Thus, for the first time, the switch must be aware of the fact that it is not dealing with a standard analog device, but a more sophisticated device with different requirements.

These digital interfaces can be stand-alone devices or integrated into the new generation of station equipment. In some cases, this integration is only a physical integration, i.e., housing, power supply, etc., being shared, and there is no integration on the access lines. In this arrangement, two or more wire pairs running to the PBX support voice and data on distinctly separate pairs terminating at different line interfaces. Thus, the PBX treats them as two distinct connections, resulting in added cost of lost voice capacity as in the case outlined earlier.

A more cost-effective solution is realized if data and voice devices share the line card at the PBX as well as the local-access wires. This local-access integration also results in the phone and DDI sharing electronics, thus making this

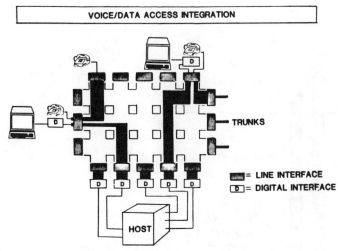

TRUNKS

▬ = LINE INTERFACE
D = DIGITAL INTERFACE

HOST

Fig. 3. Local access-integrated PBX.

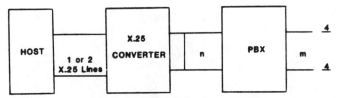

Fig. 4. Use of *X*.25 converter box with PBX.

an attractive implementation as shown in Fig. 3. This implementation yields an increase in port capacity since the new line cards can now handle voice and data ports simultaneously. The data, however, are still switched in the circuit mode and the PBX switching bandwidth is not efficiently utilized (a 9.6 kbit/s connection through the 64 kbit/s PCM stream yields 15 percent efficiency). A more balanced approach to voice/data switching requires the introduction of true packet-switching capabilities integrated in a PBX. These capabilities are now emerging in the third phase of voice/data integration.

The integration of packet switching in a PBX brings with it the concept of a virtual connection. A virtual connection is a logical association of two endpoints. The two endpoints can exchange information any time they desire to do so after a virtual connection. Therefore, the long intervals of idle time, which are so typical for data communication, do not consume any switching capacity. Moreover, the bandwidth of the local-access line can be allocated to multiple connections as required, instead of being dedicated to serve just one voice and one data call.

Virtual connections have several attractive features. They do not care what application they are being used for. They represent a universal transport mechanism which is independent of format, speed, or content. In principle, they can be used for voice, data, text, facsimile, and new applications with still unknown service characteristics. They consume transmission and switching resources only when required. This dynamic allocation of resources reduces the total resource requirements substantially.

The dynamic resource allocation introduces potential delays due to the competition for resources among multiple connections. In the data world, these delay considerations are well understood and efficient system engineering guidelines exist to minimize their impact.

The integration in the PBX can be effected by separating the voice PCM samples from data stream at the line-card level and switching it via conventional switching means—a noncontention PCM bus, whereas the data stream can be switched in a contention mode via a data bus.

This dual-bus architecture, with one bus for the switch-

ing of voice in a dedicated mode and one bus for switching of data in a contention mode, provides the user with the best of both worlds. It guarantees voice quality due to its priority handling of PCM samples and it brings the flexibility of virtual connections to every station connected to the PBX and the problem of lost voice capacity is thus resolved.

V. DATA COMMUNICATIONS USING PACKET SWITCHING

With the advent of packet switching and subsequent standardization of the applicable *X* series of recommendations (*X*.3, *X*.25, *X*.28, and *X*.29) a formal standardized method was made available offering, among other things, a multiplexing method, as well as universal applicability. Despite its initial slow acceptance, it is now provided by all DP equipment vendors. The standardization of *X*.25 also brought with it entrepreneurs that will afford retrofittability to the installed equipment by offering hardware that can concentrate traffic in one *X*.25 pipe as well as allow asynchronous terminals to talk to the host machines as shown in Fig. 4.

The equipment configuration could still be engineered to provide the level of service that the customer desired. This approach meant that the number of host ports went down at the cost of the *X*.25 converter boxes.

ROLM and INTECOM have attempted to integrate the *X*.25 functions in their PBX's in different ways. Both implementations are capable of supporting *X*.25, but the number of ports in each implementation is limited and this addition has an effect on the voice-carrying capacity of the PBX [2], [3].

The GTE OMNI SII and SIII series of PBX's have implemented the *X*.25 packet-switching approach in an evolutionary and innovative way. The main goals of the architecture are to
• use the standard OMNI-PBX cabinets, power, and backplane;
• provide *X*.25 based capabilities;
• minimize impact on the existing OMNI-PBX hardware and software;
• minimize the effect on the OMNI-PBX's voice-handling capability;
• present the PABX as a "unified" system to the user;
• provide an architecture that is extensible, for future product evolution.

The architecture chosen is shown in Fig. 5. To provide the communication capabilities needed to support data switching without affecting voice capacity, a packet trans-

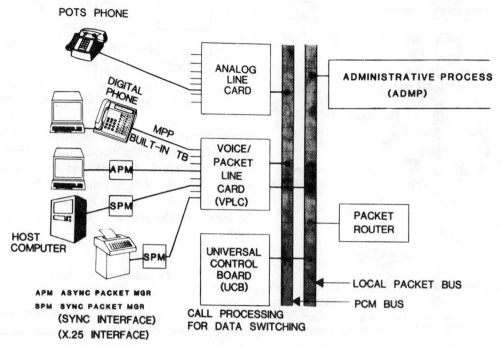

POTS PHONE

DIGITAL
PHONE

MPP
BUILT-IN TB

APM

SPM

HOST
COMPUTER

SPM

APM ASYNC PACKET MGR
SPM SYNC PACKET MGR
(SYNC INTERFACE)
(X.25 INTERFACE)

ANALOG
LINE
CARD

VOICE/
PACKET
LINE
CARD
(VPLC)

UNIVERSAL
CONTROL
BOARD
(UCB)

CALL PROCESSING
FOR DATA SWITCHING

ADMINISTRATIVE PROCESS
(ADMP)

PACKET
ROUTER

LOCAL PACKET BUS
PCM BUS

Fig. 5.   Dual-bus architecture of OMNI PBX's.

port system (PTS) has been designed. The PTS consists of a packet router (PR) and the appropriate number of local packet buses (LPB). This bus structure has been added to the backplane in the OMNI PBX. Communication within the PTS is in the form of self-routing entities known as minipackets. Each uniquely addressable device, communicating via the PTS, is assigned a packet line address (PLA). The PLA provides the internal "address" of the component to which it is assigned.

The assignment of a specific PLA is performed automatically by the data subsystem, and is based on the hardware configuration of the switch. It has no relationship to the "subscriber number" which the user sees. Devices communicating via the PTS use a GTE proprietary protocol, known as minipacket protocol (MPP) to ensure reliable error-free communication.

Attached to the LPB are universal controller boards (UCB's) and an administrative and maintenance processor (ADMP). These cards provide the processing power needed to supply the various features required of the data option, such as data-call setup/takedown. The modularity of this design allows additional cards to be added to a system as the need arises and provides an evolution path for future capabilities.

In addition to the UCB's and ADMP's, line cards, known as voice-packet line cards (VPLC's) attach to the LPB. These provide the ability for remote processing devices (RP's) to communicate via the PTS. "Remote Processor" is the name given to a family of devices which are located remotely from the central OMNI PBX cabinet, and which interface directly with the subscriber equipment.

Asynchronous devices (terminals, hosts, and modems) connect to the data option via remote processors, known as Asynchronous Packet Managers (APM's). APM's are colocated with their asynchronous devices. Except for call-control-related events (call setup, disconnect, etc.), APM's contain all of the processing and transmission capabilities necessary to support transmission of asynchronous data. In addition, the APM provides an X.3 packet assembler/disassembler (PAD) function. This converts asynchronous data into X.25 packets and allows a user to enter signaling information (commands) via the keyboard on the attached asynchronous device. Commands are supplied using an X.28 type command language. APM's are addressed using the X.121 numbering scheme.

Each APM supports, at most, one single active data call (known as a virtual circuit), and will interface to full-duplex devices running at speeds up to 19.2 kbits.

Each APM is connected, via a single twisted-wire pair, to a voice-packet line card (VPLC) located within the OMNI switch. APM's communicate via the packet transport system and are assigned a unique X.121 address. APM's are locally (wall) powered or powered over a separate wire pair from an auxiliary power supply. Each APM is connected to a host, terminal, or modem with an RS-232C connector and may be configured as a DTE or DCE.

PBM is a remote processor known as a Synchronous Packet Manager (SPM). SPM's are colocated with their X.25 hosts, and connect to them via an RS-232C or V.35 connector. The SPM may be configured as a DTE or DCE. Each SPM supports X.25 level 3 (packet level) and X.25 level 2 (link level, LAPB). SPM's, like APM's, are locally (wall) powered or powered over a separate wire pair from an auxiliary power supply. They interface via a single twisted-wire pair to a VPLC card located within the OMNI PBX.

Data call-processing functions are completely handled by a universal controller board which is configured with data call-processing (DCP) software. The OMNI PBX voice switch does not participate in data call procedures.

Most administrative functions for the data option are handled by an administrative and maintenance processor (ADMP), although some functions are controlled by the voice portion of the PBX. ADMP is also responsible for integrating the voice and data functions from an administrative user's point of view.

Every OMNI PBX running the data option requires a disk as its resident mass-storage device. This mass-storage device is shared by the voice and data processing portions of the switch. The disk will provide storage for code and tables used within the entire OMNI PBX.

This approach has led to typical traffic capabilities of supporting up to 256 devices all running at 9.6 kbits/s full-duplex. This traffic capacity can be further augmented by adding more buses and more processor power in a modular fashion.

VI. CONCLUSIONS

During the last few years, the PBX has gone through an evolution of data switching which turned it into a sophisticated data-switching device. With the emergence of new standards like ISDN, the integration of voice and data will be merged into the integration of other communications services. The result of this integration will be a truly integrated multipurpose communication switch.

REFERENCES

[1] *Functional Product Class Criteria — PBX*, AT&T Pub. 48002.
[2] ROLM product brochures.
[3] INTECOM IBX product brochures.

Brij Bhushan was born in India. He received the B.S. and M.S. degrees in electrical engineering from Auburn University, Auburn, AL.

He did advanced graduate work in electrical engineering at Concordia University, Montreal, P.Q., Canada, and taught various undergraduate courses in electrical engineering prior to joining the communications industry. From 1973 to 1980 he was with the Computer Communications Group of Bell Canada, where he was responsible for the Datapac Services planning. He has also served as consultant to Satellite Business Systems for satellite-based voice/data communication services. Currently, he is responsible for business planning activities for GTE Telenet, Reston, VA. His prior responsibilities at GTE included product planning for customer-premise equipment and product evolutions for evolving ISDN standards.

Mr. Bhushan is a member of the Association of Professional Engineers, Ontario, Canada, the Association for Computing Machinery, and Eta Kappa Nu.

Holger Opderbeck received the M.S. degree in physics from the University of Munich, West Germany, and the M.S. and Ph.D. degrees in computer science, from the University of California at Los Angeles.

He began his career in communications as head of the Arpanet Measurement Project at the UCLA Network Measurement Center. In 1975 he joined GTE Telenet, a common carrier company providing the first public packet-switched data communications service in the United States. There he became Director of Software Systems, responsible for the design and development of all Telenet software products. In 1979 he was promoted to Vice President of Network Products, with full responsibility for all of GTE Telenet's product development. GTE Telenet's new family of multimicroprocessor-based communications products, the first of their kind in the industry, and the public electronic mail system, Telemail, were developed under his leadership and direction. In 1981 he transferred to GTE Business Communication Systems as Vice President of Advanced Communications Development. There he was responsible for the development of all GTE business terminals, office automation products, PBX data-switching products, and the next generation of integrated voice/data switches. Currently, he is President of Opderbeck Communications Consultants (OCC), a company specializing in the design, selection, and evaluation of integrated voice/data systems.

Voice-Data Integration in the Office: A PBX Approach

Edwin R. Coover

This article posits the role of a PBX
in achieving voice-data integraton in
the office

This article posits the role of a PBX in achieving voice-data integration in the office. For realism, it makes a number of unglamorous assumptions about the typical office:

- The office already possesses personal computers, shared logic word processors, a facsimile machine, and some kind of departmental processor, and must communicate with a remotely located large-scale IBM mainframe.
- The office knowingly or unknowingly, currently supports at least three levels of file storage: individual, on the PC's; group, at the office level on the shared logic word processors and/or departmental processors; and corporate, on the remotely located IBM mainframe.
- The office manager does not have the luxury of replacing all present office equipment at one time.
- The office manager has neither the budget nor the in-house expertise to integrate all equipment immediately even if s/he could, so an incremental approach is essential.
- Lastly, the office has or is in the process of getting a modern PBX.

Such a scenario raises the question of why, regardless of method (PBX, cable LAN, host mainframe), integrate voice-data at all? The answers here are several, and, fortunately for one who must sell the idea to management, eminently quantifiable:

Eliminate equipment duplication. If one device can perform two or more tasks, multiple physical devices do not have to be bought or installed, consume space, or be serviced. To cite a typical example, if a PC can access a time-sharing service by emulating a terminal, and neither the PC nor time-sharing service is used continuously, then a PC can replace a terminal.

Implement a uniform wiring plan. Data devices that require coaxial cabling impose special pain on the office manager. They are expensive to install and expensive to move. Something must be done to prevent employees from tripping over the cabling, much less to hide it for aesthetic reasons. Yet retrofitting coax connection networks (Ethernet, broadband) into existing offices is expensive and disruptive in the extreme. By contrast, employing extant telephone wiring for data use has an irresistible appeal: ubiquity and low cost. Furthermore, as typically everyone in the office has a telephone, and nearly everyone some kind of video workstation, and personnel rearrangements are common, being able to implement most moves and changes in software at a PBX administrative console can be a substantial money-saver.

Device interconnection. Here, the problem is the necessity of transferring information files (electronic mail, word processing test, data base subsets) across physical space (countries, states, cities, blocks, floors) and between different types of devices (often with different equipment vendors). This often involves specialized equipment and a significant amount of technical understanding. Nonetheless, once the necessary equipment is in place and the requisite training accomplished, the process can become routine and the

Reprinted from *IEEE Communications Magazine*, Volume 24, Number 7, July 1986, pages 24-29. Copyright © 1986 by The Institute of Electrical and Electronics Engineers, Inc.

costs of reentering "foreign" information can be eliminated.

To further clarify the assumptions regarding the archetypical office environment described earlier, Fig. 1 summarizes the five categories of devices and their typical uses, and presents some representatives. Figure 2 attempts to summarize their communications capabilities in terms of the ISO seven-level typology. Note that in Fig. 2, "Media," technically a sublayer of the Physical Layer or Level 1, is listed separately in order to emphasize the wiring aspect of the overall connectivity problem. Finally, the term "modern PBX" used to refer to a digital circuit switch of current manufacture (AT&T's Systems 75 and 85, NEC's IMS 2400, Rolm's CBX II, Northern Telecom's SL-1, Inte-Com's S/80, and the like) whose primary mission is voice switching, but which can be augmented to provide a variety of data services as well.

Having set the scenario and limitations, how might such a PBX-implemented, incremental voice-data integration strategy for the office proceed? Specifically, what roles might a PBX play?

Port selector. Perhaps the simplest cure is where the PBX functions as a port selector. Should there be multiple hosts accepting ASCII/asynchronous terminal traffic, a user with an ASCII/asynchronous terminal (or PC emulating the same) reaches either host by dialing or keying a four-digit number. The PBX equipment needed to effect this integration can take several forms. One consists of an electronic phone with asynchronous data interface. The terminal or PC is hooked RS-232C to RS-232C to the voice-data set at the user station. Another form is a plug-in card for the IBM PC, which may (Northern Telecom) or may not (Rolm) allow a 2500 analog phone to be attached as well. On the port side of the PBX several arrangements are also possible. On some models, a dedicated data pair is terminated directly on a data card; on others, a multiplexed voice-data stream is demuxed and then split. On the DCE side of the PBX, the PBX and host

front-end processor (FEP) are similarly connected. Commonly, a port card with RS-232C connects with a RS-232C port on the host FEP. If distances over 50 feet are involved, an additional RS-232C connecting "line driver" (signal amplifier) may be employed. The direct advantage to this scheme over the traditional, dial-up modems is that transmission speeds up to 19.2 Kbps are possible, and, where phones are present, the station-to-switch connection can be used simultaneously for voice.

Port selector with PBX-provided coax elimination. A slightly more complicated case involves the port selector function in conjunction with high speed devices and the elimination of coaxial cable. Some PBX's support coax elimination directly. AT&T, Northern Telecom, and InteCom currently support 3270 terminals in this manner. InteCom expects to add support of Wang shared-logic word processing workstations soon. Other vendors are likely to follow. In this case, the PBX directly time-slots the data between the workstations and host. This involves a special balun (resistance balancer) from the workstation to the electronic voice-data station and high-speed data cards on both the port and DCE sides of the PBX connecting to the terminal controller. With this scheme, coaxial cable is eliminated and terminal moves and changes are facilitated.

Coax elimination using PBX wiring. A less elegant alternative solution is to use a spare twisted pair of the telephone wiring, bypass the PBX, and hook directly to a cluster controller or host FEP. In this scheme, for which IBM and Lee Data provide equipment, a special cable connects the workstation, a balun (which varies by workstation type), and a data connector, which attaches to two twisted pairs. Then, at either a wiring closet or the main distribution frame cross connects, the pairs are terminated by another balun and connected to the computer equipment. One should bear in mind that permissible device distances between terminals and controllers are altered under this scheme, as

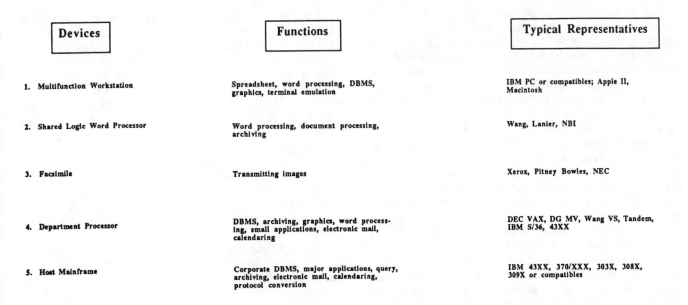

Devices	Functions	Typical Representatives
1. Multifunction Workstation	Spreadsheet, word processing, DBMS, graphics, terminal emulation	IBM PC or compatibles; Apple II, Macintosh
2. Shared Logic Word Processor	Word processing, document processing, archiving	Wang, Lanier, NBI
3. Facsimile	Transmitting images	Xerox, Pitney Bowles, NEC
4. Department Processor	DBMS, archiving, graphics, word processing, small applications, electronic mail, calendaring	DEC VAX, DG MV, Wang VS, Tandem, IBM S/36, 43XX
5. Host Mainframe	Corporate DBMS, major applications, query, archiving, electronic mail, calendaring, protocol conversion	IBM 43XX, 370/XXX, 303X, 308X, 309X or compatibles

Fig. 1. Devices, functions, and typical representatives.

	-Media-	Level 1 -Physical-	Level 2 -Data Link-	Level 3 -Network-	Level 4 -Transport-	Level 5 -Session-	Level 6 -Presentation-	Level 7 -Application-
Multifunction Workstation	Twisted pair, various coax	RS-232C; with cards, numerous options	Asynchronous; with co-processors, HDLC, SDLC, BSC	Can be used on circuit & packet-switched networks & LANs	In terminal or cluster controller emulation modes, ASCII/asynchronous, 3278, 3274; upper layers host & application-dependent			
Shared Logic Word Processor	Various coax	Various proprietary	Proprietary; optionally, HDLC & BSC	Proprietary LAN with external 3278/4 or asynchronous bridges	In terminal or cluster controller emulation modes, ASCII/asynchronous, 3278, 3274; upper layers host & application-dependent			
Facsimile (Categories I-IV)	Twisted pair, usually shielded	RS-232C, V.35	Proprietary & HDLC	Can be used on circuit or packet-switched networks	Conformity to one or more CCITT (Category I,II,III,IV) capabilities under proprietary upper layers			
Department Processor	Twisted pair, usually shielded	RS-232C, RS-449, Ethernet, proprietary channel	Asynchronous, HDLC, BSC, SDLC & Ethernet	Can be used on circuit or packet-switched networks or LANs	Limited SNA (PU 2, 2.1, LU 2, 6.2) capabilities, or pre-SNA device emulation (BSY 3274, 3276, 3777, 3780, HASP) with upper layers host determined; if 370 architecture, full SNA or pre-SNA			
Host Mainframe	Twisted pair, usually shielded, various coax	RS-232C, RS-449, Ethernet, proprietary channel	Asynchronous, HDLC, BSC, SDLC & Ethernet	Can be used on circuit or packet-switched networks or LANs	Various implementations of SNA or pre-SNA functional layers			

Fig. 2. Device communication capabilities.

the twisted pair run can only be about half the maximum distance of a coax run. To overcome this limitation, IBM offers a fiber optic channel extension kit (the IBM 3044) which allows the 3274/76 controllers to be moved closer to the terminals they support. Although the voice/data co-existence occurs only in the station-to-closet or station-to-main distribution frame wiring, and supported distances become less, this less elegant scheme both gets rid of coaxial cable and greatly eases future terminal moves and changes, although manual wiring reconnects are necessary at the closet or main distribution frame.

Port selector with out- or in-bound modem pooling. Another extension to the PBX-implemented port selector, resource sharing, has a number of advantages, providing users with a hierarchy of modem speeds, saving on long distance accesses, and centralizing the devices for maintenance. Administratively, the port selection can be implemented in several ways. In a "hardware" approach, the user can dial different numbers for different computer/speed combinations. Alternately, in a "class of service" or software approach, the user can dial a unique number for each computer, and the PBX will employ the fastest modem supportable by the connection, terminal, and host computer. For those accessing distant hosts, the PBX offers the additional advantage of economically routing dial-out data calls via its Advanced Route Selection (ARS) software. Physically, on the station side, the setup is the same as with other port selector roles: the electronic voice/data set connects the terminal with the twisted pairs via RJ-11 to the electronic voice/data set by RS-232C. A transformer that powers the line driver plugs into an electrical wall outlet. Call set-up varies by manufacturer with several sequences popular. On some, the user turns on the terminal, hits a data button on the voice-data set, and dials the station number. On others, the user turns on the terminal and types in the called

number on the keyboard. Some allow both. On the network side, the modems are connected between the trunk side data ports and the analog trunk groups.

Port selector with X.25 PAD. X.25 packet assemblers/disassemblers (PAD's) are accommodated in a manner very similar to the in- and out-bound modem pool—and are potentially modem pool users themselves. Depending on the number of simultaneous connections supported, port selection for the PAD can be a single "hardwired" number, multiple numbers, or a single number associated with a "hunt group" of lines assigned to the PAD. As with other PBX port selector services, an array of voice management features is available: camp-on, busy line call back, automatic call queuing, and recorded messages, depending on the contention/queuing philosophy.

Port selector/device emulation/protocol conversion. Incorporating protocol conversion capabilities into the PBX switch is consistent with accessing multiple hosts and reducing the number of physical devices on a user's desk. Most typically, this involves converting line-oriented asynchronous ASCII terminal streams into an IBM EBCDIC coded, 3270 full screen mode, 3270 bisynchronous, or 3270 synchronous data link control (SDLC) format.

The usual approach is for the PBX to perform the three conversions (ASCII to EBCDIC, line to screen, and stream to block) and to emulate a 3274/76 concontroller (Physical Unit 2, Logical Unit 2) to the FEP. (With the increasing popularity of IBM host-based Distributed Office Support System (DISOSS) services, such as electronic mail, revisable format document interchange, and peer-to-peer links, carrying multiple sessions via Logical Unit 6.2/Physical Unit 2.1 is likely to be added to the PBX protocol conversion repertory.) In sum, via the PBX's emulation/protocol conversion, an ASCII/asynchronous workstation may connect to various remote IBM hosts and interact as a monochrome 3278, or, in some cases, as a color 3279 terminal where the physical connection is dedicated or dial-up.

Bandwidth allocation via multiplexing. The employment of digital T1 (1.544Mbps) trunks has become increasingly popular in the larger private networks and can be expected to become more so with multiplexers that allow direct—and possibly dynamic—user bandwidth allocation. Conventional techniques place the muxes on the DCE side of the PBX and divide the bandwidth on a preallocated basis, with voice channels going into the PBX and the data into FEP's. This is likely to change for three reasons. First, modern PBX's have considerable data switching capability and may, along with their voice station wiring, furnish the connection medium to the workstations. Second, multiplexers are available that allow scheduled allocation (for instance, voice during the day and channel-speed data transfers at night) or dynamic allocation (for example, a dial-up 2 to 3 p.m. video conference, where preempted voice traffic is routed through the common carrier network). In any of these integrated voice-data contexts, the bandwidth request will begin with a voice-data station call, requiring close integration of PBX and multiplexer functions. Third, given the cost of T1 links, one-time costs in multiplexer intelligence that offer substantial and recurring utilization benefits become extremely attractive. All modern PBX's today offer T1 interfaces, and scheduled bandwidth allocation schemes are commonplace, though most often implemented by a network control group.

High-speed data services. High-speed data services with data rates over 64Kbps are, as mentioned earlier in 3270 cable replacement schemes, still the exception among modern PBX capabilities. Nor is it certain how much demand exists, beyond the 3270 cable replacement market. Relatively few present-day offices employ LAN's where the devices themselves (workstations, facsimile machines, printers)—as opposed to the signaling used on the LAN—are capable of transmitting at speeds exceeding 64 Kbps. The requirements situation may, however, change. Should the PBX makers decide to provide high-speed support, several approaches are possible. Some, such as InteCom, may have sufficient bandwidth in the main switch to support high-speed data within their present switch design. Others, such as AT&T's System 85 and Northern Telecom's Meridian, have already announced data LAN services via an attached processor concept, where data is split off at the switch backplane and passed to the extra processor. In the AT&T scheme, where data devices are remote and clustered, a fiber optic link directly connects the 327X type controllers to the attached LAN processor.

More probable is that the impetus for high speed support (3270 polling, Wang shared-logic word processors, Ethernet, IBM token ring) may come for more mundane reasons. Data devices, taken as a class, have been very inferior to voice devices in several respects. They have been expensive to install and hard to move, with IBM 3270 coax the prevalent *bête noire*. Also, the data gathering regarding their use has been extremely deficient; the emphasis has been placed, rather, on diagnosis and service routines to keep them working. Few cable-based LAN's produce easily available statistics on usage. Strongest in this area are those data PBX's that provide Station Message Detail Reporting (SMDR) records on all calls. Most voice-data PBX's

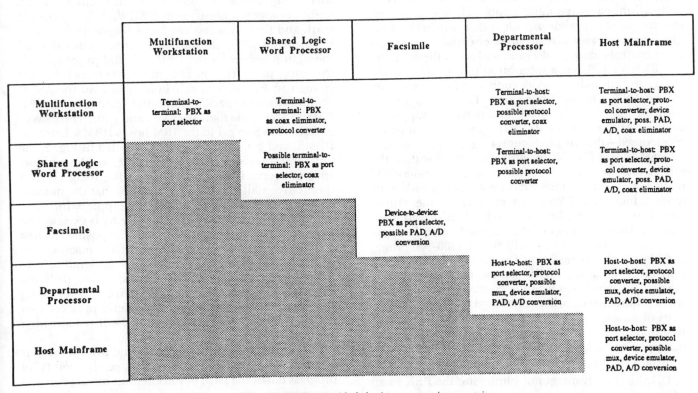

	Multifunction Workstation	Shared Logic Word Processor	Facsimile	Departmental Processor	Host Mainframe
Multifunction Workstation	Terminal-to-terminal: PBX as port selector	Terminal-to-terminal: PBX as coax eliminator, protocol converter		Terminal-to-host: PBX as port selector, possible protocol converter, coax eliminator	Terminal-to-host: PBX as port selector, protocol converter, device emulator, poss. PAD, A/D, coax eliminator
Shared Logic Word Processor		Possible terminal-to-terminal: PBX as port selector, coax eliminator		Terminal-to-host: PBX as port selector, possible protocol converter	Terminal-to-host: PBX as port selector, protocol converter, device emulator, poss. PAD, A/D, coax eliminator
Facsimile			Device-to-device: PBX as port selector, possible PAD, A/D conversion		
Departmental Processor				Host-to-host: PBX as port selector, protocol converter, possible mux, device emulator, PAD, A/D conversion	Host-to-host: PBX as port selector, protocol converter, possible mux, device emulator, PAD, A/D conversion
Host Mainframe					Host-to-host: PBX as port selector, protocol converter, possible mux, device emulator, PAD, A/D conversion

Fig. 3. PBX-provided device connection matrix.

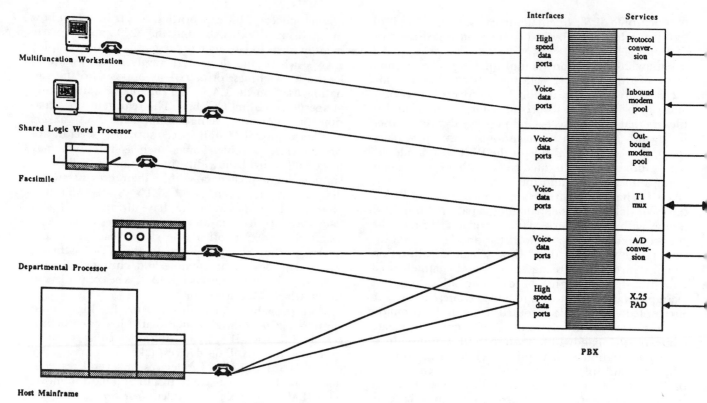

Fig. 4. PBX as voice-data integrator.

produce peg counts on feature use (such as data calls) on inside (4-digit) calls, and full SMDR records on outside (7 or more digit) calls. In sum, the mundane advantages of PBX-provided voice-data integration—the multiple use of extant wiring and the ability to collect limited usage data, impose classes of service, enforce security, and provide other low-tech, low-glamour administrative features essential to management control—may tilt decision makers in the direction of PBX's for voice-data integration in the office.

Figure 3 provides a device connection matrix wherein the PBX role is summarized. Figure 4 diagrammatically depicts the PBX functions to supported devices. As the figures illustrate, the initial predicament posed—that of interconnecting disparate devices (Wang, IBM PC's, office minicomputers) within the office, and between the office and the remote IBM mainframe—can be done today on a modern PBX with modest incremental costs. In most cases, the salient cost item is upgrading the individual's voice-data station. Although prices for integrated voice-data stations are falling, many are still in the $300–500 range, and, unlike data items located at the switch (line cards, port cards, modems, PAD's, protocol converters), they are neither shared resources nor do they service multiple users. Nonetheless, when compared with the annual costs of moves and changes for data devices, redundant terminal devices, redundant data entry, and the accompanying lack of usage statistics and management control, PBX upgrade costs can seem modest.

Despite the advantages of employing the PBX as an office voice-data integrator, several limitations need to

be stressed relative to this level of voice-data integration. Unlike voice, connectivity does not imply transparency, and the PBX data connection functionality is at a relatively low level (see Fig. 2). For example, if the user is employing an IBM PC to run Lotus 1-2-3 and wishes to access a department DEC VAX for electronic mail, and then to access the latest corporate data on a remote IBM 3081, the physical connectivity—dialing the right numbers for the DEC and IBM processors—is the easy part. He or she must be knowledgeable enough in PC DOS to exit Lotus and load the ASCII communications package, familiar enough with DEC VMS to access the mail package, and sufficiently savvy in CICS/MVS to get to the IBM host's DBMS, enter the DBMS, and get what is needed. As noted in Fig. 2, the top three protocol layers are visible, vendor-unique, and, for security reasons, often unforgiving. It is a speculative statistic, but it is unlikely that the number of computer users who regularly grapple with three different operating systems on a daily basis exceeds one percent. The return argument is that exposure to alien operating systems can be minimized via macros, particularly for such trivial functions as sending and receiving electronic mail, posting or checking the latest data base numbers, and the like. Despite the bridging strategies, highly dissimilar, upper-level protocol user interfaces ensure that training costs will remain high and usage low.

In sum, such device connectivity and primitive levels of voice-data integration represent early points of progress down the path of information integration and presentation, not to speak of cognition and understanding. They nonetheless represent a promising beginning offering clear and quantifiable benefits, and a modern **PBX** enables this progress to proceed incrementally, economically, and at an understandable velocity.

References

[1] AT&T Information Systems, *Reference Manual DIMENSION System 85 Data Management, Reference Manual DIMENSION System 85 Voice Management*, and *Reference Manual DIMENSION System 85 Hardware* (Indianapolis, IN: Western Electric, 1983).

[2] Ericsson Information Switching Systems, *MD110 General Description* (Garden Grove, CA: Ericsson, February 1983).

[3] GTE, *The GTD-4600-E Digital PBX* (McLean, VA: GTE, April 1984).

[4] Harris, *20-20 Integrated Network Switch* (Novato, CA: Harris Corporation, undated).

[5] InteCom, *General Description IBX S/80 Integrated Business Exchange* (Allen, TX: InteCom, February 1983).

[6] Mitel, *SX2000 General Description* and *SX2000 Features and Services Guide* (Boca Raton, FL: Mitel, 1984).

[7] NEC, *NEAX 2400 IMS General Description* (Melville, NY: December 1983).

[8] Northern Telecom, *SL-1 Business Communications System, Generic X11 Feature Document Business Features* (Santa Clara, CA: Northern Telecom, March, 1983), *Electronic Switched Network Feature Document* (Santa Clara, CA: Northern Telecom, March, 1984), and *SL-1XN System Description* (Santa Clara, CA: Northern Telecom, April 1984).

[9] ROLM, *CBX II Business Communications System* (Santa Clara, CA: ROLM, October, 1983) and *9000 System Data Communications Feature, System Administrator's Guide* (Santa Clara, CA: ROLM, September 1983).

[10] United Technologies Lexar, *UTX-5000 Voice/Data Switching System General Description* (Westlake Village, CA: Lexar Corporation, February 1984).

[11] Western Union, *Vega System General Description Manual* (McLean, VA: Western Union, March 1984).

[12] Ztel, *PNX System Description* (Wilmington, MA: Ztel, May 1984).

[13] S. L. Junker and W. E. Noller, "Digital Private Branch Exchanges," *IEEE Communications Magazine* (May 1983), pp. 11-17.

[14] E. R. Coover and M. J. Kane, "Notes from Mid-Revolution: Searching for the Perfect PBX," *Data Communications* (August 1985), pp. 141-150.

[15] N. Janakiraman, "An Overview of Recent Developments in the Designs and Applications of Customer Premises Switches," *IEEE Communications Magazine* (October 1985), pp. 32-45.

[16] E. E. Mier, "PBX Trends and Technology Update: Following the Leaders," *Data Communications* (September 1985), pp. 82-96.

[17] A. Sikes, "The Data PBX Solution Local for Networks [*sic*]," *Teleconnect* (December 1985), pp. 112-125.

Edwin R. Coover has taught at Indiana University, Bloomington, and is currently with the MITRE Corporation in McLean, Virginia. In the last several years he has been heavily involved in the specification of **PBX** and office automation systems. He holds Masters and Doctorate degrees from the University of Virginia and University of Minnesota, respectively.

Office Communications and the Digital PBX

I. Richer and M. Steiner

Bolt Beranek and Newman Inc., 50 Moulton Street,
Cambridge, Massachusetts 02238, U.S.A.

and

M. Sengoku

Nippon Electric Company, Tokyo, Japan

As part of a study on office automation, we have investigated two related topics: voice and data communications on local office networks, and the use of a computerized PBX as a switch in an office network. Since a computerized PBX might be an effective method for implementing a voice/data office network, we have addressed the important issues of (a) whether voice and data should be handled by the same techniques, and (b) whether these traffic types should be combined on a single network or should use distinct, but interconnected, networks. In studying these topics, we have considered end-user requirements in order to determine the economics and the possible evolution of such networks. We have also evaluated a number of technical problems, including appropriate switching techniques and network topology. Our principal conclusions are that in the near future there are valid technical and non-technical reasons for adding data traffic to the office voice networks, and that the combined network should be based on a star topology.

Keywords: Voice communications, local office networks, computerized PBX.

1. Introduction

"The Technical Office: Analysis and Research"

"Plan Today for Tomorrow's Data/Voice Nets"

"Packet Switching and Office Applications"

"PBXs will Unify Office of the Future"

"Integrated Office Information Systems"

These are the titles of some recent articles and conference papers. Almost daily, we are enticed with such titles (including the one on this paper), each over an article or paper which purports to describe the office of the future. Contained in many of these is a figure showing a box with the words "*Office Network*", and with every possible type of terminal connected to the network – telephones, facsimile devices, "*work stations*", OCR devices, automated typesetters, etc. Rarely, however, does an author dissect the magical box and explain or justify what the communications subnetwork looks like or how it handles its tasks. This dearth of *substantive* information prompted the small study on which this paper is based. The goal of the study was to attempt to deter-

Marianne Steiner is a member of BBN Information Management Corporation (IMC), where she is involved in the planning, marketing and support of office automation systems. She is presently concerned with IMC's newest product, an electronic mail software package. Prior to the formation of IMC Ms. Steiner directed consulting studies at BBN on a variety of network and communication topics including network architecture and office technology. Previously Ms. Steiner worked with the Network Product Management group at Digital Equipment Corporation and the Systems and Programming Division of the Bank of America in San Francisco, CA. Ms. Steiner has an M.E. in Information Science and an M.S. in Applied Mathematics from Harvard University. Her B.S. is from the University of Miami.

Masama Sengoku was born on February 15, 1950. He graduated from Tokyo Electric Engineering College in 1972. He joined Nippon Electric Company, Ltd. in 1972 and is now engineer of the Data Switching Systems Department, Switching Engineering Division. He was engaged in the development of the Digital Data Switching Systems. Mr. Sengoku is a member of the Institute of Electronics and Communication Engineers of Japan.

Ira Richer received the B.E.E. degree from Rensselaer Polytechnic Institute, Troy, New York, and the M.S. and Ph.D. degrees in electrical engineering from the California Institute of Technology, Pasadena, California. After holding postdoctoral positions at the Technical University of Denmark, Lyngby and at Caltech, Passadena, he joined MIT Lincoln Laboratory, Lexington, Massachusetts, where he was involved in a number of advanced communications projects that spanned orders of magnitude in both the frequency and altitude domains (ELF to UHF, and submachine to satellite). In 1977 he joined Bolt Beranek and Newman (BBN) Inc., Cambridge, Massachusetts. As a senior scientist at BBN, he consults to both commercial and government organizations on a wide variety of network and communications topics.

North-Holland Publishing Company
Computer Networks 5 (1981) 411–422

mine whether it is desirable and feasible to develop a voice/data system, and if so, what the characteristics of such a system might be. The focus was on offices in the United States in the near future (three to five years). Because our interest was in realistic, practicable possibilities, important aspects of the study were economics, evolution, and market forces as well as technical performance.

This paper presents our principal results on the gross voice and data characteristics of the future office, and on the most promising design alternatives for an office network. However, we shall first present some observations about the interaction of voice and data traffic. In the long term, merging voice and data would be of primary advantage at the management/professional level: it is at this level that voice communications are most important and that the greatest economic incentive lies. To date, there has not been much technological assistance directed at the manager/professional's job and the information flow related to it. The information flow related to the job of a professional or a manager is oriented primarily around interpersonal communications, mostly in meetings and by telephone, but also through written material. The key technology here is communications. We believe that the efficiency and convenience of communications can be enhanced through the availability of voice and data facilities within close reach of the manager's or professional's work space. In the short term, however, we have been able to identify only two specific applications which might require the integration of voice and data communications:

— *voice mail* — a system whereby a caller can leave a spoken message which can be retrieved at the recipient's convenience;

— *dictation* — verbal dictation would be stored and subsequently retrieved for transcription, perhaps by a central pool of secretaries.

We assume that these applications should integrate voice and data techniques because while voice input is more convenient, digital storage is most flexible, enabling messages or dictated text to be manipulated, filed, and retrieved. * Another possibility, of course,

is to use the ubiquitous telephone as a more general-purpose input device, for example to enter transactions or to initiate commands to a computer.

A key feature of the above applications is the inherent capability for remote access. Thus, from any telephone, a user could enter or retrieve mail or could input dictation. Of course, in the more distant future, when computers are able to generate text from voice (voice recognition) and to produce high-quality voice from text in *cost-effective* ways, many additional applications will become practical and economical (and the above applications can be augmented appropriately). For the above reasons, we expect the gradual emergence of system configurations that will support the interaction of voice and data in a single application.

The technology for the effective handling of voice communications already exists. In the remainder of this paper, we explore the details of voice and data traffic in the office, and the techniques to best handle this traffic.

2. Office Traffic

In this section we present some statistics on the voice and data traffic in an office. The primary purpose of generating these statistics is to obtain an understanding of the relative magnitudes of the various traffic types and hence of the network requirements. We first consider a hypothetical future office and then give data for Bolt Beranek and Newman Inc. (BBN), which *currently* has significant office data traffic.

2.1. Future Offices

In producing the voice traffic values for a future office, we were able to utilize some general statistics and standard industry guidelines that are available for telephone traffic. On the other hand, since data communications does not presently exist to any great extent in offices, we based our data traffic estimates upon market research reports and user surveys [2] together with some of our own assumptions regarding the data communications environment. However, *the particular assumptions we make are not at all critical to our conclusions*. In fact, in order to be conservative, we intentionally attempted to overestimate the amount of data traffic; the rationale for overestimating will become clearer in the discussion below.

---

* Dictation utilizing a conventional analog recorder together with control signals from a push-button telephone is currently planned or in use [1].

The principal terminals that we believe will participate in communications on a local office network are:
- telephones for voice communications;
- data terminals for data entry and distributed processing;
- word processors for text editing and electronic mail handling;
- facsimile devices for graphic and hand-written document delivery (primarily inter-office);
- printers for high-speed text output;
- copiers for multiple copies of on-line text documents and also possibly for internal document distribution.

These terminals would communicate with each other; with terminals and computers outside the office; with local minicomputers for data processing and special applications such as electronic mail and text processing; and possibly with local mainframes for database access, file storage, and large scale computing tasks. Note that we have excluded wideband video devices because we do not believe that their use on office networks will be very widespread in the near future.

Table 1 shows the assumed terminals' characteristics and the number of terminals that might be used in offices of three different sizes. For the purposes of this report, we characterize the size of the office by the number of telephones, since there is usually one telephone per employee, and we denote a small, medium, or large office as having 100, 500, or 2000 telephones, respectively. The average utilization and throughput values in Table 1 are based on the following assumptions:

(1) At each telephone there are 20 calls per eight-hour business day with each call lasting 3 minutes. In a typical two-way conversation, each talker uses the circuit only about half the time, and during that time has short silent intervals between talk spurts. If a mechanism is provided to detect these silences, the throughput requirements for a technique such as packet switching could be reduced by as much as 60%. However, in order to ensure reasonable speech quality and to allow for possible overhead that might be required, we have assumed that the half duplex connection is utilized 100 percent of the time. For voice communications we assumed a digitization rate of 64 kbps, consistent with standard PCM (Pulse Code Modulation) techniques. (The peak data rate is 198 kbps because data might flow in each direction.)

(2) Each word processor is connected for 200 minutes per day (for example, ten sessions of 20 minutes each), and five percent of this time is devoted to actual data communications, with the rest of the time occupied with typing, thinking, reading, and other secretarial activities.

(3) Each data terminal is on-line all day (for example, for data entry or other clerical functions); again, the traffic flows only five percent of the time. Note that word processors and data entry terminals could have a wide range of "intelligence". With much intelligence at the terminal, communications over the network would tend to be in much longer blocks than with dumb terminals; however, to a first order of approximation, the overall throughput would be similar.

(4) Each facsimile device handles 100 pages per day at one minute per page, and 100 percent of the

Table 1
Assumed Terminal and Office Characteristics

	Peak Data Rate (kbps)	Average Utilization (erlangs)	Average Throughput (kbps)	Number of Terminals		
				Small Office	Medium office	Large office
Telephone	128.0	0.13	8.0	100	500	2000
Word Processor	2.4	0.4	0.048	5	50	200
Data Entry	2.4	1.0	0.12	5	50	200
Facsimile	9.6	0.21	2.0	2	10	40
Copier	48.0	0.036	1.7	2	10	40
Printer	9.6	0.36	3.5	2	10	40

connect time is devoted to actual communications. Since facsimile will be used primarily for inter-office communications, we assume that the data rate through the office network is 9.6 kbps for communications over external voice grade telephone lines. Operation at one minute per page therefore assumes that some compression coding is used.

(5) Each copier produces copies from 1000 original documents per day (only the original need be transmitted over the network). We assume that copies would be used mostly for intra-office work and therefore that the original would be transmitted in, say, ASCII form, with 50 kbits per page.

(6) Each printer produces 100 20-page reports each day. (We have assumed here that the transfer rate to the printer is equal to the printer's data rate; an alternate configuration would have a large buffer memory and controller located with the printer at a much higher transfer rate.)

Using the data in Table 1, and assuming that the busy-hour traffic volume is twice the average, we arrive at the busy hour utilization and throughput figures shown in Table 2. The entry for interactive data includes both word processing and data entry. The utilization figures are in erlangs, which is the average number of simultaneous connections. Of course, each connection operates at the data rate appropriate to the communicating devices, and thus each interactive connection requires much less capacity than a voice connection. We see from the table that for each office size, the number of simultaneous data connections might be comparable to the number of voice conversations, but the throughput

requirements for voice are substantially greater than those for data.

The data from Table 2 can now be used to estimate the overall traffic handling requirements of the office network. Potentially, there are three relevant switching techniques: circuit switching, packet switching, or a hybrid scheme with circuit switching for voice and packet switching for data. However, because the voice traffic is so much greater than data traffic, we need not perform calculations for the hybrid approach: the results for circuit switching are essentially the same as for hybrid switching.

For circuit switching we obtained the peak number of connections required by using standard telephony (Erlang B) tables for a blocking probability of 0.01 — that is, one percent of the attempted connections would not be completed. We performed a similar calculation for the number of channels required for data traffic and then converted these channels into equivalent full duplex 64 kbps voice channels, assuming that with the overhead necessary for submultiplexing a voice channel, only 48 kbps of throughput could be obtained. (For example, 20 2.4 kbps channels over one voice channel.) The figures we generated assume that full duplex channels are required for data traffic; if the protocols used for data communications require only a half duplex channel, then the data requirements would be somewhat lower.

The sizing for packet switching was obtained from the throughput requirements of Table 2. Clearly, the total capacity must be greater than the average busy hour throughput in order to allow for peak traffic

Table 2
Traffic Volumes for Three Office Sizes

	Busy-Hour Utilization (erlangs)			Busy-Hour Throughput (kbps)		
	Small Office	Medium Office	Large Office	Small Office	Medium Office	Large Office
Voice	25.0	125.0	500.0	1600.0	8000	32000
Interactive Data	9.0	90.0	360.0	1.7	17	67
Facsimile	0.84	4.2	17.0	8.0	40	160
Copier	0.14	0.72	2.9	6.8	34	140
Printer	1.4	7.2	29.0	14.0	70	280

levels, for packet overhead, and for control information, and to ensure a utilization level of less than 100 percent. Thus, we multiplied the total throughput by a factor greater than one to arrive at the required capacity. We assumed, however, that we could take advantage of more statistical averaging as office size increased. Thus, the multiplicative factors used were 1.4, 1.3, and 1.2 for small, medium and large offices, respectively. Note that because there are no real-time high bandwidth devices, response time is not a factor in the sizing calculation.

The overall switching requirements are shown in Table 3. The figures show the number of full duplex, 64 kbps voice channels that would be required for the various alternatives. We now briefly draw some conclusions from the data presented above; we will elaborate on these conclusions in the discussion in subsequent sections. The most striking conclusion we draw from the data above is that voice traffic is substantially greater than data traffic, even though we intentionally attempted to overestimate the data requirements. (It is interesting to note that a similar conclusion about the relative magnitudes of voice and data traffic in long distance information transfer was reached by Cerf and Curran [3].) A related observation is that the peak data throughput in an office is actually quite small, and even for a large office is less than 1 Mbps. The major implication of this conclusion for the design of an office network is that *if a single communications network handles both voice and data, then the network should be optimized for voice.* In addition, in terms of raw throughput, a voice switch for a small office can handle the data traffic for a much larger office. Table 3 also shows that a packet-switching communications network needs only half the capacity of a circuit-switching network. Essentially all of the saving is obtained because we have assumed that a packet switch will take advantage of the half duplex nature of voice traffic, whereas a circuit switch must allocate a full duplex channel to each voice conversation.

As a final point, we remark that the bit rate of high quality, ILI-generated digital voice will be lower than 64 kbps (perhaps 16 kbps) in the not-too-distant future. When these techniques become standardized, they can be used to reduce the required network capacity in almost direct proportion to the decrease in voice digitization rate. Nevertheless, the ratio of voice to data traffic will still be high, and the conclusions stated above will therefore still be valid.

Table 3
Number of full duplex 64 kbps channels required for different size offices for packet and for circuit switching.

	Small Office	Medium Office	Large Office
Circuit Switching			
Voice Only	36	144	527
Voice & Data	39	156	562
Packet Switching			
Voice Only	18	82	300
Voice & Data	1	83	306

2.2. Bolt Beranek and Newman Inc.

In this section we present statistics for current voice and data traffic at BBN's Cambridge facilities. * There are two major reasons for presenting these statistics. First, there is a lot of data traffic at BBN: most reports and documents are generated on-line (*all* secretaries have terminals that link to BBN's computers for editing, storage, and retrieval of text); in addition, *most* staff members and secretaries use an electronic mail system in their everyday business activities. Thus, although BBN may not be a typical office, it represents one possible model for a future office, and the volumes of voice and data traffic provide us with a useful benchmark. Second, we can obtain actual statistics, rather than mere conjectures, of traffic flow: BBN's computerized PBX produces detailed statistics on numbers and types of calls and on call durations, and we can obtain reasonable estimates of data traffic from our knowledge of the BBN working environment. Note that we shall ignore BBN traffic that would not normally flow in a business office – for example, communications involved in preparing computer programs used in BBN's research and development activities.

The configuration at BBN is basically two distinct star networks, one for voice and one for data. For the purposes of this study, the pertinent components of the data network are a central switch, terminals for secretaries and professional staff, mainframes and minicomputers, and printers. There are approximately 800 telephone extensions in Cambridge; however, in order to provide a direct comparison with a medium-size office of the previous section, *all the*

---

* The data we present is based on measurements and observations made in mid-1979.

figures below are linearly scaled so as to represent an office with 500 extensions.

2.2.1. Voice Traffic

There are two methods of determining the switch requirements necessary to handle voice traffic. As was done in the previous section, the conventional method is to obtain information on the numbers and durations of busy hour internal and external calls, and then to size the switch accordingly. The second method is to observe the number of switch connections at various times and to use the peak value to size the switch. We actually used both methods and arrived at the same results for BBN's traffic: the switch should be capable of providing 70 simultaneous voice channels.

2.2.2. Text Processing

At BBN, there are 40 secretaries, each of whom has a terminal that is on-line approximately three hours per day. However, to allow for peak hour usage, we shall assume that with circuit switching, a dedicated circuit for each terminal must be provided. We shall also assume that all terminals operate at 2.4 kbps (although most terminals at BBN operate at lower speeds), so that two 64 kbps voice circuits can handle all word processing traffic. We estimate the actual data flow by assuming that the average typing speed is 60 words per minute; that approximately 50 percent of the three-hour connect time is used for text input; that because of editing functions, the total traffic is three times the input traffic; and that peak traffic is about twice the average. The total peak data rate is then 2.2 kbps.

2.2.3. Electronic Mail

This medium is heavily used at BBN. We assumed the following average statistics: * half of the employees at BBN use the electronic mail system; each user spends 20 minutes per day reading mail and an additional 20 minutes composing two ten-line messages per day; each message is sent to three recipients; the input/output and peak to average traffic ratios are the same as for word processing. The resulting requirements are three voice channels for circuit-switched connections and a peak data rate of about 1.0 kbps.

---

* Recent measurements at BBN have shown that these estimates are quite accurate.

2.2.4. Printers

There are seven printers (including high quality output terminals) of various data rates, but with a total maximum data rate of approximately 30 kbps. Because these devices are on-line essentially all day, we shall use this value as an estimate of the peak traffic.

Table 4 summarizes the results for BBN traffic and shows the number of full duplex voice channels required to handle voice and data traffic on a circuit-switching and on a packet-switching basis. We see that BBN's traffic requirements are roughly half those of the medium size office of the previous section although, of course, the ratio of packet- to circuit-switching requirements is the same because of the dominance of voice traffic. Furthermore, for all types of devices, the data traffic at BBN is substantially smaller than that projected in Section 2.1. In summary, the BBN data reinforce the conclusions that were drawn in that section.

2.2.5. Facsimile and Copiers

Although these devices are not part of BBN's data network, we include the statistics for completeness and also to show that the resulting traffic is negligible in comparison with the data traffic given above.

At BBN there are two facsimile machines that together handle about 35 input and 35 output pages per day. During the busiest minute, both machines would be operating, and therefore, the peak data rate is just twice the bit rate of the machines, or 4.8 kbps; hence only 0.1 voice channel is needed for this traffic. (Of course, BBN's facsimile traffic will probably grow as the use of this technique becomes more widespread.)

The copiers at BBN produce about 60,000 copies per month (this excludes BBN's Copy Center, which is used primarily for reproducing long documents and for making many copies; we presume that such a copy center would exist even if copiers were on the network). If the copiers were linked to a data network, then the original copy need be transmitted only once, and if we assume an average of ten copies of each original, with the peak usage twice the average, then the peak traffic is only 1.0 kbps.

2.2.6. Voice Mail

As a final calculation that might be of interest since we are considering voice/data applications in a future office, we shall make some projections on the resource requirements needed to handle a voice mail system. We envision that such a system would use a

Table 4
BBN Traffic (Scaled to 500 Telephones)

	Number of terminals	Required Number of full duplex 64 kbps circuits	Peak throughput (kbps)
telephone	500	70	4500
text processing	40	2	2.2
electronic mail	50 *	3	1.0
printer	7	1	30.0
Requirements for a Voice/Data Network			
circuit-switching		76	
packet-switching		46	

mailbox approach and might have a few of the basic features of a text oriented mail system, but that the voice system would be used only for short messages to individuals who did not answer their telephones or whose telephones were busy. In addition, the voice system would be used for some of the text messages currently transmitted via the electronic mail system. On the basis of statistics gathered by BBN's computerized PBX, we estimate that approximately 1500 call attempts (including internal and external calls) either receive no answer, or receive a busy signal, or are picked up by BBN's Message Center. If we assume that about two thirds of these are either repeated calls or would not be forwarded, then 500 messages per day would be stored by the voice mail system, or about one message per person per day, a reasonable quantity. In addition, perhaps five percent of the present text messages might be sent using the voice system; these messages would be those that are neither sensitive, nor multi-destination, nor very long. Since this amounts to only 25 messages per day, the total is negligible in comparison with that above, and we shall neglect these messages in our calculations.

If we assume that each message lasts about 30 seconds of real time, that each message flows once into storage and once to the recipient, and that the peak traffic is twice the average, then the peak utilization and throughput are 2.1 erlangs and 130 kbps, respectively, for this application. If this traffic were consolidated with the other traffic, three additional voice channels would be required for circuit switching, or two additional channels for packet switching.

However, now consider the storage requirements

for these messages. According to the above data, approximately 250 minutes worth of messages are stored *each day* if the digitization rate is 64 kbps, so that approximately 100 megabytes of storage are needed! Clearly, standard pulse code modulation (PCM), which produces this high bit rate, is an inappropriate technology for a voice mail system in a moderate size office. We might note that some possible alternatives are:

– Use of vocoder techniques to remove silent periods and to compress the data by at least an order of magnitude; the vocoder could be dedicated to this application and thus a single device could be shared by all users;

– Use of conventional analog, audio recording techniques (however, unless convenient and nonsequential retrieval methods are provided, analog techniques would be undesirable);

– Use of video disk technology to provide high capacity storage and convenient message access.

3. Design Alternatives

In this section we analyze alternatives related to three high-level design issues. First, we evaluate whether a single network should handle both voice and data, or whether there should be two separate networks, one for voice and one for data, with a communications path between the two. Based upon this evaluation, we then discuss which network topology is preferable – star, ring, bus, or distributed. Finally, we address the switching technique for the preferred topology.

We shall consider these alternatives in light of the following observations:

– Intra-office voice networks are pervasive;

– Intra-office data networks are becoming more necessary and useful; they will be essential to tie together the currently developing variety of office systems to achieve full automation of office processes;

– In a typical business office, voice communications predominate; the ratio of data traffic to voice traffic is extremely low even in highly automated offices;

– At present, there are few applications which combine the use of voice and data in a cost-effective way; in the future, however, combined voice/data applications will become cost-effective and hence more prevalent.

3.1. Separate Networks Versus a Combined Network

On the basis of the observations given above, we can conclude that in the near future, there will be strong interest in intra-office data networks and some interest, but perhaps less utility, in unified voice/data networks. We can find no one strong argument for a single integrated voice/data office network. However, there certainly are reasons for constructing a network that will provide some connection between voice and data devices. Since voice traffic volume is so much greater than data traffic volume and since we assume that an intra-office voice network will always exist, the potential for carrying the data on the already-existent voice network is, at least superficially, extremely appealing, but some concrete justifications are clearly required.

Before outlining the relative merits of separate and combined networks, we present a few thoughts about the traffic patterns in a future office. The data flows in the office will be both for internal and external communications: almost all devices will be involved in some intra-office communications, and many will also utilize some outside communications. Initially the traffic flows within a newly automated office may be somewhat static, but this will change as the variety of devices and applications grows; then the interconnections will become quite dynamic, partially because we anticipate that most communications among terminals will be mediated by a computer or some type of controller (for example, a buffering unit that manages facsimile input/output). In summary, the future terminal will connect to a variety of hosts or terminals, depending upon which provides the

particular specialized service required. Also, for data communications external to an office, we believe that with the increased use of distributed processing, an increased fraction of connect time will be devoted to actual communications. In these ways, future data connections will become increasingly similar to current voice connections.

The relative advantages of separate and of combined networks are summarized in Table 5. In evaluating the potential advantages of separate networks in greater depth, we can invoke the following counter-arguments to the three points given in the table:

1. When designing a network (or a product), one should plan for *future* needs (for which a combined network is a better match).

2. Since the volume of data traffic is much less than that of voice, for a given level of performance the data-handling capabilities of a combined network

Table 5.
Relative advantages of separate and combined voice and data networks

Separate Networks	Combined Network
1. At present, there is not much voice-data cross traffic, and the flow patterns of the two are different.	1. In the future, there will be more voice-data cross traffic, and the flow patterns of data will become more similar to those of voice.
2. Separate networks can each be optimized for its own traffic.	2. Data access to external resources is more direct with a combined network (since voice terminals implicitly have such access already).
3. Data and voice have different requirements for delay, throughput, error control, and reliability.	3. With a combined network, a customer might want to purchase a single product with modularity; the customer can then begin with a voice network and later add data capabilities at lower incremental cost.
	4. It may be possible to use existing in-building telephone wiring to carry data traffic.
	5. Since the volume of data traffic is much less than voice, it is incrementally less expensive to provide the capacity for initial as well as for expanded data requirements on a combined voice/data network.

can be sub-optimum without much increase in total cost.

3. There should be no problem in meeting the delay, throughput, and error requirements of both voice and data because (a) if properly designed, the delay through a local network will be very small for all traffic; (b) the volume of data is negligible compared with voice; and (c) existing protocols can be used to handle error control.

The one remaining issue is the different reliability requirements of voice and data. The reliability of the voice network is usually critical to an organization, and telephone systems are designed with this principle in mind. On the other hand, because data handling needs are generally less predictable and more complex, data networks tend to be less reliable. If the addition of data handling capability to a voice network increases the likelihood that the voice traffic will be disrupted, then a combined network will not be accepted in the marketplace. We believe that this is an important issue. However, we also believe that it should be possible to incorporate mechanisms into a combined network that ensure a high degree of reliability. For example, voice and data connections and traffic could be handled differently in order to ensure that if a failure occurs in the data portion, the voice portion is not affected. Also, significant spare capacity could be provided for data traffic in order to avoid problems that might occur when operating near saturation. In other words, it is our opinion that the reliability issue should be manageable with proper design. Thus, in the office environment, the potential advantages of separate networks, as listed in Table 5, either are not significant or can be overcome, and the itemized technical and economic advantages of a combined network outweigh those of separate networks. Our overall conclusion, therefore, is that future office networks should be based upon combining voice and data.

3.2. Network Topology

We now consider the possible topological structure of a combined voice/data network. Four basic alternatives are a star, over which all communications flow through a central controller; a ring, in which data flows sequentially around a loop; a bus, in which data can be broadcast to all devices; and a general distributed topology in which several paths exist between communicating nodes, but not all nodes are connected directly to each other. In evaluating these alternative topologies for local office networks, we rely on the projected office traffic statistics presented in the previous sections, and in particular on the high ratio of voice traffic to data traffic.

We must emphasize strongly that here we are considering the "physical" topology – the arrangement for connecting devices to the "network". In particular, a ring topology, for example, necessarily implies that data flows from one device controller to the next, whereas a star configuration implies that all data flows through a single controller. However, a star controller can take advantage of any of the above alternatives inside its central controller, so that, in principle, a physical star topology could use a central controller that internally uses a ring transmission technique. In fact, within the constraints of distance between a device and its network interface, the contoller for a star network might be able to utilize hardware identical to that developed for other physical topologies.

Within the time frame we are considering, we assume that intra-office voice-only networks will be star networks. Today's voice network in a typical office is centered around a central PBX; a large facility may be organized around multiple PBXs which are interconnected. The market, customer, and technical inertia for the continuing use of star networks for voice is very strong: techniques for central switching are well-proven, and the installation base is enormous. Voice communications have vastly improved over decades of use and continued development; extremely high performance and reliability standards have been achieved, and PBXs are a proven technology for delivering the required quality of service.

None of the other three topologies have been commercially used for intra-office voice networks; however, various data networks have been designed around these topologies. Ring and bus networks are specifically applicable for local area networks, while a distributed topology is applicable for both local and long distance networking. We shall not further consider the general distributed network as a *primary* design alternative for a local office network. In general, a main advantage of this design is that it can parallel the physical topology of the organization. In a large organization, multiple controllers (in the case of a star network), or multiple bus/ring structures will be required to support the volume of traffic or the physical separation of facilities; as such, these networks may evolve to distributed topologies. Other general advantages of distributed topologies are (1) statistical averaging of traffic through network nodes and lines, and (2) high reliability because multiple paths are available. Within a local office environment, however, communications bandwidth is not the costly resource, so this averaging advantage is not relevant. High reliability can be achieved through other means with other designs, so this not a strong advantage. As a primary design, therefore, a distributed topology requires switching complexity with no strong countervailing advantages; however, as an evolutionary capability from single star, bus, or ring networks it might be important.

The characteristics of star and bus/ring networks are compared in Table 6. At the present level of analysis, we believe that the flexibility and the evolutionary considerations listed in Table 6 are perhaps the strongest reasons to develop star network technology (i.e. PBX technology) to support both data and voice. The technology exists now for voice, it is widely used and understood, and the gain for both vendors and users appears to be great, relative to the (probably) low investment. The vendor who can offer a switch for both voice and data can gain an additional market segment, and the user organization can acquire full communications support, probably for a lot less expense than with separate facilities. Product compatibility would be the goal, so that voice "controllers" could be expanded to support data; expansion should be modular so the user can isolate voice and data functionality, or combine it.

A related advantage of a star configuration is that it might be possible to use in-building PBX wiring, thereby reducing not only the cost, but also the time and inconvenience of installing a voice/data network. If an organization owns its own PBX and hence the associated wiring, then these existing wires could also carry data traffic (by a multiplexing technique, for example). Also, if an organization plans to replace a Bell System PBX with a non-Bell unit, then new wiring would generally be installed; in this case, a pair of cables (rather than a single cable) could be routed to each office at little additional cost, the second cable being available for a (possible) data terminal.

3.3. Switching Techniques for a Voice/Data Computerized PBX

In the previous section we presented arguments showing that a combined voice/data network using a star topology is a preferable approach for designing an office communications network. Since most of the traffic on such a network will be voice, we shall call the network's central switch a "computerized PBX" (CPBX), even though this future switch may bear little resemblance to present-day, digital telephone switches. In this section we present some design considerations for the choice of switching technique internal to an office CPBX.

Because of its use in existing PBXs, circuit switching is clearly a prime candidate for use in a CPBX. We use the term "circuit switching" in its broadest sense, namely to signify any switching technique which *pre-allocates* (and hence guarantees) certain resources to a voice or data connection. Thus, circuit switching includes, for example, both space and time division multiplexing. The alternative to circuit switching is "packet switching", where again we shall use the term in a broad sense to denote a method which does not pre-allocate specific resources to users. There are many possibilities here, such as simple ALOHA or carrier sense multiple access (which can be used if the *internal* CPBX topology is a bus). Clearly, the switching technique and the internal CPBX configuration are not independent decisions.

Before comparing these two switching alternatives, wer first note that there are some considerations which do not significantly influence the choice of switching technique, the most basic being performance. For some networks, the performance requirements dictate certain aspects of the switching technique. For example, if many interactive users are to share a single satellite channel, circuit switching (i.e., pre-allocation of bandwidth) is clearly inappropriate, and therefore a variety of "demand assignment" techniques have been proposed. However, for an office network with a single CPBX (or even with several CPBXs), some performance issues disappear. For example, the delay and the error rates should be small regardless of the switching technique that is used. In addition, many of the complexities associated with multi-node packet networks (such as routing and message reassembly) do not occur in a CPBX-based local network. Finally, with circuit switching approaches in which the internal data rate of the switch is much greater than the user data rate (as in time division multiplexing), the hardware must provide some buffering and must construct small blocks of data for transmission through the switch; thus, these approaches must perform some of the same functions performed in a packet switch. In summary, the arguments noted above cannot be

Table 6
Comparison of star and bus/ring topologies for a combined voice/data network

	Star	Bus/Ring
Reliability		
Controller	limiting resource – impact of failure is great; can be overcome by redundancy	impact of failure should be only a single station outage
Transmission		
Medium	impact of failure is a single station outage	limiting resource – risk of failure is small, but may be difficult to repair; redundancy is not practical
Growth		
Capability	limited by controller; large infrequent additions may require overall reconfiguration	limited by bus/ring capacity; each new connection requires new controller
Flexibility	controller can utilize techniques and hardware developed for any physical technology	can have local, specialized functionality
Economics	economy of scale within controller; additional devices may be required for physically long lines	cost of controllers is major factor in assessing viability
Evolutionary		
Considerations	voice networks are star today (strong market inertia); data traffic is very much less than voice, so it may be minimal cost to add data	none exist – would require massive conversions
Maintainability	more convenient because centrally located; but single complex switch may be more difficult to troubleshoot	distributed maintenance is burdensome (e.g., synchronization of nodes, remote troubleshooting)

invoked *a priori* in order to choose one switching technique over the other.

We now outline the relative advantages and disadvantages of circuit and packet switching. However, because we have not performed a detailed comparison, we must be careful to distinguish between *potential* and clear-cut (or inherent) benefits. In other words, there are certain limitations that existing circuit or packet switching techniques possess for the application under consideration; but if we were to design a new switching technique especially for a voice/data CPBX, we might be able to overcome those limitations. With this point in mind, we can list several benefits associated with circuit switching:

– it is a proven technology (it already exists for voice)
– because of its widespread use, circuit switching hardware components are more common and should be relatively low priced
– the processing software is less complex than with packet switching (e.g., with packet switching, the switch will need congestion control mechanisms, more sophisticated buffer management capabilities, and silence recognition for voice traffic).

Some of the potential advantages of circuit switching are that it uses less buffer memory (with packet switching there is always some chance that a transmission will be delayed, and hence some additional buffers are needed); that it is easier to isolate voice and data traffic, thereby providing the potential for achieving the required reliability of voice connections in a combined voice/data network (as discussed in Section 3.1); and that support for existing protocols is more readily achieved (since, in effect, a "wire" is dedicated to the connection, the switch appears transparent to the communicating devices). The principal disadvantage of circuit switching is its much greater throughput requirements. This greater bandwidth means that more processor hardware may be needed.

Clearly, the above points are not conclusive for selecting a switching method. On the contrary, we believe that the decisive factor is *cost*, and more detailed analysis is required to evaluate this factor. In a typical CPBX installation, the switch constitutes a significant fraction of the overall system cost, and hence the switching technique should be chosen primarily on the basis of how much the resulting CPBX would cost. In order to properly perform a cost analysis it is necessary to conduct a more detailed study of the traffic characteristics (e.g., flow patterns, message sizes) and of digital voice technology, to develop candidate switching techniques well-matched to the requirements, and to carefully evaluate the hardware and software requirements of these techniques.

4. Summary of Conclusions

In the study reported on here, our goal was to determine the feasibility of integrating voice and data on a single office network. We considered briefly the functional requirements for combining voice and data, and then we analyzed the traffic characteristics of the office in order to determine the magnitude of voice traffic and of data traffic. Subsequently, we considered design alternatives for an office network and its main switching components.

We believe that the requirement for using systems based on both voice and data technologies is most prominent among management and professional level personnel. We have concluded that voice is the preferred input medium for this group of personnel, and digital information is the most convenient and flexible form for processing, storing, and retrieving information. The two most apparent applications for combining voice and data in the immediate future are voice mail and voice dictation, both using digital storage and retrieval techniques. In the more distant future, the widespread availability of computer voice recognition and generation systems capabilities will spur innovation of many more applications which combine voice and data.

To understand the relative magnitudes of the various traffic types that might flow within an office in the future, we generated projections of traffic volumes for voice traffic, text processing communications, electronic mail messages, and communications to/from printers, intelligent copiers and facsimile machines. These traffic projections were based upon market research reports and user surveys, together with some of our own assumptions regarding the data communications environment. We intentionally attempted to overestimate the data traffic in order to be conservative. Nevertheless, voice traffic is shown to be substantially greater than data traffic. The major conclusion we draw from this data is that if a single communication network handles both voice and data, then the network should be optimized for voice. In other words, data traffic should be added to voice networks.

In considering design alternatives for local office networks, we reached several conclusions:

— Future office network designs should be based upon combining voice and data. We find few advantages to separating voice from data, while we believe there are strong technical and economic benefits in a combined network.

— The star topology is deemed the most immediately suitable structure for a combined voice/data intra-office network; such a network would be based around a switch similar to that of the computerized PBX which is currently oriented to voice. Internally, the CPBX could utilize any physical topology.

— Traffic characteristics of both data and digital voice must be studied in more detail; the results of such further study would then provide the basis for identifying candidate switching techniques well matched to the requirements, and for evaluating the resource requirements of these alternative switching techniques. It would then be possible to choose a CPBX design on the basis of delivered performance as well as cost of the switch.

— The circuit-switching schemes currently used within the voice CPBXs may or may not be optimal when switching both voice and data. In order to determine the optimal switching technique, the merits of each must be understood on the basis of resources required in the switch and on the basis of delivered performance; this would then provide the basis for a cost analysis of the switching facilities. Cost is a major decision factor since the switch constitutes a major portion of the cost for a star network.

References

[1] "Country Government Cuts Costs with PBX System," Telecommunications, April 1980, pp. 43–44.
[2] See, e.g., "Managing Global Communications," Creative Strategies International, 1979.
[3] V.G. Cerf and A. Curran, "The Future of Computer Communications," Datamation, May 1977, pp. 105–114.

PBX VS. LAN

HARVEY KAUFMAN

ABSTRACT

The subject of the LAN vs the PBX is usually approached from the viewpoint of promoting one or the other as dominant in the eventual role as Hub in the integrated office of the future. The PBX has been developed to address the needs of voice communications. The LAN has been developed as an approach more suited to the characteristics of data communications. Given the current limitations imposed by technology, it is reasonable to project that each technology will continue to evolve, and that they will increasingly coexist in distributed integrated networks for some time to come.

INTRODUCTION

The PBX, which has been evolving over a period of many years, has encountered a dramatic increase in development activity over the past ten years. The advantages that have accrued from this activity have included improved functional performance and enhanced economics while still addressing the unchanging need for full duplex, real time connectivity for voice communications.

Those digital device and microprocessor developments that have brought about new generations of PBX, also accelerated the trend to distributed processing and spurred the ever increasing demand for data communications. Because economics is the ultimate determinant in the successful application of technology, the data community has sought to develop telecommunications techniques that would permit more efficient use of transmission facilities than has been achieved within the real time constraints of a voice communication environment.

Because data does not require real time communications, store and forward techniques can be employed which permit a substantial increase in the utilization of shared transmission facilities. These techniques utilize the simultaneous physical connection of numerous terminals to a common transmissions while looking for information addressed to it. The conventional set up time encountered establishing a connection in a circuit switch is virtually eliminated. Pursuing the potential for economic advantage in the exploitation of differences between voice and data involves optimizing the shared use of a common transmission facility which in turn requires the use of a suitable contention scheme. This is necessary in order to permit the various terminals to communicate as desired without introducing an unacceptable level of interference by one transmission of another. This form of optimization requires knowing how long it will take for a signal to travel the full length of the transmission line and return, which in turn necessitates defining the maximum length of the cable. It is this requirement for placing a finite limit on propagation time that results in the "local" aspect of a "Local Area Network."

Reprinted from *Proceedings of the 1985 Symposium on New Developments in Local Area Networks*, 1985, pages 1-11. Copyright © 1985 by The Institute of Electrical and Electronics Engineers, Inc.

It is feasible to switch data in a digital PBX, subject to a number of limitations including circuit bandpass and connection time. It is also possible to switch voice in a LAN, with the primary limitations of concern being throughput and the store and forward effects on voice quality and intelligibility. Because each approach can technically switch both voice and data, proponents of the two types of system each promote theirs as the future central element in an environment of integrated voice and data.

In order to evaluate whether, in fact, either will dominate the "integrated" environment, at least in the near future, it is necessary to consider the functional priorities of each, and to define what "combined voice and data" actually means.

PBX DESIGN PRIORITIES

The designer of a PBX would like, for economic reasons, to build a system that has a zero fixed cost and a linear expandibility to infinity. Approaches to this objective are seen in "families" of switches that utilize common circuit packages, and more recently in highly modular architectures that permit expansion of port sizes over a very broad range with little or no loss of hardware.

Within this concept, the designer must keep certain functional priorities in hand in the process of evolving a system optimized for voice communications. These generally include:

a. Connectibility

It is the primary function of the PBX to meet the interface standards of the public switched network in order to assure universality of voice networking. This means that the transmission characteristics of the matrix path should be transparent when inserted into the public network, and signaling systems must be network compatible. In a typical PBX application, approximately one third of the traffic is incoming, one third is outgoing, and only one third is intraswitch.

b. Availability

The system must meet public expectations with regard to "up time." The visibility of voice system failure is very high, and performance is observable both from inside and outside the organization. Tolerance levels for system outage are in the same range as for power failure, and design objectives for maximum down time (in larger systems) is two hours in 40 years. Mean time to repair objectives are in the order of 20 minutes.

c. Real Time

Real Time Connectivity is necessary to voice communications both for reasons of intelligibility and to provide transparency to conventional conversation. Even the simple delay encountered in satellite connections has a negative impact on the using public. Error rate is of relatively little significance because of the considerable redundancy in analog voice communications.

d. Bandpass

Bandpass for voice communications must be adequate to permit "telephone quality" voice from end to end. Although not objectively defined, this may be interpreted to indicate a transmission transparency that is adequate to allow recognizability of the speaker's voice.

e. Size Flexibility

The size requirements for a PBX must accommodate virtually all employees of a company, a number that is larger and far more variable than for data. The PBX must also provide universal voice service with universality of features and functions for all users. It is not practical to require that a user's work arrangements be configured to accommodate the functional constraints of a limited telecommunications facility or to inhibit the flexibility for reconfiguring. PBX's need the extensive capability of flexibility for reconfiguring systems that is offered by the star topology of a centralized control type circuit switch. Loops and buses can be accommodated, but move and reconfiguration activity can be significantly more costly and disruptive of communications after completion of the original installation than for a star.

PRIMARY FUNCTIONS OF A LAW

The objective of a LAN is to permit machines, rather than people to intercommunicate. This can be terminal to terminal, terminal to host, host to terminal, or host to host.

Terminals speak at greater speeds than do people, but usually for very brief periods compared to voice. It is, therefore, an objective of a LAN design to effect the economics achievable from having numerous "connections" share a common transmission path in such a way that communications between the two terminals essentially use only as much of the time as necessary for their communication. This presumably leaves the bandpass of the path available for others during the silent periods. Although Time Division Multiplexing (TDM) also time shares a common path, the real time and bandpass requirements of voice cause the total bandpass of a transmission line to be subdivided into a limited number of specific "time slots," each of a predetermined length and repetition rate, and each dedicated to the communicating terminals until completion of a session.

The short, bursty nature of the data communications compared to voice, and particularly the tolerance to storage of the data communication until a path is available, allow the LAN to accommodate a greater number of users on a shared path than can be done with circuit switching. This is accomplished by permitting one originating terminal to transmit on to the bus at any given time, after first determining that there is no transmission present with which it would interfere. If there is a transmission present, the terminal waits until it senses a clear path.

All connected terminals in a LAN are attached to and listening to the common transmission medium, obviating the need for establishing physical connection for a communication. In this environment, each packet of information transmitted onto the bus by the originating terminal contains the address of the destination terminal, and each destination terminal must read the address of each packet and extract only its own information.

Having this type of addressing function work requires that all inputs, regardless of source, be translated into the standard system packet information format. Each LAN port is therefore interfaced with an encoding/decoding device known in packet switching as Packet Assembler Disassembler (PAD). Different PADS can be connected to each of the various ports of the LAN. Although the LAN also offers transparent communications, such as the Datagram, the connection of dissimilar devices through different PADS offers an efficient means for protocol conversion that is not so easily accomplished in a circuit switching PBX.

LAN DESIGN PRIORITIES

In addressing the objectives of providing connectivity between machines, minimizing minimum set up times, effecting protocol conversions, and providing dynamic allocation of bandwidth, the LAN designer, like the PBX designer, has to maintain a list of priorities to be addressed in optimizing his design.

a. Connectibility

    As with the PBX, the ability to provide working connections between terminals is the primary function of the LAN. Connectibility, however, is not so much concerned with providing transparency between similar users over a public switched network, but rather in providing the perception of transparency between terminals that may or may not employ the same connection protocols. These terminals are to be located within some limited, pre-defined geographic area.

b. Throughput

    The throughput capability of a LAN is a form of traffic measurement. Because of the way a LAN is used, the throughput capability is of greater relative significance than is traffic capability to a circuit switching PBX. Throughput relates to the accommodation of data speed, to the need for computer time, to the numbers of terminals that can be accommodated, and even to the extent to which error correction can be provided. Bit error rate is a far more significant parameter for data than it is for voice.

    Throughput is affected by many parameters of the LAN. These include the raw data rate, the length of the maximum transmission run (propagation time), addressing scheme, error correction, and other overhead items that require the use of bandwidth. The extent of the impact these factors can have on throughput are described in a review published in the June 1985 issue of Data Communications of the IBM

Technical Paper that appeared at the Fifth International Conference on Distributed Computing (1). According to this review, IBM's forthcoming token ring LAN has a raw data rate of 4 megabits per second, but has an upper limit of 200 kilobits per second throughput on data files that can be passed between two devices over the ring.

STORAGE CAPACITY

In communications between terminals on a LAN, the originating terminal operates on the assumption that it has unimpeded access via the transmission medium. The designer must therefore provide buffer capacity at each interface for the storage of the transmitted data, forwarding packets from the buffer to the destination terminal as it gains access to the transmission medium. The selection of buffer capacity becomes a significant cost/performance decision to be made by the designer of the system.

INTEGRATED VOICE AND DATA

What is the impetus to integrate voice and data, and what does integration mean in this context?

The impetus, of course, is economics. It is not necessarily the economics of finding the cost of a single unified switch to be less that that of two separate switchng arrangements, but more realistically that of being able to make use of an existing twisted pair infrastructure. It is the same incentive that existed for the development of integrated multiline key equipment by the various PBX manufacturers. Although there had originally been a significant resistance to the implementation of systems employing non-standard, proprietary station equipment, the growing desire for so-called universal cable systems has largely displaced concerns with becoming more captive to the PBX supplier. There is an increasing trend towards extending the digital information to the end terminal, and the subsequent opportunity to expand the utilization of end to end digital capability. What comes with end to end digital communications is a considerable flexibility in the kinds and numbers of simultaneous communications that can be provided between terminals. In an ISDN environment, circuit switching, packet switching and packetized control and signalling data will be merged into a single transmission.

In larger campus type environments, the design and configuration of a new cabling system presents a far greater challenge than do the selection of PBX and data equipment. Machines can be individually replaced fairly readily and there is generally an active market for the used equipment being displaced. The forecasting of future needs, however, particularly with regard to data functions, is not something easily developed, and a real concern with the cost and potentially disruptive effects of move and change activities are enough to intimidate the most intrepid of communications planners.

One result is a strong motivation on the part of end users to seriously promote the idea of a single network controller, the implication of which is the presence of a single, universal, low cost cable distribution system. The reality of being able to accomplish this objective of a universal voice/data system with today's technology would depend upon the user's ability to tolerate the compromises necessitated by the economics involved. There will undoubtedly be some incidence of "merged" systems, though these are likely to prove the exception rather than the rule based on the differing priorities of performance between voice and data applications.

THE PBX AS A DATA SWITCH

The current PCM voice standards call for 64 kilobits per second of bandpass derived from an 8 khz sampling rate and an 8 bit format. A standard network compatible PCM switching matrix is therefore constructed to provide some quality of 64 kilobit paths for the shared use of terminals connected to the port interfaces of that matrix.

A request for service requires that one end of a 64 kilobit path be connected to the port address associated with the originating terminal, and the other end be connected to the port address associated with the terminating terminal. The result is a 64 kilobit point-to-point connection between the two ports.

In order to use this matrix for establishing a data connection, it would be necessary for the originating terminal to provide the system with a request that identifies the physical location of the terminating port on the matrix. In doing so, it would encounter the delays associated with the dialing procedure itself, and with the conventional delays encountered with the sharing of common equipment, such as registers, in a high traffic environment. Once having established a connection, the time slot becomes dedicated between the two points, and is unaffected by other traffic in the network. Throughput, however, remains subject to the 64 kilobit limitation of the circuit path.

Cost is the major potential disadvantage to the use of circuit switching voice PBX's for data. The penalties in cost relate both to the significant software functions that are required to provide the full range of features and functions associated with voice communications and the allowances for hardware necessary to the ultimate need for providing analog terminations. Circuit switches designed purely for data switching are less expensive to build, and are available at approximately one third the cost per port of a voice switch. Although a separate data circuit switch may involve separate local loop cabling, the overall cost could be less than would result from doubling the port size of a combined voice/data PBX.

Assuming that the bandpass limitations and point-to-point constraints of circuit switching are not limiting, then the relative costs of increasing the port size of a voice switch must be compared to the cost of providing a separate digital data switch and providing two extra twisted pairs to the star configured cabling plant providing local distribution. A voice PBX which provides simultaneous voice and data capability to all stations requires twice the number of station ports than for voice only.

Systems that utilize the voice infrastructure for data as well, must also accept the limitations that go with the use of twisted pair wiring.

Although the use of twisted pairs is a stated objective of merged systems, there is not the same capacity for data rate/distance as there is for coaxial or fiber optic cables. Even with the considerable activity taking place in the area of data compression techniques which reduce the required bit rate for the transfer of a given amount of information, these factors have no effect on the conductive characteristics of the twisted pair medium itself.

THE LAN AS A VOICE SWITCH

The LAN seeks to overcome the circuit switch limitations imposed on data by a PBX. It seeks to eliminate path set up time, and replace the fixed bandpass with a dynamic bandpass allocation. It approaches these objectives by the use of packet switching techniques where all transmissions are made in bursts of fixed bit length. In addition to the data being sent, each burst or packet includes address information so that it may be identified by the destination terminal.

There are different approaches to the LAN, but generally only one terminal transmits at a time, sending one packet and then waiting for availability of the bus to send the next packet. The storing of the data to be forwarded upon availability of the bus is a form of queuing which permits a very high utilization of the bandpass of the transmission path. The store and forward technique works because the receiving terminal is a machine that can collect and assemble completed messages over a period of time without losing intelligibility.

The heavier the traffic becomes on the LAN, the longer the delay time between the delivery of packets and the lower the effective throughput per virtual connection.

It is fundamental to digital telecommunications systems that once the information to be transmitted is encoded into digital format, the system need not differentiate between the different kinds of information represented by the transmitted data. It follows that voice can be packet switched as well as raw data. It does, however, become necessary to identify voice traffic, and to differentiate its treatment in a LAN. Delays of more than a few milliseconds of a packet representing voice communications result in unacceptable distortion in the analog reconstruction and therefore packets delayed more than the specified threshold must be dropped. This necessitates making a decision as to how or whether to replace the dropped packets.

Because of the real time requirements for voice communications, voice packets in a LAN would need to be given priority over data. When this is done, the throughput capacity for data is heavily impacted.

The use of a LAN for voice only is definitively described in a paper entitled "A Local Area Network as a Telephone Local Subscriber Loop" published in the December 1983 issue of the IEEE "Journal on Selected Areas in Communications." (2) The authors describe simulations of LAN's used for voice only traffic, looking at a 1 kilometer bus operating at 1 megabit and at 10 megabits per second, with each circuit carrying 64 kilobits per second of full duplex traffic.

The significance of this study, relative to the subject of the PBX vs the LAN, lies in the summary and conclusions.

"Two local area network protocols have been compared as to their ability to support interactive telephone conversations on digital voice terminals. Examination of the percent lost packet versus the offered traffic revealed that a stable network would be operated such that less than two percent of the voice packets would be lost during the busy hour. This would be controlled by distributed call-blocking. Listener tests showed that as high as 2 percent dropped packets could be accepted by the user. When used as a multidrop local subscriber loop to a PABX, a 1 megabit/second LAN can support 24 subscribers with a CSMA/CD protocol and 29 with GBRAM. A 10 megabit/second LAN can support 314 subscribers with CSMA/CD and 431 with GBRAM. Implementation awaits the right economic situation."

It is evident that a 30 subscriber limit would be overly restrictive for an economically feasible packet based voice PBX. Although a ten megabit LAN can theoretically support upwards of 400 voice subscribers, that number would be significantly less if any nominal volume of data traffic were to be superimposed on the same LAN. Even should a suitable application be identified for the larger version, twisted pair wiring would not support the 10 megabit transmission.

FOURTH GENERATION PBX

Trade and advertising references to "Fourth Generation" PBX's indicate the emergence of new PBX designs that successfully combine the advantages of packet and circuit switches into a single vehicle. Though such implications may be technically accurate, these systems may or may not offer significant economic advantages over alternative voice and data telecommunications networks. The architectures vary significantly, but the design approach appears to lie in the provision of a decentralized system comprising multiple nodes that communicate with each other via a wide band transmission medium such as coaxial cable.

The intention is to geographically distribute the several nodes in such a manner that all station cables may be held to a maximum length which would permit the high bit transmission rates associated with combined voice and data transmission. In addition, packet data is applied to a separate cable or to a dedicated band in a broad band configuration. This approach eliminates the need for the cost of a separate port in the matrix of a circuit switch.

The data in this configuration is, however, limited to asynchronous transmissions because of the inability of a synchronous virtual connection to tolerate the widely variable delays associated with varying traffic in the packet switching network. In order to offer synchronous capability, these systems share the circuit switched matrix with voice for synchronous connections.

CONCLUSION

The conclusion that must be drawn at this time, is that the optimizing of voice and data transmissions imposes divergent demands on design priorities, requiring that there be continuing development and application of each for the foreseeable future. Unlike voice, data can impose a wide variety of demands on transmission networks. To the extent that data is compatible with voice delivery networks, and so long as the economics of a given application provide justification, there will be an area of common ground where voice and data will share a common switching system.

Within the present constraints of hardware costs, this will likely be in the form of limited data switching provided by a PABX in conjunction with voice switching. These economics are most likely to exist where:

A. The PBX is useful for contention, permitting larger numbers of terminals to compete for a lesser number of host ports on a dial up basis.

B. The numbers of terminals are a small enough percentage of the total stations that the economics favor expansion of the PBX over the provision of a separate system.

C. The majority of requirements are for casual access as opposed to continuous on-line operations, and where the terminal user is likely to want access to a number of different hosts on a dial selective basis.

Packet switches can sometimes incorporate voice on a limited basis, for purpose of economics as in a wide area international packet switching network. They are unlikely, however, to include PBX type voice requirements in addition to data unless substantial increases are achieved in bandpass that will permit accomplishment of acceptable quality, real time voice communications.

Efforts to reduce the costs in the face of increasing demand for access to distributed data bases have led to efforts toward dealing with the bandpass constraints imposed by voice networks. In the local area environment, it may well be that a new generation of PABX system will have to evolve before a real integration of voice and data can occur within a common local switching system. A convenient way of viewing this PABX evolution is view the four subsystems that make up the PABX system and see where developments in the recent past have been directed towards the alleviation of limitations.

"Generation One" can be thought of as comprising all manual and electromechanical PBX systems that have gone before. From this viewpoint, "Generation Two" can be considered the displacement of the wired logic control subsystem by stored program control, which resulted in dramatically increasing the feature, maintenance and cost control capabilities of the PBX.

"Generation Three," the displacement of analog matrix subsystems with network compatible digital PCM systems becomes economically feasible with the increasing power of stored program controls. The fourth generation followed with the extension of both digital information and distributed intelligence to the terminal subsystem, spurring the ongoing activities toward achieving end to end digital communications.

The communications industry is currently immersed in the development of terminal subsystems as means for expanding the value added capabilities offered by the switching system and is now encountering limitations imposed by the as yet unaddressed subsystem, the cable distribution plant.

A logical extension of the above view is that "Generation Five" will come about with the displacement of the traditional twisted pair distribution by something with far greater capabilities. The new medium would need to be cost effective, offer considerably increased bandpass, and offer some kind of isolation from the potentially disruptive effects on high bit rate transmission by external electrical interference.

Although the performance requirements are nicely addressed by fiber optics, the transducer per circuit costs in an electronic switch environment appear as a significant deterrent to the simple displacement of copper. A fifth generation system could come about with the commercial availability of an optically switching PABX, an occurrence which would not only contribute to elimination of bandpass constraints on the distribution subsystem, but which could dramatically alter the bandpass capabilities of the circuit switch itself.

In the meantime, awaiting the arrival of some such dramatic event, the development of both PBX and LAN can be expected to continue in parallel. Although there will be some merge of functions in appropriate applications, the two will coexist, and will be called on to intercommunicate to an ever greater degree in our increasingly distributed and diverse telecom-environment.

REFERENCES

1. E.E. Mier, "IBM Leaks Performance Details of Forthcoming Token Ring Network," Data Communications, June 1985, pp. 50, 52.

2. J.M. Musser, T.T. Liu, L. Li, and G.J. Boggs, "A Local Area Network as a Telephone Local Subscriber Loop," IEEE Journal on Selected Areas in Communications, Vol. SAC-1, No. 6, Dec. 1983, pp. 1046-1054.

BIOGRAPHY

Harvey Kaufman, Vice President
Telecom Plus International, Inc.
48-40 34th Street
Long Island City, NY 11101

Harvey Kaufman graduated from Harvard University in 1953. He attended the U.S. Army Signal Corps School at Fort Monmouth, New Jersey in 1954, and in 1955 was assigned to the Electronic Warfare Division at White Sands Proving Ground.

Upon separation from the service he joined the General Electric Company at Schenectady, New York, serving in a number of design and application engineering assignments in the Transformer and Rectifier Departments in Lynn, Mass., Fort Wayne, Indiana, and Lynchburg, Virginia. In 1958 he was assigned to the Communications Products Department as a Special Terminal Systems Engineer where he remained until mid 1960. During this period, he served as Director and Program Chairman of the Lynchburg Society of Engineering and Science.

In June 1960, he transferred to the Semiconductor Products Department in Upstate New York. He served there as Manager for High Reliability Program Marketing until 1964, and as Product Manager for medium power devices until 1969, during which period he was a contributing author to the General Electric SCR Manual. From 1969 to 1972 he was Manager, Overseas Business Development with responsibility for offshore licensing of semiconductor patents and technology.

In 1972 he joined NEC Telephones, Inc., a subsidiary of Nippon Electric Company, Ltd., which had recently been formed for purposes of addressing the newly emerging telephone interconnect market. He was Northeast Regional Manager from 1972 to 1976, and Director, Large Systems Marketing, until September, 1979, when he joined Telecom Plus International in New York City as Vice President, Applications Engineering, and later as Vice President, Strategic Planning. He was named Executive Director Marketing of Siemens Information Systems Inc., Control Systems and Networks Group following their acquisition of Tel Plus Communications in March 1987.

Section 5: The Network Interface

5.1 Overview

The purpose of a local network is to provide a means of communication for the various attached devices. To realize this purpose, the interface between the network and devices must be such as to, permit cooperative interaction. For circuit-switched local networks (digital switches and digital PBXs), the problem is straightforward. The switch provides a transparent connection service that looks like a point-to-point link.

For packet-switched local networks (LANs and HSLNs), a number of issues are raised that relate to the allocation of protocols to the attached devices and to the network. Packet switching implies that the data to be sent over the network by a device are organized into packets that are sent through the network one at a time. Protocols must be used to specify the construction and exchange of these packets. At a minimum for a local network, protocols at layers 1 and 2 are needed to control the multiaccess network communication (For example, these layers would comprise the logical link control (LLC), medium access control (MAC), and physical control functions specified IEEE 802 and introduced in Section 2)

Thus, all attached devices must share these common local network protocols. From a customer's point of view, this fact structures into three alternatives the ways in which devices attach to a LAN or an HSLN: (1) homogeneous/single-vendor approach, (2) "standards" approach, and (3) standard network interface approach.

A homogeneous network is one in which all equipment (network plus attached devices) is provided by a single vendor. All equipment shares a common set of networking and communications software. The vendor has integrated a local network capability into its product line. Customers need not concern themselves with details of protocols and interfaces.

Undoubtedly, many customers will adopt this approach. The single-vendor system simplifies maintenance responsibility and provides an easy path for system evolution. On the other hand, the flexibility to obtain the best piece of equipment for a given task may be limited. Relying on a vendor, without consideration of the vendor's network architecture, for easy accommodation of foreign equipment is risky.

Another approach that a customer may take is to procure a local network that conforms to a standard and to dictate that all equipment be compatible with that standard. The local network would consist of a transmission medium plus an expandable set of "attachment points." This approach, although attractive, has some problems. The IEEE standard for LANs, although final, has not yet been widely implemented. Worse, from the point of view of the present discussion, is that the standard is loaded with options, so two devices claiming to be "IEEE compatible" may not be able to coexist on the same network. The ANSI standard for HSLNs is still in draft form. Thus, there is little hope that incompatible systems will fade away anytime soon.

The promise of local network standards does not lie in the solution of the interconnect problem. Rather, standards offer the hope that the prospect of a mass market will lead to cheap silicon implementations of local network protocols. However, the interconnect problem is an architectural issue, not a protocol issue.

Now, consider that a LAN or an HSLN consists of not only a transmission medium but also a set of intelligent devices that implement the local network protocols and provide an interface capability for device attachment. We will refer to this device as a network access unit (NAU). The NAUs, collectively, control access to and communications across the local network. Subscriber devices attach to the NAU through some standard communications or I/O interface. The details of the local network operation are hidden from the device.

The NAU architecture is commonly used by independent local network vendors (those who sell only networks, not the data processing equipment that uses the network). It holds out the promise that interface options provided by virtually all vendors for communications and I/O operation can be used to attach to a local network.

5.2 Network Access Unit

Typically, the NAU is a microprocessor-based device that acts as a communications controller to provide data transmission service to the attached device. The NAU transforms the data rate and protocol of the subscriber device to that of the local network transmission medium and vice versa. Data on the medium are available to all attached devices, whose NAUs screen data for reception based on address. In general terms, NAUs perform the following functions: (1) accept data from attached device, (2) buffer the data until medium access is achieved, (3) transmit data in addressed packets, (4) scan each packet on medium for the device's own address, (5) read packet into buffer, and (6) transmit data to attached device at the proper data rate.

The hardware interface between the NAU and the attached device is typically a standard serial communications interface, such as RS-232-C. Almost all computers and terminals support this interface. For higher speed, a parallel interface, such as an I/O channel or direct memory access

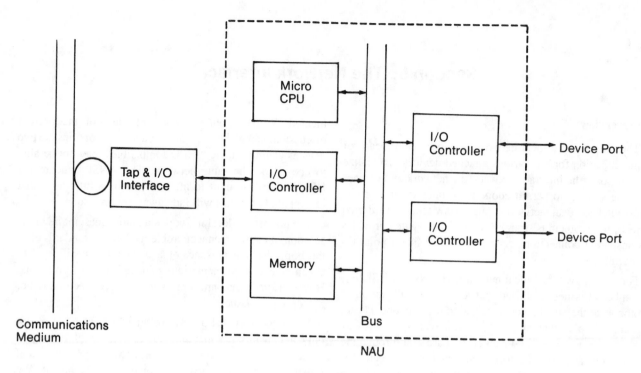

Figure 5.1

(DMA) interface, can be provided.

The NAU can be either an outboard or an inboard device. As an outboard device, the NAU is a stand alone unit, which may have one or more serial communications ports for device attachment. High-speed parallel ports are also used. As an inboard device, the NAU is integrated into the chassis of the data processing device, such as a minicomputer or terminal. An inboard NAU generally consists of one or more printed-circuit boards attached to the device's bus.

Figure 5.1 presents a generic architecture for an outboard NAU. The NAU consists of a number of modules connected by an internal system bus. One I/O controller module controls the interface to the local network medium. Typically, this module will contain the medium access control logic and the physical I/O logic to drive the medium transceiver or modem. Other I/O controllers contain the physical and link layer logic for controlling attached devices. A given controller might handle one or multiple device ports.

The operation of the NAU is controlled by a microprocessor, which makes use of an internal memory to store programs and data. The microprocessor generally executes a simplified operating system and a set of application programs specific to the local network function. For example, the system needs to be able to engage in a dialogue with attached devices to set up and tear down connections to other LAN addresses. Higher-layer protocols, such as a transport protocol, may also be implemented in the NAU.

The architecture for an in-board NAU is similar to that of Figure 5.1. In this case, the device I/O controllers are replaced by an I/O controller that attaches directly to a host computer system bus. Such a controller often employs DMA to exchange data with the host computer's main memory.

From a customer's point of view, an NAU with standard interface options solves, at least at the electrical level, the interconnect problem. From a designer's point of view, the NAU is a useful architectural concept. Whether a network is homogeneous or not, and whether the interface provided to the local network is standard or not, there must be some distributed logic for controlling local network access. Conceptualizing this logic as an NAU clarifies some of the communications architectural issues associated with networking applications on a local network.

The NAU must, at minimum, implement the LAN or HSLN protocols. The articles in this section explore the issue of what, if any, additional communications service the NAU might provide.

5.3 Article Summary

The first article examines the important issue of the protocol implications of using an NAU architecture. Specifically, some sort of protocol is needed between the host and the NAU. The nature of this protocol, and the related design and standardization issues, are explored. The next article, "Core Modules Speed System Design," looks at the implementation of such a host-NAU architecture. Again, the issue of how the host and the NAU cooperate and interact is discussed.

"Tutorial: RS-232-C Data Switching on Local Networks" describes the use of an NAU for terminal handling. This seemingly simple case is shown to require considerable functionality. The final article, by Cerruti and Voce, looks at the opposite extreme in terms of performance requirements: the mainframe. The interface described in this article is appropriate (and common) for mainframe attachment to a high-speed local network (HSLN).

William Stallings, Comp/Comm Consulting, Great Falls, Va.

Interfacing to a LAN: Where's the protocol?

Users must be assured that their network devices are compatible. To accomplish this requires the use of a host-to-front-end protocol—but there is no standard.

LANs

The IEEE-802 standards and the FDDI optical-fiber local area network standard, soon to be adopted, solve many of the problems caused by the use of different protocols and interfaces for LANs. The acceptance of these standards by both vendors and customers means that customers have a wide variety of standardized LAN equipment to choose from. However, one significant area in need of standardization has been overlooked, and it has to do with the way in which customer equipment is connected to the LAN.

In IEEE-802 jargon, the following protocols are needed to connect to a LAN: physical, medium access control (MAC), and logical link control (LLC). These protocols specify the logic needed for end-to-end functionality. The next-higher layer (usually the network layer) must be able to invoke the services of the LLC in order for user applications to employ a LAN.

In considering the implementation of a network-LLC interface, two possibilities arise: (1) network and LLC both execute in the host processor; or (2) LLC and below are offloaded onto a front-end processor (FEP).

The FEP approach is attractive for several reasons: It relieves the host of the network processing burden and thus enhances efficiency. Also, the FEP can be procured from a different vendor than the supplier of the attached devices, so that the user has more flexibility in selecting equipment to attach to the network: It is not necessary that the attached equipment support the particular type of local network that the user has implemented; it is only necessary that the FEP and the attached devices share a common, standardized interface. The potential drawback of the FEP approach is that a new protocol is needed, known as a host-to-front-end protocol (HFP).

Before exploring the implementation of an HFP and the standards-related issues it raises, we need to look at the protocol architecture requirements of a local network.

As Figure 1 shows, a LAN communication architecture involves the three layers mentioned earlier—physical, MAC, and LLC. The physical layer provides for attachment to the medium. The MAC enables multiple devices to share the medium's capacity in an orderly fashion. And the LLC provides for data link control across the network.

The figure also indicates that higher layers of software will make use of the LLC. Put another way, the LLC provides the service of transmitting frames of data across the LAN, and that service is invoked by a higher layer of software. The IEEE-802 standards and the optical-fiber ring standard from ANSI 3T9.5—the Fiber Distributed Data Interface (FDDI)—use this three-layer architecture.

The three LAN layers correspond to the lowest two layers (physical and data link) of the ISO's Open Systems Interconnection (OSI) model (see "Of local networks, protocols, and the OSI reference model," DATA COMMUNICATIONS, November 1984, p. 129). The next layer, then, would be the network layer. In the context of a LAN, most functions traditionally associated with the network layer are not needed. For example, the LLC layer provides for the routing and addressing needed to transmit protocol data units from source to destination. Also, if the connection-oriented LLC service is used, the LLC layer provides for logical connections, flow control, and error control. Above that, the recently approved ISO connectionless network-layer standard, which provides an internetworking protocol, is needed so that the hosts on the LAN can be connected, via a gateway, to hosts on other subnetworks (see "Internetworking in an OSI environment," DATA COMMUNICATIONS, May 1986, p. 118).

Figure 2a shows this architecture. The LLC layer moves frames of data from one station on the LAN to another. The network layer provides internetworking capability. The transport layer provides end-to-end reliability. Thus, the user of the transport layer is guaranteed that its data will be

1. Three layers. *The logical-link-control layer provides for data link control across the network. Higher layers of software will make use of the LLC.*

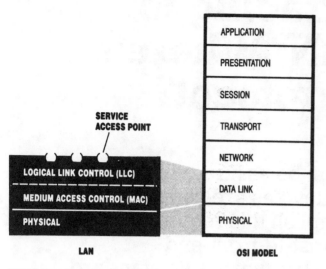

delivered with no losses and no misorderings. Above the transport layer are user-oriented layers (session, presentation, application) that handle communication functions beyond reliable data transfer.

We can trace the operation of this architecture on a single unit of user data in Figure 2b, which is keyed to event times marked on Figure 2a. At some time t0, the session entity presents a block of data to the transport entity. The transport entity encapsulates this data with a transport header and passes the resulting unit to the network-layer entity (t1), which adds its own header and passes the resulting unit to the LLC (t2). The LLC in turn adds its own header and passes the resulting unit to the MAC (t3). MAC produces a frame that includes both a MAC header and a MAC trailer, and this frame is transmitted across the LAN (t4). The MAC frame includes a destination station address, and the frame will be copied by the station with that address (t5). The user's block of data then moves up through the layers, with the appropriate headers and trailers stripped off at each layer (t6, t7, t8, and t9).

The FEP

The preceding discussion and Figure 2 assume that all layers of the architecture are implemented in the same processor. That is not always the case. Often, some of the lower layers are offloaded onto a front-end processor.

Consider a local network as consisting of not only a transmission medium, but also a set of intelligent devices that implement the network protocols and provide an interface for attaching subscriber devices (terminals or computers). We will refer to these intelligent devices as FEPs. The FEPs collectively control access to and communications across the local network. Subscriber devices attach to the FEP through some standard communications or Input/Output interface. The details of the local network operation are hidden from the devices.

continued

2. Internetworking architecture. *To interconnect hosts via a gateway (a), an internetworking protocol is needed. Its operation can be traced on a single unit of user data (b). The user's data moves up through the layers, with the appropriate headers and trailers stripped off at each layer (t6, t7, t8, t9). The transport layer provides end-to-end reliability.*

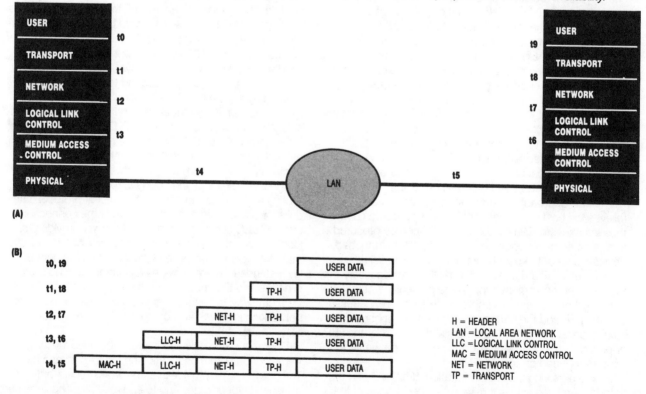

H = HEADER
LAN = LOCAL AREA NETWORK
LLC = LOGICAL LINK CONTROL
MAC = MEDIUM ACCESS CONTROL
NET = NETWORK
TP = TRANSPORT

3. Missing on the link. *A serial communications link is assumed between the front-end processor and any attached devices. Thus, a physical-layer protocol and a link-* *layer protocol are needed to exchange data across that link. One more protocol—not yet provided—is also needed: a host-to-front-end protocol, or HFP.*

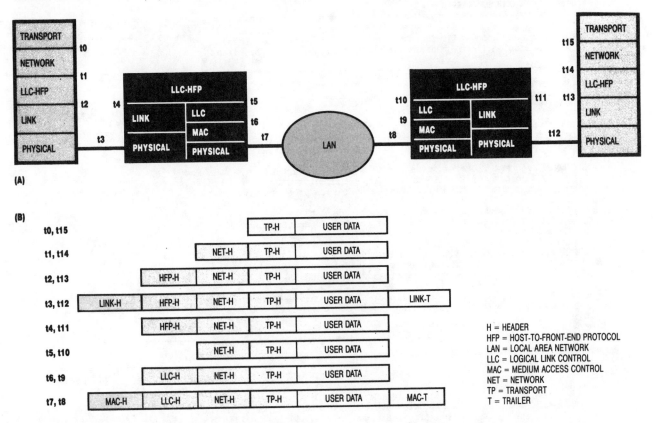

(A)

(B)

t0, t15				TP-H	USER DATA	
t1, t14			NET-H	TP-H	USER DATA	
t2, t13		HFP-H	NET-H	TP-H	USER DATA	
t3, t12	LINK-H	HFP-H	NET-H	TP-H	USER DATA	LINK-T
t4, t11		HFP-H	NET-H	TP-H	USER DATA	
t5, t10			NET-H	TP-H	USER DATA	
t6, t9		LLC-H	NET-H	TP-H	USER DATA	
t7, t8	MAC-H	LLC-H	NET-H	TP-H	USER DATA	MAC-T

H = HEADER
HFP = HOST-TO-FRONT-END PROTOCOL
LAN = LOCAL AREA NETWORK
LLC = LOGICAL LINK CONTROL
MAC = MEDIUM ACCESS CONTROL
NET = NETWORK
TP = TRANSPORT
T = TRAILER

The FEP architecture is commonly used by independent local network vendors (those who sell only networks, not the data processing equipment that uses the LAN). Thus, as noted, in many cases the FEPs in a local network configuration are supplied by a different vendor than the supplier of the terminal and computer equipment.

The FEP is a microprocessor-based device that acts as a communications controller to provide data transmission service to one or more attached subscriber devices. It transforms the data rate and protocol of the subscriber device into that of the local network transmission medium and vice versa. Data on the medium is available to all attached devices—each FEP screens the data for reception based on the attached address or addresses.

In general terms, the FEP performs the following functions:

■ Accepts data from attached device.
■ Buffers the data until medium access is achieved.
■ Transmits data in addressed packets.
■ Scans each packet on medium for own address.
■ Reads packet into buffer.
■ Transmits data to attached device.

The FEP can either be an outboard or an inboard device. As an outboard device, it is a standalone unit. The hardware interface between the outboard FEP and the attached device is typically a standard serial communications interface, most commonly RS-232-C. Almost all computers and terminals support this interface. As an inboard

device, the FEP is integrated into the chassis of the data processing device—for example, a minicomputer or terminal. An inboard FEP generally consists of one or more printed-circuit boards attached to the device's bus. Communication is typically by means of direct memory access (DMA) across the bus.

The FEP approach is becoming increasingly popular, since a customer can mix a variety of vendor equipment on a LAN but use a single-vendor FEP product to simplify network management. In the highly competitive microcomputer area, a variety of vendors offer LAN FEPs that connect to the popular system bus organizations (Multibus, for example).

The device-FEP interface
Remember that the discussion centering on the scenario of Figure 2 assumes that all of the protocol layers are integrated and executed on a single processor. Now assume instead that the LLC and below reside on an FEP.

The architecture of this approach is not as straightforward as you might have expected. Additional layers are needed to link an FEP and its attached station. Figure 3 assumes a serial communications link between the FEP and the attached device. Thus, a physical-layer protocol and a link-layer protocol are needed to exchange data across that link. One more protocol is also needed. This protocol has no universally accepted name, but it is often referred to as HFP. To identify this protocol as referring to a

Table 1: Logical link control service primitives

UNACKNOWLEDGED CONNECTIONLESS SERVICE

```
L-DATA.request (local-address,remote-address,l-sdu,service-class)
L-DATA.indication (local-address,remote-address,l-sdu,service-class)
```

CONNECTION-ORIENTED SERVICE

```
L-DATA-CONNECT.request (local-address,remote-address,l-sdu)
L-DATA-CONNECT.indication (local-address,remote-address,l-sdu)
L-DATA-CONNECT.confirm (local-address,remote-address,status)

L-CONNECT.request (local-address,remote-address,service-class)
L-CONNECT.indication (local-address,remote-address,status,service-class)
L-CONNECT.confirm (local-address,remote-address,status,service-class)

L-DISCONNECT.request (local-address,remote-address)
L-DISCONNECT.indication (local-address,remote-address,reason)
L-DISCONNECT.confirm (local-address,remote-address,status)

L-RESET.request (local-address,remote-address)
L-RESET.indication (local-address,remote-address,reason)
L-RESET.confirm (local-address,remote-address,status)

L-CONNECTION-FLOWCONTROL.request (local-address,remote-address,amount)
L-CONNECTION-FLOWCONTROL.indication (local-address,remote-address,amount)
```

ACKNOWLEDGED CONNECTIONLESS SERVICE

```
L-DATA-ACK.request (local-address,remote-address,l-sdu,service-class)
L-DATA-ACK.indication (local-address,remote-address,l-sdu,service-class)
L-DATA-ACK-STATUS.indication (local-address,remote-address,service-class,status)

L-REPLY.request (local-address,remote-address,l-sdu,service-class)
L-REPLY.indication (local-address,remote-address,l-sdu,service-class)
L-REPLY-STATUS.indication (local-address,remote-address,l-sdu,service-class,status)

L-REPLY-UPDATE.request (local-address,l-sdu)
L-REPLY-UPDATE-STATUS.indication (local-address,status)
```

front-end whose highest layer is LLC, it shall be called an LLC-HFP.

To understand the need for an HFP, consider again the case of an integrated architecture (Fig. 2). At t2, the network entity passes a block of data to the LLC for transmission. How does the LLC know what to do with this data block? That information is contained in the link control primitive (command) used by the network layer to invoke the LLC. The link control primitives are listed in Table 1. For example, if the unacknowledged connectionless service is used, the network entity would use the following primitive and associated parameters to invoke the LLC:

L-DATA.request (local-address,remote address, 1-sdu, service-class) where:

local address	=	local LLC service access point
remote address	=	destination station (MAC) address and destination LLC service access point
1-sdu	=	block of data being passed to LLC for transmission

service class = desired priority

Exactly how this information is passed to an LLC entity will depend on the implementation. For example, if the LLC is invoked by a subroutine call, the L-DATA.request call is compiled into a machine-language subroutine branch, and the parameters of the call are placed somewhere in registers or memory, to be picked up by the called routine. The details are not, and should not be, part of the LLC standard. The internal implementation of this interface depends on the machine language and operating system and upon optimized design choices.

The subroutine-call approach works fine if the network and LLC entities execute in the same processor. But in the case of the example in Figure 3, they run on separate processors. A way is needed for the network and LLC entities to exchange primitives and parameters, and that function of the LLC-HFP-LLC-HFP provides a way for the network and LLC entities to communicate. In the host, the LLC-HFP entity presents an interface with the network entity that mimics the LLC. This setup allows the network entity to use calls such as L-DATA.request as if the LLC and network were running on the same processor. In the FEP, the LLC-HFP behaves like any other LLC user. *continued*

4. Adding transport. *An attractive and increasingly popular approach is to house all layers, up through transport, in the front-end processor. This architecture—depicted here—relieves the host of all processing associated with establishing and maintaining a reliable end-to-end connection. Thus, a host-to-front-end protocol is mandated.*

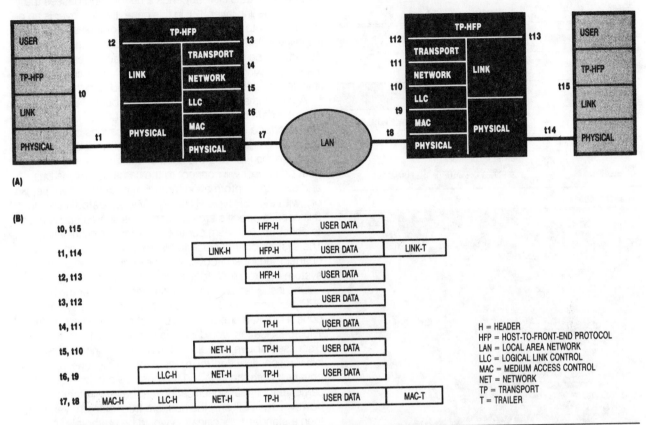

Table 4: ISO transport service primitives

```
T-CONNECT.request (Called Address,Calling Address,Expedited Data Option,Quality of Service,Data)
T-CONNECT.indication (Called Address,Calling Address,Expedited Data Option,Quality of Service,Data)
T-CONNECT.response (Quality of Service,Responding Address,Expedited Data Option,Data)
T-CONNECT.confirm (Quality of Service,Responding Address,Expedited Data Option,Data)

T-DISCONNECT.request (Data)
T-DISCONNECT.indication (Disconnect Reason,Data)

T-DATA.request (Data)
T-DATA.indication (Data)

T-EXPEDITED-DATA.request (Data)
T-EXPEDITED-DATA.indication (Data)
```

that a transport entity can have multiple users. The first six primitives listed in the table are used to establish and subsequently tear down a logical connection between transport SAPs. Most of the parameters are self-explanatory. The quality-of-service parameter allows the transport user to request specific transmission services, such as priority and security levels. The remaining primitives are concerned with data transfer. The expedited version requests that the transport entity attempt to deliver the associated data as rapidly as possible. Note the similarity of these primitives to those for the LLC.

Although placement of the transport layer and those below in the FEP is becoming popular, making desirable a standard specification for TP-HFP and a transport-level system control block is not in sight. (For current and projected LAN standards activity, see "LAN standards.")

The exact functions performed by the HFP will depend on the architecture employed. For example, an LLC-HFP will need to pass different primitives and parameters than a TP-HFP. In any case, some format, such as that indicated in Table 2 or 3, is needed. Other characteristics of an HFP are relatively independent of the protocol layer involved. Specifically, the HFP must be:

■ Reliable, to ensure no loss of messages. *continued*

Table 2: LLC-HFP header and primitives

HEADER	
FIELDS	**FUNCTION**
SERVICE ACCESS POINT	SPECIFIES USER OF LLC SERVICES
PRIMITIVE CODE	SPECIFIES WHICH LLC PRIMITIVE IS BEING INVOKED
PARAMETER COUNT	SPECIFIES NUMBER OF PARAMETERS
PARAMETER	THIS FIELD OCCURS ONCE FOR EACH PARAMETER AND CONSISTS OF TWO SUBFIELDS
LENGTH	SPECIFIES THE LENGTH IN OCTETS OF THE VALUE SUBFIELD
VALUE	SPECIFIES THE VALUE OF THE PARAMETER

PRIMITIVE CODES

```
 1  L-DATA.request
 2  L-DATA.indication
 3  L-DATA-CONNECT.request
 4  L-DATA-CONNECT.indication
 5  L-DATA-CONNECT.confirm
 6  L-CONNECT.request
 7  L-CONNECT.indication
 8  L-CONNECT.confirm
 9  L-DISCONNECT.request
10  L-DISCONNECT.indication
11  L-DISCONNECT.confirm
12  L-RESET.request
13  L-RESET.indication
14  L-RESET.confirm
15  L-CONNECTION-FLOWCONTROL.request
16  L-CONNECTION-FLOWCONTROL.indication
17  L-DATA-ACK.request
18  L-DATA-ACK.indication
19  L-DATA-ACK-STATUS.indication
20  L-REPLY.request
21  L-REPLY.indication
22  L-REPLY-STATUS.indication
23  L-REPLY-UPDATE.request
24  L-REPLY-UPDATE-STATUS.indication
```

Table 3: LLC-HFP system control block format

WORD	NAME	DESCRIPTION
1	STATUS	NETWORK INTERFACE UNIT (NIU) OR HOST STATUS INFORMATION, SUCH AS WHETHER OR NOT READY TO RECEIVE DATA
2	DIRECTIVE	MANAGEMENT-RELATED COMMANDS AND ACKNOWLEDGMENTS
3	COMMAND POINTER	POINTS TO AN AREA OF MEMORY THAT CONTAINS ONE OR MORE COMMANDS. EACH COMMAND CONSISTS OF A COMMAND CODE AND A LIST OF PARAMETERS.
4	FRAME POINTER	POINTS TO A BUFFER CONTAINING A BLOCK OF DATA BEING PASSED BETWEEN THE LLC AND THE LLC USER
5-8	ERROR COUNTERS	ERROR-RELATED STATISTICS

The operation of Figure 3's architecture can now be traced. At t1, the network entity passes the user's data plus a network header to LLC-HFP, using the L-DATA.-request call. LLC-HFP appends a header and passes the result to the link layer (t2). In this case, the link layer is an ordinary point-to-point data link control protocol, such as the High-level Data Link Control (HDLC). Table 2 suggests a format for the header. Note that the header identifies which user is invoking the services of the LLC, the primitive being invoked, and the parameters associated with that primitive.

Again, this scenario assumes an outboard FEP and the use of a data link protocol, such as HDLC, across the host-FEP interface. If the FEP is a communications board, then there will be no link and physical layer protocols as such between the FEP and the host. In most cases, the FEP and host processor will connect to the same backplane bus and exchange information through a common main memory, with the FEP typically using DMA, as stated earlier. In this case, a specific area of memory is shared and is used to construct a system control block for communication. The system control block fulfills the same function as the header mentioned above. As an example, Table 3 gives the system control block format used in an Intel product.

One issue remains to be examined. Whether the host-FEP exchange is achieved by a header or by a system control block, a specification of that exchange is needed. The specification would include not only the formats discussed above, but also such protocol functions as initialization, flow control, management functions, and recovery. If both the FEP and the host are provided by the same vendor, that specification can be proprietary. If, however, the FEP and the host are from different vendors, then a standard specification would be preferable. As stated, it is likely that FEPs will be from a different vendor than the vendor for the attached devices. Indeed, there may be attached devices from a number of different vendors. Thus, the case for a standard for the host-FEP exchange is a strong one. Unfortunately, no such standard exists or, as far as is known, is even contemplated by IEEE 802, ANSI X3T9.5, or the ISO.

A transport-level FEP

With today's microprocessors, it makes sense to offload even more of the processing burden from the host. An increasingly popular approach is to house all layers up through transport in the FEP. This relieves the host of all processing associated with establishing and maintaining a reliable end-to-end connection.

Figure 4 depicts this architecture. Note the similarity to Figure 3—the same reasoning applies here. In this case, the user of the transport layer executes on a different processor than does the transport entity. Hence, a transport-level host-to-front-end protocol (TP-HFP) is needed to allow the transport user to exchange primitives and parameters with the transport entity. The TP-HFP header will contain a code specifying which primitive is being invoked and a list of parameter lengths and values. In the case of an inboard FEP, the primitives and parameters can be exchanged by means of a system control block.

Table 4 lists the primitives for the ISO transport protocol standard. The ISO transport protocol standard, like the LLC, has the concept of a service access point (SAP), so

LAN standards

The key to the development of the local area network market is the availability of a low-cost interface. The cost to connect equipment to a LAN must be much less than the cost of the equipment alone. This requirement, plus the complexity of the LAN protocols, dictates a very large scale integration solution. However, chip manufacturers will be reluctant to commit the necessary resources unless there is a high-volume market. A LAN standard would ensure that volume and also enable equipment from a variety of manufacturers to intercommunicate.

That is the rationale of the IEEE 802. Its standards are being processed by the International Organization for Standardization (ISO). The standards are in the form of a three-layer communications architecture, which is matched against the ISO's better-known Open Systems Interconnection (OSI) reference model in Figure 1.

The logical link control (LLC) layer provides for the exchange of data between service access points (SAPs), which are multiplexed over a single physical connection to the LAN. The LLC provides for both a connectionless, datagram-like and a connection-oriented, virtual-circuit-like service. Both the protocol and the frame format resemble those of the High-level Data Link Control (HDLC).

The medium access control (MAC) layer provides for the regulation of access to the shared LAN transmission medium. For each MAC specification (carrier-sense multiple access with collision detection, and token ring), a physical layer specification tailored to the topology and MAC algorithm of the corresponding MAC protocol is provided.

The IEEE-802 standards are designed for low-to medium-speed LANs, up to 20 Mbit/s. Work on higher-speed LANs has been performed within the ANSI X3T9 technical committee on I/0 interface standards. A subcommittee, called X3T9.5, has developed a proposed standard called the Fiber Distributed Data Interface (FDDI), which will soon be adopted as an ANSI standard. FDDI specifies the MAC and physical layers and assumes the use of the IEEE-802 LLC layer. The MAC layer is a token-ring specification, similar to that of IEEE 802. The physical layer specifies a 100-Mbit/s optical-fiber ring.

■ Connection-oriented, to maintain the state of a dialogue with each user of the HFP.
■ Multiplexed, to allow multiple higher-level users.
■ Individually flow-controlled by the user.

Overall, the HFP must examine each command that it receives, verify the parameters associated with the command, and reformat as necessary for communication. ■

William Stallings is president of Comp/Comm Consulting. He has a B. S. E. E. from Notre Dame and a computer science Ph. D. from M. I. T. This article is based on material in the second edition of his book, Local Networks, *recently published by Macmillan. He is also author of* Data and Computer Communications *(Macmillan, 1985).*

Core modules speed system design

Systems integrators and manufacturers can easily connect LANs to even proprietary-bus-based systems.

Systems integrators and equipment manufacturers using nonstandard, proprietary buses can save considerable time in adding local-area-networking capability by adopting a core-module approach. Essentially, the module comprises the core hardware and software elements of a network controller—the elements that would be required for any bus scheme. The interface circuits for each particular bus then can be added.

Because the core module isolates the host-computer software from the network, the core-module software that works today with, say, Ethernet will also work in the future with a token

Subhash Bal, VP Marketing
Duane Murray, Technical Marketing Manager
Kevin White, Hardware Engineering Manager
Excelan Inc.
2180 Fortune Dr.
San Jose, CA 95131

bus. And, by combining the core-module concept with high-level protocol software, systems integrators can implement a communications subsystem to link multiple computers into a distributed computer system. No matter what bus is used on each networked computer, the same core-module design can serve and allow each computer to communicate—a technique that saves the effort of designing a custom controller for each computer (Fig. 1).

To maintain compatibility with the ISO OSI reference model, a good network interface should include provisions for multilevel protocols. An overview of the necessary hardware and software elements will indicate how the core module fits into the scheme of designing a network interface, and show what problems systems integrators can avoid when they employ the concept.

The first but not necessarily the least complex parts of the interface are the

physical- and link-layer protocols encompassed by networking standards such as IEEE 802.3 (Ethernet). Conformance to these layers gives a computer the basic ability to connect to a network.

Much more important for sophisticated networking are network and transport, the next two layers in the ISO model. The protocols in these layers deal with the normal functions of a computer's operating system and application software. A crucial aspect of designing a network interface is deciding where to run the software that implements these protocols. (Ideally, all seven levels should run on the core module.)

The remaining layers in the ISO model generally fall into territory covered by the computer's operating system and application software. For that matter, the network- and transport-layer software could run as an applica-

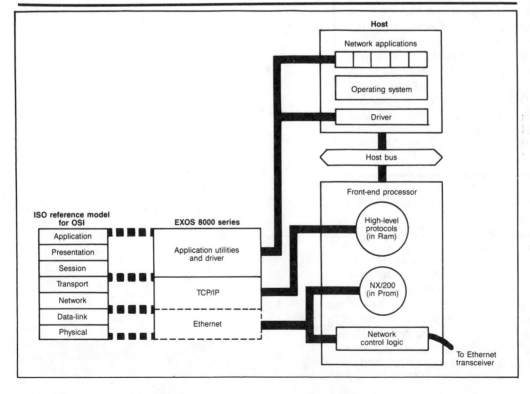

1. An overview of core-module functions shows the hardware and software functions needed to interface a computer with a network. The goal of the core-module approach is to establish the network interface so that it doesn't vary from computer to computer, thus minimizing redesign requirements.

Core modules

tion on the computer.

There are, however, some good performance reasons for delegating virtually all networking tasks to a separate processor on the network interface. First, the overhead associated with networking can make a significant impact on overall computer performance. For example, a single user needing network access can easily lower the performance of a multiuser computer.

The second reason for delegating network tasks to a separate processor lies in the efficiency of message handling. Informal tests reveal that an 80186-based interface board handles networking protocols at the same rate as a VAX 11/750. If a number of applications are vying for a large computer's processing time, that computer's response to networking needs will be even slower. In fact, a network interface's network and transport layers can act as a bottleneck in message handling. Even though IEEE 802.3 networks transmit and receive at 10 Mbits per second, for instance, the effective transfer rate, as seen by communicating hosts, can be much lower due to the time taken by message-handling protocol software.

A processor dedicated to networking chores, on the other hand, ensures that the 60 Kbytes or more of program code needed for the network and transport layers doesn't slow system throughput and, therefore, maximizes the effective transfer rate. An optimized communications-processor board in a front-end processor mode can significantly improve network performance at greatly reduced cost without burdening the host cpu.

Developing a network interface that deals with all the tasks up to the transport layer is a complex job that can take years—particularly if the job involves proprietary system buses for which off-the-shelf hardware is not available from multiple sources. This application is where the core-module concept shows its worth. Instead of developing custom hardware and software to handle the physical, link, network, and transport layers, systems integrators can buy a prepackaged unit or license a design from an outside source.

This off-the-shelf approach to an otherwise closed proprietary system —intrinsic to the core-module concept—is another good reason for delegating as many networking tasks as possible to the interface. If the network and transport software runs on the core module instead of the host, it is possible to standardize the code because it always runs in the same environment (Fig. 2). Any networking software running on the host, on the other hand, must conform to whatever hardware and OS environment the host provides. Stabilizing the software by keeping it on the core module spreads the development cost over many system types and reduces the cost and time investment to each system designer. In addition, upgrades become easier, because protocol code is isolated to a single environment.

The challenge to adopting the core-module concept lies in the interface between the module and the host— especially if the host employs a proprietary or nonstandard bus. Whether a systems integrator configures the network controller as a self-contained board or puts the circuitry and software on the same board as the host cpu, the same principle holds true: If the module won't adapt easily to a wide variety of situations and still maintain networking efficiency, the concept loses much of its value.

Fortunately, it is possible to design a core module that meets these requirements. One such device is the Excelan EXOS 200 (Fig. 3). The core-module family includes the EXOS 200 circuit design, available via sample boards and as a license agreement; the NX/200 real-time OS, which runs on the core module; and the EXOS 8010, 8030 and 8040 host-resident software, which runs under Unix, RSX-11M, and VMS, respectively.

The core module—a DMA peripheral.
The most important feature of the core module is its ability to work independently of any host. The greater its independence, the easier it can adapt to many different types of host systems. Thus, the core module communicates with the host via direct-memory access (DMA), just as any other peripheral controller does. When the host has a message to send, it stores the message and the destination address in a specific area of host memory. The core module receives a message from the network; the module stores the message in host memory via DMA.

This use of DMA implies that the host bus must permit multimasters, because the core module must take control of the bus to perform DMA. Many personal-computer buses—usually those on single-user systems—do not allow multimasters. With some modification, however, the core-module concept proves useful even for such machines.

Some other computers also require modifications to the basic core module. A computer running Unix 4.2 BSD, for example, has networking functions built into the operating system. In such situations, it is usually best to run the core module in link-level mode; then the host, instead of the core module,

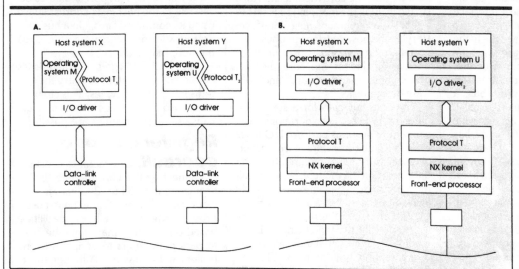

2. Running network protocols on the host computer requires custom software for each machine (a); upgrades must be made on an individual basis. In contrast, running the protocol software on a core-module-based front-end processor provides a consistent environment from one host to another (b). The software, therefore, has to be designed only once, and only one version has to be supported.

performs protocol processing. However, the core module can still provide advantages over a dumb controller, due to the module's buffering; the core module decouples the network from the host to some extent.

Another feature of the core module is the incorporation of an operating system to organize tasks handled by the module's general-purpose processor. Because these tasks must execute as events demand, the unit requires a very dependable real-time operating system.

In addition to the general-purpose processor used for protocol handling, the core module needs a networking processor to deal with the details of physical- and link-layer tasks. Just as the core module offloads networking functions from the host, the networking processor takes on the dedicated activities required to deal with a network.

Excelan employs Intel's 82586 networking processor, which implements the IEEE 802.3 standard. The 82586 interfaces with the core's 80186 general-purpose processor via dual-port memory. The design's standard memory complement is 128 Kbytes, but systems integrators could increase memory to 512 Kbytes if the system is to handle special tasks. It is possible, for instance, to allocate a large amount of RAM to buffer large host files before or after network transmission. The host interface must adapt to many hosts.

The most crucial aspect of core-module integration for designers is the interface between the host and the module. Because the module's design is fixed, systems integrators need only be concerned with the host-driver software needed to deal with message transfers to and from application programs. Before considering these drivers further, it's important to understand the core module's interface functions.

The most basic level at which the core module must interface with the host involves the host's bus structure. Most multimaster bus structures feature three buses: an address bus, a data bus, and a control bus. Typically, the address bus is 16 to 32 bits wide and the data bus is 8, 16, or 32 bits wide. The control bus usually has read and write command lines, some sort of interrupt line, and bus-arbitration lines. Some bus structures have their address and data lines time-multiplexed; others permit block transfers of data. Buses have vectored interrupts, multiplexed interrupts, and even memory-mapped interrupts. Bus arbitration can be synchronous, asynchronous, polled,

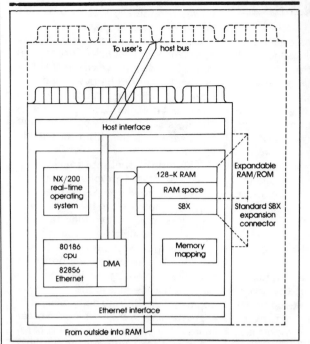

3. A core-module design acts as part of a complete network interface. The module encompasses all the functions that can be made constant from one computer to another. Systems integrators must add some circuitry to adapt the module design to a specific bus.

serial, parallel, nested, etc. To simplify integration, the core module is designed to implement as many of these schemes as possible using a minimum of circuitry.

To deal with wide address buses—and thereby work with large host-memory capacities—the core module has a 32-bit address bus. This width encompasses virtually all available computers that need networking capability. Those computers that employ fewer than 32 address bits can connect to the appropriate number of module address bits. The 18 Unibus address lines, for example, connect to the lower 18 lines of the module.

Systems integrators can create a 32-bit address by using a 16-bit microprocessor and expanding the processor's address bus via mapping registers. Even if the host has a 16-bit address bus, the core-module interface should include the mapping registers to establish a common host interface. Varying the host interface to physically accommodate various hosts destroys the universality of the core module, and complicates hardware- and software-design tasks.

The data bus calls for a somewhat different set of considerations. Because most systems perform I/O tasks in 8- and 16-bit transfers, it isn't generally necessary to accommodate 32-bit data buses on the module. When 32-bit microprocessors become more widely available, the systems integrator can expand the host interface to double width. But, for the time being, a 16-bit module data bus can handle almost all host-computer requirements. This approach keeps costs down and capabili-

ties more in line with system needs.

To summarize—a generic bus interface must contain, minimally, a 32-bit address bus, a 16-bit data bus, read/write command lines, and an interrupt line. The interrupt is used to notify the host software that the core module requires some action. If the actual host bus needs only a subset of these features, the systems integrator can add a small amount of custom circuitry external to the core module to make up the differences.

The host also must be able to reset, wake, and command the core module. The core can access commands in host memory to satisfy the last requirement, but the first two demand some sort of slave interface on the core module. Because not all systems have interrupt lines that the host can activate, an I/O port is probably the best choice for these functions. This port should be accessible to the host in its address space using its command lines. On a bus such as the VMEbus, the port should be memory-mapped.

The final I/O port characteristics depend on the custom circuitry the systems integrator provides. This circuitry must also handle bus arbitration because so many schemes are possible.

Register acts as a doorbell.
One factor to consider in connecting the core module to the host is the method used to initiate network transactions. Some host buses provide extensive mailbox capabilities based on registers that allow the host to pass parameters to peripheral controllers and vice versa. Although these methods can simplify message passing,

they aren't available on all hosts. Thus, an off-the-shelf core module can't make much use of such specialized schemes.

A more universal way for the host and module to communicate is via a very basic, two-register design. One register acts essentially as an I/O-port doorbell for the host to tell the core module that it should do something. Instead of passing parameters (as with a mailbox), the doorbell register simply interrupts the core-module processor; parameters are passed via the host's memory space.

The second register acts as a doorbell for the module to interrupt the host. This register doesn't pass networking parameters either, but it is useful for passing basic core-module status information, such as self-test results.

A cache arrangement can prove beneficial for some host interfaces; the core module permits this method as an option. The cache approach suits buses—such as the Q-bus—that have multiplexed data and address lines. Cache memory can minimize the load placed on this type of bus by transferring message data in bursts. A 16-word cache can send a small block of data over the bus with only one address for the entire block. Otherwise, the core module sends an address with each word, which uses a multiplexed bus almost twice as much as with the cache.

Core module handles all the details.

Before examining the software aspects of the host interface, consider how the host and core module pass messages. When the host wants to send a message over the network, it stores the message at a predesignated address in main memory along with the address of the message's network destination. The host then writes the appropriate value into the doorbell register to tell the core module a message is ready.

The core module handles the rest of the job. Using DMA, it retrieves the message from host memory. It then performs all protocol conversions necessary to transmit that message over the network. Some of the housekeeping tasks the module must handle include all response/acknowledge signaling and checksum calculations.

Receiving a message from the network is equally simple from the host's point of view. Via the second doorbell register, the core module informs the host that a message has arrived. The module then uses DMA to load the message into a predesignated part of host memory.

The core module can perform automatic "scatter and gather" of packets to and from host memory as a way of simplifying the host's job. The level of software on the core module is high enough so that the host software might not even have a notion of packets; to the host, a chunk of memory might represent a file or a track buffer for a disk drive. The core module can grab data from the memory in packet chunks as the module loads its own memory and write data into a memory block from packets scattered throughout module memory.

To shield the host from the need to respond to network traffic in real time, the core module can furnish some onboard packet buffering. This allows the module to handle a burst of network packets without host intervention. The amount of buffering required is a function of the network's peak load with respect to the amount of packet-processing overhead. The greater the buffering, the larger the peak traffic can be. However, buffering does not help if the average network load exceeds the packet-processing power of the core module or the host.

Files stored on a host disk must be transferred to the host's main memory before being sent as a network message. The core module can't retrieve messages directly from disk because this capability would place restrictions on the host OS's disk-buffer locations. Most systems use complex operating systems that allocate memory in efficient ways; systems integrators don't want to restrict the OS to one buffer-memory location. Such a requirement would also demand links to a system's OS—a chore that a good core module should not include. Disk controllers generally handle the disk-to-memory transfer without host-cpu involvement, and the core module takes care of the memory-to-module transfer, also without host involvement.

In the messages and addresses to and from the core module, not all computers employ the same byte order within words (Fig. 4). In particular, Motorola's byte order differs from DEC's. If every host had to adapt to one byte order, a core module wouldn't be universal.

The easiest way for systems integrators to solve this problem is to put an optional byte-swapping facility in the core-module interface. Also, the systems integrator can choose to do byte swapping in hardware or software. The hardware method is faster, but for designs that must fit into a relatively small amount of space—on a Eurocard, for example—the software method might prove more practical.

The byte-swapping facility is one core-module function that requires some knowledge of host characteristics. Other factors include the memory locations where the host will store mes-

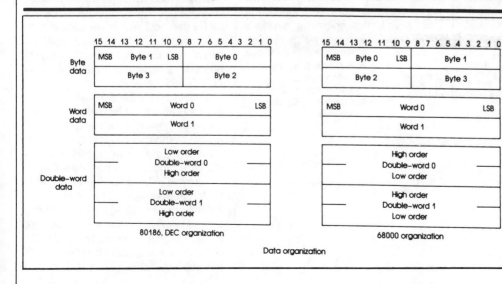

4. Because computers differ in the byte order they recognize, a truly universal core module must be able to interpret whatever byte order occurs. As shown, the word order in double-word data also varies.

sages; whether the core module should operate as a front-end processor or in link-level mode; and what type of interrupt the host accepts (e.g.: memory mapped, I/O-mapped, or bus-vectored). Similarly, the host needs information about the core module's operation.

All these parameters can be set up in an initialization procedure. When the host wishes to initialize the core module, it resets the module and writes the address of a configuration message to the doorbell register—the only case in which parameters are passed via the doorbell register. To get the rest of the necessary parameters, the core module can then read the message via DMA. By incorporating a pattern of known data types in the message, the module can even derive the byte order automatically.

After the core module is initialized, the host and the module communicate exclusively via messages stored in host memory. If the core module is to act as a front-end processor, the host uses this method as part of the initialization procedure to download the transport- and network-layer code that runs on the module.

The network and transport protocols provided with the core module come from the Arpanet standard—currently the only established protocols for these ISO-model layers. There's no reason the core module should be restricted to Arpanet protocols on the network and transport layers, however. If an application required it, integrators could develop software to implement one of the emerging sets of protocols or a proprietary set.

Host-based drivers complete interface.

The final element in the host/core-module interface—and the most important for

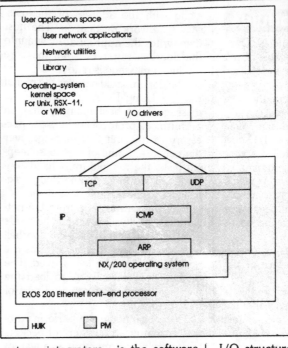

5. The software that supports networking runs mostly on the core module. The host generally runs network-related software only to connect the operating system and application programs with network services.

systems integrators—is the software that runs on the host. The value of the core module is that it runs independently of the host in almost every respect, but the host must still communicate with the module. Therefore, software drivers are needed to execute a number of housekeeping functions on the host.

Driver development can begin at a low level with simple I/O drivers. Then, integrators can upgrade the basic software to make message handling more transparent to users. For example, drivers can accept message destinations, such as "Nancy," and translate them to the proper network addresses. (The complete software structure can appear as illustrated in Fig. 5.)

For transparent capabilities under operating systems such as Unix, it's beneficial to put a knowledge of protocol commands and replies in the drivers so the core module can integrate cleanly with the operating system's

I/O structure. The network I/O can then look like a typical Unix I/O stream that's transparent to users. The protocol knowledge that's useful to put in the drivers includes message semantics, definitions of data structures, and descriptions of values.

A look at the core-module concept shows that the only tasks systems integrators have to be concerned with are physically adapting the bus width and writing host drivers. It isn't necessary to write drivers for some operating systems because off-the-shelf software is available from Excelan.

If the options designed into the core module don't solve all of a specific system's problems, the systems integrator can add other functions on an expansion card via a 16-bit iSBX connector. The connector can interface with other equipment, such as a terminal for debugging purposes, by adding an RS-232 interface card. (The NX/200 OS contains debugger software that's useful for protocol and driver-software development.) The expansion capability can also be used to create gateways to non-802.3 networks, such as X.25 or HDLC facilities.

For configuration purposes, the core module can almost be treated as an extremely powerful integrated circuit (Fig. 6). With that thought in mind, systems integrators can readily interface the core module to a host by satisfying the circuit's hardware and software I/O requirements. When one considers the years required to develop a custom networking interface, configuring a core module becomes the way to get powerful networking systems to market quickly. ☐

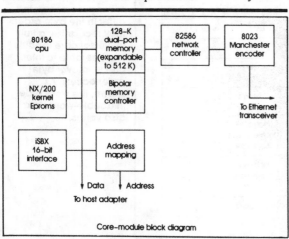

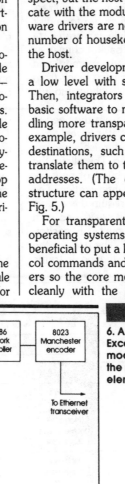

6. A block diagram of Excelan's core-module design shows the major hardware elements.

Robert Olsen, William Seifert, and Jonathan Taylor,
Interlan Inc., Westford, Mass.

Tutorial: RS-232-C data switching on local networks

Small, specialized controllers--known as terminal servers—establish virtual circuits to link devices to the likes of Ethernet.

During the last two years, vendors, engineers, and designers have used controllers to connect standalone minicomputers and microcomputers to local networks. As a result of their efforts, users are now witnessing the increasing availability of networking software that provides information exchange between compatible and, in some cases, incompatible computers. Computer-to-computer applications include interprocess communications, file transfer, remote file access, and electronic mail.

With recent advances in semiconductor and software technology, smaller, more specialized nodes can be economically connected to local networks, especially to Ethernet because of its potential as a standard. Nodes that offer a specific service to network users and applications are called "terminal servers."

A terminal server connects RS-232-C-compatible devices to a local network. Though it is called a terminal server, the unit is not limited to terminals. As depicted in Figure 1, a terminal server can also handle computer ports, modems, serial printers, microcomputers, and any other data processing device that is RS-232-C-compatible.

Using packet-switching technology, a terminal server provides a means by which users at a data processing installation can access computer and peripheral resources by virtual-circuit links. Virtual circuits appear as direct physical connections between devices. However, they are electronically created, maintained, and terminated by protocol procedures working within the terminal server. Compared to physical circuits, virtual circuits offer users the important advantages of being electronically switchable, enabling communications over extended geographic distances, and resolving communications incompatibilities between sender and receiver (see "Charting channel capacity"). Other benefits include:

■ *Overcoming device incompatibilities:* RS-232-C devices with different data rates, frame format, flow-control mechanisms, connectors, and signal pin assignments can be readily interconnected. This means, for example, that a hard-copy terminal that operates at 1.2 kbit/s can be logically connected to a computer port set for 9.6-kbit/s operation. Once the terminal server has been configured to the operating characteristics of the directly attached device, it will resolve device incompatibilities in a manner that is completely transparent to either device.

■ *Multiplexed device communications over extended geographic distances:* With an Ethernet terminal server, RS-232-C device communications is multiplexed onto a coaxial-cable transmission line. This permits a substantial reduction in the amount of RS-232-C twisted-pair point-to-point wiring that would otherwise be needed. Devices attached to the terminal server can communicate over distances up to 2,500 meters (1.5 miles) over a single Ethernet, a distance considerably further than that specified by EIA RS-232-C or RS-423. With the aid of a gateway server, geographically distant devices can be interconnected.

■ *User commands for electronically connecting and disconnecting devices:* The speed and ease by which connections are made with a network terminal server lets RS-232-C devices become shared resources. A terminal user can, for example, issue a command to the terminal server to establish a connection to a computer port on the network. When the user is finished using the computer, the computer port then becomes available to other users on the network. This circuit-switching facility can yield a considerable cost saving by encouraging more productive use of existing computer ports, serial printers, modems, and terminals.

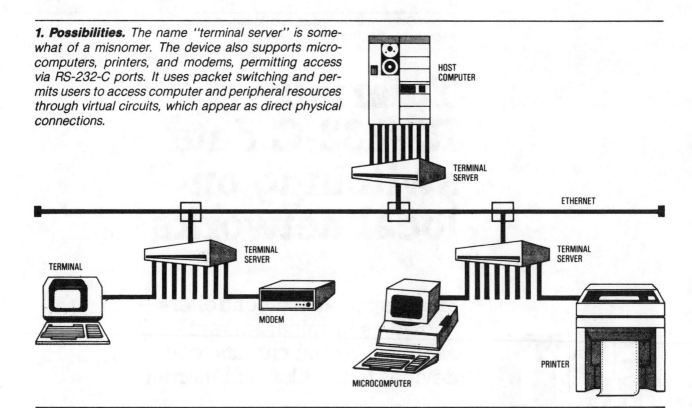

1. Possibilities. *The name "terminal server" is somewhat of a misnomer. The device also supports microcomputers, printers, and modems, permitting access via RS-232-C ports. It uses packet switching and permits users to access computer and peripheral resources through virtual circuits, which appear as direct physical connections.*

HOST COMPUTER

TERMINAL SERVER

ETHERNET

TERMINAL SERVER

TERMINAL

MODEM

TERMINAL SERVER

MICROCOMPUTER

PRINTER

Applications

A network terminal server can solve many of the data communications problems found within a typical data processing installation. Widely used applications of a terminal server are:

■ *Port Switching*—For data processing installations with terminal users requiring access to multiple host computers, a terminal server provides switched virtual-circuit connections. The user issues a "call" command and references the target host by a symbolic name, say, "VAX750." Although access security is generally provided in most computer operating systems, a terminal server provides a password security mechanism to protect against unauthorized user connections to devices on the network that do not contain such security provisions.

■ *Port contention*—For data processing installations that have more terminal users than host computer ports, a terminal server provides users with a way of contending for the limited processor resources. When a terminal user requests a connection to the host computer and its ports are busy, the terminal server will "rotor" to find an open port. If all ports are in use, the user may "camp on" the computer and wait for the first available port. As users log off the computer, ports are freed for use by other terminal users.

The terminal server can handle situations where the user logs off but forgets to disconnect from the host, where the user disconnects but forgets to log off the host, or where the user forgets to both log off and disconnect.

■ *Resource sharing*—For data processing installations where efficient use of expensive RS-232-C devices is desired, the terminal server eliminates the need for physically unplugging and plugging RS-232-C devices

together and matching the communications attributes of each device. A terminal server provides user commands for electronically interconnecting devices.

■ *Microcomputer networking*—At many data processing installations, managers prefer that corporate databases be centrally located and controlled by a large host computer. For distributed microcomputing to be effective, users need to store and retrieve files at the host computer and to transfer files between microcomputers. The terminal server provides users with the universal connectivity they require: microcomputers to the host, microcomputer to microcomputer, and microcomputers to printers or other peripheral devices.

■ *Simplified RS-232-C wiring*—A terminal server can resolve RS-232-C wiring problems. Instead of running a large number of point-to-point wires between terminals and computer ports, an Ethernet terminal server multiplexes RS-232-C communications onto a high-bandwidth coaxial cable that can handle thousands of concurrent virtual circuits, and which can span thousands of feet as well.

How it works

A terminal server can contain, for example, four or eight RS-232-C ports. Up to four units (32 ports) might be connected together at their transceiver cable interface so that they share a common transceiver unit connection on Ethernet. This would simplify transceiver-cable wiring problems that occur at such network locations as computer rooms, where a large number of transceiver units are required, although each must be spaced no more than 2.5 meters apart to comply with Ethernet specifications.

To ensure integrity of network operation, a terminal server can place users into two classes; users and network managers. A network manager (a privileged user) may, from any location on the network, configure the operating characteristics of any individual terminal server port (by knowing the password previously assigned to that port), issue the "configure" command, and respond to a series of configuration prompts. Port attributes selected include data rate, frame format, use of modem control lines, use of flow control, device logical names, device operation, and device passwords. The "configure like" command eases the network manager's job of configuring a large number of similar devices attached to the network.

As part of the configuration process, the network manager must specify the connection requirements of the attached device. A terminal server can classify attached RS-232-C devices into one of four types: command device, target device, command/target device, and auto-call device. A command device can issue commands to the terminal server. Typical com-

issues the command "call VAX750." The terminal server then broadcasts onto the Ethernet a packet with a "where's VAX750?" message, which is received by all other terminal servers on the network.

Terminal servers with ports having that name respond with their network address information. When multiple ports on the network share a common logical name, the server searches for the first free port in that logical name group. By distributing this name service, the server does not depend on the existence and proper operation of any master station or service.

Once a connection has been established, the terminal server ensures delivery of a byte stream between sending and receiving devices. Communications services provided by the terminal server include:
■ *Flow control performed on the incoming byte stream:* This is an essential function in a virtual circuit connection. A device operating at 9.6 kbit/s must be able to respond to the terminal server's flow control for it to

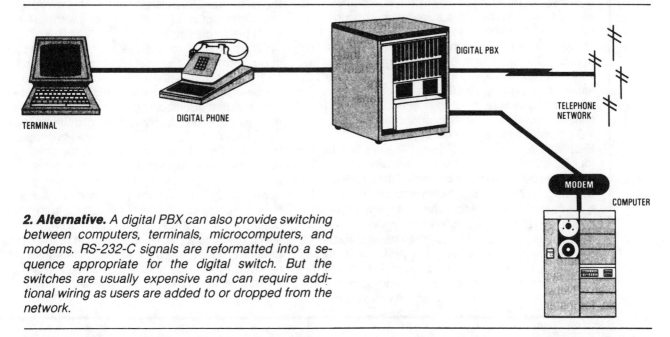

2. Alternative. *A digital PBX can also provide switching between computers, terminals, microcomputers, and modems. RS-232-C signals are reformatted into a sequence appropriate for the digital switch. But the switches are usually expensive and can require additional wiring as users are added to or dropped from the network.*

mand devices would include terminals, microcomputers, and auto-answer modems. A target device serves as the target of a virtual-circuit connection request. Typical target devices are host computer ports, auto-dial modems, and serial printers. A command/target device issues terminal server commands and also is the target of an incoming virtual-circuit connection request. This type of operation is suited for such devices as computer ports, auto-dial/auto-answer modems, and statistical multiplexers. An auto-call device requests, at initialization time, a permanent virtual-circuit connection to a prespecified target device.

A switched virtual-circuit connection is established by a user issuing the "call" command and referencing the target port either by its physical address or by one of it logical names. The terminal server uses Ethernet's broadcast delivery technique to provide an entirely decentralized port name/location service. When a user wants a connection to his VAX-11/750, he simply

successfully communicate with lower-speed devices.
■ *Byte stream assembled into packets for transmission:* A 20-millisecond packet-assembly timer assembles bytes into a packet. For the interactive terminal user, typically one byte (or character) is transmitted in a packet. However, for a 9.6-kbit/s block-mode output from a computer, about 20 characters will be assembled into an Ethernet packet.
■ *Reliable packet transmission:* To deliver packets reliably, a set of protocols such as the Xerox Network Systems Internet Transport Protocols is used. These transmission protocols allow the terminal server to sequence packet transmissions, check for transmission errors, detect missing packets, identify duplicate packets, and institute any recovery procedures required. In addition, the protocols invoke packet flow control between network stations, as well as providing complete support for internetwork communications.
■ *Received packets disassembled into an outgoing*

Charting channel capacity

A terminal server may use Ethernet as the transmission channel for connecting RS-232-C devices by virtual circuits. Although this approach to data switching is becoming increasingly popular, it is still a relatively new concept to most users, and many wonder how many RS-232-C devices Ethernet can support. This number is impossible to calculate because even if all network traffic statistics were known (and remained stationary), today's quantitative analysis tools are not sophisticated enough to handle the complexity of most problems users face. Because of this, analysts often resort to simulation techniques to get the answers they are looking for.

Users without enough programming resources or time to perform a network simulation can use the following technique for determining the number of virtual circuits that can share the channel capacity of the Ethernet (the terminal server used here is the Interlan NTS10). This technique is applied to four timesharing applications in which it is assumed that all the users run the same application concurrently. While the likelihood of this occurring is remote, the analysis provides useful insight into Ethernet's channel capacity. The four applications examined are:

■ Half-duplex block-mode device-to-device transfers at 9.6 kbit/s and a 100 percent duty cycle
■ Inquiry/update terminal-to-host applications
■ Interactive terminal-to-host applications
■ Data-entry terminal-to-host applications

Each analysis makes a different assumption about four RS-232-C device transmission statistics:

■ Average *size* of an input character stream (A to B)
■ Average *rate* of an input character stream (A to B)
■ Average *size* of an output character stream (B to A)
■ Average *rate* of an output character stream (B to A)

To calculate channel loading, an understanding of the terminal server transmission protocol is useful. The Xerox Network Systems Internet Transport Protocols, for instance, which provide end-to-end delivery of packets between terminal servers, include:

■ RIP—routing information protocol for internetwork routing of packets
■ SPP—sequenced packet protocol for end-to-end delivery of packets
■ PEP—packet exchange protocol for transmission of short message and responses
■ ECHO—protocol for verifying the existence and proper operation of terminal server nodes on the network
■ ERROR—protocol for delivering transmission error messages

The byte stream from an RS-232-C device is transmitted over the network using SPP. This protocol carries with it 12 bytes of sequencing information (for flow control and reliability checking) preceded by 30 bytes of addressing information by the network-level datagram protocol; the SPP is then encapsulated into an Ethernet frame with 4 bytes of trailer (32-bit cyclic redundancy check). As the frame goes onto the wire, a 9.6-microsecond minimum interframe spacing is required (12 bytes), along with a 64-bit (8-byte) preamble sequence.

For assembling the RS-232-C device's byte stream into packets, the terminal server uses a 20-millisecond (ms) packet assembly timer. When a byte is transmitted to the server from a device, it is held for 20 ms so that additional bytes can be assembled into a single packet for transmission onto Ethernet. After the 20-ms time period expires, a packet containing at least one byte of user information is transmitted. For interactive terminals attached to the server, each packet transmitted onto the network will generally contain only one byte of keyboard data. For sustained transmissions, such as output from a computer port, the number of bytes (or ASCII characters) assembled into a packet is a function of the device's data rate. If that rate is 9.6 kbit/s, a character will be received every 1.04 ms by the terminal server port, and an average of 19.2 bytes of user data will be sent in each packet.

byte stream: The outgoing bytes must be transmitted at the appropriate data rate for the attached device.
■ *Device flow control recognized on the outgoing byte stream:* This prevents the attached device from being overrun by the transmitted byte stream.

Alternatives

A terminal server installation is in many respects an application of distributed RS-232-C data switching. Three alternative approaches to data switching are port selectors, PBXs, and host-to-host networks with remote terminal access (for a comparison, see table).

Port selectors have been in use for more than a decade. Terminal lines and computer ports are wired to the central location, where the port selector resides. Circuit switching is performed by time-division multiplexing of the input RS-232-C signals from all active lines and ports. The input digital signals are successively sampled, transmitted over an internal bus, and received at the appropriate output port, where they are reproduced exactly, sample by sample.

Compared with a terminal server's distributed switching approach, the port selector has two major drawbacks:

■ The port selector's star topology mandates the use of more linear feet of wiring than is required by an equivalent installation based on distributed terminal servers. This means that wiring an installation is costly, including adding and relocating operators and equipment.

■ The port selector contains no intelligence for doing speed, frame-format, and flow-control conversions. This means that a calling terminal must be properly preconfigured with the communications requirements of the computer port being called. For such equipment as interactive terminals and computer ports, this is

Scorecard for Ethernet virtual circuits

	BLOCK MODE 9.6 KBIT/S, 100%	INQUIRY, UPDATE	INTERACTIVE	DATA ENTRY
AVERAGE SIZE OF INPUT CHARACTER STREAM	19.2 BYTES (19.2 BYTES PER PACKET)	10 BYTES (1 BYTE PER PACKET)	10 BYTES (1 BYTE PER PACKET)	5 BYTES (1 BYTE PER PACKET)
AVERAGE RATE OF INPUT CHARACTER STREAM	50 BYTES PER SECOND	2 BYTES PER MINUTE	5 BYTES PER MINUTE	1 BYTE PER SECOND
AVERAGE SIZE OF OUTPUT CHARACTER STREAM	0	1,920 BYTES (19.2 BYTES PER PACKET) PLUS ECHO OF INPUT	192 BYTES (19.2 BYTES PER PACKET) PLUS ECHO OF INPUT	ECHO OF INPUT
AVERAGE RATE OF OUTPUT CHARACTER STREAM	0	2 BYTES PER MINUTE	5 BYTES PER MINUTE	0
TOTAL CHANNEL BANDWIDTH CONSUMED PER VIRTUAL CIRCUIT	50.880 KBIT/S	3.531 KBIT/S	1.856 KBIT/S	1.344 KBIT/S
NUMBER OF VIRTUAL CIRCUITS PER ETHERNET	138	1,982	3,771	5,208

For the analysis, an assumption is made that is generally accepted in the Ethernet technical community: that Ethernet can be loaded to about 70 percent channel capacity before the channel access time (carrier deference, collision resolution) introduces packet transmission delays that become perceptible to an interactive terminal.

In the use of this 30 percent channel derating factor, the other four Internet Transport Protocols are absorbed, as they tend to be infrequently used in comparison with SPP.

Within SPP, system packets are transmitted whenever flow control and acknowledgment information cannot be piggybacked within traffic going in the opposite direction on the virtual circuit. Operational experience with the terminal server shows that about 25 percent of the packets transmitted are system packets. One is sent as an acknowledgment for every three RS-232-C data packets received.

Results of the analysis are shown in the table. The block-mode application is a sustained 9.6 kbit/s device-to-device half-duplex transfer at 100 percent duty cycle (no flow control). It is important to note that for such an application, greater channel-access delay can be tolerated.

The inquiry/update application assumes infrequent user keyboard transmissions that occur in full-duplex and that also result in a full CRT screen update (1,920 characters) from a host computer that outputs at 9.6 kbit/s.

The interactive application assumes an environment in which a user is editing a file.

The data-entry application assumes an environment consisting of keyboarders working at 50 words per minute.

Each analysis assumes that no other activity is occurring on the network. If such activity is present, then additional channel derating is required.

---

generally not an insurmountable problem, as the terminal user can experimentally change his data rate to match that of the computer. But for equipment (and users) that are less readily adaptable, severe connection problems will arise. For example, how does the off-site terminal user dialing in via an auto-answer 1.2-kbit/s modem use the port selector to access the same computer resources as his on-site counterparts have use of? Clearly he cannot, unless all on-site resources are also configured to operate at only 1.2 kbit/s.

Retrofitting

PBXs have historically been oriented toward the switching of analog voice circuits by using a time-division multiplexing technique called pulse amplitude modulation. More recent PBX offerings have an all-digital internal design (Fig. 2). Incoming analog voice signals

are digitized by a codec chip located inside either the switch or the handset. The codec samples the voice signal at 8 kHz into 8-bit values that are then transmitted onto an internal bus and received at an output voice circuit. For the PBX to be capable of performing RS-232-C data switching, the digital PBX must be retrofitted:

■ A box is required at each user device. This box reformats the RS-232-C data into a digital format appropriate for the switch and also functions as a short-haul modem to the switch.

■ A line card must be installed at the switch for handling incoming data streams from a number (generally 16) of the remote boxes.

■ New software must be loaded into the PBX. At the present time, PBX data switching costs range from $750 to $1,200 per line.

Compared to the terminal server, the digital PBX has

Charting the alternatives

CRITERIA	PORT SELECTOR	DIGITAL PBX	HOST TO HOST REMOTE TERMINAL ACCESS	NETWORK TERMINAL SERVER
SWITCHING LOCATION	CENTRALIZED	CENTRALIZED	DISTRIBUTED	DISTRIBUTED
EASE OF WIRING DEVICES TO SWITCHING EQUIPMENT	DIFFICULT FOR DISPERSED TERMINALS AND HOSTS	EASY FOR TERMINALS LOCATED NEAR TELEPHONE WIRES; DIFFICULT FOR HOST	EASY; CONNECT TERMINALS TO LOCAL HOST AND ATTACH HOST TO NETWORK	EASY; ATTACH SERVER UNIT ON NETWORK AND CONNECT LOCAL RS-232-C DEVICES TO SERVER
CONNECTIVITY OF SWITCHING EQUIPMENT	GENERALLY FULL CONNECTIVITY, THOUGH SOME EQUIPMENT DOES NOT PROVIDE TERMINAL-TO-TERMINAL AND HOST-TO-HOST CONNECTIONS	FULL CONNECTIVITY	TERMINAL ACCESS LIMITED TO DEVICES SUPPORTED BY THE NETWORK SOFTWARE PACKAGE. NO DEVICE-TO-DEVICE COMMUNICATIONS	FULL CONNECTIVITY
SWITCHING TECHNIQUE	GENERALLY TDM CIRCUIT SWITCHING. DEVICE PARAMETERS MUST BE IDENTICAL ON EACH END OF THE CIRCUIT CONNECTION	TDM CIRCUIT SWITCHING. DEVICE PARAMETERS MUST BE IDENTICAL ON EACH END OF THE CIRCUIT CONNECTION	PACKET SWITCHING	PACKET SWITCHING
SWITCH PERFORMANCE	NO DELAY. USE OF HIGH DATA RATES CAN ADVERSELY AFFECT SWITCHING CAPACITY	NO DELAY. USE OF HIGH DATA RATES CAN ADVERSELY AFFECT SWITCH CAPACITY	GENERALLY, THE DELAY IS IMPERCEPTIBLE UNLESS EITHER HOST BECOMES HEAVILY LOADED. FLOW CONTROL IS PERFORMED FOR ATTACHED DEVICES MAKING BLOCK-MODE TRANSFERS	END-TO-END DELAY IS IMPERCEPTIBLE TO THE INTERACTIVE TERMINAL USER. FLOW CONTROL IS PERFORMED FOR A HIGH-SPEED DEVICE COMMUNICATING WITH A LOWER-SPEED DEVICE
USER MAINTAINABILITY	YES, WITH TRAINING. RANGES FROM DIAGNOSTICS TO BOARD-LEVEL REPLACEMENT. A SET OF SPARE BOARDS IS REQUIRED	NO. MAINTAINED ONLY BY VENDOR	YES, WITH TRAINING. RANGES FROM DIAGNOSTICS TO BOARD-LEVEL REPLACEMENT. A SET OF SPARE BOARDS IS REQUIRED	YES, SOME TRAINING IS REQUIRED. RANGES FROM DIAGNOSTICS TO LOW-COST UNIT REPLACEMENT. ONE SPARE UNIT IS REQUIRED
COST PER CONNECTION	$200 to $300 PER LINE ON EQUIPMENT WITH RELIABILITY OPTIONS AND OPERATION TO 9.6 KBIT/S	$750 to $1,000 PER LINE	$2,000 to $5,000 PER HOST	$300 TO $400 PER LINE

three major disadvantages:

■ Digital PBXs are not as economical for data switching. If users already have an adequate PBX telephone service, purchasing a digital PBX for the additional task of data switching is difficult to justify financially. Even if a new voice PBX installation is in order, the data options of the voice/data digital PBX currently cost two to three times that of a terminal server installation.

■ Like the port selector, few digital PBXs contain (at this time) any intelligence for handling incompatibilities between sending and receiving data devices. The digital PBX simply performs a circuit-switching function and leaves device compatibility concerns to the user.

■ Contrary to popular belief, digital PBXs do not necessarily eliminate local network wiring problems just because the phone lines are already in place. In many instances, an additional wire pair is needed to implement the digital PBX. Although some wiring can be eliminated by handling voice and data simultaneously, considerable obstacles remain to connecting data-only devices in a distributed network architecture. As people and equipment are added to or moved around in an organization, the cost of rewiring the PBX must be considered.

Host-to-host

There is considerable activity underway in the area of networking standalone host computers. In addition to remote-file-access and electonic-mail software pack-

ages, host-to-host remote terminal access (RTA) capabilities are now becoming available. RTA provides the terminal user with the ability to interact with any computer on the network that runs the same network software package. Because RTA is usually a component of a more complete networking software package that also has host-to-host file transfer and electronic mail, it can be an economical way to obtain distributed RS-232-C terminal-to-host data switching.

Nevertheless, compared with the terminal server, RTA has considerable limitations:

■ RTA is generally restricted to local-terminal-to-remote-application connectivity. No device-to-device connection is supported. More important, RTA only works between computers running the same network software package, often written for one specific computer. Support for other hosts and terminals is generally not possible.

■ RTA, like the terminal server, uses packet switching to establish virtual-circuit connections. Because RTA is generally implemented on a multitasking, multiuser host, periods of heavy loading can introduce annoying delays in the reception of character echoes from the remote application. For the same reason, block-mode transmissions from an attached intelligent device, such as a microcomputer, may be heavily flow-controlled by the local and remote hosts, resulting in substantial loss in device-to-remote-application communications bandwidth. ■

Michael W. Cerruti and Maurice Voce, Intel Corp., Phoenix, Ariz.

Zap data where it really counts— Direct-to-host connections

Attaching directly to a mainframe channel, bypassing the front-end, can pay off for high-speed links to LANs, or to other mainframes.

Throughput

Connectivity used to mean mainly the interconnection of terminals and host processors. Now, of course, it has evolved into a much grander issue, encompassing not only terminal applications, but also the need to connect diverse islands of automation—consisting of microcomputers, minicomputers, and mainframes, plus various network topologies and a wide range of peripherals.

For increasing numbers of users, a key component of this broad connectivity challenge is making a connection to a mainframe, such as an IBM System/370. The host connection not only opens extensive databases to authorized users, but also provides access to the programs resident in the mainframe. Host access also lets users exploit the mainframe's considerable processing power for performing data-intensive tasks.

In addition, a mainframe connection allows multiple network workstations to simultaneously run the same complex application program resident on a mainframe, and to accomplish tasks cooperatively with it.

For example, to make reservations and seat assignments for individual airline flights, travel agents can use workstations in their offices in cooperation with a remote airline mainframe. After logging onto the network, the agent identifies the customer's flight number, then sends the necessary data to the remote mainframe for processing (Fig. 1).

The mainframe in turn provides information to the agent regarding the type of craft involved and kinds of seats available. Based on that information, the agent can readily book reservations, enter and check locally maintained accounting data, and then return the selection information to the central mainframe where it can be stored and then retrieved by the airline for its use.

This type of cooperative interaction, here between an airline mainframe and processors at travel agencies, is becoming increasingly common. Among the benefits offered, one is to relieve the central mainframe of performing the entire processing task itself—and thus avoid becoming overloaded—while travel agents can be provided with locally maintained data required to run their business. Further, with this cooperative interaction, the various workstations share in accomplishing work efficiently—usually within a more reasonable time frame than is possible if the mainframe did the entire job.

Connectivity crisis

Whatever the application, the need to boost organizational productivity by pooling resources and distributing information effectively between users and the mainframe is becoming an important part of the overall connectivity picture. But at the same time that users are recognizing the potential of the mainframe connection—or perhaps because of this recognition—a phenomenon that some observers have termed a "connectivity crisis" is occurring in many networks.

Many users purchased their computers believing that they would connect easily with mainframes and other processors; others selected their equipment without giving the issue of mainframe connectivity any consideration. The crisis is felt when users realize that they were not sold "instant" connectivity when they invested in their computing devices. Further, when users realize that traditional methods for connecting diverse tools to the mainframe are not always as easy or as efficient as anticipated, the crisis deepens.

The mainframe connection has been traditionally accomplished by linking to a mainframe or I/O (input/output) channel through telecommunications solutions. (As used here, telecommunications refers to remote access.) Principally, these links have been used to connect terminals, remote peripherals, and remote mainframes to the central

1. Cooperative processing. *A mainframe connection allows multiple network workstations to run the same complex application programs resident on the mainframe.*

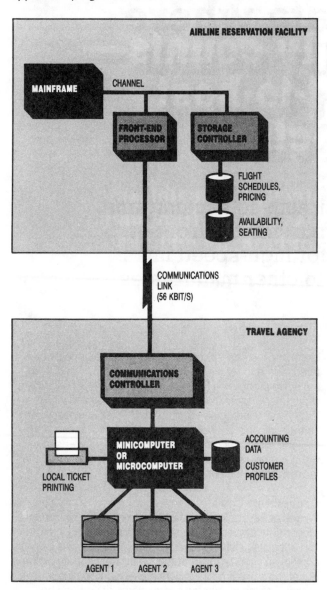

devices, instead of an inflexible center around which all other tools must be configured with comparatively greater effort or difficulty.

As Figure 2 shows, telecommunications solutions use terminal emulation hardware and software and associated communications processors to connect to the mainframe. Generally, they are limited to maximum data transfer rates of 56 kbit/s. This rate is inadequate to sustain acceptable interactive response times (the goal is no more than three seconds) on networks supporting hundreds of users or applications that involve the transfer of large amounts of information in real time.

The bottleneck
The problem with telecommunications solutions is that they require 12 to 13 minutes, on average (in the case of a 56-kbit/s digital facility), to move a 1-Mbyte file between mainframe and microcomputer on a network. Although higher transmission speeds such as T1 are available, they are still limited to transferring data in terminal mode, which limits the transfer block size.

Such high data transmission speeds saturate the processing bandwidth of the front-end communications con-

2. Old solutions. *Telecommunications uses terminal-emulation hardware and software and associated communications processors to connect to the mainframe.*

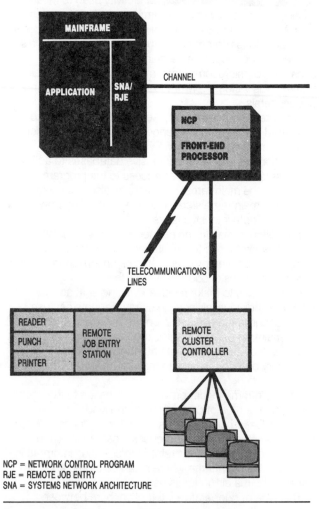

NCP = NETWORK CONTROL PROGRAM
RJE = REMOTE JOB ENTRY
SNA = SYSTEMS NETWORK ARCHITECTURE

mainframe. In such applications, telecommunications connections allow remote users to move screen images of data interactively. File transfers, however, are handled somewhat less efficiently. Addressing these non-time-critical data transfers with the traditional telecommunications link has nevertheless been quite successful.

Telecommunications connections are optimized for terminal-oriented messages. In today's computing environment, however, a broader orientation is needed if diverse computer networks and peripherals are to be connected in a more symmetrical peer-to-peer relationship with the user's mainframe.

The connection must also be broad enough in scope to support different sizes of data, satisfying diverse users with differing data transfer requirements. In addition, the connection should be easy enough to implement so that the mainframe becomes an accessible server for the various

3. Connectivity needs. *A chemical company's accounting department transfers to the mainframe via a cluster controller. The processing plant connects via LANs.*

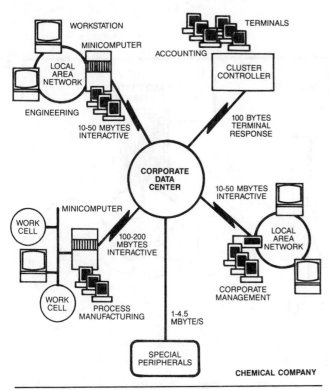

works, terminals, and other computing devices. In this way, the group can perform real-time processing tasks, access applications on the mainframe, and share data with other groups in the company. This user group represents medium-sized data exchanges of 100- to 200-kbyte blocks.

The company's engineering organization connects to the mainframe chiefly via other computers such as departmental minicomputers used for local data "crunching." The engineering group relies on the mainframe for the temporary or permanent storage of data that later can be extracted for further analysis. The transferred blocks of data can be as large as 50 Mbytes and require data transfers approximating local disk-transfer rates (250 kbyte to 1 Mbyte per second; for these comparisons, one byte equals 8 to 10 bits).

In our scenario, a fourth group, the corporate management team, connects via local area network attachments to the corporate mainframe so that the group can tap into its shared databases and programs. These users, like those of the engineering staff, require the equivalent of disk-transfer rates for large amounts of data: 50 or more Mbytes at a time.

Yet with a telecommunications link to the mainframe, all four groups, which represent very different sets of expectations, connections, and distances from the mainframe, must rely on the same connectivity performance characteristics.

Ultimately, because a telecommunications link favors terminal-type connections, the result is that data transmission can be slowed down to an unacceptable level when bulk file transfers or time-critical batch transmissions are required. Thus this link is likely to fail to efficiently meet the mixed demands of the different user groups in the chemical plant scenario—and in organizations with a similar dichotomy of local communications and mainframe-access configurations.

Reconsidering the problem

It is clear that connectivity is not just a matter of installing cable—it involves much more than fitting a computing tool or new user into a wiring scheme. Instead, connectivity must, by definition, also include the capability of connecting diverse applications with varying data transfer requirements to a range of mainframes. It must also provide organizations with a "comfortable," user-oriented way of interacting with the mainframe.

What has been lacking is a connectivity approach removing the mainframe from its position at the center of the network universe, making the mainframe an accessible server, and featuring direct attachment to the mainframe by varied user communities at channel speeds (3 Mbyte/s maximum).

Connecting to the mainframe means opening the machine's architecture so that the mainframe becomes a productive, integral part of the user's world, not a monolith around which everything else must be designed and configured. What is needed to realize such a connectivity scenario is a bidirectional bridge directly between the IBM mainframe and diverse users that can be incorporated into existing architectures in order to protect the user's investment in already-installed devices. Replacement costs are thus avoided.

troller, thereby greatly increasing the cost of the connection. As a result, users face a bottleneck that can hamper throughput and, subsequently, productivity. Moreover, the mainframe link must be able to accommodate ever higher transmission speeds such as 100 Mbit/s supported on new fiber-based LANs (local area networks).

Chemistry lesson

To understand the demands placed upon a mainframe link by users with different types of mainframe attachments and varying data transfer requirements, consider a typical chemical company (Fig. 3).

The accounting department is one of the company's major data users. The department is in the same building as the mainframe, but beyond the maximum allowable distance for local attached devices. The department connects to the corporate mainframe primarily by terminals and remote peripherals, and it shares data and applications running on the mainframe.

Accounting, in a transaction mode, typically sends small data blocks (2 kbytes) to the mainframe. It uses standard telecommunications links, such as synchronous data link control over leased lines, for such small data transfers, and its users find this transmission method adequate. When the department has to transfer larger data blocks, however, accounting finds transmission considerably slower (the previously mentioned 12 to 13 minutes per megabyte). Such batch transmissions are typically performed during off-peak hours.

A second company group, those in the processing plant, connect to the corporate mainframe via local area net-

4. Meeting the needs. *Shown is a mainframe computer with an open-architecture channel adapter attached directly to a mainframe channel, operating at channel speed. It al-* *lows the user to readily connect multiple devices through standard protocols, such as IEEE 796, without changing software at the application level.*

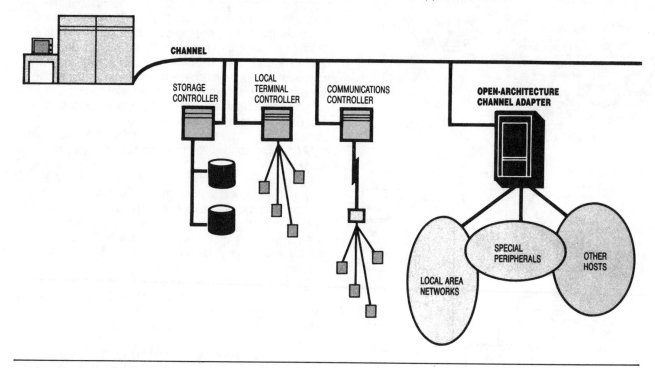

Recognizing the growing need to make the mainframe easier to access as a node on a network, IBM now offers built-in connectivity on its new 9370 computers. The 9370's integrated communications controllers enhance local area network-to-mainframe connectivity by opening the latest IBM mainframe architecture to a broad range of users. Architecturally speaking, that was accomplished by enabling the built-in controllers to interface directly to local area networks and to other computers, without having to go through front-end processors. But these built-in connectivity devices are not available for the entire family of IBM computers. Therefore, they do not meet the connectivity challenges posed by "closed" System/370-type mainframe architectures.

Another product that has attempted to address System/370-type connectivity is the multisource channel adapter, a device that provides a pathway for connecting to the mainframe various computing tools, such as local area networks and high-speed peripherals. Until recently, however, most channel adapters have been designed with proprietary interfaces. That has restricted users to connecting only those products offered by the channel-adapter vendor, thus severely limiting user choice of those computing tools. In addition, most of the adapters have been special-purpose connectivity products capable of handling only one type of connection, and have not supported general attachment for multiple devices.

A nonproprietary open-architecture channel adapter can bring less limiting solutions to users and serve as a connectivity "platform." It can go beyond the terminal orientation of telecommunications links. Shown in Figure 4 is an open-architecture channel adapter, which is an interface device that attaches directly to the mainframe

channel at channel speed. It allows the user to readily connect multiple applications through standard protocols, such as IEEE 796, without changing software at the application level.

Channel-attached connectivity devices act as high-speed (3-Mbyte/s) interfaces between various types of IBM-compatible mainframes and local area networks, minicomputers, other mainframes, microcomputers, and specialized peripherals such as optical disks. Such connectivity allows original equipment manufacturers (OEMs) to customize their applications by using programmable interfaces.

Enhancing performance

Channel-attached connectivity opens an IBM mainframe to a wide array of non-IBM devices, networks, and computers. This would be similar to IBM—in a departure from its tradition—"going public" with the bus architecture of its comparatively low-cost microcomputer so that vendors could build applications for a variety of environments (such as LANs and archiving tapes) by using add-in printed-circuit boards.

An immediate benefit of the open-architecture channel adapter application is that peripheral manufacturers who wish to supply products for the mainframe are spared the expense of developing connectivity technology and can focus on product development.

The adapters can also connect mainframes to minicomputers, such as the DEC (Digital Equipment Corp.) VAX, so that VAX users can exploit the resources of both computers. The adapters also allow users to connect various LAN topologies to the mainframe.

The adapter allows multiple connections through a

single channel attachment, minimizing the number of channel attachments. And it handles combinations of applications concurrently, so that disparate elements—such as LANs, optical disks, and minicomputers—can share the mainframe economically. The ability to connect diverse applications concurrently lets users multiplex the bandwidth of the channel for slower devices. Adapters that provide a buffer for data flowing at channel speeds to slower applications offer an effective way to enhance channel throughput. The open-architecture channel adapter allows users to define their application priorities by user or message type—that is especially important when multiple applications coexist in a single adapter.

When evaluating potential adapter vendors, users should be on the lookout for vendor-sponsored development

---

Connectivity guidelines

Some general connectivity rules for effecting a high-speed direct-to-mainframe link apply to a number of different applications and to evolving technological changes:

1. The channel adapter should support industry standards such as those adopted by the International Organization for Standardization (ISO) and the IEEE. Examples: the Open Systems Interconnection (OSI) model and token ring and Ethernet networks.

2. Tools for network management should be provided.

3. An important feature to consider is the ability to support multiple device types so that the channel adapter looks to be whatever the mainframe deems is appropriate for the type of function being connected. This avoids the expense and performance inefficiency of multiple layers of protocol conversion software on the mainframe.

4. Look for a channel adapter that can be readily configured with a wide range of adapter boards to support standard applications. This will reduce development time in obtaining specific application solutions. It also enables a simple connectivity to support a number of different connections, such as to a Digital Equipment VAX minicomputer, an Ethernet or token ring LAN, a Manufacturing Automation Protocol application, or an ASCII terminal. These multiple mainframe-connectivity applications could also be run simultaneously.

5. Where there is a time-critical element to the data flow, such as in engineering and scientific environments, look for a high-speed interface of at least 3-Mbyte/s transmission in a data streaming mode (not limiting transmission to a predetermined amount).

6. Choose a vendor carefully, because the vendor's experience, technical knowledge, service, and support are key to the connectivity's success. Pick a vendor whose record shows long-term reliability. Look for a vendor who can help develop and test applications, perhaps by providing a development laboratory. And not least, make sure the vendor can provide training and field support for the entire connection, including the application.

---

facilities. Where such resources exist, users have access to technically knowledgeable personnel who can help with testing implementations, providing important assistance with application development.

Another vendor-evaluation criterion is vendor experience in providing mainframe-related products and support. The vendor's commitment to ongoing research and development, and its long-term viability, are more obvious points for consideration (see "Connectivity guidelines").

Besides standard connections, the open-architecture channel adapter is designed to deliver tools and methodologies for those users requiring customized applications. The tools include libraries of application routines and development environments that allow simulation of a final configuration during the implementation cycle. Methodologies include protocols that make tasks easier to perform, such as a disciplined methodology for interfacing to the adapter's control unit.

Evolving expectations

The open-architecture channel adapter enables a user to connect several applications concurrently—an efficient approach—which makes the mainframe accessible to many different users and applications. That technology is based on industry standards such as IBM's OEM interface or Federal Information Processing Standard 60.

Attaching to megabyte-per-second channels becomes even more critical as channel speeds steadily increase. Amdahl has already announced a 4.5-Mbyte/s channel. And there is speculation that IBM will move into fiber optics, which should drive channel rates even higher—to at least 12 Mbyte/s.

The speed associated with local area network technology is also on the rise. Standard LAN technology currently offers 1.25 Mbyte/s (the equivalent of 10 Mbit/s) capability. Thus the 3-Mbyte/s data-transfer rate offered by channel-attached adapters is more than adequate for most LAN applications.

However, as LAN speeds increase further, the bottleneck will be moved back to the channel. Users must assure themselves that the connectivity interface between the LAN and the mainframe is adaptable enough to accommodate improved performance on both sides in a constant evolutionary game of catch-up.

The emergence of new peripheral devices requiring connection to the mainframe will also continue. The adapter's channel-speed performance will be a boon for interfacing between the mainframe and advanced devices treated as peripherals, such as aircraft simulators, optical disks, and CAD/CAM (computer-aided design/computer-aided manufacturing) workstations. ■

Mike Cerruti is strategic marketing manager for Intel's System Interconnect Operation. He has worked with mainframe software and channel connect technology for the past 15 years. Maurice Voce is product marketing manager for Intel's System Interconnect Operation. He has had more than seven years' system engineering and marketing experience ranging from mainframes to personal computers and networks. Voce holds a B.S. in mathematics and computer science from UCLA.

Section 6: Performance

6.1 Overview

This section looks at the performance of packet-switched local networks. The performance of a LAN or an HSLN depends on a number of key factors, the most important of which are as follows: (1) Network characteristics, which include propagation delay between devices and data rate of the transmission medium, (2) medium access control protocol, and (3) load (traffic) on the network.

The objectives of this section are to report some results from comparative analysis, to provide guidance in assessing overall network performance, and to give the reader a feel for the complexity of the problem.

6.2 Article Summary

The first article, ''Local Network Performance,'' demonstrates that two basic characteristics of a local network,

propagation delay and data rate, set an upper bound on performance independent of the medium access control protocol. The article then develops simple performance models for CSMA/CD, token bus, and token ring.

The next article, by Bux, is a description (rather than analytic) report on the delay characteristics of token bus, token ring, and CSMA/CD. The article also examines the end-to-end performance of a file server and timing problems in local network access units. Next, Sastry also examines the performance of token bus, token ring, and CSMA/CD, with the emphasis on throughput rather than delay.

The final article, by Mitchell, looks at the important (to the user) issue of end-to-end performance.

307

I n recent years, there has been a proliferation of local network products and an intensification of local network R&D activity. Nevertheless, the vast majority of systems conforms to one of two topologies and one of a handful of medium-access control protocols:[1]

- Bus Topology
  ..CSMA/CD
  ..Token Bus
- Ring Topology
  ..Token Ring
  ..Slotted Ring
  ..Register Insertion

Because the number of truly different local network configurations is manageably small, a comparative analysis of local network performance is possible.

The question of performance is of concern in the design or selection of a local network for a specific application. Given a certain collection of devices, with certain traffic characteristics, a fundamental requirement is that the local network has adequate capacity for the expected load. Table I, based on studies by the IEEE 802 Local Network Standards Committee, indicates the type of load that may be offered to a local network by various devices. We would like the local network to be able to sustain a throughput that keeps up with the load, and does so without undue delays.

This paper aims to show which factors are significant in determining local network performance and to summarize recent comparative studies. The first section below shows that two basic characteristics of a local network, propagation delay and data rate, set an upper bound on performance independent of the medium-access control protocol. Next, some simple models are developed for comparing three protocols: CSMA/CD, token bus, and token ring. These are protocols for which standards have been developed [2], and it is likely that most local network products will use a variant of one of them. Finally, some comparative studies are summarized. The results cover CSMA/CD, token bus, and token ring, as well as two other ring protocols — slotted ring and register insertion.

The Effect of Propagation Delay and Transmission Rate

In analyzing local network performance, the two most useful parameters are the data rate (R) of the medium, and the average signal propagation delay (D) between stations on the network. The propagation delay reflects the length of the medium and, in the case of the ring, the number of repeaters and their delay characteristics. In fact, it is the product of these two terms, $R \times D$, that is the single most important parameter for determining the

---

[1]For the unacquainted reader, these topologies and protocols are defined briefly in an appendix; further details can be found in Stallings [1].

Reprinted from *IEEE Communications Magazine*, Volume 22, Number 2, February 1984, pages 27-36. Copyright © 1984 by The Institute of Electrical and Electronics Engineers, Inc.

Local Network Performance

William Stallings

Significant factors in determining local network performance based on recent studies

February 1984—Vol. 22, No. 2
IEEE Communications Magazine

TABLE I*
Workload Generated from Each Source Type

Type of Source	Peak Data Rate (kb/s)	Duty Factor (%)
Heat/Vent/Air Conditioning/Alarm/Security	0.1	100
Line Printer	19.2	50–90
File Server/Block Transfer	20 000	0.1
File Server/File Transfer	100	10–30
Mail Server	100	30–50
Information Server/Calendar	9.6	1.5
Information Server/Decision Support	56	20–40
Word Processor	9.6	1–5
Data Entry Terminal	9.6	0.1–1.0
Data Enquiry Terminal	64	10–30
Program Development	9.6	5–20
Laser Printer	256	20–50
Facsimile	9.6	5–20
Voice/Immediate	64	20–40
Voice/Store and Forward	32	30–50
Video/Noncompressed	30 000	50–90
Video/Freeze Frame	64	50–90
Video/Compressed	400	20–40
Graphics/Noncompressed	256	1–10
Graphics/Compressed	64	10–30
Optical Character Reader	2.4	50–90
Gateway	1000	0.1–1.0
Host/0.5 MIPS	128	20–40
Host/5 MIPS	1000	20–30

*In Stallings [1].

performance of a local network. Other things being equal, a network's performance will be the same, for example, for both a 50-Mb/s, 1-km bus and a 10-Mb/s, 5-km bus. It will be seen that many widely-used metrics of LAN protocol performance, such as channel utilization and normalized service times, will remain constant if the $R \times D$ product is held constant.

Note that the data rate times the delay product is equal to the length of the transmission medium in bits, that is, the number of bits that may be in transit between two nodes at any snapshot in time. Several examples: assuming a velocity of propagation of 2×10^8 m/s, a 500-m Ethernet system (10 Mb/s) has a bit length of 25; both a 1-km HYPERchannel (50 Mb/s) and a typical 5-km broadband local network (5 Mb/s) run about 250 bits.

A useful way of viewing this is to consider the length of the medium as compared to the typical packet transmitted. This allows one to distinguish protocols geared for a local network from those designed for a multiprocessor backplane bus, which needs to accommodate a maximum of a few bits in transit; and from those for a satellite link, which should accommodate several entire packets in transit. Intuitively, it can be seen that this will make a difference. Compare local networks to multiprocessor computers. Relatively speaking, things happen almost simultaneously in a multiprocessor system; when one component begins to transmit, the others know it almost immediately. For local networks, the relative time gap leads to the need for

a complex medium-access control protocol. Compare local networks to satellite links. To have any hope of efficiency, the satellite link must allow multiple packets to be in transit simultaneously. This places specific requirements on the link layer protocol, which must deal with a sequence of outstanding packets waiting to be acknowledged. Local network protocols generally allow only one packet at a time to be in transit, or, at the most, a few for some ring protocols. Again, this affects the access protocol.

The length of the medium, expressed in bits, compared to the length of the typical packet is usually denoted by a:

$$a = \frac{\text{Length of Data Path in Bits}}{\text{Length of Packet}}$$

$$a = \frac{RD}{L}$$

where L is the length of the packet. But D is the propagation time on the medium (worst case), and L/R is the time it takes a transmitter to get an entire packet out onto the medium. So,

$$a = \frac{\text{Propagation Time}}{\text{Transmission Time}}$$

Typical values of a range from about 0.01 to 0.1. Table II gives some sample values for a bus topology. In computing a for ring networks, repeater delays must be included in propagation time.

The parameter a determines an upper bound on the utilization of a local network. Consider a perfectly efficient access mechanism that allows only one transmission at a time. As soon as one transmission is over, another node begins transmitting. Furthermore, the transmission is pure data — no overhead bits. What is the maximum possible utilization of the network? It can be expressed as the ratio of total throughput of the system to the capacity or bandwidth:

TABLE II
Values of a

Data Rate	Packet Size	Cable Length	a
1 Mb/s	100 bits	1 km	0.05
1 Mb/s	1000 bits	10 km	0.05
1 Mb/s	100 bits	10 km	0.5
10 Mb/s	100 bits	1 km	0.5
10 Mb/s	1000 bits	1 km	0.05
10 Mb/s	1000 bits	10 km	0.5
10 Mb/s	10 000 bits	10 km	0.05
50 Mb/s	10 000 bits	1 km	0.025
50 Mb/s	100 bits	1 km	2.5

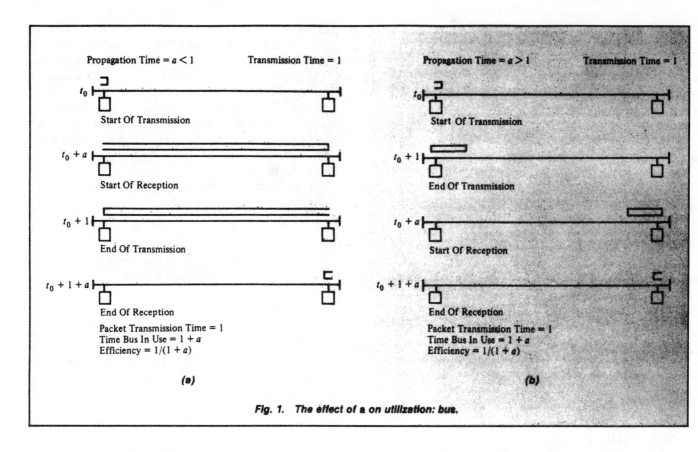

Fig. 1.   The effect of a on utilization: bus.

$U = \text{Throughput}/R$

$= \dfrac{L/(\text{Propagation} + \text{Transmission Time})}{R}$

$= \dfrac{L/(D + L/R)}{R}$

$= \dfrac{1}{1+a}$ (1)

So, utilization varies inversely with a. This can be grasped intuitively by studying Fig. 1; this shows a baseband bus with two stations as far apart as possible (worst case) that take turns sending packets. If we normalize the packet transmission time to equal one, then the sequence of events can be expressed as follows.

1) A station begins transmission at t_0
2) Reception begins at $t_0 + a$
3) Transmission is completed at $t_0 + 1$
4) Reception ends at $t_0 + 1 + a$
5) The other station begins transmitting

Event 2 occurs *after* event 3 if $a > 1.0$. In any case, the total time for one "turn" is $1 + a$, but the transmission time is only 1, for a utilization of $1/(1 + a)$.

The same effect can be seen to apply to a ring network in Fig. 2. Here we assume that one station transmits and then waits to receive its own transmission before any other station transmits. The identical sequence of events outlined above applies.

The implication of (1) for performance is shown in Fig. 3. The axes of the plot are:

- S, the throughput or total rate of data being transmitted on the medium, normalized to the bandwidth of the medium.
- G, the offered load to the local network; the total rate of data presented for transmission, also normalized.

The ideal case is $a = 0$, which allows 100% utilization. It can be seen that, as offered load increases, throughput remains equal to offered load up to the full capacity of the system $(S = G = 1)$ and then remains at $S = 1$. At any positive value of a, the system saturates at $S = 1/(1+a)$.

So we can say that an upper bound on utilization or efficiency is $1/(1 + a)$, regardless of the medium-access protocol used. Two caveats: First, this assumes that the maximum propagation time is incurred on each transmis:...,. Second, it assumes that only one transmission may occur at a time. These assumptions are not always true; nevertheless, the formula $1/(1 + a)$ is almost always a valid upper bound, because the overhead of the medium access protocol more than makes up for the lack of validity of these assumptions.

The overhead is unavoidable. Packets must include address and synchronization bits. There is administrative overhead for controlling the protocol. In addition, there are forms of overhead peculiar to one or more of the protocols. We highlight these briefly:

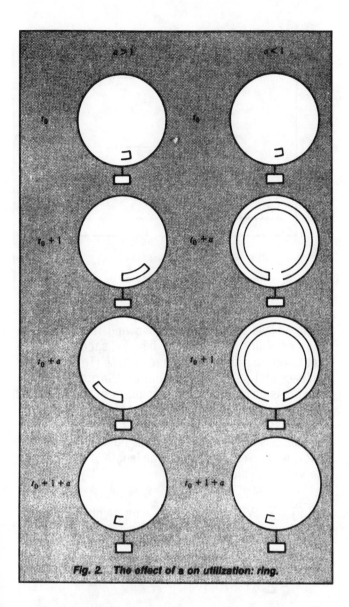

Fig. 2. The effect of a on utilization: ring.

- CSMA/CD — Time wasted due to collisions; need for acknowledgment packets.[2]
- Token bus — Token transmission; acknowledgment packets.
- Token ring — Time waiting for token if intervening stations have no data to send.
- Slotted ring — Time waiting for empty slot if intervening stations have no data to send.
- Register insertion — Delay at each node of time equal to address length; from the point of view of a single station, the propagation time, and hence a, may increase due to insertion of registers on the ring.

There are two distinct effects here. One is that the efficiency or utilization of a channel decreases as a increases. This, of course, affects throughput. The other

---

[2]Strictly speaking, acknowledgments are not part of the access protocol but of a higher-level link protocol. However, the ring protocols under discussion allow for acknowledgment by having the sender remove its own packet from the ring. Thus this overhead is avoided.

effect is that the overhead attributable to a protocol wastes bandwidth and hence reduces effective utilization and effective throughput. For the most part, we can think of these two effects as independent and additive. However, we shall see that, for CSMA/CD, there is a strong interaction such that the overhead of the protocol increases as a function of a.

In any case, it would seem desirable to keep a as low as possible. Referring back to the defining formula, for a fixed network, a can be reduced by increasing packet size. This will only be useful if the length of messages produced by a station is an integral multiple of the packet size (excluding overhead bits). Otherwise, the large packet size is itself a source of waste. Furthermore, a large packet size increases the delay for other stations. Of course, variable-length packets may be used; in that case, performance tends to reflect average packet length [3].

Simple Performance Models of Token-Passing and CSMA/CD

In this section, we will give some insight into the relative performance of the most important LAN protocols — CSMA/CD, token bus, and token ring — by developing two simple performance models. It is hoped this will aid in understanding the results of more rigorous analyses to be presented later.

For these models, we assume a local network with N active stations, and a maximum normalized propagation delay of a. To simplify the analysis, we assume that each station is always prepared to transmit a packet. This allows us to develop an expression for maximum achievable throughput (S). While this should not be construed as the sole figure of merit for a local network, it is the single most analyzed one, and does permit useful performance comparisons.

First, let us consider token ring. Time on the ring will alternate between data packet transmission and token passing. Refer to a single instance of a data packet followed by a token as a cycle and define:

C = average time for one cycle
T_1 = average time to transmit a data packet
T_2 = average time to pass a token.

It should be clear that the average cycle rate is just $1/C = 1/(T_1 + T_2)$. Intuitively,

$$S = \frac{T_1}{T_1 + T_2} \qquad (2)$$

That is, the throughput, normalized to system capacity, is just the fraction of time that is spent transmitting data.

Refer now to Fig. 2; time is normalized such that packet transmission time equals 1 and propagation time equals a. For the case of $a < 1$, a station transmits a packet at time t_0, receives the leading edge of its own packet at $t_0 + a$, and completes transmission at $t_0 + 1$. The station then emits a token, which takes an average time

a/N to reach the next station. Thus, one cycle takes $1 + a/N$ and the transmission time is 1. So, $S = 1/(1 + a/N)$.

For $a > 1$, the reasoning is slightly different. A station transmits at t_0, completes transmission at $t_0 + 1$, and receives the leading edge of its frame at $t_0 + a$. At that point, it is free to emit a token, which takes an average time a/N to reach the next station.[3] The cycle time is therefore $a + a/N$ and $S = 1/(a(1 + 1/N))$. Summarizing,

$$\text{Token } S = \begin{cases} \dfrac{1}{1 + a/N} & a < 1 \\[2ex] \dfrac{1}{a(1 + 1/N)} & a > 1 \end{cases} \tag{3}$$

The above reasoning applies equally well to token bus where we assume that the logical ordering is the same as the physical ordering and that token-passing time is therefore a/N.

For CSMA/CD, we base our approach on a derivation in Metcalfe [4]. Consider time on the medium to be organized into slots whose length is twice the end-to-end propagation delay. This is a convenient way to view the activity on the medium; the slot time is the maximum time, from the start of transmission, required to detect a collision. Again, assume that there are N active stations. Clearly, if each station always has a packet to transmit, and does so, there will be nothing but collisions on the line. Therefore we assume that each station restrains itself to transmitting during an available slot with probability P.

Time on the medium consists of two types of intervals. First is a transmission interval, which lasts $1/2a$ slots. Second is a contention interval, which is a sequence of slots with either a collision or no transmission in each slot. The throughput is just the proportion of time spent in transmission intervals (similar to the reasoning for (2)).

To determine the average length of a contention interval, we begin by computing A, the probability that exactly one station attempts a transmission in a slot and therefore acquires the medium. This is just the binomial probability that any one station attempts to transmit and the others do not:

$$A = \binom{N}{1} P^1 (1 - P)^{N-1}$$
$$A = NP(1 - P)^{N-1}$$

This function takes on a maximum over P when $P = 1/N$:

$$A = (1 - 1/N)^{N-1}$$

Why are we interested in the maximum? Because we want to calculate the maximum throughput of the medium. It should be clear that this will be achieved if we maximize the probability of successful seizure of the

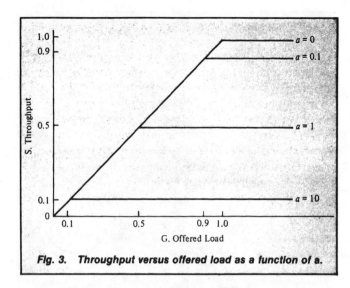

Fig. 3. Throughput versus offered load as a function of a.

medium. This says that the following rule should be enforced: During periods of heavy usage, a station should restrain its offered load to $1/N$. (This assumes that each station knows the value of N. In order to derive an expression for maximum possible throughput, we live with this assumption.) On the other hand, during periods of light usage, maximum utilization cannot be achieved because G is too low; this region is not of interest here.

Now we can estimate the mean length of a contention interval, w, in slots:

$$E[w] = \sum_{i=1}^{\infty} iPr[i \text{ slots in a row with a collision or no transmission followed by a slot with one transmission}]$$

$$= \sum_{i=1}^{\infty} i(1 - A)^i A$$

The summation converges to

$$E[w] = \frac{1 - A}{A}$$

We can now determine the maximum utilization, which is just the length of a transmission interval as a proportion of a cycle consisting of a transmission and a contention interval:

$$\text{CSMA/CD } S = \frac{\frac{1}{2}a}{\frac{1}{2}a + \dfrac{1 - A}{A}} = \frac{1}{1 + 2a\dfrac{1 - A}{A}} \tag{4}$$

Figure 4 shows normalized throughput as a function of a for various values of N and for both token-passing and CSMA/CD. For both protocols, throughput declines as a increases. This is to be expected; but the dramatic difference between the two protocols is seen in Fig. 5, which shows throughput as a function of N. Token-passing performance actually improves as a function of N, because less time is spent in token-passing. Conversely, the performance of CSMA/CD decreases be-

---

[3]The station could transmit at $t_0 + 1$ (tailgating). This is not allowed in the IEEE 802 Standard to simplify control.

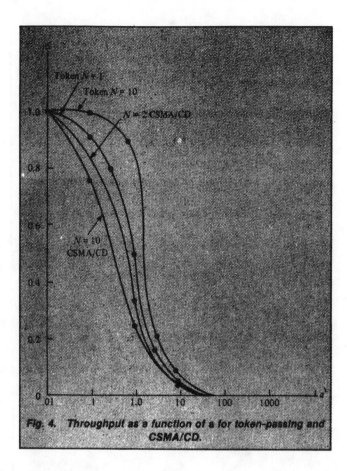

Fig. 4. *Throughput as a function of a for token-passing and CSMA/CD.*

cause of the increased likelihood of collision or no transmission.

It is interesting to note the asymptotic value of S as N increases. For token:

$$\text{Token} \quad \lim_{N \to \infty} S = \begin{cases} 1 & a < 1 \\ 1/a & a > 1 \end{cases} \quad (5)$$

For CSMA/CD, we need to know that $\lim_{N \to \infty} (1 - 1/N)^{N-1} = 1/e$. Then

$$\text{CSMA/CD} \quad \lim_{N \to \infty} S = \frac{1}{1 + 3.44a} \quad (6)$$

Comparative Results from Analytic and Simulation Models

Although there have been a number of performance studies focusing on a single protocol, there have been few systematic attempts to analyze the relative performance of the various local network protocols. In what follows, we look at the results of several carefully-done studies that have produced comparative results.

CSMA/CD, Token Bus, and Token Ring

The first study was done by a group at Bell Labs, under the sponsorship of the IEEE 802 Local Network Standards Committee [5]. Naturally enough, the study analyzed the three protocols being standardized by IEEE 802: CSMA/CD, token bus, and token ring. The analysis is based on considering not only mean values but second

moments of delay and message length. Two cases of message arrival statistics are employed. In the first, only one station out of one hundred has messages to transmit, and is always ready to transmit. In such a case, one would hope that the network would not be the bottleneck, but could easily keep up with one station. In the second case, 100 stations out of 100 always have messages to transmit. This represents an extreme of congestion and one would expect that the network may be a bottleneck. In the two cases, the one station or one hundred stations provide enough input to fully utilize the network. Hence, the results are a measure of maximum potential utilization.

The results are shown in Fig. 6. It shows the actual data transmission rate versus the transmission speed of the medium for the two cases and two packet sizes. Note that the abscissa is not offered load but the actual capacity of the medium. Three systems are examined: token ring with a one-bit latency per station, token bus, and CSMA/CD. The analysis yields the following conclusions:

- For the given parameters, the smaller the mean packet length, the greater the difference in maximum mean throughput rate between token-passing and CSMA/CD. This reflects the strong dependence of CSMA/CD on a.
- Token ring is the least sensitive to workload.
- CSMA/CD offers the shortest delay under light load, while it is most sensitive under heavy load to the workload.

Note also that in the case of a single station transmitting, token bus is significantly less efficient

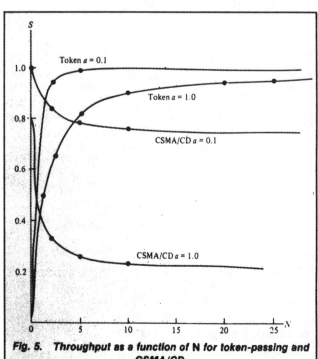

Fig. 5. *Throughput as a function of N for token-passing and CSMA/CD.*

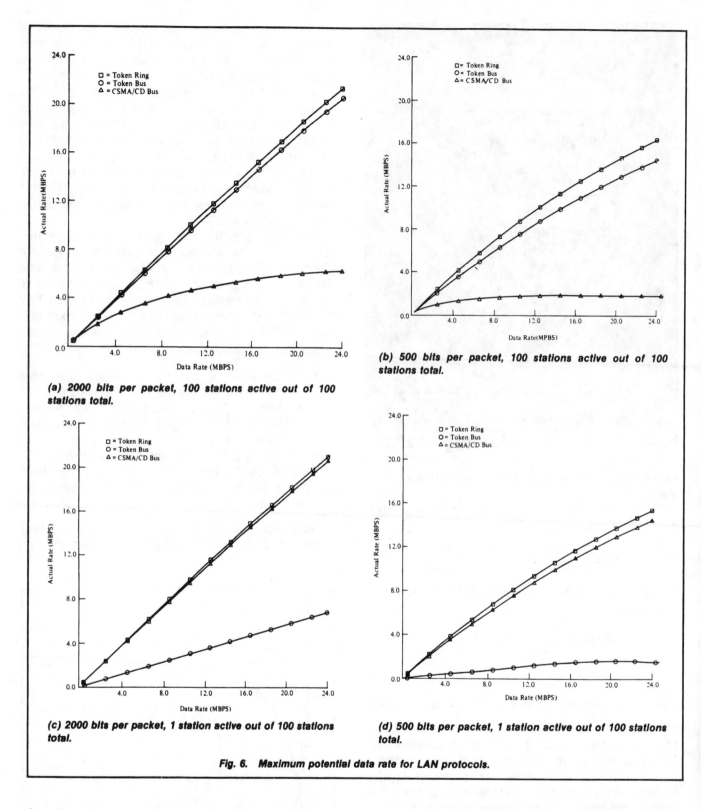

(a) *2000 bits per packet, 100 stations active out of 100 stations total.*

(b) *500 bits per packet, 100 stations active out of 100 stations total.*

(c) *2000 bits per packet, 1 station active out of 100 stations total.*

(d) *500 bits per packet, 1 station active out of 100 stations total.*

Fig. 6. *Maximum potential data rate for LAN protocols.*

than the other two protocols. This is so because the assumption is made that token-passing time equals the propagation delay, and that the delay in token processing is greater than for token ring.

Another phenomenon of interest is seen most clearly in Fig. 6(b). For a CSMA/CD system under these conditions, the maximum effective throughput at 5 Mb/s is only about 1.25 Mb/s. If expected load is, say, 0.75 Mb/s, this configuration may be perfectly adequate. If,

however, the load is expected to grow to 2 Mb/s, raising the network data rate to 10 Mb/s or even 20 Mb/s will not accommodate the increase. The same conclusion, less precisely, can be drawn from the simple model presented earlier.

The reason for this disparity between CSMA/CD and token-passing (bus or ring) under heavy load has to do with the instability of CSMA/CD. As offered load increases, so does throughput until, beyond its maxi-

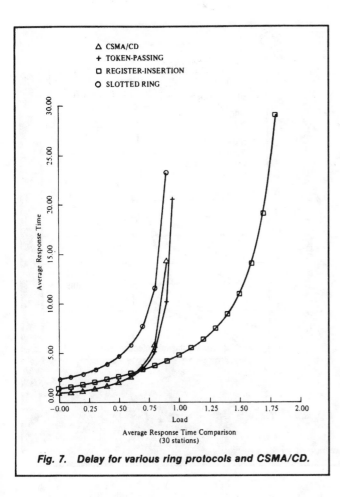

Fig. 7. Delay for various ring protocols and CSMA/CD.

(Legend in figure)
△ CSMA/CD
+ TOKEN-PASSING
□ REGISTER-INSERTION
○ SLOTTED RING

Average Response Time
Load
Average Response Time Comparison
(30 stations)

techniques, few have attempted pairwise comparisons, much less a three-way analysis. The most systematic work in this area has been done by Liu and his associates [6]. Liu made comparisons based on analytic models developed by others for token ring, slotted ring, and CSMA/CD, plus his own formulations for register insertion. He then obtained very good corroboration from simulation studies.

Figure 7 summarizes the results. They are based on the assumption that $a = 0.005$ and that register insertion ring packets are removed by the destination station, whereas slotted-ring and token-ring packets are removed by the source station. This is clearly an unfair comparison since register insertion, under this scheme, does not include acknowledgments, but token ring and slotted ring do. The figure does show that slotted ring is the poorest performer, and that register insertion can carry a load greater than 1.0. This is because the protocol permits multiple packets to circulate.

Bux [7] performed an analysis comparing token ring, slotted ring, and CSMA/CD. This careful analysis produced several important conclusions (see Fig. 8). First, the delay-throughput performance of token ring vs. CSMA/CD confirms our earlier discussion. That is, token ring suffers greater delay than CSMA/CD at light load but less delay and stable throughput at heavy loads. Further, token ring has superior delay characteristics to slotted ring. The poorer performance of slotted ring seems to have two causes: 1) the relative overhead in the small slots of a local-area ring is very high, and 2) the time needed to pass empty slots around the ring to guarantee fair bandwidth is significant. Bux also reports several positive features of slotted ring: 1) the expected delay for a message is proportional to length (that is, shorter packets get better service than long ones), and 2) overall mean delay is independent of packet length distribution type. Bux has recently extended his analysis to include register insertion [8], achieving results comparable to Liu's.

It is difficult to draw conclusions from the efforts made so far. The slotted ring seems to be the least desirable over a broad range of parameter values, owing to the considerable overhead associated with each small packet. For example, the Cambridge ring, which is the most widely commercially-available ring in Europe, uses a 37-bit slot with only 16 data bits!

As between token ring and register insertion, the evidence suggests that, at least for some sets of parameter values, register insertion gives superior delay performance. Interestingly, there seems to be no commercially-available register insertion product, with the exception of the IBM Series 1 loop, where performance is not an issue. On the other hand, token ring in the United States, with a boost from the IEEE 802 Standard and IBM, and slotted ring in Europe, where many firms have licensed the Cambridge slotted ring, seem destined to dominate the ring marketplace.

The primary advantage of register insertion is the

mum value, throughput actually declines as G increases. This is because there is an increased frequency of collisions: more packets are offered, but fewer successfully escape collision. Worse, this situation may persist even if the input to the system drops to zero. Consider: for high G, virtually all offered packets are retransmissions and virtually none get through. So, even if no new packets are generated, the system will remain occupied in an unsuccessful attempt to clear the backlog; the effective capacity of the system is virtually zero. Thus, even in a moderately loaded system, a temporary burst of work could move the network permanently into the high-collision region. This type of instability is not possible with the other protocols.

CSMA/CD and Ring Protocols

It is far more difficult to do a comparative performance of the three major ring protocols than to do a comparison of bus and token-ring protocols. The results depend critically on a number of parameters unique to each protocol. For example:

- Token Ring — size of token, token processing time
- Slotted Ring — slot size, overhead bits per slot
- Register Insertion — register size

Thus it is difficult to do a comparison, and although there have been a number of studies on each one of the

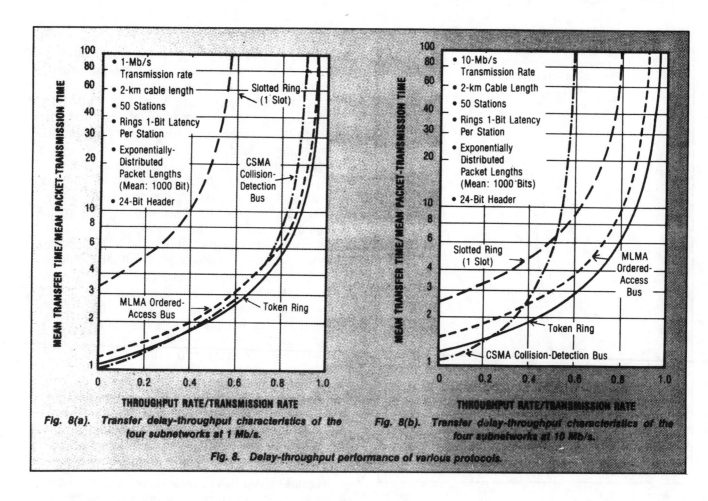

Fig. 8(a). *Transfer delay-throughput characteristics of the four subnetworks at 1 Mb/s.*

Fig. 8(b). *Transfer delay-throughput characteristics of the four subnetworks at 10 Mb/s.*

Fig. 8. *Delay-throughput performance of various protocols.*

potentially high utilization it can achieve. In contrast with token ring, multiple stations can transmit at one time. Further, a station can transmit as soon as a gap opens up on the ring; it need not wait for a token. On the other hand, the propagation time around the ring is not constant, but depends on the amount of traffic.

A final point in comparing token ring and register insertion: Under light loads, register insertion operates more efficiently, resulting in slightly less delay. However, both systems perform adequately. Our real interest is under heavy load. A typical local network will have $a < 1$, usually $a << 1$, so that a transmitting station on a token ring will append a token to the end of its packet. Under heavy load, a nearby station will be able to use the token. Thus almost 100% utilization is achieved, and there is no particular advantage to register insertion.

References

[1] W. Stallings, *Local Networks: An Introduction*, New York: Mac-Millan, 1984.
[2] W. Myers, "Toward a local network standard," *IEEE Micro*, pp. 28–45, Aug. 1982.
[3] F. Tobagi, "Performance analysis of carrier sense multiple access with collision detection," *Computer Networks*, pp. 245–259, Oct./Nov. 1980.
[4] R. M. Metcalfe and D. R. Boggs, "Ethernet: distributed packet switching for local computer networks," *Commun. Ass. Comput. Mach.*, pp. 395–404, July 1976.
[5] B. Stuck, "Calculating the maximum mean data rate in local area networks," *Computer*, pp. 72–76, May 1983.
[6] M. T. Liu, W. Hilal, and B. H. Groomes, "Performance evaluation of channel access protocols for local computer networks," *Proc. COMPCON Fall '82*, pp. 417–426, 1982.
[7] W. Bux, "Local-area subnetworks: a performance comparison," *IEEE Trans. Commun.*, pp. 1465–1473, Oct. 1981.
[8] W. Bux and M. Schlatter, "An approximate method for the performance analysis of buffer insertion rings," *IEEE Trans. Commun.*, pp. 50–55, Jan. 1983.

Appendix — Local Network Terms

Bus — The common name for a local network with a linear or tree topology, in which stations are attached to a shared transmission medium. Transmissions propagate the length of the linear medium or throughout all the branches of the tree, and may be received by all stations.

Ring — A local network in which stations are attached to repeaters connected in a closed loop. Data are transmitted in one direction around the ring, and can be read by all attached stations.

Medium Access Control Technique — A distributed control technique, shared by stations attached to a local network, that determines which device may transmit on the medium at any time.

CSMA/CD — Carrier Sense Multiple Access with Collision Detection. A medium access control technique for bus local networks. A station wishing to transmit first senses the medium and transmits only if the medium is idle. The station continues to sense the medium during transmission and ceases transmission if it detects a collision.

Token Bus — A medium-access control technique for bus local networks. Stations form a logical ring, around which a token is passed. A station receiving the token may transmit data, and then must pass the token to the next station in logical order.

Token Ring — A medium-access control technique for ring local networks. A token circulates around the ring. A station may transmit by removing the token, inserting a packet onto the ring, and then retransmitting the token.

Register Insertion — A medium access control technique for ring local networks. Each station contains a register that can temporarily hold a circulating packet. A station may transmit whenever there is a gap on the ring and, if necessary, hold an oncoming packet until it has completed transmission.

Slotted Ring — A medium access control technique for ring local networks. The ring is divided into circulating slots, which may be designated empty or full. A station may transmit whenever an empty slot goes by, by marking it full and inserting a packet into the slot.

Dr. William Stallings is a frequent lecturer on data communications topics. He is the author of *Local Networks: An Introduction* (MacMillan, 1984); *Local Network Technology* (IEEE Computer Society Press, 1983); *A Manager's Guide to Local Networks* (Prentice-Hall, 1983); and *Data and Computer Communications* (MacMillan, forthcoming).

Dr. Stallings received a Ph.D. from M.I.T. in computer science in 1971. Currently, he is senior communications consultant with Honeywell Information Systems, Inc. He is involved in the planning and design of communications network products and in the evaluation of communications requirements for Honeywell customers. He has been vice-president of CSM Corp., a firm specializing in data processing and data communications technology for the health-care industry. He has also been director of Systems Analysis and Design for CTEC, Inc., a firm specializing in command, control, and communications systems. ∎

MAXIMUM MEAN DATA RATE IN A LOCAL AREA NETWORK
WITH A SPECIFIED MAXIMUM SOURCE MESSAGE LOAD

A. R. K. Sastry

Rockwell International Science Center
1049 Camino Dos Rios
Thousand Oaks, California 91360

ABSTRACT

This paper considers the collective impact of various parameters of a local area network (LAN) such as propagation delay, interface delay, transmission rate, message length, etc., on the maximum mean data rate (throughput). Due to the interaction of these parameters, the realizable maximum throughput rate depends on the degree of synchronization between instants of time at which the network access and the data to be transmitted become available. If a source is blocked (not allowed to generate data when transmission of a previous message unit is pending), the realizable maximum throughput rate is less than or equal to the nominal maximum throughput rate chosen in the design, while both would be equal for the non-blocked case. The reduction in the throughput for the blocked case can be avoided by introducing a buffer of suitable size at the input of the network interface.

INTRODUCTION

A sub-committeee of the IEEE Project 802 (Local Area Network Standards) recently considered [1]-[3] estimation of the maximum mean data rate as an additional means of characterizing the traffic handling capabilities for the three local area network (LAN) schemes: token-passing ring, token-passing bus, and Carrier Sense Multiple Access with Collision Detection (CSMA/CD). This involves computation of the maximum mean data rates under two extreme traffic conditions, i.e., when (1) only one station is active and (2) all stations are active (which represents the worst-case congestion). The analyses of maximum mean data rates in [1] and [2] assume that each active station is always ready with another message (a data packet or frame) as soon as a previous message is transmitted, irrespective of the LAN transmission rate. It would be more meaningful from a user point of view to examine the implications for a given maximum total message rate. As shown in this note, such an analysis not only identifies the minimum transmission rate required for a particular LAN configuration but also brings out more clearly the impact of the interaction of various network parameters, which might partially explain the observed

discrepancies between the theoretical and measured performance [4].

ANALYSIS

Figure 1 shows a user-oriented representation of the throughput (actual useful data delivered) characteristics of a LAN as a function of its transmission (clock) rate.

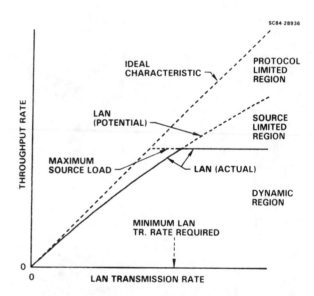

Fig. 1. User–view of qualitative performance of a local area network (LAN) for a given maximum total source data input load.

For a given transmission rate, R bits/s, a given LAN will have a maximum potential throughput rate, M^* bits/s. In most practical situations, for a designed value of M^*, the actual maximum throughput rate, M, $(M \leq M^*)$, is limited by the maximum source data rate, i.e., it would be operating in a "source-limited" region. In this region, the actual total throughput rate depends on the availability of a new packet at each station's interface as soon as it finishes transmitting the previous packet. This availability for a specified source work load results from an intricate relationship among the individual source data rate, the interface delay, the one-way propagation delay, size of the message unit, and the access scheme.

Consider N identical stations (sources) in a LAN, all of them being active, each continuously generating and delivering data (worst congestion case) at a rate of r bits/s to its interface unit connected to the medium. The interface unit handles packet assembly/disassembly functions and any other signal processing, participates in the execution of the medium access protocol, and transmits/receives packets to/from the LAN medium at a transmission rate of R bits/s. Let T_i be the time taken by the interface unit for performing these functions (interface delay) for the transmission of each packet. Also, let T_m be the transmission time for the packet consisting of D data bits and T_p be the largest one-way propagation delay. Then, for a token bus scheme, the maximum mean throughput rate [2], M_b, in bits/s is given by

$$M_b = \frac{D}{(T_m + T_p + T_i)}. \tag{1}$$

We will assume that each station is allowed to transmit only one packet when it holds the token and that the token transmission time and processing times are absorbed in T_i. If a station is synchronously ready with an additional D data bits to be transmitted by the time the token comes back to it, we have

$$\frac{D}{r} = N[T_m + T_p + T_i]. \tag{2}$$

From (1) and (2), we get $M_b = Nr$. However, in a source-limited condition,

$$\frac{D}{r} \geq N[T_m + T_p + T_i], \tag{3}$$

which would mean that the interface unit is not ready with D bits by the time it gets back the token and thus has to pass on the unused token to the next station. Under identical conditions, the same situation would prevail at each station involving a delay of $(T_p + T_i)$. Let $[x]$, denoting the largest integer that is less than x, represent the number of times a station has to pass on an unused token following transmission of a packet and before getting ready with another D bits at its interface. x can be obtained from,

$$\frac{D}{r} = N[T_m + x(T_p + T_i)], \tag{4}$$

noting that (3) and (4) imply that $x \geq 1$.

(i) Blocked case:

Even when the next D data bits are ready and are formed into a packet, the interface unit cannot transmit the packet immediately. It will have to wait until it gets the token again before initiating transmission. Letting $X = [x] + 1$, the waiting time is given by $(X - x)N(T_p + T_i)$. If during this waiting time the source is prevented

from sending further data bits (by locking a keyboard of an interactive terminal, for example) there would not be any need for buffering at the interface. Let us call this a "blocked" operation. As shown in Fig. 2a, X would then be a constant for each packet transmission cycle at a given station. We thus have,

$$\frac{D}{r} \leq N[T_m + X(T_p + T_i)], \tag{5}$$

and

$$M_b = \frac{D}{T_m + X(T_i + T_p)}. \tag{6}$$

Notice that X has a minimum value of 1, for which Eq. (6) becomes identical to Eq. (1). Also, using (5),

$$M_b \leq Nr, \tag{7}$$

which means that while Nr could be used for selecting R or vice versa, the actual allowed source load should be bounded by M_b to avoid excessive and accumulating delays. Proceeding similarly and using the basic relationships for token ring and CSMA/CD [2], the corresponding maximum mean throughput rates in bits/s, M_r and M_c respectively, can be shown to be

$$M_r = \frac{D}{T_m + X(T_i + T_p/N)} \tag{8}$$

and

$$M_c = \frac{D}{T_m + (2e - 1)(T_s + T_j) + XT_i}, \tag{9}$$

where, in Eq. (9), T_j is the transmission time for 48 bit collision detection reinforcing jamming pattern, T_s is the slot time equal to $\max[51.2 \ \mu s, 2T_p]$, and T_i is the interface delay or interframe gap, whichever is higher. $2e$ collisions per successful transmission of each packet are assumed [2]. In Eq. (8) for token ring, notice that the propagation delay is T_p/N unlike in the token bus in which the entire value of T_p appears for each token transfer. When T_p is small, the difference in performance of the two schemes narrows substantially. Both M_r and M_c are also upper bounded by Nr as in (7).

(ii) Non-blocking case:

If each station is allowed to continue generation of source data bits instead of being blocked during the time

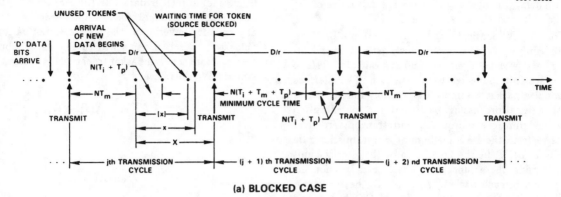

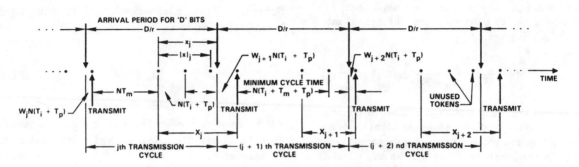

(a) BLOCKED CASE

(b) NON-BLOCKING CASE

Fig. 2. Timing relationships between data arrival and transmission processes at the interface unit of a continuously active station (source). (a) source blocked (b) not blocked.

the previous packet is waiting for the token, we would need a buffer of at least D bits long at the interface. From Fig. 2b, it can be seen that if $w_j N(T_i + T_p)$ is the waiting time in the jth transmission cycle $(w_j < 1$ for all $j)$, we can write

$$[x]_j N(T_i + T_p)$$

$$= \frac{D}{r} - NT_m - [w_j + (1 - w_{j+1})]N(T_i + T_p) \quad (10)$$

where x is as defined in (4). If $(x - [x]) \geq (1/k)$ with $w_j = 0$, $k = 2,3,4...$, $[x]$ would change by ± 1 once in every k successive transmission cycles. Considering that $[x]$ can only assume integral values and that $w_j < 1$ for all j, we can deduce from (10) that

$$-1 \leq \{[x]_{j+1} - [x]_j\} \leq 1, \quad (11)$$

$$w_j = w_{j+k}, \quad (12)$$

and

$$(\sum_{l=j}^{j+k-1} [x]_l) N(T_i + T_p)$$

$$= \frac{kD}{r} - (kNT_m) - kN(T_i + T_p), \quad (13)$$

for all j. Thus, for example, if $k = 2$, it follows from (11)-(13) that X assumes only two values X_1 and X_2 such that

$$(X_1 + X_2)N(T_i + T_p) = \frac{2D}{r} - 2NT_m, \quad (14)$$

with

$$X_1 = \frac{(D/r) - NT_m}{N(T_i + T_p)} - \frac{1}{2}, \quad (15)$$

and

$$X_2 = \frac{(D/r) - NT_m}{N(T_i + T_p)} + \frac{1}{2}, \quad (16)$$

or vice versa. X_1 and X_2 occur alternately in successive packet transmission cycles and differ by 1, except when $[x] = 0$, i.e., when the the system is not in the source-limited condition, for which case $X_1 = X_2 = 1$. It is clear from (11)-(14) that $\sum_{l=j}^{j+k-1} X_l$ is a constant for any k consecutive transmission cycles and (kD/r) data bits would be transferred during that time. Thus, using (13), and substituting kD, kT_m, and $\sum_{l=j}^{j+k-1} X_l$ in place of D, T_m, and X, respectively, in Eqs. (6), (8), and (9), we get the maximum mean throughput rate, M, for all k as

$$M = Nr \leq M^*, \quad (17)$$

with M and M^* having subscripts $b, r,$ and c for token bus, token ring and CSMA/CD respectively. Notice that Eq. (17) is independent of k. The corresponding bounds M^* for the three schemes can be obtained from Eqs. (6), (8), and (9) using $X = 1$.

When only a single station is active, the token bus scheme will have lower potential throughput rate than the other two schemes since the rest of the $N-1$ stations have to pass on the unused token, causing a minimum delay of $N(T_i + T_p)$ for each packet. Expressions (1)-(9) can be modified using the formulae for the active single station case [2], considering the total maximum message rate as r. When a LAN is designed to carry the total message load when all stations are active, it would certainly be able to carry the message load when only one station is active. In the next section, we will consider only the worst congestion case, which is more important from the point of view of understanding the capability limits of a LAN.

NUMERICAL RESULTS

To illustrate the impact of the interaction of various network parameters on the maximum mean throughput rate, M, some numerical results are presented in Figs. 3-5. The number of overhead bits per data packet is assumed

to be 96 bits. Values of various other parameters are indicated in the figures. Figure 3 gives M as a function of the LAN transmission rate R. The dotted curves correspond to the case $X = 1$, which indicates the throughput potential of the respective LANs. When the total maximum message load is held at 10 Mbits/s, token ring and token bus enter the source-limited region after crossing the minimum required R, which are about 11 and 12.5 Mbits/s, respectively. In this region, $M = Nr$ for the non-blocked case. However, for the blocked case, the throughput $M \leq Nr$ exhibits a series of ramps that have progressively decreasing slopes, with the steps occurring whenever x just exceeds integral values. For CSMA/CD, the throughput curve is far below the net offered load, indicating its inability to carry the load even when R is 20 Mbits/s. In a token passing ring, though the token transfer time is expected to be only one bit, data manipulation within the interface could involve significant delays [4]. For this reason, an interface delay of 10 μs is used in this example for the token ring.

Figures 4 and 5 show the effect of propagation delay and interface delay, respectively, on the maximum mean throughput for a fixed LAN transmission rate of 10 Mbits/s. The results are shown at two different total maximum source loads, such that the nature of variation

SC84-28938

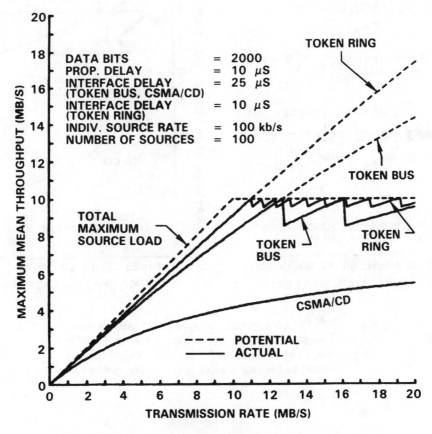

Fig. 3. Maximum mean throughput rate, M, as a function of the LAN transmission rate, R.

in the source-limited region can be seen for CSMA/CD also. For all the three schemes, the step sizes of ramps increase with increase in propagation delay and interface delay and decrease for lower total message rates. Token ring exhibits the smallest step size at low interface and propagation delays, but at higher interface delays all the three schemes have comparable step sizes. However, at high propagation delays, as is to be expected, token ring is the least affected. In Figs. 4 and 5, unlike in Fig. 3 (variation with R), the ramps have negative slopes and the steps occur when the decreasing values of x just take on integral values. Thus, in the source-limited region, Nr is only a design tool for the blocked case, with the actual allowable maximum source load being $M \le Nr$ (from the ramps), unlike for the non-blocking case for which $M = Nr$. In the protocol-limited region, $M = M^*$ for both blocked and non-blocked cases. By providing an ad-

ditional buffer (other than that required for processing the earlier D data bits) of length $N(T_i + T_p)$ at the interface, blocking and hence the throughput reduction as depicted by the ramps, can be avoided. Though attention in this analysis is only on deriving the maximum mean throughput rates, a similar phenomenon is also to be expected under actual dynamic message conditions, since most networks are likely to operate under source-limited regions. This could possibly explain part of the observed discrepancy between the predicted and measured performance of a token passing ring [4]. Analytical treatment of the interactions of various parameters under dynamic loading conditions (unlike the extreme conditions considered in this paper) would be quite complex. Simulation and experimental measurements seem to be more desirable approaches.

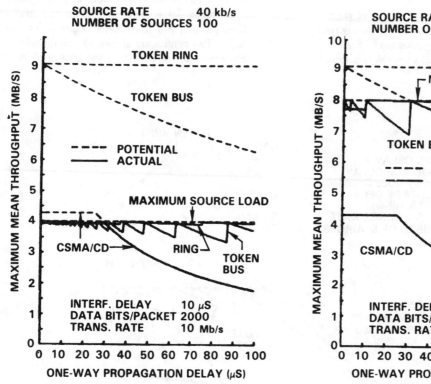

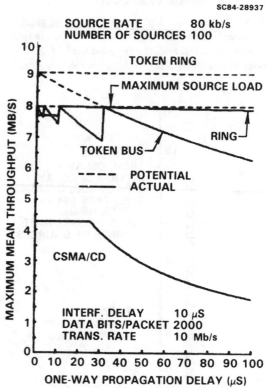

Fig. 4. Effect of propagation delay on the maximum mean throughput rate, M, for a fixed LAN transmission rate, R, of 10 Mb/s, under protocol–limited (dashed curves) and source–limited (solid curves) conditions.

322

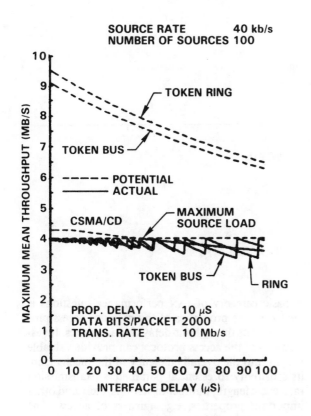

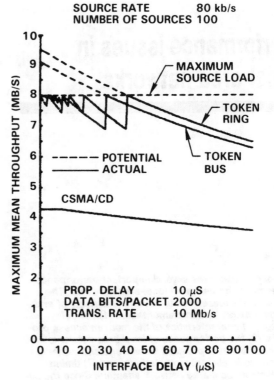

Fig. 5. Effect of interface delay on the maximum mean throughput rate, M, for a fixed LAN transmission rate, R, of 10 Mb/s, under protocol–limited (dashed curves) and source–limited (solid curves) conditions.

CONCLUSIONS

Lack of synchronism between allowed transmission times and availability of messages can reduce the maximum mean throughput in a source-limited regime with a specified maximum total source message load. The extent of reduction depends on the actual values of such parameters as individual source rate, propagation delay, interface delay, LAN transmission rate, and the protocol. Thus, actual allowable total maximum message rates will have to be lower than the design values used in generating the throughput curves. This reduction in throughput could be avoided by adding a buffer at the protocol interface.

REFERENCES

[1]. E. Arthurs et al, IEEE Project 802 Local Area Network Standards: Traffic-Handling Characteristics Committee Report, Working Draft, IEEE Computer Society, Silver Spring, Md., June 1982.

[2]. B. W. Stuck, "Calculating The Maximum Mean Data Rate in Local Area Networks," IEEE Computer, pp. 72-76, May 1983.

[3]. W. Stallings, "Local Network Performance," IEEE Communications Magazine, vol. 22, No. 2, pp. 27-36, February 1984.

[4]. J. Sventek, W. Greiman, M. O'Dell and A. Jansen, "Token Ring Local Area Networks: A Comparison of Experimental and Theoretical Performance," Symposium Record, IEEE/NBS Computer Networking Symposium, pp. 51-56, December 1983.

Performance issues in local-area networks

by W. Bux

This paper discusses several important performance problems in the design of local-area networks. The questions discussed relate to various aspects of architecture, design, and implementation: (1) the delay-throughput characteristics of the medium access protocols, (2) the performance of local-area networks on which a file server provides file storage and retrieval services to intelligent workstations, and (3) timing problems in local-area network adapters. Since the paper does not primarily address the performance analyst, it is descriptive in nature; analytic details are omitted in favor of a more intuitive explanation of the relevant effects.

The performance evaluation of local-area networks (LANs) is a multifaceted problem because of the complex interaction among a potentially large number of system components. Therefore, modeling of LANs needs to be performed at various levels, similar to the hierarchical approaches in the analysis of equally complex systems, such as wide-area data networks, telephone networks, or computer systems. This paper summarizes some of the performance analysis work done at the IBM Zurich Research Laboratory in the context of a LAN research project. It discusses various aspects of LAN architecture, design, and implementation. The paper does not primarily address the performance-evaluation specialist; its intention is, instead, to provide a sound intuitive understanding of performance problems that are peculiar to LANs. Theoretical details are omitted, but an extensive list of references to the appropriate literature is given in which the interested reader can find additional detailed information. For an introduction to LANs in general, the reader is referred to Clark,[1] Dixon,[2] or Kuemmerle.[3]

A basic category of LAN performance questions is related to the properties of the medium access protocol, i.e., its throughput-delay characteristics. Investigations of the access protocol can provide valuable insight into the overall efficiency of the mechanism, its sensitivity to essential parameters (transmission rate, cable length, number of stations, etc.), and other important properties, e.g., fairness of access. The second section of this paper is devoted to an overview of the performance characteristics of important LAN medium access protocols.

Models of the above type are suitable to assess the performance characteristics of different access mechanisms (which usually imply a certain network topology) and thus are helpful in finding a good network design. Such models, however, are not appropriate for determining application-oriented performance measures. If one is interested, for example, in the quality of a file service, higher-level protocols, i.e., Logical Link Control, Network, Transport, and Session protocols have to be modeled. Moreover, implementation choices, such as the user-system-to-network interface or buffer management, may have an important effect on the quality of service seen by a user. In the third section, we describe a model of this category, i.e., a file server providing file storage and retrieval services over a LAN to a set of intelligent workstations.

Figure 1 LAN architecture reference model

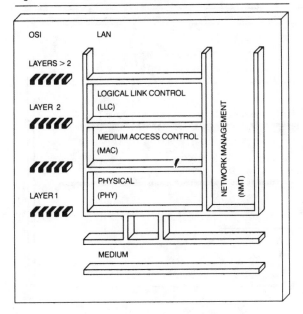

In order to answer detailed questions about the performance of specific components of a system, modeling at a rather deep level of detail may be necessary. A typical example is discussed in the fourth section, where a model of an adapter to a LAN is described. This model was used to study the timing problems associated with the reception of a continuous stream of information.

With these three categories of models, we cover a rather broad spectrum of performance issues related to LANs; nevertheless, there are various important topics we do not address in the present paper. Examples are problems related to the interconnection of local subnetworks, an area where flow and congestion-control problems arise. Furthermore, specific applications, for example, transmission of voice and images, raise challenging performance problems. Additional important areas are traffic measurement methodologies and the traffic-related aspects of network management and configuration.

Delay-throughput characteristics of medium access protocols

The groups concerned with LAN standardization, the Institute of Electrical and Electronics Engineers (IEEE) Project 802 and the European Computer Manufacturers Association (ECMA) TC24, have adopted a LAN architecture model that describes the relation-

ship of LAN architecture and the Open Systems Interconnection (OSI) Reference Model.[3-14] As shown in Figure 1, the OSI data-link layer is split into two sublayers, the medium-dependent "Medium Access Control" (MAC) sublayer and the medium-independent "Logical Link Control" (LLC) sublayer. Peculiarities of the various local-network techniques are thus restricted to the medium, the physical layer, and the MAC sublayer. Consequently, the quality of service at the MAC-to-LLC interface differs between different local-area networks. An important aspect of this service is the delay-throughput characteristic, which will be treated in this section.

We focus on the discussion of the three methods that have been standardized: Carrier-Sense Multiple-Access with Collision Detection (CSMA/CD), token ring, and token bus.[5-9,11-13]

CSMA/CD. Carrier-sense multiple-access with collision detection can be viewed as the offspring of CSMA methods developed for broadcast systems, mainly ground-radio packet-switching systems. Immediate detection of collisions is difficult in radio systems, whereas a rather simple collision-detection technique can be employed on bus systems, at least, if baseband transmission is used. Collision detection helps to improve performance in a short-delay environment. CSMA/CD was first described in Reference 15 as the access protocol of Ethernet.[16] In the meantime, ECMA and IEEE Project 802 have produced standards specifying a CSMA/CD-based local-area network.

The following brief description of the CSMA/CD protocol follows the specification in the existing standards.[5-7,11]

Medium access protocol. The protocol can conceptually be divided into a transmission and a reception part.

In the transmission part, when a station has a frame ready for transmission, it monitors the cable to determine whether any transmissions take place. When the medium is found utilized, transmission is deferred. When the medium is clear, frame transmission is initiated (after a short interframe delay, e.g., 9.6 microseconds).

If multiple stations attempt to transmit at the same time, interference can occur (see Figure 2). Overlap of different transmissions is called a collision. In this case, each transmitting station enforces the collision

Figure 2 CSMA/CD: example of operation (from Ref. 21)
©1981 IEEE

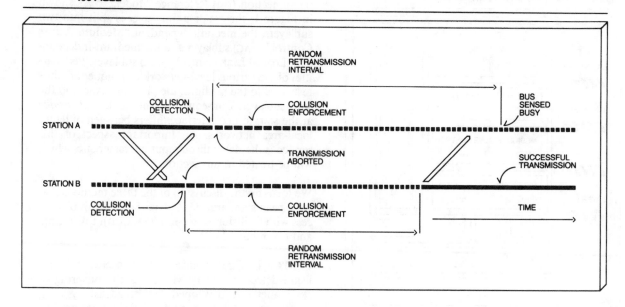

by transmitting a bit sequence called the jam signal. This ensures that the duration of the collision is sufficient to be noticed by all other stations involved in the collision. Then stations schedule a retransmission attempt for a randomly selected time in the future. Retransmission is attempted repeatedly in case of subsequent collisions. Repeated collisions indicate a heavily utilized medium; therefore stations adjust their retransmission activity to the traffic load perceived. This is accomplished by expanding the mean of the random retransmission time on each retransmission attempt.

The scheduling of the retransmissions is determined by a process called "truncated binary exponential backoff." Retransmission times are an integral multiple of the so-called slot time. The slot time must be equal to or greater than the maximum round-trip signal propagation time of the system. For the 10-million-bit-per-second baseband CSMA/CD system, a slot time of 51.2 microseconds has been standardized. The number of slot times to be delayed before the nth retransmission attempt is taken from a discrete distribution that assumes all integer values between 0 and 2^n with equal probability. If ten retransmissions of the same frame fail, the attempt is abandoned, and an error is reported.

The CSMA/CD access mechanism requires transmission of frames of a minimum length. If the frame size is less than the minimum required, a transmitting station must append extra, so-called "pad" bits after the end of the LLC-supplied data. Standardized minimum frame length for a CSMA/CD system with a baseband of 10 million bits per second is 512 bits.

In the reception part, all active stations synchronize with the preamble of an incoming frame and then decode the received signal. The destination-address field of the frame is checked to decide whether the frame should be received by this station. If so, the relevant parts of the frame are copied. The station also checks the validity of the received frame by inspecting the frame check sequence and proper octet-boundary alignment.

Performance characteristics. The performance of CSMA and CSMA/CD systems has formed the subject of numerous studies. The groundwork for the understanding of the performance properties of CSMA was laid in References 17 and 18. CSMA/CD performance has been studied in References 15 and 19 through 23 for different variants of the access principle. To provide a basic understanding of the delay-throughput characteristic of the standard CSMA/CD protocol, an analysis based on the work by Lam[22] appears attractive because the approach is rather straightforward, the underlying assumptions are close to the standardized CSMA/CD protocol, and the results are simple to evaluate numerically.

Figure 3 CSMA/CD delay-throughput characteristic (exponentially distributed information-field lengths)

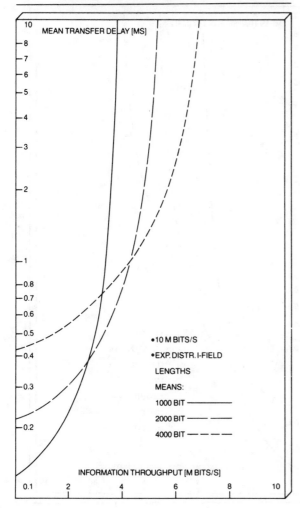

The assumptions underlying the analysis in Lam[22] are as follows. The traffic offered to the network is a Poisson process with a constant and state-independent arrival rate. Each station is allowed to store at most one frame at a time. The generation of a new frame is equivalent to increasing by one the number of stations ready to transmit a frame. Frame transmission times are generally distributed.

The following assumptions are made regarding the medium access protocol: (1) Following a successful transmission, all ready stations transmit within the next slot. (2) Following a collision, stations use an adaptive retransmission algorithm in such a way that the probability of a successful transmission within

any of the slots subsequent to a collision is constant and equal to $1/e$ (= 0.368). For a large number of stations, this assumption is well justified.[15-22] (3) Operation is assumed to be slotted in time, i.e., transmission attempts are made only at the beginning of a slot.

Under the above assumptions, the mean queuing delay of the frames was determined in Lam.[22] The examples shown below have been computed with the aid of this solution; however, we modified the analysis in the following three points:

1. It has been assumed in Lam[22] that after every successful transmission, a time interval equal to the end-to-end signal propagation time expires before stations sense end-of-carrier and start to transmit. This represents a slightly pessimistic view of the operation as described in the previous subsubsection. For our results, we assumed that end of transmission is detected with zero delay by all stations.
2. A consequence of assuming a slotted channel is that, even if the channel utilization approaches zero, frames have to wait for half a slot length on the average. Such a delay, of course, does not occur on a nonslotted system, such as the one described in the last subsubsection. We therefore reduce the mean delay according to Lam[22] by half the slot length.
3. As pointed out above, the CSMA/CD access protocol requires a minimum frame length of at least the slot length measured in bits. This fact has not been taken into account in Lam.[22] However, it can be easily incorporated through an appropriate modification of the distribution function of the frame transmission times.

In Figures 3 to 5, we show basic results for delay and throughput of CSMA/CD systems. As parameters for these examples, the values standardized for the 10-million-bit-per-second baseband CSMA/CD system have been used.[5-7,11]

Figure 3 shows the mean transfer delay of the transmitted frames as a function of the information throughput. The frame transfer delay is the time from the generation of a frame until its successful reception at the receiver. The information throughput is defined as the number of bits contained in the LLC-Information field of the frames transmitted per unit time. An exponential distribution for the information-field lengths is assumed. As described above, padding bits are added when the frame length is shorter than the minimum required. We observe from the figure that the delay-throughput characteristic depends strongly on the mean length of the information field. The shorter the frame length, the smaller the delay at small throughput values, but also the smaller the maximum throughput and hence the steeper the increase of the delay curves. The reason for this behavior is that with a decreasing ratio of frame transmission time to slot length, the protocol overhead increases significantly in terms of the fraction of time lost for collisions and their resolution.

In Figure 4, the behavior of the same system, however, for constant information-field lengths of 1000, 2000, and 4000 bits is shown. It can be seen that the delays are smaller than for the exponential distribution. However, the general tendency is the same, in particular, the location of the vertical asymptotes; i.e., the maximum throughput is very insensitive to the information-field length distribution. Generally, the type of this distribution can have an impact on the maximum throughput because of the minimum frame-length requirement. As comparison of Figures 3 and 4 shows, this impact is relatively small for the information-field lengths considered.

How the maximum throughput depends on the transmission speed, given a slot length equal to the standardized value of 51.2 microseconds, is shown in Figure 5. For the different values of the mean information-field length, an area for the maximum throughput is indicated in this figure. The upper and lower boundaries of these areas are determined by two different considerations regarding the situation in the first slot following a successful transmission. In the above-described approach to determine the mean delays, a constant, state-independent frame arrival rate has been assumed. If, under this assumption, the traffic load reaches the system capacity, the probability of a collision after a successful transmission will approach one. As described above, the probability of a successful transmission in one of the subsequent slots is equal to $1/e$. Under this assumption, the lower bound of the maximum throughput regions in Figure 5 has been determined.

A more optimistic assumption is that in an overload case, the probability of a successful transmission in the first slot after a successful transmission is equal to $1/e$. Under this assumption, the average time between subsequent successful transmissions is one slot length shorter than for the more pessimistic assumption first described. The optimistic assump-

Figure 4 CSMA/CD delay-throughput characteristic (constant information-field length)

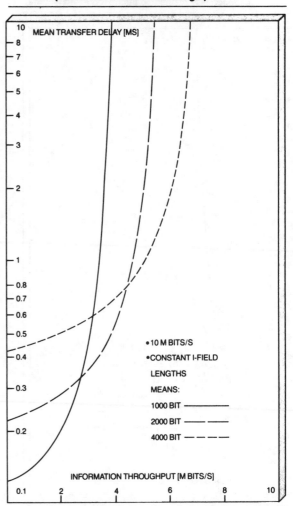

Figure 5 CSMA/CD maximum information throughput versus transmission rate for 51.2-microsecond slot length

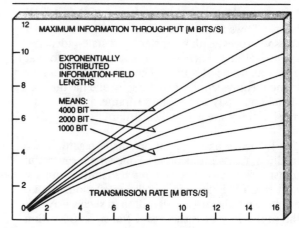

Figure 6 Token-ring queuing model (from Ref. 32, reprinted with permission of North-Holland Publishing Company)

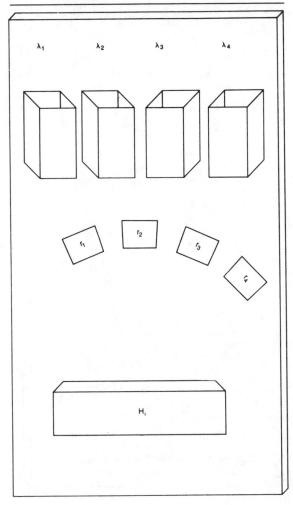

tion underlies the analysis given by Metcalfe and Boggs.[15] This solution has been used to determine the upper bound of the shaded areas in Figure 5. It can be seen that, even under the optimistic assumption, the efficiency of the CSMA/CD protocol decreases significantly with increasing speed, especially in the case of a 1000-bit mean information-field length. Measurements performed on an Ethernet showed a mean frame length of 976 bits.[24]

Token ring. Compared to the other LAN techniques, token rings have a relatively long technical history. Experimental systems showed the feasibility of the ring technique long before alternative methods, e.g., CSMA/CD or token-passing bus systems, were consid-

ered.[25-27] However, because of a lack of applications, token rings were not implemented on a broad basis. With the advent of local-area networks, the token-ring principle was reconsidered and found to provide an attractive solution because of its favorable attributes regarding wiring, transmission technology, performance, and the potential for low-cost implementation.[1-3,27-30] Moreover, recent work showed that what had been considered a potential problem of token rings, namely, lack of reliability, can be overcome by a suitable access protocol and an appropriate wiring strategy.[28,29] The above arguments led the standards groups concerned with LAN standardization to consider token rings as one of the candidates for a LAN standard.

The following description is based on the specification of the token-ring operation given in the existing IEEE-802 and ECMA standards.[8,13]

Medium access protocol. A token ring consists of a set of stations serially connected by a transmission medium, e.g., twisted-pair cable. Information is transferred sequentially from one active station to the next. A given station (the one having access to the medium) transfers information onto the ring. All other stations repeat each bit received. The addressed destination station copies the information as it passes. Finally, the station which transmitted the information removes it from the ring.

A station gains the right to transmit when it detects a token passing on the medium. The token is a control signal comprised of a unique signaling sequence that circulates on the medium following each information transfer. Any station, upon detection of a token, may capture the token by modifying it to a start-of-frame sequence, and then appends appropriate control and address fields, the LLC-supplied data, the frame check sequence, and the frame-ending delimiter. On completion of its information transfer and after appropriate checking for proper operation, the station generates a new token which provides other stations the opportunity to gain access to the ring.

A token-holding timer controls the length of time a station may occupy the medium before passing the token.

Multiple levels of priority can be provided on a token ring through an efficient priority mechanism. This mechanism is based on the principle described in Bux et al.[28] whereby higher-priority stations can interrupt the progression of lower-priority tokens and frames by making "reservations" in passing frames. This scheme requires that stations do not issue a new token before having received back the header of their transmitted frame. This so-called "single-token" rule[21,28] also leads to improved reliability of the access protocol because each transmitting station can check the proper functioning of the ring at the beginning of its transmission.

Performance characteristics. The basic operation of a token ring can be described by a performance model as shown in Figure 6. The active stations are represented by their transmit queues. These queues are serviced in a cyclic manner symbolized by the rotating switch that stands for the token.

The time needed to pass the token from station i to station $(i + 1)$ is modeled by a constant delay r_i. On an actual ring, the delay r_i corresponds to the propagation delay of the signals between stations i and $(i + 1)$ (approximately five microseconds per km cable) plus the latency caused within station i by the repeater and by actions such as alteration of the token bit. The station latency is usually in the order of one bit time.

In token rings, the sender is responsible for removing the frames it transmitted from the ring. Therefore, the location of frame destinations on the ring relative to the location of the sender does not affect the ring performance.

Queuing models applicable to token rings have been extensively studied, primarily in the context of polling systems.[20,21,27,31–42] However, analytic results, and especially those that lend themselves to numerical evaluation, are scarce. This is particularly true for models in which the transmission time of a station per access opportunity is limited through a bound on either the token-holding time or the number of frames to be transmitted per token.

Subsequently, we discuss some fundamental results for the token-ring delay-throughput characteristic obtained through simulation and analysis (where applicable).

As pointed out above, a fundamental performance characteristic of any LAN medium access protocol is its sensitivity to transmission speed and distance. Figures 7 and 8 show how token rings perform for various speeds and distances. Figure 7 shows the

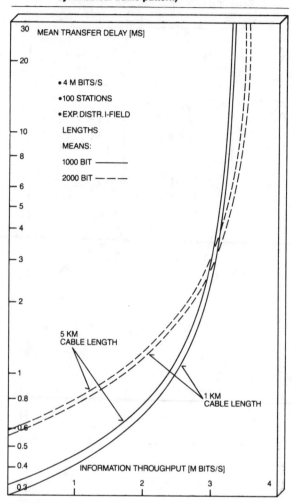

Figure 7 Token-ring delay-throughput characteristic (four-million-bit-per-second transmission rate; symmetrical traffic pattern)

mean frame transfer delay as a function of the information throughput for four-million-bit-per-second rings with one- and five-kilometer (km) cable lengths. It is assumed that all 100 stations generate the same amount of traffic; other traffic patterns lead to very similar results for the delay averaged over all stations. A further assumption is that frames are generated according to Poisson processes. Stations follow the single-token rule described in the last subsubsection; i.e., they wait until the header of their frame has returned before generating a new token. Only one frame per access opportunity can be transmitted. It can be seen that increasing the ring length from one to five km has virtually no impact on the delay-throughput characteristic.

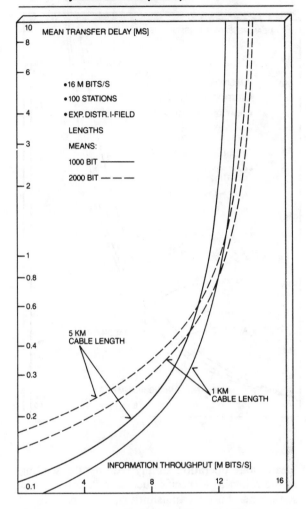

Figure 8 Token-ring delay-throughput characteristic (16-
million-bit-per-second transmission rate;
symmetrical traffic pattern)

Under the same assumptions, except for a transmission rate of 16 million bits per second, Figure 8 shows the same performance measures as the previous one. Increasing the cable length from one to five km leads to more noticeable differences here, primarily because of the single-token rule; however, the overall effect is still minor.

Overall efficiency of an access protocol is the most basic performance property; a further important criterion is the quality of service given to individual stations, especially in case of unbalanced traffic situations. This service can differ significantly, depending on the rule defining the time a station is allowed to transmit per access opportunity. As mentioned in

the last subsubsection, the standards specify the use of a token-holding timer that limits the time a station is allowed to transmit continuously. To demonstrate the impact of this timer, we subsequently consider two extreme cases, a very short timer, such that stations can only transmit one frame per token (Figure 9), and a very long timer, such that stations can always empty their transmit queues completely on each transmission opportunity (Figure 10).

For both examples, Poisson arrival processes have been assumed. However, the arriving data units are not single frames but entire messages, the lengths of which are distributed according to a hyperexponential distribution with a coefficient of variation equal to two. In cases where a message is longer than the maximum information-field length of a frame (256

Figure 9 Token-ring delay-throughput characteristic (one-
million-bit-per-second transmission rate,
asymmetrical traffic pattern, short token-holding
time-out) (from W. Bux, F. Closs, K. Kuemmerle, H.
Keller, and H. R. Mueller, "Architecture and Design
of a Reliable Token-Ring Network," *IEEE Selected
Areas in Communications* SAC-1, No. 5, 756–765
(November 1983).
©1983 IEEE

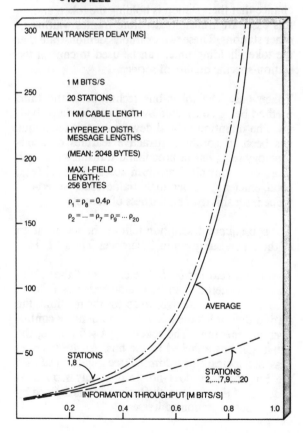

bytes), the message is segmented. In both examples, the assumed traffic pattern is very unbalanced: two of the 20 stations (Nos. 1 and 8) each generate 40 percent of the total traffic; each of the other 18 stations generates only 1.1 percent of the total traffic.

For the single-frame-per-token operation, Figure 9 shows the mean transfer delay of the messages (not frames!) as a function of the total information throughput. Of course, the delay averaged over all stations increases with increasing ring throughput. The same is true for the delay of the messages transmitted by the heavy-traffic stations 1 and 8. However, the delay experienced by the light-traffic stations remains rather small even for very high utilizations. In this sense, the token-passing protocol combined with a single-frame-per-token operation provides fair access to all users.

From Figure 10, it can be seen that the relationship of the delay experienced by light and heavy users is reversed when the token-holding time is long. Here, the mean message transfer delay of light-traffic stations is even higher than the one of heavy-traffic stations. This is due to the fact that messages generated at a heavy-traffic station have a relatively good chance that their station is holding the token and, in this case, are transmitted before frames waiting in other stations. These two examples demonstrate that the token-holding timer can be used to control the station-specific quality of service.

Token bus. The token-bus technique is the third method being considered by the LAN standards bodies. The intention behind developing this technique has been to combine attractive features of a bus topology (e.g., use of broadband transmission) with those of a controlled medium access protocol (e.g., good efficiency under high traffic load, speed-distance insensitivity, and fairness of access).

The subsequent description follows the specification of the token bus given in References 9 and 12.

Medium access protocol. The essence of the token-bus access method can be characterized as follows. A token controls the right to access the medium; the station that holds the token has momentary control over the medium. The token is passed among the active stations attached to the bus. As the token is passed, a logical ring is formed (see Figure 11). Since the bus topology does not impose any sequential ordering of the stations, the logical ring is defined by a sequence of station addresses.

Figure 10 Token-ring delay-throughput characteristic (one-million-bit-per-second transmission rate, asymmetrical traffic pattern, long token-holding time-out)

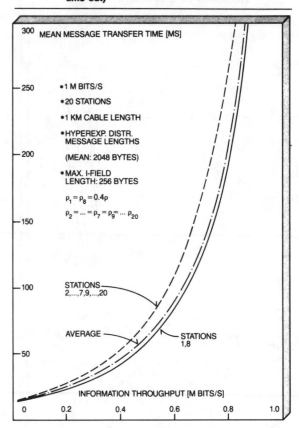

Steady-state operation simply requires the sending of the token to a specific successor station when a station has finished transmitting. A more difficult task is establishing and maintaining the ring (initialization, station insertion in, or removal from, the logical ring). Each participating station knows the addresses of its predecessor and its successor. After a station has completed transmitting data frames, it passes the token to its successor by sending a special MAC control frame, called an "explicit token." The maximum transmission time of any station is controlled by a token-holding timer.

After having sent the token, the station monitors the bus to make sure that its successor has received the token and is active. If the sender detects a valid frame following the token, it will assume that its successor has the token and is transmitting. If the sender does not sense a valid frame from its successor, it must assess the state of the network and, if necessary, take appropriate recovery actions to re-

---

Conceptually, token passing on buses and rings is very similar.

---

establish the logical ring. Details about establishment and re-establishment of the logical ring are specified in References 9 and 12.

The token-bus access method also allows defining of a priority mechanism, which is not further discussed here.

Performance characteristics. Conceptually, token passing on buses and rings is very similar; hence, the same type of performance model can be used to describe the two techniques. It is obvious, however, that the model parameters are rather different; this is particularly the case for the token-passing over-

head. In a token ring, the time to pass the token from one station to the next consists of the signal propagation time between the two stations (approximately five microseconds per km cable) plus the delay caused within a station. As pointed out in the previous subsubsection, the latter delay can be kept as small as one bit time. In contrast to this, on a token bus, passing the token from a station to its successor requires the transmission of an explicit-token frame, which in the standard for the token bus is 152 bits long. To this the signal propagation delay between the two stations has to be added. The third component of the token-passing overhead is the reaction time of the station, i.e., the time a station needs from reception of a token until it has prepared either a token or a data frame for transmission.

In Figure 12, we show the delay-throughput characteristic of one-million-bit-per-second token-bus systems with 100 and 200 stations attached. Further assumptions are: two km cable length, exponentially distributed information-field lengths with means of 1000 and 2000 bits, and zero reaction (processing) delay in the stations. For this example, the traffic is assumed to be completely symmetrical; i.e., all stations generate the same amount of traffic. Furthermore, for this and the following example, a token-holding time is assumed that is sufficiently long for stations always to be able to completely empty their

Figure 11 Token bus: logical ring on physical bus

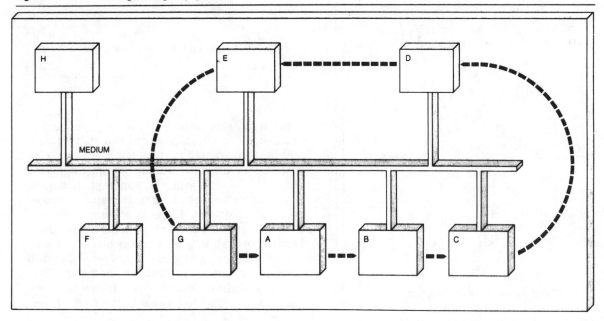

transmit queues at each transmission opportunity. The figure shows that the mean transfer delays are remarkably high compared with one and two milliseconds, respectively, the time it takes to transmit an information field of average length. This is due to the relatively large token-passing overhead of the token-bus technique.

As the next figure demonstrates, the token-passing overhead is reduced in case of asymmetric traffic. The parameters assumed for Figure 13 are a rate of five million bits per second (which is another one of the standardized speeds), a two-km cable length, 100 stations, and exponentially distributed information-field lengths with a mean of 1000 bits. Three different

Figure 13 Token-bus delay-throughput characteristic (mean transfer delay averaged over all stations for different symmetrical and asymmetrical traffic patterns)

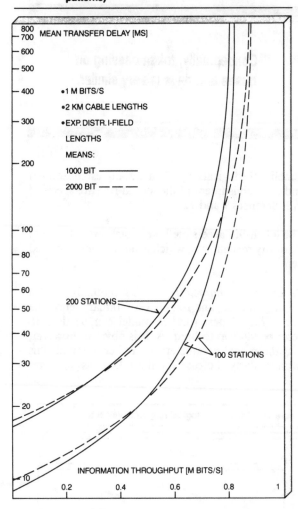

Figure 12 Token-bus delay-throughput characteristic (one-million-bit-per-second transmission rate, symmetrical traffic pattern)

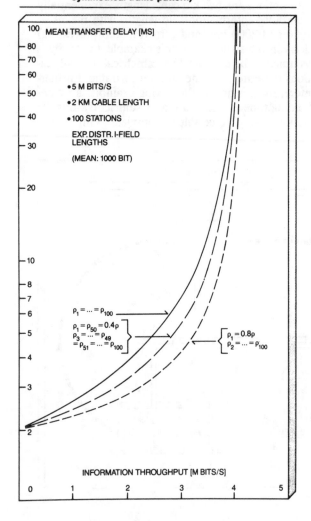

traffic patterns are assumed: (1) a totally symmetrical situation, (2) a situation where two stations each generate 40 percent of the total traffic, the rest being generated by the other stations in equal amounts, and (3) a situation with one station generating 80 percent of the traffic while again the rest is generated by the other stations. For each of these traffic patterns, the figure shows the mean frame transfer delay averaged over all stations as a function of the total ring information throughput. We observe that with increasing asymmetry of the traffic, the average delay decreases slightly, because—per frame transmission—the overhead to forward the token is smaller. It should be noted, however, that this is only true

334

when the token-holding time-out is sufficiently long; for a short token-holding time-out, the effect is reversed.

Other local network techniques. In addition to the three "standard" approaches discussed previously, various alternative LAN techniques have been developed and used. Among the most attractive techniques are slotted rings,[27,43] buffer-insertion rings,[27,44,45] buses with controlled-type access,[37,46–49] or buses employing a combination of random and controlled access.[37,49–53] Because of a lack of space, we cannot discuss these methods in detail; for the interested reader, we subsequently list references in which performance questions related to the above systems are discussed.

The performance of slotted rings is discussed in References 21, 31, 54 and 55. Analyses of buffer-insertion rings can be found in References 56 through 58. Controlled and hybrid-access schemes for buses have been analyzed in References 21, 49, and 59 through 64.

End-to-end flow and error control

Introduction. Models of the type discussed in the previous section are useful in understanding the quality of service provided by the local network at the MAC-to-LLC interface. Apparently, the performance characteristics seen at this interface are not the ones experienced by a user at the application level. To determine application-oriented performance measures, additional levels of architecture need to be modeled, such as an end-system-to-end-system protocol providing means for flow and error control.

The need for flow control arises in cases of a speed mismatch between the communicating partners, limited buffer sizes in the end systems and/or network adapters, and applications where, e.g., one station provides a certain service simultaneously to multiple workstations.

Means to detect and recover from errors are needed for various reasons: (1) Data units can be corrupted by transmission errors; (2) Frames may be lost because of buffer overflow in the receiving end system and/or its adapter; (3) Timing problems in the receivers may cause loss of frames (see the following major section on LAN adapter design).

Protocols providing the functionality needed for flow and error control in LANs are, for example, Class 4

of the ISO/ECMA Transport Protocol,[65,66] or the Type 2 Logical Link Control protocol defined by the IEEE Project 802.[10] Depending on this choice, end-to-end flow and error control is performed in layers corresponding to either layers 4 or 2 of the OSI reference model.

In the next subsection, a scenario consisting of a file server and workstations attached to a local-area ring network is described. The subsection after that de-

---

Flow control is implemented by a window mechanism.

---

scribes a model developed to study performance issues of such systems.[67] Results of this study are summarized in the subsequent subsection.

Network operation. The configuration of the local-area network under consideration is shown in Figure 14. It consists of user systems (file server and workstations) attached to a token-ring network through ring adapters. Each adapter has a number of transmit/receive buffers. It also contains a processor whose major tasks are to control the data transfer between the ring and the transmit/receive buffers, to manage these buffers, and to control the interface to the user system.

File transfer is performed over a logical connection between the file server and the workstation. The file server can manage multiple connections simultaneously. The protocol under consideration is a subset of the IEEE 802.2 Type 2 Logical Link Control protocol.[10] It provides procedures for connection establishment, connection termination, flow control, and error recovery.

A file is transmitted as a series of Information (I-) frames. For the file transfer environment, information flow on a given connection is unidirectional; i.e., on one connection, I-frames are either sent from the file server to a workstation, or vice versa.

Flow control. Flow control is implemented by a window mechanism; i.e., a sender is permitted to

Figure 14 File-service scenario

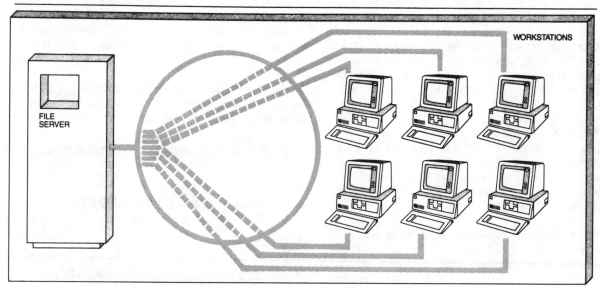

WORKSTATIONS

FILE SERVER

transmit up to W (the window size) I-frames without having to wait for an acknowledgment. The receiver uses Receive Ready (RR-) frames to acknowledge correctly received I-frames and to indicate to the sender that more I-frames can be transmitted.

Error recovery. Any I-frame received with an incorrect Frame Check Sequence (FCS) is discarded. If a received I-frame has a correct FCS, but its send sequence number is not equal to the one expected by the receiver, the receiver will return a Reject (REJ-) frame. The receiver then discards all I-frames until the expected I-frame has been correctly received. The sender, upon receiving a REJ-frame, retransmits I-frames starting with the sequence number received within the REJ-frame.

In addition to REJECT recovery, a time-out mechanism is used. At the instant of transmission of an I-frame, a timer will be started if it is not running already. When the sender receives an RR-frame, it restarts the timer if there are still unacknowledged I-frames outstanding.

When the timer expires, the station performs a "checkpointing" function by transmitting an RR-frame with a dedicated bit (the "P-bit") set to one. The receiver, upon receiving this frame, must return an RR-frame with the "F-bit" set to one. When this RR-frame has been received by the sender, it either proceeds with transmitting new I-frames or retrans-

mits previous I-frames depending on the sequence number contained in the RR-frame received.

Simulation model. A simulation model employed to study the above scenario is illustrated in Figure 15 and subsequently described.[67]

Medium access protocol. The token-ring protocol for medium access is modeled by a multiqueue, single-server submodel with cyclic service (cf. the earlier section on performance characteristics of the token ring). A queue in this submodel represents the frames waiting in the transmit buffers of an adapter.

Ring adapter and system interface. The adapter transmit buffers contain frames to be transmitted onto the ring. The adapter receive buffers temporarily hold frames received from the ring until they can be transferred to the user system. When upon arrival of a frame no receive buffer in the adapter is available, the frame is lost and has to be recovered through the LLC protocol. Transmission errors are assumed to have negligible effect and are not included in the model. Furthermore, it is assumed that timing problems associated with the receive operation, such as the ones described in the next major section, do not exist here.

The adapter processor, together with the system interface, is modeled by a single server with two queues: the receive buffer queue in the adapter and

Figure 15 File-service performance model

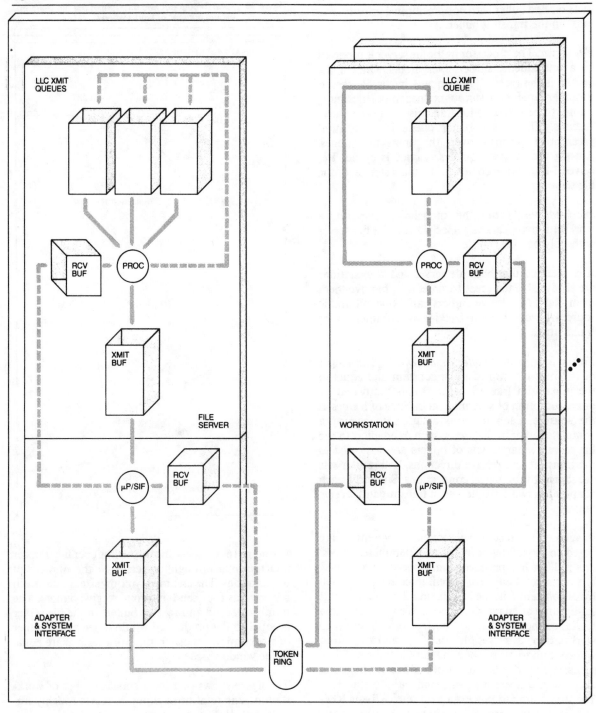

the transmit buffer queue in the user system (see Figure 15). The service time corresponds to the sum of the time to set up a transfer by the adapter processor and the data-transfer time across the system interface. The adapter processor handles frames in its receive buffer with nonpreemptive priority over those in the transmit buffer.

File server. The processor in the file server is modeled by a multiqueue, single-server model. One of the queues is the receive-buffer queue in the file server; the others are for the various connections, containing frames to be prepared for transmission to the workstations. The receive-buffer queue is given nonpreemptive priority over the transmit queues. Among the transmit queues, service is cyclic. Received I-frames are copied to the mass storage of the file server.

Workstations. From the modeling viewpoint, a workstation appears as a special case of a file server with only one file transfer.

It is assumed that both file server and workstations are always able to accept I-frames (i.e., remove them from the LLC receive buffers) and that all traffic sources always have a backlog of I-frames to be transmitted.

Frame lengths and buffer management. The length of I-frames is assumed to be constant and equal to the maximum frame length. This is motivated by our assumption of a permanent backlog of frames at the sources. Each frame is assumed to occupy a complete buffer in the user system or adapter. In the file server, separate sets of buffers are dedicated to the transmit and receive directions; both buffer sets are shared by all logical connections. Similarly, each adapter has two separate sets of transmit and receive buffers.

Results. The results subsequently presented are based on the following selection of parameter values: one million bits per second ring speed, two million bits per second effective system interface speed, 500 bytes constant I-frame length, and 20 microseconds set-up time at adapter processor. We shall refer to a logical connection for file transfer from file server to workstation as a "get-file transfer," and that from workstation to file server as a "put-file transfer." The scenario considered consists of a file server handling an equal number of get-file and put-file transfers. The mean time to process an I-frame (RR- or REJ-frame) at the file server is assumed to be 10 milliseconds (2 milliseconds). The corresponding values for a workstation are 50 and 10 milliseconds. Each adapter/user system has the same number of transmit and receive buffers.

Figure 16   Total throughput and throughput per file transfer versus number of workstations

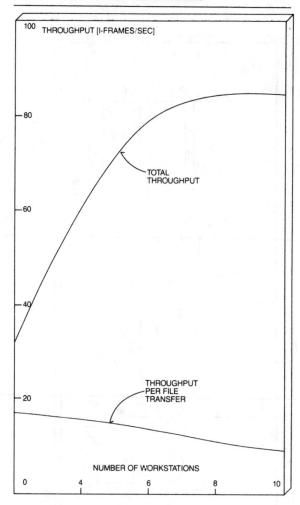

In Figure 16, we show the throughput per file transfer and the total throughput versus N, the number of workstations. The assumed window size is four. Each adapter has four send and four receive buffers. The number of send and receive buffers in the file server is equal to the product of window size and number of workstations; those in the workstations are equal to the window size.

The figure shows that for a small number of workstations, the total throughput increases roughly linearly with N. The reason is that, as long as N is small, the workstations are the bottleneck, and the addition of a workstation does not cause much interference at the file server. When N is large, the bottleneck is shifted from the workstations to the file server. The

338

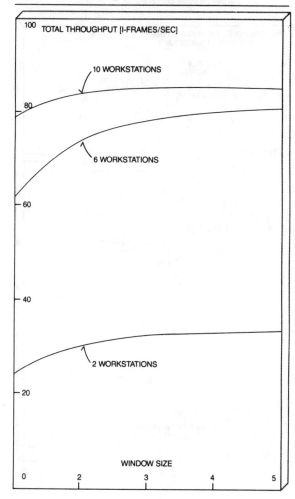

Figure 17 Total throughput versus window size

considered: $N = 2$, 6, and 10 workstations. The assumptions regarding the buffer sizes are identical to the ones underlying Figure 16.

For the case of small W, both the workstation and the file-server processors are not busy all the time. An increase in W (e.g., from one to two) therefore results in a noticeable improvement in total throughput. However, when W is larger, either the file server or the workstation processor is busy almost all the time; hence, increasing the window size does not cause an increase in total throughput.

Consider now the effect of file-server buffer size on performance. In Figure 18, we plot the loss probabilities at the file-server adapter versus the number of file-server receive buffers for a configuration with $N = 10$ workstations. The window size is four. Results are shown separately for put-file transfers (loss

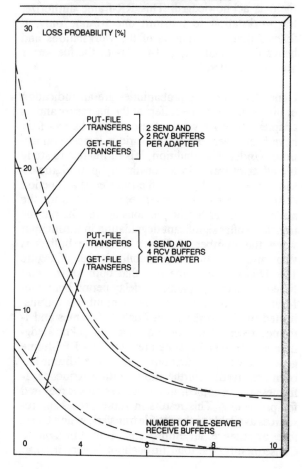

Figure 18 Loss probability at file-server adapter versus number of file-server receive buffers

processor of the file server is working at close to full capacity; increasing N does not result in an improvement in total throughput. Since the file-server processor is shared by the various file transfers, the throughput per file transfer is a decreasing function of N.

The ring is not heavily utilized; its utilization increases from 14 percent when $N = 2$ to 34 percent when $N = 10$. Also, the loss probability due to buffer shortage at the file-server adapter is less than 0.2 percent for all cases.

We next study the effect of window size W on the total throughput. In Figure 17, we show the total throughput for different values of W. Three cases are of I-frames) and get-file transfers (loss of RR- and REJ-frames). The results show that a significant fraction of frames is lost when the number of file-server receive buffers is small, but the loss probability decreases quickly with this number. The loss probability also decreases with an increasing number of buffers in the adapter, because in an overload situation, the adapter receive buffers function as an "extension" of the file-server receive buffers.

In view of the fact that the five workstations involved in put-file transfers may have a total number of 20 I-frames simultaneously outstanding, it is surprising that the loss probabilities are rather small already for six file-server receive buffers. This result can be explained as follows. In the implementation of the LLC protocol, each I-frame is separately acknowledged by an RR-frame. Since the file-server processor gives priority to frames received from its adapter, the preparation of frames for transmission is delayed. When the processor is ready to prepare an RR-frame for a put-file transfer, a number of I-frames for this connection may have been received, but only one of them is acknowledged. This RR-frame authorizes the workstation to transmit one I-frame only. It follows that the windows of the workstations and hence the arrival rate of I-frames to the file server are self-regulated.

Generally, high loss probabilities are an indication of insufficient receive buffers at the file server and its adapter. In other words, these receive buffers may have been over-sold to the various logical connections. Under this condition, it is of interest to study the effect of frame losses on throughput. Figure 19 shows the throughput per file transfer as a function of the number of file-server receive buffers for the same scenario as for the previous figure. The put-file transfers suffer significant degradation in throughput when the number of file-server receive buffers is small and hence the loss probability is high (cf. Figure 18). This is due to the fact that both REJECT and time-out recovery result in a delay period before an I-frame with the correct sequence number is retransmitted by the workstation. For lost I-frames and I-frames received out of sequence, no acknowledgments have to be generated (except for a REJ-frame generated when the first out-of-sequence I-frame has been received). Furthermore, out-of-sequence I-frames are not copied, and hence less time is required for processing. This results in more processing resources available to the get-file transfers, which therefore experience an improvement in throughput. Consequently, the total throughput is very insensi-

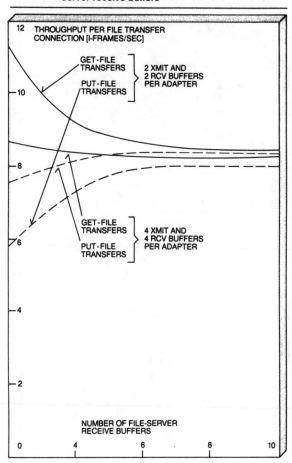

Figure 19 Throughput per file transfer versus number of file-server receive buffers

tive to frame losses because the throughput degradation of the put-file transfers is compensated by the throughput increase of get-file transfers.

Local-area network adapter design

In a local-area network, user systems are attached to the transmission medium through network adapters, also called network controllers. An essential feature of an adapter is that it is able to receive frames arriving with no or very small gaps between them. If adapters were frequently unable to receive such frames, the performance of the local network—as seen by the user—would be unacceptable. Subsequently, we describe a study, the goal of which was to understand the timing problem associated with the reception of back-to-back frames.[68,69]

Figure 20   Structure of local-area network adapter (from
Ref. 68)
©1982 IEEE

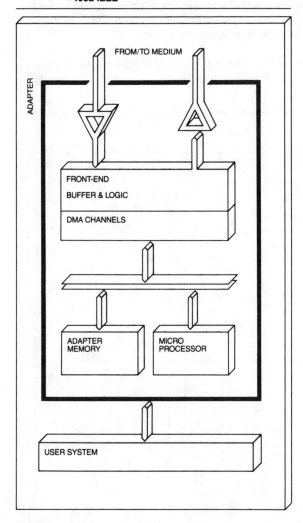

Adapter operation. The structure of the network adapter under consideration is shown in Figure 20. It contains the circuitry necessary to transmit data onto and receive data from the transmission medium and memory for buffering both outgoing and incoming frames. It also has one or more direct memory access (DMA) channels for data transfer between the transmission medium and the adapter memory. Furthermore, the adapter contains a processor that manages the frame buffers and DMA channel(s), and controls the interface to the user system.

When a frame is received, its destination address is compared with the address of the adapter to determine whether the frame is to be copied. If so, the frame is transferred into the adapter memory, provided a DMA channel has previously been set up by the processor. Arriving frames can get lost if no receive buffer is available or if a buffer is available but the processor was unable to set up a DMA early enough. At the end of each DMA transfer, an interrupt to the processor is generated. When servicing this interrupt, the processor searches for a free receive buffer and then sets up the DMA channel to receive into the acquired buffer.

The design goal is that a DMA channel is enabled when the first bit of a frame is received. Obviously, the chance of achieving this goal is higher, the smaller the DMA set-up time and the more DMA channels provided. In addition, one may employ a FIFO buffer at the adapter front-end to temporarily store incoming data in case no DMA channel is enabled. A further possibility to achieve zero (or very small) frame-loss probability is to define the medium access protocol in such a way that a minimum gap is guaranteed between subsequent frames. In this paper, we do not consider the latter possibility, although the analysis can be modified to cover this case.[69]

Data flow on transmit operations is essentially the reverse of the receive operation described above. Since our study concentrates on the most critical part of the adapter operation, namely, frame reception, we do not elaborate on details of the transmit operation.

An alternative to the adapter structure under consideration is a design where received frames are transferred (by DMA) directly into the user system memory without being buffered in the adapter. This, of course, places more constraints on the architecture and performance of the attaching station; an advantage is, however, that intermediate buffering is not needed in the adapter. It should be noted that in such a system, basically the same problem has to be solved regarding the reception of back-to-back frames. Again, a DMA channel must be enabled when the first bit of a frame needs to be buffered.

The model subsequently developed is oriented towards the adapter structure shown in Figure 20. However, the basic mechanism modeled is general enough for the analysis of this model also to be applicable to other adapter structures, e.g., one without buffers.

Performance model. The major assumptions underlying this study are as follows. Frame losses due to shortage of receive buffers are negligible, either because sufficient receive buffers are provided or because the frames received can be moved very rapidly to the user system. A fixed number of DMA channels is always dedicated to the receive direction. We shall restrict our discussion to the situation where a series of frames arrives back-to-back at an adapter. Upon arrival of the first frame, all DMA channels are assumed to be enabled.

The structure of our model is shown in Figure 21; its operation can be described as follows. When the first bit of a frame is to be copied, the state of the front-end buffer is checked; if the front-end buffer is not empty, the frame will be lost. Otherwise, two different situations may occur:

• At least one DMA channel is enabled: In this case, the frame is transferred via one of the enabled

Figure 21 Adapter performance model (from Ref. 68)
©1982 IEEE

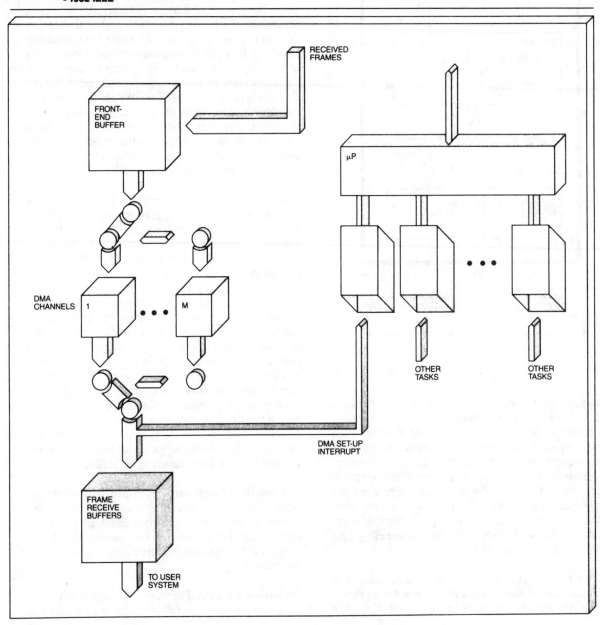

Table 1 Probabilities PB(*n*) (in percent) that *n*th back-to-back frame has been lost (one DMA channel; *B* is in bytes)

| | Speed (million bits per second) | | | | | |
| | 4 | | 8 | | 16 | |
	$B = 0$	$B = 10$	$B = 0$	$B = 20$	$B = 0$	$B = 40$
PB (1)	0	0	0	0	0	0
PB (2)	100	0	100	0	100	0
PB (3)	0	0	0	15.0	32.6	65.4
PB (4)	100	0	100	12.7	67.4	27.2
PB (5)	0	0	0	10.8	54.6	17.4
PB (6)	100	0	100	11.4	56.1	41.0
PB (7)	0	0	0	11.6	58.8	32.2
PB (8)	100	0	100	11.5	55.7	26.1

DMA channels into a receive buffer at medium transmission speed.

- No DMA channel is enabled: At medium transmission speed, the frame is written into the front-end buffer. If the front-end buffer is filled before a DMA channel is enabled, the frame will be lost. Otherwise, the newly enabled DMA channel will transfer the contents of the front-end buffer into a receive buffer at DMA channel speed, which is higher than the medium transmission speed. Once the front-end buffer has been emptied, the remainder of the frame is, of course, transferred at medium transmission speed.

An interrupt to the processor is generated at the end of the DMA operation. When servicing this interrupt, the processor acquires a free receive buffer and sets up the DMA channel with the starting address of this buffer. It is assumed that processing of the interrupt takes a constant time and that this interrupt has preemptive priority over the other processing tasks. Our model takes into account that, at interrupt generation time, the processor may still be busy processing an earlier interrupt of the same type, or—in an even worse situation—that previously generated interrupt requests from other DMA channels may still be waiting to be processed.

Analysis. It is relatively straightforward to determine conditions under which back-to-back frames are always successfully received (see Wong and Bux[68,69]). In practice, these conditions may not be met for reasons of hardware/software constraints or cost. If this is the case, knowledge of the probabilities of (a) losing the *n*th back-to-back frame and (b) being able to receive *n* back-to-back frames successfully will be very useful in designing an adapter. We subsequently

outline how analytic results for these probabilities can be obtained.

The basic approach is to study the time-dependent behavior of a two-dimensional stochastic process $(i(t), j(t))$ defined as follows: $i(t)$ measures the occupancy of the front-end buffer at time t, expressed in terms of the time it takes to transfer the buffered data to the adapter memory at DMA speed; $j(t)$ is the total amount of unfinished work of the adapter processor (relevant to the DMA set-up task). Since the DMA set-up time is constant, the number of enabled/disabled DMA channels can be simply deduced from $j(t)$ at any point in time. Figure 22 shows a sample path of this process and the corresponding states of the DMA channels.

Define an "observation instant" to be a point in time immediately after the last bit of a frame has been copied, under the condition that a DMA channel is available. It is not difficult to see that the process $(i(t), j(t))$ possesses the Markov property[70] at these observation instants. Furthermore, one can determine whether or not a frame has been lost from the state of the process at the previous observation instant. We can therefore obtain answers to our basic performance questions if the state probabilities at the observation instants are known.

Details of the analysis are given in Reference 68; Reference 69 also describes efficient numerical algorithms to compute the relevant performance measures.

Results. For the subsequent results, the transmission speeds considered are 4, 8, and 16 million bits per second. The DMA channel speed D is assumed to be 32 million bits per second. Frame lengths are distributed according to the discrete analog of a truncated hyperexponential distribution;[69] the mean and coefficient of variation of this distribution are 100 bytes and 1.2, respectively. The choice of these values is motivated by the measurement data reported in Shoch and Hupp.[24]

Adapter model with one DMA channel. Consider first the case of one DMA channel. In Table 1, we show the probabilities PB(*n*) that the *n*th frame in a sequence of back-to-back frames is lost for a DMA set-up time of 20 microseconds and different medium transmission speeds. The front-end buffer size B is either zero or equal to the product of DMA set-up time T and ring transmission speed R.

IBM SYSTEMS JOURNAL, VOL 23, NO 4, 1984

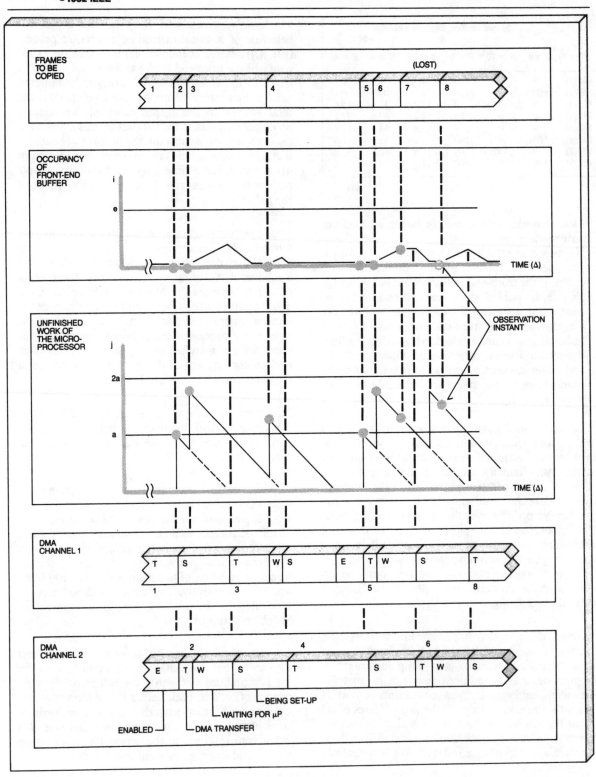

Table 2 Probability NB(n) (in percent) that first n back-to-back frames have been successfully received (one DMA channel; 16-million-bit-per-second transmission rate)

	DMA Setup Time (microseconds)				
	4	8	12	16	20
NB (1)	100.0	100.0	100.0	100.0	100.0
NB (2)	100.0	100.0	100.0	100.0	100.0
NB (3)	100.0	78.6	58.2	44.2	34.6
NB (4)	100.0	61.6	33.8	19.2	12.0
NB (5)	100.0	48.5	19.7	8.7	4.2
NB (6)	100.0	38.1	11.5	3.8	1.4
NB (7)	100.0	20.0	6.7	1.7	0.5
NB (8)	100.0	23.5	3.9	0.8	0.2

Table 3 Probability NB(n) (in percent) that first n back-to-back frames have been successfully received (16-million-bit-per-second transmission rate)

	DMA Channels		
	2	2	3
	No F/E buffer	40-byte F/E buffer	No F/E buffer
NB (1)	100	100	100
NB (2)	100	100	100
NB (3)	67.4	100	100
NB (4)	45.4	95.4	100
NB (5)	30.6	90.1	98.7
NB (6)	20.6	85.1	97.1
NB (7)	13.9	80.4	95.5
NB (8)	9.4	75.9	94.0

Apparently, the adapter performs poorly when front-end buffering is not employed. Every other frame is lost for medium speeds of 4 and 8 million bits per second. The results for the case of 16 million bits per second are different because more than one frame may arrive during DMA set-up.

If front-end buffering is employed, all frames are successfully received at the four-million-bit-per-second transmission speed. However, frame loss is observed when the speed is doubled. For the case of 16 million bits per second, the use of front-end buffering results in only a slight improvement in the loss probability. This is an indication that the DMA set-up process is too slow and the processor is the system bottleneck. This observation leads us to subsequently study the adapter performance as a function of the DMA set-up time.

In Table 2, we show the results for NB(n), the probability that the first n frames in a sequence of back-to-back frames have been successfully received for different values of the DMA set-up time T. The medium transmission speed is 16 million bits per second. The front-end buffer size is equal to T * R. All frames have been successfully received when T = 4 microseconds. For other values of T, frames may be lost, and the results in Table 2 show the performance degradation when T is increased.

Adapter model with two or more DMA channels. Finally, we consider the effectiveness of using more than one DMA channel to prevent loss of frames. For the case of a transmission speed of 16 million bits per second, Table 3 shows results for three different designs: (1) two DMA channels, no front-end buffer; (2) two DMA channels, 40-byte front-end buffer; (3) three DMA channels, no front-end buffer. The DMA set-up time is 20 microseconds.

We observe substantial improvements offered by the use of front-end buffering or the use of an additional DMA channel. The addition of an extra DMA channel is slightly more effective than front-end buffering in alleviating the timing problem associated with DMA setup. Any further increase in the number of DMA channels is not expected to improve performance significantly.

Acknowledgment

The last two major sections of this paper are based on joint work by J. W. Wong and the author. The token-ring simulation results in the second major section were produced by H. L. Truong. Both contributions are gratefully acknowledged. The author would also like to thank K. Kuemmerle for many helpful discussions and for reviewing the manuscript. Much of this paper also appears in *Lecture Notes in Computer Science* (Editors: D. Hutchinson, D. Shepherd, and J. Mariani), published by Springer-Verlag, Heidelberg, Germany, and is reprinted with their permission.

Cited references

1. D. D. Clark, K. T. Pogran, and D. P. Reed, "An introduction to local area networks," *Proceedings of the IEEE* **66**, 1497–1517 (1978).
2. R. C. Dixon, N. C. Strole, and J. D. Markov, "A token-ring network for local data communications," *IBM Systems Journal* **22**, Nos. 1 & 2, 47–62 (1983).
3. K. Kuemmerle and M. Reiser, "Local-area communication networks—An overview," *Journal of Telecommunication Networks* **1**, 349–370 (1982).
4. *ECMA TR/14: Local Area Networks Layers 1 to 4 Architecture and Protocols* (September 1982).

5. *Standard ECMA-80: Local Area Networks (CSMA/CD Baseband) Coaxial Cable System* (September 1982).

6. *Standard ECMA-81: Local Area Networks (CSMA/CD Baseband) Physical Layer* (September 1982).

7. *Standard ECMA-82: Local Area Networks (CSMA/CD Baseband) Link Layer* (September 1982).

8. *Standard ECMA-89: Local Area Networks Token Ring* (September 1983).

9. *Standard ECMA-90: Local Area Networks Token Bus (Broadband)* (September 1983).

10. *IEEE Standard 802.2, Logical Link Control.*

11. *IEEE Standard 802.3, CSMA/CD Access Method and Physical Layer Specifications.*

12. *IEEE Standard 802.4, Token-Passing Bus Access Method and Physical Layer Specifications.*

13. IEEE Project 802 Local Area Network Standards, *Draft IEEE Standard 802.5, Token Ring Access Method and Physical Layer Specifications,* Working Draft (February 1984).

14. International Organization for Standardization, *Data Processing—Open Systems Interconnection—Basic Reference Model,* Draft Proposal ISO/DP 7498 (February 1982).

15. R. M. Metcalfe and D. R. Boggs, "Ethernet: Distributed packet switching for local computer networks," *Communications of the ACM* **19**, 395–404 (1976).

16. *The Ethernet—A Local Area Network Data Link Layer and Physical Layer Specifications,* Version 1.0, Digital Equipment, Intel, and Xerox Corporations (September 30, 1980); available from Digital Equipment Corporation, Maynard, MA, from Intel Corporation, Santa Clara, CA, and from Xerox Corporation, Stamford, CT.

17. L. Kleinrock and F. A. Tobagi, "Packet switching in radio channels: Part I—Carrier sense multiple access modes and their throughput-delay characteristics," *IEEE Transactions on Communications* **COM-23**, 1400–1416 (1975).

18. F. A. Tobagi and L. Kleinrock, "Packet switching in radio channels: Part IV—Stability considerations and dynamic control in carrier sense multiple access modes," *IEEE Transactions on Communications* **COM-25**, 1103–1120 (1977).

19. G. T. Almes and E. D. Lazowska, "The behavior of Ethernet-like computer communications networks," *Proceedings of the 7th Symposium on Operating Systems Principles,* Asilomar Grounds, CA (1979), pp. 66–81.

20. E. Arthurs and B. W. Stuck, "A theoretical performance analysis of polling and carrier sense collision detection systems," *Proceedings of the IFIP Conference on Local Computer Networks,* North-Holland Publishing Company, Amsterdam (1982), pp. 415–438.

21. W. Bux, "Local-area subnetworks: A performance comparison," *IEEE Transactions on Communications* **COM-29**, No. 10, 1465–1473 (1981).

22. S. S. Lam, "A carrier sense multiple access protocol for local networks," *Computer Networks* **4**, 21–32 (1980).

23. F. A. Tobagi and V. B. Hunt, "Performance analysis of carrier sense multiple access with collision detection," *Computer Networks* **4**, 245–259 (1980).

24. J. F. Shoch and J. A. Hupp, "Measured performance of an Ethernet local network," *Communications of the ACM* **23**, 711–721 (1980).

25. D. J. Farber, J. Feldman, F. R. Heinrich, M. D. Hopwood, D. C. Loomis, and A. Rowe, "The Distributed Computer System," *Proceedings of the 7th IEEE Computer Society International Conference,* IEEE, Piscataway, NJ (1973), pp. 31–34.

26. W. D. Farmer and E. E. Newhall, "An experimental distributed switching system to handle bursty computer traffic," *Proceedings of the ACM Symposium on Problems in the Optimization of Data Communications,* Pine Mountain, GA (1963), pp. 31–34.

27. B. K. Penney and A. A. Baghdadi, "Survey of computer communications loop networks: Parts 1 and 2," *Computer Communications* **2**, 165–180 and 224–241 (1979).

28. W. Bux, F. Closs, P. A. Janson, K. Kuemmerle, and H. R. Mueller, "A reliable token-ring system for local-area communication," *Conference Record of NTC '81,* IEEE, Piscataway, NJ (1981), pp. A2.2.1–A2.2.6.

29. W. Bux, F. Closs, P. A. Janson, K. Kuemmerle, H. R. Mueller, and E. H. Rothauser, "A local-area communication network based on a reliable token-ring system," *Proceedings of the International Symposium on Local Computer Networks,* North-Holland Publishing Co., Amsterdam (1982), pp. 69–82.

30. J. H. Saltzer and K. T. Pogran, "A star-shaped ring network with high maintainability," *Computer Networks* **4**, 239–244 (1980).

31. A. K. Agrawala, J. R. Agre, and K. D. Gordon, "The slotted vs. the token-controlled ring: A comparative evaluation," *Proceedings of COMPSAC 1978,* Chicago (1978), pp. 674–679.

32. W. Bux and H. L. Truong, "Token-ring performance: Mean-delay approximation," *Proceedings of the 10th International Teletraffic Congress* (Montreal, Canada), North-Holland Publishing Company, Amsterdam (1983), pp. 3.1-3/1–3.1-3/6.

33. W. Bux and H. L. Truong, "Mean-delay approximation for cyclic-service queueing systems," *Performance Evaluation* **3**, 187–196 (August 1983).

34. R. B. Cooper, "Queues served in cyclic order: Waiting times," *Bell System Technical Journal* **49**, 399–413 (1970).

35. M. Eisenberg, "Queues with periodic service and changeover times," *Operations Research* **20**, 440–451 (1972).

36. O. Hashida, "Analysis of multiqueue," *Review of Electrical Communications Laboratories* **20**, 189–199 (1972).

37. J. F. Hayes, "Local distribution in computer communications," *IEEE Communications Magazine,* pp. 6–14 (March 1981).

38. A. R. Kaye, "Analysis of a distributed control loop for data transmission," *Proceedings of the Computer Communications, Networks, and Teletraffic Symposium,* Brooklyn Polytechnic, New York (1982), pp. 47–58.

39. A. G. Konheim and B. Meister, "Waiting lines and times in a system with polling," *Journal of the ACM* **21**, 470–490 (1974).

40. P. J. Kuehn, "Multiqueue systems with nonexhaustive cyclic service," *Bell System Technical Journal* **58**, 671–698 (1979).

41. I. Rubin and L. F. DeMoraes, "Polling schemes for local communication networks," *Conference Record ICC '81,* IEEE, Piscataway, NJ (1981), pp. 33.5.1–33.5.7.

42. G. B. Swartz, "Polling in a loop system," *Journal of the ACM* **27**, 42–59 (1980).

43. M. V. Wilkes and D. J. Wheeler, "The Cambridge Digital Communication Ring," *Proceedings of the Symposium on Local Area Communication Networks,* Boston (1979), pp. 47–61.

44. E. R. Hafner, Z. Nenadal, and M. Tschanz, "A digital loop communications system," *IEEE Transactions on Communications* **COM-22**, 877–881 (1974).

45. C. C. Reames and M. T. Liu, "A loop network for simultaneous transmission of variable length messages," *Proceedings of the 2nd Annual Symposium on Computer Architecture,* Houston, TX (1975), pp. 7–12.

46. L. Fratta, F. Borgonovo, and F. A. Tobagi, "The Express-net: A local area communication network integrating voice and data," *Proceedings of the International Conference on the Performance of Data Communication Systems and their Applications,* North-Holland Publishing Co., Amsterdam (1981), pp. 77–88.

47. J. O. Limb and C. Flores, "Description of Fasnet, a unidirectional local area communications network," *Bell System Technical Journal* **61**, 1413–1440 (September 1982).

48. E. H. Rothauser and D. Wild, "MLMA: A collision-free multiaccess method," *Proceedings of IFIP Congress 77*, North-Holland Publishing Co., Amsterdam (1977), pp. 431-436.

49. F. A. Tobagi, "Multiaccess protocols in packet communication systems," *IEEE Transactions on Communications* **COM-28**, 468–488 (1980).

50. J. Capetanakis, "Tree algorithms for packet broadcast channels," *IEEE Transactions on Information Theory* **IT-25**, 505–515 (1979).

51. J. Capetanakis, "Generalized TDMA: The multi-accessing tree protocol," *IEEE Transactions on Communications* **COM-275**, 1476–1484 (1979).

52. J. F. Hayes, "An adaptive technique for local distribution," *IEEE Transactions on Communications* **COM-26**, 1178–1186 (1978).

53. W. M. Kiesel and P. J. Kuehn, "CSMA-CD-DR: A new multiaccess protocol for distributed systems," *Conference Record NTC '81*, IEEE, Piscataway, NJ (1981).

54. G. S. Blair, "A performance study of the Cambridge Ring," *Computer Networks* **6**, 13–20 (1982).

55. G. S. Blair and D. Shepherd, "A performance comparison of Ethernet and the Cambridge Digital Communication Ring," *Computer Networks* **6**, 105–113 (1982).

56. W. Bux and M. Schlatter, "An approximate method for the performance analysis of buffer insertion rings," *IEEE Transactions on Communications* **COM-31**, 50–55 (1983).

57. M. T. Liu, G. Babic, and R. Pardo, "Traffic analysis of the distributed loop computer network (DLCN)," *Proceedings of the National Telecommunications Conference*, IEEE, Piscataway, NJ (1977), pp. 31:5-1–31:5-7.

58. A. Thomasian and H. Kanakia, "Performance study of loop networks using buffer insertion," *Computer Networks* **3**, 419–425 (1979).

59. W. Bux, "Analysis of a local-area bus system with controlled access," *IEEE Transactions on Computers* **C-32**, 760–763 (1983).

60. M. Fine and F. A. Tobagi, "Performance of round-robin schemes in unidirectional broadcast local networks," *Proceedings of the ICC '82*, IEEE, Piscataway, NJ (1982), pp. 1C.5.1–1C.5.6.

61. V. C. Hamacher and G. S. Shedler, "Access response on a collision-free local bus network," *Computer Networks* **6**, 93–103 (1982).

62. O. Spaniol, "Modelling of local computer networks," *Computer Networks* **3**, 315–326 (1979).

63. O. Spaniol, "Analysis and performance evaluation of HYPER-CHANNEL access protocols," *Proceedings of the 2nd International Conference on Distributed Computing Systems*, IEEE, Piscataway, NJ (1981), pp. 247–255.

64. F. A. Tobagi and R. Rom, "Efficient round-robin and priority schemes for unidirectional broadcast systems," *Proceedings of IFIP WG 6.4 International Workshop on Local Area Networks*, Boston (1979), pp. 47–61.

65. *Standard ECMA-72: Transport Protocol*, 2nd Revision (September 1982).

66. International Organization for Standardization, *Data Processing—Open Systems Interconnection—Connection Oriented Transport Protocol Specification*, Draft Proposal ISO/DP 8073 (June 1982).

67. J. W. Wong and W. Bux, *Performance Evaluation of Logical Link Control in a Local-Area Ring Network*, to appear as an IBM Research Report (1984).

68. J. W. Wong and W. Bux, "Analytic modeling of an adapter to local-area networks," *Proceedings of GLOBECOM 82*, Miami, IEEE, Piscataway, NJ (1982), pp. C.2.3.1–C.2.3.6.

69. J. W. Wong and W. Bux, *Analytic Modeling of an Adapter to Local-Area Networks*, Research Report RZ-1175, IBM Corporation, Research Division, P.O. Box 218, Yorktown Heights, NY 10598.

70. L. Kleinrock, *Queueing Systems*, Vols. I and II, John Wiley & Sons, Inc., New York (1976).

Reprint Order No. G321-5230.

Werner Bux *IBM Research Division, Thomas J. Watson Research Center, P.O. Box 218, Yorktown Heights, New York 10598.* Dr. Bux joined the IBM Zurich Research Laboratory as a Research Staff Member in 1979. He is currently on assignment to the Research Center in Yorktown Heights. His work for the past several years has been in the area of architecture and performance evaluation of local-area networks. He has also been involved in local network standardization through his work in TC24 of the European Computer Manufacturers Association (ECMA). Dr. Bux received the M.S. and Ph.D. degrees in electrical engineering from the University of Stuttgart, Stuttgart, West Germany, in 1974 and 1980, respectively.

End-To-End Performance Modeling of Local Area Networks

LIONEL C. MITCHELL, MEMBER, IEEE, AND DAVID A. LIDE

Abstract—This paper presents a generic modeling framework for synthesizing existing modeling techniques into a hierarchical structure for representing the end-to-end path between subscriber devices on local area networks (LAN's). The modeling framework is based on analytical queueing network models in a hierarchical decomposition along the layers of communications protocols in the LAN. The methodology can be used during the various phases of LAN system design as well as for capacity planning during the operational phase. The level of system detail that can be examined using the methodology ranges from the architectural level to the component level. A survey of existing LAN models is given and their applicability to the heirarchical framework is discussed. The methodology is described and a case study is presented.

I. INTRODUCTION

THE widespread use of LAN systems in government and industry has brought with it a diversity in communication protocol architectures. Protocols such as X.25, TCP, and Xerox Network Service (XNS) have been used to implement reliable transport service between subscriber devices as well as between subscriber device and Network Interface Unit (NIU) and between NIU's. The flow control throttling mechanism of these protocols plus the long path length for some functions (e.g., CRC in software) performed by these protocols provides the motivation to model these aspects of the LAN in detail to determine performance characteristics. There is a commensurate motivation to represent the subscriber devices at a corresponding level of detail in the LAN system model since performance requirements are stated in terms of end-to-end response time and throughput.

The queueing network model is an effective tool for ascertaining the performance characteristics of LAN's. The queueing network provides the framework for representing the hardware resource capacities, the software/firmware and message resource demands, and the workload demand frequencies of the subscriber devices and the NIU's in the LAN as well as the contention among the NIU's for channel access. A natural decomposition of LAN communication path elements has evolved in the modeling of LAN's along the layers of the different communication protocols. The Media Access Control (MAC) protocol constitutes the primary level of the hierarchical decomposition. The protocols which affect communica-

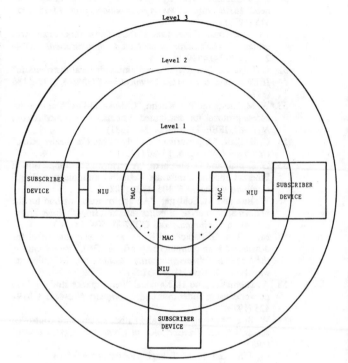

Fig. 1. Hierarchical LAN model.

tions between the NIU's and between the subscriber devices constitute a second level. The communications between application programs in the subscriber devices constitute a third level. In this hierarchical structure, each level depends on the next lower level to complete its "service." The three-level hierarchy is illustrated in Fig. 1. The hierarchical model is solved approximately using the Chandy, Herzog, and Woo theorem [7] on decomposition. Many models have been developed which examine the MAC protocol; however, few to date have examined all three levels in a common framework using analytical and approximation techniques exclusively. The methodology presented in this paper provides a generic approach for representing the delay components which affect end-to-end performance. The methodology can be used to model a wide variety of protocols used in LAN systems.

In Section II of this paper, a survey of existing LAN models and techniques is given. This discussion includes different MAC protocol models as well as hierarchical models (for Levels 2 and 3) which have been solved by analytical and simulation techniques. The hierarchical modeling methodology synthesis is described in Section

Manuscript received October 7, 1985; revised February 19, 1986.
The authors are with Computer Technology Associates, Inc., McLean, VA 22102.
IEEE Log Number 8609932.

III. The assumptions and solution techniques of the hierarchical model are given. A case study is presented in Section IV in which a LAN model is described and results are presented.

II. LAN MODEL SURVEY

Early LAN models were associated with the development of the MAC protocols. Analytical models were developed to predict maximum system throughput. These early models and subsequent models were extended to provide packet delay results. In Level 2 models, the Network Interface Unit (NIU) details were combined with the delay results of Level 1 models to predict delay between NIU's for a fully populated LAN. These models treated subscriber unit delay cursorily if at all. Some models have focused on the complete thread between subscriber devices for the purpose of predicting user response time. These Level 3 models use the results from the Level 2 and Level 1 models to obtain end-to-end delay and throughput metrics.

A survey of models for the different levels of the hierarchy is given in this section. The models presented are exemplary of the types of LAN models which appear in the literature.

A. Level 1 Model Survey

Level 1 in the LAN modeling hierarchy corresponds to the Media Access Control (MAC) protocol. Models have been developed for carrier sense protocols (e.g., CSMA and CSMA/CD), ALOHA, token ring, and token bus. These models compute the time for a station to gain access to the channel and transmit a packet. Several examples of Level 1 models and their application in the hierarchical modeling methodology are given below.

Some of the earliest MAC protocol models were developed by Kleinrock and Tobagi [14]–[16], [42]. These models examined the Carrier Sense Multiple Access (CSMA) protocols without collision detection. LAN throughput equations for nonpersistent, 1-persistent, and p-persistent were developed. These analytic models assume a Poisson traffic source from an infinite number of stations, each generating a small proportion of the total traffic. This is a reasonable assumption for a large number of interactive terminals. Packet delay equations can be derived from the throughput equations of these models. The resulting packet delay can be used as the mean service time for the MAC server in a Level 2 model.

Other similar analytical models have been developed for nonpersistent, p-persistent, and 1-persistent CSMA/CD protocols. In addition to the persistent difference, these models differ in the way that the time line is modeled (i.e., continuous versus slotted) and in the representation of the backoff algorithm. The mean packet delay expressions from these models may be used to quantify the mean service rate of the MAC server in a Level 2 model. The reader is referred to [8], [11], [20], and [39] [41] for the details of these models.

A finite population model of 1-persistent CSMA/CD has

been developed by Lazowska et al. [19] with the hierarchical modeling scheme in mind. The model computes the service rate of the MAC protocol as a function of the number of stations on the LAN. This variable rate function can be used in a Flow-Equivalent Service Center (FESC) in a Level 2 system model.

O'Reilly describes a simulation model of a slotted 1-persistent CSMA/CD model in [28]–[30]. The average packet delay results from this model can also be used in a Level 2 model.

Several models have also been developed to analyze the delay/throughput characteristics of token protocols. In [35], three polling protocols are modeled: gated, exhaustive, and reservation. The Markov chain models are used to derive results for mean message delay for the gated and exhaustive protocols and upper and lower bounds for the mean message delay for the reservation protocol. In [24], a token bus protocol similar to IEEE 802 Standard [12] is modeled analytically and approximate average packet delay results are derived. Berry and Chandy use an $M/G/1$ model in [2] to compute delay and queue length statistics for a token ring protocol. This model showed good results when compared to simulation results. The single packet delay expressions from these models can be used to quantify the service time for the MAC server in a Level 2 model.

In [21], the Hyperbus[1] virtual token protocol is modeled using a discrete-time Markov chain. A packet delay expression is derived from which the service time for a MAC server in a Level 2 model can be quantified.

Tobagi presents a Markovian model of the slotted ALOHA protocol in [41]. Packet delay and interdeparture time distributions are derived and expressions for their moments are given. The expression for the mean packet delay can be used to determine the service time for the MAC server in a Level 2 model.

Bux provides a comparison of MAC protocols in [4]. The models of the token ring, slotted ring, CSMA/CD, and ordered-access bus all assume a finite number of stations, each with a Poisson arrival rate and a general packet size distribution. An expression for mean packet transfer time is given for each model. The mean packet transfer time can be used for the MAC service time in a Level 2 model.

B. Level 2 Model Survey

Level 2 in the LAN modeling hierarchy corresponds to the path between subscriber devices on the LAN. This includes the protocol processing and data transfer within the network Interface Units (NIU's) as well as the MAC protocol functions. It also includes the interface between the NIU and its attached subscriber device and any protocol processing in the subscriber device.

Maglaris amd Lissack present an analysis of NIU architectures in [22]. They use open queueing network models and a separate Level 1 model to represent the MAC protocol (CSMA). These models represented the

---

[1]Hyperbus is a trademark of the Network Systems Corporation.

NIU hardware and protocol software, but ignored flow control mechanisms. This Level 2 model could easily be extended to include the third hierarchical level of the present methodology. If the Level 3 model is an open queueing network, then the subscriber device queueing servers could be added to the open chain of the Level 2 model. This model can be solved exactly by Jackson's theorem; decomposition is not necessary. If the Level 3 chain is closed, then it is not necessary to solve the Level 2 model separately (i.e., it becomes part of the Level 3 closed chain model which is solved exactly). The absence of the closed chain representation of flow control in the Level 2 model obviates the third level of the hierarchy.

A closed queueing network model was used by the same authors in [23] to represent the flow-controlled path between subscriber devices. The population size of the closed chain was equal to the number of subscriber devices attached to an NIU. The flow control protocol was assumed to have a window size of one. Approximate mean value analysis [31] was used to solve the model. Single packet requests and responses were assumed. The CSMA "service" time was determined from a Level 1 MAC Protocol model. Delay within the subscriber devices was represented by a delay server (i.e., as a think time). The results from this model (with think times equal to zero) could be used in an FESC model in a Level 3 model.

Mitchell and Lide model reliable protocol connections between NIU's and between NIU's and subscriber devices using a closed queueing network model [27]. A Level 1 MAC protocol model (nonpersistent CSMA/CD) was used to compute service time for the MAC server in the Level 2 model. The model represents acknowledgment packets explicitly. The population sizes of the closed chains are the window sizes for the different flow control protocols being represented. Approximate MVA [31] was used to solve the model. The results of this Level 2 model could be used in a Flow-Equivalent Service Center (FESC) node in a Level 3 model.

C. Level 3 Model Survey

Level 3 in the LAN modeling hierarchy corresponds to the path between application programs in subscriber devices. This model incorporates the Level 2 model communication delays in computing end-to-end delay and throughput. The delay attributable to the application processes may be due to CPU processing, disk and/or tape data access, and data transfer over internal computer buses.

The models of end-to-end LAN threads presented in [25] and [26] use an open queueing network approach. The packet delay computed by the Level 1 model is used in the MAC server of the queueing network model which includes the NIU and subscriber device servers as well as the interface servers. Protocol and application processing and I/O activities are characterized in the NIU and subscriber devices. Because these models do not represent flow control protocols, the three-level hierarchy reduces to two levels.

In [1], Bernard uses a hierarchical model of interconnected LAN's to compute end-to-end delay. In the model of a single LAN, the MAC protocol is reduced to a single variable rate server with the exponential service rate as a function of the number of NIU's. Execution time of the communication software is assumed to be insignificant relative to application processing time and is ignored. The application processor queues of the LAN stations are aggregated into a single queue with an exponential service rate proportional to the number of active stations. This single LAN representation is comparable to the present hierarchical methodology. The primary differences are that NIU's are not represented at all; and the entire set of LAN subscriber devices is represented by a single FESC node. Also, no representation is made of flow control procedures.

Wong *et al.* present a hierarchical modeling scheme in [45] which is directly comparable to the present methodology. The three levels in that approach are basically the same as the ones described here. A hybrid analytical/simulation solution technique is used to solve the hierarchical model. Data packets and acknowledgments (ACK's) are both modeled explicitly, and it is assumed that each data packet is acknowledged separately. The Level 1 MAC model is solved analytically to determine the FESC node service rates for the Level 2 model for data and ACK packets. The Level 2 model is solved by simulation. It includes servers for the MAC protocol and the subscriber device/NIU interface. The protocol processing times in the subscriber devices and the NIU's are assumed to be zero. Markov chain analysis is used to solve the Level 3 model. A single, aggregate server is used in the Level 3 model to represent the application process in the subscriber device. The results from the hybrid model were compared to results from a detailed simulation model. The differences presented ranged between 1 and 12 percent with an average of 5 percent. Their findings showed that the greatest error occurred for a large number of stations and a large flow control window size. The present methodology differs from that described in [45] in solution techniques and in level of system detail modeled. We represent explicitly the details of the protocol software in the subscriber devices and NIU's.

Goldberg *et al.* present an end-to-end model of a token ring LAN in [10]. The system configuration modeled consisted of four VAX 11/750's, each with a set of directly connected terminals. The product-form queueing model represents the terminals as delay servers, the CPU as a processor sharing server, the disks as FCFS servers, and the network as a single FCFS server. This is comparable to subscriber device representation in the present methodology. The model ignores the communication protocols in the hosts and NIU's and approximates the details of the multiple access protocol with an FCFS single server. Also, there is no representation of flow control as contrasted with the present methodology. The model is solved by a variation of the MVA which accommodates an asynchronous background activity. Measurement data were used as input to the model, and predicted results were compared to experimental results. The range of differences between the model predictions and the measured results was approximately 10–25 percent.

Other communication system models serve as prime inspiration in our LAN modeling methodology, although they are not representative of LAN systems. Reiser [31] analyzed computer communication networks with a window flow control protocol using a closed queueing network model. The analysis assumes that messages arriving to a system when the window is "closed" are discarded (i.e., a loss system). In [32], Reiser extends the technique to a no-loss system by assuming that each message has an exponential sojourn time (i.e., the chain delay). Varghese *et al.* in [44] analyze a similar model without the exponential assumption. They use an approximation approach validated by a simulation model. The approximate model results were within 10 percent of the simulation model results.

III. METHODOLOGY

The goal of the hierarchical LAN modeling methodology is to provide a generic basis for computing end-to-end response time and throughput for a LAN system where reliable protocols are implemented. The methodology draws on queueing network techniques (both exact and approximate) that have previously been applied to the modeling of computer and communication systems. It can be applied for open and closed chains in the Level 3 model.

The methodology relies primarily on the decomposition technique [7]. Decomposition provides a good approximation for nonproduct-form networks where the number of cycles in the subnetwork (e.g., Level 2) is large [36]. The error introduced when the number of cycles is equal to one can be greater than 25 percent (overestimation) as shown by Varghese *et al.* in [44] for small networks with small population size and high utilization. Their results suggest, however, that the error decreases as population size increases. They used an approximation technique which showed errors less than 10 percent for the same networks when compared to simulation results. In the present methodology, if we represent the feedback loops due to the subscriber device and NIU execution of multiple layers of protocol, then the number of cycles increases. If we use this detailed representation of the protocols and the flow control window size is large, then we would expect the error due to decomposition to be reasonably small. We have not, to date, validated this hypothesis with simulation or measurement results.

The methodology also relies on the independence assumption of service times at the various queues. This is justified where the mix of message sizes (which determine service time at some of the servers) is diverse [13].

The notation for the hierarchical models is given in Table I. A description of the models for each level followed by a step-by-step description of the solution algorithm is given below.

TABLE I
LAN HIERARCHICAL MODEL NOTATION

Hierarchy Level	Symbol	Description
1	d_{MAC}	MAC Protocol Delay
1	λ_N	Total LAN Load
1	λ_N'	Background Load on LAN
1	NS	Number of LAN Stations
2	N	Number of Servers
2	M	Number of Chains
2	W_j	Chain j Population ($j = 1, \cdots, M$)
2	μ_i'	Server i Service Rate ($i = 1, \cdots, N$)
2	μ_i	Adjusted Service Rate for Server i
2	$\lambda_j(K)$	Chain j State Dependent Throughputs ($K = 1, \cdots, W_j$)
2	$p_{ij}(K)$	Server i, Chain j State-Dependent Queue Length Probabilities
2	$d_{ij}(K)$	Server i, Chain j State-Dependent Delays
2	$A_j(K)$	Chain j ACK Delay
2	B	Number of Background Device Chains
2	b_j	Background Device Chain j Throughput ($j = 1, \cdots, B$)
2	$C_b(i)$	Set of Background Device Chains Visiting Server i
2	$S_b(j)$	Set of Servers in Background Device Chain j
2	$S_A(j)$	Set of Servers Providing Service to ACK Packets in Chain j
3	D	End-to-End Chain Delay
3	D'	End-to-End Chain Delay Adjusted for ACK's
3	W_T	Population Size for Closed, End-to-End Chain
3	λ_T	Throughput for End-to-End Chain
3	$\lambda_T(K)$	State-Dependent Throughputs for Subscriber Device Subnetwork ($k = 1, \cdots, W_T$)
3	$\mu_{Ti}(K)$	State-Dependent Service Rates for FESC Node i in End-to-End Chain
3	μ_{Ti}	Fixed Service Rate for Node i in End-to-End Chain
3	N_T	Number of Servers in End-to-End Chain

A. Level 1 Model Description

In the Level 1 model, the performance of the MAC protocol is determined for all stations on the LAN. By analyzing a multiple access protocol, such as the 1-persistent CSMA/CD illustrated in Fig. 2, we can determine the average delay d_{MAC} for a single packet from a random station on the LAN. Other MAC models (see Section II-A) could also be used. This delay includes the transmission and propagation times as well as the waiting time for packets at other stations. It does not include time spent waiting on other packets in the same station. The Level 1 model delay d_{MAC} becomes the mean exponential service time in queueing servers for the MAC protocol in the Level 2 model. The total LAN load λ_N used by the Level 1 model is the sum of the throughput of the end-to-end chain λ_T, the background LAN load λ_N', and the sum of the background device chains b_j. For finite population Level 1 models, the number of stations NS is also an input parameter. Note that the MAC server in the Level 2 model may be a fixed rate of variable rate server depending on the type of Level 1 model used.

The Level 2 model which uses the results of the Level

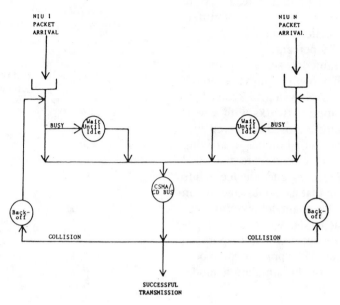

Fig. 2. 1-persistent CSMA/CD model.

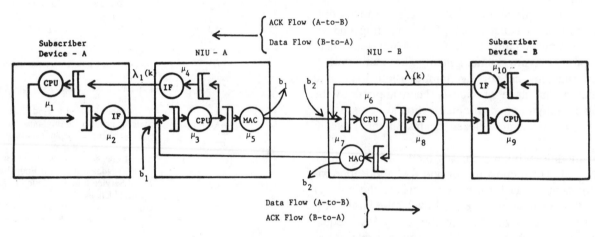

Fig. 3. Level 2 model of a single end-to-end flow control protocol.

1 MAC protocol model represents the MAC protocol as an FCFS queue. The restriction on the service time is that it must be exponentially distributed. The service time determined from the MAC protocol model may not necessarily be exponential. If the mix of packet sizes is sufficiently diverse, then the exponential assumption may not be unreasonable. In general, queueing network models are robust enough to reproduce reasonably accurate results even when the exponential service time assumption is violated [5]. An alternative to the exponential assumption is to use an approximate solution algorithm such as [31] which uses general service times; however, some error may be introduced due to the approximation nature of that algorithm.

B. Level 2 Model Description

In the Level 2 model, a closed queueing network model is constructed of the resources of a thread between two devices of interest. The closed chains in this Level 2 model represent the different levels of flow control. The chain populations are the window sizes for the different

levels. Acknowledgments (ACK's) are represented explicitly and each data packet is assumed to be separately acknowledged. Also, each direction of data flow between a pair of subscriber devices is represented by a separate set of closed chains. In addition, a set of background traffic chains which use some of the resources in the subscriber devices and/or NIU's may be introduced in the Level 2 model to represent other activities. If these chains are closed, iteration is required to determine their throughput. This is subsequently described. The background flows are included implicitly in the Level 2 model by the "load concealment" technique [34].

An example of a single end-to-end flow control protocol Level 2 model is given in Fig. 3. The single Level 2 chain, with throughput λ_1, flows through the CPU and IF servers in subscriber device A into the CPU and MAC servers in NIU-A. The chain continues into the CPU and IF servers in NIU-B and, then, through the CPU and IF servers in subscriber device B. The reverse path of the chain can be traced from subscriber device B into NIU-B, NIU-A, and subscriber device A to complete the

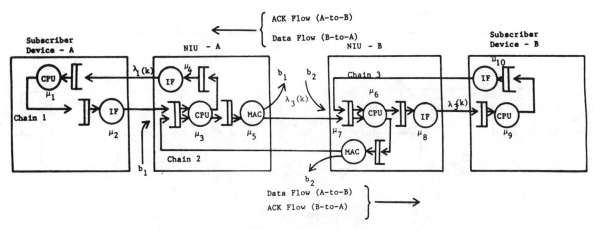

Fig. 4. Level 2 model of multiple flow control protocols.

closed chain. The forward path of the chain represents the data packet, and the reverse path represents the ACK packet. Two background chains are shown for the NIU's. These chains pass through the CPU and MAC servers of each NIU. This might correspond to traffic from another subscriber device attached to the same NIU.

An example of a Level 2 model with multiple levels of flow control is represented in Fig. 4. The three chains in Fig. 4 represent, respectively, the flow control protocols between subscriber device A and NIU-A, between NIU-A and NIU-B, and between NIU-B and subscriber device B. Two background chains are also shown.

The Level 2 queueing model consists of N servers with service rate μ_i, $i = 1, \cdots, N$, and M chains with population size w_j, $j = 1, \cdots, M$. The raw service rates μ_i' are adjusted by load concealment for the servers affected by background chains. For example, the service rates of the CPU and MAC servers of both NIU's in Figs. 3 and 4 are adjusted due to the background device chains. The MAC service rate must be adjusted in the Level 1 model; the CPU service rate is adjusted at Level 2. This model is solved using a product-form or approximate algorithm for population size $k = 1, \cdots, w_j$ for each chain j. The solution yields the chain throughputs $\lambda_j(k)$, the queue length probabilities for the servers $p_{ij}(k)$, and the delays for the servers $d_{ij}(k)$. The chain throughputs become the state-dependent service rates of the servers in the Level 3 model. The queue length probabilities and delays for the servers are used to determine the contribution to total chain delay due to the ACK packet. This delay $A_j(k)$ is defined by

$$A_j(k) = \sum_{i \in S_A(j)} \sum_{k=1}^{w_j} p_{ij}(k)\, d_{ij}(k) \quad \text{for } j = 1, \cdots, M$$

(1)

where $S_A(j)$ is the set of servers providing service to the ACK. These ACK delays are used in the Level 3 model to adjust the end-to-end chain delay.

The performance metrics computed for this Level 2 model are for packets that are internal to the closed chains. When there are w_j packets in chain j (i.e., the flow control window is closed), then any other packets arriving at that chain must wait until an ACK is received before joining the chain. This is analogous to the passive queue of memory partition models [6] for computer systems. Therefore, the closed chains of the Level 2 model become the basis for FESC nodes of the Level 3 model.

C. Level 3 Model Description

In the Level 3 model, a single closed or open chain model is constructed of the queues of the subscriber devices and the FESC nodes representing the closed chains from the Level 2 model. The single chain in this model represents the path between pairs of communicating subscriber devices. An example Level 3 model is illustrated in Fig. 5. The servers of each subscriber device are represented by a CPU and a set of disks. The three FESC nodes represent the three levels of flow control protocols that were shown in Fig. 4. The Level 3 model consists of N_T servers with service rates μ_{Ti} for fixed rate servers and $\mu_{Ti}(K)$ for state-dependent servers where $i = 1, \cdots, N_T$. The throughput for the end-to-end chain is λ_T, and the population size for a closed chain is W_T. This model is solved using a variable-rate algorithm for end-to-end delay D. This value is adjusted by the sum of the ACK delays defined in (1) to give D'. For a closed chain Level 3 model, iteration is required to determine the LAN traffic load λ_N used in the Level 1 model. A second level of iteration is required if closed background device chains are present in the Level 2 model.

The same level of detail that has been incorporated in computer models [3], [6], [36] can be incorporated in the subscriber device representation (e.g., memory management and channel models) in a Level 3 model. It should be apparent that the queues of the subscriber devices in the Level 3 model could also be aggregated into FESC nodes. This is exact for a product-form representation of the subscriber device.

D. Hierarchical LAN Model Solution Algorithm

The following steps are performed in computing end-to-end delay D' and throughput λ_T.

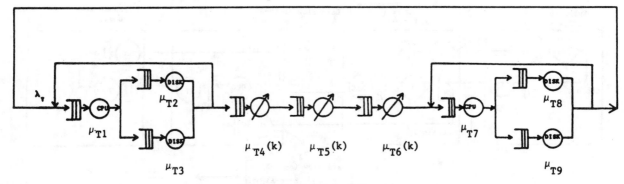

Fig. 5. Closed chain level 3 model.

Step 1: Determine an initial value for the total network throughput λ_N based on the λ_T, λ_N', and b_j values (these are known if the Level 3 chain and the background chains are open). Also, initialize d_{MAC} for use in Step 3.

Step 2: Solve the Level 1 model for average packet delay d_{MAC} using λ_N.

Step 3: If $|d_{\text{MAC}}(\text{old}) - d_{\text{MAC}}(\text{new})| < \epsilon_1$, then GO TO 10.

Step 4: Adjust the raw service rates μ_i' for the background devices chain throughputs b_j in the Level 2 models:

$$\mu_i = \mu_i' - \sum_{j \in C_b(i)} b_j \quad \text{for all } i \in S_b(j). \quad (2)$$

Note that the sum of the b_j terms must be less than μ_i'. This step requires iteration if the background device chains are closed.

Step 5: If the subscriber device queues are to be aggregated in the Level 3 model, then solve this subnetwork using a product-form solution algorithm for closed chain throughputs $\lambda_T(K)$ for $K = 1, \cdots, W_T$.

Step 6: Solve the Level 2 model using a product-form or approximation solution algorithm for chain throughputs $\lambda_j(K)$, server delays $d_{ij}(K)$, and queue length probabilities $p_{ij}(K)$ and for ACK delays $A_j(K)$ using (1).

Step 7: Solve the Level 3 model for LAN throughput $\lambda_j(K)$ and $\lambda_T(K)$, determined from Steps 5 and 6.

Step 8: If $|\lambda_N(\text{old}) - \lambda_N(\text{new})| < \epsilon_2$, then GO TO 4.

Step 9: GO TO 2.

Step 10: Adjust the Level 3 model chain delay D by the ACK delays determined in Step 6:

$$D' = D - \sum_{j=1}^{M} A_j(K). \quad (3)$$

The end-to-end chain throughput λ_T is also available from the final Level 3 model computations.

IV. CASE STUDY

We have used the hierarchical LAN modeling methodology in the design and analysis of production as well as experimental LAN systems. In this section, we present some results from a typical analysis. The configuration analyzed, shown in Fig. 6, consists of a single host device with n terminals. We also consider background loads on

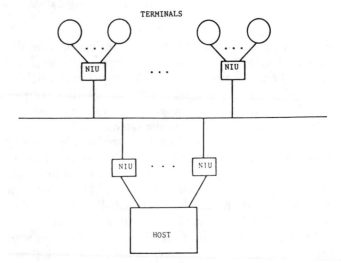

Fig. 6. Ethernet time-sharing configuration.

the LAN from other devices without explicitly representing those devices. The objective is to compute delay and throughput for an interactive application (e.g., database queries). Delay is defined as the interval from the last character of the request until the first character of the response. The host NIU's are interfaced directly to the host channel. The host channel delays are negligible relative to the other delay components and are not represented. The interface between the terminals and the terminal NIU is asynchronous (i.e., a character at a time). This interface delay is not included for the request because that time is overlapped with the request message input time. The interface delay for the response is also ignored since the delay definition is given in terms of the first character of the response. The terminal think time is assumed to include the request message data input time and the response message data display time.

The MAC protocol of this system is the 1-persistent CSMA/CD Ethernet[2] protocol [9]. The flow control protocol Xerox Network Service (XNS) is implemented between the NIU's [46]. Each NIU is modeled by servers for a microprocessor and a transceiver to represent the protocol processing and packet transmission, respec-

---

[2]Ethernet is a trademark of the Xerox Corporation.

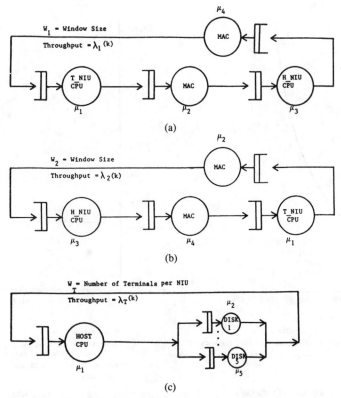

Fig. 7. Level 2 models of Ethernet time-sharing configuration. (a) To-host submodel. (b) From-host submodel. (c) Host submodel.

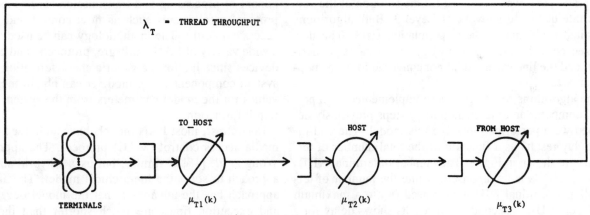

Fig. 8. Level 3 model of Ethernet time-sharing configuration.

tively. The host components represented are the CPU and five disks.

The equations from [20] are used to determine d_{MAC} for the Level 1 model. The data and ACK packet sizes are averaged to determine the network packet size. An open chain is used in the Level 1 model to represent a background load on the LAN. The Level 2 models are illustrated in Fig. 7. The NIU processing service time is determined from the processor execution rate and the protocol software path length. Separate models are used to represent the flow-controlled path for the request and the response. The load concealment technique [34] is used to adjust the service rates for the common servers in both

models (i.e., service rates are adjusted both for direction as well as for multiple chains in common queues). Normalized convolution [33] was used iteratively to solve the two models as well as the host subsystem model. Host service times are characterized by processor execution rate, disk transfer rate, software path lengths, and data record size. The representation of the host is a product-form network; therefore, the decomposition is exact. The Level 3 model is illustrated in Fig. 8. This model includes the terminal server with infinite server (IS) discipline, a pair of FESC nodes for the terminal-to-host connection of interest, and an FESC node for the host. The population of the Level 3 closed chain is the number of terminals for

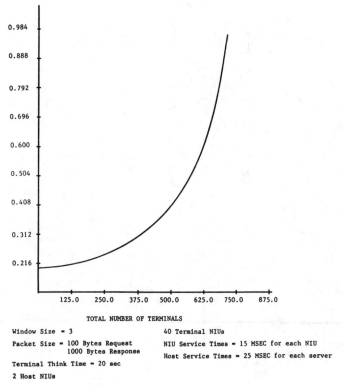

Fig. 9. Delay versus number of terminals.

Window Size = 3

Packet Size = 100 Bytes Request
              1000 Bytes Response

Terminal Think Time = 20 sec

2 Host NIUs

40 Terminal NIUs

NIU Service Times = 15 MSEC for each NIU

Host Service Times = 25 MSEC for each server

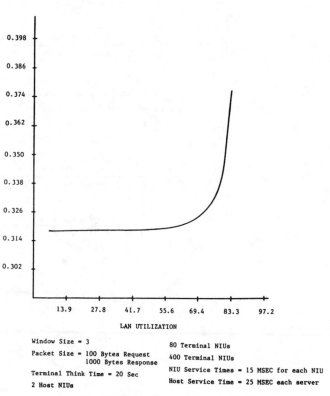

Fig. 10. Delay versus background load.

Window Size = 3

Packet Size = 100 Bytes Request
              1000 Bytes Response

Terminal Think Time = 20 Sec

2 Host NIUs

80 Terminal NIUs

400 Terminal NIUs

NIU Service Times = 15 MSEC for each NIU

Host Service Time = 25 MSEC each server

the thread of interest. The Level 3 model is also solved by normalized convolution. Besides the normalized convolution algorithm another algorithm, the improved Linearizer [17], was examined for the solution of the variable rate queueing network of Level 3. Both algorithms exhibited problems for large population sizes. The normalized convolution algorithm became unstable numerically, and the linearizer would not converge for large population sizes.

The algorithms referenced were implemented on a personal computer and the methodology steps previously described were performed to solve this model. The end-to-end delay results as a function of the total number of terminals are shown in Fig. 9. The number of terminal NIU's and host NIU's is held constant while the number of terminals per terminal NIU is increased (up to a maximum of 32 per NIU). A second set of results shows delay for a fixed number of terminals with a background load on the LAN. The results in both cases are as expected. In the former case, the host is the bottleneck. The LAN utilization is very low because of the small message sizes and relatively long terminal think times. In the latter case, the LAN saturates at high utilization, causing the delay to tend to infinity.

V. Summary

A hierarchical modeling methodology was presented for quantifying end-to-end performance in local area network (LAN) systems. We have used this technique to model Hyperbus and token ring LAN's in addition to CSMA/CD. The methodology embodies a systematic and generic approach to quantifying end-to-end delay. The motivation

of the methodology is the requirement to examine all components of delay to determine their contribution to user response time. The methodology treats each component of processing and transmission service as well as protocol mechanisms such as flow control and multiple access explicitly. The methodology can be used to model a wide variety of LAN hardware, protocols, and computer devices since it allows a generic characterization of these system components. The modeler can obtain most of the values for the model parameters from the system description information.

In contrast, most LAN models have addressed only the media access control (MAC) protocol. The approach by Wong et al. [45] is similar, but uses a hybrid simulation approach to solve the hierarchical model. The analytical approach has the advantage that the model development and execution times are much shorter than those of a comparable simulation model. The execution time of the queueing network and MAC protocol algorithms on a microcomputer is on the order of a few minutes. The analytic approach also allows easy substitution of different Level 1 model algorithms into the model hierarchy.

The primary strength of the methodology is that it provides a three-level generic decomposition approach for computing end-to-end performance metrics for different types of LAN systems (i.e., different flow control and MAC protocols can be accommodated). The modeling framework is also amenable to analytical/simulation hybrid solution techniques.

The primary limitation to the methodology is the restriction that user messages cannot be fragmented into multiple packets for transmission across the LAN. The modeling of transport layer protocols (responsible for packet fragmentation/reassembly) such as TCP and XNS represents points of fission and fusion in the model. The solution to this problem has not been addressed to any extent in the literature using analytical techniques. A technique suggested in [45] is currently being pursued. The problem can also be solved using simulation (e.g., see [38]).

We are currently developing a microcomputer-based queueing network package, Performance Analysis Tool Box (PATB), for modeling distributed systems. We expect to incorporate a LAN modeling capability in PATB.

We have also been involved in defining experimental conditions and procedures for measurement data collection in a LAN testbed and hope to validate the models with the empirical data. The test bed environment consists of a few computer/NIU device pairs, the appropriate length of cable, and an artificial traffic generator (ATG). In this scheme, the "real" devices are instrumented to send and receive an emulated traffic stream and collect statistics on delay and throughput. The ATG is used to emulate a fully populated network by transmitting packets according to a script (e.g., see O'Reilly [28]–[30]). The practical problems associated with this scheme concern the "real" device drivers and the script of the ATG. The device drivers must be able to asynchronously send and receive packets such that multiple packets may be in the "pipeline" concurrently. This corresponds to the queueing network representation of the LAN thread. The script which drives the ATG should represent the conditions (i.e., busy and idle periods) of a fully populated LAN as faithfully as possible. However, this script may become distorted if the ATG obeys the rules of access of the MAC protocol in transmitting the artificial traffic. Conversely, if the ATG does not obey the MAC protocol rules, then the packets from the "real" devices may be unduly affected.

Acknowledgment

The authors would like to thank Prof. Leon-Garcia and the anonymous referees for their comments and suggestions on this paper.

References

[1] G. Bernard, "Interconnection of local computer networks: Modeling and optimization problems," *IEEE Trans. Software Eng.*, vol. SE-9, July 1983.

[2] R. Berry and K. Chandy, "Performance models of token ring local area networks," *ACM Perform. Eval. Rev.*, Aug. 1983.

[3] S. Bleistein et al., "Analytic performance model of the U.S. en route air traffic control computer systems," *ACM Perform. Eval. Rev.*, vol. 13, Aug. 1985.

[4] W. Bux, "Local-area subnetworks: A performance comparison," *IEEE Trans. Commun.*, vol. COM-29, Oct. 1981.

[5] J. Buzen and P. Denning, "Measuring and calculating queue length distributions," *IEEE Computer*, Apr. 1980.

[6] K. Chandy and C. Sauer, "Approximate methods for analyzing queueing network models of computer systems," *ACM Comput. Surveys*, vol. 10, Sept. 1978.

[7] K. Chandy et al., "Parameteric analysis of queueing networks," *IBM J. Res. Develop.*, vol. 19, Jan. 1975.

[8] E. Coyle and B. Liu, "Finite population CSMA/CD networks," *IEEE Trans. Commun.*, vol. COM-31, Nov. 1983.

[9] Digital Equipment Corp., Intel Corp., Xerox Corp., *The Ethernet, A Local Area Network: Data Link Layer and Physical Functional Specifications*, Version 1.0, Sept. 30, 1980.

[10] A. Goldberg et al., "A validated system performance model," in *Performance '83*. Amsterdam: North-Holland, 1983.

[11] J. Gunn, "Throughput and delay calculations for CSMA and CSMA/CD," in *Fall 1984 Symp. Proc.*, Washington Oper. Res./Management Sci. Council.

[12] "Token-passing bus access method and physical layer specifications," *IEEE Project 802 Local Area Network Standards*.

[13] L. Kleinrock, *Communication Nets: Stochastic Message Flow and Delay*. New York: McGraw-Hill, 1964.

[14] L. Kleinrock and F. A. Tobagi, "Carrier sense multiple access for packet switched radio channels," in *Proc. IEEE Int. Conf. Commun.*, Minneapolis, MN, June 1974.

[15] ——, "Random access techniques for data transmission over packet switched radio channels," in *AFIPS Conf. Proc., 1975 Nat. Comput. Conf.*

[16] ——, "Packet switching in radio channels: Part I—Carrier sense multiple-access modes and their throughput-delay characteristics," *IEEE Trans. Commun.*, vol. COM-23, 1975.

[17] A. Krzesinki and J. Greyling, "Improved lineariser methods for queueing networks with queue dependent centres," *ACM Perform. Eval. Rev.*, vol. 12, Aug. 1984.

[18] S. Lam, "A carrier sense multiple access protocol for local networks," in *Computer Networks 4*. Amsterdam: North-Holland, 1980.

[19] E. Lazowska et al., *Quantitative System Performance*. Englewood Cliffs, NJ: Prentice-Hall, 1984.

[20] D. Lide, "An analytical model of the 1-persistent CSMA/CD protocol," unpublished paper.

[21] ——, "An analytical model of the NSC hyperbus protocol," unpublished paper.

[22] T. Lissack et al., "Impact of microprocessor architectures on performance of local network interface adapters," presented at Local Networks and Distributed Office Systems, London, England, May 1981.

[23] B. Maglaris and T Lissack, "Performance evaluation of interface units for broadcast local area networks," in *CompCon Proc.*, Fall 1982.

[24] D. Menasce and L. Leite, "Performance evaluation of isolated and interconnected token bus local area networks," *ACM Perform. Eval. Rev.*, 1984.

[25] L. Mitchell, "Optimization of maximum packet size in a local area network," in *CompCon Proc.*, Fall 1983.

[26] ——, "A methodology for predicting end-to-end responsiveness in a local area network," presented at the *Comput. Networking Symp.*, 1981.

[27] L. Mitchell and D. Lide, "LAN thread models for datagram and reliable transport services," in *Fall 1984 Symp. Proc.*, Washington Oper. Res./Management Sci. Council.

[28] P. O'Reilly and J. Hammond, "An efficient algorithm for generating the busy/idle periods of a channel using CSMA and loaded by an arbitrary number of stations," in *CompCon Proc.*, 1982.

[29] ——, "An efficient simulation technique of performance studies of CSMA/CD local networks," *IEEE J. Select. Areas Commun.*, vol. SAC-2, Jan. 1984.

[30] P. O'Reilly et al., "Design of an emulation facility for performance studies of CSMA-type local networks," in *Local Computer Networks*, IEEE, 1982.

[31] M. Reiser, "A queueing network analysis of computer communication networks with window flow control," *IEEE Trans. Commun.*, vol. COM-27, Aug. 1979.

[32] ——, "Admission delays on virtual routes with window flow control," in *Performance of Data Communication Systems and Their Applications*. Amsterdam: North-Holland.

[33] ——. "Mean-value analysis and convolution method for queue-dependent servers in closed queueing networks," in *Performance Evaluation 2*. Amsterdam: North-Holland, 1981.

[34] ——, "Performance evaluation of data communication systems," *Proc. IEEE*, vol. 70, Feb. 1982.

[35] I. Rubin and L. DeMoraes, "Polling schemes for local communication networks," in *Proc. ICC'81*, IEEE, 1981.

[36] S. Salza and S. Lavenberg, "Approximating response time distributions in closed queueing network models of computer performance," in *Performance '81*. Amsterdam: North-Holland, 1981.

[37] C. Sauer and K. Chandy, "Approximate solution of queueing models," *IEEE Computer*, Apr. 1980.

[38] C. Sauer et al., "Queueing network simulations of computer com-

munications,'' *IEEE J. Select. Areas Commun.*, vol. SAC-2, Jan. 1984.

[39] R. Sherman *et al.*, ''Concepts, strategies for local data network architectures,'' *Data Commun.*, July 1978.

[40] F. Takagi and L. Kleinrock, ''Throughput analysis for persistent CSMA systems,'' *IEEE Trans. Commun.*, vol. COM-33, July 1985.

[41] F. Tobagi and V. Hunt, ''Performance analysis of carrier sense multiple access with collision detection,'' in *Proc. LACN Symp.*, May 1979.

[42] F. Tobagi, ''Distribution of packet delay and interdeparture time in slotted ALOHA and carrier sense multiple access,'' *J. ACM*, vol. 29, Oct. 1982.

[43] F. A. Tobagi and L. Kleinrock, ''Packet switching in radio channels: Part II—The hidden terminal problem in carrier sense multiple-access and the busy tone solution,'' *IEEE Trans. Commun.*, vol. COM-23, 1975.

[44] G. Varghese *et al.*, ''Queueing delays on virtual circuits using a sliding window flow control scheme,'' *ACM Perform. Eval. Rev.*, 1983.

[45] J. Wong *et al.*, ''Hierarchical modeling of local area computer networks,'' in *Nat. Telecommun. Conf. Proc.*, Dec. 1980.

[46] *Xerox System Integration Standard: Internet Standard Protocols*, Xerox Corp., Dec. 1981.

Lionel C. Mitchell (M'80) was born in Portersville, AL, on January 28, 1949. He received the B.S. degree in mathematics and the M.S. degree in statistics and operations research, both from Auburn University, Auburn, AL, in 1971 and 1976, respectively.

From 1976 to 1979 he was an instructor in the Department of Mathematics and Computer Science at the West Virginia Institute of Technology. He was Manager of System Performance Analysis at Contel Information Systems from 1979 to 1984, where he was involved in performance analysis of local area and wide area network systems. He currently leads the Computer and Communication Systems Performance Evaluation group at Computer Technology Associates. He is the principal investigator of an internal R&D project for developing a microcomputer-based performance analysis tool.

Mr. Mitchell is a member of the Association for Computing Machinery, the Computer Measurement Group, and the Washington Operations Research/Management Science Council.

David A. Lide was born in London, England, on December 29, 1959. He received the B.A. degree in mathematics from the University of Pennsylvania, Philadelphia, PA, in 1981 and the M.Sc. degree in operations research from the London School of Economics, London, England, in 1982.

From 1982 to 1984, he was with Contel Information Systems, where he was involved in design and analysis of local area networks. He is currently with Computer Technology Associates, where he is engaged in the modeling and analysis of computer and communication systems. He is the codesigner and principal implementor of CTA's proprietary performance analysis modeling package. His current interests include computer performance analysis and the development of computer-aided design tools.

Section 7: Internetworking

7.1 Overview

In many cases, a local network will not be an isolated entity. An organization may have more than one type of local network at a given site to satisfy a spectrum of needs. An organization may have local networks at various sites and may need them to be interconnected for central control or distributed information exchange. Plus, an organization may need to provide a connection for one or more terminals and hosts of a local network to other computer resources.

7.2 Article Summary

"Beyond Local Networks" provides an overview of the key issues involved in extending communication for an attached device beyond the scope of its local network.

The next article is an extract from a document by the IEEE 802.1 subcommittee. It presents a systematic analysis of the various internetwork situations that might arise involving local networks.

The article by Schneidewind looks at the issue of long-haul interconnection and the use of gateways. The final two articles are concerned with connecting multiple LANs and examine the use of bridges.

How bridges and gateways make it possible to switch data among dissimilar networks.

Reprinted from *Datamation*, date © 1983 by Cahners Publishing Company.

BEYOND LOCAL NETWORKS

by William Stallings

The story of local networks is by now a familiar one to data processing managers. The proliferation of small computers throughout large organizations has created the need for some means of connecting them and enabling them to share data and access to costly peripherals. The local network alone, however, hardly solves all of a manager's interconnection problems.

Like it or not, more than one local network will probably be required to service the wide-ranging mix of computers found in typical corporations. Word procesors in one department, personal computers in another, and mainframes in the back room all need their own kinds of local networks, whether they are sold under that name or not. From simple twisted-pair cabling to hyperfast coax, local networks of many sorts are finding their way into offices and labs, necessitating a new level of communications expertise: internetworking protocols.

This networking of networks takes place within single buildings and across continents as corporations strive to provide company-wide access to electronic files, services, and resources. Electronic mail systems, for instance, gain value geometrically as new users are brought on-line, a procedure that often requires differing local networks to be linked efficiently and transparently.

These various interactions are depicted in Fig. 1. There are a number of local networks, some of which may be in the same building, some not. Local networks may be linked point-to-point (e.g., with a private or leased line) or through a packet-switched network. Devices on the local networks, plus those on the long-haul net, may communicate. The figure shows two types of devices for linking networks, the bridge and the gateway. A bridge is a relatively simple device for linking two local networks that use the same protocols. The gateway is more complex and intended for heterogeneous cases.

To understand the action of the bridge, first consider how communication takes place among stations attached to a single local network. Fig. 2 is an example using a bus-topology local network; the principle is similar for the ring and tree topologies.

Data on a local network are transmitted in packets. So, for example, if station X wishes to transmit a message to station Y, X breaks its message up into small pieces that are sent, one at a time, in packets. Each packet contains a portion of X's message plus control information, including Y's network address. Based on some medium-access protocol (e.g., CSMA/CD or token passing), X inserts each packet onto the bus. The packet propagates the length of the bus in both directions, reaching all other stations. When Y recognizes its address on a packet, it copies the packet and processes it.

Now, suppose two local networks using the same protocols are to be linked. This is accomplished in Fig. 3 using a bridge that is attached to both local networks (frequently, the bridge function is performed by two "half-bridges," one on each network). The functions of the bridge are few and simple: it reads all packets transmitted on network A, and accepts only those addressed to stations on B; it buffers each accepted packet for retransmission on B, using the medium access protocol; and it does the same for B-to-A traffic.

The bridge makes no modifications to the content or format of the packets it handles, nor does it encapsulate them with an additional header. If any modifications or additions were made, we would be dealing with a more complex device—a gateway. This is discussed later. Essentially, the bridge provides a transparent extension to the local network. It appears to all stations on the two local networks that there is a single network, a composite of the two separate nets. All stations may be addressed in the same fashion.

For similar but geographically separate local networks, the desirability of a bridge is clear. It provides a simple and efficient means of interconnecting devices in a number of locations. But the bridge is useful even when all devices are local to each other, for the following reasons:

Reliability. The danger in connecting all data processing devices in an organization to one network is that a fault on the network may disable communications for all devices. By using bridges, the network can be partitioned into self-contained units.

Performance. In general, performance on a local network declines with an increase in the number of stations or the length of the wire. A number of smaller networks will often give improved performance if devices can be clustered so that intranetwork traffic significantly exceeds internetwork traffic.

Security. A bridge architecture can enhance network security. For example, sensitive data (accounting, personnel, strategic planning) could be isolated on a single local network. The bridge can prevent those data being sent out to other networks.

Convenience. It may simply be more convenient to have multiple networks. For example, if a local network is to be installed in two buildings separated by a highway, it may be far easier to use a microwave bridge link than to attempt to string coaxial cable between the two buildings.

**GATEWAYS
MORE
COMPLEX**
When connecting different types of local networks, a gateway is required. As with bridges, paired half-gateways are commonly used, each being attached to its respective local network. A gateway is generally a more complex device than a bridge, for it must accommodate differences between local and long-haul networks. These differences include the following:

● Addressing schemes. The networks may use different end-point names, addresses, and directory maintenance schemes.

● Maximum packet sizes. Packets from one network may have to be broken into smaller pieces to move on another network. This process is referred to as fragmentation.

● Interfaces. The interface to a local network is usually defined through various protocols, including one governing access to the network wire itself. Long-haul networks generally use different protocols (X.25, etc.) than local nets.

● Time-outs. Generally a connection-oriented transport service (e.g., a file transfer, as opposed to electronic mail) will await in acknowledgement until a time-out expires, at which time it will retransmit its segment of data. Generally, longer times are required for successful delivery across multiple networks. Internetwork timing procedures must facilitate successful transmission that avoids unnecessary retransmissions.

● Error recovery. Internetwork services should not depend on or be interfered with by the nature of the individual network's error recovery capability.

● Status reporting. Networks can report status and performance differently, yet it must be possible for the gateway to provide such information on internetworking activity.

● Routing techniques. Intranetwork routing may depend on fault detection and congestion

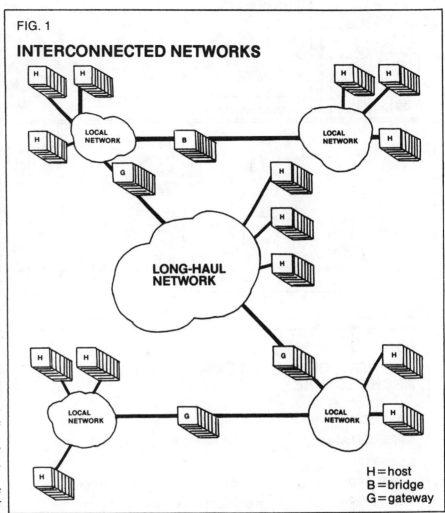

FIG. 1

INTERCONNECTED NETWORKS

H = host
B = bridge
G = gateway

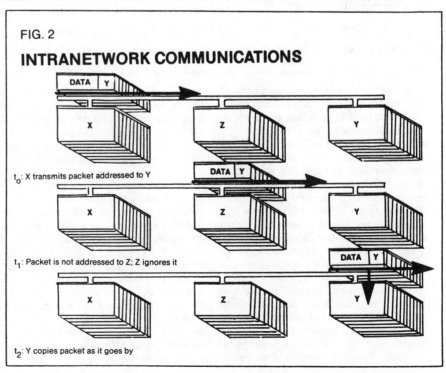

FIG. 2

INTRANETWORK COMMUNICATIONS

t_0: X transmits packet addressed to Y

t_1: Packet is not addressed to Z; Z ignores it

t_2: Y copies packet as it goes by

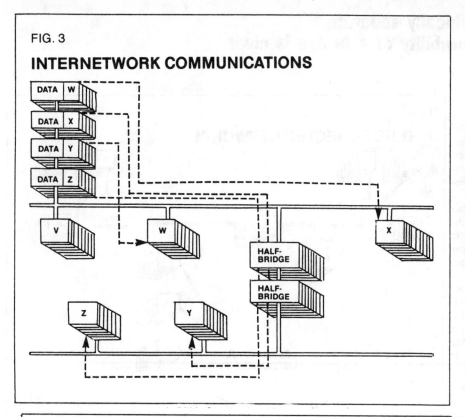

FIG. 3

INTERNETWORK COMMUNICATIONS

DATA W
DATA X
DATA Y
DATA Z

V W HALF-BRIDGE HALF-BRIDGE X

Z Y

FIG. 4

THE ROLE OF IP IN A COMMUNICATIONS ARCHITECTURE

7 APPLICATION	Application services
6 PRESENTATION	Formatting and data presentation
5 SESSION	Connection control
4 TRANSPORT	End-to-end transmission service
IP	Internetwork routing and delivery
3 NETWORK	Internetwork routing and delivery
2 DATALINK	Reliable point-to-point transmission
1 PHYSICAL	Physical and electrical connection

control techniques peculiar to each network. The internetworking facility must be able to coordinate these to route data adaptively between stations on different networks.

● Access Controls. Each network will have its own user access control technique. These must be invoked by the internetwork facility as needed. Further, a separate internetwork access control technique may be required.

● Connection, connectionless. Individual networks may provide connection-oriented (e.g., virtual circuit) or connectionless (datagram) service. The internetwork service should not depend on the nature of the connection service for the individual networks.

A number of approaches have been tried for accommodating these differences among networks. At one extreme, a special-purpose gateway, known as a protocol converter, can be built for each particular pair of networks. Typically, a protocol converter ac-

cepts a packet from one network, strips off the control information to recover the data, and then retransmits the data using the protocols of the other network. The disadvantage of this approach, of course, is that a different gateway must be built for each pair of networks.

At the other extreme is the X.75 protocol, which is an extension of the X.25 packet-switch network interface standard that makes it possible to set up a virtual circuit between two stations on the same network. In effect, X.75 provides a logical connection between disjoint stations by stringing together virtual circuits across several networks. The drawback of this approach is that all of the networks must use X.25, a standard not used by most local networks. Furthermore, public-access networks, such as Telenet and Tymnet, do not accommodate X.75 links to private networks.

A more promising approach is the internet protocol (IP), initially developed for Arpanet. Versions of IP have been standardized by both the Department of Defense and National Bureau of Standards. The philosophy of IP is that the gateways and stations share a common protocol for internet traffic, but that the stations and networks are otherwise undisturbed. In terms of the usual open system interconnection (OSI) model for communications architecture, IP fits between the network (routing) and transport (end-to-end delivery) layers (Fig. 4).

IP provides what is known as a datagram service; that is, it will handle each packet of data independently. Multiple packets may arrive out of sequence. If a connection-oriented service is required, communicating hosts must share a common higher-layer protocol. Fig. 5 depicts the operation of IP for data exchange between host A on a local network and host B on a local network through an X.25 long-haul packet-switched network, and shows the format of the data packet at each stage. Each host must have the IP layer, plus some higher layers, in order to communicate. Intermediate gateways need only protocol software up to the IP level.

The data to be sent by A are encapsulated in a datagram with an IP header specifying a global network address (host B). This datagram is then encapsulated with the local network protocol and sent to a gateway that strips off the local network header. The datagram is then encapsulated with the X.25 protocol and transmitted across the network to a gateway. The gateway strips off the X.25 fields and recovers the datagram, which is then wrapped in a local network header and sent to B.

IP makes no assumptions about the underlying network protocol. Each host or gateway that uses IP interfaces with its network in the same fashion as for intranetwork communication.

OPERATION OF AN IP CATANET

A collection of interconnected networks using IP is often referred to as a catanet. Consider two hosts, A and B, on different networks in the catanet. Host A is sending a datagram to host B. The process starts in host A. The IP module in host A constructs a datagram with a global network address and recognizes that the destination is on another network. So the first step is to send the datagram to a gateway (example: host A to gateway 1 in Fig. 5). To do this, the IP module appends to the IP datagram a header appropriate to the network that contains the address of the gateway. For example, for an X.25 network, a layer 3 packet is formed by the IP module to be sent to the gateway.

Next, the packet travels through the

network to the gateway. The gateway unwraps the packet to recover the original datagram. The gateway analyzes the IP header to determine whether this datagram contains control information intended for the gateway, or data intended for a host farther on. In the latter instance, the gateway must make a routing decision. There are four possibilities:

1. The destination host is directly connected to one of the networks to which the gateway is attached.

2. The destination host is on a network that has a gateway that directly connects to this gateway. This is known as a "neighbor gateway."

3. To reach the destination host, more than one additional gateway must be traversed. This is known as a "multiple-hop" situation.

4. The gateway does not know the destination address.

In case 4, the gateway returns an error message to the source of the datagram. In the first three cases, the gateway must select the appropriate route for the data, which it then inserts into the appropriate network with the appropriate address. For case 1, the address is the destination host address. For cases 2 and 3, the address is a gateway address.

Before actually sending data, however, the gateway may need to fragment the datagram to accommodate a smaller packet size. Each fragment becomes an independent IP datagram. Each new datagram is wrapped in a lower-layer packet and queued for transmission. The gateway may also limit the length of its queue for each network it attaches to so as to avoid having a slow network penalize a faster one. Once the queue limit is reached, additional datagrams are simply dropped.

The process described above continues through as many gateways as it takes for the datagram to reach its destination. As with a gateway, the destination host recovers the IP datagram from its network wrapping. If fragmentation has occurred, the IP module in the destination host buffers the incoming data until the entire original data field can be reassembled. This block of data is then passed to a higher layer which is responsible for the proper sequencing of a stream of datagrams and for end-to-end error and flow control.

The internet protocol is most easily understood by looking at its header format (Fig. 6). Data to be transmitted are inserted into a datagram with the IP header. The header is largely self-explanatory. Some clarifying remarks:

Lifetime: in the NBS version, this field indicates the maximum number of gateways a datagram may visit so as to prevent endlessly circulating datagrams. DoD specifies this field in units of seconds, for the same purpose, and also to permit reassembly to be aborted at time-out.

Checksum: this is computed at each gateway for error detection.

Address: specifies a hierarchical address consisting of network identifier plus host identifier.

Options: the only option NBS has defined so far is a security field to indicate the security level of the datagram. In addition, DoD defines source routing, which allows the source host to dictate the routing; record route, used to trace the route a datagram takes; and internet time stamp.

FIG. 5

DATA ENCAPSULATION WITH IP

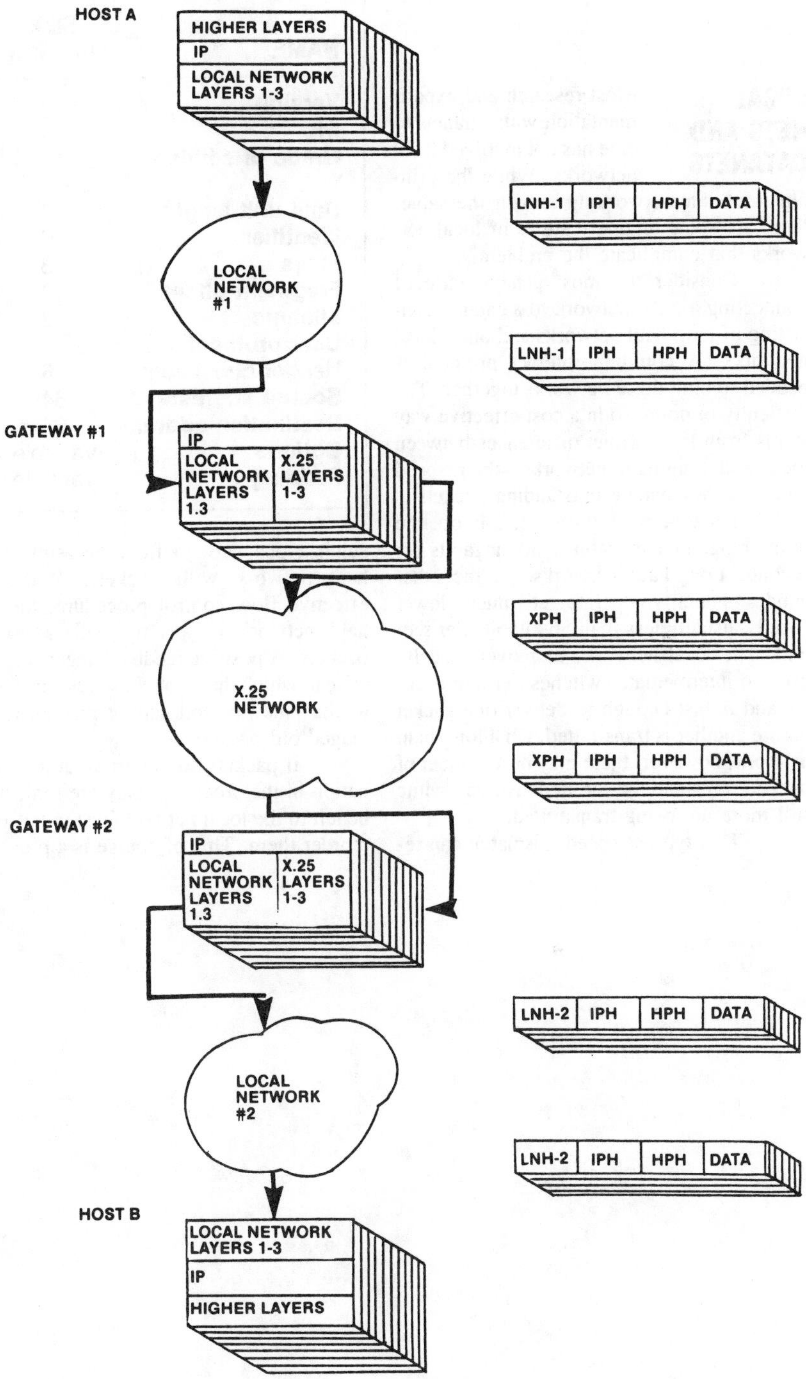

HPH = Higher Layer Protocol Header
IPH = Internet Protocol Header
LNH = Local Network Protocol Header
XPH = X.25 Protocol Header

LOCAL NETS AND CATANETS

Most research and experimentation with catanets to date has not involved local networks. While the principles of internetworking remain the same, there are some unique features of local networks that complicate the problem.

Consider the most general case of connecting a local network to a catanet consisting of long-haul networks and other local networks. A common internet protocol is needed to bind these networks together. The difficulty of doing so in a cost-effective way stems from two distinct differences between local and long-haul networks—their speed and how they handle outstanding packets.

Local network links typically operate in the range of 1 megabit to 50 megabits per second. Long-haul networks, on the other hand, generally operate at much lower speeds, usually less than 56 kilobits per second. The local network, moreover, usually uses no intermediate switches to route packets and is fast enough to deliver one packet before another is transmitted. On a long-haul network, however, there may be a number of packets outstanding, or undelivered, while still more are being transmitted.

This type of speed mismatch can re-

sult in a local network flooding a slower long-haul network with packets. Without an effective flow control procedure, the long-haul network may simply discard excess packets. A positive feedback mechanism can arise in which the local net sends new packets to the gateway and retransmits unacknowledged old packets.

If packets do not arrive at their destination in the order that they are sent, it may be left to the local network host to buffer and reorder them. This of course is a processing

burden on local network hosts.

In conclusion, the manager of local networks needs to be careful when connecting dissimilar networks, for although the technology has made major advances, there are still several pitfalls to avoid. ✱

Dr. William Stallings is a senior communications consultant with Honeywell Information Systems in McLean, Va. He is author of *Local Networks: An Introduction* (Macmillan, 1983).

FIG. 6
IP HEADER FORMAT

NAME	SIZE (in bits)	PURPOSE
Version	4	Version of Protocol
IHL	4	Header length in 32-bit words
Grade of service	8	Specify priority, reliability, and delay parameters
Data unit length	16	Length of datagram in octets
Identifier	16	Unique for protocol, source, destination
Flags	3	Includes more flag
Fragment offset	13	Offset of fragment in 64-bit units
Lifetime	8	Number of allowed hops
User protocol	8	Protocol layer that invoked IP
Header checksum	16	Applies to header only
Source address	64	16-bit net, 48-bit host
Destination address	64	16-bit net, 48-bit host
Options	Variable	Specifies additional services
Padding	Variable	Ensures that header ends on 32-bit boundary

6. **NETWORKING**

Reprinted from *IEEE Draft Standard P802.1: Section 6: Internetworking, Revision C*, February 1984, pages 1-40. Copyright © 1984 by The Institute of Electrical and Electronics Engineers, Inc. All rights reserved.

6.1 Introduction

For the purposes of this section a sub-network is defined as a Local Area Network, Metropolitan Area Network, or Wide Area Network. The architecture, services, protocols, management and addressing of LANs and MANs, but not of WANs is within the scope of IEEE 802. The interconnection of all three types of sub-network and the interconnection of LAN or WAN components is also within the scope of IEEE 802 as follows:

(1) Inter-network connection

This concerns the interconnection of LANs and MANs with each other, with WANs, and via WANs.

(2) Intra-network connection

This concerns the interconnection of the components of LANs and MANs (i.e. segments or lesser LANs and MANs)

Collectively these two areas of standardisation are referred to as networking. The terminology and concepts underlying IEEE 802 networking are presented in section 6.2.

In order to describe the networking architecture of IEEE 802 it is necessary to address two subjects: the architecture of the gateways which interconnect sub-networks (or their components), and the secenarios which describe the broad styles of interconnection. These two topics are discussed in sections 6.3 and 6.4.

6.2 Networking Terminology and Concepts

6.2.1 A system is an integrated collection of data communications resources. A real system is one which is implemented in hardware and software. An abstract system is one which is described in implementation-independent architectural terms. A distributed system is one whose layer components are separated by identified interface mechanisms.

An open system is a real system whose external appearance conforms to the 7-layer OSI Reference Model. An end system is a an abstract system whose external appearance conforms to the 7-layer OSI Reference Model. An open system contains one or more Transport Entities, but an end system contains exactly one. Both distributed open systems and distributed end systems are possible.

A gateway is a real system whose external appearance conforms to the Reference Model but which contains only layers 1 up to less than 7. A relay is an abstract system whose external appearance conforms to the Reference Model but which contains only layers 1 up to less than 7. A gateway or relay is named according to the (sub-)layer in which it performs its function; its specialised operation is not known to the (sub-)layer above or the (sub-)layer below.

Gateways or relays may be classified according to their function. The routing type performs a mapping between two identical service interfaces and performs a routing decision. It thus effects a (potentially) dynamic mapping between Service Access Points (SAPs) or connections. The converting type performs a mapping between two identical services interfaces but without any routing decision. It thus maps SAPs or connections on a fixed basis only. The interfacing type operates like the converting type but applies to the case where the system has been distributed, and the interface mechanism is a recursive use of OSI.

Other terms used outside IEEE 802 are explained below in order to avoid confusion. The term protocol converter is widely used but loosely defined. To contrast it with the gateway concept described in this document, a protocol converter is defined to perform a mapping between two protocols via their common protocol features. It thus differs from a gateway in that the mapping is performed on an intimate basis and not via a general, protocol-independent service interface. The term communications server is also sometimes used without precision. It is here defined as a system which supports shared access over a Local Area Network to communications facilities. The term interworking unit is used in ISO to denote a system which effects the interconnection of sub-networks. The term switching node, used particularly in the Network Layer, refers to a routing gateway. The term bridge, used particularly in the Link Layer, refers to a converting gateway or protocol converter where both protocols are the same. The term repeater, used particularly in the Physical Layer, refers to a protocol converter where both protocols are the same.

The terminology defined above is summarised in the diagram overleaf. The next section describes a categorisation of gateways and relays according to the positioning of the relay function.

Please see also ISO TC97/SC6 N2965 for details of the internal Organisation of the Network layer.

6.2.2 Relay Function Positioning

A relay function is deemed to operate in a sub-layer of its own. Because the relay maps identical service interfaces onto each other, relaying can take place under one of two conditions:

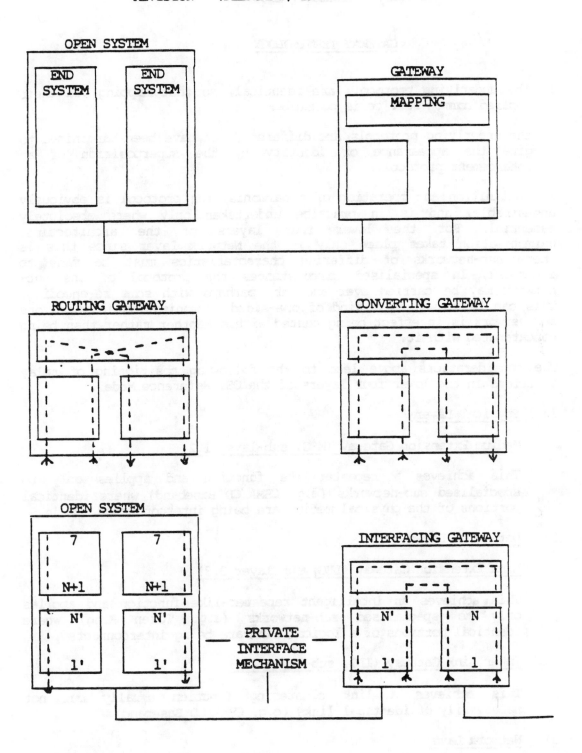

GATEWAY TERMINOLOGY

1) the underlying protocols are identical, so that mapping via their implied common service is possible.

2) the underlying protocols are different, but have been harmonised to give the appearance of identity by the superposition of an enhancement protocol.

The definition and operation of a harmonisation protocol is obviously undesirable, and is in practice undertaken only where absolutely essential. For the lower four layers of the architecture, harmonisation takes place only in the Network Layer since this is where sub-networks of differing characteristics must be made to interwork. In specialised circumstances the protocol of one sub-network may be carried over another, perhaps with some re-encoding. This can be viewed as a kind of one-sided harmonisation in which one sub-network is in effect being nested within another rather than being concatenated with it.

The considerations above lead to the following positioning of relay functions in the lower four layers of the OSI Reference Model:

1) **Physical Layer**

   Medium Extension Gateway (MEG, sub-layer 1.2)

   This achieves a repeater-like function and applies only to specialised sub-networks (e.g. CSMA/CD Baseband) where identical portions of the physical medium are being interconnected.

2) **Data Link Layer**

   Link Extension Gateway (LEG, sub-layer 2.3)

   This achieves an intelligent repeater-like function and applies only to specialised sub-networks (e.g. Token Ring) where identical portions of a logical link are being interconnected.

   Inter Link Gateway (ILG, sub-layer 2.4)

   This achieves a link clustering function usually but not necessarily of identical links (e.g. CSMA/CD Baseband).

3) **Network Layer**

   Network Extension Gateway (NEG, sub-layer 3.2)

   This allows one sub-network to constitute part of another (e.g. if X.25 were carried over a LAN, thus treating the LAN as part of a larger X.25 network).

Inter Network Gateway (ING, sub-layer 3.4)

This treats all sub-networks as equal and combines them to form
the appearance of a single uniform network.

4)   Transport Layer

Distributed System Gateway (DSG, sub-layer 4.2)

This hides the distribution of a system from the outside view and
provides maximum decoupling of networking environments (e.g. for
LAN-WAN interconnection).

The relaying possibilities defined above are summarised in the diagram
overleaf. This shows the conventional ISO/IEEE 802 sub-layering, with
the relaying sub-layers interposed. The next section presents a
general model for the structure of a gateway.

6.2.3   Generalised Model

A relay function may be visualised as a kind of patchboard. In the
case of a connectionless service the "sockets" are Service Access
Points (SAPs), and in the case of a connection-oriented service the
"sockets" are Connection End-Points (CEPs). The logical equivalent of
"jumper leads" is the mapping function performed by the relay. The
relationship between "sockets" may be intermittent (as in the
connectionless case), dynamic (as in the connection-oriented case with
adaptive routing) or static (as in the connection-oriented with fixed
or no routing). Although a relay function has many inputs and outputs
and in general is bi-directional, it is convenient to show it in
diagrams as if it interfaces only two services in one direction.

From the architectural point of view, a relay function sees a number
of underlying SAPs. If the service is connection-oriented it also
sees CEPs within these SAPs. On the basis of mapping information (eg.
routing tables) and address information passed up from the underlying
service or through a relay protocol, the relay function establishes
the appropriate service-to-service mapping. The service primitives
themselves are mapped in a trivial one-for-one fashion, although the
relay function may perform some buffering.

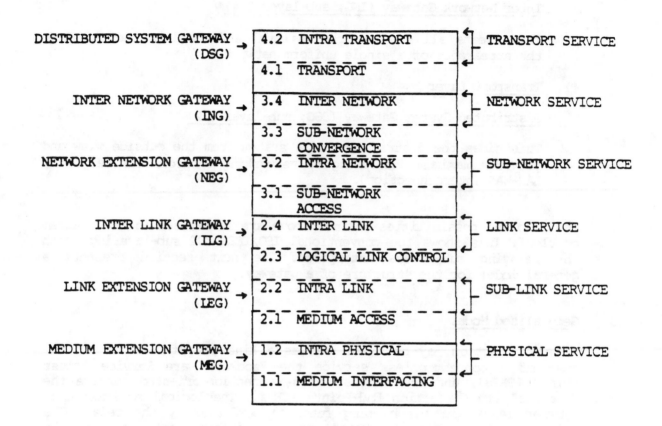

DISTRIBUTED SYSTEM GATEWAY (DSG) →
INTER NETWORK GATEWAY (ING) →
NETWORK EXTENSION GATEWAY (NEG) →
INTER LINK GATEWAY (ILG) →
LINK EXTENSION GATEWAY (LEG) →
MEDIUM EXTENSION GATEWAY (MEG) →

4.2	INTRA TRANSPORT	TRANSPORT SERVICE
4.1	TRANSPORT	
3.4	INTER NETWORK	NETWORK SERVICE
3.3	SUB-NETWORK CONVERGENCE	
3.2	INTRA NETWORK	SUB-NETWORK SERVICE
3.1	SUB-NETWORK ACCESS	
2.4	INTER LINK	LINK SERVICE
2.3	LOGICAL LINK CONTROL	
2.2	INTRA LINK	SUB-LINK SERVICE
2.1	MEDIUM ACCESS	
1.2	INTRA PHYSICAL	PHYSICAL SERVICE
1.1	MEDIUM INTERFACING	

RELAYING POSSIBILITIES

A gateway requires to participate in management operations. For example, it may supply statistics or accounting information, and may request directory assistance or access clearance. A gateway is therefore often combined with an open system so that it can communicate with management applications. Section 5 of IEEE 802.1 defines the relevant management architecture.

It is also conceivable that a gateway may perform relaying at a number of levels simultaneously. It is therefore possible to specify a generalised model of a gateway which can be subset to describe any particular implementation of it.

The "patchboard" model introduced above emphasises that the relay function can itself be thought of as a kind of sub-network. This leads to the interesting notion of a half-gateway which handles one particular realisation of the service being mapped. A gateway could then consist of a number of half-gateways interconnected in some standard fashion.

These considerations lead to the generalised diagram overleaf of how a gateway is structured. At any level, the relay function determines whether inbound traffic is local (i.e. destined for higher layers of the gateway) or remote (i.e. requires to be sent out again along another path). Any particular input message will either be re-transmitted at one level of the gateway or will ultimately be consumed by an application in the gateway itself. The level at which a message is re-transmitted or consumed depends entirely on its destination address.

6.2.4   Common Functions

A gateway, by virtue of the fact that it supports standard services and protocols, shares many design features with OSI systems in general. The distinctive characteristics of a gateway derive from its role as a relay and as a focus for management activities. The discussion of specific gateway types later in this document is therefore organised as follows:

General Characteristics

1) architecture - how the gateway is structured and how it relates to other systems

2) applicability - how the gateway may be used and what its strengths and weaknesses are

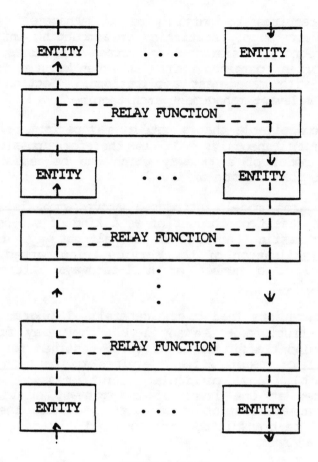

GATEWAY MODEL

Relay Characteristics

3) routing - how SAPs/CEPs are related

4) mapping - how service primitives are related

5) configuration control - how the structure of the sub-network
is set up and maintained.

6.3   Gateway Classification and Architecture

This section takes each of the gateway types introduced in section
6.2.2 and describes their architecture and characteristics in more
detail.

6.3.1   Medium Extension Gateway (MEG)

6.3.1.1 Architecture

A Medium Extension Gateway (MEG) contains a converting relay function
situated in the Intra Physical sub-layer (1.2). It is transparent to
the systems connected to the physical medium. Because a MEG sits at
the physical medium level it can be considered as connectionless in
operation.

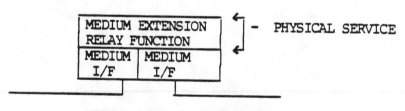

MEDIUM EXTENSION GATEWAY

6.3.1.2 Applicability

An MEG is used to expand the topography of the communications link, by
allowing segments of physical medium to be joined without signal
degradation. For example, an MEG may regenerate clocking information
and data waveforms.   An MEG is also used to expand the topology of
the communications link by allowing branching of the physical medium.

The characteristics of an MEG are obviously very technology-dependent.
One example is the repeater used between segments of a CSMA/CD
Baseband network.

6.3.1.3 Routing

An MEG conveys information between its input and output channels in a
fixed fashion. The data flow is unconstrained, i.e. input on one
channel is sent to all others. An MEG commonly joins only two segments
of the physical medium.

6.3.1.4 Mapping

Physical signals are mapped one-for-one. They may, however, be re-generated or re-transmitted unchanged. The MEG implicitly contains a limited amount of buffering in that input will be delayed a small number of bit-times before being re-transmitted. The initial part of a synchronising preamble may be lost if the relay function is not re-generative.

6.3.1.5 Configuration Control

An MEG contains no configuration control facilities. Failure of an MEG will usually result in part of the communications medium becoming unavailable and should be detected by higher layers of protocol.

6.3.2   Link Extension Gateway (LEG)

6.3.2.1 General Characteristics

A Link Extension Gateway (LEG) contains a converting relay function situated in the Intra Link sub-layer (2.2). The relay function does, however, have a certain flavour of routing in that it acts to block transmission of superfluous messages. An LEG is transparent to the systems connected to the logical link. It is aware, however, of the address spaces for each partial link (two or more) which it interfaces. This information is used to filter out irrelevant messages as they are considered for re-transmission on the next part of the link. An LEG is thus an "intelligent" repeater. Because an LEG operates very close to the physical medium it can be considered as connectionless in operation.

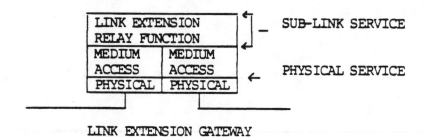

LINK EXTENSION GATEWAY

6.3.2.2 Applicability

Because the relay function of an LEG sits above the medium-specific drivers, it is in principle technology-independent. In practice, however, the tight coupling needed for efficiency means that an LEG is closely integrated with the specific sub-network technology. An LEG therefore joins like sub-links.

The most suitable area of application for an LEG is in partitioning a LAN or extending it beyond the normal physical limits. If a LAN carries distinct categories of traffic between distinct categories of stations it may be useful to separate them. This may be necessary for security reasons (e.g. part of the LAN is not in a secure environment and requires encryption techniques) and for load-sharing reasons (e.g. a single LAN has become over-loaded and requires expansion). An LEG is particularly beneficial where traffic within portions of the link is high and traffic between portions is low. This is because the utilisation of each part and hence the collision rate can be reduced.

6.3.2.3 Routing

An LEG requires knowledge of how link addresses are partitioned between portions of the link. The easiest solution is to divide the link address into two parts: the link partition number and the relative terminal number. An LEG inspects the partition number of an incoming message and does the following :

1) if the destination partition number is that of the originating partition then ignore the message, else

2) if the destination partition number is that of one of the other partitions attached to the gateway then re-transmit the message on that partition, else

3) re-transmit the message on all of the other attached partitions, excluding a partition which matches the source partition number.

This routing algorithm is of the type known as flood-routing. In general it is inefficient and can lead to indefinitely looping messages with certain topologies (see the example overleaf). However, the algorithm works for many simple types of network including buses, stars, unrooted trees, rings and cliques (i.e. networks with maximal connectivity). It fails if between two systems but not directly connected to them is a pair of partitions or gateways which have alternative paths between them. The algorithm will eventually find a path (if any) to the destination. The cost of transmitting multiple copies can be traded against the cost of source re-transmission by making a random choice in step 3) above instead of re-transmitting on all permissible outboard partitions.

The algorithm can be implemented efficiently and requires only limited information to be fixed in the gateways (i.e. the attached partition numbers). Since partitions which are not at the extremities of the sub-network are used to carry inter-partition traffic, the scheme proposed will operate satisfactorily only if transit traffic is sufficiently low to be carried on top of the normal partition load.

6.3.2.4 Mapping

An LEG buffers a complete message before forwarding it (if at all). In principle, the fate of the message is known once its header has been received, so that discarding or re-transmission could begin at once. In practice, the complexity of doing this and the marginal benefits for high-bandwidth LANs mean that overlapped processing is not performed.

An LEG must always be prepared to buffer one message per attached partition. For contention-based or token-based technologies it will not be possible to re-transmit a message immediately if another transmission on the target partition is in progress or if a collision ensues. There is no explicit flow control through an LEG. In the event of buffer congestion the LEG discards incoming messages until the blockage clears.

6.3.2.5 Configuration Control

An LEG contains primitive configuration control facilities: the partition numbers of attached links are set up in a simple way (e.g. on thumbwheel switches). Failure of an LEG may result in part of the communications link becoming unavailable and should be detected by higher layers of protocol. The LEG routing algorithm permits alternative paths to exist (within certain constraints), so failure of an LEG may be invisible except for some performance degradation.

6.3.3 Inter Link Gateway (ILG)

6.3.3.1 Architecture

An Inter Link Gateway (ILG) contains a routing relay function situated in the Inter Link sub-layer (2.4). It is visible to the systems connected to the links inasmuch as the sub-layer has to convey "global" interlink addresses in its protocol. These addresses are only global in the sense that they are unique to within a cluster of links. An ILG differs from an LEG in the following respects:

1) its relay function is truly technology-independent

2) it can operate in connectionless or connection-oriented mode

3) it allows each link to have independently administered link addresses

4) it permits each link to operate its own link protocol

5) it offers more comprehensive facilities, e.g. better routing and diagnostics.

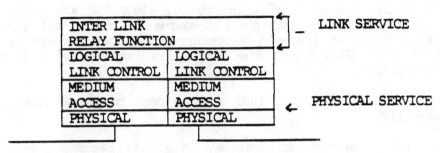

INTER LINK GATEWAY

6.3.3.2 Applicability

The technology-independence and efficiency of the ILG relay function makes it ideal for LAN to LAN interconnection, particularly where LAN characteristics such as data rate differ. An ILG, however, only interfaces LANs which support the same service interface (basically, connectionless and connection-oriented). The most suitable area of application for an ILG is in connecting nearby LANs which are similar and which have been (or are required to be) kept totally independent.

6.3.3.3 Routing

An ILG requires knowledge of how to reach the communications link to which the destination is attached. This knowledge is conveyed in interlink address parameters of an Interlink Protocol. The Interlink Protocol is a stripped-down version of the Internet Protocol. The simplest form of addressing is to divide the interlink address into two parts: the link number and the relative link address. An ILG inspects the link number of an incoming message and looks it up in a locally held routing table. This indicates the link over which to re-transmit the message. If the link is an intermediate hop the routing table gives the next link address to be used. If the link is the final one (identified as such because the gateway is directly connected to it), the link address is as given in the relative part of the interlink address.

Although the mechanics of this routing algorithm are quite simple, a lot of complexity lies in the procedures to create and update routing tables. This is properly a management matter and is described in section 5 of IEEE 802.1. The properties required of a routing table are as follows:

1) the routing table must indicate the best choice of next gateway for each link

2) if a link or the next gateway on a link becomes unavailable then the routing tables in all gateways must be updated in a time that is small compared to the total retry period of the systems attached to the links

Although the mechanics of this routing algorithm are quite simple, a lot of complexity lies in the procedures to create and update routing tables. This is properly a management matter and is described in section 5 of IEEE 802.1. The properties required of a routing table are as follows:

1) the routing table must indicate the best choice of next gateway for each link

2) if a link or the next gateway on a link becomes unavailable then the routing tables in all gateways must be updated in a time that is small compared to the total retry period of the systems attached to the links

3) the routing tables in all gateways must be mutually consistent; that is, they must not lead to loops or dead-ends

4) however, in the connectionless case temporary loops, occassional loss and duplication of messages is permitted on the assumption that the systems attached to the links can tolerate this.

6.3.3.4 Mapping

A connectionless ILG behaves very like an LEG and the same considerations of buffer management, flow control, etc. apply (see section 6.3.2.4). A connection-oriented ILG is presumed to have flow control facilities available in its underlying protocols. These will manifest themselves as locally significant flow control service primitives. Such flow control will be exercised in both directions across the interface. A connection-oriented ILG contains a limited amount of buffering per connection: this is just enough to keep transmitting on one connection while more data is requested on the other connection (by sending credit, Receive Ready or whatever).

6.3.3.5 Configuration Control

An ILG participates in control of the network configuration by being aware of neighbouring ILGs and links. An ILG may be (de-)activated in its entirety, or with respect to only one attached link. ILGs help to make their network self-organising by dynamically declaring their existence when they become active and by updating routing tables dynamically. The only information an ILG needs on awakening is:

1) a knowledge of its own link address for each link to which it is attached

2) a knowledge of the addresses (or preferably, multicast address) whereby it can contact its neighbours

3) a knowledge of the identifying numbers for its attached links.

access procedures of the greater sub-network when communicating via the NEG to systems on the latter. Communication which is entirely within the lesser sub-network uses its "native" access procedures.

As shown overleaf, the NEG must support the services of the greater sub-network over the lesser sub-network. The obvious way to do this is to carry the protocols of the greater sub-network over the lesser. In some cases (e.g. X.25 Packet and Link Layers directly over a LAN or MAN Link and Physical Layers) this would be quite feasible. However, if the protocols of the lesser sub-network are comparatively rich this approach becomes inefficient. In general, then, the services of the greater sub-network are supported by mapping them onto those of the lesser sub-network. This requires a (hopefully) small enhancement protocol to be run over the lesser sub-network. An alternative view of this same architecture is that the greater sub-network service has been exposed and distributed using the lesser sub-network. The NEG architecture is shown in the diagrams overleaf.

An NEG is similar in some ways to an LEG (see section 6.3.2) except that it operates with larger units: sub-networks instead of sub-links. It differs, however, in the following respects:

1) its relay function is truly technology-independent

2) it can support connectionless or connection-oriented sub-networks, including the case where the lesser and greater sub-networks are of differing type

3) it is unsymmetrical

4) it offers more comprehensive facilities, e.g. access control and accounting.

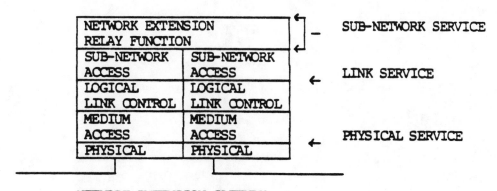

NETWORK EXTENSION GATEWAY

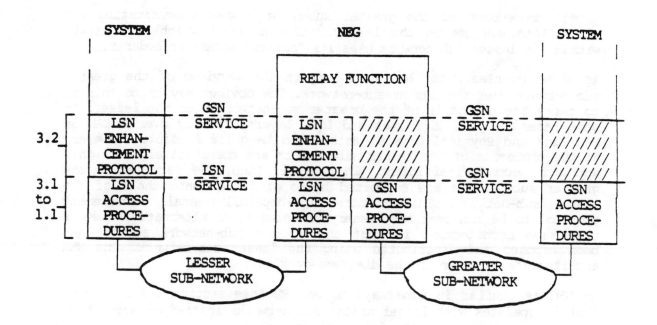

Key

GSN = Greater Sub-network

LSN = Lesser Sub-network

NEG = Network Extension Gateway

NEG ARCHITECTURE

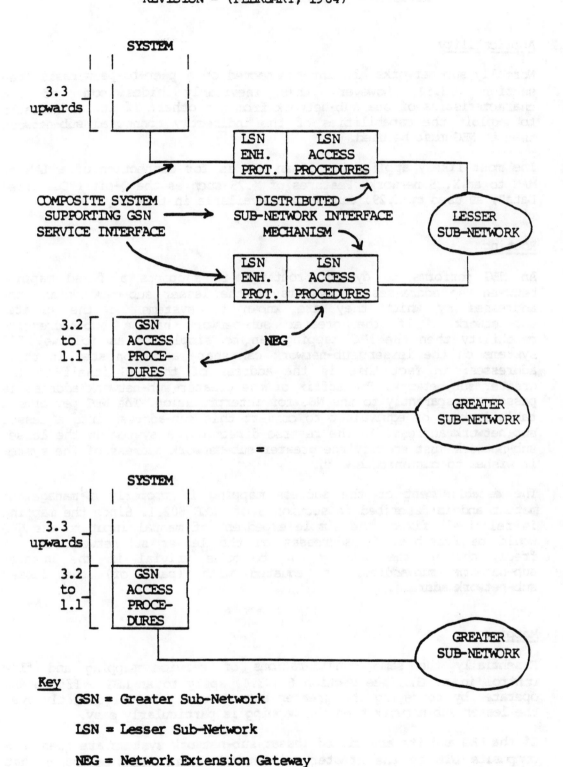

Key

    GSN = Greater Sub-Network

    LSN = Lesser Sub-Network

    NEG = Network Extension Gateway

ALTERNATIVE VIEW OF NEG ARCHITECTURE

6.3.4.2 Applicability

Normally sub-networks are interconnected on a peer-to-peer basis (see section 6.3.5). However, this inevitably hides some of the characteristics of one sub-network from the other. If it is desirable to exploit the capabilities of the indirectly connected sub-network then an NEG must be used.

The most likely application of an NEG is for connection of a LAN or MAN to an X.25 network. Features of X.25 such as the Q-bit ("Qualified Data", as used by X.29) can be made available in this way.

6.3.4.3 Routing

An NEG performs no dynamic routing: it supports a fixed mapping between the addresses of systems on the lesser sub-network and the addresses by which they are known to systems on the greater sub-network. If the greater sub-network has a sub-addressing capability then the NEG mapping can be simplified as follows. All systems on the lesser sub-network can share a common stem in their addresses: in fact this is the address of the NEG itself on the greater sub-network. The suffix of the greater sub-network address is passed transparently to the NEG for interpretation. The NEG performs a table look-up or equivalent to convert this sub-address into a lesser sub-network address. In the reverse direction, a system on the lesser sub-network must specify the greater sub-network address of the system it wishes to communicate with.

The establishment of the address mapping is properly a management matter and is described in section 5 of IEEE 802.1. Since the mapping is relatively fixed, the simple expedient of manual input to the NEG would be feasible. If addresses on the lesser sub-network can be freely chosen, the mapping can be made trivial if the greater sub-network sub-address is equated with (part of) the lesser sub-network address.

6.3.4.4 Mapping

Essentially the same considerations of service mapping and flow control in an ILG (see section 6.3.3.4) apply to an NEG. If the NEG operates by conveying the greater sub-network protocol directly over the lesser sub-network then the mapping is particularly easy.

If the NEG and its associated lesser sub-network systems are seen as a composite DTE by the greater sub-network, care must be taken that failure of one of the lesser sub-network systems is not seen as failure of the whole. For example, misoperation of one logical channel in the case of X.25 may lead to all logical channels being restarted. If the greater sub-network protocol were in fact supported by the lesser sub-network systems and the NEG were transparent to by the lesser sub-network systems and the NEG were transparent to this, an error by one system could affect all others. It is therefore essential that the NEG perform relaying at the <u>service</u> not protocol level even though the same protocol may be used on both sides.

The NEG maintains separate connections on each side in the connection-oriented case, and ensures close synchronisation between each such pair. Initially an NEG receives a Connection Request from a system on one sub-network. The destination address is extracted and used to determine the target system in the other sub-network; the Connection Request is then forwarded. In the reverse direction the NEG passes the Connection Confirm back. The process of disconnection is similar. The NEG also handles other cases such as refusal of the sub-network connection by itself or by the remote system. If one sub-network connection should fail (after recovery actions, if applicable) the NEG releases the other sub-network connection. During connection establishment the NEG participates in the negotiation of service options (such as the use of X.25 Fast Select) and quality-of-service characteristics (such as X.25 throughput class). As an implementation-dependent matter the NEG may negotiate a convenient choice of sub-network protocol parameters to assist its operation (such as X.25 packet size and window size). This requires the parameters to be privately visible through the sub-network service interface.

An interesting case arises when the greater sub-network service is connectionless but the lesser sub-network service is connection-oriented. The NEG must then decide when to open and close the lesser sub-network connections. For connections established by the NEG this is done by monitoring the length of the output queue for the sub-network connection. When the queue size exceeds a certain limit a new connection is opened, and when the queue size drops to zero for a certain time the connection is closed.

6.3.4.5 Configuration Control

The NEG needs to know the configuration of just the lesser sub-network, and that only in respect of the address mapping. As mentioned earlier, the configuration details may be simply set up manually or may be set up dynamically through some management "grope" facility. In the connection-oriented case the NEG is normally aware of the presence and operability of the lesser sub-network systems through the operation of the connection-oriented protocol. In the connectionless case the NEG may need supplementary management assistance to achieve the same effect. As part of its configuration control capability, an NEG allows lesser sub-network systems to be brought "on line" or taken "off line" and allows the configuration status to be interrogated. See section 5 of IEEE 802.1 for further information on network management.

Failure of an NEG will isolate the lesser sub-network, although the lesser sub-network can continue to function autonomously. Because all inter-network traffic is channelled through the NEG, it is important that the NEG should be designed for resilience or should be replicated. Resilient operation by replication can be achieved provided the systems are able to tolerate loss and duplication of sub-network data; this is true, for example, of systems which implement the connectionless Internet Protocol and the Class 4 Transport Protocol.

An Inter Network Gateway (ING) contains a routing relay function situated in the Inter Network sub-layer (3.4). It is very similar to an ILG (see section 6.3.3) except that it operates with larger units: networks instead of links. An ING differs from an ILG in the following respects:

1) it is concerned with global, end-to-end interconnection

2) it supports the interconnection of sub-networks with differing service and addressing characteristics

3) it offers more comprehensive facilities, e.g. access control and accounting.

Like an NEG (see section 6.3.4) an ING is used for sub-network interconnection. However, an ING is symmetrical and interconnects sub-networks on a peer-to-peer basis. This requires each sub-network to be brought to the level of a common service (the global Network Service) by means of a Harmonisation Protocol. Such a protocol or mapping is specific to a sub-network and the type of common service desired (connectionless or connection-oriented).

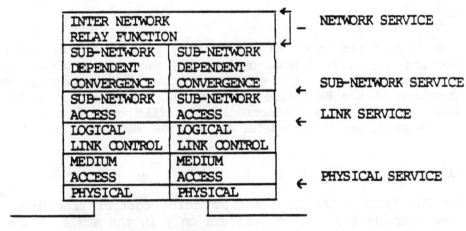

INTER NETWORK GATEWAY

6.3.5.2 Applicability

An ING is applicable to the global interconnection of any kind of OSI sub-network. It completely supports all the end-to-end routing and relaying requirements of the Network Layer. However, it needs a common agreement as to what type of Network Service is to operate globally (connectionless or connection-oriented). This is currently a contentious issue which is bound up with a number of factors:

1) the relationship between LAN and OSI standardisation

1) the relationship between LAN and OSI standardisation

2) the relationship between private and public networking in the scope of OSI

3) the relative advantages and disadvantages of connectionless and connection-oriented internetworking

4) the conformance requirements of the Transport Protocol.

It is therefore not clear at present whether the ING will be the sole means of OSI global interconnection. A strongly favoured complementary approach is described in section 6.3.6.

6.3.5.3 Routing

An ING performs routing in exactly the same way as an ILG (see section 6.3.3.3). The only difference is that the full Internet Protocol is used.

6.3.5.4 Mapping

The relay function of an ING is very similar to that of an ILG (see section 6.3.3.4). However, an ING must cope with the differing service levels of the sub-networks it interconnects; this is the function of the Harmonised Network sub-layer (3.3). An ING must also deal with carrying connectionless traffic over a connection-oriented sub-network, as described for an NEG (see section 6.3.4.4).

6.3.5.5 Configuration Control

An ING follows the same configuration control procedures as an ILG (see section 6.3.3.5) and differs only in the scale of the routing to be done.

6.3.6   Distributed System Gateway (DSG)

6.3.6.1   Architecture

Logically, this should be called a Transport Extension Gateway (TEG) for consistency with the naming of other gateway types. However, the name Distributed System Gateway (DSG) has already gained currency in standardisation work and is more descriptive of the function of the gateway.   Currently the OSI Reference Model excludes any form of relaying in the Transport Layer. It is important to realise that a DSG does not contradict this principle because it is concerned with the internal construction of an OSI system in an open and distributed manner. The design of a DSG is therefore strictly outside the scope of OSI.   However, ISO are actively studying the requirements for limited relaying in the Transport Layer: this would be for conversion between different Transport Protocol Classes. Should this become established as a valid OSI concept then the term TEG will be applied to this subtly different form of Transport gateway.

A Distributed System Gateway (DSG) contains a converting relay function situated in the Intra Transport sub-layer (4.2). Since the function of a DSG is to support the lower four layers of an OSI system on behalf of distributed components supporting the upper three layers, a DSG is not symmetrical. The DSG arranges that it and its distributed system components are viewed as a single OSI system from outside. The DSG is therefore invisible externally. By choosing the system distribution mechanism to be a LAN carrying layer 4 to 1 protocols it is possible to give the DSG the appearance of symmetry: to the systems on the LAN the external OSI world itself appears as a single OSI system. This is paradoxical but not contradictory. The paradox arises because the OSI architecture has been used recursively: an OSI system has been built using OSI internally. A residual asymmetry remains in the DSG to deal with the case where two distributed system components wish to be regard externally as a whole.

For the purposes of understanding the DSG concept it is important to clarify some terminology:

Distributed : consisting of logically or physically separated components.

End System : an abstract system which contains all 7 layers of the OSI architecture but only one Transport Entity.

OSI System : a real system which contains all 7 layers of the OSI architecture.

There is still considerable debate in ISO on the precise definition of an End System. The definitions given above follow the view that an End System is the atomic architectural concept out of which OSI Systems are built. An alternative view of this same architecture is that the

The positioning of encryption in the OSI Reference Model is still the subject of debate in ISO. The Transport Layer is a good choice, although it is not clear whether encryption just below the Transport Service (i.e. per transport connection) or just above the Network Service (i.e. per group of multiplexed transport connections) would be better. Pending technical resolution of this issue, it is assumed that the first option will be adopted. A DSG is ideally positioned to operate encryption because it sits on the boundary of "transport network" zones.

A DSG is very similar to an NEG (see section 6.3.4) except that it operates with larger units: sub-"transport networks" instead of sub-networks. It differs, however, in the following respects;

1) it is architecturally part of an OSI system and is not separately visible

2) it is (nearly) symmetrical

3) it offers more comprehensive facilities, e.g. provisions for encryption.

ECMA have actively studied the characteristics of a DSG and this is contained in an ECMA Technical Report. With minor terminological differences, the material of this section is based on the ECMA work.

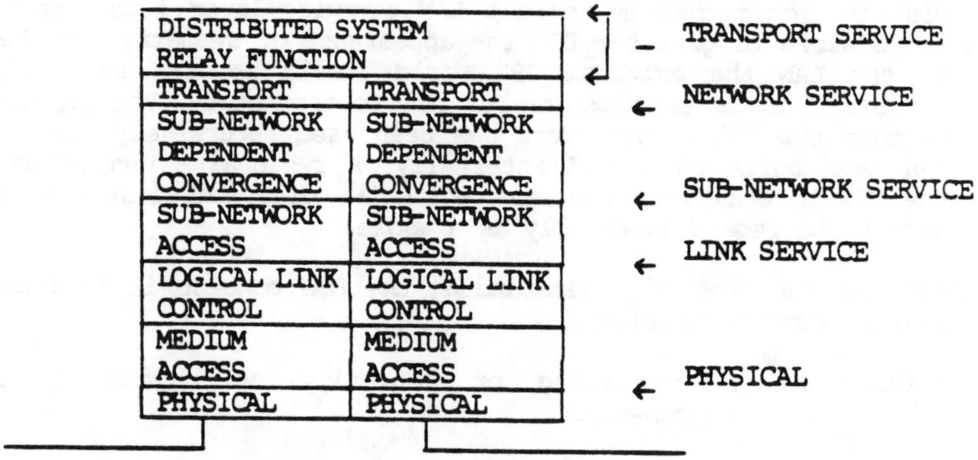

DISTRIBUTED SYSTEM RELAY FUNCTION		TRANSPORT SERVICE
TRANSPORT	TRANSPORT	NETWORK SERVICE
SUB-NETWORK DEPENDENT CONVERGENCE	SUB-NETWORK DEPENDENT CONVERGENCE	SUB-NETWORK SERVICE
SUB-NETWORK ACCESS	SUB-NETWORK ACCESS	LINK SERVICE
LOGICAL LINK CONTROL	LOGICAL LINK CONTROL	
MEDIUM ACCESS	MEDIUM ACCESS	PHYSICAL
PHYSICAL	PHYSICAL	

DISTRIBUTED SYSTEM GATEWAY

6.3.6.2 Applicability

As a means of system distribution, only a LAN can sensibly be considered because of the bandwidth and transit delay requirements. As discussed in section 6.3.5.2 there are many interlinked issues in current discussions by ISO of LANs and their place in OSI. The use of a DSG to decouple LAN and WAN considerations and to allow optimised solutions to be devised for LANs is very attractive. A DSG is most likely to be used with a single LAN interface and a variety of WAN interfaces. Its amenability to encrypting traffic on vulnerable parts of a route strengthens its attractiveness.

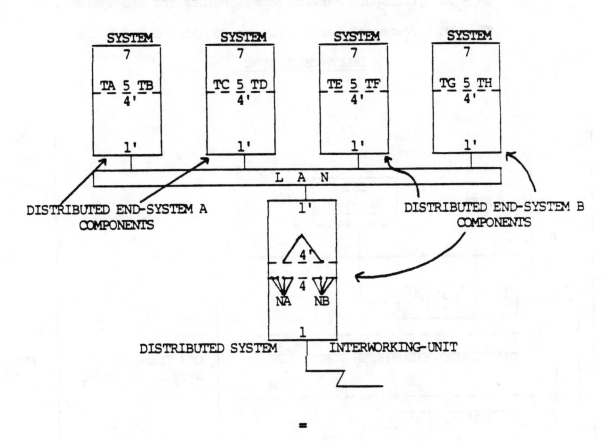

DISTRIBUTED END-SYSTEM A COMPONENTS

DISTRIBUTED END-SYSTEM B COMPONENTS

DISTRIBUTED SYSTEM   INTERWORKING-UNIT

=

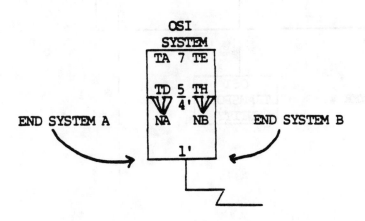

END SYSTEM A

END SYSTEM B

Key

    NA - NB = Network Service Access Points for End Systems A and B

    TA - TD = Transport Service Access Points for End System A

    TE - TH = Transport Service Access Points for End System B

DSG ARCHITECTURE

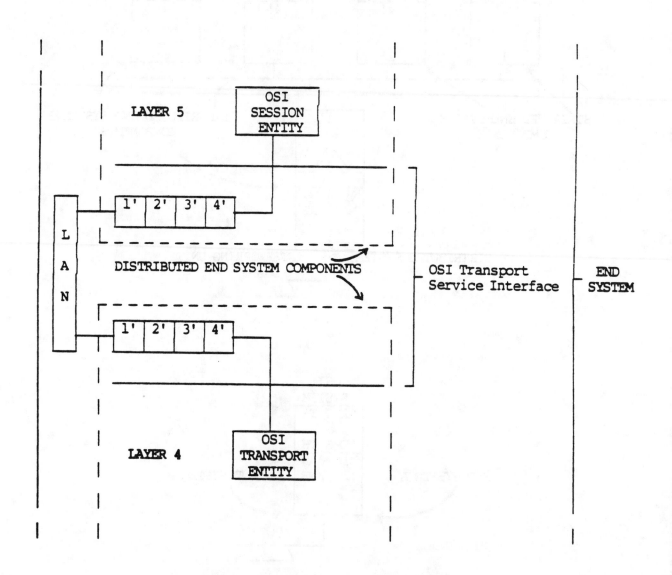

ALTERNATIVE VIEW OF DSG ARCHITECTURE

6.3.6.3 Routing

A DSG performs no dynamic routing: it supports a fixed mapping between the addresses of systems on the LAN and the addresses by which they are known to the outside world. The Network Service Access Points of a distributed OSI System formally lie in the DSG. They do, however, have their counterparts in the Network Service Access points of the distributed system components. To avoid an address translation in the DSG for LAN-bound messages, the Network Address of the distributed system components is chosen to be that by which they are known externally. The Inter Network Entity of the DSG is aware that these addresses are locally handled by the DSG and passes up any incoming messages for the corresponding Network Service Access Points. In fact, the Inter Network Entity of a DSG will normally pass all incoming traffic up in this way; in this respect a DSG is like an end system. However, an implementation might well combine the functions of a DSG and an ING. Some incoming traffic would then be local (handled by the DSG) and some would be remote (routed onwards).

The local traffic passes on upwards through the Transport Layer to the relay function of the DSG. The Transport Service Access Points of a distributed OSI system formally lie in the distributed system components. They do, however, have their counterparts in the Transport Service Access Points of the DSG. To avoid an address translation in the DSG for LAN-bound messages, the Transport Address of the distributed system components is chosen to be that by which they are known externally.

There is one exception to these addressing rules, and that arises when a number of distributed system components wish to be regarded externally as one End System instead of individual End Systems. In this case, the DSG must determine which distributed system component actually contains the intended Transport Service Access Point. This information is embodied in a translation table for the appropriate Network Service Access Point. Since there are many Network Service Access points in the distributed system components corresponding to one in the DSG, the DSG must determine both the Network Address and the Transport Address for the intended component. This address translation table may be set up using management facilities, much as routing tables and other directories are set up.

Address handling for messages leaving the LAN via the DSG is essentially the same as the above, except that the case of a distributed End System does not normally arise. One potential difference arises if the LAN carries only the null Internet Protocol, as is likely to be the case with early implementations. In this case the Transport Protocol must carry the full Transport Address. If the full Internet Protocol is used across the LAN to the DSG, the Transport Protocol carries only the Transport Selector when hierarchic addressing is in use.

6.3.6.4 Mapping

Service mapping in a DSG is analogous to that in an NEG (see section 6.3.4.4). Transport Protocol Class conversion is straightforward with the exception of Class 0 because a common service is supported. The relay function of the DSG can therefore operate above the normal Transport Service level. Each of the paired transport connections operates as usual and is subject to its own flow control, error recovery, etc. The complication with Class 0 is that it does not support expedited data or (dis)connection user data; neither of these omissions presents any real difficulty, however. If a system expects to use Class 0 then it will not expect to use expedited data. When the DSG receives a Connection Request which specifies Class 0 (hence, non-use of expedited data) it will request non-use in the corresponding Connection Request it sends out. Since non-use of expedited data is the mandatory selection then the Connection Confirm must agree to its non-use. A similar argument applies to a Connection Request to a Class 0 system. If a Connection Request passed on from a Class 0 system results in a Connection Confirm with user data, there is a basic incompatibility between the two Transport Service Users. In such a case the DSG must break both transport connections. A similar argument applies to a Connection Request with user data being sent to a Class 0 system. If an attempt is made to send user data with a Disconnect Request to a Class 0 system, the DSG must complete the disconnection (apparently as normal) but not fowarding the user data. Delivery of user data on disconnection is not, in any case, guaranteed.

The relay function of the DSG will, as a normal Transport Service User, participate in the negotiation of service options (such as use of expedited data) and quality-of-service characteristics (such as throughput and transit delay). The DSG must support both use and non-use of expedited data, but must not influence the end-to-end decision as to whether it should be exployed or not.

The relay function of the DSG may also coordinate the choice of Transport Protocol parameters on each transport connection. This requires the parameters to be privately visible through the Transport Service interface. For IEEE 802 purposes, a DSG will support the following architecture on the LAN side:

1) class 4 Transport Protocol (normal and extended header formats; non-use of Checksum, Alternative Protocol Class, Quality of Service, Version Number, Security, and Acknowledge Time parameters)

2) connectionless Internet Protocol (or its null form)

3) IEEE 802.2 Type 1 Logical Link Control

4) IEEE 802.3/4/5/6 Medium Access as appropriate

The DSG supports this protocol structure on the LAN side but is prepared to deal with other protocols, classes and options externally: these are at least the minimal conformance options but may include other features as an implementation-dependent decision. The DSG proposes the Transport Protocol class and options above when forwarding a Connection Request from the LAN, but is prepared to negotiate externally down to the Conformance values. The DSG may choose to simplify its buffering by an appropriate choice of Transport Protocol Data Unit size on each side. In practice, however, this is likely to be a difficult optimisation.

Because a DSG will frequently be used to access systems which also obey the connectionless Internet Protocol and Class 4 Transport Protocol, it is desirable that the DSG be able to support a null conversion efficiently. More explicitly, it is desirable that a DSG should be able to operate as an ING as well. The architecture of a multi-level gateway implementation such as this is discussed in section 6.2.3 Transparent operation of a DSG as an ING is contingent on a common set of Transport Protocol options and parameter values being acceptable. For LAN-WAN interconnection, it is quite likely that differing choices of credit window size and sequence number space size will be made.

6.3.6.5 Configuration Control

A DSG has the system configuration control capabilities of an NEG (see section 6.3.4.5) and the sub-network configuration control capabilities of an ING (see section 6.3.5.5). Resilience to DSG failure is particularly critical since the DSG supports the Transport Service, which is where all end-to-end requirements of reliability and quality must ultimately be met. As for NEGs, resilience may be achieved by replicating DSGs. For this to be feasible, however, even more stringent constraints are necessary:

1) data must be acknowledged end-to-end; that is, the DSG must never acknowledge data on one transport connection before the corresponding acknowledgement on the other transport connection has been received; this does not, of course, imply that the Transport Protocol Data Unit size on each connection must be the same

2) the replicated DSGs must be able to take over each other's transport connections; this needs shared store or files which give the current status of each connection

3) a means of switching the transport connection from one DSG to another must be supported; this can be done by a LAN-attached system without the change-over being externally visible.

6.3.7 Review of Gateway Characteristics

This section reviews the characteristics of the gateways described earlier for the purposes of comparison. The table below summarises the properties of the various gateways and the diagrams overleaf give examples of how they may be used.

CHARACTERISTICS	sub-section	MEG	LEG	ILG	NEG	ING	DSG
described in section 6.?.?	-	.3.1	.3.2	.3.3	.3.4	.3.5	.3.6
relay function sub-layer?	.1	1.2	2.2	2.4	3.2	3.4	4.2
relay function type?	.1	C	C/R	R	C	R	C
relay function symmetrical?	.1	Y	Y	Y	N	Y	Y/N
relay service connectionless?	.1	Y	Y	Y	Y	Y	Y
relay service connection-oriented?	.1	N	N	N	Y	Y	Y
LAN-LAN interconnection?	.2	Y	Y	Y	N	Y	N
LAN-WAN interconnection?	.2	N	N	N	Y	Y	Y
LAN-WAN interconnection?	.2	N	N	N	Y	Y	N
WAN-WAN interconnection?	.2	N	N	N	Y	Y	N
routing algorithm type?	.3	-	fl-ood	min. cost	-	min. cost	-
relay and underlying services can differ?	.4	N	N	N	Y	Y	Y
degree of configuration control?	.5	0	2	7	5	8	9
resilience by replication?	.5	N	N	N	Y	N	Y

Key

MEG = Medium Extension Gateway
LEG = Link Extension Gateway
ILG = Inter Link Gateway
NEG = Network Extension Gateway
ING = Inter Network Gateway
DSG = Distributed System Gateway

C = Converting (relay)
R = Routing (relay)
Y = Yes
N = No
digit = facility level
    (0 = lowest, 9 = highest)

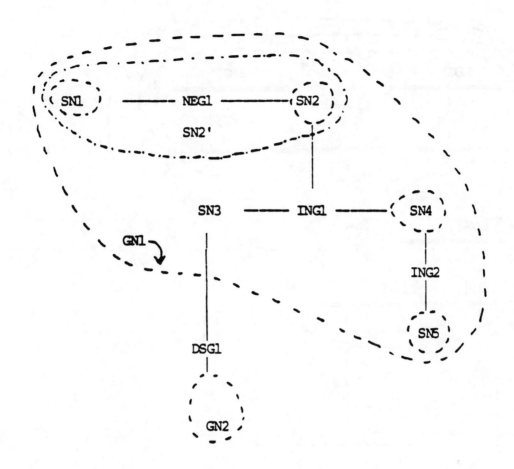

Key

DSG = Distributed System Gateway

GN = Global Network

ING = Inter Network Gateway

NEG = Network Extension Gateway

SN = Sub-Network

EXAMPLE OF INTER-NETWORK CONNECTION

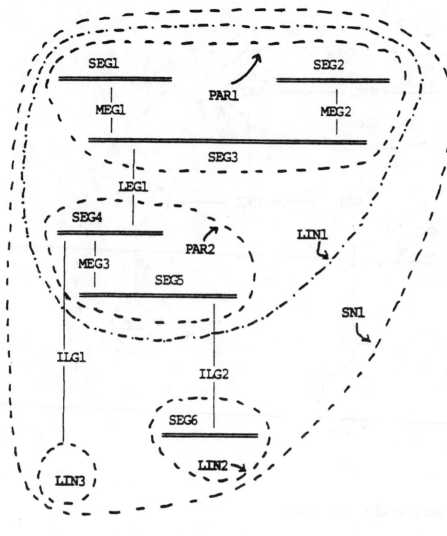

Key

    ILG = Inter Link Gateway

    LEG = Link Extension Gateway

    LIN = Link

    MEG = Medium Extension Gateway

    PAR = Partition

    SEG = Segment

    SN = Sub-Network

6.4   Inter-network and Intra-Network Connection

6.4.1   Introduction

The gateways described in section 6.3 are applicable to networking as follows:

```
Distributed System Gateway (DSG) }
Inter Network Gateway      (ING) } inter-network connection
Network Extension Gateway  (NEG) }

Inter Link Gateway         (ILG) }
Link Extension Gateway     (LEG) } intra-network connection
Medium Extension Gateway   (MEG) }
```

The detailed implementation of intra-network connection is beyond the scope of IEEE 802.1 and is described in sections 802.3, 802.4, 802.5 and 802.6 as appropriate. The architecture of inter-network connection is, however, LAN or MAN technology-independent and is discussed further in this section.

The basic classification used to describe inter-networking is the OSI Scenario Category (OSC). The most fundamental distinction to be made between network services is whether they are connection-oriented (CO) or connectionless (CL). For IEEE 802 the use of Type 2 Logical Link Control (LLC) results in CO operation, and the use of Type 1 Logical Link Control (LLC) results in CL operation. On this basis, the following combinations of sub-network services yielding the global network service are of interest:

OSC	SUB-NETWORK 1 SERVICE	SUB-NETWORK 2 SERVICE	GLOBAL NETWORK SERVICE
1	CO	CO	CO
2	CL	CL	CL
3	CO	CL	CO
4	CL	CO	CL

In addition, OSC5 covers the CL/CO case where interworking within the Network Layer is not possible.

6.4.2 <u>OSC1: CO + CO -> CO</u>

For this case, a connection-oriented ING shall be used (see section 6.3.5). A typical example of the protocols handled by the gateway is a follows:

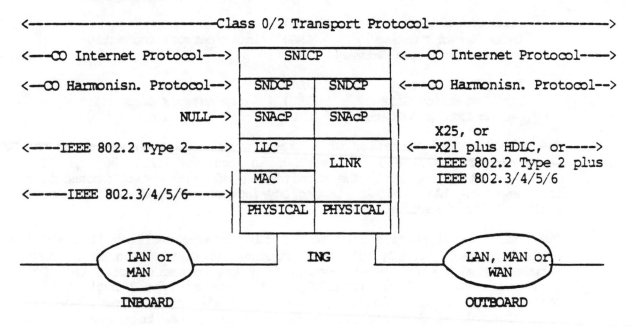

6.4.3 <u>OSC2: CL + CL -> CL</u>

For this case, a connectionless ING shall be used (see section 6.3.5). A typical example of the protocols handled by the gateway is as follows:

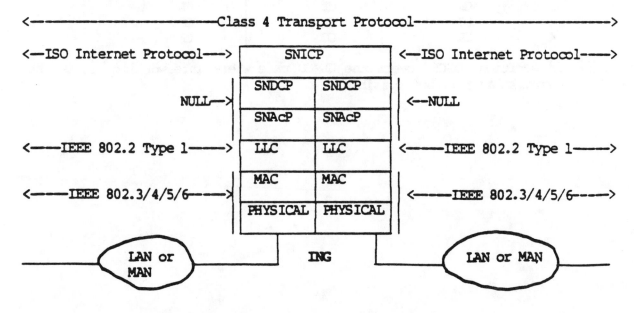

INBOARD   OUTBOARD

6.4.4   **OSC3: CO + CL -> CO**

This scenario requires a comprehensive CO enhancement protocol to be operated over the inboard LAN or MAN.

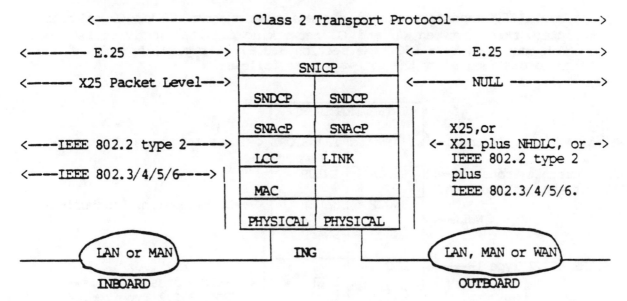

6.4.5   **OSC4: CL + CO -> CL**

This scenario requires a CL de-enhancement protocol to be operated over the outboard LAN, MAN or WAN. A typical example of the protocols handled by the gateway is as follows:

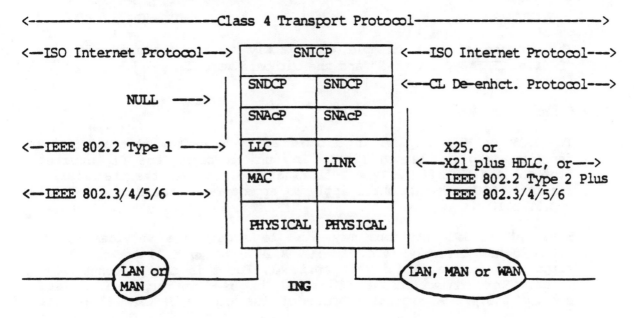

INBOARD   **OUTBOARD**

6.4.6   <u>OSC5: CL, CO</u>

This senario applies when a Distributed System is to be interworked with a CL Network.

Unless ISO mandate that all systems must support CL or CO or both, interworking between CL and CO networking domains involving LANs or MANs may be by a DSG (see section 6.3.6). A typical example of the protocols handled by the gateway is as follows:

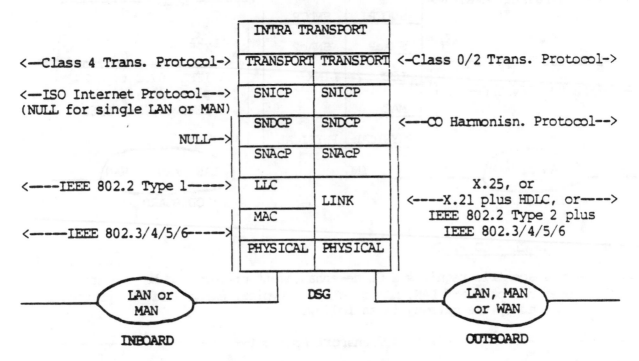

	INTRA TRANSPORT	
<—Class 4 Trans. Protocol->	TRANSPORT	TRANSPORT	<-Class 0/2 Trans. Protocol->
<—ISO Internet Protocol—-> (NULL for single LAN or MAN)	SNICP	SNICP	
	SNDCP	SNDCP	<—-CO Harmonisn. Protocol—->
NULL—>	SNAcP	SNAcP	
<—-IEEE 802.2 Type 1—->	LLC	LINK	X.25, or <----X.21 plus HDLC, or----> IEEE 802.2 Type 2 plus IEEE 802.3/4/5/6
	MAC		
<—-IEEE 802.3/4/5/6—->	PHYSICAL	PHYSICAL	

LAN or MAN   DSG   LAN, MAN or WAN

INBOARD   **OUTBOARD**

The inverse of this example would apply if the inboard side were CO (i.e. IEEE 802.2 Type 2) and the outboard were CL.

6.4.7   <u>Other Cases</u>

Two LANs or MANs may be interconnected by a dedicated transmission facility (e.g. a leased line). In such a case, the CL Internet Protocol and IEEE 802.2 Type 2 LLC shall be run over the transmission facility. OSC2 or OSC5 shall apply as appropriate (see sections 6.4.3 and 6.4.6).

Some LAN or MAN stations may wish to access the services of an outboard WAN directly (e.g. to run X.29 over an X.25 network). The support of such a facility is optional. For this case a connection-oriented or connectionless NEG shall be used as appropriate (see section 6.3.4). A typical example of the protocols handled by the gateway is as follows:

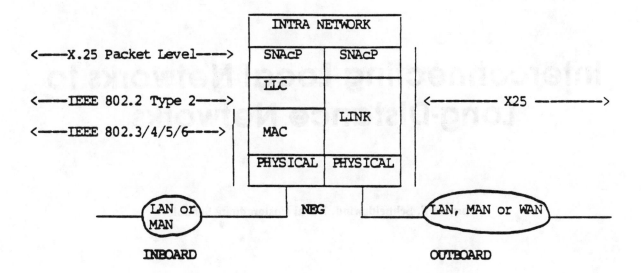

The approaches to interconnection—network access, network services, and protocol functions—are related and overlap. User requirements and existing specifications determine which one the designer emphasizes.

Interconnecting Local Networks to Long-Distance Networks

Norman F. Schneidewind, Naval Postgraduate School

The demand for broad yet specific network services is an urgent one, and as both local and long-distance networks proliferate, the need for better connections between these disparate systems is becoming critical.

A local network is a data communications system that allows communication between a number of independent devices. These devices can be computers, terminals, mass storage devices, printers, plotters, or copying machines.[1] The network may support a wide variety of applications, such as file editing and transfer, graphics, word processing, electronic mail, database management, and digital voice. Local networks are usually owned by a single organization and operated within a restricted geographical area, most often within a mile radius, at a moderate to high data rate such as 10 million bits per second. A long-distance network, on the other hand, is usually owned by a communications carrier and operated as a public utility for its subscribers, providing services such as voice, data, and video.

An emerging service of long-distance networks is providing the interconnection for local networks and other long-distance networks. Interconnection can provide

- local network to local network communication,
- local network to long-distance network communication, and
- long-distance network to long-distance network communication.

These interconnection possibilities, though exciting, inevitably present designers with the problem of resolving network incompatibilities. There are inherent differences in network characteristics as the result of the diversity of networks that exist to serve the various user communities. These differences have been accentuated by the failure of some networks to adopt standard protocols, by the variety of existing protocols and protocol standards, and by the wide range of incompatible options within existing protocol standards. In addition, designers are faced with a confusing mix of unregulated vendor products (e.g., IBM's System Network Architecture), local networks (e.g., Ethernet), regulated common carrier networks (e.g., Telenet), and newly deregulated communication services (e.g., American Bell).

The changing network scene

To set the stage for discussing the interconnection problem, let's review the evolution of computer networks to their current level of complexity.

Early connections. Before the advent of local networks, network services—supported by a single long-distance network—were viewed as shown in Figure 1. This view had the following major characteristics:

- terminal to computer communication,
- computer to computer communication, and
- terminal to terminal communication.

The orientation was one of data communication rather than networking. The long-distance network provided the terminal or remote-job-entry user with access to

Reprinted from *Computer*, September 1983, pages 15-24. Copyright © 1983 by The Institute of Electrical and Electronics Engineers, Inc.

remote computers or terminals. This mode of operation was typical of, for example, earlier versions of Arpanet, Decnet, and SNA and of the services provided by data communications carriers such as AT&T and MCI. The network provided access to hardware and software resources that were not available locally.

Emergence of networking. Rapid advances in technology, coupled with the development of local network architectures and protocols, led to the implementation of multiple mini/microcomputer-based workstations. The workstations are tied together by a physical communications medium and supported by protocols for network

access and for message transmission and reception. Initially, the terminal was the focal point of activity, accessing hosts in a resource-sharing network such as Arpanet or using a long-distance communications network such as AT&T for connection to a remote computer. Now, the emphasis has shifted to complete, self-contained local networks that access long-distance networks to communicate with other networks and, at the same time, provide communication among the local-network workstations. Thus, contemporary network services feature both inter-local and intra-local network communications (see Figure 2). As far as the long-distance network is concerned, the entire local network looks and functions like a single terminal. Indeed, this is an interconnection design goal.

Interconnection issues

Local and long-distance networks have significant differences that must be addressed when planning and designing networks consisting of one or more local networks interconnected by one or more long-distance networks.

The differences between local and long-distance networks, summarized in Table 1, lead to major interconnection issues:

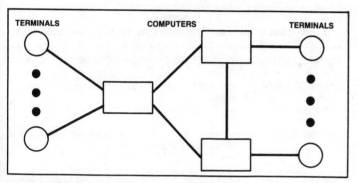

Figure 1. Previous view of computer networks.

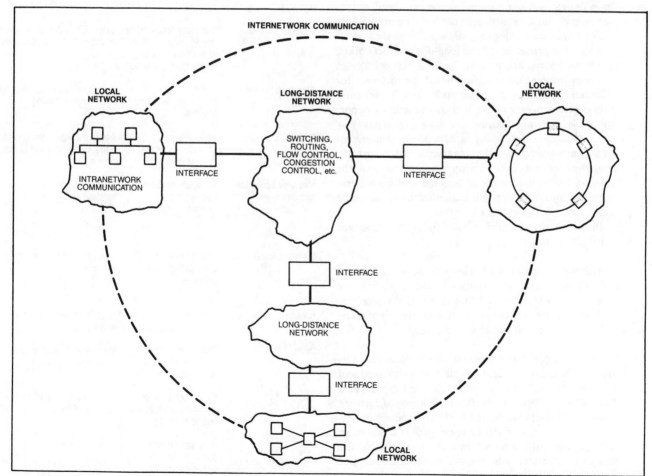

Figure 2. Contemporary view of computer networks.

- How should a local network be physically attached to a long-distance network?
- How should one local network access and communicate with another local network?
- To what extent should protocol and network architecture standards used in one network be used in another network?
- How is the difference in bandwidth, as it affects acknowledgment handling and flow control, to be resolved?
- How is the difference in delay time, as it affects user response time, to be reconciled?
- How should network addressing capability be provided? (A single local network can, of course, have a simpler address structure than a long-distance network, but communication among multiple local networks is the most difficult addressing problem of all.)

Decisions regarding these interconnection issues must be made before, not after, the networks are implemented.

A variety of situations and factors can affect the type of interconnection provided. Sometimes the networks already exist and their specifications are known—for example, when an existing local network is connected to an existing long-distance network to communicate with other local networks. In other situations, however, one or more of the networks must still be specified. A common design problem involves developing specifications for nonexistent local networks that are to communicate via one or more existing long-distance networks.

Thus, the properties of the long-distance network(s) are usually given and part of the local network design problem involves the specification of the interface for connecting the two types of networks. For the designer, this situation presents both a challenge and an opportunity: a challenge because few user organizations—other than communications carriers or the Department of Defense—can control the characteristics designed into long-distance networks; an opportunity because the designer can influence the effectiveness of both intra-local and inter-local communication by the approach he uses to specify the network interface.

In designing the interface, the following important principle applies:

> The more a local network is designed to increase the effectiveness of intra-local network communication, the more the cost of the interface to a long-distance network increases and the more the effectiveness of inter-local network communication decreases.

This principle is an outgrowth of the significant differences in the characteristics that distinguish local and long-distance networks (Table 1). These differences lead to a high-cost, complex interface if each type of network is tailored to the particular needs of its user communities. On the other hand, if the local network is designed to achieve compatibility with a long-distance network, the cost of the interface falls, but local-network throughput and response time suffer. The usual way of resolving this trade-off is to lean heavily in the direction of maximizing

local network effectiveness, at the expense of interface cost, because the interface represents a one-time cost while the local network must provide effective service for its users over the lifetime of the network.

The ISO architecture

A significant development in the standards area that exerts considerable influence on network design and intercommunication methods is the International Standards Organization model of architecture for open systems interconnection.[2] (See Figure 3.) The extent to

Table 1.
Comparison of local and long-distance network characteristics.

CHARACTERISTIC	LOCAL NETWORK	LONG-DISTANCE NETWORK
Typical Bandwidth	10 million bits per second.	56,000 bits per second.
Acknowledgment	One message acknowledged at a time.	N messages acknowledged at a time.
Message Size and Format	Small (simple header). No need to divide message into packets.	Large (complex header). Need to divide message into packets.
Network Control	Minimum requirement due to small number of links and nodes and simple topology.	Extensive due to large number of nodes and links and complex topology.
Flow/Congestion Control	Minimum due to high bandwidth and simple topology.	Extensive due to low bandwidth and complex topology.
Error Rate	Relatively low. Operated in benign environment.	Relatively high. Operated in noisy environment of telephone network.
Message Sequence and Delivery	Minimum problem due to simple topology (e.g., bus or ring).	Major problem due to complex topology (e.g., mesh).
Standard Architecture	Usually only two or three bottom layers provided.	Frequent use of all or many ISO layers.
Routing	None required due to simple topology.	Major problem due to complex topology.
Delay Time	Small due to short distance and medium (e.g., coaxial cable).	Large due to distance and medium (e.g., satellite).
Addressing	Simple intra-network communication due to simple topology. Complex inter-network communication due to the use of long-distance network(s).	Complex because of many nodes and links.

which local and long-distance networks adhere to the ISO model has an important bearing on the nature and complexity of the interconnection. The use of many, or all, ISO layers is particularly important for long-distance networks because of their

- complex topology,
- wide geographical coverage,
- large number of nodes and links,
- extensive switching and routing,
- numerous points requiring flow control and congestion control,
- relatively long delays in end-to-end transmission, and
- long distance process-to-process communication requiring complex acknowledgment schemes.

Local networks, on the other hand, have much simpler characteristics and thus less need for the various ISO protocol services. Warner[3] has suggested that forcing a local network design *in total* into the ISO mold could result in significant overhead in terms of (1) a large message size to accommodate multiple headers for the many ISO layers, (2) complicated and unnecessary message acknowledgment procedures, and (3) extraneous hardware and software to support the ISO transport and network layers. However, not using ISO in the local network risks loss of compatibility with ISO-based networks, one of

which could be a long-distance network that must interface with the local network.

Approaches for solving the interconnection problem

The three basic approaches to interconnection—network access, network services, and protocol functions—are related and frequently overlap. Bear in mind that a combination of the approaches, described and compared below, may be necessary to interconnect diverse networks effectively.

Network access. The network access approach involves making electrical and physical connections of local networks and user communities via the long-distance network. The predominate considerations in this approach are ones of physical access and interfacing—for example, signal levels, pin connectors, cable length, and transmission medium. But it also emphasizes local-network compatibility with the long-distance network at the bottom three layers of the ISO model. All three layers are needed. *Any* network communication requires the data link layer for reliable internode communication, and a long-distance network requires the switching and routing functions of the network layer.

The main concern in this approach is the user's ability to *access* additional users and resources at a reasonable cost by the most convenient, feasible method. Whether or not the network services obtained as a result of the connection are ideal for the application is of secondary concern.

A number of situations could motivate user interest in the network access approach. Frequently, the motivation is convenience; the service needed—say, for example, an X.25-compatible network—might simply be readily available. Another possibility is that the user's objective is limited. He might not be interested in obtaining computer-based services such as database management, financial forecasting, or engineering computation; perhaps he only wants the services of a *transmission medium* for providing connectivity to other users. Then, the need is for a communications facility whose primary function is the *transport* of data. A data communications carrier is frequently the long-distance network that provides this level of service. A third possibility is that the user's terminal equipment is only compatible with certain networks, so the ability to provide interconnection at the lowest physical level outweighs other considerations.

Ordinarily, the network access approach is used when both the local networks and the long-distance network already exist. Since network characteristics cannot be created or modified, the user's options are limited, and he must be content with a low-cost network that is hardware-compatible with his local networks.

Network services. High-level user services can be obtained with the network services approach to interconnection. Some services, such as database management, could be related to the application and presentation layers of the ISO model; others, such as a high-level com-

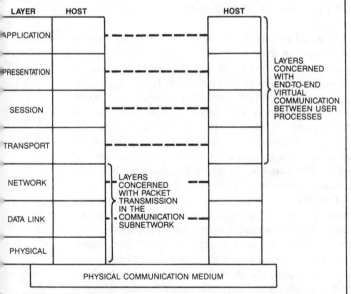

LAYER	FUNCTION
Application	Communication between cooperating user processes
Presentation	Formatting and display of user data
Session	Coordination and administration of user process data exchange
Transport	Reliable end-to-end transfer of data over virtual circuits
Network	Routing and switching of packets in the communication subnetwork
Data Link	Reliable packet transfer between nodes in the communication subnetwork
Physical	Transmission of bits between nodes in the communication subnetwork

Figure 3. ISO model seven-layer architecture.

munication service like electronic mail, could be related to the transport and network layers.

Obviously, any interconnection approach involves connections between local networks and a long-distance network and thereby provides inter-local network access. However, in contrast to the first approach, the network services approach stresses obtaining specific network services for the user organization, and the details of physical and electrical interfacing, while important, become secondary issues. Necessarily, this approach emphasizes compatibility between local networks and a long-distance network at the higher level layers of the ISO model.

What conditions motivate a user to consider this approach? One situation is when the long-distance network provides a data management or processing service that is not available in the local networks. Often only a large-scale network (e.g., Arpanet) has the host hardware and software capable of providing a desired service. A second situation arises when a high-level, inter-local network communication service is desired. For example, the user organization may want to tie its local networks together, or connect to other organizations' local networks to provide remote interactive processing involving session control and sequenced, error-free message delivery. Typically, this type of service would be obtained from a long-distance network that provides a virtual circuit service. Since the objective is to obtain a specific type of network service, naturally the long-distance network is an existing one. However, the local networks may or may not exist. If they do, protocol conversion will probably be required at the interface between the local networks and the long-distance network. If they don't exist and if ease of interfacing is a primary objective, the desired service may prompt the local network designer to attempt maximum compatibility with the layers and protocols of the long-distance network.

In general, a data communication network is appropriate for the network access approach, but a resource-sharing or value-added network is germane to the network services approach.

Protocol functions. The third method of achieving interconnection provides one set of protocol functions for the local network and another set for the long-distance network, where some functions, or corresponding network layers, are common to both networks. When crossing network boundaries, a transition or "conversion" is made between protocols. The boundary points are typically implemented in hardware with gateways (an interface between two networks) and front-end processors.

This method is used when the user's *primary* objective is to optimize local network communication, by using only those layers and protocols necessary for local network operation, while also providing communication between local networks via the long-distance network. Although the user will not be indifferent to physical access and network services, the dominant objective is to marry two diverse types of networks, which are inherently incompatible, and still retain the effectiveness of each. Protocol conversion is necessary to achieve this objective. The degree of conversion is a function of the dif-

ferences between the layers and protocols in the two types of networks.

When would a user organization be able to capitalize on this approach? The most likely situation is when the local networks have not been implemented and the user has the opportunity to influence both intra-local network and inter-local network effectiveness by virtue of the protocol functions provided in the local networks; the long-distance network may or may not have been implemented (i.e., it may also be in the planning or development stage). Regardless of the status of the long-distance network, the user organization would, in most instances, have negligible influence over the design of the long-distance network due to the size and dominant position of the long-distance network organization.

In some cases, one protocol can be translated into another. In others, protocols can be held in common among the communicating parties.

This approach is seldom viable when the local networks exist; the likely degree of protocol conversion required, in terms of message format, message size, acknowledgment method, naming, addressing, error control, etc., would make it infeasible.

Comparison of approaches

As stated by Cerf and Kirstein,[4] the common objective of all interconnection methods is to allow all subscribers a means of accessing a host on any of the interconnected networks. They go on to declare that achieving this objective requires that data produced at a source in one network be delivered and correctly interpreted at the destination(s) in another network. This reduces to providing interprocess communication across network boundaries. In some cases, it is enough to translate one protocol into another. In others, protocols can be held in common among the communicating parties.

The efficiency of achieving this objective depends on which approach is utilized. It is not necessary to implement all ISO layers in the local network to achieve effective intra-local network communication, nor is implementation necessary to connect to a long-distance network. However, the number, types, and characteristics of the layers utilized determine the efficiency of inter-local network communication (i.e., communication over the long-distance network).

The network access approach certainly achieves *physical* access to hosts, but the interconnection does not provide access to all the services available in the long-distance network. This approach does not *fully* achieve the requirement of delivering data from the source and having it correctly interpreted at the destination, because complete compatibility between local network protocols and long-distance network protocols may not be possible. For example, it might achieve a datagram service, which requires only the first three ISO layers, but might not be able to realize virtual circuit service, which requires use of the transport layer.

The network services approach does, on the other hand, *completely* satisfy the requirement regarding data delivery and interpretation, but not necessarily efficiently. In this approach, it may be necessary to adopt inefficient local network protocols to achieve compatiblity with the long-distance network. This is the case if the protocols are held in common among the communicating parties, where the "communicating parties" are the local network and the long-distance network.

Table 2.
Comparison of network interconnection approaches.

APPROACH	CHARACTERISTIC	ADVANTAGES	DISADVANTAGES
Network Access	Achieves physical access and protocol compatibility in lower layers of ISO model (e.g., physical, data link, and network layers of X.25).	Relatively inexpensive. May obtain compatibility with international standards.	Only provides compatibility with lower layers of network architecture. Restricted to services of network access method.
Network Services	Obtains use of specific types of services (e.g., virtual circuit service) to satisfy user needs.	The network service is matched to the user need as opposed to simply obtaining physical access to a network. Reduces software development expense.	Restricted to using the same (perhaps inefficient) protocols in all interconnected networks. May be restricted to using a single type of service.
Protocol Functions	Matches number and types of protocols to each type of network.	Uses only those protocols that are necessary in each type of network. High performance. Low overhead.	Expensive software development. Complex network interface.

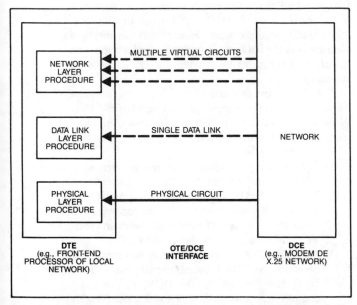

Figure 4. Structure of the X.25 interface (adapted from Reference 5).

The protocol functions approach solves the problem of local-network communications efficiency, but at high hardware and software costs. Its use of the protocol translation technique necessitates a complex network interface.

In general, no matter which approach is utilized, the owner of the local network is responsible for designing the interface and arranging the connection with the owner of the long-distance network, using the specifications of that network as a guide. This work will take place over an extended period of time, and involves development, design, implementation, and maintenance. The three approaches are summarized and compared in Table 2.

Examples of interconnection approaches

Network access. Rybczynski[5] provides an example of the network access approach to interconnection vis-a-vis the X.25 interface standard. X.25 is a standard device-independent interface between X.25-compatible packet networks and user devices operating in the packet mode. The interface point occurs between the user's data terminal equipment, or DTE, and the data communications equipment, or DCE, of an X.25 packet switching network (e.g., GTE-Telenet). Although the DTE is often thought of as an individual terminal or host, it could just as well be a front-end processor of a local network. The DCE could be a modem associated with the communication channel of an X.25 packet-switching node. Multiple local networks connected in this fashion would provide inter-local network communication and the services offered by the X.25 long-distance network. The interface between the DTE and DCE occurs at the first three layers of the ISO model, as shown in Figure 4.

The characteristics of these layers* are as follows:

Physical layer
- full duplex,
- point-to-point, and
- synchronous.

Data link layer
- data link control procedures compatible with the high-level data, link control (HDLC) protocol,
- single data links,
- data transfer,
- link synchronization,
- detection of and recovery from errors, and
- reporting of errors to a higher layer.

Network layer
- packetizing of user and control data,
- network addressing, and
- multiple virtual circuits.

From a practical standpoint the user organization must provide the appropriate hardware and software in

---

*The X.25 designations for the ISO network and data link layers are "packet" and "frame," respectively; X.25 also uses "level" rather than the ISO term "layer." The ISO terminology is used here to maintain consistency.

its network access unit (e.g., a front-end processor) in the physical, data link, and network layers to be compatible with X.25. This means, for example, providing software to implement HDLC in the data link layer and an RS-232-C hardware interface in the physical layer.

This approach to interconnection emphasizes physical access and the use of the long-distance network as a communications medium for the exchange of messages between local networks. The interconnected local networks must adopt the standards of the long-distance network and install the lower level protocols (e.g., physical, data link, and network layers of X.25) of the long-distance network. This will be beneficial or detrimental for the operation of the local networks, depending on whether the protocol characteristics (acknowledgement, addressing, etc.) enhance or degrade the performance of the local networks. Since this approach only addresses the lower level protocols, the user must provide the upper layer protocols. Also, since network performance is primarily a function of upper-layer characteristics, achievable performance will be uncertain. The major advantage of this approach is its low cost, since the required protocol software exists for many computers.

DDN, the defense data network, illustrates the limitations of the network access approach, specifically with regard to X.25. Although using X.25 is not currently a DDN requirement, it may be added to permit communication with network nodes in the NATO community.[6] The switching nodes used in the DDN (BBN Model C/30s) are designed to be compatible with X.25 in all three layers. However, layer 3 of X.25, the network layer, is not compatible with the layer-3 host-IMP protocol used to support communication between a local network and the DDN. Without the installation of a gateway (i.e., the protocol functions approach), it will not be possible for hosts in the DDN to communicate with hosts in NATO. Thus, although X.25 protocol software exists in DDN, offering the *potential* for a low-cost interconnection, no local network can presently connect to DDN using X.25 protocols; it would not be compatible with all the DDN protocols. Achieving this compatibility would require a protocol converter for translation between the host-IMP and X.25 network layer protocols.

Network services. Another example using X.25 illustrates the relationship between network access and network services. In this example, the real significance of achieving X.25 network access compatibility is to obtain X.25 network services such as switched virtual circuits, permanent virtual circuits, and datagrams.

SVCs and PVCs. Switched virtual circuits, or SVCs, provide a temporary logical circuit between two host processes. A call request action by the process that wants to open a connection is required. An SVC will compete for the use of available network resources, and possibly experience delay in establishing the circuit, but has the advantage of using these resources efficiently. On the other hand, a permanent virtual circuit, or PVC, guarantees network access to the user, obviating the call request procedure, and provides a data path between a fixed pair of network endpoints. The SVC and PVC services are

analogous to the switched network and leased lines services offered by data communications carriers.

Datagrams. A datagram service provides transmission of packets in a network where each packet is independent of other packets. There is no guarantee of sequenced delivery of packets constituting a message, nor guarantee of any type of delivery, for that matter. A datagram service is fast and uses network resources efficiently—for example, the destination node can pass a message to a host without waiting to reassemble all of its packets or tieing up valuable buffer space for this purpose. If the user desires guaranteed sequenced delivery, it must be provided by the transport layer residing above the network layer, which is charged with datagram delivery.

It is one thing for users to tolerate an occasional lost packet but quite different to forego sequential delivery.

A datagram service is useful in certain applications where no higher layers are necessary to complete the job of message delivery and where all the data to carry out a function can be contained in a single packet—for example, transaction processing such as a file update, where each update represents an independent action, and narrative message transmission, where each message can be considered an independent entity. In some applications—digitized voice, for example—a datagram service is used primarily because of its speed.

Most practical applications of datagram services require the transport layer to sequence datagrams for delivery to a host process. It is one thing for all the data in a packet to be self-contained (e.g., a Fortran compile command) or to tolerate an occasional lost packet (e.g., digitized voice) but quite different, from the standpoint of the user's operation, to forego sequential delivery; the user wants a Fortran compile done next or the parts of a voice conversation to reach the listener in sequence. (Subsequent sections show how the Department of Defense uses the datagram concept in combination with upper layer functions to provide the desired network services.)

DoD DDN. An application where X.25 takes on great importance is the Department of Defense's Defense Data Network.[6] As related by Corrigan,[7] planners of DDN were confronted with the following situation:

(1) For the most part, vendor protocols are incompatible across different manufacturers' equipment.

(2) However, the DDN must allow for various vendor protocols because many DoD user communities, using a great variety of vendor hardware and software, must be accommodated in the DDN.

(3) Although the Arpanet architecture and protocols, on which the DDN is based, provide many of the capabilities desired for the DDN, they are not completely compatible with the various vendor protocols.

(4) X.25 has been adopted by manufacturers but has not been implemented in the DDN.

Cerf and Lyons[8] point out that, although X.25 is a network access standard for connecting to packet-switched networks, it has the following deficiencies relative to its use in the DDN:

(1) Although datagram service is part of the standard, it has not been implemented in any network. The datagram mode is essential to real-time military applications, such as tactical operations and packet voice.
(2) The availability of only virtual circuit service in X.25, with its required sequencing, introduces intolerable delays in certain real-time applications. In many applications, total data integrity is not essential, but minimum delay is mandatory. Certain military applications require a broadcast mode, which is not compatible with sequenced delivery in a virtual circuit.

Given the diversity of network characteristics, the network services strategy may be good for inter-local network operations but not for intra-local network performance.

Thus, the DoD is faced with a dilemma: compatibility with X.25 is important because many vendors and communications carriers have adopted it, but X.25 does not fully meet DoD's requirements. The DoD's response to this problem is fourfold[8]:

(1) The Internet protocol[9] has been developed for the DDN and is now operational on Arpanet. IP provides a datagram service for those applications which require fast, nonsequenced delivery and addressing and routing capabilities for transmission of datagrams across multiple networks.
(2) The Transmission Control Protocol[9] has been developed for the DDN and is now operational on the Arpanet. Using the services of IP, and the additional capabilities of sequenced delivery, flow control, and end-to-end acknowledgment, TCP provides a virtual circuit service for applications that require interactive terminal to remote host processing.
(3) As a long-range goal, DDN compatibility with X.25 is planned.
(4) The Defense Communications Agency is working with the international standards bodies (e.g., ISO and CCITT) to promote acceptance of TCP/IP in the civilian community and to urge these bodies to give more weight to military requirements, such as real-time response, security, precedence message handling, and survivability, in their standards efforts.

From the above, it can be seen that achieving interconnection among diverse networks can very likely involve a combination of approaches: network access (e.g., X.25). network services (e.g., datagram and virtual circuit), and political and standards activity (e.g., ISO).

The important factor in the network services approach to interconnection is obtaining services available in the long-distance network for the user organization's local networks. Given the diversity of network characteristics, this strategy may be good for inter-local network operations but not for intra-local network performance. Such penalties as high software overhead, due to unneeded flow control, routing, and addressing capabilities, are especially prevalent if all layers of the long-distance network are incorporated into local network communication operations. Even inter-local network efficiency can be poor if service is limited to one type (e.g., fixed-routing virtual circuit service). However, this approach has the significant advantage of providing clean interfaces at the network boundaries, due to the use of the same protocols in all networks. The implication of this is reduced software development costs compared to methods that tailor the protocols to the characteristics of each interconnected network.

Protocol functions. An example illustrating the protocol functions approach is the Navy's Stock Point Logistics Integrated Communications Environment system. The SPLICE concept is being developed as a result of growing demands for automated data processing at Navy stock points and inventory control points. SPLICE is designed to augment the existing Navy stock point and inventory control point ADP facilities, which support the Uniform Automated Data Processing System-Stock Points. The hardware for the UADPS-SP consists of Burroughs medium-size systems. At present there are 20 new application systems being developed that require considerable interactive and computer communication support. These new application systems will utilize minicomputers capable of supporting foreground interactive and computer communication requirements.

Two major objectives led to the development of SPLICE: first, the increased need for the use of interactive database processing to replace the current batch-oriented system; second, the need to standardize the current multitude of interfaces. To reduce total system cost, SPLICE will be developed using a standard set of minicomputer hardware and software. Standardization is particularly important because SPLICE will be implemented at some 60 geographical locations, each having a different mix of application and terminal requirements. The SPLICE processors will be co-located with the host Burroughs system at each Navy stock point and with Burroughs and Univac systems at the inventory control points. A "foreground-background" concept will be implemented with SPLICE minicomputers, which will serve as front-end processors for the Burroughs systems via a local area network interface. The Burroughs computers will provide background processing functions for large file processing and report generation.

The SPLICE project[10] has the following characteristics:

• intra-local area network communication,

- inter-LAN communication over the long-distance DDN,
- conflicting requirements—LAN vs. long-distance network—for communication,
- mandated communications protocols, required for compatibility purposes, that have little relevance to LAN communication,
- local and remote interactive and batch processing, and
- off-loading of certain processing (e.g., database management) from mainframes to minicomputers.

The network configuration (Figure 5) shows the integration of the three interconnection methods—network access, network services, and protocol functions. Network access is achieved via the hardware of the front-end processor in conjunction with the access line and the host-IMP protocol, a network access protocol used in the Arpanet and adapted to the DDN. Basic network services consist of a virtual circuit service for interactive processing and other operations that require reliable, sequenced end-to-end message delivery, plus a datagram service for operations which involve the transmission of independent messages (e.g., the sending of a message in the electronic mail system). The datagram service, implemented in the internet protocol (IP) and operating in the network layer,* supports the transmission control protocol (TCP), operating in the transport layer, to provide a virtual circuit service. The datagram service is used to obtain efficient bandwidth utilization and flexibile message routing. This flexibility is achieved because the messages can be transmitted as independent packets without being constrained to follow a single path and to follow one another in sequence. The TCP sequences the messages

*Some authors classify this as an eighth layer—the internet layer—situated between the transport and network layers.

and provides reliable end-to-end delivery. The protocol functions approach provides only those protocols in the local area network that are needed to support this type of communications environment. Due to the great differences between local and long-distance network characteristics, protocol requirements differ significantly. This point is illustrated in Table 3, which delineates differences in the utilization of ISO layers and protocols in LAN and DDN communication.

Sending and receiving messages on the DDN will use all seven layers of the ISO model, as shown in Table 3. The LAN has no need for the services normally provided by the transport and network layers, because routing, switching, and traditional flow control and congestion control services are unnecessary. The presentation layer, implemented in the terminal management module, will accept data from the application process and convert it to LAN format. Conversely, it will accept messages in LAN format and convert them to the appropriate application process format.

**Table 3.
Use of ISO layers in LAN design.**

LAYER	LAN COMMUNICATION PROTOCOL/MODULE	DDN COMMUNICATION
Application	Application Process Modules	Same as for LAN
Presentation	Terminal Management	Terminal Management
Session	Session Services	Session Services
Transport	— —	TCP
Network	— —	IP
Data Link	Local Communications	Specified by the DDN (Various Protocols)
Physical	Local Communications	

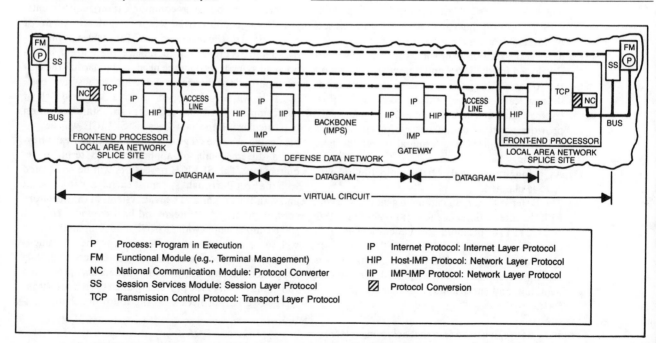

P — Process: Program in Execution
FM — Functional Module (e.g., Terminal Management)
NC — National Communication Module: Protocol Converter
SS — Session Services Module: Session Layer Protocol
TCP — Transmission Control Protocol: Transport Layer Protocol
IP — Internet Protocol: Internet Layer Protocol
HIP — Host-IMP Protocol: Network Layer Protocol
IIP — IMP-IMP Protocol: Network Layer Protocol
▨ — Protocol Conversion

Figure 5. Relationship between local area networks and the Defense Data Network.

To simplify the LAN design, the following message formats are used:

(1) TCP format will be provided to the DDN by the NC module (see Figure 5) whenever communication on the DDN is necessary. A much simpler format will be used for intra-LAN communication.

(2) End-to-end virtual circuit connections and breaking of complete messages into fragments, services normally provided by the transport layer, will be implemented in each of the LAN modules. "End-to-end" in this context refers to the logical communication linkage between two modules separated by a relatively short distance; in some cases the two modules could be in the same hardware unit.

To maximize compatibility and minimize software development, the protocols in the two networks are selected to match as closely as possible, consistent with satisfying the requirements of vastly different communications environments (e.g., routing in the DDN and no routing in the LAN).

The protocol functions approach is used where the inter-local network services and performance provided by the long-distance network (e.g., combination of virtual circuit and datagram services) are satisfactory. It is also used where optimization of intra-local network performance is desired. This is accomplished by using only those layers and protocols that are compatible with and can take advantage of the characteristics of local networks (e.g., single message acknowledgment made possible by high bandwidth). Of course, the user organization must be willing to pay the relatively high software cost of this tailored approach.

It is apparent from the discussion and examples that users may have diverse networking requirements and that local and long-distance networks have opposing characteristics. For most applications, this means that it will be necessary to use a combination of the three approaches to achieve an effective interconnection.■

Acknowledgment

This work was sponsored by the Fleet Material Support Office and the Naval Supply Systems Command.

References

1. A Status Report, IEEE 802 Local Network Standard, Draft B, Local Network Standards Committee, IEEE Computer Society, Oct. 19, 1981.

2. H. Zimmermann, "OSI Reference Model—The ISO Model of Architecture for Open Systems Interconnection," *IEEE Trans. Communications,* Vol. COM-28, No. 4, Apr. 1980, pp. 425-432.

3. Clifford Warner, "Connecting Local Networks to Long Haul Networks; Issues in Protocol Design," *Proc. Fifth Conf. Local Computer Networks,* IEEE Computer Society, Oct. 1980, pp. 71-76.

4. V. G. Cerf and P. T. Kirstein, "Issues in Packet-Network Interconnection," *Proc. IEEE,* Vol. 66, No. 11, Nov. 1978, pp. 1386-1408.

5. A. Rybczynski, "X.25 Interface and End-End Virtual Circuit Service Characteristics," *IEEE Trans. Communications,* Vol. COM-28, No. 4, Apr. 1980, pp. 500-510.

6. Defense Data Network Program Plan, Defense Communications Agency, Jan. 1982, revised May 1982.

7. Michael L. Corrigan, "Defense Data Network Protocols," *Conf. Record, EASCON 82, 15th Annual Electronics and Aerospace Systems Conf.*, Washington, DC, Sept. 1982, pp. 131-135.

8. V. G. Cerf and R. E. Lyons, "Military Requirements for Packet-Switched Networks and Their Implications for Protocol Standardization," op cit., pp. 119-129.

9. Jonathan B. Postel, "Internetwork Protocol Approaches," *IEEE Trans. Communications,* Vol. COM-28, No. 4, Apr. 1980, pp. 604-611.

10. N. Schneidewind, "Functional Approach to the Design of a Local Network: A Naval Logistics System Example," *Compcon Spring 83 Digest of Papers*, IEEE Computer Society, Mar. 1983, pp. 197-202.

Norman F. Schneidewind is a professor of computer science at the Naval Postgraduate School, where he teaches in information systems and computer science and does research in computer networks and software engineering. Schneidewind is the principal investigator on the Navy's SPLICE computer network project. He has held various technical and management positions in computer system development at SDC, PRC, CUC, Sperry Univac, and Hughes Aircraft.

Schneidewind is a senior member of the IEEE; a member of the Executive Board of the IEEE-CS Technical Committee on Software Engineering, the IEEE Committee on Communications and Information Policy, and the Software Engineering Standards Subcommittee; chairman of the Software Maintenance Workshop; and IEEE-CS representative to the Annual Simulation Symposium.

He received the BSEE from the University of California, Berkeley; MSCS from San Jose State University; and MSOR (Engr), MBA, and DBA from the University of Southern California; and holds the Certificate in Data Processing.

George T. Koshy, Booz, Allen & Hamilton Inc., Lexington, N

Understanding multiple LANs: The why and how of linking up

A consultant argues for the proliferation of multiple LANs in an organization that is bridged at the Data Link Layer.

In the late seventies and early eighties, computer users and vendors realized that they required networks to tie their diverse equipment together and to make their data processing more efficient. Controversy was fervent among vendors regarding the most appropriate single medium as well as the most appropriate single technique to access the medium. Today, such discussions have subsided because vendors and users alike have learned that neither one medium nor one access scheme will satisfy all needs at all times.

The emerging trend is toward the existence of multiple local area networks (LANs) within one organization—each one catering to the needs of a specific operation or a functional group. Multiple LANs within an organization need to be interconnected so that all users can communicate with all others if necessary. The devices that perform the interconnection are called bridges, providing high throughput and low delay so that users do not experience any significant performance degradation when communicating with other users attached to the conglomerate of LANs.

Why have multiple LANs?

This article consists of two parts. In the first part, the need for the existence of multiple LANs is described in detail. The second part deals with one issue of the architectural layer at which the interconnection should take place.

Local area networking products available today do not conform to a single standard. They exist on a variety of media, such as twisted pair, coaxial cable, and optical fiber; use two signaling schemes (baseband and broadband); and work with a variety of media access techniques, such as carrier-sense multiple access with collision detection (CSMA/CD), token

passing, time-division multiplexing, and so on. There is wide support among all segments of the computer industry for the Institute of Electrical and Electronics Engineers (IEEE) 802 standards, and it is expected that within the next few years most LAN products will conform to one of these standards.

Currently, IEEE 802 standards support the following schemes:
- CSMA/CD on baseband cable.
- CSMA/CD on broadband cable.
- Token-passing bus on broadband cable.
- Token-passing bus on baseband cable.
- Token-passing ring on baseband cable.

Although they do not offer a single scheme, the IEEE 802 standards have reduced the number of options for new products.

A number of LANs may coexist in a single organization for several reasons:
- Number of stations.
- Security.
- Area of coverage.
- Media access schemes.
- Organizational growth.
- Maintenance.

The following is a detailed description of these reasons.

Number of stations. In any media access scheme the performance deteriorates with an increase in the number of stations. In CSMA/CD, the greater the number of stations, the greater the probability of collisions that reduce the effective throughput. In a token-passing scheme, the effect of the number of stations on the throughput and delay is more straightforward. The token has to pass through more stations. This reduces the time available for transmission of data and increases the time a station needs to wait in order to receive the token. In a token-passing ring network, adding more stations increases the perimeter of the ring that will reduce the throughput and increase the delay.

Security. The establishment of multiple LANs may improve the security of communications. It is desirable to keep different types of traffic that have different security needs on physically separate media. At the same time, the different types of users with different levels of security need to communicate through controlled and monitored mechanisms. Multiple LANs, rather than a single LAN, are necessary under such circumstances. For example, a LAN used by personnel or for in-house financial projections should be separate from one used for customer service or on the factory floor.

Area of coverage. In many situations, one LAN is not capable of covering all areas of a user organization, due to inherent limitations of certain media access schemes, performance, and geographical locations. Certain media access schemes put a limit on the maximum distance of the LAN. The most obvious example is CSMA/CD, which imposes a limit on the maximum distance for a given minimum frame size and transmission speed. This restriction is necessary for the effective detection of collisions. Increasing the minimum packet size increases the maximum distance, but this affects the effective throughput because frames will have to be stuffed with nondata characters. Reducing transmission speed also increases the distance, but this reduces the throughput and the number of stations that may be attached to the LAN. So a CSMA/CD scheme operates on the basis of a set of fixed values for these parameters.

For example, IEEE 802.3 specifies the speed, 10 Mbit/s; the minimum frame size, 512 bits; and the maximum distance, 1.5 kilometers (km), or 0.9 miles. In this LAN, the maximum distance between the coaxial cable and the stations, such as computers or terminal concentrators, is only 50 meters (64 feet).

Broadband LANs also do not cover all areas of large organizations. Even though CATV broadband cable can cover areas of 10s of kilometers, these LANs have restrictions, covering a maximum distance up to only a few kilometers. For example, a standard IEEE 802.3 broadband CSMA/CD LAN covers an area within a radius of 1.4 km (0.87 miles) from the headend.

Media access schemes. The nature of media access schemes makes it necessary in many cases for multiple LANs with different media access schemes to be set up. Each of the common access schemes has its individual merits and demerits that make it suitable for certain environments and unsuitable for others. For example, CSMA/CD performs well under light loading but cannot provide deterministic delays. The token-passing scheme on a bus topology provides deterministic delays but introduces relatively larger delays at low levels of loading. Token-passing rings also provide

deterministic delays but are more vulnerable to failures in cables and stations. They have an advantage in that they can use optical fiber and run up to a few hundred bit/s.

The access scheme chosen for a LAN will depend on these characteristics, and an organization within one local area may have LANs of many different types. A manufacturer might use the General Motors-sponsored Manufacturing Automation Protocol (MAP) for its factory-floor communications, employing a token-passing bus LAN based on a broadband cable. Devices such as programmable contollers and robot controllers, which are directly involved in manufacturing operations, are attached to the broadband cable. The mainframe computers and peripherals at the same company might be tied together on a 10-Mbit/s token-passing ring, and the office computers and peripherals may be on a CSMA/CD bus. In this case, most communications would be confined within one type of LAN, but occasionally the office computers might need to talk to the mainframe or get information from the computers on the factory floor.

Traffic partitioning. Traffic originated at different sources must be partitioned into a number of groups, each with certain dominant characteristics. In most LANs, two major services are terminal-to-host communications and host-to-host communications. Terminal-to-host communications are characterized by small frame sizes and relatively fewer numbers of these frames. Host-to-host communications typically involve large frames and continuous generation of these frames. These two types of traffic should be put on different LANs having different characteristics. For example, terminal-to-host communications may be put on a channel operating at less than 1 Mbit/s, and host-to-host communications may be on a channel operating at 5 to 10 Mbit/s.

There are also administrative reasons for traffic partitioning. Divisions or groups within a large organization may require independence from each other. For example, a LAN for accounting and personnel departments should be separate from a second LAN used for the engineering department. Traffic can be monitored in different departments and users charged for their connect time for billing purposes. With multiple LANs, each department can grow and change its functions without affecting other sections of the company and without being affected by other sections of the company.

Organizational growth. Organizational growth could be the single most important reason for the existence of multiple LANs within an organization. If a department only has a small number of computers and peripherals, and this arrangement does not change significantly, then there is little incentive to create a LAN. If, however, the departmental computing resources are expected to change and grow, there is evey reason to have a LAN: With a LAN, the department's equipment will not have to be reconfigured every time there is a change in hardware or software. In cases like these, the motivation for establishing a LAN becomes a business rather than technological decision. This reason could be useful in convincing nontechnically oriented managers of the value of LANs.

Once a LAN is in place, the changing nature of most businesses results in the procurement of many different types of computers and peripherals for many different reasons. In most large organizations, a stable environment as far as computer networking is concerned is almost nonexistent. There will always be some part of an organization that is putting new computers into service or trying out a new piece of software or hardware. In such an environment it is advisable to divide the network into smaller sections that are independently managed, making it possible to run pilot tests without endangering the company's everyday operations.

Maintenance. Equipment that is modular in structure is easier to maintain. The same is true with networks. Even today's typical small networks of a few mainframes or minicomputers coupled with 10s of terminals are not easy to manage; networks are expected to grow into thousands of computers and terminals in the next few years, and it will be extremely difficult to manage such large networks as single entities. The solution is to divide the network into manageable sizes. Consider as an example an office complex wired with a baseband LAN using bus topology and the CSMA/CD access scheme. When the LAN does not function due to a faulty transceiver or controller on the station, it affects the entire user community. It is then difficult to locate the fault. If, on the other hand, the LAN consists of a number of separate segments, the improper operation due to a faulty component would be confined to that segment only. Such an arrangement also makes it easier to isolate the faulty component.

Mechanisms for interconnection

Having said that most large organizations will probably have multiple LANs within a limited geographical area, let us look at the possible means of providing the required interconnection between different LANs, whether local or remote. The interconnection between distant LANs will be more common than the interconnection between local LANs. The requirements and available means are different in these two situations; consequently, the solutions are also different.

LANs that are separated by long distances (perhaps up to thousands of miles) are typically interconnected using point-to-point lines operating at a few kilobits per second. These lines, which are leased from common carriers, are characterized by high cost and high incidence of bit errors (1 in 10^5).

Another common way to interconnect LANs as well as individual stations is via a Public Packet-Switching Network (PPSN). The PPSNs employ protocols that are different from the LANs, and their effective rate of data transmission is in the range of 10s of kilobits per second.

Private branch exchanges are usually used for long-distance connections and cannot usually handle enough throughput for efficient local communications.

1. OSI and 802. *Two IEEE sublayers correspond to one OSI Data Link Layer. The MAC sublayer handles addressing and identification of station networks.*

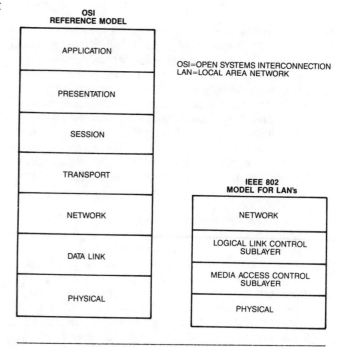

OSI=OPEN SYSTEMS INTERCONNECTION
LAN=LOCAL AREA NETWORK

For this reason, such considerations are not relevant to this discussion.

A long-haul network may be required to provide the interconnection of hundreds of host computers and 10s of LANs. In order to guarantee delivery in the event of link outages, there may be alternate paths in the topology. The links may use different speeds and transmission technologies. These factors make the routing of information among the stations and LANs attached to a long-haul network involve complex algorithms.

Local LANs may be interconnected using the same algorithms as those for long-haul interconnection. The Department of Defense's TCP/IP (Transport Control Protocol/Internet Protocol) is a good example. But many significant features of LANs make such complex algorithms unnecessary for interconnection when the LANs are close to each other. If the number of LANs is small and they are geographically close (within a few miles), they need not use expensive, low-speed lines leased from common carriers. Small numbers and geographical proximity can contribute to relatively fewer instances of lost connectivity that is due to hardware failures.

In such cases, interconnecting paths can be of a simple topology and would, therefore, not require an optimal path. Interconnecting devices that are all located within a limited geographical area can be easily managed.

Because the interconnection of local LANs is different from that in long-haul networks, the question arises: At which architectural layer does the interconnection take place?

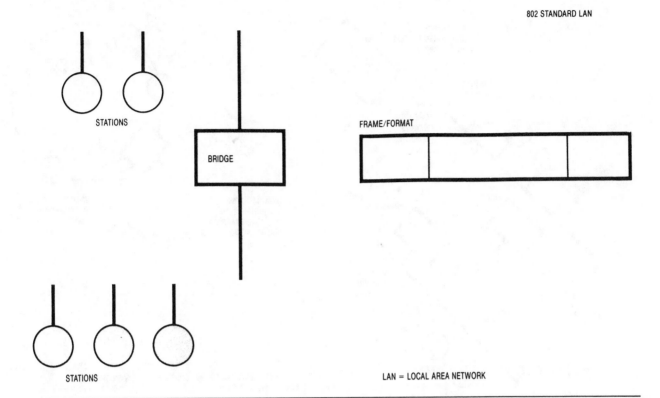

2. Two LANs and a bridge. *A bridge makes decisions about switching frames between local area networks based on the address of a station. It provides the inter-connection between LANs. Bridges can use different sorts of algorithms to determine the best method of net-work interconnection.*

802 STANDARD LAN

STATIONS

BRIDGE

FRAME/FORMAT

STATIONS

LAN = LOCAL AREA NETWORK

Traditionally, interconnection is at the OSI (Open Systems Interconnection) Network Layer, Layer 3, but the simplicity of algorithms suggests that the interconnection can take place at the Data Link Layer, Layer 2.

Decisions at the Data Link Layer

Figure 1 shows the OSI reference model and IEEE 802 model for LANs. In the IEEE model, the Data Link Layer consists of a logical link control (LLC) sublayer and a media access control (MAC) sublayer. The MAC sublayer involves addresses for stations to be identified in a network. Figure 2 shows two LANs connected through an interconnection device called a bridge. The bridge can make a decision about switching frames between the LANs on the basis of the address of a station. A number of simple algorithms may be used for making this decision. From a practical standpoint, the fact that interconnection between local LANs takes place at the MAC sublayer means that higher through-put will be achieved due to the relative simplicity in decision-making algorithms that are used at the MAC sublayer compared with other layers.

Bridges as defined above are possible between similar LANs. Even though IEEE 802 does not have a single standard, the similarities between the various standards are such that bridging between them is possible.

Figure 3 shows a configuration for a campus. It consists of four separate LANs—two baseband CSMA/CD networks, two broadband token-passing

bus networks on one CATV cable, and one token-passing ring network. One 10-Mbit/s CSMA/CD baseband network connects the office machines, and the other 10-Mbit/s CSMA/CD baseband network runs the computer-aided design (CAD) room. A 20-Mbit/s token-passing ring creates the network for the mainframe computers and peripherals in the computer room. One 5-Mbit/s token-passing bus network ties together all data-gathering equipment requiring deterministic delays.

The LAN that is made up of a 10-Mbit/s broadband token-passing bus acts as a backbone interconnecting the other four LANs. Each bridge provides the interconnection between the backbone and one other LAN: thus Bridge 1 connects the backbone and one baseband LAN; Bridge 2 connects the backbone and the other baseband LAN; Bridge 3 connects the back-bone and the token-passing ring; and, finally, Bridge 4 connects the backbone and the 5-Mbit/s token-passing bus LAN.

Algorithms for bridges

Among the many possible algorithms for decision making in bridges, two are significant for the present discussion. These two in particular have been proposed to the IEEE 802 committees. One, proposed by Digital Equipment Corp. (DEC), uses a nonsource routing scheme. Alternatively, IBM has proposed a source-routing scheme. Other proposals have been variations on these two methods.

3. Campus LANs. How four different local area networks are configured on a typical campus using four bridges. Two baseband CSMA/CD (carrier-sense multiple access with collision detection) LANs are connected to two broadband token-passing LANs on one CATV cable and to one token-passing ring network.

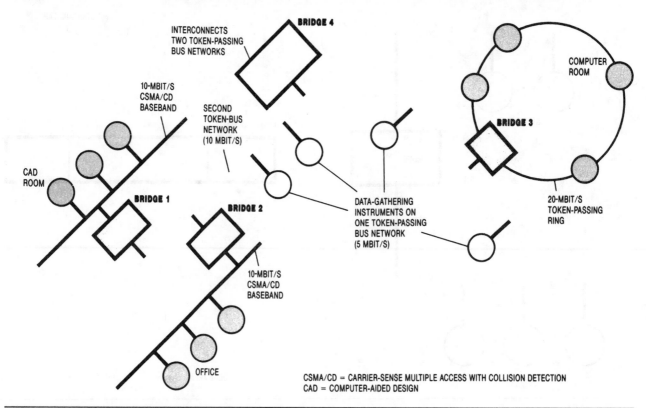

INTERCONNECTS
TWO TOKEN-PASSING
BUS NETWORKS

10-MBIT/S
CSMA/CD
BASEBAND

SECOND
TOKEN-BUS
NETWORK
(10 MBIT/S)

CAD
ROOM

BRIDGE 1

BRIDGE 2

BRIDGE 4

BRIDGE 3

COMPUTER
ROOM

20-MBIT/S
TOKEN-PASSING
RING

DATA-GATHERING
INSTRUMENTS ON
ONE TOKEN-PASSING
BUS NETWORK
(5 MBIT/S)

10-MBIT/S
CSMA/CD
BASEBAND

OFFICE

CSMA/CD = CARRIER-SENSE MULTIPLE ACCESS WITH COLLISION DETECTION
CAD = COMPUTER-AIDED DESIGN

The DEC learn-and-decide scheme is shown in Figure 2. Here, the bridge connecting the two LANs maintains a database of the addresses of stations on each side. This database is empty to begin with and watches all frames that go by on the two LANs, learning the relative locations of the stations. This information is put into the database. When a new frame is picked up by the bridge, it searches the database for the destination address contained in the frame. The forwarding of the frame to the other side is based on the results of this search.

This simple algorithm requires no extra effort by end stations to switch frames through bridges, so that operation of the bridges is transparent. With this method, bridges do need to search the database for every frame before the next frame arrives. This DEC-proposed algorithm raises challenging design issues because the database entries are addresses that are up to 48 bits long.

The IBM algorithm works when the source station originating the frame sends the routing information within the frame itself. This enables the bridge to make the switching decision. For example, the frame might contain an ordered list of the addresses of the LAN segments through which the frame has to travel before it reaches its destination. This algorithm makes it easy for the bridge to make its switching decisions but requires the involvement of the end station. This means that bridge operations are not transparent to end stations.

The terms bridge and gateways are both used to refer to devices that perform the interconnection in networks. They should be treated as two separate types of devices. Both perform the general function of interconnection, but they do so at different levels in the architecture. Bridges, as proposed in this article, interconnect LANs using simple algorithms at the Data Link Layer. Gateways interconnect LANs and hosts in a long-haul network of arbitrary topology and use complex algorithms belonging to the Network Layer.

How is the distinction between gateways and bridges relevant to the user? The algorithmic simplicity of bridges enables them to have better performance characteristics, such as throughput and delay, compared with gateways. Gateways typically have throughput in the 56-kbit/s range, while it is not too difficult to accomplish throughput in the vicinity of 5 to 7 Mbit/s with bridges. Gateways need only be used when LANs are separated geographically or are not of the IEEE 802 type. In order to achieve maximum performance when a number of LANs are interconnected locally, bridges are necessary. ■

George Koshy has a B. S. in electronics and communications engineering from Kerala University, Trivandrum, India, and an M. S. from Massachusetts Institute of Technology. He has worked for more than 11 years on network hardware, software, protocols, and architecture. Prior to joing Booz, Allen, he worked for Digital Equipment Corp.

Transparent Interconnection of Local Area Networks with Bridges

Bill Hawe
Alan Kirby
Bob Stewart
Digital Equipment Corporation

ABSTRACT   A class of devices known as bridges can be used to provide a protocol-transparent interconnection of similar or dissimilar Local Area Networks (LANs). The motivation for building such devices is briefly described followed by a discussion of their desirable characteristics. We describe the architecture, operating principles, and services provided by a bridge which utilizes a flat address space and is self-configuring. This is followed by a simple resource model of the bridge. The performance of individual LANs is contrasted with the performance of a hybrid network composed of dissimilar LANs connected with bridges.

1. Introduction

As a LAN installation grows, it may exceed the design parameters of an individual LAN. Restrictions such as physical extent, number of stations, performance, and media may be alleviated by the interconnection of multiple LANs. Further, as new LAN architectures are introduced, a simple method of connecting these to existing LANs would be valuable. The traditional method of providing this interconnection borrows techniques from Wide Area Network technology, requiring the use of a common internetwork protocol or protocol translation gateways. We will discuss a class of devices which address these problems in an alternative manner suited to the LAN environment.

1.1 Bridges.   A *bridge* (also referred to as a *Data Link relay* [3] is a device which interconnects LANs and allows stations connected to different LANs to communicate as if both stations were on the same LAN (figure 1). For example, node A could send frames to nodes Q, X, or P in the same manner in which it sends frames to node B. The collection of LANs and bridges will be referred to

as an *extended LAN*. Any local network (or collection of local networks) that carries traffic between two other local networks operates as a *backbone* with respect to those networks. In its simplest form, a backbone is an interconnecting local network where all of its stations are bridges.

The extended LANs proposed here require no routing or internet information to be supplied by the sending stations. Bridges differ from devices such as amplifiers and repeaters in that they are intelligent filtering devices which store-and-forward frames. Bridges therefore are used to interconnect LANs. Repeaters, on the other hand, are used to interconnect cable segments within a LAN. Bridges also differ from internet routers, which are explicitly addressed by source nodes and which make their forwarding decisions based upon a Network Layer address supplied by the sending node. In terms of the ISO model, a bridge functions within the Data Link Layer (figure 2). Conceptually, a bridge is an n-port device (where $n \geq 2$). However, for simplicity, the rest of this paper will refer to two port bridges.

Bridges make use of Data Link Layer addresses to make forwarding decisions. They have no knowledge of any other address space,

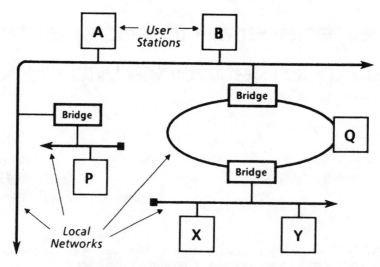

Figure 1. Bridged network configuration.

such as a network or internet address space. Because of this characteristic, bridges are relatively insensitive to the higher layer protocols used by the communicating stations. As will be seen later, the bridge is a useful component in the construction of networks which contain more traditional devices such as routers and gateways which operate above the Data Link Layer.

1.2 Useful Properties. Bridges connecting LANs have several useful properties:

- *Traffic Filtering*—Bridges isolate LANs from traffic which does not need to traverse that LAN. For example, in figure 1, traffic between nodes A and B is not sent on the LANs to which P and Q are connected. Because of this filtering the load on a given

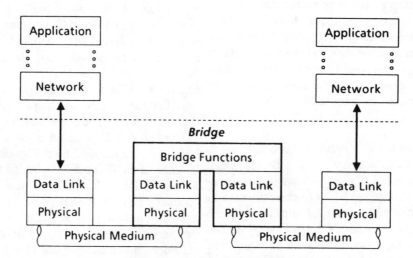

Figure 2. Bridges & data links.

LAN can be reduced, thus improving the delays experienced by all users on the extended LAN.

- *Increased Physical Extent*—LANs are limited in physical extent (at least in a practical sense) by either propagation delay or signal attenuation and distortion. Since the bridge is a store-and-forward device, it forwards frames after having gained access to the appropriate LAN via the normal access method. In this way, the extended LAN can cover a larger extent than an individual LAN. The penalty for this is a small store-and-forward delay.

- *Increased Maximum Number of Stations*—Because of physical layer limitations or stability and delay considerations most LAN architectures have a practical limit on the number of stations on a single LAN. Since the bridge contends for access to the LAN as a single station, one bridge may "represent" many nodes on another LAN or extended LAN.

- *Use of Different Physical Layers*—Some LAN architectures support a variety of physical media (baseband coax, broadband coax, or optical fiber) which cannot be directly connected at the physical layer. Bridges allow these media to co-exist in the same extended LAN.

- *Interconnection of Dissimilar LANs*—LANs of different architecture are typically interconnected with routers or gateways. Often, these devices are complex with only moderate throughput. This may be inappropriate for a LAN environment. It is possible to build a bridge in which its LANs are dissimilar (within constraints to be discussed later). For example, such a bridge would allow stations on an IEEE 802.3 (CSMA/CD) LAN to send frames to stations on 802.4 (token bus) or 802.5 (token ring) [6], [7], [8].

1.3 Desirable Characteristics

There are a number of characteristics which an ideal extended LAN should possess. These are goals, all of which, unfortunately, cannot be simultaneously satisfied. These are:

- *Minimize Traffic*—Only traffic generated by user stations should exist on the individual LANs (i.e., no traffic resulting from complex routing algorithms). Further, this traffic should traverse only those LANs necessary to best reach its destination.

- *No Duplicates*—The bridges should not cause duplicate frames to be delivered to the destination(s).

- *Sequentiality*—The combination of LANs and bridges should not permute the frame ordering as transmitted by the source station.

- *High Performance*—In the LAN environment, users expect high throughput and low delay. The extended LAN should preserve these characteristics. In practice, this means that the bridges should be able to process frames at the maximum rate at which they can be received. Since many LANs operate in the multi-megabit per second range, this requires a fast switching operation.

- *Frame Lifetime Limit*—Frames should not be allowed to exist in the extended LAN for an unbounded time. Some higher layer protocols may operate poorly if frames are unduly delayed. This is especially true for protocols designed to depend on the low delay characteristics of a LAN.

- *Low Error Rate*—LANs typically have a low effective bit error rate. Higher layer protocols are often designed with this in mind. This allows the protocols to operate more efficiently since they can assume that errors are infrequent. Extended LANs should not increase this error rate substantially.

- *Low Congestion Loss*—Individual LANs minimize congestion by employing access control schemes which prevent excessive traffic from entering the LAN. Extended LANs are more vulnerable to congestion loss since the bridges may be forced to drop frames when the frames queued to be transmitted match the available buffers. This phenomenon should be minimized by proper design (placement/sizing) of the extended LAN.

- *Generalized Topology*—For purposes of traffic splitting and reliability, it would be useful to allow arbitrary interconnection of LANs via bridges.

1.4 Bridge Types.

There are two categories of bridges which are transparent at the Data Link Layer. These are distinguished by the method used to make the forwarding decision.

The best known technique for forwarding is based upon the use of hierarchically organized address space in which the Data Link address of a station is dependent upon its physical location in the extended LAN [16]. This address space is partitioned into fields [8] describing on which LAN in the hierarchy of LANs the station resides. Such a scheme permits the use of a very simple forwarding process in the bridge.

However, there are several problems associated with such a scheme. First, the topology is restricted to a rooted tree (where the LANs are edges and the bridges are nodes). Second, the end nodes must be told their own addresses. This might be accomplished manually or perhaps with a dynamic binding. However, a dynamic binding scheme would require the existence of a protocol to accomplish the binding. In any case, when a station physically moves, its address must change. The difficulty of joining previously disjointed LANs may be significant if manual address administration is used. Third, the depth of the physical hierarchy is pre-defined by the number of fields in the address space.

For the remainder of this paper, we will concentrate on a different type of bridge which uses a flat address space and an adaptive learning algorithm to locate stations. Such a bridge requires no relationship between the address of a node and its location in the extended network. Further, nonrooted tree topologies may be supported. This type of bridge can also operate on a mixed hierarchical/flat address space, giving it significant flexibility in both operation and configuration. Also, such bridges are particularly well-suited to use with IEEE 802 LANs which exhibit consistent global address space administration.

2. Routing Algorithms

The bridge uses *backward learning* [1] with flooding as its backup strategy. Backward learning depends only on local information, inherently available by observing the traffic. Loops are prevented by restricting the topology to a branching tree. The bridge routing algorithm is thus isolated and adaptive. This results in bridges that are simple to install and use.

The bridge routing algorithms depend on a unique address for every station within the extended network. These source and destination addresses are part of the Data Link header. The bridge must receive *all* frames on each local network to which it is connected, *regardless* of a frame's destination address. Also, the bridge must be able to forward a frame with the frame's original source address, not the bridge's source address. These assumptions are the basis for the following descriptions.

Each bridge independently constructs and maintains its own routing data base. The routing data base contains one entry for each station address the bridge knows. Each entry provides an association between a station address and the bridge's local identification of the channel leading to that station. Each entry also contains an age field, used to delete obsolete entries.

Forwarding a frame requires looking up the destination in the routing data base. If the bridge finds the destination, it forwards the frame on the indicated channel, unless that channel was the source for the frame, in which case it discards the frame. If the bridge does not find the destination, it floods the frame on all channels except the one on which it was received. To avoid excessive flooding at startup, a restarted bridge does not forward frames for several seconds, allowing the update process to establish an initial routing data base. Finally, whenever the forwarding process uses an entry, it resets the entry's age.

The bridge updates the routing data base by recording the source address of each received frame, along with the source channel identification and an initialized age. The bridge does not know or care if a channel represents a single LAN or an extended LAN. In order to avoid obsolete entries in the routing data base, and to ensure correctness when stations move, the bridge removes entries that have not been used for several minutes. The timing of this process is not critical. The event occurs infrequently and is therefore low overhead.

In order to avoid frame congestion (and thus frame loss) waiting for a forwarding decision, the forwarding process must be very fast and of high priority. In particular, if there is a requirement to handle worst case traffic loads, the forwarding process must make a forwarding decision within the minimum frame interarrival time from all channels. This avoids instability in the queue for the forwarding process. The update process may be of lower priority, but must make progress so that a bridge does not continue to flood indefinitely. Although the forwarding and update functions are presented here as separate processes, in practice they are somewhat interwoven, being closely allied in the processing of an incoming Data Link protocol header.

To avoid looping, the interconnect topology is restricted to a branching tree. The bridge takes a simplistic approach to avoiding incorrect topologies by sending frames to itself during its listen-only period. If a frame sent on one channel returns on another, the bridge has detected a loop and refuses to begin forwarding. Although this will not detect loops when incorrectly placed bridges start up together, it is a simple way of detecting the most likely case of a new bridge being installed in the wrong place.

3. Services Across Bridges

Bridge routing algorithms should allow accurate and efficient forwarding of data. A bridge only relays data frames. It does not forward Data Link specific control information such as a token. The transparent forwarding of data can take two forms: *pass through* and *translation*.

Pass through is the simplest form of forwarding. It is possible only when the incoming and outgoing LANs have identical frame formats. In this case, the bridge forwards frames unchanged.

Translation is necessary when the LANs have different frame formats. Translation is only possible, however, if the formats are sufficiently similar. In this case the bridge forwards a frame that appears to have originated within the outgoing LAN, but is actually a transformation of the frame from the incoming LAN.

At best, translation involves simple transformations such as different framing, transposing fields, or directly mapping control values. At worst, it requires invention or loss of fields representing unmatched services. For example, in forwarding from a LAN that supports priority to one that does not, the translation process loses the priority information. When forwarding in the opposite direction, the bridge must insert some default priority.

Another potential incompatibility is in frame sizes. One LAN may require a minimum size where another does not, or one LAN may support larger frame sizes than another. In the minimum size case, translation requires adding or removing padding. This works best where padding mechanisms are part of the Data Link protocol; otherwise, some bridge dependent convention must be chosen or translation becomes impossible. Frames that are too large, on the other hand, must be either segmented and reassembled, or simply discarded. Although the former is possible, it is best to accept a maximum extended network frame size and discard oversized frames. This keeps bridge operation simple and fast.

Translation implies the need for address space size compatibility. It also may introduce issues when mapping one space into another. All stations must, therefore, have a unique representation in the address space of any LAN within the extended LAN. A globally administered address space in the extended LAN alleviates this problem.

Certain Data Link specific operations can affect bridge operation in an undesirable manner. For example, if the operation of accepting a frame removed it from the medium (as it could in a ring), a bridge may have difficulty operating in a receive-all manner. Any bridge will change the semantics of a Data Link Layer acknowledgment. From the sender's point of view, a Data Link Layer acknowledgment will have a different meaning depending on whether the destination was reached on the same LAN or through a bridge. In the former case, the acknowledgment means the frame arrived at the destination. In the latter case, it merely means it arrived at the bridge.

3.1 Higher Level Protocols. Higher level protocols have no direct cognizance of the existence of bridges. The protocols may make assumptions about delay, error rate, etc. However, bridges could affect the validity of these assumptions thus removing some transparency. This may adversely affect the operation of the protocols.

By their nature as store-and-forward devices, bridges necessarily introduce delay. It is important that this delay be kept to a minimum. This topic, along with the related topic of congestion control, is treated more fully later in the performance discussion.

Bridges must also avoid introducing frame corruption. A bridge must not subvert the protection of the Data Link's frame check sequence. The most straightforward way for a bridge to preserve the protection is to pass along the frame check as received. This is possible with pass-through forwarding, as long as hardware controller implementations allow it. Passing the frame check through is not possible for translating bridges. In this case, the bridge should take measures such as error detection on the memory and buses to avoid introducing undetectable corruption.

3.2 Incompatible LANs. Bridges can interconnect incompatible LANs, but not as effectively as similar LANs. When LAN addressing, services, or formats are so different that translation is impossible or impractical, the bridge has another option. Bridges can use a simple interbridge protocol to encapsulate incompatible frames. These frames can then be carried through a LAN (or extended LAN) to another bridge for decapsulation and forwarding back into their native environment. This service remains transparent to the source and destination LANs, making them a closed group that "tunnels" through another network. The stations in one closed group cannot communicate with stations in a different closed group, but at least physical coverage can be extended.

Encapsulation has the interesting benefit of preserving all original information, including frame check. On the other hand, it increases bridge complexity and does not attain the degree of compatibility in pass-through or translation forwarding.

4. Resource Models

In order to characterize performance in extended LANs, one must have a model for the resources that can be consumed. Additionally, one must understand the processes which generate work for those resources. In an extended LAN, the resources that affect performance are the Data Links, the buffering capacity, and processing capabilities in the bridges. Figure 3 depicts these resources.

There are also resources in the end stations which affect performance. These are buffer pool sizes, internal bus bandwidths, CPU, and disk speeds, etc. However, for the purposes of this analysis, we ignore those resources since we will focus on the LAN channels themselves. We assume that those other resources

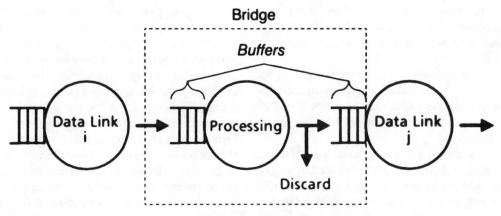

Figure 3. Bridge (2 port) resource model.

are not bottlenecks. In doing so, we imply they do not affect the performance of the LAN channels. This allows the channels to be modeled as "open" queueing systems. Therefore, the traffic sources operate independently of the state of the channel.

In reality, a LAN (or any other network) operates as a "closed" queueing system. This means that the load carried by the LAN at any instant cannot be separated from the performance of the other resources. For example, limited buffering capacity in a low cost end station may result in a large amount of frame loss when receiving traffic from a high performance server. The resultant retransmissions increase the effective load on the LAN channels and any bridges that might be present (not to mention the CPUs). To account for these effects, all resources must be modeled. To avoid this complexity though, we assume the LANs will be the bottlenecks. In the analysis, the system is configured with enough end stations to support the modelled throughput.

4.1 Special Considerations At Bridges. Bridges contend for the resources of a given LAN along with other stations. In some cases, a backbone may contain only bridges. A *subnet* contains end stations and one or more bridges to connect it to a backbone or other subnets. The policies used for the allocation of resources on a subnet or backbone will affect the fairness as perceived by the stations.

In an extended LAN, a bridge acts essentially as a concentrator for N stations. That is, the traffic that actually flows through the bridge is due to N stations. However, it may only be allocated bandwidth on a given LAN as if it were a single station. It may require allocation of resources as if it were N stations since it likely generates more traffic than any one station. One may therefore wish to operate bridges at a higher priority than user stations. This can be done in several ways. On token access LANs, the token holding times, token priorities, etc. can be adjusted to give bridges more of the LAN resources. On CSMA/CD LANs, the collision resolution or backoff algorithms could similarly be adjusted to favor bridges

when necessary. On the other hand, under a static allocation of priorities, a bridge with only one station's traffic flowing through it will essentially give that station more than its fair share of resources. The ideal scheme then would be for the allocation to adjust to the demand based on the nature of the stations generating it.

5. Performance Considerations

The performance of an extended LAN is determined by a number of design parameters, including the expected capacity of the backbone and subnets, the overall system capacity, the applied load, frame loss rates, etc. The designer must not only be concerned with providing adequate performance for current usage but must also allow for growth.

Ideally the system is designed to be sufficiently robust to respond to changes in the user population as well as their characteristics. As an example, [9] contains workload information from measurements of users in a program development environment. This can be used directly to estimate the applied load due to N of those users. To do so, however, requires that one also model *all* layers of protocol involved in transferring this information across the extended LAN.

In order to achieve the highest level of performance while at the same time maintaining the desired flexibility in the configuration, low cost to interface, etc., the network designer must understand the tradeoffs in using different LAN technologies in different parts of the extended LAN. Here we consider the differences in the performance of a few popular LAN technologies. In doing so, we consider the parameters which are most important in affecting performance.

Backbone services may require that a large physical extent be covered. Additionally, the backbone may carry several classes of traffic (voice, data, video, etc.), perhaps on separate logical networks. These are reasons that often lead designers to use broadband media as a backbone. Here we are concerned primarily with services supporting high speed frame distribution.

Subnet services usually require high performance as well as ease of configuration, wiring, etc. Subnet operation should not be compromised by stations (such as personal computers) coming up or going down frequently. The entire extended network or subnet should not need to be manually reconfigured to respond to these frequent events.

Another consideration is congestion loss. This can occur in an extended LAN when buffering resources are exhausted in a bridge. This typically is due to transient traffic overloads. There are two reasons. One is when the forwarding process fails to keep up with incoming traffic. The other is when the effective capacity of an outbound LAN is less than the rate of traffic being forwarded on that LAN. In general, it is desirable that frame loss be due to congestion on the outbound LANs, not because of inability to process frames. This simply defines which server will be the bottleneck. It also implies that the forwarding process should operate at a rate at least as great as the total arrival rate on the inbound LANs.

5.1 CSMA/CD Channels.
The performance of CSMA/CD channels is determined by several factors. (See [4], [6] and [13] for examples of CSMA/CD systems.) These factors include the number of stations, their locations, the applied load, the propagation delay between stations, and the signaling rate of the channel. As with any channel, the capacity will be diminished by the bandwidth consumed in overhead functions. Overhead includes interframe spacing, addressing and control information in frames, frame checks, and wasted bandwidth due to collisions.

Insight into the bandwidth wasted per collision can be obtained from examining the parameter a [17]. a is the ratio of the average 1-way propagation delay (between *communicating* stations) to the mean frame transmission time. It represents the fraction of a frame that is exposed to a collision. Note that the 1-way propagation delay is a function of the proximity of stations to one another. (Only in the worst case is this half the maximum round trip delay.) For a given frame size and signaling rate, the closer the stations, the lower it will be. When smaller fractions of a frame are exposed to collisions, there is less band-

width lost per collision. This results in increased efficiency (or capacity) of the channel [15]. Figure 4 shows the general relationship of a to delay.

In general, reducing a can be accomplished by moving stations closer together, sending larger frames, or reducing the signaling rate. The signaling rate is typically fixed (for example, 10 Mbps in the Ethernet). The frame size is a function of the workload, and the station separation a function of the configuration. The presence of bridges may affect a by reducing the effective propagation delay between stations on the same channel since it may be shorter. This will improve the performance of that channel.

The Physical Layer technology will also affect the performance. It has the obvious impact on propagation delay with the implications mentioned above. The geometry of the cable plant will also affect the propagation delay. Star geometries such as those used in fiber optic CSMA/CD systems typically result in increased propagation delay between stations. CSMA/CD on a broadband system is likewise affected. For example, in a broadband CSMA/CD system with collision detection implemented in the stations, the signal must flow up to the headend and back down to the stations before carrier is detected. This means that the slot time will be approximately two times the round trip propagation delay from the furthest station up to the headend.

The implications of the effect that the cable plant geometry has on performance are seen in figure 5. This compares the performance of 10 Mbps CSMA/CD channels on baseband or broadband media. This information is the result of a detailed simulation of the channel [5]. The nodes are spread uniformly across the extent of the network. The maximum extent is 2.8 kilometers. Collision detection is performed at the stations. The mean delay versus offered load is shown for both media for two frame sizes, and includes deferring, collisions, backoffs, transmission, and propagation delays. Each of the curves shown has a different value of a since the frame size and "effective" propagation delay is different for each. Note that as the frame size increases, the lost bandwidth in going from baseband to broadband

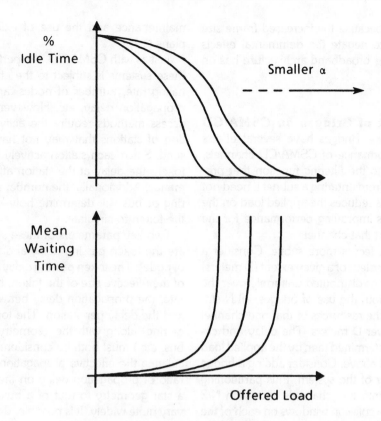

Figure 4. Effect of a on CSMA/CD performance.

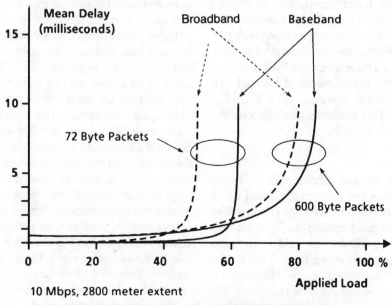

10 Mbps, 2800 meter extent

Figure 5. Broadband vs. baseband CSMA/CD performance.

is reduced, because the increased frame size has begun to negate the detrimental effects this particular broadband architecture has on a.

5.2 Effect of Bridges on CSMA/CD Channels.

Bridges have several effects on the performance of CSMA/CD channels. One is due to the filtering function that prevents traffic from entering a subnet it need not traverse. This reduces the applied load on the channel thus improving performance for the local users of that channel.

Another effect is more subtle. Consider a CSMA/CD system of a given extent (D meters) with N stations distributed uniformly over the extent. Without the use of bridges, all N stations share the resources of that one channel extended over D meters. The delay and capacity are determined then by the applied load as described above. Consider adding a bridge in the center of the system, thus partitioning the system into two channels each with N/2 stations. The collision windows on each of the partitions have been cut in half. This reduces a as described above. The net effect then is not only to reduce the load applied to a given channel (through filtering), but also to improve the overall efficiency or capacity of that channel since the extent it must cover is smaller. In other words, the channel gets more efficient while at the same time the load applied to it is reduced. Given these factors along with performance information characterizing the behavior of the channels under load, one can investigate the performance of bridged networks using these channels. (See [5], [12], [15] and [17] for examples of single channel performance).

5.3 Token Access Channels.

Token rings and buses use a token to control which station has the right to access the channel. The token is circulated among the stations with each generally allowed to hold it for some maximum predetermined time. Token rings use point-to-point technology between stations and require a physical ring topology. The ring may actually be wired in a star configuration (geometry) to allow for centralized maintenance and the use of existing wiring plans [14].

Just as with CSMA/CD, the performance of these systems is subject to the effects of signaling rate, number of nodes, applied load, propagation delay, etc. However, the token access methods require the active participation of stations that may not have traffic to send. Since each station actively handles the token, the delay at the station affects performance. Additionally, the number active in the ring or bus will determine how long it takes the token to circulate.

Two key parameters of these systems then are the token passing delay and the number of nodes. The token passing delay is a function of the effective size of the token, the signaling rate, the propagation delay between stations and the delay per station. The topology (bus or ring) along with the geometry (star, ring, bus, etc.) must both be considered when calculating the effective propagation delay. The ratio of propagation delay on the channel in a star geometry to that of a bus or ring can vary quite widely. It is possible, depending on the environment, for this effect to be large.

The number of nodes has other effects on system performance. One is that the reliability of the system will decrease as more nodes are added is because it is more likely that a given interface, link, etc. may fail. The wiring strategies mentioned above attempt to address this, and other, configuration problems [14].

Token access protocols typically perform well at heavy load and are often used for real-time systems where a worst case delay (in the absence of bit errors) is to be calculated. Unfortunately, they are not suited for large numbers of nodes for the reasons mentioned above.

As one of the many possible examples of how a system could be configured, consider the use of token access protocols for backbone services. The number of stations need not be large since most would be bridges connecting subnets to the backbone. Large populations of user stations could then be partitioned across subnets using CSMA/CD since it is more flexible to the changing environment at the user stations. Presumably, the backbone would offer good performance at heavy load as long as the number of bridges is not too large [2]. Figure 6 depicts the performance of a 10 Mbps

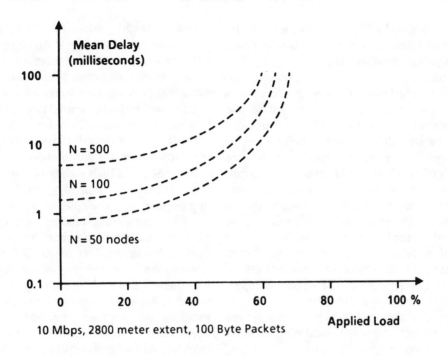

Figure 6. Broadband token bus performance.

broadband token bus using an exhaustive service policy. L is the network extent in kilometers and N is the number of nodes. This uses the model found in [2] which is based on the work in [11].

Performance degradation because of network reconfiguration could be a problem with these protocols. When used as a backbone this may not be serious since the bridges are not expected to go on/off line very often.

6. Performance of Extended LANs

It is important to size the capacity of an extended LAN. Given the characterization of user demands, this is expressed in the number of users that it can "support." The difficulty with using the number of users as the independent variable is that one must account for the resource consumption from all layers of protocol. This is difficult to do in general.

Another problem is that the performance requirements may vary for different higher level protocols. Some may be delay sensitive. For example, terminal access protocols which return echoes end-to-end are quite sensitive to the delay. Other terminal access protocols which allow local editing and echoing are not as de-

lay sensitive. File transfer protocols are not sensitive to the delay but require high throughput. Therefore, to determine the capacity of an extended LAN one must investigate both delay and throughput as applied to the requirements of a particular protocol and application which uses it.

Certain LANs place constraints on the configuration that are due to either Physical Layer limitations (such as the distance over which the line drivers can operate) or the interaction between the Data Link Layer access method and the propagation delay. For example, the Ethernet places a limit on the maximum number of repeaters between any two communicating stations [4]. This constraint assures that the propagation delay budget (which is assumed by the access method protocol) will not be exceeded in any configuration. In an extended LAN, one may also wish to place constraints on the configuration based on the performance expectations of higher layer protocols. For example, a constraint may be that there be no more than N bridges between two stations that use a delay sensitive protocol. In general though, the rules may need to be more complex when an extended LAN is configured with dissimilar LANs. This is because the individual LANs may provide different delay/throughput characteristics.

Another problem when attempting to determine capacity is estimating the amount of traffic that remains local to a given subnet and the amount that leaves a subnet. The worst case occurs when all of the traffic must be forwarded off a subnet through one or more levels of backbones. This creates the largest demand on the resources of the backbone(s). One way to handle this is to assume that all of the locally generated traffic must also be carried by the backbone. Increasing the load will then define the system saturation point. At that point, the resources of the subnets will likely be under utilized. The additional capacity of the subnet can be used for local-only traffic. This defines the limits for the system with respect to the ratio of local to transit traffic that is possible.

6.1 An Example.

To illustrate one of the many ways extended LAN concepts can be applied, consider a hypothetical configuration. The purpose of the example is to demonstrate the concepts of the architecture, not to represent a real application. A 10 Mbps broadband token bus extending 16 kilometers is used as a backbone for N 10 Mbps baseband CSMA/CD subnets, each extending 2.8 kilometers. This forms a two-level extended LAN. Figure 7 depicts this configuration.

The processing delay (for the forwarding process only) in the bridges can be neglected if it is a small part of the store-and-forward delay. This assumption is made here. We assume that there are two main classes of traffic to be carried by this extended LAN. One class is terminal/host traffic. (For examples, see [5] and [9].) The other traffic class is comprised of remote file access and transfer.

File traffic on a LAN may have greatly varying characteristics depending on the system architecture. For example, in a client/server system where there is sufficient memory in the file server, there can be a good deal of caching done at the server. This means that accesses done to the file server may return data for a brief period at a rate limited only by the I/O speeds of the server. Less memory at the server, more file transfers than file accesses, or more users sharing the server, will result in arrival rates limited by head contention on the disks at the server.

Terminal traffic can also have greatly varying characteristics. This depends on the nature of the user behavior as well as the terminal communications model. For example, the terminal access protocols may perform echoing over the channel, or it may be done locally at the point the terminal interfaces to the extended LAN. In the case of echoes carried over the channel, the responsiveness of the channel is very important since it may be visible on almost every user keystroke.

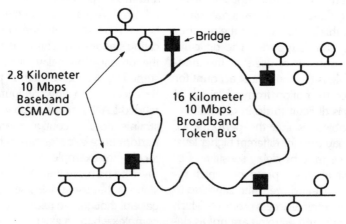

Figure 7. Example of extended LAN.

We select two of the several possibilities for file and terminal traffic outlined above. We assume that disk traffic is characterized as a Poisson process with a mean arrival rate λ_d frames/sec. We assume that frames associated with these sources have a mean size of x_d bytes. The arrival rates and frame sizes include all protocol overheads. We also assume that traffic from terminal access is a Poisson process with a mean of λ_t frames/sec and a mean size of x_t bytes. This also includes all protocol overheads. We use a hybrid model that uses simulation and analytical methods to estimate performance. The CSMA/CD portions of the system are simulated in detail [5] and the token bus performance is computed analytically [2]. Since we also apply the independence assumption [10] and are interested in merely illustrating the example, this hybrid is adequate. However, a more detailed overall model is ultimately required to understand performance fully. This is because we are unable to investigate effects such as congestion loss at bridges with this approach. The amount of loss will depend on traffic patterns, bridge processing speeds, bridge and end station buffering capabilities, higher layer protocol parameters (window sizes, timers, etc.) and higher layer congestion avoidance algorithms (such as dynamic window sizing).

As mentioned previously, it is important to consider both delay and throughput when sizing the capacity of a LAN or an extended LAN. In doing so here, we increase the number of users while observing the delay and utilization of the components of the extended LAN. When the utilization of any resource in the extended LAN reaches 0.9, the user population is no longer increased. (Note that this is utilization not offered load. The offered load is less than 0.9 when this occurs because of the overheads described earlier.) Similarly, if the *mean* delay across the extended LAN exceeds a threshold (T seconds) the user population is no longer increased. We assumed that there are sufficient resources (computers, etc.) added to the extended LAN to support the user population while maintaining the I/O rates for each user class (λ_d and λ_t). This allows the system to be viewed as an open queueing network.

Figure 8 shows several aspects of extended LAN performance. For this figure, $\lambda_d = 25$ frames/sec and $\lambda_t = 5$ frames/sec. $x_d = 600$ bytes, $x_t = 100$ bytes, and $T = 10$ milliseconds. We show three different partitionings of the user population. This includes 10, 20 and 30% of the user stations generating file traffic as defined. The remainder generate terminal traffic also as defined. Plotted in figure 8 are the utilizations of a given CSMA/CD subnet and the token bus backbone. (Note that the utilization will include overhead such as collisions or token passing.) We make the

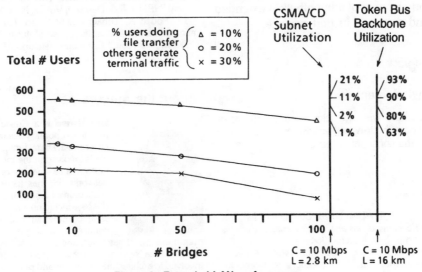

Figure 8. Extended LAN performance.

worst-case assumption here that the user population is divided evenly across the subnets and (as another worse case assumption) that all the subnet traffic must also enter the backbone. This places a lower bound on the supported user population.

Figure 8 demonstrates that there are two regions of performance. One region is where the bandwidth of the backbone is not sufficient to allow for more users. This occurs for small numbers of bridges. The other region is where the token passing delay on the backbone is too large to allow the extended LAN to meet the mean delay goal (*T* seconds). This occurs when the number of bridges is large.

7. Conclusion

We have shown the usefulness of flat address-space, learning bridges in extending LANs. These extended LANs can make use of desirable characteristics which an individual LAN cannot provide. For this architectural approach, we have stated the requirements placed on the bridges including their LAN interface operation, the routing algorithms, etc. We have also described topological constraints and mentioned issues regarding the number of bridges in the extended LAN. Finally, we have discussed the performance aspects of several LANs as well as those issues relating specifically to extended LANs. We have also provided an example of a hypothetical extended LAN and discussed its performance.

Acknowledgment

The authors wish to acknowledge the major technical contributions of Mark Kempf and George Koshy to the concepts in this paper.

References

1. P. Baran, "On Distributed Communication Networks," *IEEE Transactions on Communications Systems*, Vol. CS-12, pp. 1–9, March, 1964

2. Werner Bux, "Local-Area Subnetworks: A Performance Comparison," *IEEE Transactions on Communications*, Oct., 1981

3. R. Callon, "Internetwork Protocol," *Proceedings of the IEEE: Special Issue on Open Systems Interconnection*, Dec., 1983

4. Digital, Intel and Xerox, *The Ethernet: A Local Area Network, Data Link Layer and Physical Layer Specifications*, Version 2.0, Nov., 1982

5. Bill Hawe and Madhav Marathe, "Predicting Ethernet Capacity—A Case Study," *Proc. of Computer Performance Evaluation Users Group Conference*, Washington, D.C., Oct., 1982

6. IEEE Project 802 Local Area Network Standards, "IEEE Standard 802.3 CSMA/CD Access Method and Physical Layer Specifications," Approved Standard, July, 1983

7. IEEE Project 802 Local Area Network Standards, "Draft IEEE Standard 802.4 Token Passing Bus Access Method and Physical Layer Specifications," Draft E, July, 1983

8. IEEE Project 802 Local Area Network Standards, "Draft IEEE Standard 802.5 Token Ring Access Method and Physical Layer Specifications," Working Draft, Sept. 23, 1983

9. Raj Jain and Rollins Turner, "Workload Characterization Using Image Accounting," *Proc. of Computer Performance Evaluation Users Group Conference*, Washington, D.C., Oct., 1982

10. L. Kleinrock, *Queueing Systems, Volume II*, John Wiley & Sons, 1976

11. A.G. Konheim and B. Meister, "Waiting Lines and Times in a System with Polling," *Journal of the ACM*, Vol. 21, pgs. 470–490, 1974

12. Madhav Marathe, "Design Analysis of a Local Area Network," *Computer Networking Symposium*, Washington, D.C., Oct., 1980

13. R.M. Metcalf and D.R. Boggs, "Ethernet: Distributed Packet Switching for Local Computer Networks," *Comm. of the ACM*, July 1976

14. Jerry Saltzer, "Why a Ring?", *Proc of 7th Data Comm. Symp.*, Mexico City, Mexico, Nov., 1981

15. John F. Shoch and Jon A. Hupp, "Measured Performance of an Ethernet Local Area Network," *Comm. of the ACM*, Vol. 23, No. 12, Dec. 1980

16. Norman C. Strole, "A Local Communications Network Based on Interconnected Token-Access Rings: A tutorial," *IBM J. Res. Develop*, Vol 27, No 5, Sept., 1983

17. Fouad A. Tobagi and V. Bruce Hunt, "Performance Analysis of Carrier Sense Multiple Access with Collision Detection," *Computer Networks*, Vol. 4, No. 5, Oct/Nov, 1980

About the Authors

Bill Hawe is a Consulting Engineer in Corporate Research and Architecture at Digital Equipment Corp. He is involved in the modeling and performance analysis of computer networks. He has focused on the evaluation of Local Area Networks (LANs), including simulation modeling of Ethernet and VLSI LAN controllers, analytical models and measurements of gateways, and state descriptive models of Local Area Networking software. Recently, he has been involved in architectural definition and performance analysis of high-performance interconnects for LANs. He participates in the IEEE Project 802 LAN Standards Committee and is also a member of the IEEE 802 performance modeling working group. Prior to joining Digital, he taught courses in computer science, distributed process control, computer networks, and logic design at Southeastern Massachusetts University. While there, he also implemented an X.25 packet switching architecture for personal computers.

Alan Kirby is manager of the Advanced Development group for Networks and Communications at Digital Equipment Corporation. This group is responsible for the development and acquisition of computer communications related hardware and software technologies. His present work relates to high-performance LAN technology, LAN interconnect architecture, and network security. Before joining Digital, Mr. Kirby was Manager of Network Development at National CSS, Inc. There, he was involved in the design and development of a proprietary packet switching network. He received his B.S. degree at Worcester Polytechnic Institute and M.S. degree at the Polytechnic Institute of New York.

Bob Stewart has been with the Networks and Communications group at Digital Equipment Corporation for nearly eight years. For much of that time, he was responsible for the Network Management architecture, as well as two implementations of network management in RSX DECnet. During his time in the Architecture Group, he was the network management contributor for Digital, working with Xerox and Intel on the Version 2 Ethernet Specification. In 1982, he transferred to the Advanced Development Group. Following a study of the Xerox Network System protocols, he became leader of the project which resulted in the extended network bridge architecture. Before coming to Digital, he spent about a year as a software developer with Sycor, a manufacturer of intelligent terminals. Prior to that, he was with Comshare, a time-sharing company, for six years as an operator software developer. He received an A.S. degree from Michigan Christian College, followed by two years in Computers and Communication Science at the University of Michigan. He has also taught commercial courses in network architecture and has a personal interest in home computer software development.

SECTION 8: DESIGN ISSUES

8.1 Overview

The previous sections have not, by any means, exhausted the concepts and issues of interest for local networks. There is a whole host of design issues that have been only briefly mentioned or not touched on at all. This section introduces four of the most important design issues and provides a representative article on each one. The four issues are: (1) network control, (2) reliability and availability, (3) security, and (4) network services.

The need for network control is based on the fact that a computer network is a complex system that cannot create or run itself. The manager of the network must be able to configure the network, monitor its status, react to failures and overloads, and plan intelligently for future growth.

In many LANs and HSLNs, a network control center (NCC) is provided. Typically, this device attaches to the network through a network access unit (NAU) and consists of a keyboard/screen interface and a microcomputer. Except for the smallest networks (less than 10-20 NAUs), an NCC is vital. It supports key operations, administration, and maintenance functions. All of the functions of an NCC involve observation, active control, or a combination of the two. They fall into three categories: (1) configuration, (2) monitoring, and (3) fault isolation.

Configuration functions deal with system initialization and related functions. Examples include down-line loading of software and parameters to an NAU; providing a name/address directory service; and starting up and shutting down of network components. Monitoring functions relate to the collection, analysis, and reporting of network performance and status. Fault isolation functions are automated aids for operator alert and fault identification and location.

As local networks grow in size and capability, the loss of the network becomes more and more costly. Thus, network design must have as a goal high component reliability and high system availability. The key to enhanced availability is to design the network so that individual component failures have little or no effect on the overall network. One of the articles in this section explores ways of achieving this for broadband LANs.

Network security can be defined as the protection of network resources against unauthorized disclosure, modification, use, restriction, or destruction. Security has long been an object of concern and study for both data processing systems and communications facilities. With local networks, these concerns are combined.

Consider a full-capacity local network, with direct terminal access to the network and data files and with applications distributed among a variety of processors. The local network may also provide access to and from long-haul communications and may be part of a catenet. The complexity of the task of providing security in such an environment is clear.

The subject is broad and encompasses physical and administrative controls as well as automated ones. In this section, we include a paper that looks at one important aspect of security: The ability of a network to support users who have various levels of access rights to data.

Finally, we consider the subject of network services. At minimum, a local network must provide a data transfer service for attached devices. There are a variety of other "value-added" services, some of which are discussed in the accompanying article.

8.2 Article Summary

The first article, by Soha, looks at one aspect of a network control center, performance monitoring and reporting. The article looks at key characteristics of LANs that can be monitored and discusses implementation approaches.

"Reliability Mechanisms of the FDDI High Bandwidth Token Ring Protocol" is a detailed discussion of the reliability features built into the FDDI standard. This technique covers the physical layout of the ring, the use of backup cable, MAC protocol mechanisms, and station management protocol elements.

The next article, "Local Area Military Network," looks at a promising approach to local network security, the trusted network access unit. The article explains the requirement, examines alternative approaches, and explores the trusted interface unit concept in detail.

Finally, the article by Summers examines in some detail the issue of resources sharing on a personal-computer LAN. The article looks at potential functions, user and system interfaces, and design and implementation approaches.

A DISTRIBUTED APPROACH TO LAN MONITORING USING INTELLIGENT HIGH PERFORMANCE MONITORS

Michael Soha

As Local Area Networks (LAN's) continue to grow in acceptance, they are quickly becoming the local data communication backbone of corporations. Their popularity is a result of the high bandwidth offered (> 1 Mbps) and the multiaccess nature of the medium. At the lowest level, LAN's are used to interconnect computers, terminals and peripherals, allowing these devices to easily intercommunicate via a high bandwidth backbone [1]. At a higher level they are used to interconnect members of a distributed system. In systems such as the V-Kernel [2], the LAN supports the distribution of work among servers dedicated to specific functions.

The monitoring of a LAN needs to be done for several reasons. First, the LAN typically represents the data communication backbone for a facility; consequently, it must be viewed as a vital resource and managed as such. Secondly, monitoring allows for early detection of potential error conditions, allowing problems to be corrected before they degrade performance. Finally, monitoring is required for diagnosing failures.

Introduction

This article discusses a distributed approach to LAN monitoring which uses intelligent high performance monitors. These monitors are intelligent in that they do not require specification of what the monitor should examine; the monitor simply receives every packet and learns the required information to provide a meaningful presentation of the LAN statistics. The monitor's design guarantees that every LAN packet will be processed regardless of the LAN traffic rate. The techniques employed by this monitoring system are applicable to all 802 LAN's.

A summary of the LAN environment and its characteristics is provided. The architecture of the decentralized monitoring system and the specifics of an implementation are presented. Our experience with this system in monitoring Ethernets [3] and 10 Mbps 802.3 LAN's [4] is reviewed and the complementary use of bridges to support LAN maintenance is introduced. Finally, the benefits of this approach are summarized.

The LAN Environment

The LAN environment comprises two levels: first, the characteristics of the individual LAN, and secondly, the attributes which result from LAN's being bridged together.

LAN Characteristics

Local Area Networks have inherent characteristics which separate them from typical store-and-forward networks. These include: a geographic extent of a few kilometers, bandwidth greater than 1 Mbps, multiaccess (support for multiple stations), and broadcast communication (a message transmitted by a station can be directed to and received by a group of nodes).

LAN's also exhibit characteristics of usage which are not necessarily inherent to the LAN's themselves, but are artifacts of their usage. These characteristics are:

1) Public Data Highways—Many vendors have developed protocols that operate over LAN's due to their general applicability of supporting data communication. Frequently, several protocols from different vendors coexist

Reprinted from *IEEE Network*, Volume 1, Number 3, July 1987, pages 13-20. Copyright © 1987 by The Institute of Electrical and Electronics Engineers, Inc.

on the same LAN.

2) *Dynamic User Environment*—LAN's are typically used by an organization to support the communication needs of several groups. The ownership and management of stations may be distributed among several groups. For example, a workstation may be powered down at certain times of the day, or simply disconnected from the LAN. Also, as users become more sophisticated, they may introduce a service (and/or station) that they deem useful. This can range from a new application on a personal computer to a new distributed service (print server). In summary, the availability of stations or services on the LAN will be dynamic.

These usage characteristics of LAN's are in contrast to the environment supported by store-and-forward networks composed of point-to-point links. Since a store-and-forward network relies on direct connection between the station and the switch, the network manager has control over who is connected to the network. LAN's, however, are in the hands of the users, since LAN attachments are designed to be user installable.

Bridged LAN's

Bridges are useful for providing connectivity for separate LAN's and also for alleviating the limitations imposed by the individual LAN segments. A data link bridge allows 802 LAN's to be transparently connected; that is, stations on different LAN's can communicate as if they were on the same LAN [5,6,7,8]. The data link bridge dynamically learns local and remote stations, thus allowing the bridge to filter local traffic and forward only frames that are destined for a remote LAN segment.

Since bridges are packet store and forward devices, the limitations of geographic extent and number of supported stations apply only to the individual LAN segments, not the bridged LAN. The filtering of local traffic by bridges allows bandwidth to be reused on remote LAN segments. Bridges also allow the transparent interconnection of dissimilar 802 LAN's.

Characteristics of a Bridged LAN

The characteristics of a bridged LAN are similar to those of the individual LAN segments; however, these characteristics have been extended. Specifically, bridged LAN's can span a greater geographic extent, support more users, and provide a greater aggregate bandwidth. The extension of these LAN characteristics results in an amplification of the usage characteristics. The number of protocols observed on a bridged LAN becomes the aggregate of the protocols in use on each individual LAN, and the dynamics of the user environment for the bridged LAN will be the sum of those observed on each LAN segment.

In terms of monitoring, bridges will filter local traffic, thus localizing it to LAN segments. Consequently, one must monitor all segments if a global view of the bridged LAN is desired.

System Description

As a result of our work on data link bridges [8], it became apparent that a high performance learning monitor could be built. The two basic goals of the design were: to develop a monitor that would guarantee the reception of all valid packets regardless of the traffic rate, and to have the monitor learn the necessary information required for a meaningful presentation of statistics. The performance requirement led us to distribute the monitoring system among two elements: monitors that perform the initial collection and learning of the LAN data, and management nodes which perform the data reduction and support the user interface. This monitoring system is shown in Fig. 1.

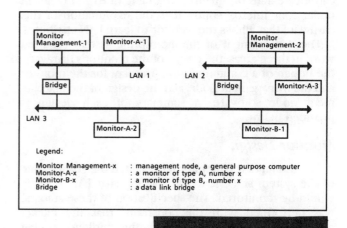

Fig. 1. A Decentralized Monitoring System Employing Intelligent Monitors.

The monitors, which can have their firmware downline loaded, perform initial data reduction functions. They receive every packet, learn specific packet attributes, and categorize each packet based on these attributes. Periodically, monitors report, via the LAN, a summary of their statistics. This report can be addressed to a specific management node or to a group of management nodes via a multicast address. The monitor also supports requests for counters that are not included in the summary statistic report.

The management node performs data reduction on the statistics provided by the monitors. This information is then provided to the user. The type of data reduction performed can vary from the development and support of real time LAN statistics to archiving of data for trend analysis. The user interface can also vary from an interactive display for viewing tabular or graphic data to an event driven interface where alarms are directed to a specific system. The management nodes are also used to control the monitors (starting, stopping, or zeroing counters).

The different types of monitors depicted in Figure 1 (Monitor-A, Monitor-B) represent a key characteristic of our monitoring system. We recognize that several classes of statistics may be required; however, instead of building a multifunction, general purpose monitor, the monitors are designed first to guarantee the integrity of their statistics. In order to ensure that every packet will be processed regardless of the LAN traffic rate, only the counters that can be maintained in minimum packet time are supported. The consequence of this design philosophy is to develop multiple types of monitor firmware which can be downline loaded as needed.

Specifications of an Implementation

A decentralized LAN monitoring system was developed based on the hardware used for data link bridges. The data link bridge [Ref 8] comprises two 10 Mbps 802.3 [4] interfaces, a microprocessor, buffer memory, and specialized hardware to assist in the learning of 48 bit data link addresses. This specialized learning hardware can locate a 48-bit quantity in a table of 8192 entries in under four microseconds. It is the exploitation of this hardware that allows the monitor to learn LAN attributes.

The development of the monitoring system required work in three areas: the design of the monitor's firmware, the design of a communication protocol for the monitor and the management node, and the design of the management node software. A summary of each design is provided below.

Monitor Design

The design of the monitor represented the cornerstone of the system since it would specify what LAN statistic would be monitored. The specification of these statistic was performed with the constraint that the packet processing had to be completed within minimum packet time. The minimum packet time for a 10 Mbps 802.3 LAN is 67.2 microseconds (14,881 packets/second).

The monitor supports CSMA/CD LAN's and is capable of monitoring 802.3 [4] and Ethernet [3] packets. In addition to maintaining general network counters such as network utilization, packet rate, and error counts, the monitor categorizes each packet based on information it has learned from the LAN. Specifically, the monitor learns source addresses, multicast addresses, Ethernet type fields and identifies IEEE 802 packets (Fig. 2). The monitor supports the learning of up to 1024 source addresses, 64 type fields (two of which are reserved for IEEE 802.3 packets), and 32 multicast addresses. Packets are also categorized based on four programmable packet size categories. The packet format assumed by the monitor is shown in Fig. 2.

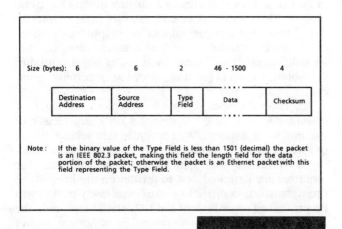

Fig. 2. LAN Packet Format.

The processing performed on each packet is summarized via the flow chart in Fig. 3, with a description of the counters being provided below. The monitor's counters are kept as running totals and are sized for long term operation without wrap around. All counters are

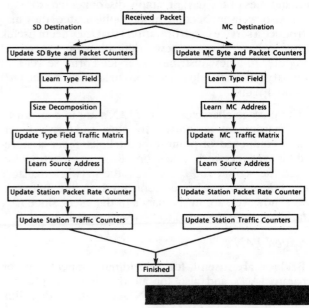

Fig. 3. Flow Chart Depicting Packet Processing of the Monitor.

four-byte unsigned integers, with the exception of the byte counters, which are 6-byte unsigned integers. Packets that are in error (bad checksums or illegal packet sizes) can be forwarded to the management node(s).

General counters—These counters provide gross level statistics on the LAN utilization. They include: separate byte counters for both single destination (SD) and multicast (MC) destined packets, separate packet counters for both SD and MC packets, and a count of packets with checksum errors.

Type Field Traffic Matrix—This matrix provides a network view of the type fields (protocols) currently in use on the LAN. For each Single Destination (SD) packet, a categorization based on type field and packet size is performed. This matrix supports up to 64 type fields and four packet size categories.

Multicast Packet Matrix—These counters identify the multicast addresses in use on the LAN and associate them with one or more type fields. This matrix supports the categorization of up to 32 MC addresses into one or more of the 64 type fields.

Station Packet Rate Counters—These resettable counters provide packet rate counts based on the source address. There are 1024 counters, one for each source address.

Station Traffic Counters—These counters perform the same function as the Type Field Traffic and Multicast Packet Matrices combined; however, the statistics are maintained for every source address on the LAN. Specifically, the Station Traffic Counters categorize packets based on the source address, type field, and packet size for SD packets with a single count being provided for MC destined packets.

Communication Protocol

Our monitoring system uses a connectionless datagram protocol for the support of communication between the monitors and the management nodes. This protocol offers both solicited and unsolicited communication. The reporting of summary statistic is supported by unsolicited messages. The monitors, which are distributed throughout the bridged LAN, gather information from the network, compress it, and periodically broadcast summary statistics. Solicited communication is used by the management nodes for requesting additional counters and issuing control messages to the monitors. The communication protocol is also used to update the management nodes databases of learned source addresses, MC addresses and type fields. This updating is done automatically by the monitor.

The two LAN ports of the monitor allow the user flexibility in how the monitor is installed on a LAN. One LAN port can be used for both LAN monitoring and the reporting of statistics, thus leaving the second disabled; or both LAN ports can be used where the monitor reports on one and monitors the second. By splitting the monitoring and reporting functions between two ports, the monitor can be used unobtrusively.

Management Node

The management nodes are general purpose computers (with a LAN interface) that reside on the LAN. A management node can support one or more monitors and conversely, a monitor can respond to one or more management nodes, thus allowing for redundant management nodes and/or monitors.

The management node supports an interactive user interface. The user can view a variety of LAN statistics ranging from a utilization graphic for the previous two days to a tabular display of all the type fields sent by a specific node. The majority of these statistics are refinements of the counters maintained by the monitors. The twelve statistics/actions provided to the user are summarized below, with items 1-5 being developed from the periodic summary statistic message.

1) *General Counters*—A group of counters including: network utilization, packet rate, percent of packets which are MC, count of packet with checksum errors and number of learned source addresses, learned type fields, and learned MC addresses.

2) *Timestamps of Peaks*—Time of day stamps corresponding to peak values of utilization, packet rate, and percent of packets which are MC are maintained. Peaks are calculated over short intervals (0.5 seconds) and also over a programmable interval (less than 5 minutes).

3) *Utilization Graphs*—Graphic plots of the network utilization, as measured every 0.5 seconds, over intervals ranging from five minutes to 48 hours (see Fig. 4).

4) *Type Field Traffic Matrix*—A decomposition of the network traffic based on the type field of the packet. For each type field, a total packet count is provided, with its relative percentage in terms of total received packets. In addition, the SD packets associated with this type field are further decomposed based on packet size with a single counter being provided for MC destined packets.

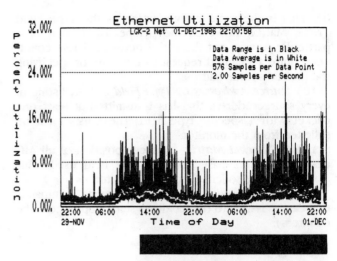

Fig. 4. *Utilization Plot of a Bridged LAN Comprising Over 600 Nodes.*

Figure 5 provides a condensed version of this matrix by showing the top ten type fields in use on a LAN.

5) *Top Users*—A listing of the top ten stations in terms of packets transmitted. Two listings are provided, one representing the top users based on total packets sent and a second reflecting the top users based on the last summary statistic report from the monitor.

6) *Station Address List*—A listing of all source addresses learned by the monitor (up to 1023 stations with one overflow entry). This information is provided automatically via the database updates.

7) *MC Address List*—A listing of all MC addresses learned by the monitor (up to 31 MC addresses with one overflow entry). This information is provided automatically via the database updates.

Stations : 682		Type Fields : 25					MC Addresses : 28
Type Field	Packet Count	% of Traffic	Single Destination - Packet Sizes (%)				MC Dest (%)
			≤ 64	≤ 300	≤ 600	> 600	
60-04 LAT	55580913	53.25	41.71	47.40	0.07	0.00	10.82
60-03 DECNET	40171191	38.49	25.45	11.81	1.72	14.63	46.38
60-07 SCA	3893625	3.73	33.14	50.41	1.35	3.71	11.39
60-06 C-USE	1698030	1.63	1.89	7.62	0.00	8.91	81.59
80-38 BRIDGE	965513	0.93	0.00	0.00	0.00	0.00	100.00
60-02 RC-MOP	754596	0.72	4.08	3.50	0.00	0.00	92.42
08-00 TCP-IP	650353	0.62	27.92	52.24	0.52	0.65	18.67
60-00 DEC-XP	321830	0.31	0.02	0.00	0.00	0.00	99.99
06-00 XEROX	148752	0.14	27.44	15.78	27.98	0.00	28.80
60-01 DL-MOP	93179	0.09	33.88	45.28	0.00	0.58	20.26
Other	98875	0.09					

note : see Table 1. for description of Type Fields

Fig. 5. *Type Field Traffic Display.*

8) *Type Field List*—A listing of all type fields learned by the monitor (up to 61 type fields, two entries for 802 packets and one overflow entry). This information is provided automatically via the database updates.

9) *Station Traffic Counters*—A decomposition of all packets sent by the specified source address (see Figure

6). This is the same categorization as the Type Field Traffic Matrix; however, the perspective is that of a particular source, not the entire network. These counters require a solicited request to the monitor specifying the desired source address.

10) *Source Addresses by Type Field List*—A listing of every source address that has transmitted at least one packet with a specific type field. These lists must be solicited from the monitor.

11) *MC Packet Matrix*—A decomposition of all MC destined packets based on the type field used. This matrix must be solicited from the monitor.

12) *General Maintenance*—Management commands that can be issued to the monitor (start, stop or zero the counters).

Stations : 682		Type Fields : 25		MC Addresses : 28		
Address : AA-00-04-00-DC-11		Name : NETRIX		Protocol Types : 6		
Type Field	Packet Count	Single Destination - Packet Sizes				MC Dest.
		≤ 64	≤ 300	≤ 600	> 600	
60-04 LAT	42620	10115	1130	34	0	31341
60-03 DECNET	254195	84847	7105	86	68136	94021
60-02 RC-MOP	1245	0	0	0	0	1245
08-00 TCP-IP	121650	105415	11006	0	0	5229
90-00 LP-BCK	16	0	16	0	0	0
08-06 TCP-AR	75	5	0	0	0	70

note : see Table 1. for description of Type Fields

Fig. 6.   Station Traffic Display.

LAN Monitoring

The LAN environment has certain attributes which should be recognized by designers of monitoring systems. These are:

1) The monitoring can be done passively by receiving all messages since each packet on an 802 LAN traverses the entire LAN (provided one does not violate physical or data link parameters of the 802 LAN with the introduction of the monitoring node).

2) The use of bridges will require that each LAN segment be monitored for a global view of the bridged LAN.

3) As a result of the LAN usage characteristics, a monitor should be capable of adapting to the LAN in terms of station or services. That is, one should not design a monitor to look for specific information; rather, the monitor should be able to learn the salient attributes of the LAN users.

4) LAN's carry large amounts of traffic (our facility LAN carries 10 million packets/work-day). In order to support the monitoring of ALL traffic, sophisticated data reduction should be done at the collection site (monitor).

The distributed LAN monitoring system, as already discussed, has been used to monitor Ethernets and 10 Mbps 802.3 LAN's. Several applications of our monitoring system based on our experience are presented in the following sections.

Monitoring of an Operative LAN

There are basic functions required for the monitoring of an operative LAN. A monitor should:

1) provide metrics demonstrating that the LAN is operative
2) provide auditing on how the LAN is being utilized,
3) provide information for preventive maintenance.

performance metrics

The metrics for performance monitoring include network utilization and network packet rate. Both of these metrics are provided, as well as their peak statistics with time stamps. Utilization Graphs (Fig. 4) are also available which can be used for trend analysis. In Fig. 4, the LAN utilization, which is sampled every half second, is displayed as data points comprising 576 samples. The monitor also provides statistics of packets received with checksum errors.

This system also provides a second level of performance metrics by monitoring the operation of stations and protocols (type fields). These statistics are provided via the Station List, the Type Field Traffic Matrix (Fig. 5), and the MC Packet Matrix. The Top Users statistics are useful in confirming that the nodes that should be using the majority of the LAN bandwidth, are indeed using it.

The monitoring system has proved very useful in the validation of high performance systems. A basic problem with other LAN monitors is that they simply do not support maximum LAN traffic rates (just under 15,000 packets/second for Ethernets and 10 Mbps 802.3 LAN's). For this type of test, the two ports of the monitor would be employed; one for monitoring the testbed and the second for reporting its statistics to the management node.

auditing metrics

Auditing is provided in terms of network utilization, packet rate, and errors counts via Time Stamps of Peaks and Utilization Graphs. The accounting of LAN stations and protocols can be obtained from the Station List and the Type Field Traffic Matrix. The MC Packet Matrix also provides useful auditing information.

The identification of a LAN service can be performed if the service employs a specialized protocol which can be identified via its type field. Our experience has shown that the majority of specialized LAN services will indeed use a unique protocol. For example, as shown in Figure 5, one sees several Digital Equipment Corporation protocols in operation on the LAN, each with its own type field.

This monitoring system also categorizes the traffic of each station, via the Station Traffic Counters. As shown in Figure 6, these counters categorize each packet sent by the source based on type field and packet size.

Given the problem of a new service (type field) appearing on the LAN, a LAN manager can identify the source(s) using this service by requesting the Source by Type Field List. This list will identify all the source addresses that have transmitted at least one packet with the specified type field. The Station Traffic Counters can then be requested for each source address, providing

TABLE I
DESCRIPTION OF TYPE FIELDS

Digital Equipment Corporation Protocols:		
Type Field		Use
60-00	DEC-XP	Reserved for Experimental Work
60-01	DL-MOP	Downline Load Protocol
60-02	RE-MOP	Maintenance Protocol
60-03	DECNET	Network Layer Protocol for Routing
60-04	LAT	Local Area Transport for LAN (Terminal Servers)
60-06	C-USE	Reserved for Customer Use
60-07	SCA	System Communication Architecture
80-38	BRIDGE	Bridge Management Protocol
Others:		
Type Field		Use
08-00	TCP-IP	DARPA - Transmission Control and Internet Protocol
08-06	TCP-AR	DARPA - Address Resolution Protocol
06-00	XEROX	XEROX Corporation - NS IDP
90-00	LP-BACK	Ethernet Standard - Loopback

Notes: Type Fields are shown in hexadecimal notation
DARPA: Defense Advanced Research Projects Agency

additional information on the traffic issued by each source.

metrics for LAN preventative maintenance

The goal of preventative maintenance is to identify anomalies before they manifest themselves to the user community. An anomaly to a LAN manager is simply something unexpected on the LAN. This could be a new station (source address), MC address, or type field. These events are monitored and can be time stamped.

Anomalies involving the manner in which the LAN is being used also warrant attention. These events include extreme excursions in LAN utilization or abnormal traffic patterns of a particular node. Excursions in LAN utilization are tracked via Time Stamps of Peaks and Utilization Graphs. The odd behavior of a node could vary from an excessive packet rate, as indicated via the Top Users, to an excessive number of type fields or MC addresses being sent, as identified via the Station Traffic Counters.

Diagnosing Failed LAN's

In dealing with failed LAN's, it is important to detect and monitor the situation even when communication is precluded on the LAN. Our monitoring system can be configured to monitor one LAN port and report on the other LAN port. If a separate LAN is dedicated for communicating with monitors, this system can support the real time monitoring of failed LAN's (assuming that the dedicated LAN has not failed).

Discussion of failed LAN's is aided by separating problems into two categories: Physical Channel and Media Access Unit (MAU) errors, and other errors (Data Link and above).

physical channel and MAU errors

Physical channel and MAU errors typically manifest themselves as a high number of channel error conditions and usually result in a complete loss of communication. These errors are associated with the cable plant and/or the media access unit. Channel error conditions include events such as a damaged cable plant; problems with the MAU can range from illegal packet sizes to a station transmitting corrupted packets.

Eliminating this type of problem involves detection, isolation, and correction. Our monitor provides detection of the condition by counting channel levels errors (frame check sequence errors) and capturing illegal frames. The isolation of the error is supported via bridges. The actual location and correction of the error will be dependent on the type of error: damaged cable plants will require specific physical channel test equipment, such as Time Delay Reflectometers; some types of MAU failures can be identified by examining the captured illegal packets at the management node.

The use of data link bridges provides an increase in the survivability of the LAN and assistance in locating the failure. For example, assume LAN 3 of Figure 1 is physically damaged. This type of failure would likely result in a complete loss of communication on LAN 3; however the operation of LAN's 1 and 2 is left unaffected since the bridge only forwards valid frames that are known to be remote. The isolation of the error condition to LAN 3 aids problem location.

The concept of using a bridge to enhance the survivability of a LAN at first appears to be counter intuitive, since it represents additional hardware. However, there are several reasons why bridges enhance the survivability of the LAN. First, bridges are simple, they have been built comprising a single printed circuit board and a power supply [8]. Consequently their failure modes are limited. Secondly, bridges support a redundant topology, allowing for back-up bridges [8,9]. Finally, bridges become part of the cable plant and thus remain relatively static as compared to stations being introduced onto a LAN. Their location and performance become well known, whereas the user community represents an ever changing environment. Thus, with a LAN failure, bridges represent one of the few known facts of the LAN environment.

other LAN errors

A LAN will provide degraded performance when problems occur at the data link, network, or transport layer. This monitoring system detects/identifies certain types of data link errors, such as misaligned address; however, these represent the minority. Experience indicates that problems associated with the higher layers (network, transport and above) make up the majority of Ethernet problems. Our experience has shown that such problems are actually due to the incorrect installation or misuse of the service (protocol); the LAN (data link layer and below) has not failed.

Our monitoring system provides the global view required for detecting and debugging problems with n-party protocols. N-party protocols support the distributed computation of a service and can be used to support such services as network layer routing or distributed name services. By monitoring all LAN traffic, one can identify anomalies in the n-party protocols that manifest themselves only at the global level.

For the general support of problems above the data link, two types of monitors are required: intelligent data link monitors (as described in this paper) and specialized monitors which understand the specifics of the protocol in question. The use of intelligent data link monitors provides a complete view LAN in terms of stations and services. The view is important since it can be used to accurately state the problem. Given this perspective, specialized monitors can then focus on specific aspects of the LAN.

Conclusions

The importance of LAN monitoring is just being acknowledged. As LAN's increase in size and complexity, LAN managers will demand sophisticated monitoring tools. This paper reviewed a novel approach to LAN monitoring which supports current and future LAN's. This LAN monitoring system can be applied to other 802 LAN technologies such as Token Buses [10] and Token Rings [11]. Specifically, the techniques employed by this system assume LAN characteristics which are basic to all IEEE 802 LAN's. The benefits of our approach are summarized below.

Distributed—The distribution of LAN monitoring allows one to monitor bridged LAN's. Coupled with the centralized management, this approach offers a truly scalable LAN management architecture.

Natural Separation of Work—The separation of work between the monitors and the management nodes exploits the specific attributes of the respective systems. Monitors provide a high performance engine for collecting LAN data. The management nodes support the functions required to reduce and interpret this data (real time display, trend analysis, archiving).

Intelligent Monitors—The monitor receives every packet and categorizes LAN traffic based on information it has obtained from the LAN. Consequently, the network manager need not know what is on the LAN or how the LAN is being used.

High Performance—The monitor's designs guarantees that ALL traffic will be captured and categorized. Given the large amount of traffic carried by a LAN (our facility's LAN carries 10 million packets/work-day), the categorization of traffic at the monitor is very helpful in minimizing the work required at the management nodes.

Autonomous Operation—The monitors operate autonomously in collecting and reporting the LAN data. The counters maintained by the monitors are sized for long term operation (approx. 50 days assuming a continuous packet rate of 1000 packets/second).

Downline Load of Monitors—The monitoring firmware can be downline loaded into the monitor hardware. Consequently, a single monitor hardware base can serve many monitoring functions by the loading of different firmware.

Monitor becomes a Front End—The monitor operates at maximum LAN speeds and periodically reports statistics to the management nodes. Therefore, regardless of the load on the LAN, the load on the management node remains static.

Dual LAN Ports—The two LAN ports of the monitor can be used to split the monitoring and reporting functions of the monitor. This configuration is useful for unobtrusive monitoring of heavily loaded LAN's. If a separate LAN is reserved for communication with the monitors, real time monitoring (and detection) of failed LAN's can be supported.

Future Work

This design was based on a philosophy of guaranteed performance, thus resulting in a fixed function monitor. This approach has the benefit of providing high performance, however its basic disadvantage is that functional tradeoffs must be made during the design process. There is a potential for multiple types of monitors. This is not a major concern however, since the monitor is downline loadable and relatively inexpensive.

Because of the performance constraint, numerous tradeoffs were made with respect to the monitoring statistics. At the highest level, this design concentrated on the perspective of who is on the LAN (source addresses) and what type of traffic is present (protocol type). An equally viable perspective is that of a traffic flow monitor; this monitor would categorize packets based on the source and destination addresses. Tradeoffs were also required at a lower level in the design. For example, due to the plethora of Ethernet traffic, the protocol type database was tailored to Ethernet packets, versus IEEE 802.2 [12] source access points [SAP's]. Consequently, one sees the opportunity for enhancements to the current design, and also the potential to build other types of downline loadable monitors.

Acknowledgments

The author would like to acknowledge Bob Shelley who helped refine the design and was responsible for the design of the monitor firmware; its functionality is a direct result of his highly efficient code. The author would also like to thank George Varghese for his critical reviews of the manuscript.

References

[1] B. E. Mann, C. Strutt, and M. F. Kempf "Terminal servers on ethernet local area networks," *Digital Technical Journal*, Digital Equipment Corporation, No. 3, Sept. 1986.

[2] D. R. Cheriton, "The V kernel: a software base for distributed systems," *IEEE Software*, vol. 1, April 1984.

[3] Digital Equipment Corporation, Intel Corporation, Xerox Corporation, "The ethernet—a local area network—data link layer and physical layer specifications," Version 2.0, Digital Equipment Corporation, Maryland MA, AA-K759B-TK, Nov. 1982.

[4] IEEE Computer Society, "Carrier sense multiple access with collision detect (CSMA/CD) access method and physical layer specifications," ANSI/IEEE Standard 802.3 (ISO/DP 8802/3), IEEE 1985.

[5] B. Hawe, A. Kirby, and B. Stewart, "Transparent interconnection of local area networks with bridges," *Journal of Telecommunications*, vol. 3, no. 2, Summer 1984.

[6] B. Stewart and B. Hawe, "Local area network applications," *Telecommunications*, vol. 18, no. 9, Sept. 1984

[7] B. Hawe, B. Stewart, and A. Kirby, "Local area network connections," *Telecommunications*, vol. 18, no. 4, April 1984.

[8] W. R. Hawe, M. F. Kempf, and A. J. Kirby, "The extended local area network architecture and LANBridge 100," *Digital Technical Journal*, Digital Equipment Corporation, no. 3, Sept. 1986.

[9] R. Perlman, "An algorithm for distributed computation of a spanning tree in an extended LAN," Digital Equipment Corporation, Technical submission to IEEE 802 LAN Standards Committee, San Diego, CA, Oct. 29, 1984.

[10] IEEE Computer Society, "Token-passing bus access method and physical layer specifications," ANSI/IEEE Standard 802.4 (ISO/DP 8802/4), IEEE 1985.

[11] IEEE Computer Society, "Token ring access method and physical layer specifications," ANSI/IEEE Standard 802.5 (ISO/DP 8802/5), IEEE 1985.

[12] IEEE Computer Society, "Logical link control," ANSI/IEEE Standard 802.2.-1985 (ISO/DIS 8802/2), IEEE 1984.

Michael Soha works in the Advanced Development Group for Communications and Distributed Systems at Digital Equipment Corporation. As a principal engineer, his work includes current and future LAN technologies, LAN interconnect architecture, and High Performance LAN monitoring. Prior to joining Digital, he worked for The MITRE Corporation. There, he was involved with the development of MITRENET, a CSMA/CD LAN technology, and also consulted on several DOD communications projects. He received his B.S. degree from the University of New Hampshire (UNH), and has done post graduate work in computer architecture at UNH.

Reliability Mechanisms of the FDDI High Bandwidth Token Ring Protocol *

Marjory J. JOHNSON

Research Institute for Advanced Computer Science, NASA Ames Research Center, Moffett Field, CA 94035, USA

The Fiber Distributed Data Interface (FDDI) is an ANSI draft proposed standard for a 100 megabit per second token ring using fiber optics as the transmission medium. The FDDI design represents an extensive effort to incorporate reliability mechanisms as an integral part of the design. These mechanisms provide fault detection and isolation functions, monitoring functions, and configuration functions. The purpose of this paper is to discuss these reliability mechanisms, and to compare and contrast them with reliability mechanisms which have been incorporated in other local area network architectures.

Keywords: Token ring, FDDI protocol, local area networks, reliability mechanisms.

Marjory J. Johnson is currently a scientist at the Research Institute for Advanced Computer Science (RIACS). She received the Ph.D. degree in mathematics from the University of Iowa in 1970. Since then she has been an Assistant Professor of Mathematics at the University of South Carolina and an Associate Professor of Computer Science at the University of Missouri-St. Louis. She has also been a systems analyst at NCR Corporation, studying microcomputer systems and communication networks. At RIACS she is studying networking requirements for the Space Station.

* This work was supported by the National Aeronautics and Space Administration under NASA Contract NAS2-11530 to the Universities Space Research Association (USRA).

North-Holland
Computer Networks and ISDN Systems 11 (1986) 121–131

1. Introduction

The study of reliability reported herein was motivated by a study of reliability needs of the local area network (LAN) for the Space Station. Functions supporting its reliability should be automated, for even though the Space Station will be manned, the crew will be busy with assigned tasks and will have little time for routine computer maintenance and repair.

The Fiber Distributed Data Interface (FDDI) is an ANSI draft proposed standard for a 100 megabit per second fiber-optic token ring. Because it is designed specifically for high bandwidth and for fiber optics, it is an attractive candidate for use on the Space Station. The purpose of this paper is to describe and evaluate the reliability mechanisms that have been incorporated in the FDDI protocol.

One aspect of reliability is transmission management functions, such as flow control, congestion control, buffer management, acknowledgement schemes, and error recovery, all of which are included in the Open Systems Interconnection (OSI) network model. Functions of this type are not discussed further in this paper. Another aspect of network reliability is management of the various OSI layers, something called "computer network control" in [18]. Additional network management functions are necessary for LANs, since their broadcast nature means that activities of a single station (i.e., network interface unit) affect the entire network. These functions, which are not part of the basic OSI model, fall into three categories: fault detection and isolation, monitoring, and configuration [18]. ** Automation of these

** The need for these functions is now widely recognized in the literature. Both IEEE and ANSI are addressing network management functions in their development of LAN standards. The IEEE 802 LAN documents include a general document, 802.1, currently under development, which treats network management as an extension of OSI layer management. The ANSC X3T9.5 committee, the ANSI committee which is developing FDDI, is developing a separate Station functions is desirable, so that they can be accomplished in a manner transparent to the user.

For each of the three network management categories identified above, this paper presents a discussion of the general nature of the functions in that category, followed by a discussion of the specific mechanisms provided by FDDI. The final section compares the reliability mechanisms of FDDI with those in other LAN architectures. Related work includes a paper which discusses error handling in the IEEE 802.4 token-passing bus [16] and a paper which discusses the physical configuration and the reliability of the access protocol of an IBM token ring whose design is similar to that of the IEEE 802.5 token ring [1].

2. FDDI Token Ring

In this section we present a brief description of the FDDI media access protocol. FDDI is one of only a very few LAN access protocols designed specifically for high bandwidth and for fiber optics. (See [2], [15], and [20] for discussions of others.) It represents the only current effort to develop a standard for a 100 megabit per second fiber-optic LAN. Consequently, the FDDI effort is attracting attention throughout the computer and communications industry.

The FDDI access protocol is based on the IEEE 802.5 token ring, modified to support the higher data rates. (As explained in [11], "There is more to high speed protocol design than taking a low speed protocol and changing the numbers in it.") A key difference between the FDDI and 802.5 Media Access Control (MAC) protocols is the method of passing the token after transmission. The FDDI method is for a station to issue the token immediately after it completes transmission of its last frame, whereas the 802.5 method is for a station to wait until the first frame it sent propagates back around to it before issuing a new token. Other modifications are presented in [11]. The designers originally conceived of FDDI either

as a network to interconnect supercomputers or to connect high speed computers with peripheral devices in a computer center environment, where high speed data transfer is essential, or as a backbone network to connect smaller LANs. However, other configurations (including a frontend network) are now considered likely.

The FDDI protocol provides two classes of service, synchronous service and asynchronous service. Synchronous service is for applications, such as real-time control, that require access to the channel within a specified time period. Each station is allotted a percentage of the bandwidth for its synchronous transmission needs. Synchronous frames can be transmitted by a station whenever it receives the token. Asynchronous transmission is permitted only if the token is rotating quickly enough, as indicated by an internal station parameter, called Late_Ct. Thus, synchronous transmission receives highest priority. Multiple levels of priority may be assigned for asynchronous traffic.

Access to the network and scheduling of the network is controlled by timers that interact in a relatively complex manner. Each station has its own set of timers and its own Late_Ct parameter. As part of the ring initialization process, the stations negotiate a value for the Target Token Rotation Time (TTRT), a parameter which specifies the expected token rotation time. Each station requests a value that is fast enough to support its synchronous traffic needs. The shortest requested time is assigned to T_Opr, and then this value is used to load each station's Token Rotation Timer (TRT). A station's Late_Ct is incremented each time its TRT expires, and it is cleared each time the station receives the token. The token is considered to arrive at a station on time if its TRT has not expired since the station last received the token, i.e., if Late_Ct = 0. Otherwise, the token is considered to be late.

The amount of time that a station may hold the token and transmit frames is governed by its TRT, its Token Holding Timer (THT), its synchronous bandwidth allocation, and its parameter Late_Ct as follows:

1. If the token is on time, i.e., if Late_Ct = 0, then the current value of TRT is placed in THT, and TRT is reset to T_Opr. Both asynchronous and synchronous frames may be transmitted.

2. If the token is late, i.e., if Late_Ct ≠ 0,

Management (SMT) document [7]. Similar to the IEEE work, the X3T9.5 committee is developing Station Management as an extension of OSI layer management. By definition, Station Management is an entity within each station which "monitors station activity and exercises overall control of station activity [17]."

Late_Ct is cleared, but the TRT is not reset. Only synchronous frames may be transmitted in this case.

3. TRT is enabled during transmission of all frames, synchronous and asynchronous. THT is enabled only during transmission of asynchronous frames.

4. The length of time an individual station may transmit synchronous frames may not exceed its synchronous bandwidth allocation. The length of time that a station may transmit asynchronous frames is governed by its THT; no asynchronous frames may be transmitted after its expiration. No frames of either class may be transmitted after expiration of the station's TRT.

For more information about the protocol see [4], [11], [12], [14], and [17].

3. Fault Detection, Isolation, and Correction Functions

Ideally, failure of any device attached to the network should not cause failure of the entire network, only the function or service offered by that individual device. To facilitate ease of maintenance and repair, the network should be self-diagnosing, i.e., the network should continuously monitor itself to detect faults. When a problem is detected, the network should be able to determine the nature of the problem and to isolate the fault to a single component or to a small group of components.

There are two major types of errors in a LAN, protocol-related errors and errors caused by failure of a physical resource. The FDDI protocol features several mechanisms which automatically detect the presence of errors of either type and which automatically initiate ring recovery. If the error is protocol-related, the ring recovery process will correct it; otherwise, the ring automatically physically reconfigures itself so as to bypass the failed resource.

3.1. Physical Reconfiguration

A major concern with a token ring architecture is that a break in the ring, caused either by a failed link or a failed station, will cause failure of the entire network. FDDI provides a solution to this single-point-of-failure problem by providing a redundant ring and optical station bypasses, as follows.

The FDDI draft proposed standard specifies that the network should consist of both a primary ring and a secondary ring, rotating in opposite directions. The secondary ring may be used only as a backup ring, or transmission may be scheduled for both rings under normal operations, thus doubling the effective transmission rate of the ring. There are two types of stations, Class A stations and Class B stations. Class A stations are attached to both rings. Class A stations may be equipped with an optical bypass, so that they may be switched out of the ring in the event of failure. Class B stations have only one physical connection to the network. Consequently, a Class B station must be connected to the network via a Class A connection, called a concentrator. "Traffic into a Class A node is made to go back and forth to the attached Class B nodes before it flows to the next Class A node further downstream [6]." Class B nodes may be electronically bypassed within the concentrator if the station fails or is switched off. In the event of link failure on the primary ring or the secondary ring or both, the network is automatically reconfigured (actually wrapped around) using a combination of the operational links of both rings. Multiple link failures may divide the original ring into two or more isolated smaller rings. Diagrams in [14] and [17] illustrate how the network reconfigures itself after failure of one or more links connecting Class A stations. Station Management (SMT), the control entity within each station, automatically manages the necessary reconfiguration. Failure of a link which attaches a Class B station to a concentrator is, of course, equivalent to failure of the Class B station.

3.2. Frame Stripping

A commonly cited problem with a token ring access protocol is a frame which circulates forever on the ring. If the token is issued only after the frame is stripped from the ring, normal operation of the ring would be disrupted until the problem was corrected. This will not occur with FDDI, since the token is issued by a station immediately after it finishes transmitting. However, it is still undesirable for a frame to continue circulating around the ring. The destination station would have to handle the duplicate frames, and counters in all the stations would be affected.

The FDDI protocol provides for frame removal in an orderly way. The station which transmits a frame is responsible for stripping it from the ring. Normally, when a station is not transmitting, it repeats whatever it receives on the ring. When it recognizes its own address in the source address field of a frame, it absorbs the rest of the frame and pumps idle symbols onto the ring instead. This actually leaves a truncated frame on the ring, since the fields at the beginning of the frame will have already been repeated. All other stations will recognize the frame as a remnant and will disregard it when they encounter the idle symbols before an ending delimiter, and this remnant will be absorbed from the ring when it encounters a transmitting station. Even if the station which transmits a frame fails before the frame circulates back around to it, the frame will eventually be removed from the ring when it encounters a transmitting station; normal operation of the ring is not disrupted.

3.3. FDDI Timers

Each station on the ring needs to be able to determine the status of the network, i.e., whether or not the ring is operational. Sensing transmission on the line isn't sufficient evidence to conclude that the ring is operating properly, because this transmission could represent random noise or a jabbering transmitter. To indicate proper operation of the ring, the transmission must be meaningful and each station must be given an opportunity to transmit within a reasonable amount of time.

Two timers included in the FDDI MAC protocol, the Valid Transmission Timer (TVX) and the Token Rotation Timer (TRT), are used to maintain proper operation of the ring by detecting problems and by forcing initiation of ring recovery when necessary. Each station has its own TVX and TRT. These timers work as follows.

The Token Rotation Timer's fault detection and recovery functions are closely related to its ring-scheduling function. The TRTs in all the stations work together to ensure that the amount of time required for the token to circulate around the ring is bounded above by twice T_Opr. Expira-

tion of a station's TRT when the token isn't late, i.e., when Late_Ct = 0, is a means of hurrying the token along, by preventing the station from transmitting asynchronous frames when it receives the token. Expiration of a station's TRT when the token is already late, i.e., when Late_Ct ≠ 0, indicates a serious ring problem, and forces the station to initiate ring recovery. It is proved in [13] that under normal ring operation, the token is guaranteed to return to a station before its TRT expires a second time. That is, expiration of a station's TRT when Late_Ct ≠ 0 will occur only if there is a serious problem and ring recovery is indeed necessary. Thus, the TRT detects and attempts automatic correction of errors which make the token appear to be lost.

The Valid Transmission Timer maintains proper operation of the ring by ensuring that the transmission on the channel is meaningful. This timer is reset each time that a "nonrestricted" token is received or that a valid frame is received. (Tokens for general operation of the ring are "nonrestricted." Stations may hog the channel through the use of a special mechanism called a "restricted" token.) Expiration of a station's TVX forces the station to initiate ring recovery. The default value of the TVX is large enough so that expiration will only occur if the invalid transmission is of a long-term nature. This means that random noise on the line won't initiate ring recovery.

Station Management may request that the station capture the token before a frame is placed in the transmission queue. Upon capture of the token, the station transmits idle symbols as a filler until it has a frame ready for transmission. To prevent expiration of the TVX during this time, Station Management can send void frames. Void frames are interpreted and counted as valid frames, but they are not copied into MAC's receive buffer. Hence, receipt of a void frame will reset a station's TVX, but it will not contribute any congestion in the individual stations.

The default value of the TVX is much shorter than the default value of the TRT. If the token is garbled, then the TRT would eventually expire. However, the TVX will detect the transmission problem much earlier, thus improving the efficiency of the ring. In addition, the TVX will detect a problem that the TRT will not. When stations are finished using a restricted token to hog the ring, the last one is supposed to issue a nonrestricted token. If it erroneously issues a restricted token, expiration of the TVX prevents this token from circulating forever and effectively blocking access to the ring.

3.4. FDDI Ring Recovery Process

Ring recovery is the process of restoring ring operation by negotiating a TTRT value and by issuing a new token. A unique station is selected in a distributed manner to issue this new token.

Ring recovery is initiated if a serious problem with ring operation is detected. For example, ring recovery is initiated if too long a time passes between successive receipts of valid transmissions (either tokens or frames), if the token is lost, or if there is a jabbering transmitter or a deaf receiver. Recovery will be successful if the problem is related to the access protocol; recovery will not be successful if the problem is caused by a physical break in the ring. Specific mechanisms that trigger the recovery process include expiration of various timers, receipt of frames indicating that a station on the ring has detected abnormal operating conditions, or a SMT command to initiate recovery. Ring recovery will also be required if a station's parameter settings are inconsistent with the operational parameters of the network as a whole, e.g., if a station requires a faster token rotation time to support its synchronous needs than is currently being supported by the network.

The Claim Token Frame is the mechanism by which ring recovery is attempted. Stations on the ring are linearly ordered by the requested TTRT, with ties resolved by station address. The station with highest precedence is the station which requires the fastest token rotation time. If two stations request the same TTRT, then the station with the higher address takes precedence. The claim token arbitration procedure, if it is successful, selects the highest precedence station to issue the new token. It works as follows. When ring recovery is intiated at a station, the station's transmitter continuously sends Claim Token Frames. The information field of these frames contains that station's requested value for the Target Token Rotation Time (TTRT). The station continues to send these Claim Token Frames until either the Claim arbitration is resolved or the process is preempted. If a station receives a Claim Token Frame from a lower precedence station, then it either starts or continues to transmit its own Claim Token Frames. If a station receives a Claim Token Frame from a higher precedence station, then it defers and repeats all subsequent Claim Token Frames. Hence, at most one station (necessarily, the highest precedence station on the ring) will succeed in receiving its own Claim Token Frames. If this happens, the arbitration is resolved, and this highest precedence station issues a token to restart ring operation.

If ring recovery is successful, the ring is restored to normal operation within only a few milliseconds. Ring recovery consists of two components, pinpointing the highest precedence station on the ring and setting station parameters when the new token is issued. Since Claim Token Frames are short, requiring 0.00256 ms transmission time, and since at most two cycles of sending them would be necessary (depending on the location of the highest precedence station relative to the station which initiated the recovery process), very little time would be required by the first component. Two initial token rotations are then required before normal ring operation is resumed, i.e., before asynchronous transmission is allowed. The purpose of the first token rotation is to set station parameters and to align timers. Only synchronous transmission is allowed during the second token rotation. Hence, the second component of ring recovery also requires little time.

Claim arbitration should be successfully resolved if there is no physical break in the ring, unless the arbitration is interrupted prematurely. Events that would terminate the arbitration process are either a MAC_Reset signal (discussed in Section 5.5) or receipt of a Beacon Frame (described below). Hence, if recovery is initiated because of a token-related problem, such as a lost token, then the ring will be reinitialized automatically and in a distributed manner.

3.5. FDDI Beacon Frame

The Beacon Frame is used to indicate a problem of a disruptive nature, requiring physical reconfiguration of the network. An important difference between the Claim Token Frame and the Beacon Frame is that the source of the problem is pinpointed with the Beacon Frame, whereas it is not with the Claim Frame. This is because the Claim Frame process, if it runs to completion, leaves the highest precedence station on the ring in control. In contrast, any station which receives a Beacon Frame defers and repeats the frames it receives. Thus, the station immediately downstream from the problem will be the only station to persist in sending Beacon Frames, and will be designated in the source address of the frames. Thus, the situation that is being "beaconed" is located in the transmitter of the upstream station, the receiver of the station which is sending the Beacon Frames, or the link in between.

Beacon Frames are transmitted if there is a change in ring topology. When a break in the ring occurs, causing the token to appear to be lost, ring recovery will be attempted first. However, recovery will fail, because no station will be able to receive its own Claim Token Frames. If a station's TRT expires while it is sending its own Claim Token Frames, then that station begins to transmit Beacon Frames. If a station receives its own Beacon Frames, then that station sends Claim Token Frames again to attempt ring recovery. If there is indeed a break in the ring, then no station will receive its own Beacon Frames. Station Management will automatically physically reconfigure the ring to bypass the failure.

Another type of topology change occurs when a Class A station is inserted into the ring. The station insertion process has not been completely developed. The description in the current version of the Station Management document states that after either a Class A or a Class B station is inserted into the ring, it will transmit Beacon Frames. In this way it could announce its existence and identity to all other stations on the ring. The ring recovery procedure would follow, to negotiate TTRT, to set T_Opr values, and to determine which station would issue a token to resume operation of the ring.

Beacon Frames are also transmitted upon command from SMT. SMT continuously monitors network performance. If it detects a significant degradation of performance, SMT can issue a Beacon Frame to purge the ring of all traffic. The beaconing station remains in control of the network and can transmit recovery information to other stations on the ring, using an "immediate" service class, a class to be used only for recovery purposes. When this service class is used, it is not necessary to capture the token before transmitting.

4. Monitoring Functions

It is an "unsettling fact that current performance models do not appear to predict the performance of real-world network implementations [19]." This is because of simplifying assumptions which must often be made in order to obtain analytical results. Thus, the only way to determine the true performance of a network is on-line collection and analysis of statistics about network traffic.

Monitoring functions are typically divided into three areas: performance measurement, performance analysis, and artificial traffic generation [18]. Performance measurement and analysis are necessary to determine both performance of the access protocol and performance of the network in general. Artificial traffic generation is necessary so that network performance can be observed under a controlled load. This can be a useful tool in the laboratory before the network becomes operational. After the network is in place, artificial traffic generation can help to detect potential problems before they become serious, and it can help in planning for future growth of the network.

FDDI monitoring functions monitor performance of the access protocol only. Monitoring of general network performance is considered to be outside the scope of the standard, since it is not necessary for interoperability of stations in the network.

4.1. Performance Measurement

Several mechanisms have been provided by the MAC protocol for the gathering of statistics and the communication of status information from MAC to Station Management. As stated above, the objective of FDDI monitoring is fault detection and isolation, not determining general network performance.

4.1.1. FDDI Frame Status Indicators

Frame status indicators (four bits long) are located at the end of every frame. Error Detected (E), Address Recognized (A), and Frame Copied (C) indicators are mandatory; others may be added if desired. Each station has flags which correspond to the mandatory indicators. These three indicators are initially reset. The first station to detect an error in a frame which makes the frame invalid (i.e., either an error indicated by the Frame Check Sequence, an invalid frame control field, or an invalid frame length), sets the corresponding E indicator and reports the error to MAC. Once the E indicator has been set, all subsequent stations transmit it as set, but do not report the error. The Address Recognized indicator is set by a station which recognizes the destination address of the frame as its own; all other stations transmit it as received. The Frame Copied indicator is set by a station which recognizes the destination address of the frame as its own and copies the frame into its receive buffer; all other stations transmit the indicator as received.

These status indicators serve a dual purpose. First, they provide a link layer acknowledgement to the sending station. However, since an error may occur in the transfer of the frame from MAC to Logical Link Control, the sending station cannot be assured that its frame was received even if the A and C indicators are set. Also, if the destination address is a group address, the A and C symbols being set only reflects that one of the intended stations received and copied the frame. Second, these indicators help in fault detection and isolation. If a station on the ring recognizes the destination address as its own, but the A flag has already been set, this indicates a duplicate address problem. Comparison of the error counts in the various stations is an aid in detecting and isolating faults, since errors are reported only by the first station to detect the error. Also, a frame with the A indicator set, but not the C indicator, indicates a possible congestion or buffer management problem.

4.1.2. FDDI Station Flags

Each station has three flags, the Address Recognized Flag, the Frame Copied Flag, and the Error Recognized Flag, corresponding to the three mandatory status indicators at the end of each frame. Additional flags in each station record necessary book-keeping information to regulate normal ring operation and information used in ring initialization or ring recovery to indicate which station will issue the new token. All the flags (except one which indicates token class) are cleared

when the station receives the first symbol of the starting delimiter of a token or frame and then they are modified according to information in the frame itself.

4.1.3. FDDI Station Counts

The MAC entity in each station maintains some counters "to aid in problem determination and fault location [4]." These counters include Frame_Ct, a count of all frames received, Error_Ct, a count of all frames received with one or more errors that were previously undetected (this count is incremented when the Error Detected status indicator is set by a station), Lost_Ct, a count of all instances when a format error, such as an invalid physical symbol or a symbol that violates the defined format of a frame, is detected when MAC is in the process of receiving a frame or token (MAC strips such frames from the ring, so that they won't be counted by subsequent stations), and Late_Ct, a count of the number of times TRT has expired since the last receipt of a token. Under normal ring operation, Late_Ct should never be greater than 1. The only time a station's Late_Ct can exceed 1 is if its TRT expires while it is transmitting Beacon Frames, because Late_Ct will not get cleared while the transmitter is in this state. The magnitude of Late_Ct is then a measure of the severity of the problem.

Comparison of the counter values within the various stations would be an effective means of fault detection and isolation.

4.2. Performance Analysis

FDDI performance analysis is directed towards detecting and isolating network faults. The Station Management entity in each station is responsible for analyzing status information provided by MAC. MAC reports errors and significant status changes to SMT when they occur. Events to be reported include receipt of a frame that will initiate the ring recovery process, receipt of a frame that signals a disruption of normal ring operation, overflow of station counters, inability to copy a frame addressed to the station, expiration of protocol timers, indication that another station on the ring is responding to this station's address, and any other events as agreed upon between MAC and SMT.

SMT could perform comprehensive data analysis based on these reported statistics. Via peer communication between SMT entities in various stations, the stations could obtain a global picture of network performance. If Station Management detected a potential problem, it could then take whatever action might be appropriate.

4.3. Artificial Traffic Generation

SMT can transmit a frame with a bad frame check sequence, for diagnostic purposes. Other than this, there is no direct provision for artificial traffic generation in FDDI.

5. Configuration Functions

Configuration functions include physical management of stations, address management, station reset, and network reconfiguration. No human intervention should be required for these tasks. The FDDI Station Management, Media Access Control, and Physical Layer Protocol adequately provide for these functions.

5.1. Insertion and Removal

Insertion of a station into the ring is managed automatically by Station Management. This process was discussed in Section 3.5.

Failure of a Class A station which is not equipped with an optical bypass automatically causes reconfiguration of the network. The ring will be wrapped around to physically omit the failed station. Removal of multiple stations from the ring will split the original ring into two or more isolated subrings. A Class B station is either connected to the network or electronically bypassed via a switch in the associated concentrator.

5.2. Address Management

It is SMT's responsibility to assign station addresses and to resolve duplicate address problems. The existence of duplicate addresses is indicated if a station receives a frame with a destination address that it recognizes as its own, but the Address Recognized indicator is already set. This information is reported to SMT, so that SMT can resolve

the problem. SMT's actions are not specified at this point, but it might send a frame to the other station to try to resolve the problem. Or, SMT might remove the station from the ring and then reinsert it with a different address.

5.3. Neighbor Notification

It is useful to know the physical topology of the entire network, for both configuration and fault isolation purposes. The global topology of a ring can be easily constructed if each station knows the identity of its upstream neighbor. A neighbor notification procedure is periodically initiated by the active monitor in the IEEE 802.5 token ring. However, the monitor is not essential to the procedure, and neighbor notification could be handled similarly in the FDDI token ring.

5.4. Changing Station Parameters

Each station on the ring contains internal parameters whose settings determine the operational characteristics of that station and of the ring as a whole. Such parameters include timing values used in the negotiation of TTRT, the station's synchronous bandwidth allocation, and parameters identifying events that should be reported to SMT. These parameters can all be assigned by SMT. Change of some parameters might necessitate recovery of the ring, while others might not be so serious. SMT can also clear counters in MAC, so SMT might gather information from MAC and then clear counters on a periodic basis to monitor network performance.

5.5. Reset

Reset of a station's MAC entity can be specifically requested by SMT, or it may be initiated as an automatic by-product of the ring recovery process. MAC reset erases all knowledge of operational parameters within the station. T_Opr is set to the maximum value supported by the station. If this happens to be the value of T_Opr for the rest of the ring, recovery will probably not be initiated. However, if the reset station's T_Opr value is larger than the one used by the rest of the stations, ring recovery is likely to be initiated by another station on the ring. TTRT (and hence, T_Opr) would then be renegotiated, so that all the stations agreed on its value. (See [13] for a more complete discussion of the consequences of station reset.)

5.6. Reconfiguration

SMT manages ring reconfiguration after resource failure or after station insertion as explained in Sections 3.1 and 3.5.

5.7. Synchronous Bandwidth Allocation

This is identified as a function of Station Management in the draft proposed standard, but no details have been provided as yet. Allocation of synchronous bandwidth must be managed so that no more is allocated than the network can support. Also, a means must be provided for dynamic reassignment of these allocations.

6. Comparison to Reliability Mechanisms in Other LAN Architectures

Reliability issues are being addressed in other LAN architectures, as well as FDDI. The IEEE 802 draft proposed LAN standards all refer to network management functions. Draft IEEE standards have been developed for a CSMA/CD bus, 802.3 [8], a token-passing bus, 802.4 [9], and a token ring, 802.5 [10]. A separate document, 802.1, is planned, which is to include a discussion of network management issues as part of its contents.

Considering that the FDDI token ring was designed as a high bandwidth modification of the IEEE 802.5 token ring, it is not surprising that similar reliability mechanisms are included in the two designs. Both specify an interface between the physical layer and network management for insertion of a station into the ring and removal of a station from the ring. Both append status indicators at the end of a frame. Both provide for automatic detection of and recovery from token-related problems, though different timers are required because of the differences in the two access protocols. Both also specify a claim frame process for ring recovery, and a beaconing process for fault isolation. The two interfaces between station (or network) management and medium access control are almost identical. The primary dif-

ference in handling ring recovery and fault isolation is the existence of a network monitor in the 802.5 design. Even though every station on the ring has the ability to act as the network monitor, there is only one "active monitor" on the ring at a time and this station has ultimate authority in the ring recovery process. FDDI recovery is completely distributed.

Neither the 802.5 nor the FDDI design for station (or network) management is complete. It is likely that the two will end up having nearly identical functions. The fundamental difference seems to be that 802.5 must include provisions for management of a network monitor, whereas FDDI control is distributed.

Reliability mechanisms provided by FDDI and by the 802.4 token-passing bus are also similar. Ring maintenance functions which are provided for by 802.4 include "ring initialization, lost token recovery, new station addition to logical ring, and general housekeeping of the logical ring [9]." 802.4 specifies an interface between MAC and Station Management, but it is substantially different from the interface provided in FDDI. Most noticeable is the lack of a primitive in 802.4 for MAC to report status to SMT.

Management primitives provided for the 802.3 CSMA/CD bus include a reset command and some access-protocol-related commands. The document also specifies a jabber inhibit capability, i.e., a "self-interrupt capability to inhibit transmit data from reaching the medium [8]," to protect the network from a faulty transmitter that won't stop transmitting. (This is also specified in 802.4.) There is little mention of a network management entity in the document. In fact, it is concluded that for a CSMA/CD access protocol, "no peer management functions are necessary for initiating, terminating, or handling abnormal conditions. Monitoring of on-going activities is done by the carrier sense and collision detect mechanisms [8]."

The goal of the 802 project is to develop a network management entity common to all the architectures specified in the various 802 standards. Conceptually, this is a reasonable goal, since there seems to be no valid reason for the scope of network management capabilities to depend on the particular access protocol, other than to assure the correct functioning of the protocol. In reality, due to the diversity of the various interfaces between MAC and network management as they now exist, development of a common network management may be a difficult task.

Reliability mechanisms are also being included in network implementations that are not being developed according to any of the above IEEE or ANSI standards. Various reliability mechanisms have been included in the design of the Fiber Optic Demonstration System (FODS), a 100 megabit per second fiber-optic star network [20]. This network uses a Carrier Sense Multiple Access with Collision Detection and contention resolution via Time Slot (CSMA/CD/TS) access protocol. FODS was developed by Sperry Space Systems Division in Phoenix, Arizona, under contract to NASA Goddard Space Flight Center, and it is also a candidate for use on the Space Station. FODS includes built-in-test equipment, which tests a backup channel, shuts down a jabbering transmitter, and automatically switches to a backup station upon failure of the primary. The claim is that FODS provides for distributed network control. Network statistics collected at each node "can be used to determine the relative health, efficiency, and loading of the network and individual nodes." An interesting feature of this project is a FODS Exerciser that generates artificial traffic, to determine performance of the network under various conditions, including error situations.

7. Conclusion

The current trend in LAN design, as illustrated by the FDDI effort, is to incorporate network management functions as an extension of OSI layer management. The emphasis is on detecting and correcting errors in the access protocol and on automating physical reconfiguration of the network. In accordance with this philosophy, monitor functions monitor the performance of the access protocol, rather than general performance of the network.

Unfortunately, the standardization of network management functions seems to be a long way away. For even though the importance of including reliability mechanisms in network design is widely accepted, there is no agreement on a specific set of network management tasks that is independent of network topology.

Acknowledgement

The author is indebted to Floyd Ross, Jim Hamstra, and Sunil Joshi, members of the ANSC X3T9.5 committee, for enlightening discussions about FDDI.

References

[1] W. Bux, F. Closs, K. Kuemmerle, H. Keller, and H. Mueller, "Architecture and Design of a Reliable Token-Ring Network," IEEE Journal on Selected Areas in Communications, Vol. SAC-1, No. 5, Nov., 1983, pp. 756–765.

[2] "Draft Proposed American National Standard for Local Distributed Data Interfaces," X3T9.5/84–16, Revision 6.0, April 10, 1985.

[3] "FDDI Token Ring Extended Media Access Control Interface," Draft Proposed American National Standard, X3T9.5/84–46, Dec. 13, 1984.

[4] "FDDI Token Ring Media Access Control," Draft Proposed American National Standard, X3T9.5/83–16, Rev 8, Mar. 1, 1985.

[5] "FDDI Token Ring Physical Layer Medium Dependent Standard," Draft Proposed American National Standard, X3T9.5/84–48, Rev 2, April 5, 1985.

[6] "FDDI Token Ring Physical Layer Protocol Standard," Draft Proposed American National Standard, X3T9.5/83–15, Rev 9, April 5, 1985.

[7] "FDDI Token Ring Station Management," Draft Proposed American National Standard, X3T9.5/84–49, Rev 1.2, Feb. 12, 1985.

[8] IEEE Project 802 Local Area Network Standards, "CSMA/CD Access Method and Physical Layer Specifications," Draft IEEE Standard 802.3, Revision D, December, 1982.

[9] IEEE Project 802 Local Area Network Standards, "Token-Passing Bus Access Method and Physical Layer Specifications," Draft IEEE Standard 802.4, Draft D, December, 1982.

[10] IEEE Project 802 Local Area Network Standards, "Token Ring Access Method and Physical Layer Specifications," Draft IEEE Standard 802.5, September 23, 1983.

[11] V. Iyer and S. Joshi, "Streamlining Protocols at High Data Rates," Proceedings of Wescon/84, Session 2, Paper 4.

[12] V. Iyer and S. Joshi, "FDDI's 100 M-bps Protocol Improves on 802.5 Spec's 4 M-bps Limit," EDN, May 2, 1985, pp. 151–160.

[13] M. Johnson, "Proof that Timing Requirements of the FDDI Token Ring Protocol are Satisfied," RIACS Technical Report 85.8, August, 1985.

[14] S. Joshi and V. Iyer, "New Standards for Local Networks Push Upper Limits for Lightwave Data," Data Communications, July, 1984, pp. 127–138.

[15] E. Lee and P. Boulton, "The Principles and Performance of Hubnet: A 50 Mbit/s Glass Fiber Local Area Net-

work," IEEE Journal on Selected Areas in Communications, Vol. SAC-1, No. 5, Nov., 1983, pp. 711–720.

[16] T. Phinney, and G. Jelatis, "Error Handling in the IEEE 802 Token-Passing Bus LAN," IEEE Journal on Selected Areas in Communications, Vol. SAC-1, No. 5, Nov. 1983, pp. 784–789.

[17] F. Ross, and R. Moulton, "FDDI Overview-A 100 Megabit per Second Solution," Proceedings of Wescon/84, Session 2, Paper 1.

[18] W. Stallings, *Local Networks: An Introduction*, MacMillan, 1984.

[19] J. Sventek, W. Greiman, M. O'Dell, and A. Jansen, "Token Ring Local Area Networks-A Comparison of Experimental and Theoretical Performance," Proceedings of Computer Networking Symposium, Dec. 13, 1983, IEEE Computer Society Press, 1984, pp. 51–56.

[20] M. Varga, "A Robust 100 MBPS Network for Avionics Application," Proceedings of the National Aerospace and Electronics Conference (NAECON), May, 1985.

LOCAL AREA MILITARY NETWORK

Deepinder P. Sidhu
Research and Development Division
SDC - A Burroughs Company
Paoli, PA 19301

ABSTRACT

A design of a local area military network is presented that can provide protection of multilevel data on the network from subscribers at different security levels. The design makes maximum use of well-understood security concepts, existing protocols, and off-the-shelf hardware. The approach mainly relies on trusted software for enforcing security in LAN interface units.

INTRODUCTION

LANs are becoming popular with the military for providing means for distributed processing within a restricted environment to subscribers at different security levels. For single-level subscribers, communication is restricted to those at the same security level. This restriction is enforced by trusted interface units (TIUs) used by each subscriber to interface to the LAN, and is based on a security level field in the header of each packet. The TIUs are trusted to enforce and check the security markings in the packets--the hosts or terminals themselves are not.

For multilevel subscribers (a multilevel secure terminal or host), communication is restricted according to the DoD security policy constraints. That is, a multilevel host can transmit at a range of levels between the minimum and maximum. The minimum and maximum are enforced by the TIU for the multilevel host, with the host trusted to choose the specific level of each packet it transmits. Likewise, the multilevel host is trusted to receive packets at the range of its levels and to properly protect the data according to the classification in the packet header. Figure 1 shows a simple multilevel LAN with single-level and multilevel subscribers.

Because the data on the network medium (e.g., coaxial cable) is not encrypted, appropriate physical protection is required. In a broadcast LAN, this would imply that the entire cable and the TIUs would have to be protected to system-high, since all packets on the network are visible at all locations. For subscribers operating at lower security levels (and in less-protected environments) it might not be feasible to protect the medium to system-high at all points, especially since both the TIU-subscriber and TIU-LAN interfaces usually consist of relatively short cables. For example, the physical and procedural controls necessary to provide a DoD Top Secret environment are extremely costly. It would be unreasonable to expect such protection to be required for all the TIUs and the entire LAN medium in a network whose majority of users are unclassified.

To allow for realistic combination of environmental controls we extend the secure LAN architecture to incorporate the concept of separate physical subnetworks whose mediums are each protected to some maximum level that may be less than the maximum level of the entire local network. The subnetworks are connected by "bridges" in such a way that the entire set of subnetworks appear as a single local network to each TIU and subscriber [Clark78]. An example of a LAN composed of several subnetworks is shown in figure 2. Where portions of the medium, TIU-subscriber link, or bridge link must pass through unprotected areas, data is encrypted using mostly standard link encryption techniques. While this paper does not address encryption as a solution to multilevel data protection, some encryption issues peculiar to this architecture will be discussed below.

The bridges implement a function similar to gateways in wide-area networks but are much simpler. Their job is to route packets between LAN subnetworks with identical protocols. They operate at a level of protocol that makes them transparent to TIUs and hosts or terminals, so that they have no effect on the hardware and software in the TIUs. The bridges perform their routing function based on fixed tables within the bridges and destination addresses in the headers of the packets. They also perform a security check to insure that information from a high level TIU on one subnetwork does not flow to a lower level subnetwork. In this way subnetworks need only be "trusted" (and physically protected) to maintain separation of data within the range of levels of subscribers on that subnetwork. Even unclassified subnetworks can be supported as shown at the bottom of figure 2.

The overall design is intended to be easily implementable with minimal changes to existing off-the-shelf technology and protocols. As such it is felt that it is a practical solution for many installations that have near-term requirements to incorporate a local area network into existing or planned data processing facilities and cannot afford to spend the time or money for more sophisticated long-term options. It is far more flexible than a "system-high" approach where all subscribers must be protected to the highest level [DoD72]. It provides a foundation for multilevel

Reprinted from *IEEE International Conference on Communications ICC '83*, 1983, pages D2.5.1-D2.5.11. Copyright © 1983 by The Institute of Electrical and Electronics Engineers, Inc.

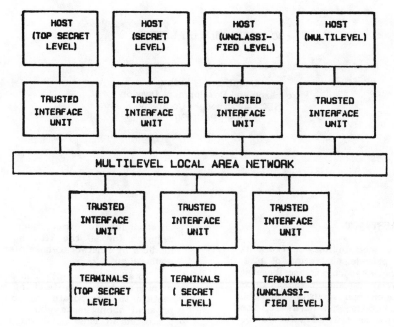

Figure 1. Simple Multilevel Local Area Network

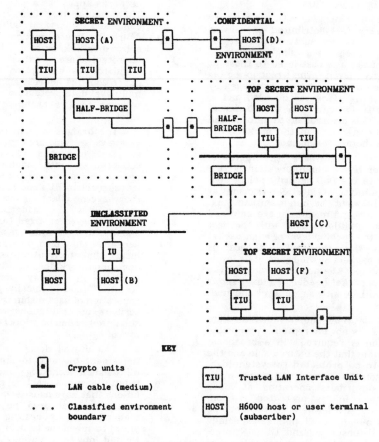

KEY

- ▪ Crypto units
- ── LAN cable (medium)
- ... Classified environment boundary

- TIU Trusted LAN Interface Unit
- HOST H6000 host or user terminal (subscriber)

Figure 2. Full Multilevel Local Area Network

communications at sites that may initially only require communication between single-level entities, but may later upgrade to multilevel hosts and terminals. A proposed implementation would take place in three phases, allowing an initial capability for single-level communication with incremental upgrade to multilevel communication. This phasing matches the anticipated availability of multilevel computers and terminals, where only single-level components are available today, followed by controlled-mode (two-level) hosts, "variable-level" terminals (to be discussed below), and finally multilevel terminals and hosts.

The concept deals with practical matters such as physical protection of the medium, terminals and hosts. It also takes into account the difficulty of certifying large pieces of hardware or software for multilevel operation by reducing to an absolute minimum the components of the system that must be trusted. No "security kernel" or sophisticated trusted mechanisms are required. The design deals with a phased implementation that will satisfy many initial needs in the near future and can later be upgraded, with no disruption of service, for more sophisticated applications as the need for multilevel service increases and a greater volume of traffic must be supported.

The next sections discuss security concepts, protocols and the architecture of the TIU and bridge. Some encryption issues are addressed at the end of this paper.

SECURITY CONCEPTS AND CONSIDERATIONS

When a person is given a security clearance, the security system is explained to him and he is then **trusted** to handle all levels of data up to his security level. Attributing the same level of trust to a computer whose hardware and software has been constructed by many people who may not have clearances is not generally done without careful examination of all aspects of the design, construction, and continuing maintenance of the computer. As a practical matter multilevel security for any of the resources to be connected to the LAN is a hard problem only beginning to be solved. Most existing computers, networks and terminals are untrusted: they are only permitted to process information at a single level. They are not certified for operation in a multilevel secure mode—or even in a controlled mode of operation.

Single-level means merely that a resource is only allowed to process data at a certain classification. In practice, a user cleared to at least that level will use an untrusted computer to maintain information for him at all levels from unclassified up to the level of the computer. The computer cannot be trusted, however, to maintain the separation of data; the user is required to manually label or verify the classification of the output from the computer. "Single level" is often considered equivalent to "untrusted", since, as long as all external interfaces to the computer (i.e., the users) are trusted, no particular trust is required of the computer itself to maintain

separation of data. Untrusted single-level systems run in a mode of operation commonly called system-high.

A **multilevel** resource is trusted to maintain separation of data at a wide range of security levels. Generally, building a large multilevel secure computer system requires a sophisticated system architecture and formal mathematical specification and verification of large parts of the system's software. These are major technological problems as mentioned earlier. However, multilevel operation of smaller special-purpose systems (such as the bridges and TIUs of the secure LAN) is achievable. Also, while a particular system may not be trusted to operate in a full multilevel mode, DoD regulations allow a limited **controlled** mode of operation in which the system is sufficiently trusted to process and protect data at two or three adjacent security levels [DoD72].

The controlled mode is similar to the operation of one of our secure LAN subnetworks whose "minimum level" is above unclassified because it is not trusted to provide the required separation. As for the single-level system-high mode, the classification of output from a system running in controlled mode is assumed to be at least at the lower level unless manually declassified.

PROTOCOL

In order to design multilevel security into any network specific protocols must be examined. To insure feasibility of implementation and operation, we are basing our design on an existing protocol that is known to be operational and thus presumably has its bugs worked out. Our goal is to minimize the modifications to the protocol so as not to affect any existing performance studies or implementation techniques. While many of the basic concepts of the approach in this paper are applicable to a number of existing LAN protocols, we have chosen to center our design around the carrier sense multiple access with collision detection (CSMA/CD) protocol that has been proposed for the IEEE standard 802 [IEEE82a, IEEE82b]. This protocol was chosen because similar protocols are fairly widely (though by no means universally) accepted in industry (Ethernet being the prime example [Ethernet80]). We are not specifying that CSMA/CD is the only protocol that can be used for a multilevel network. However, as design details are presented here it will be apparent where CSMA/CD is specific to this particular design. Certain aspects of the design would have to be modified to use another protocol. When we refer to CSMA/CD in this paper we are specifically referring to the IEEE version, although other versions (e.g., Ethernet) would probably be suitable with little change.

The recent draft (draft D) of IEEE 802 has separated the link layer into two sublayers called Logical Link Control (LLC) Sublayer and and Medium Access Control (MAC) Sublayer. The LLC sublayer is the top sublayer of the link layer and is common to the various access methods that are being considered by IEEE 802 committee for standardization. The MAC is the other sublayer of the link layer that depends on the particular access method such as CSMA/CD, Token Ring and Token Bus and are being specified separately. In the subsequent discussion of multilevel security in local area networks, we will use IEEE 802 specification of CSMA/CD access method.

We are not concerned with the issue of whether the LAN medium is a broadband or baseband cable. That is, the physical layer (layer 1 of the ISO reference model [ISO81]) is not an issue for our design, although many aspects of the physical interface (e.g., TEMPEST) must be addressed in an implementation for secure applications. Many of the other aspects of the CSMA/CD protocol not mentioned here remain unchanged from that in the proposed IEEE 802 standard.

Figure 3 shows the format (with 48 bit address fields) of the IEEE 802 CSMA/CD packet, along with the modified version for our secure LAN. The fields of the modified packet format on the right side of this figure are interpreted as follows:

Preamble: 7 octets

> Used to allow the physical signalling circuitry to reach its steady state

Start Frame Delimiter (SFD): 1 octet

> Consists of sequence 10101011, used to indicate the start of a valid frame

Destination Subnet Number: 1 octet

> Destination local subnetwork number

Destination: 5 octets

> Address on the subnetwork of the TIU receiving the frame

Source Subnet Number: 1 octet

> Source local subnetwork number

Source: 5 octets

> Address on the subnetwork of the TIU sending the frame

Security Level: 2 octets

> Security level of the data part in the frame

Length: 2 Octets

> Indicates the number of LLC data octets in the data field

LLC Data and Pad: variable (up to some maximum) number of octets

> Data in a fully transparent form, i.e., any bit sequence is allowed. If the frame size is less than the minimum frame size then the data field is extended by appending padding bits at the end of LLC data in units of octets

Frame Check Sequence: 4 octets

Contains cyclic redundancy check (CRC) value computed over all the fields

We have subdivided the source and destination address fields into two components, to provide a two-level hierarchical address based on subnetwork number and TIU number. The other change

is the addition of a security level field at the beginning of the data fields. Note that the packet and header length is unchanged from that in the standard. The logic for processing secure LAN protocol is slightly changed from that in the standard CSMA/CD protocol to process security level field in the packet at the sender and the receiver. For example, a function of the following type will be needed in the secure LAN protocol

> **function** Recognize_Security_Level
> (level: Security_Level_Value): **Boolean**
> **begin**
> Recognize_Security_Level := {*Return true if the "level" is a member of the set of security levels associated with the receiving unit*}
> **end**; {Recognize_Security_Level}

to allow only valid packets to be received by an interface unit.

The two octets in the security level field can used, in general, to specify a very large number of security levels. One scheme [Postel81a] to use these 16 bits to specify 16 security levels is as shown below:

00000000	00000000	-	Unclassified
11110001	00110101	-	Confidential
01111000	10011010	-	EFTO
10111100	01001101	-	MMMM
01011110	00100110	-	PROG
10101111	00010011	-	Restricted
11010111	10001000	-	Secret
01101011	11000101	-	Top Secret
00110101	11100010	-	(Reserved for future use)
10011010	11110001	-	(Reserved for future use)
01001101	01111000	-	(Reserved for future use)
00100100	10111101	-	(Reserved for future use)
00010011	01011110	-	(Reserved for future use)
10001001	10101111	-	(Reserved for future use)
11000100	11010110	-	(Reserved for future use)
11100010	01101011	-	(Reserved for future use)

Of course, CSMA/CD is only a sublayer of a low-level link protocol (layer 2 of the ISO reference model), and there are higher layer protocols to be considered in any full implementation. However, our solution is oriented around implementing multilevel security at the link level, with no requirement for any particular protocols at a higher layer. This further minimizes the effect of our approach on any existing software making use of and implementing those higher layers.

Focusing on the link layer alone does have its drawbacks, however. These are seen as minor in an initial scenario where a multilevel LAN would be installed to provide a basic communications capability and also to handle existing security requirements. As the traffic load increases and the type of multilevel processing becomes more sophisticated, the TIUs and bridges on the LAN would be upgraded (in fully compatible manner) so as to provide additional services. These services require the consideration of higher-level protocols, such as

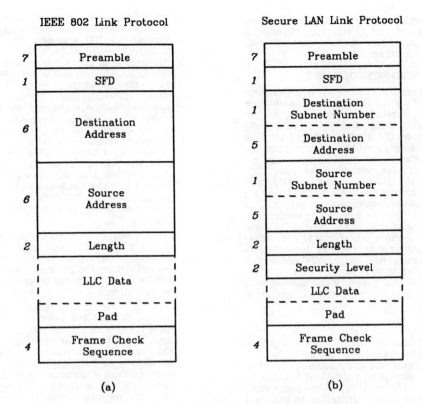

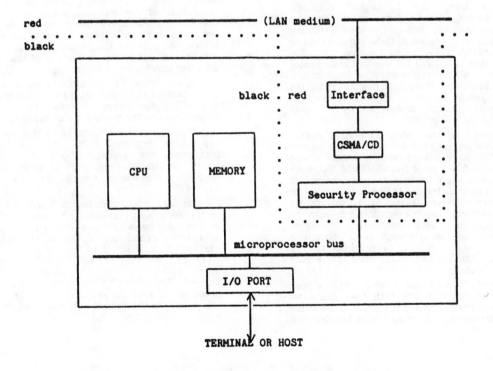

Figure 3. Local Area Network Packet Format

Figure 4. Trusted Interface Unit (TIU) Architecture

the DoD standard Transmission Control Protocol (TCP) with Internet (IP) [Postel81a, Postel81b]. Further discussion of this upgrade capability will be presented in the relevant sections.

TRUSTED INTERFACE UNIT

The TIU is responsible for enforcing the security policy based on the level(s) of its subscriber and the level of packets. TIUs come in three versions, in increasing order of complexity. Initially there would only be the need for single-level TIUs that provide the single-level type of protection for untrusted subscribers discussed earlier. Another version would provide variable-level operation. This means that the TIU is not permanently fixed to communicate at just one level, but can vary its level based on some human operator action. This type of TIU would allow, for example, a terminal to sometimes operate at one security level (to communicate with a certain set of hosts) and sometimes operate at another security level. Hosts whose levels change due to periods processing would also use a variable-level TIU. Finally, there is a multilevel TIU that properly coordinates with its terminal or host to support full multilevel operation.

Single-level TIU

The trusted interface unit shown in figure 4 allows a single-level subscriber (untrusted host or terminal) to communicate with another subscriber at the same security level, via a local network to which subscribers of several levels are connected. The TIU must be physically protected to the level of network-high, and is designed to reliably isolate the traffic at one particular security level from the traffic at all other levels.

We are using the IEEE 802 standard (CSMA/CD) physical and link layer interface on the network, and envision that off-the-shelf hardware will eventually be available, in the form of a chip or circuit board, that facilitates construction of a microcomputer-based TIU for the CSMA/CD protocol. In our security architecture we have anticipated the functions of such hardware and have made an attempt to use it to simplify the TIU implementation, though our design is by no means dependent on its availability.

The header of the CSMA/CD packet begins with a destination address, followed by the source address. The packet ends with a frame check sequence. The function of the CSMA/CD interface is to recognize valid packets received from the network and to transfer the entire packet into the TIU's memory. (We are describing the interface's function as if it were loading data into a microcomputer memory as a DMA device, although there may be variations on this approach.) When the packet has been successfully received and loaded into memory, the TIU CPU is signalled that a successful DMA transfer has occurred.

The CSMA/CD hardware is assumed to be programmed (or "burned in") with the ability to recognize one particular destination address as its own. As data arrives from the network the first few

bytes of header are examined and, if the destination is correct, the remaining data is passed through to TIU memory. If the destination is incorrect, or if a collision is detected, the rest of the packet is ignored (not passed into memory). The CSMA/CD protocol is designed so as to detect all collisions while reading the header of the packet (though this attribute is not currently specified in the standard), so that receipt of a correct destination, coupled with no collision, nearly guarantees that the remainder of the packet in memory is valid (i.e., no collision will occur) and is addressed for the current recipient. Once the packet has been read into memory, it is still possible that a frame-check error will be detected by the hardware as the last byte is read. In this case the TIU CPU is not signalled, so the data, even though now resident in memory, will be ignored.

On output to the network, a DMA transfer is initiated by the CPU and the interface handles the contention part of the protocol required to get the packet out on the network. It may also, perhaps, handle source address insertion and frame-check computation.

What is important to note is that, between the second field of the header (the source address) and the frame-check sequence, the CSMA/CD interface attaches no particular meaning to the data. For our secure local network we have added an additional field, immediately after the source address, that is the security level of the data. The secure TIU has been designed so as to totally isolate the security-relevant processing (CSMA/CD protocol handling and security field checking) from the remainder of the protocol processing, thus maximizing the flexibility of TIU functions without having to worry about verifying that remainder of the software within the TIU. This concept is particularly important if more complex protocols, such as TCP and IP, are implemented in TIUs. Of course, the security field checking mechanism and many properties of the CSMA/CD protocol handler must be verified.

In the figure we have added a security processor between the CSMA/CD interface and the rest of the TIU, so that there is a distinct trusted/untrusted separation of functions

This separation is similar to the "red/black" separation employed with crypto hardware. In fact, when the "untrusted" side is unclassified, many of the conventional physical red/black separation requirements would have to be adhered to.

On data input from the network, the function of the security processor is to look at the third field of the header, the security level, and only accept the remainder of the packet data if the security level is equal to that of the subscriber. Thus, data will only arrive in the TIU's memory if both the destination and security level are correct. On output to the network, the security processor inserts the subscriber's security level in the packet as the packet is transferred to the network from memory.

We envision the security processor to consist of hardwired logic or perhaps a single-chip computer with an on-board program. This processor has a very simple function since it only processes "good" packets, due to the outboard handling of the contention protocol by the CSMA/CD interface. Also, it need only have the throughput of the subscriber device, not that of the network, since only the subscriber's input and output need be processed. However, depending on the interface characteristics of the CSMA/CD hardware, instantaneous speed might have to be much higher.

Note that, on input from the network, security rules require that no data arrive in the memory of the TIU unless that data is of the proper level. Thus we may be forced to buffer the destination and source fields of an incoming packet within the security processor until we can be sure of the security level, instead of simply passing the fields into TIU memory "on the fly". Also, if a collision has occurred, which will always be detected during reading of the destination or source fields, we may not want to have the partially-read data in memory. Finally, there is the possibility that a packet with a frame-check error will be fully read into memory before the error is detected. There would then be a slight chance that the security level field was corrupted and that the packet should not have been accepted. The probability of this happening is extremely low, since untrusted TIU software cannot force a frame-check error to occur at will, and even if one should occur, there is little likelihood that the error will be such that both the destination and security level have precisely the required values. Furthermore, since the error is a random event, there is no way for malicious software in the TIU to modulate this type of error for covert communication. In any case, full-frame buffering in the security processor could be implemented.

The reason only single-level subscribers can be supported with the architecture outlined here is that nothing outside of the TIU CSMA/CD interface and security processor (e.g., terminals, hosts, TIU software) is trusted to maintain separation of data of different levels. This is the most common situation in today's environments.

Variable-level TIUs

A variable-level TIU is the same as a single-level TIU, except that an operator can change the level of the TIU from time to time. This is accomplished via some manual interface to the security processor (e.g., rotary switch). Procedural controls should insure that the host or terminal is appropriately sanitized when the level of the TIU is lowered. This sanitization can be accomplished automatically using a number of techniques. The variable-level TIU might also interface to special-purpose keys on a user's terminal keyboard--keys that are electrically linked to the security processor.

A more complex variable-level TIU for a terminal might allow the operator to communicate the change of security level via the normal keyboard

and screen of his terminal. This would entail, however, significantly more complex mechanisms that must be trusted. In figure 4, for example, all of the software in the TIU would have to be trusted, since that code processes keyboard input before it is seen by the security processor. Sophisticated, but well-understood, techniques to implement a logical "trusted communications path" from operator to security processor would have to be employed. Of course for a host that undergoes periods processing to handle classified data of different levels at different times, only a manual interface to the TIU security processor would be appropriate.

Multilevel TIUs

The multilevel TIU for a host or terminal is likely to contain fully trusted software. The security processor in such a TIU would only be able to limit communications to the range of levels at which the host or terminal is authorized to operate. The rest of the TIU would have to be trusted to properly identify the security level of the data to the host within that range, so that the host (which is trusted) can make the correct decisions to provide the necessary protection of the multilevel data. In terms of total functionality and complexity, a multilevel TIU is the same as a single-level TIU. The only difference is in the degree of trust given to the software and hardware in the TIU that is not in the security processor. Thus, the difficulty of building a multilevel TIU over that of a single-level TIU is dependent on software engineering techniques (e.g., verification) rather than on inherent complexity.

BRIDGE

Bridges operate strictly at the CSMA/CD protocol level. A bridge always connects exactly two subnetworks (a simplifying requirement). Its job is to pick packets from one subnetwork, check their destinations and security levels, and send them to the other subnetwork. To prevent congestion, bridges must operate at a speed fast enough to handle a reasonable load of traffic from one subnetwork to another, although multiple bridges could be used to help.

Bridge Routing Concepts

Since a subnetwork may have a number of bridges attached to it and a bridge connects two subnetworks to each other, possibility exists for multiple paths from a source to a destination at a LAN site. In such situations, a bridge might, in general, be required to decide which path to transmit a packet based on the dynamics of the load on the two subnetworks. While this may be desirable in some situations, for our bridges we will have static routing for simplicity. Therefore, suitable restrictions are needed to define only one logical path between each pair of source and destination addresses (in the presence of multiple physical paths) in the LAN. Such a unique path from a source to a destination can be ensured by requiring that only one bridge on a subnetwork can receive a packet destined for a host on a different subnetwork.

It was stated above that there is a routing table in the bridge that helps it to decide if a data packet on one subnetwork should be picked by it for broadcast into the other subnetwork. The bridge will read the destination subnetwork number in the header part of the packet and pick the packet for transmission into other subnetwork if the bridge provides logical connectivity to the destination subnetwork. This means that a bridge must store information about all the destination subnetworks that lie on logical paths through it. One convenient way of storing this information in a bridge is in the form of row vector, as shown in the example in figure 5(a), where 1 in column n means that this bridge will pick packets destined for a remote subnetwork numbered n. This structure would entail programming a different row vector into each bridge. To simplify configuration management, it may be more desirable to make the tables in all bridges identical. To accomplish this we could combine row vectors for all bridges into an MxN matrix as in the example in figure 5(b), where M is the total number of bridges and N is the number of subnetworks in the LAN.

For simplicity, the routing information in the matrix is static, i.e., it does not change with time. The design allows for future enhancements to include dynamic updating of the routing information in the bridges, but this would be at the expense of introducing considerable complexity in the trusted bridge software.

Bridge Operation

Figure 6 shows the logical operation of the bridge. Note that the destination check is made as the packet is read in from the network before it is buffered, exactly the same as is done by the CSMA/CD interface in the TIU. In the case of bridge, however, more than a single destination must be checked. The set of destinations accepted are stored in a fixed routing table that can be quickly scanned at network speeds. A two-level hierarchical addressing structure is employed to simplify this lookup and reduce the size of the table (see figure 3). Each bridge knows exactly which subnetworks it is responsible for. Thus, packets are buffered in the bridge only if they are definitely addressed to another subnetwork to which the bridge is logically linked.

The security processor in the bridge makes the appropriate security checks on the buffered packets, based only on the levels of the two subnetworks immediately adjacent to the bridge. The bridge does not check final TIU or subnetwork destinations, nor does it verify that the level of the packet is correct with respect to the source. It only checks that the received packet is labelled within the range of levels of the subnetwork from which the packet is arriving, and that that level is within the range of levels of the next subnetwork.

Outgoing packets are handled by the CSMA/CD interface from output buffers in a manner identical to outgoing packets in a TIU.

Because the bridge contains no protocol software outside of the CSMA/CD interface, and the only function it implements is a simple security level check, we see the bridge as simple enough to be fully trusted to perform its job correctly and fast enough to handle a considerable load. The buffers in the bridges smooth out temporary overloads. It is not expected that the bridges would be a bottleneck in the overall system except in times of heavy continuous traffic. For this reason the approach is recommended in environments where high traffic density is not expected in the near term. To better deal with greater traffic loads, and to provide more flexibility in addressing and routing, the bridges should provide some form of congestion control as might be implemented in a higher protocol layer such as the DoD Internet Protocol (IP). Such a change should be implemented as a future enhancement (along with corresponding changes to the TIUs to use IP) as it would significantly complicate the amount of trusted software in the bridges and TIUs.

Adding certain key aspects of IP to the bridges, in place of some portions of the CSMA/CD protocol, would allow for internet routing among the local subnetworks and through gateways to wide area networks. This means that the subnetworks would be more like separate networks and the bridges would be more like gateways. IP in the bridges and TIUs would also allow incorporation of the security level field into the header where it is specified as an option in IP, rather than usurping part of the data field of CSMA/CD. Finally, IP would allow a primitive form of congestion control—a bridge could return a control packet to a sender to turn off further transmissions due to overload in the bridge or adjoining subnetwork.

While there are many advantages to putting IP in the bridge, we do not feel at this point that the extra complexity in the TIUs and bridges is desirable in an initial configuration considering the need to trust the software. It may be very likely that an initial installation of a secure LAN would indeed require IP in the TIUs for internetworking [Skelton80], but that IP implementation would reside in the untrusted portion of the TIU and would not be interpreted by the bridges. A smooth transition to installation of IP in the bridges may involve, in part, verifying the existing IP software in the TIUs for multilevel operation.

The two half-bridges shown in figure 1 comprise a special form of bridge required when encryption is necessary between two classified subnetworks. This will be discussed further in the following section.

ENCRYPTION

In Figure 2 several locations are shown where encryption is required. At the top an encrypted line is shown between the confidential host and its TIU that resides in the secret environment. This line would probably employ conventional bit-serial link encryption at the appropriate speed (ignore, at this point the dubious need for encryption on a confidential line).

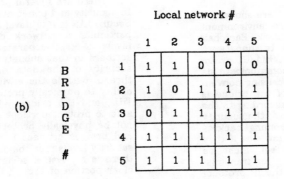

Local network #

(a)

1	2	3	4	5
1	1	0	1	0

1 (0) in column *n* means that the bridge will (not)
pick packets destined for subnetwork *n*.

Local network #

		1	2	3	4	5
B	1	1	1	0	0	0
R	2	1	0	1	1	1
I D G E	3	0	1	1	1	1
E	4	1	1	1	1	1
#	5	1	1	1	1	1

(b)

Figure 5. Fixed Routing Tables in Bridge

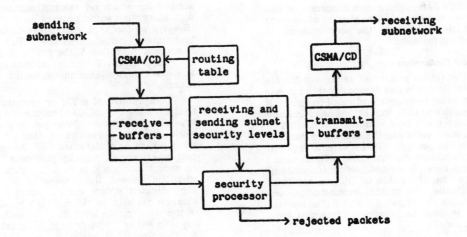

Figure 6. Functional Bridge Architecture (Half-duplex)

Another encrypted line is shown on the right side between the Top Secret subnetworks. Encryption here is employed directly between the media of the two subnetworks, without the use of a bridge. This is intended to illustrate encryption of the LAN medium where a cable may pass, for example, between two Top Secret protected buildings. We have not studied the problem of encrypting the LAN medium directly, and what affect it might have on the physical and CSMA/CD protocols. However, our design is not dependent on the ability to encrypt such media, as the subnetworks could be separate and bridges could be used instead.

Near the center of the figure 1 are shown two "split-bridges"—one in the Top Secret environment and the other on the Secret subnetwork. Each half of the bridge communicates with its subnetwork directly using the straightforward CSMA/CD protocol. The two halves of the bridge communicate via a serial line that can be encrypted using conventional means. The functionality of the bridge is allocated between the two halves according to the security requirements. For example, the security processor, which checks that incoming packets from the high side only go to the low side if they have the appropriate security level, must be located on the high side. Buffering for transmission to the low side, and part of the IP protocol handling, if implemented, could be on the low side. Note that the split bridge concept, while introduced here to deal with the encryption problem, is a general solution where two subnetworks cannot be brought into close physical proximity.

The split-bridge is considerably more complex than a single bridge, and it would not be needed in cases where encryption is not required and the media of the two subnetworks could be brought close together. A bridge between a classified subnetwork to an unclassified subnetwork would not have to be split.

LIMITATIONS AND RESTRICTIONS

The Secure LAN architecture described in this paper has a number of limitations, of varying importance depending on the environment in which the LAN is installed.

Need-to-know Protection

The architecture presented so far can handle multiple security levels and compartments but has generally ignored the control of need-to-know. If there is a requirement to implement need-to-know controls, there must be additional mechanism in each TIU to limit values of the source or destination fields in the packets. This mechanism is apt to add considerable complexity to the TIU in terms of trusted software. Need-to-know (authorization) databases can be accessible to TIUs on the local network, with the TIUs making requests for connection via these databases, but the TIU ultimately makes the decision to receive or transmit to a given subscriber.

Authentication

TIUs attached to terminals cannot verify the identity of the user—the TIUs must believe that anyone with physical access to the outboard lines on the TIU has authorization to access anything on the network within the range of security levels at which the TIU is initialized. More complex authentication mechanisms (passwords, keys, etc.) could be implemented, with external databases to assist in determining identity, but, as with need-to-know, the ultimate granter of access must be the TIU and not some external component on the LAN.

Security Threats

There are several potential problems relating to security and penetration threats. Although the Secure LAN is multilevel in the sense that, for any particular subnetwork, data of different security levels is kept separated with respect to subscribers in that subnetwork environment, overall security of the data on the subnetwork from threats outside the environment depends on the ability to physically protect the LAN medium, the TIUs, and the bridges. Link encryption may be able to protect portions of the medium that cannot be physically protected, but where the TIUs and bridges connect to the medium data of all security levels must be in the clear (red). Thus, if there is a physical security breach and a TIU or clear portion of the medium is compromised, *all* data on the subnetwork is accessible to the penetrator (including data of higher levels that the compromised TIU may not have originally passed to its subscriber). Only approaches that encrypt all data on the medium can counter such an attack.

This threat may be compounded by the fact that, because of the nature of the broadcast medium, unauthorized receipt of data by a compromised TIU or tap on the line may not be detectable (although it is probably possible to design circuitry that could detect extra taps).

A related problem is possible malfunction of the TIU resulting in receipt of data by the subscriber for which he was not authorized. End-to-end encryption would prevent such a compromise. However we feel that, through suitable engineering techniques based on the TIU architecture described in section 4, the probability of this type of failure in a TIU can be significantly reduced. The exact cost of accomplishing this is difficult to assess.

Compromise of a TIU or unauthorized access to the medium could also result in an active attack where a penetrator injects packets into the network to cause a receipt of classified data or to masquerade as a classified TIU. Numerous checks can be employed, e.g., by placing a "sensing" TIU on each subnetwork, to detect "extra" TIUs or TIUs who "lie" about their security levels. A more sophisticated active attack would be to modify existing packets on the network by altering fields in the header. We have no clear method for dealing with either active or passive attacks in general. A thorough vulnerability analysis would be required to investigate each threat, with implementation of ad hoc countermeasures for those threats deemed serious.

Security Watch Functions

Since there is no central authority granting permission for two TIUs to communicate, there is no way to remotely disable a subscriber or control access between subscribers. Authority to communicate is distributed among all the TIUs on the subnetwork. It is of course possible to add additional control functions to the TIUs to implement central authorization, disabling, auditing, etc., but these functions are only as reliable as the TIUs. Note that auditing of traffic on the LAN is possible (and fairly easy), so it would be difficult for two TIUs to carry out a covert conversation without detection by a "sensing" TIU as discussed above.

Reconfiguration

The physical subnetwork structure of the LAN is assumed to be relatively static in that it is not possible to install a subscriber of an arbitrary security level anywhere along the medium. If, in a building previously containing only a Secret subnetwork, one wanted to add a Top Secret terminal, it would be necessary to upgrade the entire subnetwork in the building to Top Secret (probably infeasible) or to link that Top Secret terminal to a TIU on the nearest Top Secret subnetwork in another building with a protected (encrypted) line (or equivalently, install new Top Secret subnetwork in the building linked to another existing Top Secret subnetwork over a bridge and protected line). Note, however, that the cost of constructing a physical Top Secret facility for a terminal will probably far outshadow the cost of the additional protected line. The cost comparison may be less obvious for adding a new Secret terminal in a previously Confidential or unclassified area.

One advantage of some LAN technology is the ability to add subscribers wherever desired (within certain physical constraints), without disruption of service. The Secure LAN retains that ability for subnetworks within a given security environment—the difficulties are experienced only when new security environments are added.

Denial of Service

Denial of service to LAN subscribers is a threat fairly easy to carry out on most LANs. Simply cutting the cable medium usually deactivates a number of subscribers. Placing random signals or some arbitrary voltage on the medium will usually deactivate all subscribers, and could even cause physical damage to TIUs. Simple overloading could be caused by a single TIU. This threat is one which is difficult to prevent completely, but our particular architecture can limit the extent of damage due to a denial of service attack. Essentially, the bridges provide a means for electrically isolating a portion of the subnetwork so that random signals cannot pass from one subnetwork to the other. Thus, there is no danger that an attack on an unclassified unprotected subnetwork, bridged to a TS network, would cause any damage to the TS

communications as long as the bridge (which is in the TS environment) remains protected and fault-tolerant to a certain extent. The subnetwork structure can even be set up with denial of service threats in mind.

While we present "denial of service" as a "problem" here because we cannot prevent it completely, our subnetwork architecture solves the problem better than other approaches using single-network bus-oriented structures (including end-to-end encryption).

CONCLUSION

This secure local area network architecture presented here is one of several means by which multilevel data on a local network can be protected. This design makes maximum use of well-understood security concepts, existing protocols, and off-the-shelf hardware. In order to assist certification for multilevel operation, a minimal amount of trusted software or firmware is required. The TIU design provides a basic trusted multilevel service that allows for implementing in additional TIU software a wide range of applications. This additional software need not be certified or verified.

The author is grateful to Mr. Bob Pollack for help in getting this paper ready for the conference proceedings. This paper is an improved and extended version of an earlier paper by the author [Sidhu82a]. Further details of this design can be found in [Sidhu82b, Sidhu83].

REFERENCES

[Clark78], Clark, D. D., Pogran, K. T., and Reed, D. P., "An Introduction to Local Area Networks," *Proc. IEEE*, Vol. 66, No. 11, pp. 1497-1517, November 1978.

[DoD72], Department of Defense Directive, DoD 5200.28 "Security Requirements for Automatic Data Processing (ADP) Systems," December 18, 1972.

[Ethernet80], The Ethernet: A Local Area Network Specification, Version 1.0, DEC, INTEL, XEROX, September 30, 1980.

[IEEE82a], IEEE Project 802, Local Area Network Standards, Draft IEEE Standard 802.3, CSMA/CD Access Method and Physical Layer Specifications, IEEE Computer Society, December, 1982.

[IEEE82b], IEEE Project 802, Local Area Network Standards, Draft IEEE Standard 802.2, Logical Link Control, (Draft D), IEEE Computer Society, November, 1982.

[ISO81], ISO/TC97/SC16, "Data Processing—Open Systems Interconnection—Basic Reference Model," Computer Networks, Vol. 5, 1981, pp. 81-118.

[Postel81a], Postel, J. (ed.), "DoD Standard Internet Protocol," Defense Advanced Research Projects Agency, 1981.

[Postel81b], Postel, J. (ed.), "DoD Standard Transmission Control Protocol," Defense Advanced Research Projects Agency, 1981.

[Sidhu82a], Sidhu, D. P., "A Local Area Network Design for Military Applications," *Proc. 7th Conf. on Local Area Networks*, Minneapolis, MN (October 11-13, 1982).

[Sidhu82b], Sidhu, D. P., and Gasser, M., "Design for a Multilevel Secure Local Area Network," MITRE Corp. Report, MTR-8702, (1982).

[Sidhu83], Sidhu, D. P., "Security in Local Area Networks," In preparation (1983).

[Skelton80], Skelton, A. P., Nabielsky, J., and Holmgren, S. F., "FY80 Final Report: Cable Bus Application in Command Centers," MTR-80W00319, The MITRE Corporation, McLean, VA, December 1980.

A Resource Sharing System for Personal Computers in a LAN: Concepts, Design, and Experience

RITA C. SUMMERS, MEMBER, IEEE

Abstract—RM is an experimental prototype that supports the use of distributed services by personal computers in a LAN. Using a service-request model, RM allows any PC on the LAN to offer and use services, which can be user-written or off-the-shelf applications. A user can start several activities that proceed concurrently and that use services offered by different machines. Program interfaces are provided for the development of distributed applications. Remote execution is supported within the service-request framework. The paper considers issues in resource sharing and discusses the choices that were made for RM. It provides an overview of RM concepts, design, and implementation, and reviews experience using the system.

Index Terms—Distributed services, personal-computer LAN's, remote execution, resource sharing, service-request models.

I. INTRODUCTION

THE RM system described in this paper supports the use of distributed services by personal computers in a LAN. Using a service-request model, RM allows any PC on the LAN to offer and use services, which can be user-written or off-the-shelf applications. It supports concurrent activities for the user, and provides program interfaces for the development of distributed applications. Remote execution is supported within the service-request framework. Existing software products can be used as services.

RM is designed to be simple to install and to use. An experimental prototype runs on IBM PC's, XT's, or AT's, without any special software or hardware (beyond the LAN connection). The prototype uses PC DOS [7] and the PC Network LAN [23]. The concepts and design apply to other hardware and to heterogeneous networks.

In contrast to other software for PC's in LAN's, where the emphasis is on file sharing, the emphasis in RM is on services, which can provide system or application function. The concepts of *service* and *service request* are reflected in the user interface, the application interface, and the internal structure. The goal is to apply these concepts in a coherent way, but still keep the prototype appropriate in scope and usability for personal computers and a simple PC operating system. Experience with the prototype indicates that the goal has been met.

The paper provides an overview of RM and considers conceptual and practical issues in resource sharing. Sec-

tion II begins with a discussion of the service-request approach for sharing, contrasting it with other approaches, then discusses alternative service-request models and describes the specific concepts and terms used in RM. The functions provided are described in Section III, and the design and implementation in Section IV. Section V describes model applications and reviews experience with the system. A final section discusses results of the project.

II. SERVICE REQUESTS FOR RESOURCE SHARING

A. Alternative Approaches to LAN Resource Sharing

Resource sharing in a LAN is based typically on either a *service-request* model or a *distributed file system* (*DFS*) model. Many software products for PC's in LAN's are built on the DFS model (for example PC LAN Program [11]).[1] Systems for high-performance workstations (for example Andrew [19]) have also chosen the DFS model as the basic paradigm for sharing. Distributed operating systems, such as LOCUS [24], go beyond distributed files to distributed processes and other distributed OS objects. When we look to larger, more dispersed systems, however, we see a growing consensus in favor of the service-request model [9].

For LAN's as well, the service-request approach has advantages over the DFS approach. Owners of data may be unwilling to trust direct sharing [6], preferring to provide services that allow specialized (and constrained) uses of the data. It makes sense for applications requiring special resources (such as hardware, programs, or databases) to run on *service machines*, freeing each user's *personal machine* for the highly interactive work that is best done close to the user. Then, administrative control of a resource corresponds to physical access to the service machine. Finally, services provided by a machine of one type of hardware and operating system can be used from a machine of a different type, and the heterogeneous machines can cooperate in executing applications. The DFS approach is attractive as an external interface because single-computer applications can be moved onto a network easily. In other words, DFS systems provide *network transparency*. Transparency is provided by supporting in a distributed environment local concepts such as file I/O [24] or operating system call [20]. The underlying mechanism for distribution, on the other hand, is typically a

Manuscript received September 15, 1986.

The author is with IBM Los Angeles Scientific Center, Los Angeles, CA 90025.

IEEE Log Number 8714953.

---

[1] The *PC Network LAN* is hardware and firmware; the *PC LAN Program* is software that provides a DFS on that or other hardware.

form of service request, such as a *remote procedure call* [3]. The supporting (but largely hidden) service-request concept is remote procedure call in Andrew, server-redirector protocol in the PC LAN Program [12], remote service call in LOCUS [34]. Service requests made by users or applications are handled differently. In LOCUS, they are done by remote tasking [5]. In Andrew, a request file is deposited in a directory that by convention contains service requests. Thus a user-level service request is implemented on top of the DFS, which in turn uses a remote procedure call.

Service requests are needed not only to support distributed files and other distributed OS function, but also at the application level. Some systems formalize service requests in programming languages (Argus [16], Emerald [4]), language interfaces (Matchmaker [13] and interfaces for OSI [14]), or system interfaces (IBM's Advanced Program-to-Program Communication [10]).

Systems supporting *remote execution* allow the user to run a program at a remote machine, or run a program in a location-transparent way. LOCUS [5] is an example of location-transparent execution on host systems, and the V-system [32] allows workstations to do remote execution. RM also provides remote execution function—by means of service requests. The PC LAN Program [11] can be used with RM to provide a DFS.[2] For RM, the service-request model shapes the user and program interfaces, as well as the internal design. RM differs from systems like LOCUS and the V-system in this emphasis and in the level at which distribution occurs. The basic operating system entities are *not* distributed; distribution is at the service-request level, which in RM is a higher level.

RM was influenced by IBM's VM (virtual machine) system [33], which inspired the name RM (for *Real Machines* and *Resource-sharing Machines*). In VM, applications are shared in two ways. Either they are executed on the user's virtual machine, by means of shared executable files, or they are executed on a (virtual) service machine. VM service machines very effectively support office systems, bulletin boards, tools delivery, and many other applications. Putting a service on a virtual or real service machine encapsulates its function and provides a controlled environment for its execution. In a LAN, application sharing through file sharing has the added cost of moving the files across the LAN, but it may lead to better LAN system performance because personal machines carry more of the computing load. The view here, however, is that service machines are relatively low-cost and can be replicated, so that execution on a personal machine is not *a priori* preferred.

B. Issues for Models of Service Requests

Given a service-request model, issues remain as to the features of the model. Requests could be passed informally, for example, using any form of interprocess communication. The choice in RM and other systems is to define explicit roles for the client and server of a request.

Additional issues are whether a virtual circuit is established between client and server, and (if not) whether the request is synchronous. The remote procedure call does not set up a virtual circuit and is usually synchronous; that is, the client is blocked until the request completes. Asynchronous remote procedure call is possible as well; the client can continue to execute and check at a later time for completion. Asynchronous remote procedure call is used in the TABS distributed transaction facility [28] and the Remote Service Call facility [27]. RM provides a virtual circuit for the duration of the request. A request can also be viewed as a unit of work, with some of the characteristics of a transaction, including authorization and accounting. An RM request is a unit of work, but this aspect is not fully developed.

A further choice has to do with the interface to requests. Requests can be invisible to users and applications, serving only as a mechanism to support transparent distribution of data and function. In RM, requests are also exposed to users and applications, providing high-level concurrency that can be supported by operating systems with different models of interprocess communication.

C. Definition of Terms

This section describes the specific concepts used in RM and introduces the terms used in the paper. The computing environment for RM consists of a set of personal computers connected on a LAN. Some of the machines offer *services* that can be used by other machines. Each *personal machine* (*PM*) provides the usual personal computer environment, plus access to services. A *service* is an application or a system function that is offered for use through service requests. Text processing, database, mail, and printing facilities are all examples of possible services.

Any machine on the LAN can use services. A machine that offers a service is called a *service machine* (*SM*). A *request* is the unit of work that starts when a service is invoked. The same SM can provide more than one service, and can handle multiple service requests at a time, even for different services. Each service is provided by one or more *server processes* at the SM that offers the service. (RM multitasking is described in a later section.) The process providing a service is called a *server* of that service. A program not written for the RM environment may be defined as a *standard service*. This feature allows existing software products (which cannot be modified) to become services.[3]

To use a service, the user either invokes the service directly or runs a program that invokes the service. In both cases, a request for the service is started. The process that invokes the service is called the *client* of the request. The locations of the client and server do not affect the way the requests are made or handled. The client process is not blocked during the carrying out of the request. It therefore may become the client of several requests at once. While handling a request for its own ser-

---

[2]RM itself does not use the PC LAN Program.

[3]See [18] for a discussion of the problem of installing pre-existing tools.

vice, a server may invoke other services, thus becoming a client for one or more subsidiary requests. A server of a service handles one request at a time. A service machine, on the other hand, may handle multiple requests at a time, for the same service or for different services, by means of multiple servers.

An *action* starts when a user directly invokes a service; the action includes the initial request and any subsidiary requests. An action is the unit of work seen by the user, whereas a request is the more elementary system unit of work. The action concept captures the user's view of concurrency—doing several chores at once.

The RM request is both a unit of work and a virtual circuit between client and server. This model is close to that of the R* distributed database system [15], which uses a virtual circuit that persists for a series of remote procedure calls. An R* computation is viewed as a tree of processes. An RM action is a tree of *requests*, since a process may exist before and after the request and may handle multiple requests serially. A similar model is used by the Gutenberg system [25].

Other systems allow one server process to handle multiple requests concurrently. Sometimes, as in Eden [2], this choice is based on the overhead of process creation in the underlying operating system. Processes in RM have relatively low cost. One request per server at a time makes services easier to write, since they need not multiplex themselves among multiple requests. RM provides features (locking, for example) that allow the multiple servers of a service to coordinate their work. Other systems that provide multiple server processes are TABS [28] and the Remote Service Call facility [27]. Both references and also [17] provide further arguments in favor of such a structure.

III. RM FUNCTIONS

A. Functions for the User

The RM user is provided with local and remote actions, action concurrency, and an unmodified view of DOS. The user sees one instance of the DOS command interpreter plus multiple actions, which may involve any combination of local and remote services. The user thus sees two kinds of work: actions, and commands carried out by DOS.[4]

After starting RM, the user may continue to use DOS in the usual way. If, on the other hand, the user chooses to work with actions, pressing a *hot-key* causes the main RM screen to be displayed. The user can then see the status of current actions, start an action, cancel an action, or switch to an action or to DOS. From another screen the user can see what services are active at other machines. From this screen the user can assign nicknames to services and can save the currently defined nicknames and their correspondences (SM and service name as defined at

the SM) in a directory for use by RM. The SM user can: define services; activate and deactivate services, thus controlling their availability for requests; see what services are active and what requests they are handling, and cancel requests.

B. Functions for Application Programs

Using Services: To invoke a service, a program issues a **SendRequest** call. If the call is successful a *request ID* is returned. A process may issue any number of **SendRequest** calls, for the same service or for different services. Each **SendRequest** starts a new request. Some servers need only the initial *request message* from **SendRequest,** while other servers need further exchange of messages. If messages are needed, the client and the server can communicate symmetrically by **Send** and **Receive.** RM uses a nonblocking **Send** and a blocking, unconditional **Receive.** A **MessageAvailable** function can be used to determine (without blocking) if a message is available to be received for a specified request. The client can end its own participation in the request by issuing **LeaveRequest,** and it can issue **CancelRequest** to instruct the server to end the request. The equivalent of a remote procedure call can be achieved by a **SendRequest** followed immediately by a **Receive** for the reply.

Providing Services: To start handling a request, a process issues a **ReceiveRequest.** Since the process is known to RM as a server of a specific service, the call does not specify a service name. **ReceiveRequest** returns the request-message and a request ID. The server of a standard service (one not written for the RM environment) does not explicitly receive requests. When a standard server begins execution, a request has already been received, and the request message is available as parameters, just as if the program had been invoked by a local user. A server ends its work on a request by issuing **EndRequest,** which also asks the client to end its participation in the request.

RM Calls and Messages: Programs communicate with RM via *RM calls* (**SendRequest,** for example). Language-specific interface routines transform the call parameters into a language-independent format and then transfer control to RM via an interrupt. A message consists of a set of program variables, which may be scattered in memory. To send a message, the program calls interface routines to define the message, then specifies the message in a **Send.** RM extracts the field data from the field variables. Similarly, to receive a message, the program specifies a message in a **Receive,** and RM stores the message data into the variables. RM does not verify that the sender and receiver of a message supply compatible message definitions, but does prevent the receipt of a field that exceeds the size of the receiving variable. Messages as long as 32K are supported.

Example Programs: Fig. 1 shows an example of a client program, and Fig. 2 shows the corresponding server. Fig. 3 shows code common to the client and server.

---

[4]Ideally, the user would see only one kind—actions. Since RM runs alongside DOS, however, many local activities do not involve services, and only those that do are considered actions.

```
(*$TITLE: 'Sample Client Program'*)
(*include the interfaces needed for an RM application*)
(*$INCLUDE:'RMINTS.PAS'*)

PROGRAM SAMP2CL ( INPUT, OUTPUT ) ;
(*Include USES statments*)
(*$INCLUDE:'RMUSES.PAS'*)
(*Include code common to client program and service program*)
(*$INCLUDE:'sample2.INC'*)


begin

   DefineMessages;
   with RequestMsgData do begin
       param1 := 'parameter 1' ;
       param2 := 2;
       param3 := true;
   end;

   SendRequest ( 'H:SAMPLE2', RequestMsg, reqid, RC);

   if RC = 0 then begin (*normal case*)
       writeln('Request sent');
       Receive (ReplyMsg,ReqId,RC);
       if ReplyMsgData.code = 0
           then writeln('request complete')
           else writeln('request failed ', ReplyMsgData.error,
                        ' ',ReplyMsgData.code ) ;
   end (*SendRequest normal*)

   else writeln('request failed ', RC ) ;

end.
```

Fig. 1. Sample client program.

```
(*$linesize:132,$pagesize:60*)
(*$TITLE: 'Sample RM Service Program'*)
(*$include:'RMINTS.PAS'*)

PROGRAM SERVICE2 ( INPUT, OUTPUT ) ;
(*$include:'RMUSES.PAS'*)

(*include code used by both client and server*)
(*$include:'sample2.INC'*)


procedure HandleRequest;

begin
   ReplyMsgData.code :=  0;
   (*Code to handle the request goes here; it would set reply
    message fields to indicate how the request completed *)
end;


begin  (* main program*)
   DefineMessages;
   ReceiveRequest(RequestMsg,ReqID,RC);
   if RC = 0
   then begin (*normal case*)
       HandleRequest;
       Send (ReplyMsg,ReqId,RC);
   end (*ReceiveRequest normal*)
   (*note that ending the program ends the request*)
END.
```

Fig. 2. Sample service program.

```
(*Code common to SAMPLE2 client and service programs*)
type
   ErrorType = (error1, error2, error3);
   SampleRequestType = record
                       param1: lstring(20);
                       param2: integer;
                       param3: boolean;
                       end;
   ReplyMsgType = record
                       Error:ErrorType;
                       Code:integer;
                       end;

var
   RC: ReturnCode ;
   ReqID : ReqIDType ;
   serv : ServiceSpecType ;
   RequestMsg, ReplyMsg : MsgType ;
   RequestMsgField,ReplyMsgField : FieldType ;
   RequestMsgData : SampleRequestType;
   ReplyMsgData: ReplyMsgType;


procedure DefineMessages;
begin
   RequestMsgField := ADS RequestMsgData ;
   ReplyMsgField := ADS ReplyMsgData ;
   DefineMsg ( RequestMsg, 1) ;
   DefineMsg ( ReplyMsg, 1 ) ;
   DefineField ( RequestMsg, 1, RequestMsgField, sizeof(RequestMsgData) ) ;
   DefineField ( ReplyMsg, 1, ReplyMsgField, sizeof (ReplyMsgData) ) ;
end;
```

Fig. 3. Code common to sample client and service programs.

Fig. 4 represents RM in execution at one machine. Multiple processes execute concurrently. Some are *application processes* that execute user programs or service programs, and some are *system processes* that execute the RM program. RM is written in Pascal [21]. In general, the procedures of RM are executed by the invoking process. An RM call moves the process from its own language environment to the Pascal environment of RM. A process also enters RM by issuing a DOS interrupt that RM intercepts. This structure, where system functions are executed by both application and system processes, can be contrasted with a structure where all system work is done by *manager* system processes. RM uses four system processes—for network control, for aspects of request management, and to manage actions. The RM structure allows the implementer of each component to choose the appropriate point to pass work to another process. It also allows application processes to be blocked during their execution of system functions, without preventing other processes from executing the same functions. (An empirical study suggests that software is less complex and performance better when the manager structure is not used [22].)

The components of RM correspond quite directly to the concepts. The main components, shown in simplified form in Fig. 5, are introduced here and are described in later sections. The *kernel* supports all other components by providing operating system features that are useful for resource sharing. The *Request component* supports the application program interface and in general manages requests. The *Service component* maintains all objects related to services, such as service definitions and lists of active services. The *Network component* sends messages

IV. DESIGN AND IMPLEMENTATION

This section explains how RM is structured and describes the main components.

RM's relation to DOS is that of an application program. RM does not duplicate DOS function or modify DOS in any way, but it does provide some functions lacking from DOS (multitasking, for example). Several DOS interrupts are taken over during RM initialization, to allow RM to gain control as needed.

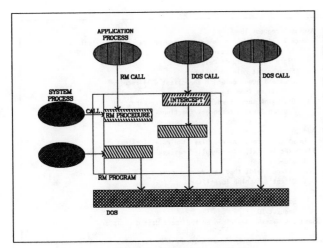

Fig. 4. RM in execution on one machine.

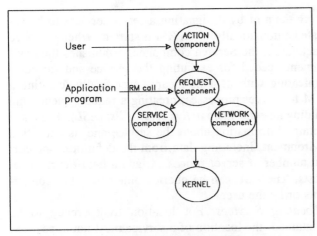

Fig. 5. Main components of RM.

between machines, using the *NETBIOS* interface provided by the PC Network LAN. The *Action component* provides the user's interface to services, allowing the user to start and control actions. More detail can be found in [1] and [31].

A. The RM Kernel

Limited multitasking, tailored to the needs of the prototype, is provided by the kernel. It includes process management, synchronization, and memory management enhancements. Kernel objects (such as processes, queues, and locks) are strictly local to a machine. Kernel functions run to completion without process switching. Only a few of the kernel functions are exposed to applications; most are used only by other components of RM.

Process Management: A process is created dynamically from a *process model (PRM)* that contains the specifications for the process. A PRM is built for each active service, and the processes created from the PRM become servers of that service. When a request arrives, and no server is available, a server process is created. **Block** and **unblock** functions support synchronization. A **pause** function allows a process to leave execution for a specified time.

Process scheduling is by process priority, which derives from the PRM and does not change. The priority of system processes can be set for each machine individually. Process switching is driven by DOS interrupts, and by **block, unblock,** and **pause.** No process switching occurs while the current process is in DOS (since DOS is not assumed to be reentrant) or in the kernel (since kernel data is designed for single access). A process switch typically occurs when a process reads the keyboard, and no character is available. The restriction on process switching in DOS limits performance, because it imposes a delay between readying and dispatching a process. An implementation that assumed more about DOS could eliminate this restriction.

Since multiple processes execute a single Pascal program, each process must have its own stack. RM provides multiple stacks [8] without modifying Pascal, but with some manipulation of internal Pascal variables. Process switching and entering RM involve changing to the process-specific stack.

Memory Management: The memory of the PC is managed partly by DOS (with RM monitoring) and partly by RM, with the amount managed by RM specified for each machine. Two kinds of elements are allocated by RM: *descriptors* and *spaces*. Descriptors are standard data structures used by RM itself (the PRM for example) and are allocated using Pascal heap allocation with RM monitoring to detect error conditions and to ensure single access. Spaces serve as the elements of *queues* and are used for messages passed by **Send** and **Receive.** RM preprocesses calls to DOS memory management to ensure that a program does not exceed the memory usage specified in its service definition.[5]

Synchronization: RM provides both synchronization of access to shared objects and synchronization of operations. *Read and write locks* [31] control access to shared objects, and *queues* synchronize operations and pass information between processes. A process is blocked if a queue is empty when the process attempts to **dequeue** from it. The process is unblocked after another process issues an **enqueue** for the queue. Queuing is either FIFO or by priority, as specified when the queue is created. There are two kinds of queues: *request queues* and *message queues*. A request queue is associated with a PRM, and so with a specific service. A **SendRequest** causes a message to be enqueued on the service's request queue, and a **ReceiveRequest** dequeues the message. The arrival of a request on the queue can trigger the creation of a new server process, if the maximum number would not then be exceeded. A message queue is associated with a single process, and is used for messages to the process from its request partner. A message is a space passed from the enqueuing process through a queue to the dequeuing process. The space is not copied; rather a pointer to the space is passed.

---

[5]Invocations of programs not defined as services are treated as requests for an "ANY-PROGRAM" service, and its definition is used to set memory limits.

Block and **unblock** are used only in the implementation of locks and queues. Other components of the system use the more structured and safer facilities of locks, queues, and service requests.

B. Request Component

The Request component at a machine manages all requests whose clients or servers are at that machine. At the client machine, a new request is given a unique request ID that includes the client machine identifier (an integer). Each request involves a pair of message queues and a pair of *request descriptors*—one each for the client and for the server. The state of a request is thus represented in data structures that may be distributed between two machines. When one of the request partners needs to change the request state, it modifies its own data structures and asks its partner to modify the partner's corresponding structures. Each machine also maintains a table of all requests of its servers and a table of all requests of its clients. The tables associate request descriptors with request identifiers. Any error detected is reflected in the *request status* field of the request descriptor, and most errors cause any subsequent calls referring to the request to fail, with a return code indicating the cause. Fig. 6 shows the steps involved in carrying out a normal **SendRequest.**

Underlying the request protocol as seen by applications is a lower-level mechanism enabling pairs of processes to communicate over a channel consisting of a pair of message queues, possibly at different machines. Such a channel is created for each request and is used to exchange both messages sent by application programs and protocol messages originating in the Request component itself. Since these messages contain different numbers of variables of different types, a message space is constructed by repeatedly calling a procedure that adds one variable to the space, and then building an index that describes the layout of the space. Local and remote messages are treated exactly the same, except that a local message goes on the partner's message queue, whereas a remote message goes on the queue of the Network component. Procedures of the Request component in general run on the thread of the application process that uses the request interface, but the component also includes a *message distribution process*. It is driven by a *message distribution queue* of messages received from other machines, and it enqueues them on the appropriate request and message queues.

C. Service Component

Defining Services: To turn an application into a service, the user provides information about the way the application behaves as a service, such as the maximum number of server processes to be created, the priority of the service, the request handling policy, and the memory requirements. The service component provides functions to create, modify, or remove these *service definitions*.

Activating and Deactivating Services: The user at a service machine controls the moment-to-moment availability of services defined at that SM, by explicitly *acti-*

```
Assign a request ID
Create a client request descriptor and put request in client table
Fill in request descriptor
    Place request ID in descriptor
    Set request role to "client"
    Create a queue on which the client will receive
        messages from the server
    Determine service machine and service name,
        using Service component functions
    Indicate that server has not been heard from yet
Add this request to the list of requests
    in which current process plays the role of client
Place the initial, user-supplied message in the message space
    data descriptor
Add message fields that server must have
    Client's machine identifier
    Service name used by client
    Effective service name
    Request ID
Send the message described by the space data descriptor
```

Fig. 6. Steps in carrying out a **SendRequest.**

vating them or by designating a set of services to be activated automatically when RM is started. When a service is activated, the Service component establishes the environment needed for executing the service and for communicating with it. This means, specifically, creating a PRM for server processes, creating a request queue, and building an entry in an *active service list* (*ASL*). The entry contains information about the service and its execution environment, including data from the definition, the current number of server processes, and a list of current requests. The ASL can be queried either by other components or by the user.

Locating Services: For location transparency to be maintained, the location of a service must not appear explicitly in a program. In principle, RM could use a centralized or distributed name service, but the simpler method chosen uses a client-machine directory (controlled by the user, as described in Section III) to find a service's location and *defined name*. The name used in the application program is converted using this directory.

D. Network Component

The Network component transmits messages between machines. These may be requests, messages sent via **Send,** or protocol messages generated by the Request component. The Network component provides a convenient, LAN-independent interface that hides NETBIOS complexities, such as interrupt handling.[6] It includes Send and Receive components, which operate independently.

Design Considerations: The PC Network LAN can transmit either a *datagram* or a *message*. In order to transmit a message, a *session* must first be established. A session provides a virtual circuit between two machines. RM uses messages, primarily because the sender of a message is notified whether it is properly delivered. Note, however, that a large "reliable datagram" would have sufficed. A session is set up when one machine executes a CALL, and the other side has previously executed a cor-

[6]An earlier version of RM used the Corvus Omninet. The Network component for PC Network supports the same interface.

responding LISTEN.[7] Message transmission is requested by a SEND and occurs if a corresponding RECEIVE is executed. To terminate the session, both sides HANG UP. NETBIOS commands refer to a *network name*. For an RM machine this name contains the RM machine ID and a protocol ID that distinguishes RM messages from others. RM accepts a CALL only from a machine whose name has the RM protocol ID. RM can thus coexist on a machine with other programs that use the network adapter. It is desirable to retain as few names and sessions as possible, as they take up adapter memory which could be used for buffering data or for additional sessions. Since a session closely resembles an RM request, consideration was given to using a session for each request. The decision was to instead start and end sessions as needed, thus reducing the use of adapter memory.

The size of a message is determined before the actual receipt, so that RM can allocate the smallest space needed. Since the NETBIOS allows a message to be received in two parts, the size is placed in a header that is received first.

NETBIOS provides WAIT and NO WAIT options for its commands. Since the WAIT option ties up the PC until the command completes, it is unsuitable for a concurrent environment. With the NO WAIT option, an interrupt occurs on completion of the command. The Network component therefore does some of its work under interrupt. Certain kernel functions—**enqueue, AllocateSpace,** and **FreeSpace,** for example—can be used under interrupt, with the interrupt routine acting on behalf of some process.

Message Transmission: A message is sent to another machine by calling the Network component, and specifying the destination machine ID and the space containing the message. (Currently, only the Request component uses this call.) A header is built, and the space is enqueued on the *message transmission queue*, which drives the *Send system process*. Multiple messages can be transmitted concurrently, but only one message at a time to any one machine. In a given machine, sending and receiving are completely independent, but the Send component in one machine cooperates with the Receive component in another.

When machine A has a message to send to machine B, it first establishes a session with B, then issues a SEND. The message header is marked to indicate whether there is another message for B in the message transmission queue. If SEND completes successfully, the message space is freed. The session is ended if there is no other message for B, or the Send process sends another message to B when one is dequeued.

The Receive component in machine B is initialized by a LISTEN, set to respond to a CALL to any name. When the LISTEN completes, a message is received in two steps. First the header is received to learn the message size. A space is allocated and a RECEIVE is then issued for the body of the message. The received message is put into the message distribution queue. If the header indicates that machine A will send another message, another RECEIVE is issued. If not, the session is ended and a LISTEN is issued, making machine B ready to receive another CALL.

Communication Layers: It can be seen that RM uses a layered structure for communication among processes and among machines. At the highest level, the Request component provides messages between client and server. The next level supports the sending of a structured *message space* between request partners. This in turn is supported by queues and (where the partners are on different machines) by the Network component and the NETBIOS. Fig. 7 shows one machine's handling of remote messages.

E. Action Component

The user's interface to services and to DOS is provided by the Action component, which consists of three subcomponents: *Action Manager, Screen Manager,* and *Remote Interaction Facility* (*RIF*).

Action Manager: The main issue in the design of the Action component is how to represent the user in the general scheme of service requests. The goal is for the user to play the role of client and thus communicate directly with the servers that carry out actions. The approach chosen is to use a system process, the Action Manager, which acts as a client on behalf of the user. As such, it invokes services and exchanges messages with servers, which may be at other machines. In addition to acting as client for each action, the Action Manager controls the sharing of the keyboard and display among actions, interprets user commands to RM, and controls the display of screens.

When the user starts an action A_1, the Action Manager issues a **SendRequest** for the specified service, thus setting up a virtual circuit with the server and creating a message queue on which all messages for A_1 will appear. The messages are received and interpreted by the Action Manager when the user switches to A_1.

The DOS command interpreter is treated as a single action that uses a predefined **Command** service. The user always starts with one action—**Command**—which is automatically started. This action behaves like any other, and can be terminated and restarted. The **Command** action corresponds to an instance of the *shell* in UNIX® [26].

Screen Manager: The Screen Manager maintains screen definitions, displays *screens*, and collects the user's inputs. A screen consists of constant information, input fields, and output fields; it also maps input and output fields to corresponding variables. A **CollectFields** function assigns the values of the input fields to the corresponding variables, displays in each output field the value of its variable, and assigns to an **ExitMode** variable the

---

[7]NETBIOS commands are capitalized here to distinguish them from RM operations.

®UNIX is a registered trademark of AT&T Bell Laboratories.

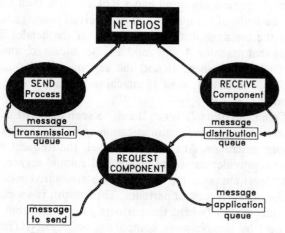

Fig. 7. Flow of network messages at one machine.

	Pascal	Assembler
Kernel	2900	900
Request component	2500	
Service component	1800	
Program management	400	
Action component	2000	900
Program interface facilities	800	
Network component	900	100
Interrupt intercepts		1300
Miscellaneous	800	
Required utilities	1400	
TOTAL	13500	3200

Fig. 8. Lines of code for main components.

value of the function key pressed by the user. This value then determines what processing is performed.

Remote Interaction Facility: A service written for RM can run at a service machine and still converse with the user at a PM (via messages to the PM's Action Manager). DOS applications, in contrast, are written to interact through standard I/O devices, typically the keyboard and display. The RIF allows such an application to interact with its user at another machine.

The first step is to gain control of the I/O operation initiated by the server. Calls to DOS for standard I/O are intercepted, and information about the I/O operation is sent to an agent at the PM, using service requests. As described earlier, each action starts a request whose client is the Action Manager at the PM and whose server is the application at the SM. The intercept routine (running on the thread of the server process) uses this request to communicate with the Action Manager, which serves as the agent. At the PM the Action Manager carries out the same I/O function.[8] It then sends any input data to the SM, again using the request circuit.

The RIF is a limited implementation. For example, it does not support the many full-screen applications that write directly into the display buffer of the PC, rather than calling DOS. However, applications such as compilers and assemblers can be supported, as can any program that does its I/O through standard files.

The method of the RIF can be compared with the remote procedure call (RPC) implementation described by Birrell and Nelson [3]. Their *user-stubs* build packets and ask the communication protocol for transmission to the remote machine, where they are passed to the *server-stubs*, which unpack the packets for the server. The RIF provides the stubs to transform local I/O into remote I/O, using the RM request circuit as equivalent of the RPC communication protocol.

----

[8]For performance reasons, the I/O function is not always strictly the same as the one issued by the server.

F. Implementation Measurements

RM consists of about 13 500 lines of Pascal and 3 200 lines of assembler code. Fig. 8 shows the lines of code for the main components. Most of RM is in one resident module, which requires about 170K bytes of storage for code and data. To this must be added the memory set aside for space allocation. Some functions are implemented as *RM utilities* that are loaded when needed. (An RM utility is a service that uses internal RM function.) Memory requirements could be reduced considerably by making other functions nonresident (with some loss of responsiveness), by producing different configurations for PM's and SM's (with some loss of function) and by improvements to the software.

On a PC-AT, the time for a "null" local service request, measured from **SendRequest** to receipt of the reply message, is about 0.1 seconds. A corresponding remote request takes about 0.5 seconds, with the LAN not otherwise used. Once a request has been started, sending a message and receiving a reply takes 0.05 seconds (local) and 0.25 seconds (remote). Since these times are small in relation to the time needed for a typical service function, performance appears very good to the user. Almost no performance tuning has yet been done, and path lengths could be reduced substantially.

V. Experience Using RM

This section describes some model applications and the use of RM to support project development work. A network of 12 machines was available, with three largely devoted to SM and file server function. One to three users were active at a time.

A. File Copy

The design of a file copy utility illustrates the flexibility of RM. Three machines can be involved: the PM whose user starts the copy, the source, and the destination. The PM can be the source or destination or neither (but not both). Two programs are used: RMCOPY at the PM and source, and RMCOPYS at the destination. RMCOPY runs as a DOS command at the PM and also as a service at the source. When RMCOPY is invoked locally it either invokes RMCOPY at the source and then terminates, or (if the machine *is* the source) invokes RMCOPYS at the destination, then transfers the file by repeated **Send** calls. RMCOPYS receives the file by repeated **Receive**s. If RMCOPY was invoked remotely, it invokes RMCOPYS at the destination, then transfers the file. A user can prevent copying to or from the PM by simply not activating RMCOPYS or RMCOPY. File copy supports the use of RM without a DFS, since data can be moved to the site of a service.

A file of 40K bytes was transferred in about 6 seconds, and one of 100K bytes in about 12 seconds, using a message size of 32K, with the LAN unused by other machines. The times are 1.5–2 times greater than corresponding times for the PC LAN Program, using the same buffer size. The results are good considering that the highest level interface is used, that acknowledgment is done by the utility (for flow control), and that considerable opportunity for tuning exists. Acknowledgment would not be needed if RM was modified to retry on space allocation failures.

B. Use of the PC LAN Program with RM

The PC LAN Program provides DFS function. It has two configurations: *server*, where files can be offered and used, and *redirector*, where files can be used but not offered. Since RM and the PC LAN redirector are both large programs, it is not possible to run both on the same machine and still have enough memory for applications. Since it *is* practical to run RM and the redirector on the same machine, all the RM machines run the redirector, and one machine (not running RM) runs the PC LAN server. Each user has a directory on the PC LAN server that is used for communication with other machines.

The PC LAN Program enhances RM with a DFS, while RM significantly adds to the function of the PC LAN Program, providing a user interface for concurrent distributed actions, interprogram communication for multiple programs at a machine (with RM managing that complexity), and execution of services concurrently with other PC activity.

C. Remote Execution of DOS Commands

The DOS command processor is defined not only as a service named COMMAND that accepts commands from the keyboard, but also as a service named REMOTE, which handles requests from clients. Using REMOTE, services can be written as command-language files. REMOTE has been used in two different versions—one using RM file copy and the other using PC LAN for remote file access. The Pascal compiler is described here as an example, starting with the RMCOPY version. The request is carried out in a directory on the SM that is associated with the client machine (the directory is created if it does

not exist). RMCOPY is invoked to copy the source file from the client machine. After the compiler runs, a file containing compiler messages and service messages is copied to the client machine. The object file remains at the SM, since it probably will be used there by a linking service. A compilation often involves included source files. An RM module, for example, may refer to ten files that specify the interfaces to other modules. These files are kept at the SM, so they need not be copied at all. The version using PC LAN works similarly, except that RMCOPY is not used. Rather, the source file is used from the user's directory on the file server, and the error message file is created in that directory.

When the PM and SM are the same speed, elapsed time for local and remote execution is about the same (since request overhead is small in relation to compile time). When the PM is a PC-XT, while the compiler runs at a faster PC-AT, remote execution is extremely effective. Remote compilation of, for example, the Request component takes less than 4 minutes (PC LAN and RMCOPY versions) compared to 8 minutes for local compilation, and the PM may be used for editing other modules during that time.

D. Other Services

Other services include: file transfer to and from a host, using one SM equipped with the necessary hardware and software; a service that starts a series of requests specified in a file; and a computational service that runs at a machine equipped with a floating point co-processor. RM utilities have been quite simple to write. For example, the utility invoked when the user inquires what services are active on other machines takes 70 lines of code.

VI. Conclusions

Experience with RM shows that a service-request model, with connection-based service requests, can be used successfully for a personal computer and a simple operating system such as DOS. This model greatly simplifies the design of a resource-sharing system, since it provides excellent support for components such as the user interface. A simple multitasking facility has been shown to be a good base for service requests. Preliminary performance results indicate that a layered approach to interprocess and intermachine communication is quite feasible, even for this level of hardware.

In contrast to current LAN software products for the PC, which emphasize file sharing, RM emphasizes application services. This kind of facility has proved effective in a program development environment. RM is easy to install and to use, and services can easily be built from existing software.

The paper has described the features implemented in the prototype. Other features (some considered in early work on RM [29], [30]) are important subjects of research. These include name service, access control, accounting, support for atomic actions, and services with permanent and recoverable data. The system provides a good base for further work in these areas.

ACKNOWLEDGMENT

R. Talmadge, M. Ebrahimi, J. Marberg, K. Perry, and U. Zernik played major roles in overall concept development and design. The kernel was written by M. Ebrahimi, D. Greening, U. Zernik, and the author, with consultation from C. Coray. K. Perry wrote the Request component, later extended by the author. J. Marberg wrote the Service component and related utilities, and the RM Call facilities. The Network component was developed by H. Lorenz-Wirzba, R. Talmadge, and G. Tsudik. The Action component was written by L. Alkalaj, H. Lorenz-Wirzba, J. Marberg, and C. Wood. G. Tsudik wrote the model applications and several utilities. L. Alkalaj did much of the system testing and enhanced several components.

The author is grateful to J. Jordan, A. Schmalz, and B. Whipple for their support, and to P. Newman and the referees for valuable comments on the paper.

REFERENCES

[1] L. Alkalaj, H. Lorenz-Wirzba, and R. C. Summers, "Action management for a LAN resource-sharing system: Providing the user's interface to services," in *Proc. 6th IEEE Phoenix Conf. Computers and Communications*, 1987, pp. 469–473.

[2] G. T. Almes, A. P. Black, E. D. Lazowska, and J. D. Noe, "The Eden system: A technical review," *IEEE Trans. Software Eng.*, vol. SE-11, pp. 43–58, Jan. 1985.

[3] A. D. Birrell and B. J. Nelson, "Implementing remote procedure calls," *ACM Trans. Comput. Syst.*, vol. 2, pp. 39–59, Feb. 1984.

[4] A. Black, N. Hutchinson, E. Jul, H. Levy, and L. Carter, "Distribution and abstract types in Emerald," *IEEE Trans. Software Eng.*, vol. SE-13, pp. 65–76, Jan. 1987.

[5] D. A. Butterfield and R. M. Matthews, "Remote tasking," in *The LOCUS Distributed System Architecture*, G. J. Popek and B. J. Walker, Eds. Cambridge, MA: M.I.T. Press, 1985, pp. 73–89.

[6] R. B. Dannenberg and P. G. Hibbard, "A Butler process for resource sharing on Spice machines," *ACM Trans. Office Inform. Syst.*, vol. 3, pp. 234–252, July 1985.

[7] *Disk Operating System Version 3.20: Reference.* Boca Raton, FL: IBM Corp., 1986.

[8] M. Ebrahimi, J. M. Marberg, R. C. Summers, and U. Zernik, "Stack management for a multitasking operating system written as a Pascal program," *IBM Tech. Disclosure Bull.*, vol. 28, pp. 4500–4501, Mar. 1986.

[9] J. N. Gray, "An approach to decentralized computer systems," *IEEE Trans. Software Eng.*, vol. SE-12, pp. 684–692, June 1986.

[10] J. P. Gray, P. J. Hansen, P. Homan, M. A. Lerner, and M. Pozefsky, "Advanced program-to-program communication in SNA," *IBM Syst. J.*, vol. 22, pp. 298–318, 1983.

[11] *IBM PC Local Area Network Program User's Guide.* Boca Raton, FL: IBM Corp., 1986.

[12] "The IBM PC Network Program," *IBM Personal Comput. Seminar Proc.*, vol. 2, pp. 23–34, Sept. 1984.

[13] M. B. Jones, R. F. Rashid, and M. R. Thompson, "Matchmaker: An interface specification language for distributed processing," in *Conf. Rec. 12th ACM Symp. Principles Program. Lang.*, 1985, pp. 225–235.

[14] A. Langsford, "The Open System user's programming interfaces," *Comput. Networks*, vol. 8., pp. 3–12, Feb. 1984.

[15] B. G. Lindsay, L. M. Haas, C. Mohan, P. F. Wilms, and R. A. Yost, "Computation and communication in R*: A distributed database manager," *ACM Trans. Comput. Syst.*, vol. 2, pp. 24–38, Feb. 1984.

[16] B. Liskov, "Overview of the Argus language and system," M.I.T. Lab. Comput. Sci., PMG Memo. 40, Feb. 1984.

[17] B. Liskov, M. Herlihy, and L. Gilbert, "Limitations of synchronous communication with static process structure in languages for distributed computing," M.I.T. Lab. Comput. Sci., PMG Memo. 41-1, Oct. 1985.

[18] S. A. Mamrak, D. W. Leinbaugh, and T. S. Berk, "Software support for distributed resource sharing," *Comput. Networks and ISDN Syst.*, vol. 9, pp. 91–107, 1985.

[19] J. H. Morris, M. Satyanarayanan, M. H. Conner, J. H. Howard, D. S. H. Rosenthal, and F. D. Smith, "Andrew: A distributed personal computing environment," *Commun. ACM*, vol. 29, pp. 184–201, Mar. 1986.

[20] F. N. Parr, J. S. Auerbach, and B. C. Goldstein, "Distributed processing involving personal computers and mainframe hosts," *IEEE J. Select. Areas Commun.*, vol. SAC-3, pp. 479–489, May 1985.

[21] *Pascal Compiler Fundamentals, Version 2.00.* Boca Raton, FL: IBM Corp., 1984.

[22] A. Pashtan, "Operating system models in a Concurrent Pascal environment: Complexity and performance considerations," *IEEE Trans. Software Eng.*, vol. SE-11, pp. 136–141, Jan. 1985.

[23] *PC Network Technical Reference.* Boca Raton, FL: IBM Corp., 1984.

[24] G. J. Popek and B. J. Walker, Eds., *The LOCUS Distributed System Architecture.* Cambridge, MA: M.I.T. Press, 1985.

[25] K. Ramamritham, D. Stemple, D. A. Briggs, and S. Vintner, "Privilege transfer and revocation in a port-based system," *IEEE Trans. Software Eng.*, vol. SE-12, pp. 635–648, May 1986.

[26] D. M. Ritchie and K. Thompson, "The UNIX time-sharing system," *Commun. ACM*, vol. 17, pp. 365–375, July 1974.

[27] M. H. Seifert and H. M. Eberle, "Remote service call: A network operating system kernel and its protocols," presented at the *8th Int. Conf. Comput. Commun.*, Munich, West Germany, Sept. 15–19, 1986.

[28] A. Z. Spector, D. Daniels, D. Duchamp, J. L. Eppinger, and R. Pausch, "Distributed transactions for reliable systems," in *Proc. 10th ACM Symp. Operat. Syst. Principles*, 1985, pp. 127–146.

[29] R. C. Summers, M. Ebrahimi, J. M. Marberg, K. J. Perry, R. B. Talmadge, and U. Zernik, "RM: A system of personal machines and service machines," IBM Los Angeles Scientific Center," Rep. G320-2734, Nov. 1982.

[30] R. C. Summers, C. Wood, J. M. Marberg, M. Ebrahimi, K. J. Perry, and U. Zernik, "RM: A resource-sharing system for personal computers," in *Proc. 1983 ACM Conf. Personal and Small Comput.*, 1983, pp. 91–98.

[31] R. C. Summers, M. Ebrahimi, J. M. Marberg, and U. Zernik, "Design and implementation of a resource sharing system as an extension to a personal computer operating system," in *Proc. 1985 ACM SIGSMALL Symp. Small Syst.*, 1985, pp. 206–216.

[32] M. M. Theimer, K. A. Lantz, and D. R. Cheriton, "Preemptable remote execution facilities for the V-system," in *Proc. 10th ACM Symp. Operat. Syst. Principles*, 1985, pp. 2–12.

[33] Special issue, *IBM Syst. J.* (Special Issue on Virtual Machine Facility/370), vol. 18, no. 1, 1979.

[34] B. J. Walker and S. H. Kiser, "The LOCUS distributed filesystem," in *The LOCUS Distributed System Architecture*, G. J. Popek and B. J. Walker, Eds. Cambridge, MA: M.I.T. Press, 1985, pp. 29–72.

Rita C. Summers (M'79) received the B.A. and M.A. degrees from the University of California at Los Angeles.

She is a Senior Staff Member at the IBM Los Angeles Scientific Center, where her current research is in distributed systems, expert systems, and computer security. She has designed and implemented time-sharing and resource-sharing systems. She received two IBM Outstanding Contribution Awards for her work on virtual memory.

She has published articles and papers on computer security, database security, and resource sharing, and is coauthor of a book on database security and integrity.

Ms. Summers is a member of the Association for Computing Machinery and the American Association for Artificial Intelligence.

Section 9: Glossary*

Many of the key terms used in this tutorial and the collected articles are defined here. Also included are some important terms from the more general field of computer networking.

ALOHA.   A medium access control technique for multiple access transmission media. A station transmits whenever it has data to send. Unacknowledged transmissions are repeated.

AMPLIFIER.   An analog device designed to compensate for the loss in a section of transmission medium. It increases the signal strength of an analog signal over a range of frequencies.

ANS X3T9.5.   A committee sponsored by the American National Standards Institute (ANSI) that is responsible for a variety of system interconnection standards. The committee has produced draft standards for high-speed coaxial cable bus and fiber optic ring local networks.

BANDWIDTH.   Refers to a relative range of frequencies, that is, the difference between the highest and lowest frequencies transmitted. For example, the bandwidth of a TV channel is 6 MHz.

BASEBAND.   Transmission of signals without modulaton. In a baseband local network, digital signals (1's and 0's) are inserted directly onto the cable as voltage pulses. The entire spectrum of the cable is consumed by the signal. This scheme does not allow frequency division multiplexing.

BRIDGE.   A device that links two homogeneous packet-switched local networks. It accepts all packets from each network addressed to devices on the other, buffers them, and retransmits them to the other network.

BROADBAND.   The use of coaxial cable for providing data transfer by means of analog or radio-frequency signals. Digital signals are passed through a modem and are transmitted over one of the frequency bands of the cable.

BUS.   A topology in which stations are attached to a shared transmission medium. The transmission medium is a linear cable; transmissions propagate the length of the medium and are received by all stations.

CATENET.   A collection of packet-switched networks connected together via gateways.

CATV.   Community antenna television. CATV cable is used for broadband local networks.

---

*Based on Glossary in *Local Networks: An Introduction,* by William Stallings, Macmillan, 1984.

CBX.   Computerized branch exchange. A term sometimes used to refer to a digital PBX that is designed specifically to handle both voice and data. See Digital PBX.

CENTRALIZED BUS ARCHITECTURE.   A bus topology in which the bus is very short and the links to attached devices are relatively much longer.

CHEAPERNET.   A baseband local area network (LAN) that uses a thinner cable and less expensive components than Ethernet or the IEEE 802.3 standard. Although the data rate is the same (10 Mbps), the network span and number of stations is less.

CIRCUIT SWITCHING.   A method of communicating in which a dedicated communications path is established between two devices through one or more intermediate switching nodes. Unlike packet switching, digital data are sent as a continuous stream of bits. Bandwidth is guaranteed, and delay is essentially limited to propagation time. The telephone system uses circuit switching.

COAXIAL CABLE.   An electromagnetic transmission medium consisting of a center conductor and an outer, concentric conductor.

CODEC.   Coder-decoder. Transforms analog voice into a digital bit stream (coder), and digital signals into analog voice (decoder) using pulse code modulation (PCM).

COLLISION.   A condition in which two packets are being transmitted over a medium at the same time. Their interference makes both unintelligible.

CONTENTION.   The condition when two or more stations attempt to use the same channel at the same time.

CRC.   Cyclic redundancy check. A numeric value derived from the bits in a message. The transmitting station calculates a number that is attached to the message. The receiving station performs the same calculation. If the answer differs, then one or more bits are in error.

CSMA.   Carrier sense multiple access. A medium access control technique for multiple-access transmission media. A station wishing to transmit first senses the medium and transmits only if the medium is idle.

CSMA/CD.   Carrier sense multiple access with collision detection. A refinement of CSMA in which a station ceases transmission if it detects a collision.

DATAGRAM.   A packet switching service in which packets (datagrams) are independently routed and may arrive out of order. The datagram is self-contained, and carries a complete address. Delivery confirmation is provided by higher level protocols.

DCE. Data circuit-terminating equipment. A generic name for network-owned devices that provided a network attachment point for user devices.

DIGITAL PRIVATE BRANCH EXCHANGE (PBX). A local network based on the private branch exchange (PBX) architecture. Provides an integrated voice/data switching service. See Private Branch Exchange.

DIGITAL SWITCH. A star topology local network. Usually refers to a system that handles only data but not voice.

DTE. Data terminal equipment. A generic name for user-owned devices or stations that attach to a network.

DUAL CABLE. A type of broadband cable system in which two separate cables are used: one for transmission and one for reception.

ETHERNET. A 10-Mbps baseband local area network (LAN) specification developed jointly by Xerox, Intel, and Digital Equipment. It is the forerunner of the IEEE 802.3 CSMA/CD standard.

FRAME. A group of bits that includes data plus one or more addresses. Generally refers to a link layer (layer 2) protocol.

FREQUENCY-AGILE MODEM. A modem used on some broadband systems that can shift frequencies to communicate with stations in different dedicated bands.

FREQUENCY CONVERTER. In midsplit broadband cable systems, the device at the headend that translates between the transmitting and receiving frequencies. Also known as a frequency translator or a central retransmission facility. See Headend.

FREQUENCY-DIVISION MULTIPLEXING (FDM). A technique for combining multiple signals on one circuit by separating them in frequency.

FSK. Frequency-shift keying. A digital-to-analog modulation technique in which two different frequencies are used to represent 1's and 0's.

GATEWAY. A device that connects two systems, especially if the systems use different protocols. For example, a gateway is needed to connect two independent local networks or to connect a local network to a long-haul network.

GRADE OF SERVICE. For a circuit-switched system, the probability that during a specified period of peak traffic an offered call will fail to find an available circuit.

HEADEND. The end point of a broadband bus or tree network. Transmission from a station is toward the headend; reception by a station is from the headend.

HIGH-SPEED LOCAL NETWORK (HSLN). A local network designed to provide high throughput between expensive, high-speed devices, such as mainframes and mass storage devices.

HOST. The collection of hardware and software that attaches to a network and uses that network to provide inter-process communication and user services.

HYBRID LOCAL NETWORK. An integrated local network consisting of more than one type of local network (LAN, HSLN, digital PBX).

IEEE 802. A committee of IEEE organized to produce a local area network (LAN) standard.

INBOUND PATH. On a broadband local area network (LAN), the transmission path used by stations to transmit packets toward the headend.

INFRARED. Electromagnetic waves whose frequency range is above that of microwave and below the visible spectrum: 3×10^{11} to 4×10^{14} Hz.

INJECTION LASER DIODE (ILD). A solid state device that works on the laser principle to produce a light source for a fiber-optic wave guide.

INTERNETWORKING. Communication among devices across multiple networks.

LASER. Electromagnetic source capable of producing infrared and visible light.

LIGHT-EMITTING DIODE (LED). A solid-state device that emits light when a current is applied. Used as a light source for a fiber-optic wave guide.

LISTEN BEFORE TALK (LBT). Same as Carrier sense multiple access (CSMA).

LISTEN WHILE TALK (LWT). Same as Carrier sense multiple access with collision detection (CSMA/CD).

LOCAL AREA NETWORK (LAN). A general-purpose local network that can serve a variety of devices. Typically used for terminals, microcomputers, and minicomputers.

LOCAL NETWORK. A communications network that provides interconnection of a variety of data communicating devices within a small area.

MANCHESTER ENCODING. A digital signaling technique in which there is a transition in the middle of each bit time. A 1 is encoded with a high level during the first half of the bit time; a 0 is encoded with a low level during the first half of the bit time.

MEDIUM ACCESS CONTROL (MAC). For bus, tree, and ring topologies, the method of determining which device has access to the transmission medium at any time. CSMA/CD and token are common access methods.

MESSAGE SWITCHING. A switching technique using a message store and forward system. No dedicated path is established. Rather, each message contains a destination address and is passed from source to destination through intermediate nodes. At each node, the entire message is received, stored briefly, and then passed on to the next node.

MICROWAVE. Electromagnetic waves in the frequency range 1-30GHz.

MIDSPLIT. A type of broadband cable system in which the available frequencies are split into two groups: one for transmission (5-116 MHz) and one for reception (168-300 MHz). Requires a frequency converter.

MODEM. Modulator/Demodulator. Transforms a digital bit stream into an analog signal (modulator) and vice versa (demodulator). The analog signal may be sent over telephone lines or could be radio frequencies or light-waves.

NETWORK ACCESS UNIT (NAU). A communications controller that attaches to a local network. It implements the local network protocols and provides an interface for device attachment.

NETWORK CONTROL CENTER. The operator inter-face to software that observes and controls the activities in a network.

NETWORK MANAGEMENT. A set of human and auto-mated tasks that support the creation, operation, and evolution of a network.

NONBLOCKING NETWORK. A circuit-switched net-work in which there is always at least one available path between any pair of idle end points regardless of the number of end points already connected.

OPTICAL FIBER. A lightwave transmission medium. Supports very high bandwidth.

OUTBOUND PATH. On a broadband LAN, the trans-mission path used by stations to receive packets coming from the headend.

PACKET. A group of bits that includes data plus source and destination addresses. Generally refers to a network layer (layer 3) protocol.

PACKET SWITCHING. A method of transmitting mes-sages through a communications network, in which long messages are subdivided into short packets. The packets are then transmitted as in message switching. Usually, packet switching is more efficient and rapid than message switching.

PASSIVE HEADEND. A device that connects the two broadband cables of a dual cable system. It does not provide frequency translation.

PASSIVE STAR. A topology in which each station atta-ches to a central node by two lines, one input and one output. A signal entering the central node on one input line is split among all output lines. The central node is passive, providing merely an electromagnetic linkage.

PBX. Private branch exchange. A telephone exchange on the user's premises. Provides a switching facility for telephones on extension lines within the building and access to the public telephone network. May be manual (PMBX) or automatic (PABX). A digital PBX that also

handles data devices without modems is sometimes called a computerized branch exchange (CBX).

PCM. Pulse code modulation. A common method for digitizing voice. The bandwidth required for a single digitized voice channel is 64 kbps.

PROPAGATION DELAY. The delay between the time a signal enters a channel and the time it is received.

PROTOCOL. A set of rules governing the exchange of data between two entities.

REGISTER INSERTION RING. A medium access con-trol technique for rings. Each station contains a register that can temporarily hold a circulating packet. A station may transmit whenever there is a gap on the ring and, if necessary, hold an oncoming packet until it has completed transmission.

REPEATER. A device that receives data on one commu-nication link and transmits it, bit by bit, on another link as fast as it is received, without buffering. An integral part of the ring topology. Used to connect linear segments in a baseband bus local network.

RING. A topology in which stations are attached to re-peaters connected in a closed loop. Data are transmitted in one direction around the ring and can be read by all attached stations.

RING WIRING CONCENTRATOR. A site through which pass the links between repeaters, for all or a portion of a ring.

SLOTTED ALOHA. A medium access control technique for multiple-access transmission media. The technique is the same as ALOHA, except that packets must be trans-mitted in well-defined time slots.

SLOTTED RING. A medium access control technique for rings. The ring is divided into slots, which may be desig-nated empty or full. A station may transmit whenever an empty slot goes by, by marking the slot full and then inserting a packet into the slot.

SPACE-DIVISION SWITCHING. A circuit-switching technique in which each connection through the switch takes a physically separate and dedicated path.

SPECTRUM. Refers to an absolute range of frequencies. For example, the spectrum of CATV cable is now about 5-400 MHz.

SPLITTER. Analog device for dividing one input into two outputs and combining two outputs into one input. Used to achieve tree topology on broadband CATV networks.

STAR. A topology in which all stations are connected to a central switch. Two stations communicate via circuit switching.

STATISTICAL TIME-DIVISION MULTIPLEXING. A method of time-division multiplexing (TDM) in which time slots on a shared transmission line are allocated to

I/O channels on demand.

SYNCHRONOUS TIME-DIVISION MULTIPLE-XING. A method of time-division multiplexing (TDM) in which time slots on a shared transmission line are assigned to I/O channels on a fixed, predetermined basis.

TAP. An analog device that permits signals to be inserted or removed from a twisted pair or coaxial cable.

TDM BUS SWITCHING. A form of time-division switching in that time slots are used to transfer data over a shared bus between transmitter and receiver.

TERMINAL. A collection of hardware and possibly software that provides a direct user interface to a network.

TERMINATOR. An electrical resistance at the end of a cable that serves to absorb the signal on the line.

TIME-DIVISION MULTIPLEXING (TDM). A technique for combining multiple signals on one circuit by separating them in time.

TIME-DIVISION SWITCHING. A circuit-switching technique in which time slots in a time-multiplexed stream of data are manipulated to pass data from an input to an output.

TIME-MULTIPLEXED SWITCHING (TMS). A form of space-division switching in which each input line is a time-division multiplexed stream. The switching configuration may change for each time slot.

TIME-SLOT INTERCHANGE (TSI). The interchange of time slots within a time-division multiplexed frame.

TOKEN BUS. A medium access control technique for bus/tree. Stations form a logical ring, around which a token is passed. A station receiving the token may transmit data and then must pass the token on to the next station in the ring.

TOKEN RING. A medium access control technique for rings. A token circulates around the ring. A station may transmit by seizing the token, inserting a packet onto the ring, and then retransmitting the token.

TOPOLOGY. The structure, consisting of paths and switches, that provides the communications interconnection among nodes of a network.

TRANSCEIVER. A device that both transmits and receives.

TRANSCEIVER CABLE. A four-pair cable that connects the transceiver in a baseband coaxial local area network (LAN) to the controller.

TRANSMISSION MEDIUM. The physical path between transmitters and receivers in a communications network.

TREE. A topology in which stations are attached to a shared transmission medium. The transmission medium is a branching cable emanating from a headend, with no closed circuits. Transmissions propagate throughout all branches of the tree and are received by all stations.

TWISTED PAIR. An electromagnetic transmission medium consisting of two insulated wires arranged in a regular spiral pattern.

VIRTUAL CIRCUIT. A packet-switching service in which a connection (virtual circuit) is established between two stations at the start of transmission. All packets follow the same route, need not carry a complete address, and arrive in sequence.

Section 10: Annotated Bibliography

As the reader should have gathered by now, the field of local networks is both broad and explosive. No bibliography can hope to be either thorough or timely. The entries in this section were chosen using the following criteria:

- *Relevance:* This tutorial is concerned with the principles and technology underlying local networks. Therefore, few of the references describe specific networks, either experimental or commercially available products.

- *Currency:* Most of the references are of rather recent origin. A good bibliography of material up to 1980 can be found in [SHOC80a].

- *Representativeness:* The interested reader can pursue the topics introduced in this tutorial by consulting the references listed here. They are, however, only representative of the available literature. The articles themselves contain further references for the truly dedicated reader.

10.1 Books

Stallings, W. *Local Networks: An Introduction, Second Edition,* New York: Macmillan, 1987.

This is, in a sense, a companion to this tutorial text, and it follows the same topical organization. It is intended as a textbook as well as a reference for professionals.

Stallings, W. *Handbook of Computer-Communications Standards, Volume I: Local Network Standards.* New York: Macmillan, 1987,

A detailed description of the 802 and FDDI standards.

Hammond, J. and O'Reilly, P. *Performance Analysis of Local Computer Networks,* Reading, Mass.: Addison-Wesley, 1986.

A detailed examination of the performance of various MAC protocols.

Mayne, A. *Linked Local Area Networks, Second Edition,* New York: 1986.

A mostly nontechnical look at networking, networking products, and networking technologies, emphasizing local networks. Includes a very extensive list of references.

Kummerle, K.; Limb, T.; and Tobagi, F., editors. *Advances in Local Area Networks,* New York: IEEE Press, 1987.

A collection of articles, mostly reprints, on various aspects of local networks.

Pickholz, R., editor. *Local Area & Multiple Access Networks,* Rockville, Md.: Computer Science Press, 1986.

A collection of original articles on various aspects of local networks.

Flint, D. *The Data Ring Main.* New York: John Wiley, 1983.

The first half of this book contains an overview of local area network (LAN) technology plus an exposition of internetworking issues. The latter, less technical, half discusses user issues and selection criteria.

Chorafas, D. *Designing and Implementing Local Area Networks.* New York: McGraw-Hill, 1984.

The majority of this book is devoted to a description of some specific vendor offerings. There is also a survey of LAN technology.

Derfler, F. and Stallings, W. *A Manager's Guide to Local Networks.* Englewood Cliffs, N.J.: Prentice-Hall/Spectrum, 1983.

A technical overview of local networks for managers, plus guidance on requirements definition, selection, and use.

Rosenthal, R. *The Selection of Local Area Computer Networks,* National Bureau of Standards Special Publication 500-96, November 1982.

An excellent guidebook for those intending to purchase a local network. Includes detailed guidance for developing a specification for vendors.

Cooper, E. *Broadband Network Technology.* Mountain View, Calif.: Sytek Press, 1984.

A comprehensive introduction to the technology and practical implementation issues for broadband LANs.

IBM Corp. *A Building Planning Guide for Communication Wiring.* G320-8059, September 1982.

This booklet describes IBM's cabling system for ring LANs. It provides detailed descriptions and instructions for cable layout and installation.

IBM Corp. *An Introduction to Local Area Networks.* SC20-8203, November 1983.

An overview of LAN and digital PBX technology, with an emphasis on IBM's token ring research.

Digital Equipment Corp. *Introduction to Local Area Networks.* EB-22714-18, 1982.

An overview of LAN technology with an emphasis on Ethernet.

Freeman, H. and Thurber, K. *Local Network Equipment.* Washington, D.C.: Computer Society Press, 1985.

This tutorial text contains reprints of articles describing a broad range of commercially available local networks.

Thurber, K.T. and Freeman, H.A. *Tutorial: Local Computer Networks (Second Edition),* Washington, D.C.: Computer Society Press, 1981.

This tutorial text contains reprints of articles describing specific LANs and HSLNs. Most of the networks described are experimental or tailor made rather than being commercially available products.

Local/Netter Designer's Handbook, Minneapolis, Minn.: Architecture Technology Corp.

This annual publication is an extensive listing of vendors of local network equipment.

Proceedings, Local Computer Network Conference.

A conference held annually in the fall in Minneapolis. Good source of current research results.

10.2 Articles

The articles are listed alphabetically with annotation. Table 10.1 provides a topical key.

ABRA86   Abraham, M. "Running Ethernet Modems Over Broadband Cable." *Data Communications,* May 1986.

A detailed look at the recent broadband option added to 802.3.

ACAM84   Acampora, A. and Hluchyz, M. "A New Local Area Network Using a Centralized Bus." *IEEE Communications Magazine,* August 1984.

A good technical description of AT&T's DataKit LAN.

AHUJ83   Ahuja, S. "S/NET: A High-Speed Interconnect for Multiple Computers." *IEEE Journal on Selected Areas in Communications,* November 1983.

Describes a 10-Mbps fiber LAN using an active star switch.

AIME79   Aimes, G.T. and Lazowska, E.D. "The Behavior of Ethernet-Like Computer Communications Networks." *Proceedings, Seventh Symposium on Operating Systems Principles,* New York: ACM, Inc., 1979.

A look at CSMA-type networks.

AKAS84   Akashi, F. and Ohteru, Y. "Efficient Local Area Network Interconnect Using a Bridge." *Proceedings, COMPCON 84 Fall,* Washington, D.C.: Computer Society Press, September 1984.

Discusses implementation and performance results for an Ethernet bridge.

ALLA83   Allan, R. "Local Networks: Fiber Optics Gains Momentum." *Electronic Design,* June 23, 1983.

A view of the state-of-the-art in multiple-access fiber LANs.

AMER82   Amer, P. "A Measurement Center for the NBS Local Area Computer Network." *IEEE Transactions on Computers,* August 1982.

Describes a rather complete set of performance measures that could be used in monitoring a LAN. Active and passive monitoring techniques are explored.

AMER83   Amer, P.D.; Rosenthal, R.; and Toense, R. "Measuring a Local Network's Performance." *Data Communications,* April 1983.

Discusses the performance measurement facility described in this tutorial. The focus is more on objectives and operational considerations rather than on means.

ARTH81   Arthurs, E. and Stuck, B.W. "A Theoretical Performance Analysis of Polling and Carrier Sense Collision Detection Communication Systems." *Proceedings, Seventh Data Communications Symposium,* Washington, D.C.: Computer Society Press, 1981.

Reports on IEEE 802 performance study.

ARTH82   Arthurs, E.; Stuck, B.W.; Bux, W.; Marathe, M.; Hawe, W.; Phinney, T.; Rosenthal, R; and Tarasou, V. *IEEE Project 802 Local Area Network Standards, Traffic Handling Characteristics Committee Report,* New York: IEEE, June 1982.

The complete report of the IEEE 802 performance study.

BAL85   Bal, S.; Murray, D.; and White, K. "Core Modules Speed System Design." *System & Software,* November 1985.

Examines implementation issues relating to the use of an NAV that supports up through the transport layer.

BASS80   Bass, C.; Kennedy, J.S.; and Davidson, J.M. "Local Network Gives New Flexibility to Distributed Processing." *Electronics,* September 25, 1980.

Describes the Ungermann-Bass baseband LAN.

BATE86   Bates, R. and Abramson, P. "You *Can* Use Phone Wire for Your Token Ring LAN." *Data Communications,* Data Communications, November 1986.

This article examines the use of telephone twisted pair and shielded twisted pair for a ring LAN. The article explores technical differences to explain why the two media offer different size and growth capabilities.

BEVA86   Bevan, M. "Image Processing May Cause Future Problems with Network Loading." *Data Communications,* March 1986.

Discusses the implications of new office equipment for local network capacity requirements.

BHUS85   Bhushan, B. and Opderbeck, H. "The Evolution of Data Switching for PBX's." *IEEE Journal on Selected Areas in Communications,* July 1985.

Looks at the different traffic requirements for voice and data on a PBX. The paper then traces the evolution of integrated voice/data capability, with an emphasis on describing the addition of packet-switching to the PBX.

BLAI82   Blair, G.S. and Shepherd D. "A Performance Comparison of Ethernet and the Cambridge Digital Communication Ring." *Computer Networks,* pp. 105–113, 1982.

The authors conclude that, under some circumstances, slotted ring is superior to CSMA/CD bus.

BOGG80 Boggs, D.R.; Shoch, J.F.; Taft, E.A.; and Metcalfe, R.M. "Pup: An Internetwork Architecture." *IEEE Transactions on Communications,* April 1980.

An early Xerox internet protocol attempt. Also contains a good discussion of the internet problem for local networks.

BOSE81 Bosen, R. "A Low-Speed Local Net for Under $100 per Station." *Data Communications,* December 1981.

Describes a low-cost LAN.

BURR83 Burr, W. "An Overview of the Proposed American National Standard for Local Distributed Data Interfaces." *Communications of the ACM,* August 1983.

Describes LDDI, a proposed 50-Mbps local network standard.

BURR84 Burr, W. and Carpenter, J. "Wideband Local Nets Enter the Computer Arena." *Electronics,* May 3, 1984.

Discusses the ANSI X3T9.5 high-speed local network (HSLN) standard and compares it with three commercial products: HYPERchannel, Loosely Coupled Network (LCN), and VAXCLUSTER.

BURR86 Burr, W. "The FDDI Optical Data Link." *IEEE Communications Magazine,* May 1986.

This article focuses on the physical medium dependent (PMD) layer of FDDI. Includes a discussion of transmitters, receivers, signaling, and the fiber cable.

BUX81 Bux, W. "Local-Area Subnetworks: A Performance Comparison." *IEEE Transactions on Communications,* October 1981.

Compares CSMA/CD, token, and slotted ring. CSMA/CD loses.

BUX82 Bux, W.; Closs, F.; Janson, P.A.; Kummerle, K.; Miller, H.R.; and Rothauser, H. "A Local-Area Communication Network Based on a Reliable Token Ring System." *Proceedings, International Symposium on Local Computer Networks,* Washington, D.C.: Computer Society Press, 1982.

Describes an experimental system that is the basis of IBM's expected product.

BUX83a Bux, W. and Schlatter, M. "An Approximate Method for the Performance Analysis of Buffer Insertion Rings." *IEEE Transactions on Communications,* January 1983.

Extends the work in [BUX81].

BUX83b Bux, W.; Closs, F.; Kuemmerle, K.; Keller, H.; and Mueller, H. "Architecture and Design of a Reliable Token-Ring Network." *IEEE Journal on Selected Areas in Communications,* November 1983.

Describes the architecture, performance, transmission system, and wiring strategy of IBM's token ring LAN. A good technical exposition.

BUX84 Bux, W. "Performance Issues in Local-Area Networks." *IBM Systems Journal,* No. 4, 1984.

This descriptive (rather than analytic) article discusses delay-throughput characteristics of medium access control protocols, end-to-end performance of a file server, and timing problems in local network adapters.

CELA82 Celano, J. "Crossing Public Property: Infrared Link and Alternative Approaches for Connecting a High Speed Local Area Network." *Proceedings, Computer Networking Symposium,* Washington, D.C.: Computer Society Press, 1982.

Discusses how to connect LANs in buildings separated by public property.

CERR87 Cerruti, M. and Voce, M. "Zap Data Where It Really Counts—Direct-to-Host Connections." *Data Communications,* July 1987.

Describes the protocol and interface issues in attaching a mainframe to a LAN via an I/O channel interface.

CHER83 Cheriton, D. "Local Networking and Internetworking in the V-System." *Proceedings, Eight Data Communications Symposium,* Washington, D.C.: Computer Society Press, 1983.

Describes the use of gateways to provide LAN internetworking using streamlined protocols for intra-LAN traffic. Contains a good discussion of LAN internetworking performance issues.

CHLA80a Chlamtac, I. and Franta, W.R. "Message-Based Priority Access to Local Networks." *Computer Communications,* April 1980.

Analyzes an HSLN protocol.

CHLA80b Chlamtac, I.; Franta, W.R.; Patton, P.C.; and Wells, B. "Performance Issues in Back-End Storage Networks." *Computer,* February 1980.

Looks at HSLN performance.

CHRI78 Christensen, G.S. "Network Monitor Unit." *Proceedings, Third Conference on Local Computer Networking,* Washington, D.C.: Computer Society Press, 1978.

Describes an NCC for an HSLN that provides a fault-isolation capability.

CHRI79 Christensen, G.S. "Links Between Computer-Room Networks." *Telecommunications,* February 1979.

Brief description of HYPERchannel.

CHRI81 Christensen, G.S. and Franta, W.K. "Design and Analysis of the Access Protocol for HYPERchannel Networks." *Proceedings, Third USA-Japan Computer Conference,* 1981.

CLAN82 Clancy, G.J., et al. "The IEEE 802 Committee States Its Case Concerning Its Local Network Standards Efforts." *Data Communications,* April 1982.

A response to the criticism that the standard has too many options and alternatives. It states the case for the need for LAN standards and offers a justification for the committee's approach.

CLAR78   Clark, D.C.; Pogran, K.T.; and Reed, D.P. "An Introduction to Local Area Networks." *Proceedings of the IEEE,* November 1978.

Despite its date, a good, wide-ranging introduction to LANS.

CONN87   Connor, G.; Scott, P.; and Vesuna, S. "Serial Data Races at Parallel Rates for the Best of Both Worlds." *Electronic Design,* January 22, 1987.

Describes a signal generator that transmits at 125 Mbps, and is suitable for the 4B/5B FDDI code.

COOP82   Cooper, E. "13 Often-Asked Questions about Broadband." *Data Communications,* April 1982.

Short and informative.

COOP83a   Cooper, E. and Edholm, P.K. "Design Issues in Broadband Local Networks." *Data Communications,* February 1983.

Primarily a comparison of mid-split and dual configurations. The article takes into consideration cost, capacity, installation, and reliability.

COOP83b   Cooper, E. "Broadband Network Design: Issues and Answers." *Computer Design,* March 1983.

Looks at implementation and maintenance issues.

COTT80   Cotton, I.W. "Technologies for Local Area Computer Networks." *Computer Networks,* November 1980.

Another good survey paper for LANS.

COYL85   Coyle, E. and Liu, B. "A Matrix Representation of CSMA/CD Networks." *IEEE Transactions on Communications.* January 1985.

A new analytical model for CSMA/CD is presented. Because of its power and simplicity, it can be used to investigate the sensitivity of CSMA/CD performance to a variety of parameters.

DAHO83   Dahod, A.M. "Local Network Standards: No Utopia." *Data Communications,* March 1983.

The author presents a case against local network standards, based on the danger of being frozen into technical obsolescence.

DALA81   Dalal, Y.K. and Printis, R.S. "48-Bit Absolute Internet and Ethernet Host Numbers." *Proceedings, Seventh Data Communications Symposium,* Washington, D.C.: Computer Society Press, 1981.

Discusses the issue of internet addressing and describes the approach advocated by the Ethernet developers.

DALA82   Dalal, Y. "Use of Multiple Networks in the Xerox Network System." *Computer,* September 1983.

Looks at the application of the XNS architecture to internetworking with an emphasis on local networks.

DAVI83   Davidson, J. "OSI Model Layering of a Military Local Network." *Proceedings of the IEEE,* December 1983.

Describes implementation experience with the layering of protocol functions between attached devices and interface units.

DC86   Data Communications. "The Big Blue Token Ring View." *Data Communications,* February and March 1986.

A series of eleven short articles, written by IBM researchers and engineers, address different technical aspects of IBM's token ring product.

DHAW84   Dhawan, A. "One Way to End the Brouhaha Over Choosing an Optimal LAN." *Data Communications,* March 1984.

Extolls the virtues of the digital PBX.

DIEN83   Diener, A.; Bragger, R.; Dudler, A.; and Zehnder, C. "Database Services for Personal Computers Linked by a Local Area Network." *Proceedings, ACM Conference on Personal and Small Computers,* New York: ACM, Inc. 1983.

Establishes a set of criteria for evaluating LAN database servers, and discusses hardware and software issues.

DINE80   Dineson, M. and Picazo, J. "Broadband Technology Magnifies Local Networking Capability." *Data Communications,* February 1980.

Describes Sytek's broadband network.

DINE81   Dineson, M.A. "Broadband Local Networks Enhance Communication Design." *EDN,* March 4, 1981.

Covers the same topics as the paper included herein, but provides more technical detail about the RF engineering of the system.

DIXO83   Dixon, R.; Strole, N.; and Markov, J. "A Token-Ring Network for Local Data Communications." *IBM Systems Journal,* Nov. 1, 1983.

A readable overview of token ring, based on IEEE 802.5 and IBM's planned product. Discusses both medium access control and the physical wiring layout.

DIXO87   Dixon, R. "Lore of the Token Ring." *IEEE Network Magazine,* January 1987.

A review of some of the important design issues in a token ring LAN, including MAC protocol, star wiring, and error isolation. The author argues the advantages of the ring.

DONN79   Donnelly, J.E. and Yeh, J.W. "Interaction Between Protocol Levels in a Prioritized CSMA Broadcast Network." *Computer Networks,* March 1979.

An analysis of the HYPERchannel protocol.

EDN82   EDN Magazine. "Credibility Problems Could Block LAN Growth." *EDN Magazine,* September 1, 1982.

A brief but sobering look at problems users have encountered with LANS.

ENNI83   Ennis G. and Filice, P. "Overview of a Broad-Band Local Area Network Protocol Architecture." *IEEE Journal on Selected Areas in Communications,* November 1983.

A detailed description of the rather powerful protocol architecture implemented in the Sytek product.

ESTR82   Estrin, J. and Carrico, B. "Gateways Promise to Link Local Networks into Hybrid Systems." *Electronics,* September 22, 1982.

Describes various approaches to designing bridges.

FARM69 Farmer, W.D. and Newhall, E.E. "An Experimental Distributed Switching System to Handle Bursty Computer Traffic." *Proceedings, ACM Symposium on Problems in the Optimization of Data Communications,* New York: ACM, Inc. 1969.

A paper describing an early token ring system.

FEIN85 Feiner, A. "Architecture, Design, and Development of the System 75 Office Communication System." *IEEE Journal on Selected Areas in Communications,* July 1985.

Describes in some detail a digital PBX from AT&T. Includes a discussion of the switching mechanism, control, and software.

FIEL86 Field, J. "Logical Link Control." *IEEE INFOCOM '86.* Washington, D.C.: Computer Society Press, April 1986.

A good summary of the LLC services and protocols. Includes the acknowledged connectionless option.

FINE84 Fine, M. and Tobagi, F. "Demand Assignment Multiple Access Schemes for Broadcast Bus Local Area Networks." *IEEE Transactions on Computers,* December 1984.

A very comprehensive survey of MAC techniques suitable for a fiber HSLN.

FINL84 Finley, M. "Optical Fibers in Local Area Networks." *IEEE Communications Magazine,* August 1984.

Surveys the various approaches to the use of optical fiber in local network architectures. A good state-of-the-art survey of U.S. and Japanese efforts.

FLAT84 Flatman, A. "Low-Cost Local Network for Small Systems Grows from IEEE-802.3 Standard." *Electronic Design,* July 26, 1984.

Describes Cheapernet, a proposed low-cost version of the IEEE CSMA/CD standard.

FLEM79 Fleming, P. *Principles of Switching.* Geneva, Il.: Lee's abc of the Telephone, 1979.

Good, fairly nontechnical description of circuit switching.

FORB81 Forbes, J. "RF Prescribed for Many Local Links." *Data Communications,* September 1981.
Broadband descriptions.

FORC85 Forcina, A.; Listanti, M.; Pattavina, A.; and Roveri, A. "A Generalized Performance Evaluation of Slotted CSMA Networks." *Proceedings, INFOCOM 85,* Washington, D.C.: Computer Society Press, 1985.

A new analysis of CSMA and CSMA/CD performance. A discrete time Markov chain is used and results encompass variable as well as fixed packet lengths.

FRAN80 Franta, W.R. and Bilodeau, M.B. "Analysis of a Prioritized CSMA Protocol Based on Staggered Delays." *Acta Informatica,* June 1980
Analysis of a high-speed local network (HSLN) protocol.

FRAN82 Franta, W.R. and Heath, J.R. *Performance of HYPERchannel Networks: Parameters, Measurements, Models, and Analysis.* Minneapolis, Minn., University of Minnesota, Computer Science Department, Technical Report 82-3, January 1982.

Summarizes results from a long-term project to analyze HSLN protocol performance.

FRAS83 Fraser, A. "Towards a Universal Data Transport System." *IEEE Journal on Selected Areas in Communications,* November 1983.

A detailed technical description of AT&T's Datakit.

FREE83 Freedman, D. "Fiber Optics Shine in Local-Area Networks." *Mini-Micro Systems,* September 1983.

An overview article with emphasis on passive-star technology.

GOEL83 Goeller, L. and Goldstone, J. "The ABCs of the PBX." *Datamation,* April 1983.

A lengthy discussion of the evolution of the PBX and its likely future direction.

GORD79 Gordon, R.L.; Farr, W.W.; and Levine, P. "Ringnet: A Packet Switched Local Network with Decentralized Control." *Proceedings, Fourth Conference on Local Computer Networks,* Washington, D.C.: Computer Society Press, 1979.

Describes an early commercial token ring product.

GRAN83 Grant, A.; Hutchison, D.; and Shepherd, W. "A Gateway for Linking Local Area Networks and X.25 Networks." *Proceedings, SIGCOMM83 Symposium,* New York: ACM, Inc., 1983.

In this approach, the local network appears as a single end point to the X.25 network.

GRAU84 Graube, M. and Molder, M. "Local Area Networks." *IEEE Computer,* October 1984.

A brief overview of the current status of LAN products.

GRNA80 Grnarov, A.,; Kleinrock, L.; and Gerla, M. "A Highly Reliable Distributed Loop Network Architecture." *Proceedings, International Symposium on Fault-Tolerant Computing,* Washington, D.C.: Computer Society Press, 1980.

Describes a technique for enhancing the reliability of a ring by using backward links.

HABE84 Haber, L. "Fiber-Optic Technology Sheds Light on Local Area Networks." *Mini-Micro Systems,* November 1984.

A survey of current products plans and standards efforts.

HAFN74 Hafner, E.R.; Nenadal, Z.; and Tschanz, M. "A Digital Loop Communications System." *IEEE Transactions on Communications,* June 1974.

An early register insertion ring.

HALL85 Hall, M. "Factory Networks." *Micro Communications,* February 1985.

Examines unique requirements for LANS in factories and describes the LAN specification in the Manufacturing Automation Protocol (MAP).

HANS81 Hanson, K.; Chou, W.; and Nilsson, A. "Integration of Voice, Data, and Image Traffic in a Wideband Local Network." *Proceedings, Computer Networking Symposium,* Washington, D.C.: Computer Society Press, 1981.

Addresses the use of a very-high speed (100 Mbps or more) local network and proposes techniques for efficient utilization.

HAUG84 Haugdahl, J. "Key Issues in Selecting Personal Computer Local Networks." *Proceedings, Ninth Conference on Local Computer Networks,* Washington, D.C.: Computer Society Press, 1984.

Examines some of the key issues involved when considering local networking personal computers.

HAWE84 Hawe, B.; Kirby, A.; and Stewart, B. "Transparent Interconnection of Local Area Networks with Bridges." *Journal of Telecommunication Networks,* Summer 1984.

A consideration of various aspects of bridges, including desirable characteristics, routing algorithms, protocol issues, and performance.

HERR79 Herr, D.E. and Nute, C.T. "Modeling the Effects of Packet Truncation on the Throughput of CSMA Networks." *Proceedings, Computer Networking Symposium,* Washington, D.C.: Computer Society Press, 1979.

A very clear and systematic analysis of various CSMA/CD protocols, including nonpersistent, 1-persistent, and p persistent.

HEYM82 Heyman, D.P. "An Analysis of the Carrier-Sense Multiple-Access Protocol." *Bell System Technical Journal,* October 1982.

One of the best and most rigorous pieces of analysis that has been published on the subject.

HEYW81 Heywood, P. "The Cambridge Ring Is Still Making the Rounds." *Data Communications,* July 1981.

Discusses commercial success of a slotted ring system.

HOHN80 Hohn, W.C. "The Control Data Loosely Coupled Network Lower Level Protocols." *Proceedings, National Computer Conference,* Reston, Va.: AFIPS Press, 1980.

A commercial HSLN product.

HOLM81 Holmgren, S.F. *Evaluation of TCP/IP in a Local Network.* MITRE Working Paper 81WOO568, September 30, 1981.

Results of an experiment to place network and transport layers in an NIU.

HOPK77 Hopkins, G.T. *A Bus Communications System.* MITRE Technical Report MTR-3515, 1977.

Describes one of the earliest broadband systems.

HOPK79 Hopkins, G.T. "Multimode Communications on the MITRE-NET." *Proceedings, Local Area Communications Network Symposium,* 1979.

Shorter version of [HOPK77].

HOPK80 Hopkins, G.T. and Wagner, P.E. *Multiple Access Digital Communications System.* U.S. Patent 4,210,780, July 1, 1980.

Contains a quite readable system description.

HOPK82 Hopkins, G.T. and Meisner, N.B. "Choosing Between Broadband and Baseband Local Networks." *Mini-Micro Systems,* June 1982.

Good discussion of pros and cons.

HOPP77 Hopper, A. "Data Ring at Computer Laboratory, University of Cambridge." In *Local Area Networking,* National Bureau of Standards Publication 500-31, 1977.

Describes a slotted ring system.

HOPP83 Hopper, A. and Williamson, R. "Design and Use of an Integrated Cambridge Ring." *IEEE Journal on Selected Areas in Communications,* November 1983.

Discusses the development process used to implement an integrated-circuit version of the Cambridge ring.

IBM82 IBM Corp. *IBM Series/1 Local Communications Controller Feature Description.* GA34-0142-2, 1982.

A very simple commercial register insertion product, one of the very few.

IYER85 Iyer, V. and Joshi, V. "FDDI's 100 M-bps Protocol Improves on 802.5 Spec's 4 M-bps Limit." *EDN,* May 2, 1985.

A comparison of FDDI and 802.5

JAJS83 Jajszczyk, A. "On Nonblocking Switching Networks Composed of Digital Symmetrical Matrices." *IEEE Transactions on Communications,* January 1983.

A discussion of the design of multistage time and space switching networks for integrated circuit implementation.

JANS83 Janson, P.; Svobodova, L.; and Maehle, E. "Filing and Printing Services on a Local-Area Network." *Proceedings, Eighth Data Communications Symposium,* Washington, D.C.: Computer Society Press, October 1983.

Examines in some detail a type of value-added LAN service that is becoming increasingly available.

JAYA87 Jayasumana, A. "Performance Analysis of a Token Bus Priority Scheme." *Proceedings, IEEE INFOCOM '87,* Washington, D.C.: Computer Society Press, March 1987.

A description and performance analysis of the 802.4 capacity allocation algorithm.

JEWE85 Jewett, R. "The Fourth-Generation PBX: Beyond the Integration of Voice and Data." *Telecommunications,* February 1985.

The author proposes that a fourth-generation PBX is characterized by an integrated LAN link, an integrated packet link, and dynamic allocation of bandwidth.

JOEL77 Joel, A.E. "What Is Telecommunications Circuit Switching?" *Proceedings of the IEEE,* September 1977.

Describes the evolution of this technology.

JOEL79a Joel, A.E. "Circuit Switching: Unique Architecture and Applications." *Computer*, June 1979.
A broad-brush treatment. Useful as an introduction.

JOEL79b Joel, A.E. "Digital Switching—How It Has Developed." *IEEE Transactions on Communications*, July 1979.
A more technical version of [JOEL77].

JOHN86 Johnson, M. "Reliability Mechanisms of the FDDI High Bandwidth Token Ring Protocol." *Computer Networks*, February 1986.
Discusses the built-in reliability mechanisms for FDDI, including fault detection, isolation and connection functions; monitoring functions; and configuration functions.

JOHN87 Johnson, M. "Proof That Timing Requirements of the FDDI Token Ring Protocol Are Satisfied." *IEEE Transactions on Communications*, June 1987.
Demonstrates that the timing requirements inherent in the FDDI MAC are consistent; that is, the token rotates fast enough to satisfy timer requirements within each station. Also examined in [SEVC87].

JOHN83 Jones, J.R. "Consider Fiber Optics for Local Network Designs." *EDN*, March 3, 1983.
Describes the uses of a fiber optic, passive star configuration that achieves the same functional effect as a baseband bus network.

JOSH85 Joshi, S. "Making the LAN Connection with a Fiber Optic Standard." *Computer Design*, September 1, 1985.
Describes the ANSI X3T9.5 FDDI standard, with an emphasis on cabling and installation issues.

JOSH86 Joshi, S. "High-Performance Networks: A Focus on the Fiber Distributed Data Interface (FDDI) Standard." *IEEE Micro*, June 1986.
A survey of the standard plus a good description of potential applications.

KANE80 Kane, D. "Data Communications Network Switching Methods." *Computer Design*, April 1980.
A brief survey of digital data switch systems.

KARP82 Karp, P.M. and Socher, I.D. "Designing Local-Area Networks." *Mini-Micro Systems*, April 1982.
Looks at network services issues for broadband systems.

KASS79a Kasson, J.M. "The Rolm Computerized Branch Exchange: An Advanced Digital PBX." *Computer*, June 1979.
Describes a commercial PBX product.

KASS79b Kasson, J.M. "Survey of Digital PBX Design." *IEEE Transactions on Communications*, July 1979.
Provides a good description of various contemporary PBX/CBX architectures.

KASS85 Kasson, J. and Johnson, H. "The CBX II Switching Architecture." *IEEE Journal on Selected Areas in Communications*, July 1985.
A description of the latest digital PBX product from ROLM. The architecture and implementation of the system are described.

KATK81a Katkin, R.D. and Sprung, J.G. "Simulating a Cable Bus Network in a Multicomputer and Large-Scale Application Environment." *Proceedings, Sixth Conference on Local Computer Networks*, Washington, D.C.: Computer Society Press, 1981.
Provides a rationale for and describes the plan for a study of HSLN performance.

KATK81b Katkin, R.D. and Sprung, J.G. *Application of Local Bus Network Technology to the Evolution of Large Multi-Computer Systems*. MITRE Technical Report MTR-81W290, November 1981.
Reports on the results of study described in [KATK81a].

KELL83 Keller, H.; Meyer, H.; and Mueller, H. "Transmission Design Criteria for Synchronous Token Ring." *IEEE Journal on Selected Areas in Communications*, November 1983.
Discusses token ring implementation issues, including cable type and layout, transmission, and synchronization with phase-locked loops.

KELL84 Kelley, R.; Jones, J.; Bhatt, V.; and Pate, P. "Transceiver Design and Implementation Experience in an Ethernet Compatible Fiber Optic Local Area Network." *Proceedings, INFOCOM 84*, Washington, D.C.: Computer Society Press, 1984.
Describes the system design of one of the few commercially-available fiber LANS.

KILL82 Killen, M. "The Microcomputer Connection to Local Networks." *Data Communications*, December 1982.
Good discussion of the technology and application of low-cost, low-speed LANs.

KLEE82 Klee, K.; Verity, J.W.; and Johnson, J. "Battle of the Networkers." *Datamation*, March 1982.
A lighthearted look at baseband versus broadband.

KOSH86 Koshy, G. "Understanding Multiple LANs: The Why and How of Linking Up." *Data Communications*, May 1986.
Examines an internetworking technique based on a bridging function at the data link layer.

KRON86 Kronenberg, N.; Levy, H.; and Strecker, W. "VAXclusters: A Closely-Coupled Distributed System." *ACM Transactions on Computer Systems*, May 1986.
A detailed examination of the DEC HSLN. Examines hardware, interface, and application software issues.

KRUT81 Krutsch, T. "A User Speaks Out: Broadband or Baseband for Local Nets?" *Data Communications*, December 1981.
A thoughtful comparison.

KUMM82 Kummerle, K. and Reiser, M. "Local-Area Communication Networks—An Overview." *Journal of*

Telecommunication Networks, Winter 1982.

A survey article.

KURO84 Kurose, J.; Schwartz, M.; and Yemini, Y. "Multiple-Access Protocols and Time-Constrained Communication." *ACM Computing Surveys,* March 1984.

Surveys multi-access protocols, including CSMA/CD. Examines the performance of such protocols, especially for real-time traffic, such as voice.

LABA78 LaBarre, C.E. *Analytic and Simulation Results for CSMA Contention Protocols.* MITRE Technical Report MTR-3672, 1978.

An important contribution to the CSMA/CD performance analysis literature.

LABA80 LaBarre, C.E. *Communications Protocols and Local Broadcast Networks.* MITRE Technical Report MTR-3899, February 1980.

A well thought-out discussion of what protocols should reside in the local network access unit.

LEE83 Lee, E. and Boulton, P. "The Principles and Performance of Hubnet: A 50 Mbit/s Glass Fiber Local Area Network." *IEEE Journal on Selected Areas in Communications,* November 1983.

Explains the principles and provides some implementation details for a fiber LAN that exists in prototype form.

LEON85 Leong, J. "Nuts-and-Bolts Guide to Ethernet Installation and Interconnection." *Data Communications,* September 1985.

A very good discussion of potential problems and their solutions.

LEVY82 Levy, W.A. and Mehl, H.F. "Local Area Networks." Series in *Mini-Micro Systems,* February, March, July 1982.

A comprehensive series of articles on LANs, HSLNs, digital switches, and PBXs. High-level discussion of architecture; list of vendors.

LEWI84 Lewis, J. and Baker, K. "Alternative to Microwave, Infrared Wins Short-Haul Run." *Data Communications,* November 1984.

Describes the use of laser for building-to-building links.

LI87 Li, V., editor. "Performance Evaluation of Multiple-Access Networks." *IEEE Journal on Selected Areas in Communications,* July 1987.

This issue contains a number of papers on local network performance.

LIMB84 Limb, J. "Performance of Local Area Networks at High Speed." *IEEE Communications Magazine,* August 1984.

An interesting look at the major LAN protocols from the point of view of traffic-handling capacity.

LIND82 Lindsay, D. "Local Area Networks: Bus and Ring vs. Coincident Star." *Computer Communications Review,* July/October 1982.

Proposes a configuration similar to AT&T's Datakit and comments on the advantages and disadvantages of this approach relative to bus and ring approaches.

LISS81 Lissack, T.; Maglaris, B.; and Chin, H. "Impact of Microprocessor Architecture on Local Network Interface Adapters." *Proceedings, Conference on Local Networks and Office Automation Systems,* 1981.

Study of local network access unit performance.

LIU78 Liu, M.T. "Distributed Loop Computer Networks." In *Advances in Computers, Vol. 17.* New York: Academic Press, 1978.

Good survey of various ring protocols.

LIU82 Liu, M.; Hilal, W.; and Groomes, B. "Performance Evaluation of Channel Access Protocols for Local Computer Networks." *Proceedings, COMPCON Fall 82,* Washington, D.C.: Computer Society Press, 1982.

Presents results of a comparative performance analysis of token ring, slotted ring, register insertion, and CSMA/CD.

LOVE87 Love, R. and Toher, T. "How to Design and Build a Token Ring LAN." *Data Communications,* May 1987.

A practical look at ring LAN installation, including cable choice, use of wiring concentrators, repeater issues, and coping with failures.

LUCZ78 Luczak, E.C. "Global Bus Computer Communication Techniques." *Proceedings, Computer Network Symposium,* Washington, D.C.: Computer Society Press, 1978.

Describes various bus protocols.

MAGL80 Maglaris, B. and Lissack, T. "An Integrated Broadband Local Network Architecture." *Proceedings, Fifth Conference on Local Computer Networks,* Washington, D.C.: Computer Society Press, 1980.

MAGL81 Maglaris, B.; Lissack, T.; and Austin, M. "End-to-End Delay Analysis on Local Area Networks: An Office Building Scenario." *Proceedings, National Telecommunications Conference,* 1981.

MAGL82 Maglaris, B. and Lissack, T. "Performance Evaluation of Interface Units for Broadcast Local Area Networks." *Proceedings, COMPCON Fall 82,* Washington, D.C.: Computer Society Press, 1982.

The above three papers provide an excellent analysis of end-to-end performance in a CSMA/CD broadband LAN.

MALO81 Malone, J. "The Microcomputer Connection to Local Networks." *Data Communications,* December 1981.

Looks at the reasons for and approaches to low cost LANS.

MAND82 Mandelkern, D. "Rugged Local Network Follows Military Aircraft Standard." *Electronics,* April 7, 1982.

Discusses MIL-STD-1553, a military LAN standard.

MARA82 Marathe, M. and Hawe, B. "Predicted Capacity of Ethernet in a University Environment." *Proceedings, SOUTHCON 82,* New York: IEEE, 1982.

Compares analysis with measured results.

MARS83 Marshall, G. "Bridges Link LANs." *Systems and Software,* May 1983.

Describes bridge operation.

MATS82 Matsukane, Ed. "Network Administration and Control System for a Broadband Local Area Communications Network." *Proceedings, COMPCON Fall 82,* Washington, D.C.: Computer Society Press, 1982.

A good discussion of desirable features in a network control center.

MAXE87 Maxemchuk, N. "Random Access Strategies for Fiber-Optic Neworks." *Proceedings, IEEE INFOCOM '87,* Washington, D.C.: Computer Society Press, 1987.

Describes and compares 12 MAC protocols that do not constrain the distance of data rate of a network. These are suitable for a bus topology fiber HSLN.

MCGA85 McGarry, S. "Networking Has a Job to Do in the Factory." *Data Communications,* February 1985.

Discusses the unique requirements for LANs that support factory automation.

METC76 Metcalfe, R.M. and Boggs, D.R. "Ethernet: Distributed Packet Switching for Local Computer Networks." *Communications of the ACM,* July 1976.

A classic paper.

METC77 Metcalfe, R.M.; Boggs, D.R.; Thacker, C.P.; and Lampson, B.W. "Multipoint Data Communication System with Collision Detection." *U.S. Patent 4,063,220,* 1977.

The Ethernet patent.

MILL82 Miller, C.K. and Thompson, D.M. "Making a Case for Token Passing in Local Networks." *Data Communications,* March 1982.

The author argues that token bus is superior to CSMA/CD both in terms of capability and cost.

MITC81 Mitchell, L. "A Methodology for Predicting End-to-End Responsiveness in a Local Computer Network." *Proceedings of the Computer Networking Symposium,* Washington, D.C.: Computer Society Press, December 1981.

Examines the issue of end-to-end local network performance. The article presents a general technique and then applies it to a specific case.

MITC86 Mitchell, L. and Lide, D. "End-to-End Performance Modeling of Local Area Networks." *IEEE Journal on Selected Areas in Communications,* September 1986.

Presents a generic modeling framework representing the end-to-end path between attached devices on a local network and for constructing performance models.

MOKH83 Mokhoff, N. "Fiber Optic LANs May Eliminate Future Bottlenecks in Office Communications." *Computer Design,* Fall 1983.

A survey of fiber-optic components and LAN configurations.

MOKH83 Mokhoff, N. "Networks Expand as PBXs Get Smarter." *Computer Design,* February 1984.

A survey of local network types, with an emphasis on the digital PBX. Issues of integrating LANs and PBXs are explored.

MOUS87 Moustakas, S. "The Standardization of IEEE 802.3 Compatible Fiber Optic CSMA/CD Local Area Networks: Physical Topologies." *IEEE Communications Magazine,* February 1987.

Assesses bus, ring, and passive star approaches.

NABI84 Nabielsky, J. "Interfacing to the 10 Mbps Ethernet: Observations and Conclusions." *Proceedings, SIGCOMM 84,* New York: ACM, Inc., June 1984.

Reports on practical experience in connecting devices to Ethernet using a variety of configurations. The performance results indicate that the 10-Mbps data rate is unnecessarily high.

NBS81 National Bureau of Standards. *A Look at Network Management.,* Report ICST/LANP-82-1, October 1981.

A survey of LAN network control issues.

NESS81 Nessett, D.M. *HYPERchannel Architecture: A Case Study of Some Inadequacies in the ISO OSI Reference Model.* Lawrence Livermore Laboratory Report UCRL-53139, April 1981.

A critical look at the HYPERchannel protocol architecture. Provides some important insights.

OKAD84 Okad, H.; Yamamoto, T.; Nomura, Y.; and Nakanishi, Y. "Comparative Evaluation of Token-Ring and CSMA/CD Medium-Access Control Protocols in LAN Configurations." *Proceedings, Computer Networking Symposium,* Washington, D.C.: Computer Society Press, 1984.

Using a Markov approach, the authors produce a set of results for the two protocols under varying assumptions.

OLSE83 Olsen, R.; Seifert, W.; and Taylor, J. "RS-232-C Data Switching on Local Networks." *Data Communications,* September 1983.

Describes in detail the use of a local network access unit for terminal handling.

PARK83a Parker, R. and Shapiro, S. "Untangling Local Area Networks." *Computer Design,* March 1983.

Survey article. Discusses pros and cons of various media, topologies, and access control schemes.

PARK83b Parker, R. "Committees Push to Standardize Disk I/O." *Computer Design,* March 1983.

Describes the functions of the ANSI X3T9.5 committee and places its HSLN standardization effort in context with its other activities.

PENN79 Penny, B.K. and Baghdadi, A.A. "Survey of Computer Communications Loop Networks." *Computer Communications,* August and October 1979.

Probably the best survey of ring protocols.

PFIS82 Pfister, G. and O'Brien, B. "Comparing the CBX to the Local Network—And the Winner Is?" *Data Communications,* July 1982.

A point-by-point comparison of the LAN to the digital PBX. The authors favor the latter.

PHIN83 Phinney, T. and Jelatis, G. "Error Handling in the IEEE 802 Token-Passing Bus LAN." *IEEE Journal on Selected Areas in Communications,* November 1983.

A description of the IEEE 802 token bus protocol, with a detailed look at error handling.

PIER72 Pierce, J.R. "Network for Block Switches of Data." *Bell System Technical Journal,* July/August 1972.

A pioneering slotted ring article.

POTT83 Potter, D. and Amand, J. "Connecting Minis to Local Nets with Discrete Modules." *Data Communications,* June 1983.

A description of an NIU implementation.

RADI84 Radicati, S. "Managing Transient Internetwork Links in the Xerox Internet." *Proceedings, Second ACM-SIGOA Conference on Office Information Systems,* New York: ACM, Inc., 1984.

Describes an approach for temporarily establishing and tearing down dial-up circuit and X.25 virtual circuit links in a LAN internet environment.

RAGH81 Raghavendra, C.S. and Gerla, M. "Optimal Loop Topologies for Distributed Systems." *Proceedings, Seventh Data Communications Symposium,* Washington, D.C.: Computer Society Press, 1981.

The authors propose a reliability-enhancing technique for rings that is optimal in terms of both availability and throughput.

RATN83 Ratner, D. "How Broadband Modems Operate on Token-Passing Nets." *Data Communications,* June 1983.

Good technical discussion of the RF modem.

RAUC82 Rauch-Hindin, W. "IBM's Local Network Scheme." *Data Communications,* May 1982.

Concise summary of IBM's ring proposal.

RAWS79 Rawson, E.G. "Application of Fiber Optics to Local Networks." *Proceedings, Local Area Communications Network Symposium,* 1979.

Looks at ways in which fiber optics is practical today. Is still valid.

REAM75 Reames, C.C. and Liu, M.T. "A Loop Network for Simultaneous Transmission of Variable-Length Messages." *Proceedings, Second Annual Symposium on Computer Architecture,* Washington, D.C.: Computer Society Press, 1975.

Good slotted-ring description.

RICH80 Richer, J.; Steiner, M.; and Sengoku, M. "Office Communications and the Digital PBX." *Computer Networks,* December 1980.

Details the requirements for intraoffice communications and discusses the satisfaction of those requirements by a digital PBX.

RODR85 Rodrigues, P.; Fratta, L.; and Gerla, M. "Tokenless Protocols for Fiber Optic Local Area Networks." *IEEE Journal on Selected Areas in Communications,* November 1985.

A review of various MAC protocols suitable for a fiber bus HSLN.

ROMA77 Roman, G.S. *The Design of Broadband Coaxial Cable Networks for Multimode Communications.* MITRE Technical Report MTR-3527, 1977.

Describes in some detail the electronic components of a broadband system and related installation issues. A good, practical account.

ROSS86 Ross, F. "FDDI—A Tutorial." *IEEE Communications Magazine,* May 1986.

A good overall tutorial.

ROSS87 Ross, F. "Rings Are 'Round for Good!" *IEEE Network Magazine,* January 1987.

A brief review of 802.5 and FDDI, plus a discussion of the benefits of the ring topology.

ROUN83 Rounds, F. "Use Modeling Techniques to Estimate Localnet Success." *EDN,* April 14, 1983.

A discussion of techniques for modeling CSMA/CD networks. A source listing of a simulation program is included.

SALT79 Saltzer, J.H. and Pogran, K.T. "A Star-Shaped Ring Network with High Maintainability." *Proceedings, Local Area Communications Network Symposium,* 1979.

Describes availability enhancements for a ring. Is similar to IBM's approach.

SALT83 Saltzer, J.; Clark, D.; and Pogran, K. "Why a Ring?" *Computer Networks,* August 1983.

Examines the benefits of a ring LAN as compared to a bus LAN.

SALW83 Salwen, H. "In Praise of Ring Architecture for Local Area Networks." *Computer Design,* March 1983.

Discusses the advantages of a token-passing ring with wiring concentrations for reliability. This is the same philosophy as that propounded by IBM.

SAND82 Sanders, L. "Interfacing with a Military Data-Comm Bus." *Electronic Design,* August 5, 1982.

Another article on MIL-STD-1553.

SAST85 Sastry, A. "Maximum Mean Data Rate in a Local Area Network with a Specified Maximum Source Message Load." *Proceedings, INFOCOM 85,* Washington, D.C.: Computer Society Press, 1985.

Considers the collective impact of various parameters such as propagation delay, interface delay, transmission rate, and message length in the maximum mean throughput of a LAN. Token ring, token bus, and CSMA/CD are compared.

SCHM83 Schmidt, R.; Rawson, E.; Norton, R.; Jackson, S.; and Bailey, M. "Fibernet II: A Fiber Optic Ethernet." *IEEE Journal on Selected Areas in Communications*, November 1983.

Describes an Ethernet-compatible fiber-optic star configuration with an active central star repeater.

SCHN83 Schneidewind, N. "Interconnecting Local Networks to Long-Distance Networks." *Computer*, September 1983.

Explores protocol-related issues in LAN-long haul internetworking. A variety of design approaches are analyzed.

SCHO81 Scholl, T.H. "The New Breed—Switching Muxes." *Data Communications*, June 1981.

Describes a modified statistical multiplexor that can be used for networking.

SCHW82 Schwartz, J. and Melling, W.P. "Sharing Logic and Work." *Datamation*, November 1982.

Describes use of a low-cost LAN in an office environment.

SEVC87 Sevcik, K. and Johnson, M. "Cycle Time Properties of the FDDI Token Ring Protocol." *IEEE Transactions on Software Engineering*, March 1987.

A rigorous examination of the timed token rotation algorithm for FDDI. The authors prove two important properties of the algorithm. Also examined in [JOHN87].

SHIR82 Shirey, R.W. "Security in Local Area Networks." *Proceedings, Computer Networking Symposium*, Washington, D.C.: Computer Society Press, 1982.

An excellent tutorial.

SHOC78 Shoch, J.F. "Internetwork Naming, Addressing, and Routing." *Proceedings, COMPCON 78*, Washington, D.C.: Computer Society Press, 1978.

Discusses internet issues, with reference to local networks.

SHOC80a Shoch, J.F. *An Annotated Bibliography on Local Computer Networks*. Palo Alto, Calif.: Xerox Palo Alto Research Center, April 1980.

A good bibliography of material up to the date of publication.

SHOC80b Shoch, J.F. and Hupp, J.A. "Measured Performance of an Ethernet Local Network." *Communications of the ACM*, December 1980.

Excellent description of a performance measurement experiment.

SHOC82 Shoch, J.; Dalal, Y.; Redel, D.; and Crane, R. "Evolution of the Ethernet Local Computer Network." *Computer*, August 1982.

A thorough and informative description of Ethernet.

SIDH82a Sidhu, D. and Gasser, M. "A Multilevel Secure Local Area Network." *Proceedings of the Symposium on Security and Privacy*, Washington, D.C.: Computer Society Press April 1982.

Describes the use of a trusted network access unit to enforce a security policy on a LAN.

SIDH82b Sidhu, D.P. and Gasser, M. *Design for a Multilevel Secure Local Area Network*. MITRE Technical Report MTR-8702, March 1982.

Describes the trusted interface unit in greater detail.

SIDH82c Sidhu, D.P. "A Local Area Network Design for Military Applications." *Proceedings, Seventh Conference on Local Computer Networks*, Washington, D.C.: Computer Society Press, 1982.

Another article on the trusted interface unit.

SKAP79 Skaperda, N.J. "Some Architectural Alternatives in the Design of a Digital Switch." *IEEE Transactions on Communications*, July 1979.

Discusses ways in which the fundamental building blocks of time- and space-division switching are used to configure digital switches.

SPAN86 Spanier, S. "FEPs Ease Migration to New LAN Protocols." *Mini-Micro Systems*, September 1986.

A general description of the use of a front-end (NAU), which supports up through the transport layer, plus a vendor survey.

STAC80 Stack, R. and Dillencourt, K. "Protocols for Local-Area Networks." *Proceedings of the Trends and Applications Conference*, Washington, D.C.: Computer Society Press, May 1980.

Concerned with protocol residency alternatives; which protocol layers should be in a local network access unit and which in the attached host. The related merits of various alternatives are discussed.

STAC81a Stack, T. and Dillencourt, K. "Functional Description of a Value-Added Local Area Network." *Proceedings, Computer Networking Symposium*, Washington, D.C.: Computer Society Press, December 1981.

Discusses various operating system and application services that can be supported across a LAN.

STAC81b Stack, T. "LAN Protocol Residency Alternatives for IBM Mainframe Open System Interconnection." *Technical Report*, Network Analysis Corporation, 1981.

A further and specific discussion of issues covered in the article in this tutorial.

STAL83 Stallings, W. "Beyond Local Networks." *Datamation*, August 1983.

An overview of the key issues involved in extending communication for an attached device beyond the scope of its local network.

STAL84a Stallings, W. "Local Network Performance." *IEEE Communications Magazine*, February 1984.

Develops a simple set of performance models for CSMA/CD and token-passing, and then surveys the results of a number of comparative LAN performance studies.

STAL84b Stallings, W. "Local Networks." *Computing Surveys,* March 1984.

A comprehensive survey.

STAL84c Stallings, W. "Digital Signaling Techniques." *IEEE Communications Magazine,* December 1984.

A discussion of various signaling techniques that can be used on baseband local networks, including Manchester and differential Manchester.

STAL87 Stallings, W. "Interfacing to a LAN: Where's the Protocol?" *Data Communications,* April 1987.

Examines the issue of attaching a device to a LAN through some sort of network access unit (NAU). The article focuses on the protocol required between the device and the NAU.

STEW84 Stewart, B.; Hawe, B.; and Kirby, A. "Local Area Network Connection." *Telecommunications,* April 1984.

A good discussion of the function and performance of a bridge.

STIE81 Stieglitz, M. "Local Network Access Tradeoffs." *Computer Design,* October 1981.

The author makes a case for token bus over CSMA/CD.

STIE85 Stieglitz, M. "X.25 Standard Simplifies Linking of Different LANs." *Computer Design,* February 1985.

Describes an approach to the use of an X.25 gateway to link a LAN to other LANs and to hosts and terminals via an X.25 wide-area network.

STRO83 Strole, N. "A Local Communications Network Based on Interconnected Token-Access Rings: A Tutorial." *IBM Journal of Research and Development,* September 1983.

Describes IBM's planned ring local network products, the basis for the IEEE 802.5 standard.

STRO87 Strole, N. "The IBM Token Ring Network—A Functional Overview." *IEEE Network Magazine,* January 1987.

A good overview.

STUC83a Stuck, B. "Which Local Net Bus Access Is Most Sensitive to Traffic Congestion?" *Data Communications,* January 1983.

Reports on an IEEE 802 performance study, with an emphasis on the approach. CSMA/CD, token bus, and token ring were examined.

STUC83b Stuck, B. "Calculating the Maximum Mean Data Rate in Local Area Networks." *Computer,* May 1983.

Same topic as [STUC83a], with an emphasis on results.

STUC84 Stuck, B. "An Introduction to Traffic Handling Characteristics of Bus Local Area Network Distributed Access Methods." *IEEE Communications Magazine,* August 1984.

A detailed examination of CSMA/CD and token bus under a variety of assumptions.

SUH86 Suh, S.; Granlund, S.; and Hegde, S. "Fiber-Optic Local Area Network Topology." *IEEE Communications Magazine,* August 1986.

A survey of the various topologies that can be used with optical fiber.

SUMM87 Summers, R. "A Resource Sharing System for Personal Computers in a LAN: Concepts, Design, and Experience." *IEEE Transactions on Software Engineering,* August 1987.

A discussion of facilities for distributed resource sharing on LANs.

SUNS79 Sunshine, C. "Network Interconnection." *Proceedings of Local Area Communications Network Symposium,* 1979.

A thought-provoking checklist of design issues for local network internetworking.

SUNS83 Sunshine, C.; Kaufman, D.; Ennis, G.; and Biba, K. "Interconnection of Broadband Local Area Networks." *Proceedings, Eighth Data Communications Symposium,* Washington, D.C.: Computer Society Press, October 1983.

Discusses a design for interconnecting large numbers of devices across multiple LANs. The key issue is routing.

SUNS85 Sunshine, C. and Ennis, G. "Broad-Band Personal Computer LANs." *IEEE Journal on Selected Areas in Communications,* May 1985.

A review of the technology of broadband LANs. This is followed by a discussion of the applicability of broadband LANs to personal computer interconnection. Finally, the IBM PC Network product is summarized.

TANG85 Tang, Y. and Zaky, S. "A Survey of Ring Networks: Topology and Protocols." *Proceedings, INFOCOM 85,* Washington, D.C.: Computer Society Press, 1985.

A brief survey of a variety of ring-based topologies and access protocols for local networks. The authors classify and compare 24 existing ring networks.

THOR80 Thornton, J. "Back-End Network Approaches." *Computer,* February 1980.

Looks at the application of high-speed local networks to back-end database applications, and describes HYPERchannel.

THUR79 Thurber, K.J. and Freeman, H.A. "Architecture Considerations for Local Computer Networks." *Proceedings, First International Conference on Distributed Computer Systems,* Washington, D.C.: Computer Society Press, 1979. (Reprinted in [THUR81])

Develops a taxonomy for local networks and classifies a number of systems.

TOBA80a Tobagi, F.A. and Hunt, V.B. "Performance Analysis of Carrier Sense Multiple Access with Collision Detection." *Computer Networks,* October/November 1980.

A detailed mathematical derivation.

TOBA80b Tobagi, F.A. "Multiaccess Protocols in Packet Communication Systems." *IEEE Transactions on Communications,* April 1980.

A widely-referenced article that surveys the performance results for CSMA/CD and related protocols.

TOBA82 Tobagi, F.A. "Distributions of Packet Delay and Interdeparture Time in Slotted ALOHA and Carrier Sense Multiple Access." *Journal of the ACM*, October 1982.
A rigorous, highly mathematical derivation.

TOBA83 Tobagi, F.; Borgonovo, F.; and Fratta, L. "Expressnet: A High-Performance Integrated-Services Local Area Network." *IEEE Journal on Selected Areas in Communications*, November 1983.
A unidirectional bus architecture and a proposed access protocol that provide good performance at high data rates. A promising approach for high-speed local networks.

TRIP87 Tripathi, S.; Huang, Y.; and Jogodia, S. "Local Area Networks: Software and Related Issues." *IEEE Transactions on Software Engineering*, August 1987.
A review of issues that affect the software requirements for LANs, including MAC protocols, system software, and application software.

TSAO84 Tsao, D. "A Local Area Network Architecture Overview." *IEEE Communications Magazine*, August 1984.
A brief overview of existing LAN architectures.

VONA80 Vonarx, M. "Controlling the Mushrooming Communications Net." *Data Communications*, June 1980.
Describes an intelligent port selector type of digital data switch. Design for redundancy is emphasized.

WAIN82 Wainwright, D. "Internetworking and Addressing for Local Networks." *IEEE Project 802 Local Network Standards, Draft C*, New York: IEEE, May 1982.
A systematic analysis of protocol issues relating to the various internetwork situations involving local networks.

WARN80 Warner, C. "Connecting Local Networks to Long-Haul Networks: Issues in Protocol Design." *Proceedings of the Fifth Conference on Local Computer Networks*, Washington, D.C.: Computer Society Press, December 1980.
Explores protocol-related issues in attempting to internetwork LANs and long-haul networks. The article highlights the relevant differences between the two types of networks.

WATS80 Watson, W.B. "Simulation Study of the Configuration Dependent Performance of a Prioritized, CSMA Broadcast Network." *Proceedings, Fifth Conference on Local Computer Networks*, Washington, D.C.: Computer Society Press, 1980.
Another look at HSLN protocol performance.

WAY81 Way, D. "Build a Local Network on Proven Software." *Data Communications*, December 1982.
Discusses the NIU-device interface.

WILK79 Wilkes, M.V. and Wheeler, D.J. "The Cambridge Digital Communication Ring." *Proceedings, Local Area Communications Network Symposium*, 1979.
A worthwhile description of a widely-used slotted ring system.

WILL81 Willard, D. "Reliability/Availability of Wideband Local Communication Networks." *Computer Design*, August 1981.
Examines a variety of techniques for enhancing the availability of broadband LANs.

WIRL85 Wirl, C. "What's the Best Way to Wire a New Building for Data?" *Data Communications*, September 1985.
A useful survey of the various media, focusing on installation issues.

WOLF78 Wolf, J.J. and Liu, M.T. "A Distributed Double-Loop Computer Network." *Proceedings, Seventh Texas Conference of Computing Systems*, Washington, D.C.: Computer Society Press, 1978.
An approach to enhancing ring availability.

WONG84 Wong, J. and Bux, W. "Analytic Modeling of an Adapter to Local Area Networks." *IEEE Transactions on Communications*, October 1984.
A study of the performance of LAN interface units with respect to their ability to absorb packets from the LAN. Some generally useful results are reported.

WOOD79 Wood, D. "A Cable-Bus Protocol Architecture." *Proceedings of the Sixth Data Communications Symposium*, Washington, D.C.: Computer Society Press, November 1979.
Looks at the protocol architecture of a broadband LAN. In this system, the layers up through transport are resident in a local network access unit.

WURZ84 Wurzburg, H. and Kelley, S. "PBX-Based LANs: Lower Cost per Terminal Connection." *Computer Design*, February 1984.
Discusses digital PBX architecture, then compares it to the LAN, and looks at integrated PBX-LAN systems.

Author Biography

William Stallings received a PhD from M.I.T. in computer science and a B.S. from Notre Dame in electrical engineering. He is an independent consultant and president of Comp/Comm Consulting of London, England. His clients have included the Government of India, the International Monetary Fund, the National Security Agency, IBM, and Honeywell. Prior to forming his own consulting firm, he has been vice president of CSM Corp., a firm specializing in data processing and data communications for the health-care industry. He has also been director of systems analysis and design for CTEC, Inc., a firm specializing in command, control, and communications systems.

Dr. Stallings is the author of numerous technical papers and the following books:

- *Data and Computer Communications, Second Edition*, Macmillan, 1988
- *Handbook of Computer-Communications Standards, Volume I: The Open Systems Interconnection (OSI) Model and OSI-Related Standards*, Macmillan, 1987
- *Handbook of Computer-Communications Standards, Volume II: Local Network Standards*, Macmillan, 1987
- *Handbook of Computer-Communications Standards, Volume III: Department of Defense (DoD) Protocol Standards*, Macmillan, 1988
- *Local Networks, an Introduction, Second Edition*, Macmillan, 1987
- *Computer Organization and Architecture*, Macmillan, 1987
- *Computer Communications: Architectures, Protocols, and Standards, Second Edition*, Computer Society Press, 1988
- *Reduced Instruction Set Computers*, Computer Society Press, 1986
- *Integrated Services Digital Networks, Second Edition*, Computer Society Press, 1988
- *Local Network Technology, Third Edition*, Computer Society Press, 1988
- *A Manager's Guide to Local Networks*, Prentice-Hall, 1983.